Principles of California Real Estate

Kathryn J. Haupt
David L. Rockwell

Rockwell Publishing Company

By Rockwell Publishing Company
13218 N.E. 20th
Bellevue, WA 98005
(425)747-7272 / 1-800-221-9347

Seventeenth edition

ISBN: 978-1-939259-60-8

PRINTED IN THE UNITED STATES OF AMERICA

Table of Contents

Chapter 1

The Nature of Real Property

I. What is Real Property?
II. Appurtenances
   A. Air rights
   B. Water rights
   C. Solid mineral rights
   D. Oil and gas rights
   E. Other appurtenant rights
III. Attachments
   A. Natural attachments
   B. Man-made attachments (fixtures)
   C. Distinguishing fixtures from personal property
      1. Written agreement
      2. Method of attachment
      3. Adaptation of the item to the realty
      4. Intention of the annexor
      5. Relationship of the parties
   D. Mobile homes
IV. Land Description
   A. Metes and bounds
   B. Government survey
   C. Recorded map
   D. Other methods of land description

Chapter Overview

Real estate agents are concerned not just with the sale of land and houses, but with the sale of real property. Real property includes the land and improvements, and it also encompasses the rights that go along with ownership of land. The first part of this chapter explains those rights, which are known as appurtenances. It also explains natural attachments and fixtures, which are sold as part of the land, and the distinction between fixtures and personal property, which ordinarily is not transferred with the land. The second part of this chapter explains methods of legal description—the different ways in which a parcel of land may be identified in legal documents to prevent confusion about its boundaries or ownership.

What Is Real Property?

There are two types of property: real property (realty) and personal property (personalty). **Real property** can be defined as land, anything affixed or attached to the land, and anything incidental or appurtenant to the land. Sometimes it is described as "that which is immovable." **Personal property**, by contrast, is usually movable. A car, a sofa, and a hat are simple examples of personal property. Anything that is not real property is personal property.

The distinction between real and personal property is very important in real estate transactions. When a piece of land is sold, anything that is considered part of the real property is transferred to the buyers along with the land, unless otherwise agreed. But if an item is personal property, the sellers can take it with them when they move away, unless otherwise agreed.

Of course, the principal component of real property is land. But this means more than just the surface of the earth. Real property also includes the **subsurface**: everything beneath the surface down to the center of the earth. It also includes the **airspace**: everything above the surface, to the upper reaches of the sky.

A parcel of real property can be imagined as an inverted pyramid, with its tip at the center of the globe and its base above the earth's surface. The landowner owns not only the earth's surface within the boundaries of the parcel, but also everything under and over the surface.

In addition to the land itself, any improvements to the land are part of the landowner's real property. **Improvements** are things that have been added to, built on, or done to the land to improve or develop it. A house, a driveway, and landscaping are all examples of improvements.

The rights, privileges, and interests associated with land ownership are also considered part of the real property. Think

Fig. 1.1 The inverted pyramid

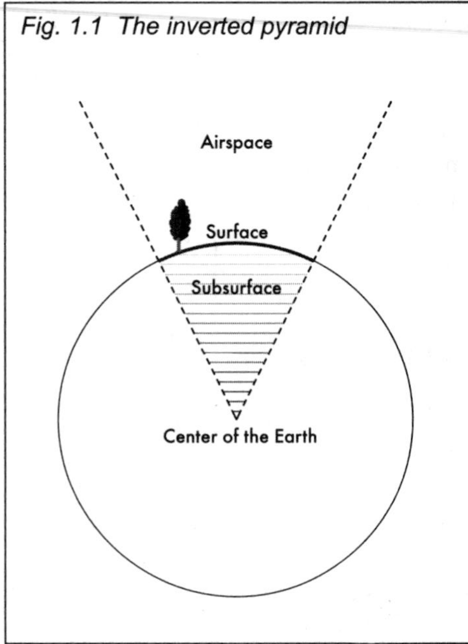

of real property as the land and improvements plus a "bundle of rights." The owner's bundle of rights includes the right to possess, use, enjoy, encumber, will, sell, or do nothing at all with the land. Of course, these rights aren't absolute; they're subject to government regulation (see Chapter 5).

Appurtenances

In addition to the basic bundle of ownership rights, a landowner has appurtenant rights. An **appurtenance** is a right or interest that goes along with or pertains to a piece of land. A landowner's property may include any or all of these appurtenances:

- air rights,
- water rights,
- solid mineral rights,
- oil and gas rights, and
- support rights.

Appurtenances are ordinarily transferred along with the land, but the landowner can sell certain appurtenant rights separately from the land. For example, the owner may keep the land but sell his mineral rights to a mining company.

Air Rights

Air rights give a landowner the right to use the airspace above her land. In theory, a landowner's air rights extend to the upper limits of the sky. In practice, however, this is no longer true. Congress gave the federal government complete control over the nation's airspace. Landowners still have the exclusive right to use the lower reaches of airspace over their property, but may do nothing that would interfere with normal air traffic.

On the other hand, sometimes air traffic interferes with a landowner's right to the normal use of his land. If aircraft overflights cause substantial harm to a landowner, he may sue the government for some form of reimbursement. The classic example is an airport built right next to a chicken farm. The noise and vibrations from overflights are so severe that the chickens no longer lay eggs. If the land can't be used for any other reasonable purpose, the value of the land is significantly diminished. The landowner may be able to force the government to condemn the property and compensate him for its fair market value. (See the discussion of inverse condemnation in Chapter 3.)

Water Rights

The right to use water can be—but isn't necessarily—an appurtenant right, tied to land ownership. Because water is vital for agriculture, industry, and day-to-day living, water rights are an important issue in many places, including many parts of California.

Water is found both on the surface of the earth and beneath the surface. (The natural level at which water can be located in a particular piece of land is called the water table.) Surface water may be confined to a channel or basin, or it may be unconfined water, such as runoff or flood water. The water beneath the surface may also be "confined" in the sense that it runs in recognizable underground streams, or it may collect in porous ground layers called aquifers.

In regard to confined surface waters, two systems govern water rights:

1. the riparian rights system, and
2. the appropriative rights system.

Riparian Rights System. Riparian rights are the water rights of a landowner with respect to water that flows through or adjacent to her property. Such a landowner, called a riparian landowner, has a right to make reasonable use of the stream's natural flow. A riparian landowner also has the right to use stream water for domestic uses, such as drinking, bathing, and watering a personal-use produce garden. However, upstream riparian owners aren't allowed to use the water in ways that could deprive downstream owners of its use; they must not substantially diminish the stream's flow in quantity, quality, or velocity.

Whether a riparian owner also owns the land under the stream depends on whether the stream is **navigable** or not. A waterway is generally considered navigable if it is large enough to be used in commerce. If a stream is not navigable, the riparian owner owns the land under the water. (If the stream is the boundary between two parcels of land, each owner owns the land under the water to the midpoint of the streambed.) If a stream is navigable, the government owns the land under the water and the riparian landowner owns the land only to the mean high water mark of the streambed. The general public has the right to use navigable waterways for transportation and recreation.

Sometimes a distinction is made between riparian water and littoral water. Riparian water is flowing water, such as the water in a river, stream, creek, or other watercourse. Littoral water, on the other hand, is standing water—a pond, a lake, or even an ocean.

Under the riparian rights system, someone who owns littoral land (land on a lakefront, for example) has essentially the same water rights as someone who owns land beside a river. Owners of littoral property have the right to use the water for domestic purposes, and they're also entitled to have the lake maintained at its natural level, to use the lake for fishing or recreation, and to have the natural purity of the lake's waters maintained. If the lake is not navigable, each littoral owner owns a portion of the lake bed adjacent to his or her property.

There's an important restriction on a riparian owner's water rights. A riparian owner is not permitted to divert water from a stream or lake for use on non-riparian land—that is, land that does not adjoin the stream or lake from which the water is taken.

> **Example:** Brown is a riparian landowner. She owns Parcel A, property that borders on the Swiftwater River. She also owns Parcel B, property that is about 300 feet inland. She cannot divert water from the Swiftwater River to irrigate the crops on her non-riparian property.

Appropriative Rights System. Riparian and littoral rights are tied to ownership of land beside a body of water. The second major type of water rights, **appropriative rights**, do not depend on land ownership. Instead, appropriative rights are based on priority of use (first in time, first in right). The appropriative rights system is also called the **prior appropriation system**.

To establish an appropriative right, someone who wants to use water from a particular lake or stream applies to the state government for a permit. It isn't necessary for the applicant to own land beside the body of water, and water taken by a permit holder doesn't have to be used on property adjacent to the water source.

If someone with an appropriative right fails to use the water for a certain period of time, she is likely to lose the appropriative right. Another person can then apply for a permit to use the water.

Water Rights in California. The appropriative rights system is primarily used in the western United States, where water resources are scarce and therefore carefully controlled. This is certainly true in California. As a result of years of legislation and litigation, California has an extremely complex body of law that regulates the use of water in the state. The basis of this body of law is the appropriative rights system, the most common method of obtaining water rights in California. California also recognizes a limited form of riparian rights. Riparian owners in California do not have the right to limitless water, but are entitled to a reasonable amount of water for beneficial uses, leaving the surplus for nonriparian appropriative users.

Stock in a **mutual water company** is considered appurtenant to real property. A mutual water company is a corporation that is created to secure adequate water supplies at reasonable rates for water users in a particular area. The stock in the company is issued to the water users.

Ground Water. Ground water is subsurface water. It may collect in porous underground layers called aquifers. Landowners have **overlying rights** in regard to the ground water in aquifers beneath their property. Overlying rights are similar to riparian rights; the landowner may make reasonable use of the ground water, but isn't allowed to transport it for use on land outside the ground water basin from which it was removed. The appropriative rights system may also be applied to ground water, but the appropriator's rights are always subordinate to those with overlying rights.

Solid Mineral Rights

Land may contain a wide range of solid minerals, such as coal, copper, gemstones, or gold. A landowner owns all of the solid minerals within the "inverted pyramid" under the surface of his property. These minerals are considered to be real property until they are extracted from the earth, at which point they become personal property.

As we mentioned earlier, a landowner can sell his mineral rights separately from the rest of the property. When rights to a particular mineral are sold, the purchaser automatically acquires an implied easement—the right to enter the land in order to extract the minerals from it.

Oil and Gas Rights

Ownership of oil and gas is not as straightforward as ownership of solid minerals. In their natural state, oil and gas lie trapped beneath the surface in porous layers of earth. However, once an oil or gas reservoir has been tapped, the oil and gas begin to flow toward the point where the reservoir has been pierced by the well. A well on one parcel of land can attract all of the oil and gas from the surrounding properties.

Ownership of oil and gas is governed by the "rule of capture." That is, a landowner owns all of the oil and gas produced from wells on her property. The oil and gas become the personal property of the landowner once they are brought to the surface. The rule of capture has the effect of stimulating oil and gas production, since the only way for a landowner to protect her interest in the underlying gas and oil is to drill an offset well to keep the oil and gas from migrating to her neighbor's wells.

Fugitive Substances. Oil, gas, and water are sometimes referred to as "fugitive substances," because they are not stationary in their natural state. As we've discussed, appurtenant rights to extract oil and gas and to use water are classified as real property; and the substances themselves become personal property once they have been captured or contained. Until that point, however, oil, gas, and water are not considered property at all under California law.

Other Appurtenant Rights

In addition to rights concerning air, water, minerals, and oil and gas, there are some other important appurtenant rights.

A piece of land is supported by the other land that surrounds it. A landowner has **support rights**—the right to the natural support provided by the land beside and beneath his property. **Lateral support** is support from adjacent land; it may be disturbed by construction or excavations on the adjacent property. **Subjacent support** is support from the underlying earth. Subjacent support may become an issue when a landowner sells his mineral rights.

Easements and restrictive covenants also create appurtenant rights. These are discussed in detail in Chapter 4.

Attachments

You've seen that the land and the appurtenances are considered part of the real property. The third element of real property is attachments. There are two main categories of attachments:

1. natural, and
2. man-made.

Natural Attachments

Natural attachments are things attached to the earth by roots, such as trees, shrubs, and crops. This includes plants that grow spontaneously, without the help of humans, and plants cultivated by people. Natural attachments are classified as part of the real property they're growing on. This means that if the property is sold, the natural attachments are transferred along with the land, unless otherwise agreed.

In accordance with that rule, when farmland is sold, unharvested crops are ordinarily treated as part of the real property and included in the sale of the land. However, if crops are sold separately from the land, they're treated as personal property as soon as they're subject to a contract of sale, even before they've been harvested.

Example: The owner of an apple orchard enters into a contract to sell her crop of apples to a juice company. The apples are now considered the personal property of the juice company, even while they're still on the trees. If the orchard owner sells the land to a third party before the apples are harvested, the apple trees will be included in the sale of the land, but the apples themselves will not be.

A special rule called the **doctrine of emblements** applies to crops planted by a tenant farmer. If the tenancy is for an indefinite period of time and the tenancy is terminated through no fault of the tenant before the crops are ready for harvest, she has the right to re-enter the land and harvest the first crop that matures after the tenancy is terminated.

Man-made Attachments: Fixtures

Things that have been attached to the land by people are called **fixtures**. Houses, fences, and cement patios are all examples of fixtures. Like natural attachments, fixtures are considered part of the real property.

Fixtures always start out as personal property. For example, lumber is personal property, but it becomes a fixture when it's used to build a fence. It is sometimes difficult to determine whether a particular item has become a fixture or is still personal property. If the item is personal property, the owner can take it away when the land is sold. But if the item is a fixture, it's transferred to the buyer along with the land unless otherwise agreed.

Adding an item of personal property to real property so that it becomes a fixture is called **annexation**. Removing a fixture from real property so that it becomes personal property again is called **severance**. (These terms may be used for natural attachments as well as fixtures.)

Distinguishing Fixtures from Personal Property

Buyers and sellers often disagree as to exactly what has been purchased and sold in their transaction. For instance, is the heirloom chandelier installed by the seller real property that's transferred to the buyer, or can the seller remove it when he moves out?

Written Agreement. The easiest way to avoid such a controversy is to put the intentions of the parties in writing. If there is a written agreement between a buyer and a seller (or a landlord and a tenant, or a lender and a borrower) stipulating how a particular item is going to be treated—as part of the real estate or as personal property—then the court will respect and enforce that agreement. The stipulation between a buyer and a seller would ordinarily be found in their purchase agreement. For example, if a seller plans to take certain shrubs from the property before the transaction closes, a statement to that effect ought to be included in the purchase agreement, since shrubbery is usually considered part of the real property.

Similarly, if the seller intends to transfer personal property, such as a couch, to the buyer, that should also be stated in the purchase agreement. In addition to the deed conveying title to the real property, a separate document called a **bill of sale** will be needed if the personal property is worth $500 or more. A bill of sale conveys title to personal property.

In the absence of a written agreement, courts apply a series of tests to classify the item in dispute. These tests include:

- the method of attachment,
- adaptation of the item to the real property,
- the intention of the annexor, and
- the relationship of the parties.

Method of Attachment. Generally, any item permanently attached to the land becomes a part of the real estate. A permanent attachment occurs when the item is:

- annexed to the land by roots, like trees or rose bushes;
- embedded in the earth, like sewer lines or septic tanks;
- permanently resting on the land, like a storage shed; or
- attached by any other enduring method, such as cement, plaster, nails, bolts, or screws.

Note that it isn't necessary for an item to be literally attached to the real property in order to be considered a fixture. There may be physical annexation even without actual attachment. The force of gravity alone may be sufficient, as in the case of a building with no foundation. Also, an article enclosed within a building may be considered annexed to the real property if it cannot be removed without dismantling it, or without tearing down part of the building.

In addition, even easily movable articles may be considered constructively annexed (legally attached) to the real property if they are essential parts of other fixtures. For example, the key to the front door of a house is a fixture. Also, fixtures that have been temporarily removed for servicing or repair remain constructively annexed to the real property. For example, a built-in dishwasher that's been sent to the repair shop is still considered to be a part of the house in which it is ordinarily installed.

Adaptation to the Property. If an unattached article was designed or specially adapted for use on a particular property, then it's probably a fixture. Examples include the pews in a church, and storm windows specifically made for a particular building.

Intention of the Annexor. The method of attachment was once regarded as the most important test in determining whether an item was a fixture, but over time courts decided that test was too rigid. It didn't allow for special situations where something permanently affixed would be more justly classified as personal property. Now the intention of the annexor is considered a more important test. Courts try to determine what the person who annexed the item to the property intended. Did she intend the item to become part of the realty or remain personal property? Each of the other tests is viewed as objective evidence of this intention. For instance, permanently embedding a birdbath in concrete indicates an intention to make the item a permanent fixture, while just setting a birdbath out in the yard does not.

Fig. 1.2 Fixture tests

- Method of attachment
- Adaptation to the property
- Relationship of the parties
- Intention of the annexor
- Agreement in writing

The acronym MARIA is often used as a memory aid for the fixture tests.

Relationship of the Parties. Intent is also indicated by the relationship between the parties: landlord/tenant, buyer/seller, borrower/lender. For example, it's generally assumed that a tenant who installs an item, such as new lighting, is doing so with the intention of removing it at the expiration of the lease. On the other hand, it's assumed that an owner making the same alteration is trying to improve the property and does not intend to remove the item. So an item that would be considered personal property if installed by a tenant might be considered a fixture if installed by an owner.

Items installed by a tenant so she can carry on a trade or business are called **trade fixtures**. Trade fixtures generally remain personal property and may be removed by the tenant unless there is a contrary provision in the lease, or unless the fixtures have become an integral part of the land or improvements. In the latter case, if the tenant wants to remove the fixtures, it is her responsibility to either restore the property to its original condition after removing them, or else compensate the landlord for any physical damage resulting from the removal. Trade fixtures that are not removed by the tenant become the property of the landlord.

Mobile Homes

The distinction between personal property and real property has special significance in relation to mobile homes, also called manufactured homes. A mobile home is mostly assembled in a factory, then transported to the property it will occupy. (This is in contrast to traditional houses that are built on the property they occupy, sometimes called site-built or stick-built homes.)

Mobile homes leave the factory as personal property but may become real property later on. As long as a mobile home is classified as personal property, a real estate broker may list and sell it only if it has been registered with the Department of Housing and Community Development. (Unregistered mobile homes are considered "new" and cannot be listed or sold by a real estate licensee who doesn't also have a mobile home dealer's license.) When a registered mobile home is sold, the real estate broker should make sure that the title and registration are delivered to the buyer, and that the Department of Housing and Community Development is notified of the transfer in writing within 10 calendar days.

To become real property, a mobile home must be permanently affixed to land. It must be installed on a foundation, the installation must be inspected and approved, a certificate of occupancy must be issued, and the vehicle registration must be canceled. The final step in the process is recording a document that identifies the property and the property owner and states that the mobile home has been affixed to the real property on a foundation system. (Recording is explained in Chapter 3.)

A mobile home can be installed on a foundation without becoming real property. It becomes real property only if all of the steps listed above are taken.

Once a mobile home has become real property, it's treated just like a site-built home. So an agent who lists or sells a mobile home and the land it's attached to must have a real estate license.

When a house attached to real property is purchased separately from the land so that it can be moved to another site, it's severed from the real property and becomes personal property. This is true whether it was originally a mobile home or site-built. Since the house is personal property, the sale is subject to sales tax. The house will become real property again when installed on its new site.

Land Description

When ownership of real property is transferred from one person to another, the legal documents used in the transaction must specify what piece of land is being conveyed. The section of a document that identifies the land is called the property description or the **legal description**.

It's essential for the description of the property to be clear and accurate. An ambiguous or uncertain description could make a contract or a deed invalid, and confusion over exactly what land was transferred could cause problems not only for the parties involved in the current transaction, but also for the parties in future transactions. To ensure accuracy, land is usually described using one of the three main methods of legal description:

- the metes and bounds method,
- the government survey method, or
- the recorded map method.

Metes and Bounds

The metes and bounds method describes a parcel by specifying the location of its boundaries. The boundaries are described by reference to three things:

- monuments, which may be natural objects such as rivers or trees, or man-made objects such as roads or survey markers;
- courses (directions), in the form of compass readings; and
- distances, measured in any convenient units of length.

Reading a Metes and Bounds Description. A metes and bounds description first specifies a **point of beginning**, which is a convenient and well-defined point on one

Fig. 1.3 Metes and bounds description

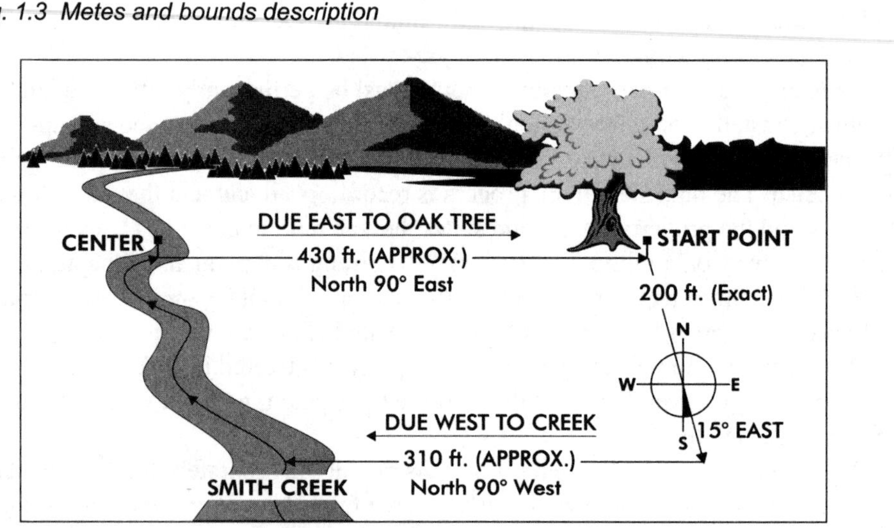

A tract of land, located in Fresno County and described as follows: Beginning at the old oak tree, thence south 15° east, 200 feet, thence north 90° west, 310 feet more or less to the centerline of Smith Creek, thence northwesterly along the centerline of Smith Creek to a point directly west of the old oak tree, thence north 90° east, 430 feet more or less to the point of beginning.

Fig. 1.4 Units of land measurement

UNITS OF MEASUREMENT FOR LAND	
UNITS OF AREA	1 Tract = 24 mi. × 24 mi. (576 sq. mi) = 16 townships 1 Township = 6 mi. × 6 mi. (36 sq. mi) = 36 sections 1 Section = 1 mi. × 1 mi. (1 sq. mi.) = 640 acres 1 Acre = 43,560 sq. ft. 1 Square Acre = 208.71 ft. × 208.71 feet
UNITS OF LENGTH	1 Mile = 5,280 ft. 1 Yard = 3 ft.

Note: To determine the area of partial sections, simply multiply the fraction of the section by 640. For example:

1 half section = ½ × 640 = 320 acres
1 quarter-section = ¼ × 640 = 160 acres
1 quarter-quarter-section = ¼ × ¼ × 640 = 40 acres

of the parcel's boundaries. A monument may be used as the point of beginning ("Beginning at the old oak tree," for example), or the point of beginning may be described by reference to a monument ("Beginning at a point 200 feet east of the northwest corner of the Sutters' barn," for example).

After establishing the point of beginning, the description then specifies a series of courses and distances. For example, "south 30 degrees east, 263.5 feet" is a course and distance.

By starting at the point of beginning and following the courses and distances given, a surveyor could walk along the parcel's boundary lines, all the way around and back to the point of beginning. A metes and bounds description must end up back at the point of beginning; otherwise, it wouldn't describe a completely enclosed tract of land.

Compass Bearings. The directions (courses) in metes and bounds descriptions are given in a peculiar fashion. A direction is described by reference to its deviation from either north or south, whichever is closer. Thus, northwest is written as north 45° west, since it's a deviation of 45° to the west of north. Similarly, south-southeast is written south 22½° east, since it's a deviation of 22½° to the east of south. Due east and due west are both written relative to north: north 90° east and north 90° west, respectively. (There are 360 degrees in a circle.)

Fig. 1.5 Compass bearings

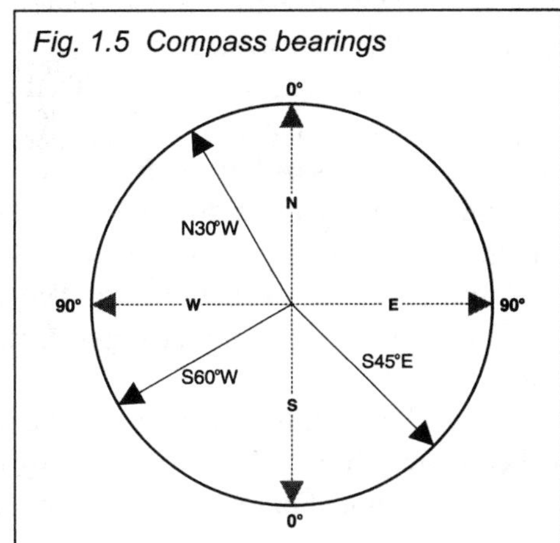

Resolving Discrepancies. To specify the direction or length of a boundary, monuments are sometimes used in conjunction with courses and distances, as in "northerly along the eastern edge of Front Street 100 feet" or "north, 100 feet more or less, to the centerline of Smith Creek."

If there's a discrepancy between a monument and a course or distance, the monument takes precedence. In the examples just given, the first boundary would be along the edge of Front Street, even if that edge does not run due north, and the second boundary would extend to the center of Smith Creek, even if the actual distance to that point is not 100 feet.

Discrepancies may also occur between other elements of a metes and bounds description. To resolve them, the following order of priority is used:

1. natural monuments,
2. man-made monuments,
3. courses,
4. distances,
5. names (e.g., "Smith Farm"),
6. areas (e.g., "40 acres").

In the case of a conflict between any two of these elements in a description, the one with higher priority prevails.

Metes and bounds descriptions tend to be lengthy, and they are often confusing. Furthermore, monuments don't always maintain their exact locations over the years. An actual survey of the property is usually necessary when dealing with a metes and bounds description.

Government Survey

In the government survey system, also called the rectangular survey system, land is described by reference to a grid of lines established by survey. (These are imaginary lines, like the lines of latitude and longitude on a globe.) This system of land description was established by the federal government after many eastern states had already been settled and described using the metes and bounds method. As a result, government survey descriptions are mainly used west of the Mississippi River.

The terminology used in the government survey system may seem confusing at first, and we recommend that you study the accompanying diagrams closely.

The system is made up of a series of large grids covering much of the United States. Each of these grids is composed of two sets of lines, one set running north/south, the other east/west. Each grid is identified by a **principal meridian**, which is the original north/south line established in that grid, and by a **base line**, which is the original east/west line. In California, there are three principal meridians: **Humboldt**, **Mt. Diablo**, and **San Bernardino**. Each has its own base line. (See Figure 1.6.)

Grid lines run parallel to the principal meridian and the base line at intervals of six miles. The east/west lines are called **township lines**, and they divide the land into rows or tiers called **township tiers**. The north/south lines, called **range lines**, divide the land into columns called **ranges**. Every fourth range line is a **guide meridian**. (See Figure 1.7.)

The area of land that is located at the intersection of a range and a township tier is called a **township**, and it is identified by its position relative to the principal meridian and base line. For example, the township that is located in the fourth tier north of

Fig. 1.6 Principal meridians and baselines

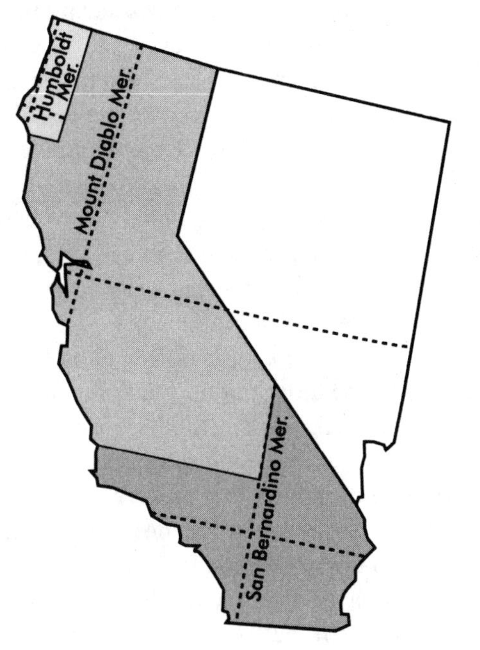

Fig. 1.7 East/west lines are township lines; north/south lines are range lines.

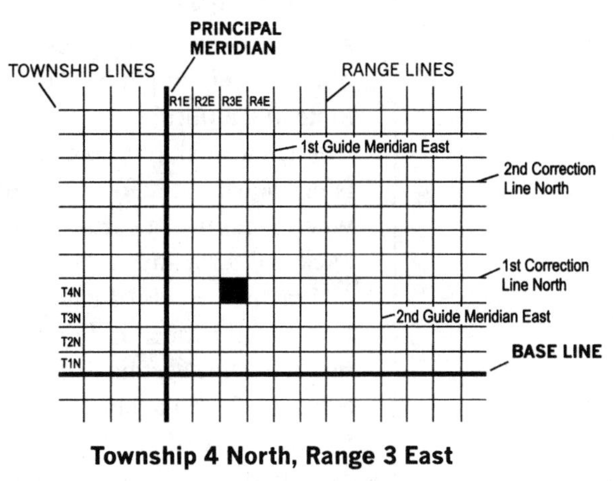

Fig. 1.8 A township contains 36 sections.

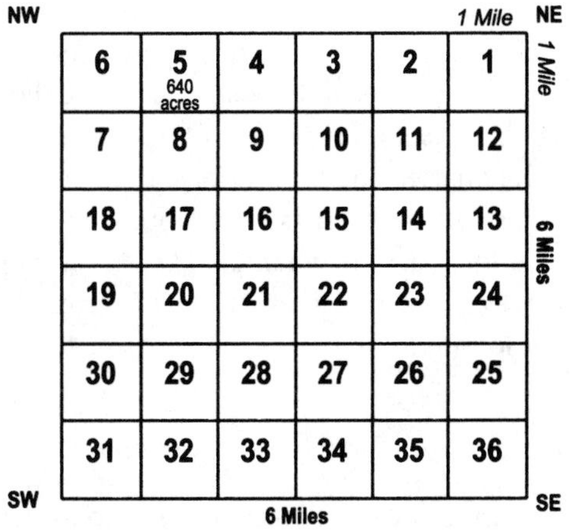

NW — 1 Mile — NE

6	5 640 acres	4	3	2	1
7	8	9	10	11	12
18	17	16	15	14	13
19	20	21	22	23	24
30	29	28	27	26	25
31	32	33	34	35	36

SW — 6 Miles — SE

1 Mile

6 Miles

Fig. 1.9 A section can be divided into smaller parcels.

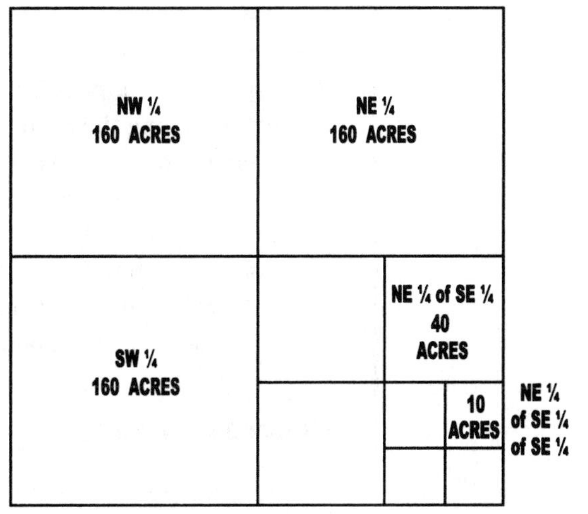

the base line and the third range east of the principal meridian is called "Township 4 North Range 3 East." (See Figure 1.7.) This is often abbreviated "T4N, R3E."

Grid systems are identical across the country, so a government survey description must include the name of the principal meridian that's being used as a reference. (Since each principal meridian has its own base line, it isn't necessary to specify the base line.) It's also a good practice to mention the county and state where the land is situated, to avoid any possible confusion. Thus, for example, a complete description of a township might be T4N, R3E of the Mt. Diablo Meridian, Sacramento County, State of California.

Each township measures 36 square miles and contains 36 sections. Each section is one square mile, or 640 acres. The sections are numbered in a special way, starting with the northeast corner and moving west, then down a row and eastward, snaking back and forth and ending with the southeast corner. (See Figure 1.8.)

Smaller parcels of land can be identified by reference to sections and partial sections, as illustrated in Figure 1.9. For example, the description for a five-acre parcel might be "the east half of the NW quarter of the NE quarter of the SW quarter of Section 12, Township 4 North, Range 3 East of the Mt. Diablo Meridian, Sacramento County, State of California." To locate a parcel of property on a government survey map, first find the section in question, then start at the end of the description and work backwards through the partial sections to the beginning. In other words, find Section 12, then the southwest quarter of Section 12, then the northeast quarter of that southwest quarter, then the northwest quarter of that northeast quarter, and finally the east half of that northwest quarter.

Even in an area where land is described using the government survey method, it may be necessary to use the metes and bounds method in conjunction with it. This is true, for example, when the parcel to be described is small or non-rectangular. The government survey method is used to identify the general location of the parcel, but then the metes and bounds method is used to specify the parcel's precise location and boundaries.

Government Lots. A government lot is a section of land of irregular shape or size that is referred to by a lot number. Because of the curvature of the earth, range lines converge, so it's impossible to keep all sections exactly one mile square. As a result, the sections along the north and west boundaries of each township are irregular in size. The quarter sections along the north and west boundaries of these sections are used to take up the excess or shortage. The quarter-quarter sections, then, along the north and west boundaries of a township are given government lot numbers.

Another situation in which government lots occur is when a body of water or some other obstacle makes it impossible to survey a square-mile section. The irregularly shaped sections are assigned government lot numbers.

Recorded Map

The recorded map method of land description is sometimes referred to as the lot and block method, or the maps and plats system. It was developed to make legal descriptions of subdivided land more convenient, and it is now the method of description used for most property in urban areas.

When land is subdivided, a surveyor uses the metes and bounds method or the government survey method (or both) to map out lots and blocks (groups of lots surrounded by streets) on a subdivision map called a **plat** or **plat map**. The plat is then recorded in the county where the land is located. (See Chapter 3 for a discussion of the recording system.)

Once a plat has been recorded, a reference to one of the lot numbers on the specified plat is a sufficient legal description of the lot. Since a precise description of the lot's location and boundaries is already on file in the county recorder's office, that description may be incorporated into any legal document simply by stating the lot number, the block number (if any), and the name of the subdivision.

> **Example:** The recorded map description for a particular single-family property is Lot 2, Block 4 of Tract 455, in the City of Fresno, County of Fresno, State of California, as per map recorded in Book 25, page 92, of maps, in the office of the recorder of said county. By looking up the plat for this subdivision in the county records, you could find the precise location and dimensions of this parcel.

Plat maps frequently contain a considerable amount of useful information beyond a detailed description of lot boundaries. For example, they may include area measurements, the location and dimensions of any easements, the location of survey markers, and a list of use restrictions that apply to the land. (Note, however, that studying a plat map is not a substitute for a title search. See Chapter 3.)

Other Methods of Land Description

There are other ways of describing land besides the three major methods of description we've discussed. When an adequate description of property is already a matter of public record—contained in a recorded document—then a simple reference to that earlier document serves as an adequate property description in a new document. (For example, "All that land described in the grant deed recorded under

Fig. 1.10 Plat map

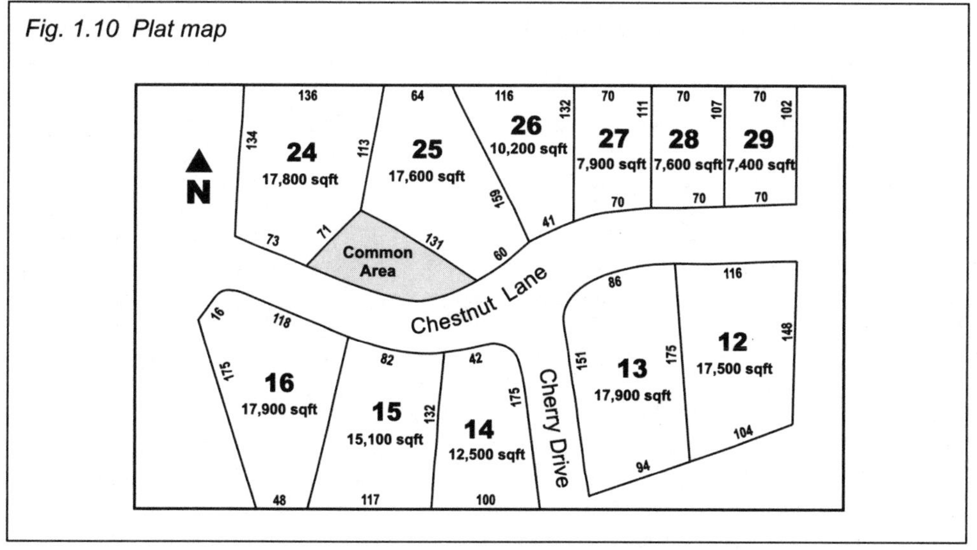

recording number 92122401503 in Orange County, California.") References to records of survey or tax assessor's maps may be used, as long as those records or maps have been recorded in the county where the property is located.

Also, generalized descriptions such as "all my lands" or "Smith Farm" can be adequate, as long as they make it possible to determine exactly what property is being described. But it's always best to use the least ambiguous description possible, to prevent future problems. This is especially true if the property owner has several properties in one area.

It should be noted that a property's street address is usually not an adequate legal description. It's also not a good idea to use the property description shown on a property tax bill.

Air Lots. Not every parcel of real property can be described simply in terms of its position on the face of the earth. Descriptions of some forms of real property must also indicate their elevation above the ground. For example, a unit on an upper story of a condominium building occupies a specific parcel of airspace, referred to as an air lot. The underlying legal description of the air lot would include its elevation.

A position above the ground is described by reference to an established plane of elevation, called a **datum**. Most large cities have their own official datum, and frequently subsidiary reference points, called **bench marks**, are also established. A bench mark is a point whose position relative to a datum has been accurately measured. A surveyor can use the bench mark as a reference when that's more convenient than using the datum.

 Chapter Summary

1. There are two types of property: real property and personal property. Real property is the land, anything affixed to the land, and anything appurtenant to the land. Movable items, such as furniture, are usually personal property.

2. Appurtenances to land include air rights, water rights, mineral rights, oil and gas rights, and support rights.

3. Attachments may be natural (growing plants) or man-made (fixtures). Personal property may be converted into real property through annexation, and an attachment may be converted back into personal property through severance.

4. In the absence of a written agreement, the tests used to distinguish fixtures from personal property include the method of attachment, the adaptation of the item to the real property, the intention of the annexor, and the relationship of the parties.

5. When real property is transferred from one owner to another, the legal documents must include an adequate description of the property. There are three major methods of legal description: metes and bounds, government survey, and recorded map.

Key Terms

Real property—Land, attachments, and appurtenances.

Personal property—Anything that is not real property. Its main characteristic is movability.

Appurtenance—A right incidental to the land that is transferred with it.

Riparian rights—The water rights of a landowner whose land borders on a stream or other surface water. Riparian rights allow only reasonable use of the water.

Littoral property—Land bordered by a stationary body of water, such as a lake or a pond.

Appropriative rights—Water rights established by obtaining a government permit, and not based on ownership of land beside a body of water.

Lateral support—The support that a piece of land receives from the surrounding land.

Subjacent support—The support that a piece of land receives from the underlying earth.

Emblements—Crops, such as wheat, produced annually through the labor of the cultivator.

Trade fixtures—Personal property attached to real property by a tenant for use in his trade or business. Trade fixtures are removable by the tenant.

Metes and bounds—A system of land description in which the boundaries of a parcel of land are described by reference to monuments, courses, and distances.

Monument—A visible marker (natural or artificial) used in a survey or a metes and bounds description to establish the boundaries of a piece of property.

Point of beginning—The starting point in a metes and bounds description; a monument or a point described by reference to a monument.

Course—In a metes and bounds description, a direction, stated in terms of a compass bearing.

Distance—In a metes and bounds description, the length of a boundary, measured in any convenient unit of length.

Government survey—A system of land description in which the land is divided into squares called townships, and each township is, in turn, divided into 36 sections, each one square mile or 640 acres.

Principal meridian—In the government survey system, the main north-south line in a particular grid, used as the starting point in numbering the ranges and township tiers. California's principal meridians are the Humboldt, Mt. Diablo, and San Bernardino meridians.

Range—In the government survey system, a strip of land six miles wide, running north and south.

Township—The intersection of a range and a township tier in the government survey system. It is a parcel of land that is six miles square and contains 36 sections.

Section—One square mile of land, containing 640 acres. There are 36 sections in a township.

Government lot—In the government survey system, a parcel of land that is not a regular section.

Recorded map—The system of description used for subdivided land. The properties within a subdivision are assigned lot numbers on a plat map, which is then recorded. The location and dimensions of a particular lot can be determined by consulting the recorded plat.

Air lot—A parcel of property above the surface of the earth, not containing any land. For example, a condominium unit on the third floor of the building occupies an air lot.

Chapter Quiz

1. Real property is equivalent to:
   a) land
   b) personal property
   c) land, attachments, and appurtenances
   d) land and water

2. The most important consideration in determining whether an article is a fixture is:
   a) physical attachment
   b) the annexor's intention
   c) adaptation of the article to the realty
   d) the intended use of the article

3. Articles installed in or on realty by tenants for use in a business are called:
   a) personalty
   b) trade fixtures
   c) emblements
   d) easements

4. A right that goes with or pertains to real property is called:
   a) an attachment
   b) an appurtenance
   c) personal property
   d) a fixture

5. A landowner's rights regarding water in a stream flowing through her land are called:
   a) riparian rights
   b) littoral rights
   c) appropriative rights
   d) easement rights

6. Minerals become personal property when they are:
   a) surveyed
   b) extracted from the land
   c) taken to a refinery
   d) claimed

7. Rights to oil and gas are determined by:
   a) the rule of capture
   b) offset wells
   c) the Bureau of Land Management
   d) the Department of the Interior

8. Whether land borders on a lake or stream is irrelevant under the system of:
   a) riparian rights
   b) capture rights
   c) littoral rights
   d) appropriative rights

9. Ted's property is damaged by sinkholes caused by old coal mining tunnels beneath his land. The rights implicated in this situation are:
   a) riparian rights
   b) subjacent support rights
   c) proximate support rights
   d) lateral support rights

10. Which of the following is most likely to be considered part of the real property?
    a) Piano
    b) Dining room table
    c) Living room drapes
    d) Kitchen sink

11. Which of the following benefits tenant farmers?
    a) Doctrine of emblements
    b) Rule of capture
    c) Overlying rights
    d) Method of attachment test

12. A section of a township contains the following number of acres:
    a) 360
    b) 580
    c) 640
    d) 560

13. A parcel that measures $^1/_4$ of a mile by $^1/_4$ of a mile is:
    a) $^1/_4$ of a section
    b) $^1/_8$ of a section
    c) $^1/_{16}$ of a section
    d) $^1/_{36}$ of a section

14. The distance between the east and west boundary lines of a township is:
    a) one mile
    b) two miles
    c) six miles
    d) ten miles

15. A township contains 36 sections that are numbered consecutively 1 through 36. The last section in the township is located in the:
    a) southeast corner
    b) southwest corner
    c) northeast corner
    d) northwest corner

Answer Key

1. c) Real property is made up of land, everything that is attached to the land (for example, fixtures), and everything that is appurtenant to the land (for example, water rights).

2. b) The intention of the party who attached the item is the primary consideration in determining whether it is a fixture. The other tests provide evidence of the party's intention.

3. b) An article installed by a tenant for use in a business is called a trade fixture, and the tenant can remove it at the end of the tenancy.

4. b) An appurtenance is a right or interest that goes with the property. Riparian rights are an example.

5. a) Riparian rights include the right to reasonable use of the water that flows through a property owner's land.

6. b) When minerals are extracted from the land, they become personal property.

7. a) The rule of capture determines ownership of oil and gas. This rule provides that the landowner owns all the oil and gas removed from a well on his property, even if the oil or gas was originally beneath someone else's property.

8. d) To obtain a water appropriation permit, it is not necessary to own riparian or littoral land.

9. b) Subjacent support rights involve support from the underlying earth.

10. d) Unlike the other items listed, the kitchen sink is a fixture, and therefore part of the real property.

11. a) The doctrine of emblements allows a tenant farmer to return and harvest crops after the lease expires.

12. c) In the government survey system of land description, one section contains 640 acres.

13. c) A section is one mile on each side, a quarter section is ½ mile on each side, and a quarter of a quarter section is ¼ mile on each side.

14. c) A township measures six miles by six miles.

15. a) Section 36 is always in the southeast corner of a township.

Chapter 2

Estates in Land and Methods of Holding Title

I. Estates in Land
  A. Freehold estates
    1. Fee simple absolute
    2. Fee simple defeasible
    3. Life estate
  B. Leasehold estates
    1. Term tenancy
    2. Periodic tenancy
    3. Tenancy at will
    4. Tenancy at sufferance

II. Methods of Holding Title
  A. Ownership in severalty
  B. Concurrent ownership
    1. Tenancy in common
    2. Joint tenancy
    3. Community property
  C. Forms of business ownership
    1. Partnerships
    2. Corporations
    3. Limited liability companies
    4. Joint ventures
    5. Trusts
  D. Condominiums and cooperatives

Chapter Overview

Real property ownership can take many different forms. An owner typically has full title to the property and full possession of it, but that isn't necessarily the case. An owner may have a more limited interest instead of full title, or may allow someone else (a tenant) to take possession of the property without taking title. In addition, a property may be owned by more than one person at the same time, which is called concurrent ownership. The first part of this chapter explains the various types of ownership interests, and also the types of interests that tenants may have. The second part of this chapter explains concurrent ownership and the different ways co-owners may hold title.

Estates in Land

In real property law, the word **estate** refers to an interest in land that is or may become **possessory**. In other words, someone has, or may have in the future, the right to possess the property—the right to exclusively occupy and use it. An estate may also be called a tenancy.

The different types of estates are distinguished by two features: the duration (how long the estate holder has the right of possession); and the time of possession (whether the estate holder has the right to possess the property right now, or not until sometime in the future).

It's important to note that while all estates are interests in land, not every interest in land is an estate. Interests that are not estates are called nonpossessory interests. For example, a mortgage gives a lender a financial interest in the property (a lien), but this interest is not an estate, because it is not a possessory interest. Nonpossessory interests are covered in Chapter 4.

Estates fall into two categories:

1. freehold estates, and
2. leasehold (less-than-freehold) estates.

A **freehold estate** is an interest in real property that has an indeterminable (not fixed or certain) duration. The holder of such an estate is usually referred to as an owner. All other possessory interests are leasehold (less-than-freehold) estates. A **leasehold estate** has a limited duration (a one-year lease is an example). The holder of a leasehold estate is referred to as a tenant; a tenant has possession of the property but not title.

Both types of estates can exist in the same piece of property at the same time. For instance, the owner of a freehold estate may lease the property to a tenant, who then has a leasehold estate in the same property. (When two or more parties have interests in the same property, their mutual relationship is referred to as "privity.")

Freehold Estates

The freehold estate got its name back in the Middle Ages—it originally referred to the holdings of a freeman under the English feudal system. Freehold estates can be subdivided into fee simple estates and life estates. There are two basic types of fee simple estates: the fee simple absolute and the fee simple defeasible.

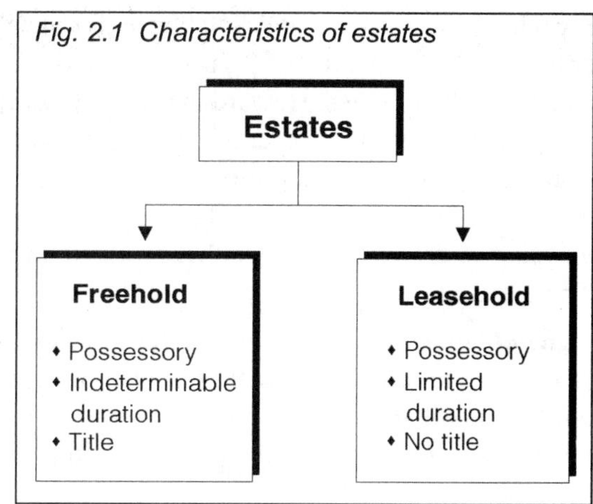

Fig. 2.1 Characteristics of estates

Fee Simple Absolute. The fee simple absolute estate is often just called the fee simple, or the fee. (The term "absolute" is used only to distinguish it from a fee simple defeasible, discussed below.) The fee simple absolute is the greatest estate that can exist in land, the highest and most complete form of ownership. It is of potentially infinite duration and represents the whole "bundle of rights."

A fee simple estate is freely transferable from one owner to another. It is also inheritable by the owner's heirs when she dies, so it is sometimes referred to as the **estate of inheritance**. A fee simple estate has no set termination point, and theoretically can be owned forever by the titleholder and her heirs. When a fee simple owner transfers title by deed, it is presumed that the grantee (the new owner) receives a fee simple absolute estate, unless the deed includes language that indicates an intent to confer a lesser estate (such as a life estate, which will be discussed shortly).

Fee Simple Defeasible. A fee simple estate may be qualified when it is transferred from one owner to another. For example, in a deed, the grantor may specify that the grantee's estate will continue only as long as a certain condition is met ("on the condition that the property is used as low-cost housing"), or until a certain event occurs ("until Aunt Jolene has a daughter"). If the requirement is not met, or if the event occurs, the new owner could forfeit title to the property. This type of qualified estate is referred to as a fee simple defeasible. The owner of a fee simple defeasible holds the same interest as the owner of a fee simple absolute, except that the defeasible interest is subject to termination.

Historically, certain types of fee simple defeasible estates would terminate automatically if the condition stated in the deed was not met. Those were abolished in California, however. The only type of defeasible estate now recognized in California is called a fee simple subject to a condition subsequent (also called a **conditional fee**). This estate does not end automatically when the condition is breached. Instead, the grantor must file a lawsuit to get the property back.

Life Estate. An estate for life is a freehold estate whose duration is limited to the lifetime of a specified person or persons.

> **Example:** Noel gives a parcel of property to Beatrice for her lifetime, calling for a reversion of title to Noel upon Beatrice's death. Beatrice is the life tenant (holder of the life estate), and the duration of the life estate is measured by her lifetime.

The measuring life may be that of the life tenant (as in the example above, where Beatrice's life is the measuring life) or it may be the life of another person. If it is for the life of another person, it may be called a life estate *pur autre vie* (which is Old

French for "for another life"). Suppose, for example, Catalina gives a parcel of property to Howard for the life of Charlie. Howard has a life estate *pur autre vie* which will end when Charlie dies. Howard is the life tenant; Charlie's life is the measuring life.

While the fee simple estate is a perpetual estate, the life estate is a lesser estate because it is limited in duration. In granting a life estate, a fee simple owner transfers only part of what he owns, so there must be something left over after the life estate terminates. What remains is either an estate in reversion or an estate in remainder. These are known as future interests.

Estate in Reversion. If the grantor stipulates that the property will revert back to her at the end of the measuring life, the grantor holds an estate in reversion. She has a future possessory interest in the property. Upon the death of the person whose life the estate is measured by, the property will revert to the **reversioner**—to the grantor or her heirs.

Estate in Remainder. If the grantor stipulates that the property should go to a person other than the grantor at the end of the measuring life, that other person has an estate in remainder and is called the **remainderman**. The only difference between reversion and remainder estates is that the former is held by the grantor and the latter by a third party. (If the grantor doesn't name a remainderman, an estate in reversion is created.) The interest that will pass to the designated party when the life estate ends is a fee simple estate.

Example: Ann deeds her property "to Barbara for life, and then to Colin." Colin is the remainderman, and he will own the property in fee simple when Barbara dies and the life estate ends.

If Ann had simply deeded the property "to Barbara for life," without naming a remainderman, then fee simple ownership of the property would revert to Ann (or, if Ann has died in the meantime, to Ann's heirs) upon Barbara's death.

Rights and Duties of Life Tenants. A life tenant has the same rights as a fee simple owner, including the right to profits or rents, and the right to lease or mortgage the property. And a life tenant also has the same duties as a fee simple owner: to pay taxes, assessments, and liens.

Because someone else has a future interest in the property, a life tenant must not commit **waste**, which means that the life tenant must not engage in acts that will permanently damage the property and harm the interests of the reversionary or remainder estate. Mismanaging or using up the property's resources (cutting down all of the trees on timberland, for example) would be a form of waste.

A life tenant may transfer or lease his interest in the property. But keep in mind that a life tenant can give, sell, or lease only what he has. In other words, a lease given by a life tenant will terminate upon the death of the person designated as the measuring life. The lease doesn't have to be honored by the remainderman. Similarly, a mortgage on a life estate loses its status as a valid lien when the person designated as the measuring life dies, ending the life estate. However, if a life tenant leases or mortgages the property and later dies, but the life estate continues because the person designated as the measuring life is still alive, the lease or mortgage remains in force.

Leasehold Estates

Less-than-freehold estates are more commonly called **leasehold estates**. (In certain legal contexts, they're sometimes called "chattels real.") The holder of a leasehold estate is the tenant, who does not own the property, but rather has a right to exclusive possession of the property for a specified period.

The leasehold is created with a **lease**. The parties to a lease are the **landlord** (the **lessor**), who is the owner of the property, and the **tenant** (the **lessee**), the party with the right of possession. The lease creates the relationship of landlord and tenant. It grants the tenant the right of exclusive possession, with a reversion of the possessory rights to the landlord at the end of the rental period.

The lease is a contract and its provisions are interpreted under contract law. We'll discuss lease contracts in more detail in Chapter 7. For now, we'll simply describe the four types of leasehold estates. They are:

1. term tenancy (estate for years),
2. periodic tenancy,
3. tenancy at will, and
4. tenancy at sufferance.

Term Tenancy. The term tenancy, or estate for years, is a tenancy for a fixed term. The name "estate for years" is misleading, in the sense that the duration need not be for a year or a period of years; it just has to be for some fixed term.

> **Example:** Bob rents a cabin in the mountains from Clark for a period from June 1 through September 15. Bob has a term tenancy because the rental term is fixed.

A term tenancy can be created only by express agreement. It terminates automatically when the agreed term expires; neither party has to give notice of termination. If either the landlord or the tenant wants to terminate a term tenancy before the end of the lease period, he or she may do so only if the other party consents. Termination of a lease by mutual consent is called **surrender**.

Unless the lease includes a no-assignment clause, a term tenancy is assignable—that is, the tenant can assign her interest to another person.

Fig. 2.2 Types of estates

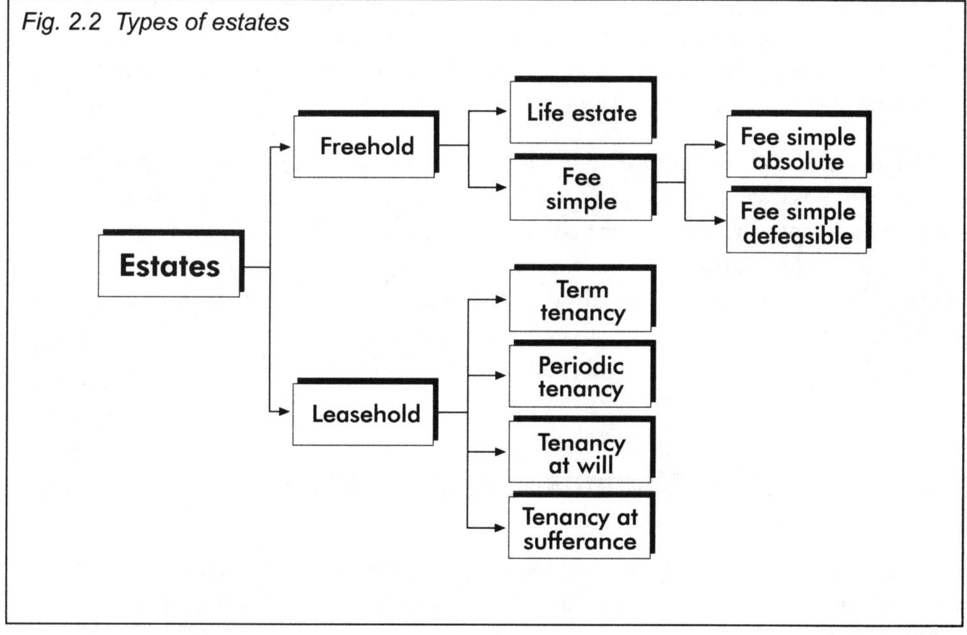

Periodic Tenancy. A periodic tenancy, sometimes called a periodic estate, has no fixed termination date. It lasts for a specific period (for example, one year, one month, or one week) and continues for successive similar periods (another year, month, or week) until either party gives the other proper notice of termination. A month-to-month tenancy is the most common example.

Unlike a term tenancy, which terminates automatically at the end of the term, a periodic tenancy automatically renews itself at the end of each period, unless one of the parties gives notice. Failure to give proper notice of termination results in the automatic extension of the lease for an additional period. (We'll discuss the amount of notice required to terminate a periodic tenancy in Chapter 7.)

Like a term tenancy, a periodic tenancy is assignable unless assignment is prohibited by the terms of the lease agreement.

Tenancy at Will. In a tenancy at will, the tenant has possession of the property with the landlord's consent for an indefinite period. A tenancy at will is created by mutual agreement between the parties and can be terminated at will by either one.

A tenancy at will often arises when a lease has expired and the parties are in the process of negotiating the terms of a new lease. Since the term of the tenancy at will is indefinite, it will continue until either party gives proper notice of termination. In California, 30 days' notice is required to terminate a tenancy at will.

Unlike a term tenancy or a periodic tenancy, which are not affected by the death of one of the parties, a tenancy at will expires if either the landlord or the tenant dies. Also, a tenancy at will is not assignable.

Tenancy at Sufferance. The tenancy at sufferance is the lowest type of estate; in fact, though it's sometimes called an "estate at sufferance," technically it isn't an estate at all. A tenancy at sufferance arises when a tenant who came into possession of the property lawfully, under a valid lease, stays on after the lease has expired without the consent of the landlord. A tenant at sufferance is also called a holdover tenant.

> **Example:** Tenant Joe has a one-year lease with Landlord Sam. At the end of the term, Joe refuses to move out. Joe initially obtained possession of the property legally (under a valid lease), but he is remaining on the property without Sam's consent. Joe is a tenant at sufferance, or holdover tenant.

Tenancy at sufferance is essentially a way of distinguishing between someone who entered into possession of the property legally, but no longer has a right to possession, and a trespasser, who never had permission to enter the land in the first place. Because a tenant at sufferance does not hold an estate (a possessory interest in the property), the landlord is not required to give the tenant notice of termination. Even so, the tenant at sufferance cannot simply be forced off the property; the landlord is required to follow the proper legal procedures for eviction.

Methods of Holding Title

Title to real property may be held by one person, which is called ownership in severalty, or it may be held by two or more persons at the same time, which is called concurrent ownership.

Ownership in Severalty

When one person holds title to property individually, the property is owned **in severalty**. The term is derived from the word "sever," which means to keep separate or apart. A sole owner is free to dispose of the property at will. Real property may be owned in severalty by a natural person (a human being) or an artificial person (such as a corporation, a city, or a state).

Concurrent Ownership

Concurrent ownership (also called **co-ownership**) exists when two or more people share title to a piece of property simultaneously. There are several forms of concurrent ownership, each with distinctive legal characteristics. Under California law, three forms of concurrent ownership are recognized:

- tenancy in common,
- joint tenancy, and
- community property.

Tenancy in Common. Tenancy in common is the most basic form of concurrent ownership. In a tenancy in common, two or more individuals each have an **undivided interest** in a single piece of property. This means that each tenant in common has a right to share possession of the whole property, not just a specified part of it. This is referred to as unity of possession.

Tenants in common may have equal or unequal interests. For example, if three people own property as tenants in common, they might each have a one-third interest in the property, or one of them might have a one-half interest and each of the other two a one-quarter interest. But no matter how small a tenant in common's ownership interest is, he is still entitled to share possession of the whole property.

A tenant in common may deed his interest to someone else, without obtaining the consent of the other co-tenants. A tenant in common may also mortgage his interest without the others' consent. At death, a tenant in common's interest is transferred according to the terms of his will, or to his legal heirs.

Creating a Tenancy in Common. A tenancy in common is created when a deed specifies that the grantees are taking title to the property as tenants in common. Also, if a deed transferring property to two or more unmarried individuals doesn't indicate how they are taking title, they take title as tenants in common. In that situation, tenancy in common is the default. (If the grantees are a married couple, the default is community property, which we'll discuss shortly.) Unless the deed that creates a tenancy in common states each co-tenant's fractional interest, the law presumes that the interests are equal.

Termination of a Tenancy in Common. A tenancy in common may be terminated by a **partition suit**, a legal action that divides the interests in the property and destroys the unity of possession. If possible, a court will actually divide the property into separate parcels. If a fair physical division isn't possible, the court will order the property to be sold and the proceeds divided among the former co-tenants in accordance with their fractional interests.

Fig. 2.3 Tenancy in common vs. joint tenancy: death of a co-owner

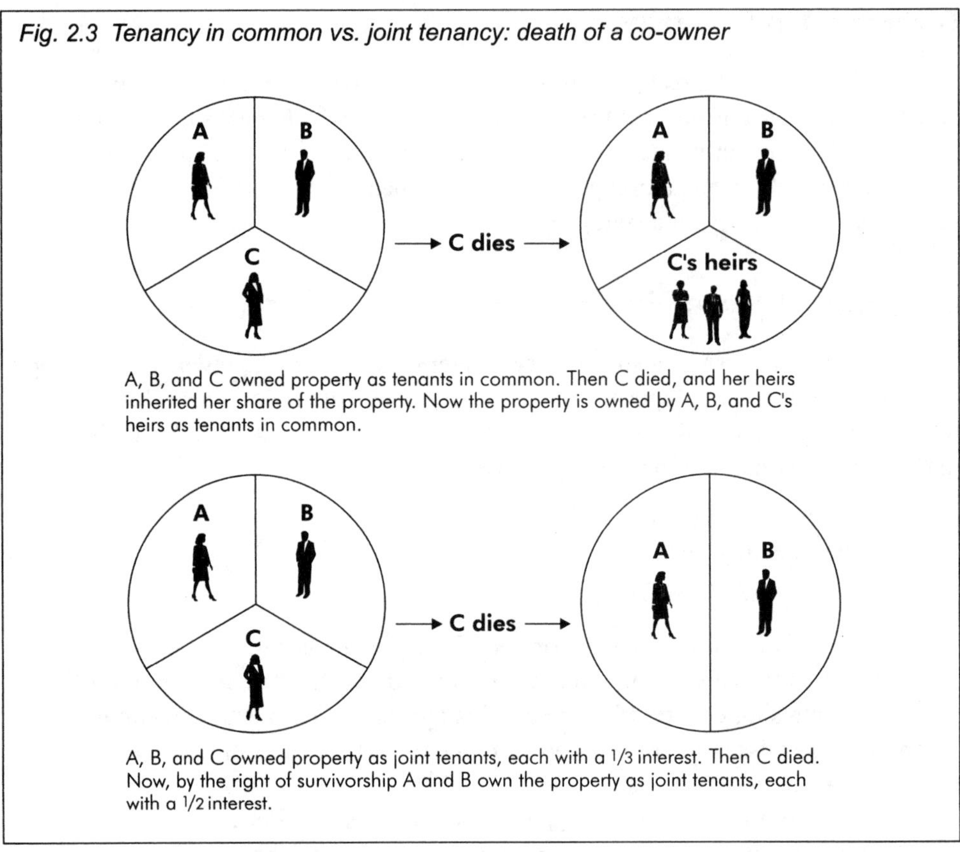

A, B, and C owned property as tenants in common. Then C died, and her heirs inherited her share of the property. Now the property is owned by A, B, and C's heirs as tenants in common.

A, B, and C owned property as joint tenants, each with a 1/3 interest. Then C died. Now, by the right of survivorship A and B own the property as joint tenants, each with a 1/2 interest.

Joint Tenancy. The second form of concurrent ownership is joint tenancy. In a joint tenancy, two or more individuals are joint and equal owners of the property. The key feature that distinguishes joint tenancy from tenancy in common is the **right of survivorship**: if one of the joint tenants dies, her interest passes automatically, by operation of law, to the other joint tenant(s). (See Figure 2.3.)

Creating a Joint Tenancy. To create a joint tenancy, the "four unities of title" must exist. These unities are:

- unity of interest,
- unity of title,
- unity of time, and
- unity of possession.

These four unities signify that each joint tenant has an equal interest in the property (unity of interest), that each received title through the same deed or will (unity of title), which was executed and delivered at a single time (unity of time), and that each is entitled to undivided possession of the property (unity of possession). If any one of these unities does not exist when the tenancy is created, a joint tenancy is not established.

Since title passes directly to the other joint tenant(s) upon the death of one joint tenant (because of the right of survivorship), property held in joint tenancy can't be willed. The heirs of a deceased joint tenant have no interest in the joint tenancy property.

Example: Jim, Sue, and Bill own property as joint tenants. Jim dies. Sue and Bill now own the entire property fifty-fifty. Jim's heirs cannot make any legal claim to the property. On his death, it ceased to be a part of his estate. Accordingly, the property is not subject to probate and could not have been willed by Jim.

Avoiding the delay and cost of probate proceedings (see Chapter 3) is one of the primary advantages of joint tenancy. Also, the survivors hold the property free from the claims of the deceased tenant's creditors and from any liens against his interest. The main disadvantage is that a joint tenant gives up the right to dispose of his property by will.

Termination of a Joint Tenancy. Like a tenancy in common, a joint tenancy can be terminated through a partition suit. But a joint tenancy also terminates automatically if any one of the four unities is destroyed. A joint tenant is free to convey her interest in the property to someone else. However, a conveyance destroys the unities of time and title. This terminates the joint tenancy with respect to the ownership of the conveying joint tenant.

Example: Aaron, Bob, and Carrie own a piece of property as joint tenants. If Aaron conveys his interest to Alice, that terminates the joint tenancy with respect to that one-third interest. Since Alice didn't receive title through the same deed or at the same time as Bob and Carrie, Alice can't be a joint tenant. Bob and Carrie are still joint tenants in relation to one another, but Alice holds title as a tenant in common.

However, if a joint tenant executes a mortgage against her interest, that doesn't break the unity of title. The joint tenancy remains intact and valid.

Community Property. The community property system of ownership is of Spanish origin; for historical reasons, it is used in several western states, including California. In those states, all the property owned by a married couple is classified either as the separate property of one spouse or as the community property of both spouses.

A spouse's separate property is the property he or she owned before the marriage, and any property he or she acquires during the marriage by inheritance, will, or gift. All other property each spouse acquires during the marriage is community property. For example, the wages earned by either spouse during the marriage are community property, and so is any property purchased with those wages. Each spouse has an undivided one-half interest in all of the community property.

The separate property of either spouse is free from the interests and claims of the other spouse; it may be transferred or encumbered without the approval or interference of the other spouse. A conveyance or encumbrance of community real property, however, requires the approval of both spouses. (Under California law, spousal approval isn't required for the transfer of community personal property, unless it's clothing, household furnishings, or a personal property residence, such as a mobile home or a live-aboard boat.)

When a married person dies, his or her separate property and a one-half interest in the community property are distributed according to the terms of his or her will. The other one-half interest in the community property belongs to the surviving spouse. (If no will exists, the property is distributed according to the rules of intestate succession. See Chapter 3.)

Since 2001, California law has allowed married couples to hold property as **community property with right of survivorship.** As in a joint tenancy, the right of survivorship means that title passes directly to the surviving spouse, rather than according to the terms of the will. This prevents a married person from willing his or her half interest in the community property to someone other than the spouse. Community property with right of survivorship offers certain tax benefits over a joint tenancy.

In 2005, California's community property laws were extended to apply to registered domestic partners as well as married couples. Domestic partners may now hold title to property as community property, or as community property with right of survivorship.

In some states that do not have a community property system, married couples may hold title to property as tenants by the entirety. A **tenancy by the entirety** resembles a joint tenancy, but is limited to married couples. Tenancy by the entirety is not recognized in community property states such as California, and it has been abolished in a number of other states as well.

Forms of Business Ownership

The discussion so far has focused on ownership by individuals, whether in severalty or concurrently. Real property can also be owned by business entities.

A **syndicate** is a group of individuals who come together and pool their resources to carry out an enterprise. The syndicate, as such, isn't a recognized legal entity. A syndicate may be a business association or a nonprofit organization, and it may be organized as a:

- partnership,
- corporation,
- limited liability company,
- joint venture, or
- trust.

The parties who create a syndicate usually decide which form of organization to use based on tax consequences and other considerations, such as the members' personal liability for the syndicate's debts. The form of organization affects how a syndicate holds title to real property.

Partnerships. A partnership is generally defined as an association of two or more persons to carry on, as co-owners, a business for profit. There are two types of partnerships: general and limited.

General Partnerships. A **general partnership** is formed by contract. Although the contract isn't legally required to be in writing, it's advisable to spell out all the terms in a written agreement. In California, if the agreement isn't in writing, the partnership will be governed by the terms of the Uniform Partnership Act. If the agreement is in writing, the terms of the written agreement will govern, instead of the Uniform Partnership Act.

The partners in a general partnership all share in the profits and management of the partnership. Unless otherwise agreed, each one has an equal share of the profits and losses, and each has an equal voice in management and control of the business.

Each general partner has **unlimited liability**, which means that a partner can be held personally liable for the debts of the partnership. In other words, if the business is unable to pay its debts, its creditors can collect the money owed from an individual partner's personal assets.

Each partner is both a principal for and an agent of the general partnership for business purposes. Thus, the authorized acts of one partner (including the execution of legal documents) are binding on the partnership. A partnership is a fiduciary relationship; all the partners have a duty to act with utmost good faith toward one another. (See Chapter 8 for a discussion of agency and fiduciary relationships.)

In general, property acquired for the partnership's business is **partnership property**. Title to partnership property may be held in the partnership's name. Alternatively, it may be held in the name of one or more of the partners, as long as the deed makes reference to the partnership.

Unless otherwise agreed, each partner has an equal right to possess and use all partnership property for partnership purposes. However, a partner is not a co-owner of the partnership property and has no transferable interest in it. Partnership property is not subject to the claims of creditors of individual partners; it can be reached only by creditors of the partnership.

When title to partnership property is held in the partnership's name, it must also be conveyed in the partnership's name. Since each partner is an agent for the partnership, any authorized partner can sign the deed.

Limited Partnerships. Many real estate syndicates in California are limited partnerships. A limited partnership has one or more general partners and one or more limited partners. Limited partnerships must conform to the statutory requirements of the California Uniform Limited Partnership Act.

The general partners in a limited partnership manage the business and have unlimited liability for the partnership's debts and obligations. By contrast, the limited partners have limited liability (that is, they cannot be held personally liable for the partnership's debts and obligations). The limited partners may advise the general partners, but they typically do not participate in management or control of the business. A limited partner who does participate in control of the business can be liable to the same extent as a general partner to someone who mistakenly but reasonably believes that the limited partner is a general partner.

Corporations. A corporation is owned by its shareholders, individuals who purchase shares of stock in the company as an investment. But the corporation is legally a separate entity from its shareholders. In the eyes of the law, a corporation is an "artificial person." It can enter into contracts, own property, and incur debts and liabilities, just like a natural person (a human individual).

Shares in a corporation are **securities**. A security is an ownership interest that represents only an investment in an enterprise, without managerial control over it. Securities are regulated by the federal government through the Securities and Exchange Commission.

A corporation is capable of perpetual existence; the death of a shareholder does not affect its operation. Corporate property is owned by the corporation in severalty, not by the shareholders. The shareholders own only a right to share in the profits of the business. They have limited liability.

The main drawback to the corporate form of organization is double taxation. First the corporation must pay income taxes on any profits it generates. Then, if the profits are distributed to shareholders as dividends, the same money is taxed again as the personal income of the shareholders. Business investors can avoid double taxation by choosing a different form of organization, such as a partnership or a trust.

A corporation formed under California law is called a **domestic corporation**. All other corporations, incorporated in other states or foreign countries, are called **foreign corporations**. Foreign corporations may conduct business in California, but they must obtain a certificate of qualification from the Secretary of State and abide by any conditions or limitations imposed.

Note that a corporation cannot co-own property in joint tenancy. Since a corporation has a potentially perpetual existence, the other joint tenant could not really have a right of survivorship. Thus, when a corporation co-owns real property with another entity or person, they hold title as tenants in common.

Limited Liability Companies. A limited liability company (LLC) can be seen as the best of both worlds. It combines many of the advantages of a corporation with many of the advantages of a partnership.

To create an LLC, two or more business owners draw up an LLC operating agreement and file articles of organization with the Secretary of State. LLC agreements can be quite flexible; the owners (referred to as members) can choose virtually any manner of allocating income, losses, or appreciation among themselves. Once the LLC is created, annual statements must be filed with the state and an annual fee must be paid.

LLC members have the flexibility of a general partnership when it comes to managing the business. Certain members may be appointed to manage the company, or all of the members may manage the company. All managing members can bind the LLC with their actions. However, unlike general partners in a partnership, an LLC's managing members are not personally liable for the company's debts and obligations. All LLC members have the same type of limited liability enjoyed by corporate stockholders or limited partners. Regardless of their level of participation in the company, LLC members risk only their initial investment in the company.

As noted earlier, a major disadvantage of the corporate form of ownership is the double taxation imposed on corporations and their stockholders. In contrast, income earned by an LLC is taxed at only one level—the member level. LLC income is taxed only as the personal income of each member, in the same manner as partnership income.

Joint Ventures. A joint venture is similar to a partnership, except that it is created for a single business transaction or for a series of individual transactions. It is not intended to be an ongoing business of indefinite duration. Joint ventures are generally governed by the same rules as partnerships. An example of a joint venture would be a property owner, an architect, and a building contractor joining together to design and construct a particular building.

Trusts. In a trust, one or more **trustees** manage property for the benefit of one or more **beneficiaries**. A trust instrument vests title to the property in the trustees, who have only the powers expressly granted in the instrument.

Trusts are sometimes used as a form of business ownership. One example is a **real estate investment trust** (REIT). Investors form REITs to finance large real estate projects. REITs qualify for tax advantages if they meet certain requirements set by the IRS. For example, they must have at least 100 investors, and at least 75% of their investment assets must be in real estate.

A qualifying REIT avoids double taxation. As long as at least 90% of its income is distributed to the investors, the trust pays taxes only on the earnings it retains. Yet the investors, like corporate shareholders, are shielded from liability for the REIT's debts. Shares in REITs are securities, subject to federal regulation.

Condominiums and Cooperatives

To end our discussion of methods of holding title, we'll look at condominiums and cooperatives, which provide alternatives to ownership of a traditional single-family home. In a sense, condos and co-ops combine aspects of individual ownership with aspects of concurrent ownership. They are popular because of their efficient use of increasingly valuable land.

Condominiums. Someone who buys a unit in a condominium owns the unit itself in severalty, but shares ownership of the common elements with other unit owners as tenants in common. **Common elements** (also called common areas) are aspects of the condominium property that all of the unit owners have the right to use, such as the driveway, lobby, courtyard, or elevator. The land itself, the roof, and shared recreational facilities are also considered common elements.

Some features may be designated as **limited common elements**, which are reserved for the owners of certain units. For example, an assigned parking space would be a limited common element. A feature such as a balcony, which is designed for use with a particular unit but is outside of the unit itself, would also be a limited common element.

Each unit owner obtains separate financing to buy his unit, receives an individual property tax bill (which includes tax liability for the owner's proportionate share of the condominium's common elements), and may acquire a title insurance policy for the unit. A lien can attach to a single unit, so that the unit can be foreclosed on separately, without affecting the other units in the condominium.

An elected governing board usually manages the condominium, collecting regular and special assessments from the unit owners for maintenance, repair, and insurance of the common elements. The regular assessments, typically collected on a monthly basis, are often referred to as condo fees or dues.

The sale of an individual unit in a condominium ordinarily doesn't require the approval of the other unit owners. The seller's interest in the common elements passes to the buyer. When selling a condominium unit, the seller is generally required to give prospective buyers a copy of the bylaws, the latest financial statement, and the CC&Rs (covenants, conditions, and restrictions) of the condominium project, including notice of any restrictions on renting the unit.

A condominium usually involves one or more multifamily residential buildings, but commercial and industrial properties can also be developed as condos. To establish a condominium, the developer must record a condominium plan and declaration. Condominium projects are generally regulated as subdivisions (see Chapter 5).

Sometimes the owner of an apartment complex will find it profitable to change the complex into a condominium. This process, called **conversion**, is regulated to protect renters who will be displaced. For instance, they must be given 180 days' advance written notice before termination of their tenancies. They must also be given an opportunity to buy their units before the units are placed on the open market.

Cooperatives. In a cooperative, ownership of the property is vested in a single entity—usually a corporation. The residents of the cooperative building own shares in the corporation, rather than owning the property itself. They are tenants with long-term **proprietary leases** on their units; they do not hold title to their units. In other words, they have leasehold estates in the property.

To establish a cooperative, the corporation gets a mortgage loan to buy or construct the building, and other funds are raised by selling shares in the corporation to prospective tenants. The rent that each tenant pays to the corporation is a pro rata share of the mortgage, taxes, operating expenses, and other debts for the whole property. The cooperative corporation is managed by an elected board of directors.

In many cooperatives, a tenant cannot transfer stock or assign her proprietary lease without the consent of the governing board or a majority of the members. This approval process is used to screen out undesirable tenants; however, discrimination in violation of fair housing laws is not allowed (see Chapter 14).

Like condominiums, cooperatives are generally regulated as subdivisions. The tenant protection rules that apply to condominium conversions generally also apply when an apartment building is converted into a cooperative.

Comparison of Condos and Co-ops. In a condominium, each unit is owned individually. In a cooperative, a corporation owns the whole project; the tenants own shares in the corporation and have proprietary leases on their units.

In a condominium, each unit owner obtains individual financing to buy the unit. In a cooperative, the corporation takes out one blanket loan for the entire project. One advantage of condominiums over cooperatives is that a condominium owner is not responsible for any default on another unit owner's loan. In a cooperative, if one tenant defaults on his share of the mortgage payments, the other tenants must cure the default or risk having the mortgage on the entire project foreclosed on. This is also true for tax assessments and other liens.

A condominium owner can usually sell her unit to anyone she chooses. In a co-op, the corporation usually must approve of the proposed purchaser.

 Chapter Summary

1. An estate is a possessory interest in real property. Someone who has a freehold estate has title to the property and is considered an owner. Someone who has a leasehold (less-than-freehold) estate has possession of the property, but does not have title.

2. Freehold estates include the fee simple absolute, the fee simple defeasible, and the life estate. A life estate lasts only as long as a specified person is alive; then the property either reverts to the grantor or else passes to the remainderman.

3. Leasehold estates include the term tenancy, the periodic tenancy, and the tenancy at will. (The tenancy at sufferance, which arises when a tenant holds over without the landlord's permission, is not really an estate.)

4. Title to real property can be held in severalty or concurrently. In California, the methods of concurrent ownership are joint tenancy, tenancy in common, and community property.

5. Real property can be owned by a syndicate, which may be organized as a general or limited partnership, a corporation, a limited liability company, a joint venture, or a real estate investment trust.

6. In a condominium, each unit is separately owned, and all the unit owners own the common elements as tenants in common. A cooperative is owned by a corporation; a resident owns shares in the corporation, and has a proprietary lease for a particular unit.

Key Terms

Estate—An interest in land that is or may become possessory.

Freehold estate—A possessory interest that has an indeterminable duration.

Less-than-freehold (leasehold) estate—A possessory interest that has a limited duration.

Fee simple absolute—The highest and most complete form of ownership, which is of potentially infinite duration.

Fee simple defeasible—A fee simple estate that carries a qualification, so that ownership may revert to the grantor if a specified event occurs or a condition is not met. Also called a defeasible fee.

Life estate—A freehold estate whose duration is measured by the lifetime of one or more persons.

Waste—Permanent damage to real property caused by the party in possession, harming the interests of other estate holders.

Term tenancy (estate for years)—A leasehold estate with a fixed term.

Periodic tenancy—A leasehold estate that is renewed at the end of each period unless one party gives notice of termination. Also called a periodic estate.

Tenancy at will—A leasehold estate that may arise after a periodic tenancy or a term tenancy terminates. Also called an estate at will.

Ownership in severalty—Sole ownership of property.

Tenancy in common—Joint ownership where there is no right of survivorship.

Joint tenancy—Joint ownership with right of survivorship.

Right of survivorship—The right by which, upon the death of a co-owner, the surviving co-owner(s) acquire his interest in the property.

Community property—Property owned jointly by a married couple (in California and other community property states).

Corporation—An artificial person; a legal entity separate from its shareholders.

Limited liability company—A form of business entity that offers limited liability and tax benefits.

Real estate investment trust—A real estate investment business that qualifies for tax advantages if certain requirements are met.

Condominium—A property that has been developed so that individual unit owners have separate title to their own units, but share ownership of the common elements as tenants in common.

Cooperative—A property that is owned by a corporation and tenanted by shareholders in the corporation who have proprietary leases for their units.

Chapter Quiz

1. A fee simple title in real estate is of indefinite duration, and can be:
   a) freely transferred
   b) encumbered
   c) inherited
   d) All of the above

2. A conveyance of title with the condition that the land shall not be used for the sale of intoxicating beverages creates a:
   a) less-than-freehold estate
   b) fee simple defeasible
   c) life estate
   d) reservation

3. Lewis was given real property for the term of his natural life. Which of the following statements is incorrect?
   a) Lewis has a freehold estate
   b) Lewis has a fee simple estate
   c) Lewis is the life tenant
   d) If Lewis leases the property to someone else, the lease will terminate if Lewis dies during its term

4. Baker sold a property to Lane, but reserved a life estate for himself and remained in possession. Later Baker sells his life estate to Clark and surrenders possession to Clark. Lane then demands immediate possession as fee owner. Which of the following is true?
   a) Lane is entitled to possession
   b) Clark should sue Baker for return of the purchase price
   c) Baker is liable for damages
   d) Clark can retain possession during Baker's lifetime

5. Cobb owns a property in fee simple; he deeds it to Smith for the life of Jones. Which of the following is true?
   a) Jones holds a life estate; Smith holds an estate in reversion
   b) Smith holds a life estate; Cobb holds an estate in remainder
   c) Smith holds a fee simple estate; Jones holds a life estate
   d) Smith holds a life estate; Cobb holds an estate in reversion

6. Johnston, a life tenant, decides to cut down all the trees on the ten-acre property and sell them as timber. Mendez, the remainderman, can stop Johnston's actions because:
   a) a life tenant is never permitted to cut down any trees on the property for any reason
   b) a life tenant cannot commit waste
   c) Mendez's interest is superior to Johnston's, since it is a possessory estate
   d) None of the above; Mendez has no legal grounds for stopping Johnston

7. Jones and Adams signed an agreement for the use and possession of real estate, for a period of 120 days. This is a:
   a) term tenancy
   b) tenancy at sufferance
   c) periodic tenancy
   d) tenancy at will

8. The four unities of title, time, interest, and possession are necessary for a:
   a) tenancy in common
   b) partnership
   c) mortgage
   d) joint tenancy

9. Which of the following is incorrect? Joint tenants always have:
   a) equal rights to possession of the property
   b) the right to will good title to heirs
   c) the right of survivorship
   d) equal interests in the property

10. A, B, and C own property as joint tenants. C dies, and then B sells her interest in the property to D. The property is now owned:
    a) as joint tenants by A, D, and C's widow E, his sole heir
    b) by A and D as joint tenants
    c) by A and D as tenants in common
    d) None of the above

11. Asher and Blake own real property together. Asher has a one-third interest and Blake has a two-thirds interest. How do they hold title?
    a) Community property
    b) Tenancy at will
    c) Joint tenancy
    d) Tenancy in common

12. All of the following statements about a corporation are true, except:
    a) A corporation has a potentially perpetual existence
    b) Each shareholder is individually liable for the corporation's acts
    c) Corporations are subject to double taxation
    d) A corporation can enter into contracts in essentially the same way as an individual person

13. A real estate investment trust is required to:
    a) invest at least 75% of its assets in real estate
    b) have at least 150 participating investors
    c) have investors accept liability for the trust's acts
    d) retain at least 50% of its income

14. In a condominium:
    a) individual units are owned in severalty, while common elements are owned in joint tenancy
    b) individual units are owned in joint tenancy, while common elements are owned in severalty
    c) individual units are owned in severalty, while common elements are owned in tenancy in common
    d) the entire building is owned in tenancy in common, with residents owning shares

15. A unit in a cooperative is owned:
    a) in severalty by its resident
    b) by the corporation that owns the building, in which the resident owns shares
    c) in tenancy in common among all residents of the building
    d) in partnership among all residents of the building

Answer Key

1. d) A fee simple owner has the full bundle of rights.

2. b) A fee simple defeasible is an estate that will fail if a certain event occurs.

3. b) Although a life estate is a freehold estate, it is not a fee simple estate.

4. d) Baker was entitled to sell his life estate to Clark. Clark can retain possession during Baker's lifetime.

5. d) Smith has possession of the property for the duration of Jones's life, so Smith has a life estate *pur autre vie.* Cobb has an estate in reversion, because the property will revert to Cobb after Jones's death.

6. b) A life tenant cannot commit waste, which means that the life tenant cannot damage the property or harm the interests of the remainderman.

7. a) A term tenancy has a set termination date.

8. d) A valid joint tenancy requires all four unities: title, time, interest, possession.

9. b) A joint tenant cannot will her interest in the property. The right of survivorship means the surviving joint tenants acquire the deceased tenant's title.

10. c) When C dies, his interest in the property goes to the other joint tenants, A and B. When B sells her interest to D, the joint tenancy is terminated and a tenancy in common is created between A and D.

11. d) Because their interests in the property are unequal, Asher and Blake must be tenants in common.

12. b) A corporation's shareholders have limited liability for the corporation's actions.

13. a) A real estate investment trust must invest at least 75% of its assets in real estate. The minimum number of investors is 100, not 150, and at least 90% of the REIT's income must be distributed to investors.

14. c) In a condominium, residents own their individual units in severalty, but own the common elements as tenants in common.

15. b) A cooperative is owned by a business entity, usually a corporation. Residents purchase shares in the corporation and receive long-term leases, rather than title to their units.

Chapter 3

Transfer of Real Property

I. Title and Alienation
II. Voluntary Alienation
  A. Patents
  B. Deeds
    1. Types of deeds
    2. Requirements for a valid deed
    3. Acknowledgment, delivery, and acceptance
    4. Nonessential terms
  C. Wills
III. Involuntary Alienation
  A. Dedication
  B. Intestate succession and escheat
  C. Condemnation
  D. Court decisions
  E. Adverse possession
  F. Accession
IV. Recording
  A. Recording procedures
  B. Legal effects of recording
V. Title Insurance
  A. Obtaining title insurance
  B. Types of title insurance

Chapter Overview

A property owner may transfer property to someone else by choice, as when an owner deeds property to a buyer or wills it to a friend. Property may also be transferred involuntarily, as in a foreclosure sale or a condemnation. This chapter describes the various types of transfers, voluntary and involuntary. It also explains how and why deeds and other documents are recorded, and how title insurance works.

Title and Alienation

A person who owns property is said to have **title** to it. Problems with a real property owner's title are called title defects or "clouds" on title. For example, if someone other than the current owner claims an interest in the property based on a transaction that took place long ago, that claim is a title defect or cloud on the owner's title. Title that is free from serious defects is called **marketable title.**

The process of transferring ownership of (title to) real property from one party to another is called **alienation**. Alienation may be either voluntary or involuntary. Voluntary alienation occurs when an owner deliberately transfers title to someone else. Involuntary alienation is a transfer of property without any action by the owner, as a result of the operation of law.

Voluntary Alienation

Voluntary alienation of real property includes the transfer of title by patent, by deed, or by will.

Patents

Title to all real property originates with the sovereign government. The government holds absolute title to all the land within its boundaries, except the land that it has granted to various other entities or persons. Title to land is transferred from the government to a private party by a document known as a **patent**. The patent is the ultimate source of title for all land under private ownership.

Deeds

The most common form of voluntary alienation is transfer by deed. With a deed, the owner of real property, called the **grantor**, transfers all or part of her interest in the property to another party, called the **grantee**. The process of transferring real property by deed is known as **conveyance**. A grantor conveys real property to a grantee by means of a deed.

Types of Deeds. There are many types of deeds. The ones used most often in California are the grant deed, the quitclaim deed, the trustee's deed, and deeds executed under court order.

Grant Deed. The grant deed is the most commonly used deed in California. A grant deed uses the term "grant" in its words of conveyance and carries two warranties:

1. the grantor has not previously conveyed title to anyone else, and
2. the grantor has not caused any encumbrances to attach to the property other than those already disclosed.

These two basic warranties apply even if they are not expressly stated in the grant deed. Additional warranties and covenants (promises) may be stated in the deed if the parties so desire.

A grant deed also conveys to the grantee all **after-acquired title** of the grantor. This means that if the grantor's title was defective at the time of transfer, but the grantor later acquires a more perfect title, the additional interest passes automatically to the grantee under the original deed.

Example: Warner conveyed her property to Meyers on June 1, by a grant deed. However, Warner did not have valid title to the property on June 1 because she held title under a forged deed. On August 12, Warner received good title to the property under a properly executed deed. Meyers automatically acquired good title to the property on August 12.

Quitclaim Deed. A quitclaim deed contains no warranties of any sort, and it will not convey after-acquired title. It conveys only whatever interest the grantor has when the deed is delivered to the grantee. It conveys nothing at all if the grantor has no interest at that time. But if the grantor does have an interest in the property, the quitclaim deed will convey it just as well as any other type of deed.

One common reason for using a quitclaim deed is to correct a technical flaw in an earlier deed. Perhaps one of the parties' names was misspelled, or the land description was inaccurate. A quitclaim deed used in this way may be referred to as a **reformation deed**. A quitclaim deed can also be used to prevent or clear away clouds on title caused by the possibility that someone other than the current owner might be able to claim an interest in the property.

A transfer of real property between family members is often made with a quitclaim deed. This type of deed is also used when the grantor is unsure of the validity of his title and wishes to avoid giving any warranties.

Example: Alvarez holds title by virtue of an inheritance that is being challenged in probate court. If Alvarez wants to transfer the property, she will probably use a quitclaim deed, because she is not sure that her title is valid.

In a quitclaim deed, words such as "grant" or "convey" should be avoided. The use of these words may imply that the grantor is warranting the title. A quitclaim deed should use only terms such as "release," "remise," or "quitclaim" to describe the transfer.

Trustee's Deed. When property is foreclosed under a deed of trust, the trustee conveys the property to the buyer at the foreclosure sale with a trustee's deed. The trustee's deed states that the conveyance is in accordance with the trustee's powers and responsibilities under the deed of trust. (Deeds of trust are discussed in Chapter 9.)

Deeds Executed by Court Order. A deed executed by court order is used to convey title after a court-ordered sale of property. A common example is the sheriff's deed used to transfer property to the highest bidder at a court-ordered foreclosure

Fig. 3.1 Grant deed

RECORDING REQUESTED BY

AND WHEN RECORDED MAIL THIS DEED AND, UNLESS OTHERWISE SHOWN BELOW, MAIL TAX STATEMENTS TO:

NAME

STREET ADDRESS

CITY, STATE ZIP

Title Order No.............. Escrow No................

This space for Recorder's use

GRANT DEED

THE UNDERSIGNED GRANTOR(s) DECLARE(s)
DOCUMENTARY TRANSFER TAX is $____________

☐ computed on full value of property conveyed, or
☐ computed on full value less value of liens or encumbrances remaining at time of sale, and

FOR A VALUABLE CONSIDERATION, receipt of which is hereby acknowledged,

hereby GRANT(S) to

the following described real property in the
County of , State of California:

Dated ____________

STATE OF CALIFORNIA
COUNTY OF ____________} SS.
On ____________before me, the undersigned, a Notary Public in and for the said State, personally appeared

known to me to be the person(s) whose name(s) is (are) subscribed to the within instrument and acknowledged that.................................. executed the same. Witness my hand and official seal.
Signature ____________

(Space above for official notarial seal)

MAIL TAX STATEMENTS TO PARTY SHOWN ON FOLLOWING LINE; IF NO PARTY SHOWN, MAIL AS DIRECTED ABOVE

Name Street Address City & State

sale (see Chapter 9). Court-ordered deeds usually state the exact amount of the purchase price approved by the court and carry no warranties of title.

Other Deeds. Two other types of deeds, the **warranty deed** and the **special warranty deed**, are rarely used in California. (Title insurance has made it largely unnecessary for buyers to rely on deed warranties.) The warranty deed gives the greatest protection to a real estate buyer. Under a warranty deed, the grantor makes five basic promises, or covenants, to the grantee. These covenants warrant against defects in the title that arose either before or during the grantor's period of ownership (tenure).

The special warranty deed contains the same covenants found in the general warranty deed, but the scope of the covenants is limited to defects that arose during the grantor's tenure. The grantor makes no assurances regarding defects that may have existed before she obtained title. This type of deed may be used by entities such as corporations, which may not have the authority to make further warranties.

Requirements for a Valid Deed. A deed will transfer title only if it meets the legal requirements for validity. To be valid, a deed must:

- be in writing,
- identify the parties,
- be signed by a competent grantor,
- have a living grantee,
- contain words of conveyance (the granting clause), and
- include an adequate description of the property.

In Writing. The **statute of frauds** is a state law that requires certain contracts and other legal transactions to be in writing. With only a few minor exceptions, the statute of frauds applies to any transfer of an interest in real property. An unwritten deed cannot transfer title; it has no legal effect.

Identification of the Parties. Both the grantor and the grantee must be identified in the deed. The name of the grantee is not required, as long as an adequate description is given; for example, "John T. Smith's only sister." The grantee may also take title under a fictitious name.

At one time, it was common for a married couple to be referred to in a deed as (for example) "John T. Smith, et ux." "Et ux." is a Latin abbreviation that means "and wife." Now it is standard practice to give the name of each spouse in full.

Signed by a Competent Grantor. In addition to requiring a deed to be in writing, the statute of frauds also requires the document to be signed by the party who is to be bound by the transfer. Thus, the grantor must sign the deed. The deed is considered to be executed at the time of the grantor's signature. If the grantor's signature is a forgery, the deed is void.

If the grantor can't sign his full name (due to disability or illiteracy), he may sign by making a mark. But a signature by mark must be accompanied by the signatures of witnesses who can attest to the grantor's execution of the deed.

A deed can also be signed by the grantor's **attorney in fact**. An attorney in fact (not necessarily a lawyer) is someone the grantor has appointed to act on her behalf in a document called a **power of attorney**. The power of attorney must include a description of the property and specifically authorize the attorney in fact to convey it. It should be recorded in the county where the property is located. Note that the law does not allow an attorney in fact to deed his principal's property to himself.

Deeds from corporations are usually signed by an authorized officer of the corporation, and the signature must be accompanied by the corporate seal.

If there is more than one grantor, all of the grantors must sign the deed. If the prior deed named more than one grantee, all of them must sign as grantors of the new deed when they convey the property to someone else.

The signatures of both spouses are required to convey community property (see Chapter 2). For this reason, it is a good idea (although not required) to state the grantor's marital status in the deed and to obtain the spouse's signature if the grantor is married, even if the property is not community property.

A grantor must be legally competent when she signs the deed. This means that the grantor must be an adult (at least 18 years old) and must be of sound mind. If the grantor is not legally competent, the deed is not valid.

Living Grantee. The grantee does not have to be legally competent in order for the deed to be valid. It is only necessary for the grantee to be alive (or, if the grantee is a corporation, legally in existence) and identifiable when the deed is executed.

Words of Conveyance. The requirement of words of conveyance, the granting clause, is easily satisfied. The single word "grant" or a similar word is sufficient. Additional technical language generally should be avoided, since it adds nothing to the validity of the deed.

Description of the Property. A valid deed must contain an adequate description of the property to be conveyed. The full legal description should always be used, although a deed can be valid without that, as long as it has a description that makes it possible to identify the property. (Land description is discussed in Chapter 1.)

Acknowledgment, Delivery, and Acceptance. In addition to a valid deed, a proper conveyance of real property also involves acknowledgment, delivery, and acceptance of the deed.

Acknowledgment occurs when the grantor swears before a notary public or other official witness that her signature is genuine and voluntary. The witness cannot be a person who has an interest in the transfer. For example, if Grandma deeds her property to Granddaughter, who is a notary public, Granddaughter should not be the one to notarize the deed.

A deed may be considered valid even if the grantor's signature is not acknowledged. However, an unacknowledged deed cannot be recorded. We'll discuss the effect and importance of recording later in this chapter.

A valid deed becomes effective, so that title is transferred, when the deed is **delivered** to the grantee. Delivery must occur while the grantor is alive.

Example: After Sam Wiggins died, a deed was found in his safe deposit box. The deed granted Sam's farm to his nephew, Frank Wiggins, but Frank knew nothing about it. The deed is void because it was not delivered during Sam's lifetime.

Delivery is more than the mere physical transfer of the document; the grantor's intent is a key element of delivery. The grantor must have the intention of immediately transferring title to the grantee. The conveyance is completed when the grantee **accepts** delivery of the deed. The grantee may accept delivery of the deed through an agent.

Example: Clark deeds his property to Martinez. Clark hands the deed to Martinez's attorney, with the intention of immediately transferring ownership to Martinez. This is considered delivery to an agent of the grantee, and the title transfer is effective.

Because delivery of a deed involves some complicated legal issues, a real estate lawyer should be consulted when there is a question concerning delivery.

Nonessential Terms. There are some elements that should be included in a deed even though they aren't legally required. There should be a **habendum clause** (also called a "to have and to hold" clause), which states the nature of the interest the grantor is conveying. Is the grantor conveying a fee simple absolute or a life estate? Unless otherwise specified, the grantor's entire interest is presumed to pass to the grantee. If there is more than one grantee, the deed should say how they will hold title. For example, is this a tenancy in common or a joint tenancy?

Many deeds have an **exclusions and reservations clause**, which is a list of any encumbrances (easements, private restrictions, or liens) that the grantee will be taking title subject to. However, valid encumbrances usually remain in force even if they aren't listed in the deed.

A **recital of consideration** is often included in a deed to indicate that the transfer is a purchase instead of a gift. (If the transfer were a gift, the grantee might be vulnerable to the claims of the grantor's creditors.) Consideration is something of value, such as money or property, exchanged by the parties to a transaction (see Chapter 6). The recital of consideration in a deed usually doesn't state the actual purchase price paid; instead, it may say something like "for good and valuable consideration."

The date of conveyance is standard, but not legally required. Other nonessential items include the grantor's seal, warranties, and technical terminology. "I hereby grant Greenacres Farm to Harry Carter. (signed) Hector Valdez" is a valid deed, assuming that Hector Valdez is legally competent. Note that the grantee does not ordinarily sign the deed.

Wills

Transfer by will is another method of voluntary alienation. A will (or testament) is a legal document in which a person specifies how his property is to be distributed when he dies. The person who makes a will is referred to as the **testator**. Someone who leaves a valid will when he dies is said to have died **testate**; someone who dies without a valid will is said to have died **intestate**.

Those who receive property through a will are called the **beneficiaries**. A gift of personal property in a will is called a **bequest** or **legacy**; a testator **bequeaths** personal property to **legatees**. A gift of real property in a will is called a **devise**; a testator **devises** real property to **devisees**. An amendment to a will is called a **codicil**.

Fig. 3.2 Will terminology

Will Terminology

Testator: One who makes a will.

Bequeath: To transfer personal property by will.

Devise: To transfer real property by will.

Executor: Appointed by the testator to carry out the instructions in the will.

Administrator: Appointed by the court if no executor was named.

Probate: Procedure to prove a will's validity.

Legal Requirements. Under California law, a will generally must be:

1. in writing,
2. signed by the testator, and
3. attested to by at least two competent witnesses.

The will must be signed by the testator in the presence of the witnesses. The witnesses must also sign an acknowledgment that the testator declared the document to be her will.

California also recognizes a type of unwitnessed will. A **holographic will** is one where all of the material provisions as well as the signature are in the testator's own handwriting. A holographic will may be valid even though it was not signed in the presence of witnesses. If any portion of an otherwise valid holographic will is typewritten or preprinted, those provisions will be disregarded by the probate court, except for statements of testamentary intent in a commercially printed will form.

Probate. Probate is the legal procedure for proving the validity of a will and carrying out the testator's directions. Note that a will does not create any interest in property until the testator has died and the will has been probated.

In California, probate proceedings are handled in superior court. Under the court's supervision, the estate property is managed and distributed to the beneficiaries by an **executor** appointed in the will. If the testator did not name an executor, the probate court will appoint an **administrator** to perform those functions. Either an executor or an administrator may be referred to as the testator's **personal representative**.

If real property devised in a will is going to be sold by the personal representative on behalf of the devisees, then the conveyance may have to be approved by the probate court. (And if a real estate broker handles the sale, the listing agreement and commission rate will also be subject to court approval.) Alternatively, if the will is being administered under the Independent Administration of Estates Act, the personal representative may sell the real property without court approval if none of the estate beneficiaries object.

Involuntary Alienation

The patent, the deed, and the will are the three most common methods of transferring property voluntarily. We will now look at the different ways interests in real property can be conveyed without any voluntary action on the part of the owner.

Involuntary alienation of real property can be the result of rule of law, adverse possession, or accession. Alienation by rule of law includes dedication, intestate succession and escheat, condemnation, and court decisions regarding real property.

Dedication

When a private owner donates real property to the public, it is called dedication. While dedication may be voluntary (for example, a philanthropist might deed land to the city for a park, as a gift), most often it is required in exchange for a benefit from a public entity.

Example: The county requires a land developer to dedicate land within a new subdivision for public streets. Otherwise, the county will deny permission to subdivide.

This type of dedication is called **statutory dedication** because it involves compliance with relevant statutory procedures. In the example above, the subdivision statutes require that land for streets and utilities must be dedicated before a parcel can be subdivided.

A second type of dedication is called **common law dedication**. The usual requirement for common law dedication is the owner's acquiescence in the public's use of her property for a prolonged period of time. If property has been used by the public long enough, a government entity can pass an ordinance accepting a common law dedication. The dedication may be treated as a transfer of ownership, or it may establish only a public easement, depending on the circumstances. (Easements are discussed in Chapter 4.)

Example: Barker owns some lakefront property. For many years, people from town have walked across a corner of his lot to gain access to the lake, and Barker has done nothing to prevent this. Barker's acquiescence to this public use could be considered a common law dedication.

Intestate Succession and Escheat

When someone dies intestate (without a valid will), the law provides for the distribution of his property by a process called **intestate succession**. The order of succession varies from state to state, but in general the property passes first to the surviving spouse, then to any surviving children, then to various other relatives. In California, a surviving spouse is entitled to all of the community property. If there is one child, the decedent's separate property is divided evenly between the surviving spouse and that child. If there is more than one child, the surviving spouse gets one-third of the separate property, and the children share equally in the remaining two-thirds.

Persons who take property by intestate succession are called **heirs**. Those who receive property by intestate succession are said to have received property by **descent** rather than by devise or bequest. Intestate succession is supervised by the probate court. The court appoints an administrator, who is responsible for distributing the property in the manner required by statute.

If a person dies intestate and the probate court is unable to locate any heirs, then the intestate person's property **escheats**. That means title to the property passes to the state government. Since the state is the ultimate source of title to property, it is also the ultimate heir when there are no intervening interested parties. To obtain title to the property, the state Attorney General must follow the appropriate legal procedures. The state may also take ownership of abandoned property through escheat.

Condemnation

The government has the constitutional power to take private property for public use, as long as it pays the owner for the property. This is called the power of **eminent domain**, and an exercise of the power is called a "taking." The legal process used to acquire property by eminent domain is called **condemnation** (see Chapter 5).

The power of eminent domain can be exercised only if two requirements are met:

- the intended use must be a **public use**—that is, it must benefit the public; and
- the owner must be paid **just compensation**, which is the fair market value of the property.

Taking property for a public park would qualify as a public use. In cases of mixed public and private benefit the question is more difficult, but generally there is no authority for the government to take one person's land for the sole purpose of turning it over to another person.

The power of eminent domain may be exercised by any government entity, and also by some semi-public entities, such as utility companies.

Inverse Condemnation. If a property owner feels that his property has been taken or damaged by a public entity, the owner may file a lawsuit called an inverse condemnation action to force the government to pay the fair market value of the property.

Court Decisions

Title to property can be conveyed by court order in accordance with statutes and common law precedents. The most common forms of court action affecting title to property are quiet title actions, suits for partition, foreclosures, and bankruptcies.

Quiet Title. As was mentioned earlier, a cloud on a property owner's title can often be cleared away by having the potential claimant sign a quitclaim deed, which releases any interest he might have. In situations where that solution is unavailable, the property owner may file a quiet title action to have the cloud removed. In a quiet title action, the court decides questions of property ownership. The result is a binding determination of the various parties' interests in a particular piece of real estate.

Example: A seller has found a potential buyer for his land. However, a title search uncovers a gap in the chain of title: the public record doesn't indicate who owned the property for a certain time period. The seller's title is unmarketable, and the buyer is unwilling to proceed with the purchase.

The seller files a quiet title action. The defendants in the action are all persons who have a potential interest in the seller's property. This includes the mystery person who held title during the gap, even though his or her name is unknown.

The seller asks the court to declare his title valid, thereby "quieting title" to the land. If no defendants appear to challenge the seller's title, the court will grant the seller's request. The buyer can then rely on the court's decision and buy the land.

Partition. Sometimes co-owners of property can't agree about what should be done with it. For example, one might want to sell the property, but the others refuse to; or they may all want to sell it, but disagree about their respective ownership shares. A suit for partition is a way to end co-ownership and divide the property. When a co-owner files a partition suit, the court decides on a fair disposition of the property, and all of the co-owners are bound by that decision. If it's impractical to divide the property itself, the court can order it sold and divide the proceeds among the co-owners.

Example: Green and Black own a vacation home together. Green has a two-thirds interest and Black has a one-third interest. After a serious argument, they both want to terminate their co-ownership, but they can't agree on how to do it. Green wants to put the property up for sale. Black wants to buy out Green's interest and keep the vacation home for himself, but Green says Black isn't offering him enough money.

Finally, Green files a suit for partition. After considering the case, the court orders the vacation home to be sold, with two-thirds of the proceeds going to Green and one-third to Black. Both of them must abide by this decision.

Foreclosure. Someone who holds a lien against real property may force the sale of the property if the debt secured by the lien isn't paid. (See Chapter 4.) Foreclosure is available for any type of lien that attaches to real property, including mortgages, deeds of trust, mechanic's liens, and judgment liens. (See Chapter 9 for more information about mortgage and deed of trust foreclosure.)

Bankruptcy. Property may also be conveyed by order of a bankruptcy court. Once a bankruptcy petition is filed, the court has the authority to distribute the eligible property of the debtor in order to satisfy creditors' claims. The debtor's real property may be sold to satisfy the claims of mortgage lenders or other creditors.

Adverse Possession

Adverse possession, another form of involuntary alienation, is the process by which possession and use of property can mature into title. The law of adverse possession encourages the fullest and most productive use of land. It provides that someone who actually uses property may eventually attain a greater interest in that property than the owner who does not use it. The specific requirements for obtaining title by adverse possession vary from state to state. These requirements are often quite technical, and they must be followed exactly in order to obtain title. Legal advice should be obtained in any transaction where title may be affected by adverse possession.

Requirements. In California, there are five basic requirements for adverse possession. Possession of the land must be:

1. actual, open, and notorious;
2. hostile to the owner's interest;
3. under claim of right or color of title;
4. continuous and uninterrupted for a specific period of time; and
5. the adverse possessor must have paid the property taxes during the required period of possession.

Actual, Open, and Notorious. Actual possession means occupation and use of the property in a manner appropriate to the type of property in question. Residence on the property is not required unless residence is the appropriate use. Thus, actual possession of farmland may be achieved by fencing the land and planting crops, while actual possession of urban property would require a residential or commercial use of the property.

The requirement of "open and notorious" possession means that the possession must put the true owner on notice that his interest in the property is being threatened. "Open and notorious" possession and "actual" possession overlap. Actual possession is generally considered to provide reasonable notice to the world that the adverse possessor is occupying the property.

Fig. 3.3 Adverse possession

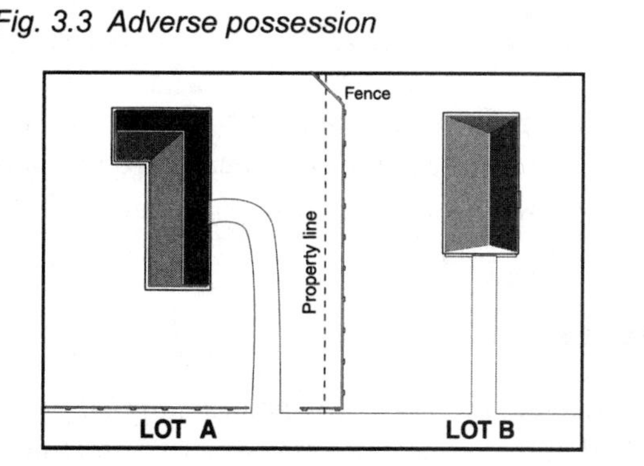

Use of property (here, the strip between Lot A's fence and the true property line) can mature into title by the process of adverse possession.

Hostile. The adverse possessor's use of the property must be "hostile" to the true owner's interest. In other words, the adverse possessor must be using the property without the owner's permission and in a manner that is inconsistent with the owner's rights. Ordinarily, if the adverse possessor uses the property (without permission) in the same way that an owner would use it, then the hostility requirement is satisfied.

Claim of Right or Color of Title. An adverse possessor must have either a claim of right or color of title. An adverse possessor with **color of title** is one who took possession of the land under an invalid deed (or other defective instrument) and has a good faith but mistaken belief that she owns it. In that situation, the adverse possessor may acquire title to all of the property described in the defective instrument, even if she occupies only part of the property.

By contrast, an adverse possessor under a **claim of right** doesn't have a deed and doesn't necessarily have a bona fide belief he owns the property; he may even know that he's trespassing. However, his actions demonstrate that he intends to claim ownership of the property nevertheless. For example, if someone moves onto apparently abandoned property, constructs a building, and begins using it, he is adversely possessing the property under a claim of right.

Continuous and Uninterrupted; Payment of Taxes. An adverse possessor must have continuous and uninterrupted possession of the property for the length of time prescribed by state statute. In California, the possession must be continuous and uninterrupted for five years, and the adverse possessor must pay the taxes on the property during that period.

In some cases, intermittent use of the property may be enough to fulfill the continuity requirement. This is true if the property is a type that an owner would ordinarily use only at certain times of year, such as seasonal farmland or summer resort property. However, the continuity requirement is not met if the adverse possessor fails to use the property for a significant period when it would ordinarily be used, or if the true owner interrupts the period of exclusive possession.

The periods of possession of successive adverse possessors can be added together to equal the statutory time period; this is called **tacking**.

Example: Tanaka adversely possesses property for four years, then transfers possession to White, who possesses the property for three years. White can claim title because the total period of adverse possession is more than five years.

Note that title to government property can never be acquired by adverse possession.

Perfecting Title. Since an adverse possessor's interest is not apparent from the public record, he must take additional steps to establish marketable title. Unless the true owner is willing to provide a quitclaim deed, the adverse possessor will have to file a quiet title action.

Accession

Accession refers to any addition to real property from natural or artificial causes. An addition to one person's property sometimes involves the involuntary alienation of another person's property. This type of involuntary alienation may occur as a result of one of these natural processes:

- accretion,
- reliction, and
- avulsion.

Accretion. Waterborne soil may be deposited on land beside a body of water. The deposited soil is called alluvion or alluvium, and the process is called accretion. When riparian or littoral land is slowly enlarged in this way, the riparian or littoral owner acquires title to the new land. A key feature of accretion is that the buildup of soil must be so gradual that the process is virtually imperceptible.

Reliction. The water in a stream or lake may gradually recede; this retreat from the land is called reliction, or sometimes dereliction. When riparian or littoral land is enlarged by the gradual retreat of the body of water, the landowner acquires title to the newly exposed land. Like accretion, reliction must be very gradual.

Avulsion. Accretion and reliction are both gradual processes. By contrast, avulsion occurs when land is violently torn away by flowing water or waves and deposited somewhere else, or when land is exposed by a sudden change in a watercourse. Avulsion doesn't necessarily result in involuntary alienation of the land that has been moved or exposed. The original owner still has title to it, if there's some way to reclaim it. If unclaimed, it eventually becomes part of the property it's now attached to.

Recording

Once an interest in property has been transferred (voluntarily or involuntarily), the new owner may protect his interest by having the deed or other document of conveyance recorded. When a document is recorded, it is placed in the public record, so that anyone who's interested can look it up and read it. The recording system provides convenient access to information regarding ownership of real property.

Recording Procedures

Recording is accomplished by filing a copy of the deed or other document at the county clerk's office (or recorder's office) in the county where the property is located. Documents are recorded chronologically, in the order in which they were filed for recording. Each recorded document is assigned a recording number.

To make it possible to locate particular documents, recorded documents have traditionally been indexed by the grantor's last name and by the grantee's last name, and sometimes by tract or property description. Computerization has made this indexing less important; in most cases, computer search functions can now be used to locate documents in the public record.

When someone is considering buying a particular piece of property, a **title search** is performed to determine the validity of the seller's title and find what other claims there are against the property. A title searcher tries to locate all of the documents in the public record that affect title to the property in question. This includes tracing the **chain of title** (the series of recorded deeds that transferred the property from one owner to the next) back in time far enough to establish whether the seller is the true owner.

Almost any document affecting title to land may be recorded: a deed, a mortgage, an abstract of judgment, a lis pendens (a notice of pending legal proceedings that may affect property), and so on. A deed or other document of conveyance must be acknowledged before it can be recorded, mainly to protect against forgeries. Also, antidiscrimination laws prohibit the recording of deeds that contain racially restrictive covenants (see Chapter 14).

The Legal Effects of Recording

Having a document recorded has two extremely important legal consequences. It provides notice of the interest conveyed in the document, and it establishes the priority of that interest.

Notice. Many legal issues depend on whether a person had notice of certain information. If someone had notice of a particular fact, that means he *knew or should have known* it, and that may affect his legal rights. There are two main types of notice: actual notice and constructive notice.

Actual notice is straightforward. A person has actual notice of a fact if she actually knows about it. She personally observed it, read about it, or was told about it. By contrast, a person has **constructive notice** of a fact if, in the eyes of the law, she should have known about it, whether or not she actually did.

Recording a document gives constructive notice to "the world" (the public at large) of the property interest set forth in the document. Anyone who acquires an interest in a particular property is legally held to know about all earlier recorded interests in that property, whether or not he actually checked the public record.

> **Example:** Jones owns Haystack Farm. She sells the farm to Chen, who immediately records his deed in the county where the farm is located. One week later, Jones sells Haystack Farm to Brown. Jones pretends she still owns the farm, and Brown simply takes her word for it, instead of checking the county records. But since Jones no longer holds title, her deed to Brown conveys no interest in the property. Brown discovers this sometime later, when he and Chen both try to assert ownership of the property.
>
> Although Brown didn't actually know about the conveyance from Jones to Chen, he had constructive notice of it; he could have found out about it by checking the public record. As a result, Brown has no claim to the property. Chen owns Haystack Farm. Brown could sue Jones to get his money back, but Jones may be difficult to find.

A grantee who fails to record his deed can lose title to a **subsequent good faith purchaser without notice**: someone who later buys the property in good faith and without actual or constructive notice of the earlier conveyance. In a conflict between two purchasers, the one who records his or her deed first has good title to the property—even if the other purchaser's deed was executed first.

> **Example:** Jones sells Haystack Farm to Chen, but Chen does not record his deed. One week later, Jones sells the same property to Brown. No one tells Brown about the previous conveyance to Chen.
>
> Since Chen's deed isn't recorded, Brown doesn't have constructive notice of Chen's interest in the property. Even if Brown does a title search, there's nothing in the public record to indicate that Jones no longer owns the property.
>
> Brown qualifies as a subsequent good faith purchaser without notice. If he records his deed before Chen records his, Brown has good title to the property.

In addition to providing constructive notice, recording also creates a presumption that the recorded instrument is valid and effective. Recording will not serve to validate an otherwise invalid deed, nor will it protect against interests that arise by operation of law, such as adverse possession.

Wild Deeds. In some situations, even though a document has been recorded, it is not part of the chain of title for the property. A deed that is outside the chain of title is called a **wild deed**. A wild deed won't necessarily be discovered in a standard title search.

Example: Atwood sells some land to Burns, but Burns doesn't record her deed. Burns later sells the land to Cooper, and Cooper does record his deed. But because the previous deed (the deed from Atwood to Burns) wasn't recorded, Cooper's deed is outside the chain of title; it's a wild deed. A title searcher investigating Atwood's title would see no indication in the public record that Atwood conveyed the property to someone else, and Cooper's wild deed might not be found.

The general rule is that a subsequent purchaser is not held to have constructive notice of a wild deed. In the example, Cooper's title is unprotected against subsequent good faith purchasers. Suppose Atwood (who knows that Burns never recorded her deed) fraudulently sells the property to Dunn, a subsequent good faith purchaser without notice of Cooper's claim. A court could rule that Dunn has good title to the property, not Cooper.

Possession and Notice. Possession of the land by someone other than the seller gives notice to the buyer that the possessor may have an interest in the property, and the buyer then has a duty to inquire into the matter further. This is sometimes called "inquiry notice" or "implied notice."

Title Insurance

Given the complexity of real property law and the high cost of real estate, it's natural that a prospective buyer will want to do everything possible to protect her interest. One means of accomplishing this is to obtain warranties of title from the seller, but warranties aren't very valuable if the seller is financially unable to back them up.

The buyer could also obtain a complete history of all the recorded interests in the property (called a **chain of title**) or a condensed history of those interests (called an **abstract of title**), and then have the history examined by an attorney who could render an opinion on the condition of the title. But the buyer would still have no protection against latent or undiscovered defects in the title. Therefore, most buyers will protect their interests with a title insurance policy.

In a title insurance policy, a title insurance company agrees to indemnify the policy holder against (reimburse her for) losses caused by defects in the title, except for any defects specifically excluded from coverage. The title company will also handle the legal defense of any claims covered by the policy.

Obtaining Title Insurance

The first step in obtaining title insurance is asking a title insurance company to perform a title search. In addition to searching through the county's public records, the title company will search through various other records that may affect the property, such as the records of the Federal Land Office.

After the title search is completed, the title company prepares a **title report** describing the condition of the title. The report lists all defects and encumbrances of record; these items will be excluded from the policy coverage. Based on the report, the parties to the transaction may arrange to have certain liens paid off or other problems resolved. Once the buyer is satisfied with the condition of the title and the transaction is ready to close, the title company issues a title insurance policy in exchange for the required premium. One premium payment, paid at closing, covers the entire life of the policy.

The protection provided by a title insurance policy may be limited in a number of ways. As was just mentioned, all defects and encumbrances of record are listed in the policy and excluded from coverage. In addition, the liability of the title company cannot exceed the face value of the policy. The extent of protection also varies according to the type of policy purchased, as described below.

Types of Title Insurance

Title insurers in California generally use policy forms published by the California Land Title Association (CLTA) and the American Land Title Association (ALTA). Title insurance policies can be categorized in two basic ways: according to what interest is being insured, and according to the extent of the coverage provided.

Interest Insured. A title insurance policy is designed to insure the particular interest that the policy holder has in the property. An **owner's policy** insures the title of the property buyer (the new owner). A **lender's policy** (also called a mortgagee's policy) protects a lender's security interest. There is also a type of policy called a **leaseholder's policy**, which insures only the validity of a lease.

An ordinary residential transaction typically involves two title insurance policies: an owner's policy to protect the buyer, and a lender's policy to protect the buyer's lender. The lender will require the buyer to pay for the lender's policy as a condition of making the loan.

Extent of Coverage. In California, as in other states, title insurers have traditionally offered two main types of coverage: standard coverage and extended coverage. In recent years, these have been joined by a third type, homeowner's coverage.

A **standard coverage** policy (sometimes called a CLTA policy) insures against defects in title, including hidden risks such as forgery. It does not insure against the interests of a person in actual possession of the property, such as an adverse possessor; against title defects known by the owner but not disclosed to the title insurer; nor against interests that would be disclosed by an inspection of the premises, such as an encroachment. (However, if a policy holder wants coverage for a specific item not ordinarily covered by a policy, it may be possible to purchase an endorsement to cover that item.)

An **extended coverage** policy (sometimes called an ALTA policy) insures against all matters covered by the standard policy, plus matters not of public record, such as the rights of parties in possession of the property, unrecorded mechanic's liens, and encroachments.

Homeowner's coverage is available only in transactions involving residential property with up to four units. Homeowner's coverage is quite broad. It covers not only everything that standard coverage does, but also most of the same matters

Fig. 3.4 Comparison of standard, extended, and homeowner's title insurance coverage

	Standard Coverage	Extended Coverage	Homeowners Coverage
Unmarketable title	X	X	X
Latent defects in title (forged deed, incompetent grantor)	X	X	X
Incorrect legal descriptions or clerical errors in recorded documents	X	X	X
Undisclosed heirs in improperly probated wills	X	X	X
Nondelivery of deeds or delivery of deeds after grantors' death	X	X	X
Unrecorded liens		X	X
Claims of parties in possession (tenants, adverse possessors)		X	X
Matters discovered by survey (incorrect boundary lines, easements, incorrect area)		X	X
Subdivision regulation violations			X
Zoning or building code violations			X
Claims that arise post-closing			X

as extended coverage, such as encroachments and unrecorded easements. And it provides some additional protection, such as coverage for violations of restrictive covenants.

As we mentioned, as a condition of obtaining a loan, buyers are generally required to purchase a lender's policy to protect the lender's security interest. The lender will almost always require this policy to be extended coverage.

On the other hand, the owner's policy—the one that protects the buyer's title—has traditionally been standard coverage. Now, however, the owner's policy in a residential transaction is more likely to be homeowner's coverage than standard coverage. In California, most residential purchase agreement forms now provide that a homeowner's policy will be obtained for the buyer, unless otherwise agreed.

Governmental Action. Note that title insurance doesn't protect a policy holder from losses due to governmental action such as condemnation or zoning changes. That's true no matter what type of coverage is involved.

Chapter Summary

1. A transfer of ownership of property from one person to another is called alienation. Alienation may be either voluntary or involuntary.

2. Property may be transferred voluntarily by patent, deed, or will. The deed is the most common way of voluntarily transferring property. To be valid, a deed must be in writing, identify the parties, be signed by a competent grantor, have a living grantee, contain words of conveyance, and include an adequate description of the property. For property to be successfully conveyed, there must be delivery and acceptance as well as a valid deed. Once the deed is delivered and accepted, it should be recorded to protect the new owner's interest.

3. When a person dies, his real property is transferred to devisees under a will, or if there is no will, to heirs by the rules of intestate succession. Property from an estate is distributed under the jurisdiction of the probate court. If a person dies without a valid will and without heirs, the property escheats to the state.

4. In addition to intestate succession and escheat, there are several other methods of involuntary alienation, including dedication, condemnation, court decisions, and adverse possession. When someone uses property openly and continuously without the owner's permission for five years, she may acquire title by adverse possession.

5. Accession refers to an addition to real property that may result from natural or artificial causes. Natural causes of accession include accretion, reliction, and avulsion.

6. Documents affecting real property are recorded to provide constructive notice of their contents to anyone interested in the property. Recording also creates a presumption that a document is valid.

7. Under the terms of a title insurance policy, the title insurance company agrees to reimburse the policy holder for losses caused by defects in title, and to defend the title against the legal claims of others. An owner's policy insures the buyer's title, a lender's policy insures the lender's lien priority, and a leaseholder's policy insures the validity of a lease.

Key Terms

Alienation—The transfer of title, ownership, or an interest in property from one person to another. Alienation may be voluntary or involuntary.

Deed—A written instrument that, when properly executed, delivered, and accepted, conveys title or ownership of real property from the grantor to the grantee.

Grant deed—The deed most commonly used in California. It carries two warranties: the covenant of the right to convey, and the covenant against encumbrances caused by the grantor.

Quitclaim deed—A deed that conveys and releases any interest in a piece of real property that the grantor may have. It contains no warranties of any kind, but does transfer any right, title, or interest the grantor has at the time the deed is executed.

Acknowledgment—A formal declaration made before an authorized official, such as a notary public or county clerk, by a person who has signed a document; he states that the signature is genuine and voluntary.

Will—The written declaration of an individual that designates how her estate will be disposed of after death.

Intestate—When a person dies without leaving a valid will, he dies intestate.

Escheat—The reversion of property to the state when a person dies without leaving a valid will and without heirs entitled to the property.

Adverse possession—A means by which a person may acquire title to property by using it openly and continuously without the owner's permission for the required statutory period.

Dedication—When a private owner voluntarily or involuntarily donates real property to the public.

Eminent domain—The power of the government to take (condemn) private property for public use, upon payment of just compensation to the owner.

Condemnation—The act of taking private property for public use under the power of eminent domain.

Accession—Any addition to real property from natural or artificial causes.

Constructive notice—Notice of a fact that a person is held by law to have (as opposed to actual notice). She had the opportunity to discover the fact in question by searching the public record.

Title search—An inspection of the public record to determine all claims and interests affecting a piece of property.

Chain of title—A complete history of all of the recorded interests in a piece of real property. Also, the series of deeds that transferred title from one owner to another.

Abstract of title—A condensed history of the recorded interests in a piece of real property.

Title report—A report issued after a title search by a title insurance company, listing all defects and encumbrances of record.

Wild deed—A recorded deed that is outside the property's chain of title.

Chapter Quiz

1. The process of transferring real property is called:
   a) avulsion
   b) quitclaim
   c) alienation
   d) dereliction

2. The government transfers title to private parties by means of a/an:
   a) patent
   b) deed
   c) quitclaim
   d) escheat

3. A grant deed warrants that:
   a) no one has adversely possessed the property
   b) the grantor has not previously conveyed title to anyone else
   c) the purchase price was fair and equitable
   d) title has been duly recorded

4. Clouds on title are usually cleared by:
   a) a suit for partition
   b) title insurance
   c) adverse possession
   d) a quitclaim deed

5. A valid deed must refer to a grantee who is:
   a) competent
   b) over 21 years old
   c) identifiable
   d) intestate

6. Conveyance requires a valid deed, plus:
   a) recording
   b) delivery
   c) acceptance
   d) Both b) and c)

7. A person who makes a will is called a/an:
   a) grantor
   b) executor
   c) testator
   d) escheat

8. An unwitnessed, handwritten will is called a:
   a) formal will
   b) holographic will
   c) nuncupative will
   d) probative will

9. The process by which possession of property can result in ownership of the property is called:
   a) fee simple
   b) succession
   c) adverse possession
   d) reliction

10. A quitclaim deed conveys:
    a) whatever interest the grantor has
    b) only a portion of the interest held by the grantor
    c) only property acquired by adverse possession
    d) None of the above

11. The main reason why a grantee should make sure the deed gets recorded is to:
    a) give constructive notice of her interest in the property
    b) show acceptance of the conveyance
    c) make the transfer of title effective
    d) prevent adverse possession

12. To be valid, a deed must:
    a) include a recital of consideration
    b) be in writing
    c) have a habendum clause
    d) transfer after-acquired title

13. When a cloud on the title cannot be cleared with a quitclaim deed, the type of judicial proceeding initiated to determine ownership is a/an:
    a) quiet title action
    b) suit for partition
    c) interpleader action
    d) reformation action

14. All of the following are requirements for adverse possession, except:
    a) actual, open, and notorious possession
    b) continuous and uninterrupted possession
    c) hostile possession
    d) tacking

15. A standard coverage title insurance policy would protect against:
    a) adverse possession
    b) encroachments
    c) a forged deed
    d) condemnation

Answer Key

1. c) The general term for a transfer of ownership of real property from one party to another is alienation.

2. a) The government transfers title to property to a private party with a patent.

3. b) A grant deed warrants that the grantor has not conveyed title to anyone else.

4. d) A quitclaim deed is commonly used to clear clouds on title.

5. c) The grantee is only required to be identifiable. He need not be competent.

6. d) To convey title successfully, the deed must be delivered and accepted.

7. c) A testator is the person who makes a will.

8. b) A holographic will is one that is handwritten by the testator and not witnessed.

9. c) Adverse possession encourages the full use of land by providing a means by which a user may acquire ownership rights.

10. a) A quitclaim deed transfers whatever interest the grantor has. If the grantor has good title, it conveys good title. If the grantor has no interest in the property, it conveys nothing at all.

11. a) Recording a deed gives constructive notice of the grantee's interest.

12. b) Under the statute of frauds, a deed must be in writing to be valid.

13. a) A quiet title action provides a binding determination of the parties' interests in a piece of real estate.

14. d) All of these are among the requirements for adverse possession, except tacking. Although an adverse possessor may use tacking to fulfill the statutory time requirement, tacking is not itself a requirement.

15. c) Standard coverage insures only against title defects concerning matters of public record (such as a forged deed), not against matters that aren't part of the public record (such as adverse possession or encroachments). No matter what type of coverage is in question, title insurance doesn't protect against government actions such as condemnation.

Chapter 4

Encumbrances

- I. Financial Encumbrances (Liens)
  - A. Types of liens
    1. Mortgages
    2. Deeds of trust
    3. Mechanic's liens
    4. Judgment liens
    5. Attachment liens
    6. Property tax liens
    7. Special assessment liens
    8. Other liens
  - B. Lien priority
  - C. Homestead law
- II. Nonfinancial Encumbrances
  - A. Easements
    1. Types of easements
    2. Creating an easement
    3. Terminating an easement
  - B. Profits
  - C. Related concepts
    1. Licenses
    2. Encroachments
    3. Nuisances
  - D. Private restrictions

Chapter Overview

An interest in real property may be held by someone other than the property owner or a tenant; such an interest is called an encumbrance. Nearly every property has encumbrances against it. Some encumbrances represent another person's financial interest in the property. Other encumbrances involve another person's right to make use of the property or to restrict how the owner uses it.

The first part of this chapter explains financial encumbrances, including mortgages and other types of liens. The second part of this chapter covers the nonfinancial encumbrances, including easements and private restrictions, and some related concepts.

Encumbrances

An encumbrance is a nonpossessory right or interest in real property held by someone other than the property owner. The interest can be financial or nonfinancial in nature. A financial encumbrance affects title only; a nonfinancial encumbrance also affects the use or physical condition of the property.

Financial Encumbrances (Liens)

Financial encumbrances are more commonly called **liens**. A lien is a security interest in property; it is held by a creditor of the property owner. If the owner doesn't pay off the debt owed to the creditor, the security interest allows the creditor to force the property to be sold, so that the creditor can collect the debt out of the sale proceeds. This is called **foreclosure**. The most familiar example of a lien is a mortgage.

A lien may also be defined as a charge imposed on real property as security for a specific act.

A creditor who has a lien against (a security interest in) the debtor's property is called a **secured creditor** or a **lienholder**. The lien does not prevent the debtor from transferring the property, but the new owner takes title subject to the lien. The creditor can still foreclose if the debt is not repaid, even though the debtor no longer owns the property.

When a lien becomes legally effective, it is said to **attach** to the property. The date of attachment can be very important, since it may affect the lien's priority in relation to other liens. (Lien priority will be discussed shortly.)

Liens may be voluntary or involuntary. A **voluntary lien** is one the debtor voluntarily gives to the creditor, usually as security for a loan. The two types of voluntary liens are mortgages and deeds of trust. **Involuntary liens** (sometimes called statutory liens) are given to creditors without the property owner's consent, by operation of law. Examples of involuntary liens are property tax liens and judgment liens.

Example: Dunn sues Bronson for injuries sustained in a car crash and wins a $125,000 judgment. The judgment can become a lien against Bronson's property.

Liens may also be classified as general or specific. A **general lien** attaches to all of the debtor's property. For instance, the judgment lien in the example is a general lien. Any property owned by Bronson could be encumbered by the judgment lien. On the other hand, a **specific lien** attaches only to a particular piece of property. A mortgage is an example of a specific lien. It is a lien against only the particular piece of property offered as security for the loan.

Types of Liens

The most common types of liens against real property include mortgages, deeds of trust, mechanic's liens, judgment liens, attachment liens, and tax and assessment liens.

Mortgages. A mortgage is a specific, voluntary lien created by a contract between the property owner (the **mortgagor**) and the creditor (the **mortgagee**). The mortgagee is usually a lender, who will not loan money unless the borrower gives a lien as security for repayment. With the lien in place, the property serves as collateral for the loan.

Deeds of Trust. A deed of trust (also called a trust deed) is used for the same purpose as a mortgage. However, there are three parties to a deed of trust rather than the two found in a mortgage transaction. The borrower is called the **trustor**; the lender or creditor is called the **beneficiary**; and there is an independent third party (often an attorney or title insurance company) called the **trustee**. The most significant difference between mortgages and deeds of trust is in the foreclosure process. Mortgages and deeds of trust are discussed in more detail in Chapter 9.

Mechanic's Liens. A person who provides labor, materials, or professional services for the improvement of real property may be entitled to claim a mechanic's lien against the property. For example, if a plumber who is involved in remodeling a bathroom isn't paid, she can claim a lien against the property for the amount owed. Eventually, if necessary, the plumber could foreclose on the lien, forcing the property to be sold to pay the debt.

A mechanic's lien is a specific, involuntary lien, attaching only to the property where work was performed or materials were supplied. Mechanic's liens are sometimes called **construction liens**. A mechanic's lien claimed by someone who provides materials (as opposed to labor) is sometimes called a **materialman's lien**.

Many improvement projects involve a complex hierarchy of contractors, subcontractors, laborers, and materials suppliers, all of whom may be entitled to claim liens. However, before a mechanic's lien can be successfully created, the lien claimant must comply with numerous statutory requirements.

Preliminary Notice. California law generally requires a mechanic's lien claimant to give a preliminary notice of his right to claim a lien to the property owner, the general contractor, and the construction lender, if any. This must occur within 20 days after the claimant starts providing labor, services, or materials. The claimant must keep proof of serving notice on the property owner; any resulting lien has no legal effect without it. This

Fig. 4.1 Lien classifications

	Voluntary	Involuntary
Specific	Mortgages Deeds of trust	Property taxes Special assessments Mechanic's liens Attachment liens
General		Judgment liens IRS liens

requirement is oriented toward subcontractors, and does not apply to persons working directly with the owner.

Claim of Lien. To establish a mechanic's lien, the claimant must record a claim of lien. The deadline for recording a claim of lien varies, depending on whether or not the property owner has recorded a notice of completion or cessation.

When a project has been completed, the property owner has 15 days in which to file a **notice of completion** for recording. Alternatively, the owner is allowed to file a **notice of cessation** after all work on the project has been stopped for a continuous period of 30 days, regardless of whether or not the project has been completed.

Once the property owner has recorded a notice of completion or a notice of cessation, mechanic's lien claimants generally must file a claim of lien for recording within 30 days. However, an original contractor has 60 days (not just 30) after the notice of completion or cessation was recorded in which to file a claim of lien. An original contractor is a general contractor or any other claimant who has a contract directly with the property owner.

If the property owner fails to record either a notice of completion or a notice of cessation, all mechanic's lien claims may be filed for recording up to 90 days after work on the project has ended.

Foreclosure. To foreclose on a mechanic's lien, the lienholder must file a court action within 90 days after the lien was recorded. Otherwise, the lien automatically becomes void and has no further force or effect.

Notice of Nonresponsibility. Sometimes construction contractors begin a project that has not been approved by the property owner. For instance, a tenant may order work to be done on the leased property without the landlord's knowledge or consent. If the tenant fails to pay for the work, the contractors, subcontractors, and suppliers could file mechanic's liens against the property, and the owner could be held responsible for the cost of the project.

There is a way for owners in this type of situation to protect themselves. Within ten days of becoming aware of an unauthorized construction project, a property owner can give notice that she will not be responsible for the work. This is done by posting a **notice of nonresponsibility** in a conspicuous place on the property, and also recording the notice. The notice must identify the property, the owner, and any tenant or purchaser of the property, and it must state that the owner will not be responsible for claims arising from the work done.

Judgment Liens. When a lawsuit is decided by a court, the judge issues a decree called a **judgment**. The decree may order the losing party to pay a certain sum of money to the winning party. The party who wins a money judgment (the judgment creditor) is entitled to a judgment lien against the property of the losing party (the judgment debtor). The lien is created by recording a document called an **abstract of judgment**.

A judgment lien is an involuntary, general lien. It attaches to all of the real property owned by the debtor in any county where the creditor records the abstract of judgment. The lien will also attach to any additional real property that the debtor acquires during the lien period (the length of time the judgment creditor has to take action on the lien). In California, a judgment lien will last for five years from the date the lien was filed. Before the five-year period is up, the judgment creditor may file an application to renew the judgment lien for another five years.

Once a judgment lien has attached, the debtor must pay the judgment to free the property from the lien. If it's not paid, the judgment creditor can foreclose, and the property will be sold by a designated official to satisfy the judgment. To order the sale, the court issues a **writ of execution**.

Attachment Liens. When someone files a lawsuit, there is a danger that by the time a judgment is entered, the **defendant** (the party sued) will have sold his property and disappeared, leaving the other party with little more than a piece of paper. To prevent this, the **plaintiff** (the person who started the lawsuit) can ask the court to issue a **writ of attachment** for specified real property owned by the defendant. The writ is recorded in the county where the property is located and creates an involuntary, specific lien against the property. An attachment lien is valid for three years and is renewable. (Note that attachment liens are available only in certain types of lawsuits.)

Also, when a lawsuit that may affect title to real property is pending, the plaintiff may record a document called a **lis pendens**, which is Latin for "action pending." While a lis pendens is not a lien, anyone who purchases the property identified in the lis pendens has constructive notice of the pending lawsuit and therefore will be bound by any judgment that results from the suit, even though that person is not a party to the lawsuit. If the need for the lis pendens disappears before the lawsuit is concluded, the lis pendens may be removed by the person who originally recorded it.

Property Tax Liens. Real property owners are required to pay general real estate taxes every year. Their property is assessed (appraised for tax purposes) and taxed according to its value. When the taxes are levied, a lien attaches to the taxed property until the taxes are paid. Property tax liens are involuntary, specific liens. (General real estate taxes are discussed in more detail in Chapter 5.)

Special Assessment Liens. Special assessments are levied to pay for local improvements, such as road paving or sewer lines, that benefit some, but not all, property owners within the county. The properties that have benefited from an improvement project are assessed for their share of the cost of the improvement. The assessment creates an involuntary, specific lien against each of those properties. (Special assessments are also discussed in Chapter 5.)

Other Liens. Many other taxes, such as income taxes, estate or inheritance taxes, and gift taxes, can result in liens against property. Liens can also arise in connection with various other types of debts, such as child support, spousal maintenance, and condominium or homeowners association assessments.

Lien Priority

It's very common for a piece of property to have more than one lien against it. (For example, most homes are encumbered with at least a property tax lien and a mortgage or deed of trust lien.) In some cases, the dollar amount of all the liens against a property add up to more than the property sells for at a foreclosure sale. When this happens, the sale proceeds are not allocated among all the lienholders in a pro rata fashion (proportionate distribution). Instead, the liens are paid according to their priority. This means that the lien with the highest priority is paid first. If any money is left over, the lien with the second highest priority is paid, and so forth. A particular lienholder might receive only partial payment, or even no payment at all.

As a general rule, lien priority is determined by the date a lien was recorded. The lien that was recorded first will be paid first, even though another lien may have been created first.

Example: Suppose Baker borrows money from two banks—$5,000 from National Bank on March 17, and $5,000 from State Bank on May 5 of the same year. Baker gives mortgages to both banks when the loan funds are received. If National Bank does not record its mortgage until July 14, but State Bank records its mortgage promptly on May 5, State Bank's lien will be paid before National Bank's in the event of foreclosure.

While "first in time (to record), first in right" is the general rule, there are some important exceptions. Certain types of liens are given special priority. In California, special priority is given to property tax and special assessment liens; they have priority over all other liens, regardless of when the other liens attached to the property. Mechanic's liens are another exception. Their priority is determined by the date that work on the entire project began, even though the claim of lien was recorded later on.

The Homestead Law

Homestead laws are state laws that give homeowners limited protection against lien foreclosure. In California, the homestead law offers protection only against judgment liens and attachment liens. It does not apply to mortgages, deeds of trust, mechanic's liens, or liens for child support or spousal maintenance.

A **homestead** is an owner-occupied dwelling, together with any appurtenant buildings and land. In California, the homestead law protects a homeowner from a forced sale of the property automatically; the homeowner doesn't have to record a document or take other formal steps to establish protection. This means that a debtor may claim the homestead exemption after the property has already become the subject of a judgment lien foreclosure proceeding.

Instead of relying on the automatic homestead exemption, a homeowner may choose to record a declaration of homestead in the county where the property is located. A declaration of homestead provides greater protection than the automatic exemption, since it applies to a voluntary sale of the property as well as a forced sale.

Exemption. Homestead property is exempt from judgment liens to the extent of the homestead exemption. Currently, the standard exemption is $75,000. The exemption for a member of a family unit is $100,000. The exemption is $175,000 if the debtor or the debtor's spouse is over 65 or unable to work because of a disability. It's also $175,000 if the debtor or spouse is over 55 and has a low income.

A judgment creditor cannot foreclose on a homestead unless the net value of the property is greater than the amount of the exemption. In other words, the property must be worth enough so that the sale proceeds would cover all of the liens against it, plus the homestead exemption amount.

When a judgment lien is foreclosed on and homestead property is sold, the sale proceeds are applied in the following manner:

1. to pay all liens and encumbrances not subject to the homestead exemption (a deed of trust, for example);

2. to the homestead claimant in the amount of the exemption ($75,000, $100,000, or $175,000);
3. to pay the costs of sale;
4. to the judgment creditor to satisfy the debt; and
5. any surplus to the homestead claimant.

Money that's paid to the former owner as a result of the homestead exemption is protected from judgment creditors after the foreclosure sale for up to six months, during which time the funds may be reinvested in another homestead property.

Termination. Homestead protection is terminated when the property is sold, when the homesteader files a declaration of abandonment, or when the homesteader files a declaration of homestead on another property. Funds from the voluntary sale of homestead property (up to the amount of the homestead exemption) are protected from judgment creditors just as the proceeds of a forced sale are protected—for up to six months, to allow the homesteader to purchase another home.

Homestead protection does not terminate automatically on the death of the homesteader. It continues for the benefit of the spouse, children, or other family members living on the property.

Nonfinancial Encumbrances

While financial encumbrances affect only title to property, nonfinancial encumbrances affect the physical use or condition of the property itself. Thus, a property owner can find the use of his land limited by a right or interest held by someone else. Nonfinancial encumbrances include easements, profits, and private restrictions. We'll also cover licenses, encroachments, and nuisances in this section; they too involve someone using another's property or affecting the owner's use of it, although they aren't actually interests in real property.

Easements

An easement is a right to use another person's land for a particular purpose. It is a nonpossessory interest in land; the easement holder has a right to use the land, but has no title or right of possession. An easement is not an estate.

Example: Keller and Drummond own neighboring lots. Keller has an easement across Drummond's property for access to the public road.

Keller has a right to make reasonable use of the easement to get to and from her property. However, she doesn't have the right to build a shed on the easement, plant a garden on it, or use it in any way other than as a driveway.

Fig. 4.2 Easement appurtenant

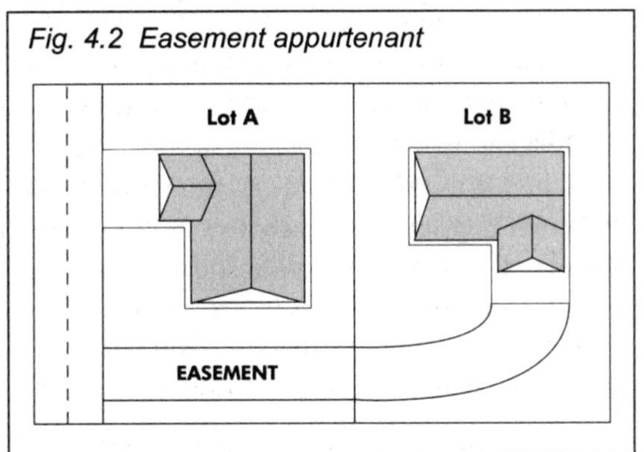

On the other hand, Drummond doesn't have the right to use the portion of his property that's subject to the easement in a way that would prevent Keller from using it as a driveway.

Types of Easements. There are two main types of easements: easements appurtenant and easements in gross.

Easements Appurtenant. An easement appurtenant (also called an appurtenant easement) burdens one parcel of land for the benefit of another parcel of land. The parcel with the benefit is called the **dominant tenement**; the one with the burden is called the **servient tenement**. The owner of the dominant tenement is called the **dominant tenant**; the owner of the servient tenement is the **servient tenant**. (Don't confuse the term "tenement," which is the land, with "tenant," which is the landowner.)

The most common type of easement appurtenant is one that gives a property owner the right to cross a neighbor's land to reach her own land, like the driveway easement in our earlier example. This type of easement is sometimes called a right of way or an easement for ingress and egress (entering and exiting). In Figure 4.2, Lot B has an easement appurtenant across Lot A. The easement provides access to Lot B from the public road. Lot B is the dominant tenement. Lot A is the servient tenement.

An easement appurtenant "runs with the land." This phrase means that if either the dominant tenement or the servient tenement is transferred to a new owner, the new owner also acquires the benefit or the burden of the easement. Refer to Figure 4.2 again. If Lot B were sold, the new owner would still have an easement across Lot A. If Lot A were sold, the new owner would still bear the burden of allowing the owner of Lot B to use the easement. A deed does not need to explicitly mention the easement for the benefit and burden of an easement to transfer along with the rest of the property.

An easement that benefits a parcel of land is called an easement appurtenant because it goes along with ownership of the land like other appurtenances (air rights, for example). The easement is appurtenant to the dominant tenement.

Easements in Gross. An easement in gross benefits a person or a company rather than a parcel of land. There's a dominant tenant, but there's no dominant tenement—no property that benefits from the easement.

Example: Wilson doesn't own any land, but he has an easement in gross that gives him the right to enter Able's land and fish in Able's pond. Able's land is the servient tenement, Able is the servient tenant, and Wilson is the dominant tenant. There's no dominant tenement, however. The easement benefits Wilson, not a parcel of land.

An easement in gross runs with the servient tenement. In the example, if Able sells his land, the new owner will have to allow Wilson to fish in the pond.

Most easements in gross are commercial (as opposed to personal easements in gross like Wilson's fishing easement). The most common example of a commercial easement in gross is an easement held by a utility company that allows company employees to enter property to install and service the utility lines.

Commercial easements in gross can be assigned—transferred from one utility company to another. With a personal easement in gross, however, the transfer or assignment of the easement rights by the dominant tenant can be an issue. In many states, a personal easement in gross is not assignable, and it's extinguished when the dominant tenant dies. But that rule doesn't apply in California. Under California law, a personal easement in gross is assignable and inheritable. Wilson could sell or will his easement in gross to another person.

Creating an Easement. Easements (whether appurtenant or in gross) can be created in any of the following ways:

- express grant,
- express reservation,
- implication,
- prescription,
- reference to a recorded plat,
- dedication, or
- condemnation.

Express Grant. An easement is created by express grant when a property owner grants someone else the right to use the property. The grant must be put into writing and must comply with all the other requirements for conveyance of an interest in land (see Chapter 3).

When granting an easement, the grantor doesn't have to specify the location of the easement. For example, a grant of an easement "across Lot A for purposes of ingress and egress" would be valid (assuming that all the other requirements for a proper conveyance are met).

A person can grant an easement only in the interest that she holds. For instance, if a tenant grants an easement in the leased property, the easement will exist only for the term of the lease.

A fee simple owner may grant an easement that will last in perpetuity (indefinitely), or for the life of the grantor, or only for a specified term.

Express Reservation. A landowner who is conveying a portion of his property may reserve an easement in that parcel to benefit the parcel of land that is retained. Like an express grant, an express reservation must be put into writing.

Example: Carmichael owns 100 acres beside a state highway. She sells 40 acres, including all the highway frontage. In the deed, she reserves to herself an easement across the conveyed land so that she will have access to her remaining 60 acres.

Implication. An easement by implication can be either an implied grant or an implied reservation. This type of easement can arise only when a property is divided into more than one lot, and the grantor neglects to grant or reserve an easement on one lot for the benefit of the other. Instead, the easement is implied by law.

For an easement to be created by implication, two requirements must usually be met:

1. it must be reasonably necessary for the enjoyment of the property, and
2. there must have been apparent prior use.

The second requirement is fulfilled if the use was established before the property was divided, and would have been apparent to prospective purchasers from an inspection of the property.

However, different rules apply if one of the parcels would be entirely landlocked without an easement. When an easement for ingress and egress is strictly necessary (not merely reasonably necessary) because there is no other way to reach the landlocked parcel, then a court may declare that there is an easement even though there was no apparent prior use. This subtype of easement by implication is called an easement by necessity.

Prescription. An easement by prescription (also called a prescriptive easement) is created through long-term use of land without the permission of the landowner. Acquiring an easement by prescription is similar to acquiring ownership through adverse possession.

An easement by prescription must meet the following requirements:

- the use must be **open and notorious** (apparent to the landowner);
- the use must be **hostile** (without the permission of the landowner);
- the use must be **reasonably continuous** for at least five years;
- the use must be under some **claim of right**; and
- if **property taxes** are assessed separately against the easement, they must be paid by the easement claimant for the five-year period.

Reference to a Recorded Plat. When a landowner subdivides her property and records a plat map, the lot purchasers acquire easements to use the roads and alleys shown on the plat.

Dedication. A private landowner may grant an easement to the public to use some portion of his property for a public purpose, such as a sidewalk. The dedication may be expressly stated, or it may be implied.

Condemnation. The government may exercise its power of eminent domain and condemn private property to gain an easement for a public purpose, such as a road. This power may also be exercised by private companies that serve the public, such as railroads and utility companies.

Terminating an Easement. An easement can be terminated in any of the following ways:

- release,
- merger,
- failure of purpose,
- abandonment, or
- prescription.

Release. The holder of an easement may release his rights in the servient tenement. This would be accomplished with a written document, usually a quitclaim deed from the easement holder to the owner of the servient tenement.

Merger. Since an easement is, by definition, the right to make a certain use of another person's land, if the dominant and servient tenements come to be owned by the same person, the easement is no longer necessary and therefore is terminated. This is called merger; ownership of the dominant tenement has merged with ownership of the servient tenement.

Failure of Purpose. If the purpose for which an easement was created ceases, then the easement terminates. For example, if an easement was created for a railroad and the railroad company later discontinued its use and removed the rails, the easement would be terminated through failure of purpose.

Abandonment. An easement is also terminated if the dominant tenant abandons it. This requires acts by the dominant tenant indicating an intent to abandon the easement. Mere nonuse is not considered abandonment.

Example: The dominant tenant builds a fence that blocks any further use of an easement for ingress and egress. Under the circumstances, it would be reasonable for the servient tenant to conclude that the easement has been abandoned.

Even though as a general rule easements are not terminated by nonuse alone (without evidence of intention to abandon), there is an exception for easements that were created by prescription: a prescriptive easement terminates automatically after five years of nonuse. Also, if any type of easement is unused for 20 years, the owner of the servient tenement can petition a court to declare the easement terminated.

Prescription. Easements can be created by prescription, and they can also be terminated by prescription. (This is true no matter how the easement was created.) An easement is extinguished by prescription if the servient tenant prevents the dominant tenant from using the easement for the statutory period (five years).

Example: The servient tenant builds a brick wall around his property. The dominant tenant can no longer use her easement for ingress and egress. If the wall remains undisturbed for five years, then the easement will be terminated by prescription.

Profits

A profit is the right to take something away from land that belongs to someone else. For example, it might be the right to take timber, peat, or gravel from someone else's land. The difference between a profit and an easement is that the easement is just a right to use another's land, but a profit allows the removal of something from the land. A profit must be created in writing or by prescription.

Licenses

Like an easement, a license gives someone the right to make some use of another person's land. However, easements and licenses are different in many ways. An easement is created in writing or through action of law. Ordinarily, a license is just spoken permission to cross, hunt or fish on, or make some other use of a landowner's property. An easement is irrevocable, but a license can be revoked at the will of the landowner. In general, easements are permanent and licenses are temporary. A license is a personal right that does not run with or pass with the land. It cannot be assigned. Since the license is revocable at the will of the landowner, it is not actually considered an encumbrance or an interest in the property.

Encroachments

An encroachment is a physical object that intrudes from one person's land onto another's without authorization, such as a fence or garage built partially over the property line onto the neighbor's land (see Figure 4.3). Most encroachments are unintentional, resulting from a mistake concerning the exact location of the property line. An encroachment is not an encumbrance, because it is not a right or interest held by the encroacher.

An encroachment may be a **trespass** if it violates the neighboring owner's rights of possession. A court can order the removal of an encroachment through a judicial

Fig. 4.3 Encroachments

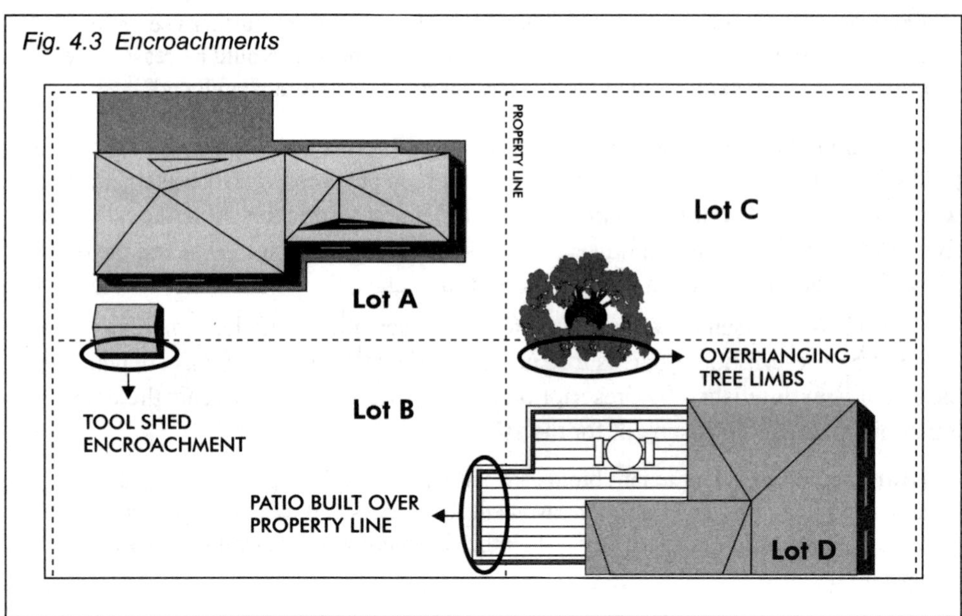

action called an **ejectment**. Alternatively, if the cost of the removal would be too great, the court could order the encroacher to pay damages to the neighbor.

There is a three-year statute of limitations on court actions for trespass on real property. That means that a property owner must file suit within three years of the time he discovered (or should have discovered) an encroachment, or the right to sue for damages or the removal of the encroachment will be lost.

Nuisances

A nuisance is an activity or a condition on neighboring property that interferes with a property owner's reasonable use or enjoyment of her own property. Common examples include odors, noise, and interference with communication signals. Like an encroachment, a nuisance isn't truly an encumbrance, but rather a violation of an owner's possessory rights.

A **private nuisance** affects only a few surrounding people. For example, rotting garbage in a neighbor's backyard would be a private nuisance. A **public nuisance** affects a larger community's health or welfare; jet noise and industrial emissions are examples. A property owner may ask a court for an injunction against a private or public nuisance, or may sue for damages.

A related concept is the **attractive nuisance** doctrine. The owner of a property with a feature that is dangerous and attractive to children, such as an unfenced swimming pool or construction site, will be held liable for any harm resulting from failure to keep out trespassing children.

Private Restrictions

Private restrictions, also called **deed restrictions** or **restrictive covenants**, are restrictions on the use of a property that were usually imposed by a previous owner. Like easements, private restrictions can "run with the land," binding all subsequent owners of the property.

Example: When the Graysons sold their property in 1940, they included a restriction in the deed stating that the poplar trees in the front yard must not be cut down. Everyone who's owned the property since then, including the current owner, has had to comply with the Graysons' wishes regarding the trees.

While restrictions are often imposed in a deed, as in the example, they can also be created by written agreement between the current property owner and a neighbor or some other party. This type of restriction can also run with the land and be binding on all future owners.

Most subdivision developers impose a list of restrictions on all lots within the subdivision, before they begin selling individual lots. This is called a declaration of restrictions, or **CC&Rs** (covenants, conditions, and restrictions). The CC&Rs typically include rules limiting all the lots to single-family residential use, requiring property maintenance, and preventing activities that would bother the neighbors. The rules are intended to ensure that the subdivision will remain a desirable place to live. The CC&Rs are recorded, and then referenced in the deeds used to convey the lots in the subdivision.

As long as a private restriction isn't unconstitutional, in violation of a law, or contrary to a judicial determination of public policy, it can be enforced in court. (An example of an unenforceable restriction is one prohibiting the sale of property to non-white buyers; see Chapter 14.)

Covenants vs. Conditions. A private restriction is either a covenant or a condition. A **covenant** is a promise to do or not do something, as in a contract. A property owner who violates a covenant may be sued, leading to an injunction (a court order directing the owner to comply with the covenant) or, less often, payment of damages for failure to comply. Violation of a **condition** can have more serious consequences. A condition in a deed makes the grantee's title conditional, so that he owns a fee simple defeasible rather than a fee simple absolute (see Chapter 2). Breach of the condition could result in forfeiture of title.

Whether a particular restriction is a covenant or a condition depends on the wording in the deed. Courts try to avoid forfeiture, which is considered a harsh remedy, so they will usually interpret a restriction as a covenant rather than a condition if there is any ambiguity. (Note that CC&Rs are virtually always interpreted to be covenants, even though the term includes the word "conditions.")

Termination of Restrictions. It is up to the property owners within a subdivision to enforce the CC&Rs. If the residents have failed to enforce a particular restriction in the past, they may no longer be able to enforce it.

Example: The subdivision's CC&Rs state that recreational vehicles may not be parked within view of the street. Over the years, however, many homeowners have broken this rule and their neighbors haven't complained. If someone tries to start enforcing the parking restriction now, a court might rule that it has been abandoned and is no longer enforceable.

A private restriction will also terminate if its purpose can no longer be achieved. For example, this might occur because zoning changes and other factors have dramatically altered the character of the neighborhood. If there's a private restriction limiting a property to single-family residential use, but most of the surrounding properties are now used for light industry, the restriction may no longer be enforceable.

Chapter Summary

1. An encumbrance is a nonpossessory right or interest in real property held by someone other than the property owner. Encumbrances may be financial or nonfinancial.
2. A financial encumbrance (a lien) affects title to property. It gives a creditor the right to foreclose and use the sale proceeds to pay off the debt. A lien is either voluntary or involuntary, and either general or specific. The most common types of liens include mortgages, deeds of trust, mechanic's liens, tax liens, judgment liens, and attachment liens.
3. A nonfinancial encumbrance affects the use or condition of the property. Nonfinancial encumbrances include easements, profits, and private restrictions.
4. An easement gives the easement holder the right to use part of someone else's property for a specified purpose. An easement runs with the land, affecting the title of subsequent owners of the property or properties in question.
5. An easement appurtenant burdens one parcel of land (the servient tenement) for the benefit of another parcel (the dominant tenement). An easement in gross burdens a parcel of land for the benefit of a person or company, not another parcel of land.
6. Licenses, encroachments, and nuisances also may affect the use or condition of property. They are not classified as encumbrances, however, because they are not interests in real property.
7. Private restrictions affect how an owner may use her own property. Like easements, private restrictions run with the land. A declaration of CC&Rs recorded by a subdivision developer is binding on the future owners of the subdivision lots.

Key Terms

Encumbrance—An interest in real property held by someone other than the property owner.

Voluntary lien—A security interest given to a creditor voluntarily.

Involuntary lien—A security interest given to a creditor by operation of law.

General lien—A lien that attaches to all of a debtor's property.

Specific lien—A lien that attaches only to one particular piece of property.

Mechanic's lien—A lien on property in favor of someone who provided labor or materials to improve it. Also called a construction lien or materialman's lien.

Judgment lien—A lien held by someone who has won a judgment in a lawsuit, attaching to property owned by the person who lost the lawsuit.

Easement—The right to use another's land for a particular purpose.

Easement appurtenant—An easement that burdens one parcel of land (the servient tenement) for the benefit of another parcel (the dominant tenement).

Easement in gross—An easement that benefits a person rather than a parcel of land.

Easement by implication—An easement created automatically because it is necessary for the enjoyment of the benefited land.

Prescriptive easement—An easement created by continuous use for the statutory period, without the landowner's permission.

Merger—When both the dominant and servient tenements are acquired by one owner, resulting in termination of the easement.

Abandonment—A way in which an easement may terminate. It requires action by the easement holder, not merely nonuse.

Profit—The right to take something (such as timber) from another's land.

License—Revocable permission to enter another's land, which does not create an interest in the property.

Encroachment—A physical object that intrudes onto another's property, such as a tree branch or a fence.

Nuisance—An activity or condition on nearby property that interferes with a property owner's reasonable use and enjoyment of his property.

CC&Rs—Covenants, conditions, and restrictions; private restrictions imposed by a subdivision developer.

Condition—A restriction on the use of land, the violation of which may result in forfeiture of title.

Covenant—A promise by a landowner to refrain from using her land in a particular manner.

Chapter Quiz

1. Real estate property tax liens are:
   a) general, involuntary liens
   b) general, voluntary liens
   c) specific, voluntary liens
   d) specific, involuntary liens

2. A lawsuit against Thatcher is pending. The court rules that a lien should be placed on his farm, holding it as security in case of a negative judgment. This is:
   a) adverse possession
   b) prescription
   c) an attachment
   d) an easement

3. A recorded document that informs potential buyers that the property may become subject to a judgment in a lawsuit is a:
   a) lis pendens
   b) writ of execution
   c) writ of attachment
   d) habendum clause

4. Which of the following has priority over a mortgage that has already been recorded?
   a) A deed of trust
   b) A judgment lien
   c) A property tax lien
   d) None of the above

5. If there were two deeds of trust against the same property and you needed to know which one had higher priority, you could find this information by checking the county records. The priority is usually established by:
   a) the printed deed of trust forms, which have the words "first deed of trust" and "second deed of trust" on their face
   b) the date and time of recording
   c) the county auditor's stamp, which says "first deed of trust" or "second deed of trust"
   d) the execution date of each document

6. When there's an easement appurtenant, the dominant tenement:
   a) can be used only for purposes of ingress and egress
   b) is burdened by the easement
   c) receives the benefit of the easement
   d) cannot be sold

7. You have the right to cross another's land to get to your house. You probably own a:
   a) dominant tenement
   b) servient tenement
   c) Both of the above
   d) Neither of the above

8. An easement in gross benefits a:
   a) dominant tenement
   b) servient tenement
   c) Both of the above
   d) Neither of the above

9. Unlike a license, an easement:
   a) is not an encumbrance
   b) is considered a possessory interest in real property
   c) runs with the land
   d) can be revoked by the owner of the servient tenement

10. Which of the following is not a method of creating an easement?
    a) Implication
    b) Express grant in a deed
    c) Dedication
    d) Spoken grant

11. The creation of an easement by prescription is similar to acquiring ownership of property by:
    a) adverse possession
    b) escheat
    c) alluvium
    d) intestate succession

12. A has an easement over B's property. If A buys B's property, the easement is:
    a) abandoned
    b) terminated by merger
    c) unaffected
    d) None of the above

13. A porch or balcony that hangs over the established boundary line of a parcel of land is called a/an:
    a) easement in gross
    b) encroachment
    c) easement appurtenant
    d) license

14. All of the following would be considered nuisances, except:
    a) fumes from a paper mill
    b) a house with regular drug-dealing activity
    c) radiation from a microwave tower
    d) a garage built on top of the property line

15. The private restrictions in a subdivision's CC&Rs:
    a) do not run with the land
    b) were imposed by the developer
    c) can terminate only with the approval of a majority of the lot owners
    d) create a lien against the property

Answer Key

1. d) Property tax liens are specific (they attach only to the taxed property) and involuntary.

2. c) In an attachment, a lien is created against the defendant's property, pending the outcome of the lawsuit.

3. a) A lis pendens provides constructive notice of a pending lawsuit that may affect the property described in the document.

4. c) Property tax liens always have priority over other liens.

5. b) The date of recording governs lien priority, rather than the date of execution of the documents.

6. c) The dominant tenement is benefited by the easement; the servient tenement is burdened by the easement. An easement appurtenant is not necessarily an easement for ingress and egress.

7. a) Since you have the right to use another's property to reach your own, you probably own a dominant tenement.

8. d) An easement in gross benefits an individual person or company (the dominant tenant) rather than any parcel of land.

9. c) An easement runs with the land, which means that future owners of the servient tenement will have to allow the easement to be used. A license does not run with the land.

10. d) Like any other interest in land, an easement must be granted in writing, unless it is created by operation of law.

11. a) An easement by prescription is obtained in much the same way as ownership by adverse possession: the use must be open and notorious, hostile, and continuous for five years.

12. b) Merger occurs when one person acquires ownership of both the dominant tenement and the servient tenement. Merger terminates the easement.

13. b) An overhanging porch or balcony is an encroachment.

14. d) A structure built on the property line is an encroachment, not a nuisance. A nuisance is an activity or condition on neighboring property that negatively affects an owner's use and enjoyment of his property.

15. b) CC&Rs are usually imposed by the developer. They run with the land, so subsequent owners of the subdivision lots must abide by them.

Chapter 5

Public Restrictions on Land

I. Land Use Controls
   A. Comprehensive planning
   B. Zoning
      1. Nonconforming uses
      2. Variances
      3. Conditional uses
      4. Rezones
   C. Building codes
   D. Subdivision regulations
      1. Types of subdivisions
      2. Laws regulating subdivisions
   E. Environmental laws
      1. NEPA
      2. CERCLA
      3. Pollution control laws
      4. CEQA
      5. California Coastal Act
      6. Alquist-Priolo Act
II. Eminent Domain
III. Taxation of Real Property
   A. General real estate taxes
   B. Special assessments
   C. Other special taxes
   D. Documentary transfer tax

Chapter Overview

Although a property owner has many rights in regard to her property, those rights are limited by certain powers of the federal, state, and local governments. This chapter examines the ways in which governmental powers affect property ownership most directly. It covers planning, zoning, and other public restrictions on land use; the taking of private property for public use; and the taxation of real property.

Land Use Controls

In the United States, the powers of government are determined by the federal and state constitutions. Thus, efforts by the federal, state, and local governments to control the use of private property raise constitutional issues. When a property owner objects to a land use law, the central question is often whether the law is constitutional—whether the federal and state constitutions give the government the power to interfere with private property rights in this way.

The basis for land use control laws is the **police power**. This is the power vested in a state government to adopt and enforce laws and regulations necessary for the protection of the public's health, safety, morals, and general welfare. A state may delegate its police power to local governmental bodies.

It is the police power that allows state and local governments to regulate the use of private property. The U.S. Constitution does not give the federal government a general power to regulate for the public health, safety, morals, and welfare. But the federal government does have authority to use its other powers (such as the power to regulate interstate commerce) to advance police power objectives.

An exercise of the police power must meet constitutional limitations. Generally, a land use law or regulation will be considered constitutional if it meets these criteria:

1. It is reasonably related to the protection of the public health, safety, morals, or general welfare.
2. It applies in the same manner to all property owners who are similarly situated (in other words, it is not discriminatory).
3. It does not reduce a property's value so much that the regulation amounts to a confiscation—an uncompensated taking of property.
4. It benefits the public by preventing harm that would be caused by the prohibited use of the property.

Government land use controls take a variety of forms: comprehensive plans, zoning ordinances, building codes, subdivision regulations, and environmental laws. All of these are intended to protect the public from problems that unrestricted use of private property can cause.

If two different government entities have passed conflicting laws based on the police power, the one with the stricter standards of health and safety will apply.

Comprehensive Planning

Unrestricted and unplanned development can have undesirable results. Incompatible uses, such as a dairy farm and a retail shopping center, could end up right next to each other. Even when neighboring uses are compatible, development may be too

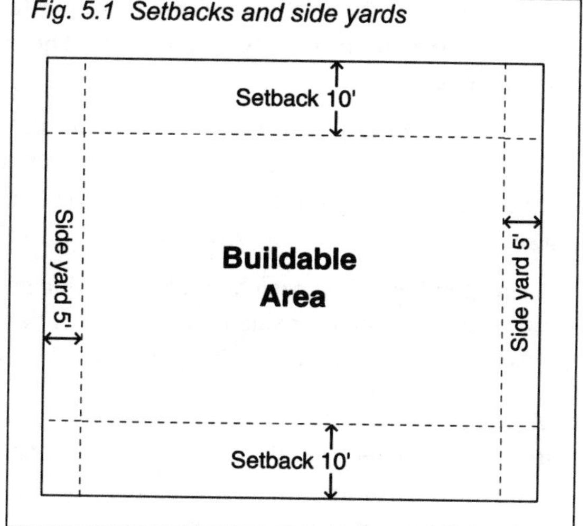

Fig. 5.1 Setbacks and side yards

dense, causing traffic gridlock, pollution, or other problems; or not dense enough, leading to urban and suburban sprawl.

To alleviate problems caused by haphazard, unplanned growth, California requires cities and counties to have a planning agency, usually called a planning commission.

The planning commission is responsible for designing and adopting a comprehensive, long-term plan for all the development within the city or county. This is often called the "master plan" or "general plan." The purpose of the general plan is to outline the community's development goals and design an overall physical layout to achieve those goals.

Once a general plan has been adopted, all development and all land use regulations for the area must conform to it. To implement the plan, the local government uses its police power to pass zoning ordinances and other laws, and may also use the power of eminent domain to acquire property for public use. (Eminent domain will be discussed later in the chapter.)

Zoning

Zoning ordinances divide a community into areas (zones) that are set aside for a particular type of use, such as agricultural, residential, commercial, or industrial use. Each of these basic classifications typically has subcategories. For instance, an industrial district could be divided into a light industrial zone and a heavy industrial zone. A residential district could be divided into single-family zones (often designated as R-1 zones) and multifamily zones (often called R-3 zones). Keeping various uses in separate zones helps ensure that only compatible uses are located in the same area. In addition, areas zoned for incompatible uses may be separated by undeveloped areas called **buffers**.

Zoning ordinances regulate the height, size, and shape of buildings, as well as their use. They also usually include setback and side yard requirements, which prescribe the minimum distance between a building and the property lines (see Figure 5.1). These regulations control population density, provide aesthetic guidelines, and help preserve adequate open space and access to air and daylight.

To be valid, zoning ordinances cannot be applied retroactively, cannot discriminate against a particular parcel of property, and cannot create a patently unfair situation.

Zoning Exceptions and Amendments. Complications inevitably arise when zoning regulations are administered and enforced. So zoning ordinances provide for certain exceptions and changes to their rules, including:

- nonconforming uses,
- variances,
- conditional uses, and
- rezones.

A zoning exception or change can be requested by an individual property owner, a developer, or a city or county government. These requests are heard by the local zoning authority.

Nonconforming Uses. A **nonconforming use** can arise when an area is zoned for the first time, or when a zoning ordinance is amended. Certain established uses that were previously lawful may not conform to the rules laid down in the new ordinance. These nonconforming uses will be permitted to continue.

Example: Smith has been lawfully operating a bakery for seven months when his property is rezoned for single-family residential use. Smith's bakery will be allowed to continue as a nonconforming use. He is not required to apply for a permit.

A nonconforming use provision in a zoning ordinance is sometimes referred to as a grandfather clause. However, even though nonconforming uses are "grandfathered in" and allowed to remain, the local government usually prefers to have all properties in a zone eventually conform to the current rules. So an ordinance might require nonconforming uses to be phased out by a certain deadline (for example, ten years after the ordinance was passed). Even in the absence of such a deadline, the owner of a nonconforming use property is often prohibited from enlarging the use, rebuilding if the property is destroyed, or resuming the use after abandoning it.

Example: Smith's bakery burns to the ground in a terrible fire. The zoning authority will not allow him to rebuild the bakery in this residential zone. He will have to sell the property and buy a suitable property located in a commercial zone.

Variances. In some cases, if a zoning law were strictly enforced, the property owner's injury would far outweigh the benefit of enforcing the zoning requirement. Under these circumstances, a **variance** may be available. A variance is authorization to build or maintain a structure or use that is ordinarily prohibited by the zoning ordinance. For example, a variance might authorize construction of a house even though the topography of the lot makes it impossible to comply with the setback requirements in the zoning law. In most communities, the property owner applies to the local zoning authority for a variance.

A variance usually won't be granted unless the property owner can show that without the variance she will be deprived of privileges available to most other property owners in the zone. A variance should not be granted simply in order to allow a property owner to make a more profitable use of her land than the zoning rules permit.

Example: Martinez owns a piece of property that she feels would be a perfect site for a four-unit apartment building. However, because of the setback requirements in the zoning ordinance, the largest structure Martinez could build there is a duplex. Martinez won't be granted a variance just because she could make much more money with a four-unit building than she could with a duplex.

Most variances authorize only minor deviations from the zoning law. A variance should not reduce the value of neighboring property, change the essential character of the neighborhood, or conflict with the community's general plan.

In California, local authorities may not grant **use variances**—variances that authorize a land use that is otherwise not permitted in a zone. For instance, a variance allowing a commercial or retail use in a single-family residential zone can't be granted.

Example: Corelli owns a lot in a single-family residential zone. Unfortunately, the land doesn't drain properly, so he isn't permitted to build a single-family home on the lot. However, the lot would make a perfect site for storage units. Corelli requests a variance, but the request is denied. The local zoning authority doesn't have the power to grant a variance that would allow a commercial use in a residential zone.

Conditional Uses. Various special uses, such as schools, hospitals, and places of worship, don't fit into the ordinary zoning categories. These uses are considered necessary to the community, yet they may have adverse effects on neighboring properties. So in most communities, the zoning authority can issue **conditional use permits** (also called special exception permits), allowing a limited number of these uses to operate in compliance with specified conditions. For example, a property owner might be given a conditional use permit to build a private school in a residential neighborhood, as long as the school meets certain requirements for parking, security, and so on.

Rezones. If a property owner believes that his property has been zoned improperly, he may petition the local zoning authority for a **rezone** (sometimes called a zoning amendment). Usually, notice must be given to surrounding landowners and a hearing must be held before a decision is made on a petition.

When an area is rezoned to a more restrictive use (for example, a change from multifamily dwellings to single-family dwellings), it's referred to as **downzoning**. An **upzone** is the opposite; the zoning becomes less restrictive. For example, an upzone would include raising the building height limits in an urban area to help meet the housing density goals of a comprehensive plan.

Zoning vs. Private Restrictions. Sometimes private restrictions impose stricter limits on property than the local zoning ordinance. For example, suppose a property is in a zone that requires lots to be a minimum of 15,000 square feet, while a private restriction on the property prevents it from being subdivided into lots smaller than half an acre (21,780 square feet). The general rule is that the more restrictive requirement must be met. In our example, the private restriction would take precedence over the zoning ordinance, because it is the more restrictive of the two. On the other hand, in cases where the zoning is more restrictive than a private restriction, the zoning will take precedence. (See Chapter 4 for more information about private restrictions.)

Building Codes

The enactment of building codes is another exercise of the police power. Building codes protect the public from unsafe or unworkmanlike construction. They are generally divided into specialized codes, such as a fire code, an electrical code, and a plumbing code. The codes set standards for construction methods and materials. A structure that was built before a new, stricter standard is enacted may still be required to meet the new standard.

Enforcement of building codes is usually accomplished through the building permit system. A property owner must obtain a permit from the city or county before constructing a new building or repairing, improving, or altering an existing building. For example, it is usually necessary to have a building permit in order to add on to a home, to convert a carport into a garage, or even to build a fence. The permit requirement allows officials to inspect the building plans to verify that building codes and zoning ordinances have been satisfied. Once the completed construction has been inspected and found satisfactory, a **certificate of occupancy** is issued.

In California, the state Housing Law sets forth minimum construction and occupancy requirements for residential construction. These requirements are enforced by local building inspectors. The construction industry is also regulated through the state Contractors License Law.

Subdivision Regulations

Another way in which state and local governments control land use is by regulating subdivisions. A **subdivision** is a division of one parcel of land into two or more parcels or lots.

Types of Subdivisions. There are various types of subdivisions in California, including standard, common interest, and undivided interest subdivisions. Subdivisions are usually residential, but they may be commercial, industrial, or recreational.

Standard Subdivisions. In a standard subdivision, each owner owns a separate parcel of land. A standard subdivision is technically defined as one with no common rights of either ownership or use among the various owners of the individual parcels created by the division.

Standard subdivisions usually consist of five or more lots that have been improved with utilities. Individuals may purchase a lot on which to build their own home, or developers may purchase several or all of the lots, build houses on the lots, and then sell the homes to individual homeowners.

Common Interest Subdivisions. In a common interest subdivision (also called a common interest development, or CID), an individual owner owns or leases a separate lot or unit along with an undivided interest in the common areas of the project. Condominium and cooperative projects are examples of common interest subdivisions. For example, a condominium owner owns her residential unit in severalty, but also has an undivided interest in the common areas of the condominium project, such as the lobby, elevators, parking lot, and recreational facilities. (See Chapter 2.)

Planned developments (sometimes called planned unit developments, or PUDs) are also common interest subdivisions. A typical planned development looks like a standard subdivision, since each lot is improved with a single-family home. But a planned development consists of lots that are separately owned, plus areas that are owned in common and reserved for the use of some or all of the individual lot owners. As in a condominium, the common areas are generally managed and maintained by an owners association. The association charges the lot owners fees to pay for the management and maintenance of the common areas.

A **timeshare** is another type of common interest subdivision. In a timesharing arrangement, buyers purchase the exclusive right to possession of the property for a specified period each year. A timeshare could be developed for any kind of housing, but it is most commonly used for resort condominiums.

Undivided Interest Subdivisions. In an undivided interest subdivision, individual owners own undivided interests in a parcel of land and have a nonexclusive right to use and occupy the property. The undivided interests are typically tenancies in common. An example of an undivided interest subdivision is a recreational vehicle park.

Laws Regulating Subdivisions. Laws that regulate subdivisions in California include the Subdivision Map Act, the Subdivided Lands Law, and the Interstate Land Sales Full Disclosure Act. The Subdivision Map Act is a "procedural" law, one that sets forth the procedures that must be followed to subdivide land. The Subdivided Lands Law is a "consumer protection" law, one that requires the subdivider to disclose certain information to lot buyers. The Interstate Land Sales Full Disclosure Act is a federal consumer protection law that applies to subdivision lots sold in interstate commerce.

Subdivision Map Act. The Subdivision Map Act establishes a set of procedures that must be followed before a subdivision can be created. It gives cities and counties the power to control the formation of subdivisions, and it sets out rules for the exercise of that power. The purpose of the Subdivision Map Act is to ensure that new subdivisions comply with the local general plan. It also ensures that adequate public utilities are provided for each new subdivision. The act applies whenever a single parcel of land is subdivided into two or more parcels (lots or units), but its most important provisions affect only subdivisions with five or more parcels.

When land is subdivided into five or more parcels, the subdivider must file a **tentative subdivision map** with the local planning agency. The tentative map includes the legal description of the property and shows the proposed lot boundaries, the location of utility easements and access roads, proposed street widths, the source of the water supply, and the provisions for control of flooding and geologic hazards. The planning agency sends copies of the map to other government agencies for their recommendations. These government agencies include transportation, health, and parks departments; school districts; city or county surveyors; and public utilities. The subdivider has the burden of demonstrating to these agencies that the off-site improvements, such as streets, curbs, sewers, and utilities, are adequate. Once these agencies report back to the planning agency, it can approve or reject the tentative map, or approve it on the condition that the subdivider take certain actions. For example, the planning agency may require the subdivider to dedicate some of the subdivision property for public streets.

Once the planning agency approves a tentative map, the subdivider has a limited period (generally 24 months, plus possible extensions) to file a **final map**, showing the subdivision in its final form. The final map must bear the signatures of the owners and of representatives of each public utility or other entity that considered the tentative map. No sale, lease, or contract for the sale or lease of any subdivided property is valid until a final map is filed.

Instead of tentative and final maps, a **parcel map** can be filed for subdivisions with two to four parcels. A parcel map doesn't have to be as detailed as a tentative subdivision map or a final map.

Subdivided Lands Law. The Subdivided Lands Law requires a subdivider to disclose certain information to buyers. It applies to most residential subdivisions with five or more lots. The five lots need not be contiguous if they are part of the same project.

The Subdivided Lands Law also applies to mobile home parks and planned developments with five or more lots; to condominiums, community apartment projects, and cooperatives with five or more units; and to some residential timeshare projects. Leases of apartments, offices, and stores within a building are exempt from the law, as are leases in mobile home parks for five years or less. Subdivisions that are entirely within the limits of an incorporated city may also be exempt if the developer complies with certain rules. Also exempt are subdivisions with parcels that are 160 acres or larger, and industrial or commercial subdivisions.

Lots or units in a subdivision covered by the act can't be sold, leased, or financed until the Real Estate Commissioner investigates it and issues a **final subdivision**

public report. A public report is issued only if the subdivision meets the requirements set forth in the Subdivided Lands Law. A report will be denied:

1. if there is any evidence that the subdivision is unsuitable for the use proposed by the subdivider, or
2. if there is no assurance that purchasers will get what they've paid for.

For example, to obtain a final public report for a residential subdivision, the subdivider must be able to show that streets and other improvements will be completed and that there will be adequate drinking water and other utilities. The subdivider also must be able to demonstrate that any deposit money will be made secure, that there are satisfactory arrangements to clear any mechanic's liens or blanket mortgage liens (for instance, with the use of impound or escrow accounts), and that when the transaction is completed, title will be conveyed to the purchaser.

When the Commissioner has determined that a subdivision has met all legal requirements, a final subdivision public report will be issued. A public report includes the following information:

- the subdivider's name and the project's name, location, and size;
- the legal interest to be acquired by the purchaser;
- the procedure for handling the purchase money;
- the amount of any taxes and assessments;
- any private restrictions;
- any unusual costs the purchaser will have to bear;
- any hazards or adverse environmental factors; and
- any unusual or potentially harmful financial or conveyancing arrangements.

The public report must be given to anyone who requests it, and all prospective purchasers must receive a copy of the report before entering into a sales agreement. They must also sign a receipt proving that they received a copy of the report. That receipt must be kept by the subdivider for at least three years.

A final public report is valid for five years, unless a material change occurs in the subdivision. Material changes include physical changes to the subdivision itself (such as new street or lot lines), changes in the documents used to transfer or finance lots, the sale of five or more lots to one party, or new conditions that affect the value or use of lots.

Often, the Commissioner issues a **preliminary report** before issuing the final report. If the developer gives a prospective buyer a copy of a preliminary report, the buyer can reserve a lot in the subdivision. But until the buyer receives the final report, he has the right to back out and have any deposit refunded in full. Preliminary reports expire after one year, but may be renewed.

If a final public report is used for advertising purposes, it must be used in its entirety. A subdivider cannot, in an advertisement, refer to any improvements or facilities that do not actually exist, unless their completion is provided for with a bond. And an artist's rendering of the subdivision cannot be used in any advertisement unless it is described as such.

If the Commissioner discovers that a subdivider is violating any provisions of the Subdivided Lands Law, the Commissioner can stop the violations or sales of the lots with a **desist and refrain** order.

Out-of-State Subdivisions. If property in a subdivision located in another state is offered for sale in California, the subdivision must be registered with the California Bureau of Real Estate. Advertising and sales contracts must have disclaimers explaining that the CalBRE hasn't inspected or approved the subdivision.

ILSA. The **Interstate Land Sales Full Disclosure Act** (ILSA) is a federal consumer protection law concerning subdivisions of vacant land offered for sale or lease in interstate commerce. It has registration requirements (requiring developers to register their projects with a federal agency) and anti-fraud provisions (requiring disclosure of information to buyers and prohibiting misleading sales practices and advertising). The anti-fraud provisions generally apply to subdivisions with 25 or more vacant lots, and the registration requirements generally apply to subdivisions with 100 or more vacant lots, but there are numerous exceptions. ILSA was originally administered and enforced by the Department of Housing and Urban Development (HUD), but that role has now been assumed by the Consumer Financial Protection Bureau.

Environmental Laws

The federal and state governments have enacted a number of laws aimed at preserving and protecting the physical environment, and many local governments have additional environmental regulations. These laws can have a substantial impact on the ways in which a property owner is allowed to use her land.

National Environmental Policy Act (NEPA). NEPA is a federal law that requires federal agencies to prepare an **environmental impact statement** (EIS) for governmental actions that would have a significant impact. NEPA also applies to private uses or developments that require the approval of a federal agency.

An EIS summarizes a proposed project's probable environmental effects (both positive and negative), and also discusses alternatives to the proposal. A planning or zoning agency will consider the EIS when deciding whether to approve the project.

CERCLA. The Comprehensive Environmental Response, Compensation, and Liability Act, a federal law, concerns liability for environmental cleanup costs. In some cases, the current owners of contaminated property may be required to pay for cleanup, even if they did not cause the contamination. The federal Environmental Protection Agency (EPA) enforces the law.

Pollution Control Laws. Federal legislation sets national standards for air and water quality and requires the states to implement these objectives. Permits are required for the discharge of pollutants into the air or water.

California Environmental Quality Act (CEQA). This California law is similar to the National Environmental Policy Act. CEQA requires state or local agencies to prepare an **environmental impact report** (EIR) for any project (public or private) that may have a significant impact on the environment. An EIR is not required only if the public agency overseeing the project rules that the project won't have significant adverse effects; this is called a **negative declaration**.

A public hearing is held for each EIR. Alternatives to the proposed action must be considered, and the developer may be required to make changes in the project to reduce its impact.

California Coastal Act. The Coastal Act established the Coastal Commission, which researches ways to protect the state's coastline and controls development along the coast. It has several regional divisions. No development is allowed in the coastal zone without a permit from the appropriate regional board.

Alquist-Priolo Act. Pursuant to the Alquist-Priolo Act, certain areas of the state are delineated as earthquake fault zones (sometimes called "special studies zones") on maps prepared by the state geologist. The zones follow traces of potentially active faults and are usually a quarter of a mile wide.

If property is located in a fault zone, an application for new development or construction generally must include a geologic report evaluating the property's earthquake risks. When property in a fault zone is sold, the seller and the seller's agent must inform buyers that the property is in such a zone.

Eminent Domain

As you've seen, the government can regulate the use of private property with a variety of laws—zoning ordinances, building codes, and so on. These laws are based on the police power, the government's power to regulate for the public health, safety, morals, and general welfare. Another governmental power that can affect land use is the power of **eminent domain**.

The power of eminent domain is the federal or state government's power to take private property for a public use upon payment of **just compensation** to the owner. A state government may delegate the power of eminent domain to local governments, and to private entities that serve the public, such as utility companies and railroads.

Condemnation is the process by which the government exercises its power of eminent domain. When a particular property is needed for a public use or purpose, the government first offers to buy it from the owner. If the owner refuses to sell for the price offered, the government files a condemnation lawsuit. The court will order the property to be transferred to the government. The owner's only grounds for objection are that the intended use of the property is not a public use, or that the price offered is not just compensation. (Just compensation is usually defined as the fair market value of the property.)

A local government can use the power of eminent domain to implement its general plan. For example, to fulfill the plan's open space goals, several pieces of private property might be condemned for use as a public park.

What constitutes a public use or public purpose can be a matter of controversy. In a 2005 case called *Kelo v. City of New London*, the U.S. Supreme Court ruled that it was constitutional for a Connecticut city to condemn private property in an economically distressed neighborhood in order to develop an urban village complex with shops, restaurants, a hotel, office space, and residences. The Court decided that the goal of the plan, economic development, fulfilled the public use requirement even though the city was going to sell the property to private owners. In 2008, in response to the *Kelo* decision, California voters passed an initiative that generally prohibits the state and local governments from exercising the power of eminent domain to take an owner-occupied residence for conveyance to a private party.

It's important to understand the distinction between eminent domain and the police power. Eminent domain involves a "taking" of private property: property is taken away from the owner, and the Constitution requires the government to pay the owner compensation. In an exercise of the police power, private property is regulated, but not taken away from the owner. The government is not required to compensate the owner for a proper exercise of the police power, even though the action (such as a zoning change) may significantly reduce the value of the property.

Fig. 5.2 Police power vs. eminent domain

	Police Power	**Eminent Domain**
Public purpose	Yes	Yes
Taking of property	No	Yes
Compensation required	No	Yes

You may also hear "condemnation" used to refer to an order by local authorities requiring occupants to vacate a building for health or safety reasons. This, however, is an exercise of police power, rather than the power of eminent domain, and does not entitle displaced persons to just compensation from the government.

Taxation of Real Property

Real property taxes affect property ownership. The taxes create liens, and if the property owner fails to pay the taxes, the government can sell the property to collect the money owed. Real property taxation has always been a popular method of raising revenue because land has a fixed location, is basically indestructible, and is impossible to conceal. While collection of other types of taxes can be difficult, collection of taxes on real property generally isn't a problem. The taxes will almost certainly be collected sooner or later, with or without the cooperation of the property owner.

In this section, we will discuss these types of taxes on real property:

- general real estate taxes (also called ad valorem taxes),
- special assessments (also called improvement taxes),
- other special real property taxes, and
- the documentary transfer tax (also called an excise tax).

General Real Estate Taxes

General real estate taxes are levied to support the general operation and services of government. Public schools and police and fire protection are examples of government services paid for with general real estate tax revenues. These taxes are levied by a number of governmental agencies, such as cities, counties, school districts, and water districts. Thus, a single property can be situated in five or six taxing districts.

Assessment. General real estate taxes are **ad valorem** taxes. That means the amount of tax owed depends on the value of the property. The valuation of property for purposes of taxation is called **assessment**.

In California, property assessment and taxation are governed by Proposition 13, an initiative passed by voters in 1978 that amended the state constitution. Property must be assessed by the county assessor at its **full cash value**. And as a general rule, the tax rate, which is set by the county's Board of Supervisors, may not exceed **one percent** of the property's full cash value.

Protection from drastic tax increases is given to those who own the same home for a long period of time. The purchase price of a home becomes its **base value**. (If a home was last purchased prior to 1975, the property's 1975 value is its base value.) As long as the same person owns the property and no improvements are made, its assessed value can't increase more than 2% per year. If the owner improves the property (by building a deck, for example), the assessed value may be increased by the amount the improvements add to the actual value.

The property's assessment is increased to the current full cash value only if there is a new owner or new construction on the property. When the property is sold or otherwise transferred, the new owner must file a **change in ownership statement** with the county recorder or assessor within 45 days of the transfer. Unless the transaction is exempt from reassessment on a change in ownership, the assessed value may be stepped up to the price paid or to the fair market value at the time of the transfer. That becomes the new base value.

If a property is transferred in the middle of a tax year, the new owner must pay a supplemental assessment for the remainder of the tax year. The supplemental assessment takes into account the difference between the previous assessed value and the new assessed value. A seller (or a seller's agent) is required to give a prospective buyer a notice explaining that the buyer may receive one or two supplemental tax bills, and that the buyer will be responsible for paying the additional taxes; the buyer's lender won't pay them out of the impound account maintained in connection with the buyer's loan.

Reassessment Exceptions. To avoid the harsh result of an increased assessment following a transfer of title when the property hasn't been sold or traded for profit, the law exempts several types of transfers from reassessment. For example, the following transfers are exempt:

- transfers where the method of holding title is changed but the ownership isn't;
- certain transfers between parents and children; and
- transfers between spouses or registered domestic partners.

Also, when a homeowner who is over 55 or severely and permanently disabled sells her home and replaces it with another home in the same county, the assessed value of the old home can be used as the assessed value of the new home. The market value of the new home must be equal to or less than the market value of the old home, and the new home must be purchased within two years after the sale of the old one. A seller who purchases a replacement home in a different county may or may not be able to transfer the assessed value of the old home to the new home. That will depend on the laws of the county where the new home is located.

Assessment Appeals. Property owners who are dissatisfied with the assessment of their property may appeal to the county. In some counties, appeals are handled by the Board of Supervisors. Larger counties have a separate Assessment Appeals Board (sometimes referred to as the board of equalization), which has the power to adjust the assessed value of property. Often, an appeal is based on the property owner's claim that the property tax burden has been applied inconsistently, because similar properties in the neighborhood have been assessed differently.

Fig. 5.3 California property tax dates

Real Property Taxes (Tax Year = July 1 – June 30)	
Taxes become lien	January 1
Taxes levied	by September 1
Tax bill mailed	by November 1
First installment due	November 1
First installment delinquent	December 10
Second installment due	February 1
Second installment delinquent	April 10

Collection of Taxes. General real estate taxes are levied annually, on or before September 1 for each tax year. The tax year runs from July 1 through June 30 of the next calendar year. The tax lien attaches to the property on the previous January 1. So the lien for the July 2014 to June 2015 tax year attached on January 1, 2014. Since the taxes aren't levied until September, the specific amount of the tax lien isn't known when the lien attaches.

A tax bill is mailed to each property owner on or before November 1 of each year. The tax bill reflects the property's assessed value, less any exemptions to which the property owner is entitled. The assessed value is multiplied by the tax rate (no more than 1%), and the result is the amount of tax the property owner must pay.

An owner may pay his taxes in two installments, or may pay the total amount when the first installment is due. The first installment is due on November 1, covers the period from July through December, and is delinquent if not paid by 5:00 pm on December 10. The second installment is due February 1, covers the period from January through June, and is delinquent if not paid by 5:00 pm on April 10. A 10% penalty is added to any delinquent payment.

If the property taxes are not paid, the tax collector can foreclose on the tax lien. First a notice of impending default is published, and the property owner is informed that he must pay the taxes by June 30. If the taxes remain delinquent after June 30, the property is considered "in default" and a five-year redemption period begins to run. (The redemption period is three years for commercial properties.) During this five-year period, the owner can keep possession of the property and has the opportunity to redeem it by paying the back taxes, interest, costs, and other penalties. If the property has not been redeemed by the end of the five-year period, the tax collector can sell the property at a tax sale and apply the proceeds to the tax debt. Any surplus from the sale is paid to the former owner or other parties who had an interest in the property.

Tax Exemptions. While the general rule is that all property is taxed at its full cash value, there are numerous total or partial exemptions. Property owned by the federal, state, or local government is totally exempt from taxation; so is most property that's used for religious, educational, charitable, or welfare purposes. The most commonly used exemption is a partial exemption for all owner-occupied homes. Currently, this allows a $7,000 reduction in a property's taxable value, so long as the property's owner used the property as a principal residence on January 1 of that tax year. An exemption is also available for veterans, though the homeowner's exemption and the veteran's exemption may not be taken on the same property in the same year.

Special Assessments

Special assessments, also called local improvement taxes, are levied to pay for improvements that benefit particular properties, such as the installation of street lights or the widening of a street. Only the properties that benefit from the improvement are taxed, on the theory that the value of those properties is increased by the improvement. For instance, street improvements are assessed against each lot that benefits from the improvements on the basis of the front footage of the lot.

A special assessment is usually a one-time tax, although the property owners may be allowed to pay the assessment in installments. When property that's subject to a special assessment is sold, the assessment is considered part of the acquisition cost of the property.

Like general real estate taxes, special assessments create liens against the taxed properties. If an owner fails to pay a special assessment, the government can foreclose on her property.

California has several statutes that authorize special assessments. One example is the Improvement Act of 1911. The act allows government entities to make street improvements and bill the affected property owners. If the bills remain unpaid for more than 30 days, bonds will be issued to pay for the improvements. Funds raised under this act can be used to pay for street paving, sidewalks, curbs, drainage systems, and other street improvements. The funds cannot be used to purchase land for development, however.

Here is a summary of the distinctions between general real estate taxes and special assessments:

1. General real estate taxes are levied to pay for ongoing government services, such as police protection. A special assessment is levied to pay for a specific improvement, such as adding sidewalks to a section of street.
2. General real estate taxes are levied against all taxable real property within a taxing district, for the benefit of the entire community. A special assessment, on the other hand, is levied against only those properties that benefit from the improvement in question.
3. General real estate taxes are levied every year. A special assessment is a one-time tax, levied only when a property is benefited by a public improvement.

Other Special Taxes

In addition to general real estate taxes and special assessments, California law also allows some other types of special taxes to be assessed against real property. These tend to be hybrids, resembling general real estate taxes in some ways (for example, they can be used to pay for ongoing services) and special assessments in others (for instance, special taxing districts may be created to cover the properties that benefit from the services or improvements funded by the taxes).

One example is the type of assessment authorized by the Mello-Roos Community Facilities Act of 1982. A Mello-Roos assessment can be used for a greater variety of improvements, facilities, and services than traditional special assessments.

The lien created by a special tax can sometimes be foreclosed on more quickly than a lien for general real estate taxes. For example, a Mello-Roos lien might be foreclosed on after payment has been delinquent for only 180 days, in contrast to the five-year redemption period allowed for delinquent general real estate taxes.

In a sale of residential property with up to four dwelling units, the seller is required to make a good faith effort to provide the buyer with a notice of the special tax from each agency that assesses such a tax against the property.

Documentary Transfer Tax

An excise tax is levied on each sale of real property in California; it is called the **documentary transfer tax**. The tax is based on the property's selling price. As a general rule, the rate is fifty-five cents per $500 of value, or fraction thereof. (In certain cities, the rate is higher.)

Example: A house is sold for $402,200.

$402,200 ÷ $500 = 804.40
805 × $0.55 = $442.75

The seller is required to pay $442.75 for the documentary transfer tax.

The documentary transfer tax does not apply to the amount of any loan the buyer is assuming or taking title subject to. If the buyer in the example above had assumed the seller's existing $325,200 trust deed, the tax would be due only on the $77,000 difference between the sales price and the assumed loan. Then the tax would be only $84.70.

Chapter Summary

1. The police power—the government's power to adopt and enforce laws for the protection of the public health, safety, morals, and general welfare—is the basis for land use control laws.

2. A general plan is a county or city's comprehensive, long-term plan for development. A local government implements its general plan with zoning ordinances and other laws.

3. Zoning ordinances provide for certain exceptions to their rules: nonconforming uses, variances, and conditional uses. They also have procedures for rezones.

4. Building codes set standards for construction materials and practices, to protect the public. The codes are enforced through the building permit system.

5. California requires subdividers to comply with both the Subdivision Map Act and the Subdivided Lands Law. In certain cases, a subdivider may also have to comply with the Interstate Land Sales Full Disclosure Act, a federal law.

6. A number of federal and state environmental laws affect land use, including NEPA, CERCLA, CEQA, the California Coastal Act, and the Alquist-Priolo Act.

7. A government entity can use the power of eminent domain to implement its general plan. When property is taken for a public use under the power of eminent domain, the government must pay just compensation to the owner. (Compensation is not required when property is merely regulated under the police power.)

8. The government's power to tax also affects property ownership. General real estate taxes are levied each year to pay for ongoing government services. Special assessments are levied to pay for improvements that benefit specific properties. The documentary transfer tax must be paid on every sale of real property in California.

Key Terms

Police power—The power of state governments to regulate for the protection of the public health, safety, morals, and general welfare.

General plan—A comprehensive, long-term plan of development for a community, which is implemented by zoning and other laws.

Zoning—A method of controlling land use by dividing a community into zones for different types of uses.

Nonconforming use—A formerly legal use that doesn't conform to a new zoning ordinance, but is nonetheless allowed to continue.

Variance—An authorization to deviate from the rules in a zoning ordinance, granted because strict enforcement would cause undue hardship for the property owner.

Conditional use permit—A permit that allows a special use, such as a school or a hospital, to operate in a neighborhood where it would otherwise be prohibited by the zoning.

Rezone—An amendment to a zoning ordinance; a property owner who feels his property has been zoned improperly may apply for a rezone.

Building codes—Regulations that set minimum standards for construction methods and materials.

Eminent domain—The government's power to take private property for public use, upon payment of just compensation to the owner.

Condemnation—The process of taking property pursuant to the power of eminent domain.

Subdivision—The division of one parcel of land into two or more parcels.

General real estate taxes—Taxes levied against real property annually to pay for general government services. They are based on the value of the property taxed (ad valorem).

Special assessment—A tax levied against property that benefits from a local improvement project, to pay for the project.

Documentary transfer tax—A tax levied when a piece of real property is sold. It is based on the selling price of the property.

Chapter Quiz

1. The police power is the government's power to:
   a) take private property for public use
   b) enact laws for the protection of the public health, safety, morals, and general welfare
   c) tax property to pay for police protection
   d) None of the above

2. Which of the following is likely to be controlled by a zoning ordinance?
   a) Use of the property
   b) Building height
   c) Placement of a building on a lot
   d) All of the above

3. Which of the following is NOT likely to be one of the goals of a land use control law?
   a) Ensuring that properties are put to their most profitable use
   b) Controlling growth and population density
   c) Ensuring that neighboring uses are compatible
   d) Preserving access to light and air

4. As a general rule, when a new zoning ordinance goes into effect, nonconforming uses:
   a) must comply with the new law within 90 days
   b) must shut down within 90 days
   c) will be granted conditional use permits
   d) are allowed to continue, but not to expand

5. An owner who feels that his property was improperly zoned should apply for a:
   a) conditional use permit
   b) variance
   c) rezone
   d) nonconforming use permit

6. A hospital is being built in a residential neighborhood. This was probably authorized by a:
   a) nonconforming use permit
   b) variance
   c) rezone
   d) conditional use permit

7. Which of these is an example of a variance?
   a) Changing a zoning ordinance to allow commercial uses in a neighborhood that was formerly zoned residential
   b) Authorizing a structure to be built only 12 feet from the lot's boundary, although the zoning ordinance requires 15-foot setbacks
   c) Allowing a grocery store to continue in operation after the neighborhood is zoned residential
   d) Approving the subdivision of a parcel of land into two or more lots

8. Which of these is NOT an exercise of the police power?
   a) Condemnation
   b) Building code
   c) Zoning ordinance
   d) Subdivision regulations

9. Eminent domain differs from the police power in that:
   a) the government is required to compensate the property owner
   b) it can be exercised only by the state government, not a city or county government
   c) it affects only the use of the property, not the title
   d) the property must be unimproved

10. The Hancocks are planning to add a room onto their house. Before construction begins, they are probably required to:
    a) request a zoning inspection
    b) submit a proposal to the planning commission
    c) obtain a building permit
    d) All of the above

11. A special assessment is the same thing as a/an:
    a) general real estate tax
    b) improvement tax
    c) real estate excise tax
    d) transfer tax

12. General real estate taxes are:
    a) used to support the general operation and services of government
    b) levied annually
    c) based on the value of the taxed property
    d) All of the above

13. Which of these is a state law that requires an environmental impact report to be prepared in certain circumstances?
    a) ILSA
    b) CERCLA
    c) CEQA
    d) NEPA

14. The documentary transfer tax is based on the property's:
    a) selling price
    b) fair market value
    c) current use
    d) highest and best use

15. Lots in a subdivision cannot be sold until a:
    a) final map is filed with the local planning agency
    b) parcel map is filed with the Office of Interstate Land Sales
    c) preliminary public report is issued by the Commissioner
    d) building permit has been issued

Answer Key

1. b) The police power is the government's power to pass laws (such as zoning ordinances) for the protection of the public health, safety, morals, and general welfare.

2. d) Zoning ordinances typically control the height and placement of buildings, as well as type of use.

3. a) Land use controls are not aimed at encouraging the most profitable use of particular properties. In some cases they prohibit more profitable uses that would be detrimental to the public health, safety, morals, or welfare.

4. d) A nonconforming use (a use established before new zoning rules go into effect, which does not comply with those rules) is ordinarily allowed to continue, but the use cannot be expanded, rebuilt after destruction, or resumed after abandonment.

5. c) A rezone is an amendment to the zoning ordinance, giving a particular area a new zoning designation.

6. d) A conditional use permit (also called a special exception permit) allows a special use, such as a school or a hospital, to operate in a neighborhood where it would otherwise be prohibited by the zoning.

7. b) A variance authorizes the improvement of property in a manner not ordinarily allowed by the zoning ordinance. Most variances permit only minor deviations from the rules.

8. a) Condemnation is an exercise of the power of eminent domain, not the police power.

9. a) When a government body takes property under the power of eminent domain, it is required to pay compensation to the owner. Compensation is not required if a property loses value due to regulation under the police power.

10. c) A building permit is generally required before an addition or remodeling project is begun, to ensure that the structure will comply with the building codes and zoning.

11. b) Special assessments are also called improvement taxes. They are typically levied to pay for a particular public improvement.

12. d) All of these statements concerning general real estate taxes are true.

13. c) CEQA is the California Environmental Quality Act. (CERCLA and NEPA are federal environmental laws, and ILSA is a federal subdivision law.)

14. a) The documentary transfer tax is levied only when title to property is transferred, and it is based on the selling price.

15. a) A final map must be filed with the local planning agency before a subdivision lot can be sold.

Chapter 6

Contract Law

I. Legal Classifications of Contracts
   A. Express vs. implied
   B. Unilateral vs. bilateral
   C. Executory vs. executed
II. Elements of a Valid Contract
   A. Capacity
   B. Mutual consent
   C. Lawful objective
   D. Consideration
   E. Writing requirement
III. Legal Status of Contracts
   A. Void
   B. Voidable
   C. Unenforceable
   D. Valid
IV. Discharging a Contract
   A. Full performance
   B. Agreement between the parties
V. Breach of Contract
   A. Remedies for breach of contract
      1. Rescission
      2. Compensatory damages
      3. Liquidated damages
      4. Specific performance
   B. Tender

Chapter Overview

Contracts are a significant part of the real estate business. Almost everyone has a basic understanding of what a contract is, but real estate agents need more than that. This chapter explains the requirements that must be met in order for a contract to be valid and binding; how a contract can be terminated; what is considered a breach of contract; and what remedies are available when a breach occurs.

Introduction

Real estate licensees deal with contracts on a daily basis: listing agreements, purchase agreements, option agreements, and leases are all contracts. Thus, it is essential for a licensee to understand the basic legal requirements and effects of contracts.

Keep in mind, however, that a real estate licensee may not draft the original language for a contract. Anyone other than a lawyer who drafts a contract for someone else may be charged with the unauthorized practice of law.

Here is a general definition of a contract: an agreement between two or more competent persons to do or not do certain things in exchange for consideration. An agreement to sell a car, deliver lumber, or rent an apartment is a contract. And if it meets minimum legal requirements, it can be enforced in court.

Legal Classifications of Contracts

There are certain basic classifications that apply to any contract, no matter what type it is. Every contract is either express or implied, either unilateral or bilateral, and either executory or executed.

Express vs. Implied

An **express** contract is one that has been put into words. It may be written or oral. Each party to the contract has stated what he or she is willing to do and has been told what to expect from the other party. Most contracts are express. On the other hand, an **implied** contract, or contract by implication, is created by the actions of the parties, not by express agreement.

Example: A written lease agreement expires, but the tenant continues to make payments and the landlord continues to accept them. Both parties have given their implied consent to a new lease contract.

Unilateral vs. Bilateral

A contract is **unilateral** if only one of the contracting parties is legally obligated to perform. That party has promised to do a particular thing if the other party does something else. But the other party hasn't promised to do anything and isn't legally obligated to do anything.

Fig. 6.1 Contract classifications

Express *Written or oral*	OR	**Implied** *Actions of the parties*
Unilateral *One promise*	OR	**Bilateral** *Two promises*
Executory *Not yet fully performed*	OR	**Executed** *Fully performed*

Example: In an open listing agreement, a seller promises to pay a real estate broker a commission if the broker finds a buyer for the property. The broker doesn't promise to try to find a buyer, but if he does find one, the seller is obligated to pay. An open listing agreement is a unilateral contract.

A **bilateral** contract is formed when each party promises to do something, so that both parties are legally obligated to perform. Most contracts are bilateral.

Example: In a purchase agreement, the seller promises to transfer title to the buyer, and the buyer promises to pay the agreed price to the seller. This is a bilateral contract. Each party has made a promise, and both are obligated to perform.

Executory vs. Executed

An **executory** contract is one that has not yet been performed, or is in the process of being performed. An **executed** contract has been fully performed. In this sense, the terms "executed" and "performed" mean the same thing.

Note, however, that "executed" also has another meaning in connection with contracts. Execution of a contract (or execution of a will, a deed, or some other legal document) can simply refer to signing it, as opposed to performing or fulfilling it. In this sense, the party or parties who have executed a document have signed it and taken any other steps needed to make it legally effective (for example, in the case of a will, having it witnessed). Which meaning is intended in a particular case will usually be clear from the context.

Elements of a Valid Contract

Four elements are needed for a valid and binding contract that will be enforced by a court:

1. legal capacity to contract,
2. mutual consent,
3. a lawful objective, and
4. consideration.

Capacity

The first requirement for a valid contract is that the parties must have the legal capacity to enter into a contract. A person must be at least 18 years old to enter into a valid contract, and he must also be competent.

Age Eighteen. Eighteen is the age of majority in California. Minors (those under the age of 18) do not have capacity to appoint agents or to enter into contracts. If a minor signs a contract, it is voidable by the minor; that is, it cannot be enforced against her.

> **Example:** A 16-year-old signs a contract to purchase a car. The car dealer cannot enforce the contract against the minor, although the minor could compel the dealer to honor the terms of the agreement.

The purpose of this rule is to prevent people from entering into legally binding agreements when they may be too young to understand the consequences.

In California, most types of contracts entered into by minors are voidable, as just discussed. However, real estate contracts entered into by minors are void. A purchase agreement signed by a minor cannot be enforced by either party.

A minor who has been legally emancipated may enter into any type of contract. For example, a 17-year-old who is married is considered emancipated and may enter into a contract to buy real estate. A minor can be emancipated in three ways: by marrying, by serving in the military, or by court order. When a minor who has been emancipated by court order enters into a real estate transaction, copies of the emancipation documents should be given to the escrow company so it will know that the minor has the capacity to carry out the transaction.

Competent. A person must also be mentally competent to have capacity to contract. If a person has been declared incompetent by a court, any contract he signs is void. If a person was probably incompetent when a contract was signed, but wasn't declared incompetent until afterwards, the contract is voidable at the discretion of the court-appointed guardian. (Note that the fact that a person is receiving psychiatric treatment doesn't necessarily mean that he's incompetent.)

A contract entered into by a person who is temporarily incompetent—for example, under the influence of alcohol or drugs—may be voidable if she takes legal action within a reasonable time after regaining mental competency.

Necessities Exception. There's an exception to these capacity rules. If a minor or an incompetent person contracts to buy necessities (such as food or medicine), he is required to pay the reasonable value of those items.

Representing Another. Often, one person has the capacity to represent another person or entity in a contract negotiation. For instance, the affairs of minors and incompetent persons are handled by parents or court-appointed guardians; corporations are represented by properly authorized officers; partnerships are represented by individual partners; deceased persons are represented by executors or administrators; and a competent adult (but not a minor) can appoint another competent adult to act on his behalf through a power of attorney. In each of these cases, the authorized representative can enter into a contract on behalf of the person represented.

Aliens. An alien (someone who isn't a U.S. citizen) has essentially the same property rights as a citizen and may acquire and convey property freely. However, aliens are subject to certain property transfer reporting requirements.

Convicts. Those convicted of crimes and serving time in prison aren't automatically deprived of all of their civil rights. As a general rule, they don't forfeit their property, nor are they prevented from obtaining or transferring real property.

Mutual Consent

Mutual consent is the second requirement for a valid contract. Each party must consent to the agreement. Once someone has signed a contract, consent is presumed, so no contract should be signed until its contents are fully understood. A person can't use failure or inability to read an agreement as an excuse for nonperformance. An illiterate person should have a contract explained thoroughly by someone trustworthy.

Mutual consent is sometimes called mutual assent, mutuality, or "a meeting of the minds." It is achieved through the process of **offer and acceptance**.

Offer. A contract offer shows the willingness of the person making it (the **offeror**) to enter into a contract under the stated terms. To be valid, an offer must meet two requirements.

1. It must express a willingness to contract. Whatever words make up the offer, they must clearly indicate that the offeror intends to enter into a contract.
2. It must be definite and certain in its terms. A vague offer that doesn't clearly state what the offeror is proposing is said to be illusory, and any agreement reached as a result is unenforceable.

Note that an advertisement that lists a property's price is not considered a contract offer; it is merely an invitation to negotiate.

Terminating an Offer. Sometimes circumstances change after an offer has been made, or perhaps the offeror has had a change of heart. If an offer terminates before it is accepted, no contract is formed. There are many things that can terminate an offer before it is accepted, including:

- revocation by the offeror,
- lapse of time,
- death or incompetence of the offeror,
- rejection of the offer, or
- a counteroffer.

The offeror can **revoke** the offer at any time until she is notified that the offer has been accepted. To effect a proper "offer and acceptance," the accepting party must not only accept the offer, but must also communicate that acceptance to the offeror before the offer is revoked. (See the discussion of acceptance, below.)

Many offers include a deadline for acceptance. If a deadline is set and acceptance isn't communicated within the time allotted, the offer terminates automatically. If no time limit is stated in the offer, a reasonable amount of time is allowed. What is reasonable is determined by the court if a dispute arises.

If a seller delivers his acceptance to a buyer in person, acceptance occurs at the time of delivery. However, the rules are slightly different if the seller mails an acceptance. Under the "mailbox rule," acceptance takes place as soon as the seller places it in the mail, even though the buyer does not receive it right away. This rule has been applied to other methods of communication, such as faxed messages.

A purchase agreement's language may override the "mailbox rule," though. For instance, the California Association of Realtors® purchase agreement states that delivery is only effective upon personal receipt, regardless of the communication method used.

If someone makes an offer and then dies or is declared incompetent before the offer is accepted, the offer is terminated.

A **rejection** also terminates an offer. Once the **offeree** (the person to whom the offer was made) rejects the offer, she can't come back later and create a contract by accepting the offer.

> **Example:** Valdez offers to purchase Carter's house for $785,000. Carter rejects the offer the next day. The following week, Carter changes her mind and decides to accept Valdez's offer. But her acceptance at this point doesn't create a contract, because the offer terminated with her rejection.

A **counteroffer** is sometimes called a qualified acceptance. It is actually a rejection of the offer and a tender of a new offer. Instead of either accepting or rejecting the offer outright, the offeree "accepts" with certain modifications. This happens when some, but not all, of the original terms are unacceptable to the offeree. When there is a counteroffer, the roles of the parties are reversed: the original offeror becomes the offeree and can accept or reject the revised offer. If he chooses to accept the counteroffer, that creates a binding contract. If the counteroffer is rejected, the party making the counteroffer can't go back and accept the original offer. The original offer was terminated by the counteroffer.

> **Example:** Palmer offers to buy Harrison's property under the following conditions: the purchase price is $450,000, the closing date is January 15, and the downpayment is $35,000. Harrison agrees to all of the terms except the closing date, which he wants to be February 15. By changing one of the terms, Harrison has rejected Palmer's initial offer and made a counteroffer. Now it's up to Palmer to either accept or reject Harrison's counteroffer.

Acceptance. An offer can be revoked at any time until acceptance has been communicated to the offeror. To create a binding contract, the offeree must communicate acceptance to the offeror in the manner and within the time limit stated in the offer (or before the offer is revoked). If no time or manner of acceptance is stated in the offer, a reasonable time and manner is implied.

The offeree's acceptance must be free of any negative influences, such as fraud, undue influence, or duress. If an offer or acceptance is influenced by any of these negative forces, the contract is voidable by the injured party.

Fraud is misrepresentation of a material fact to another person who relies on the misrepresentation as the truth in deciding to enter into a transaction.

- **Actual fraud** occurs when the person making the statement either knows that the statement is false and makes it with an intent to deceive, or doesn't know whether or not the statement is true but makes it anyway. For example, a seller who conceals cracks in the basement and then

Fig. 6.2 Mutual consent is achieved through the process of offer and acceptance.

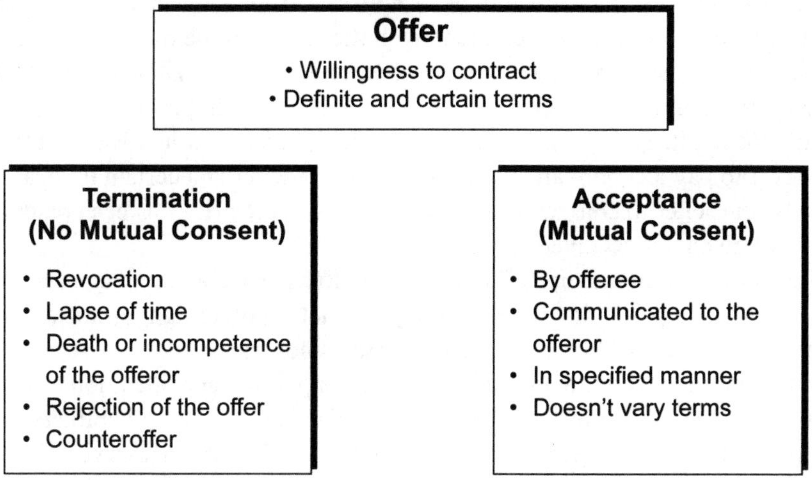

Offer
- Willingness to contract
- Definite and certain terms

Termination (No Mutual Consent)
- Revocation
- Lapse of time
- Death or incompetence of the offeror
- Rejection of the offer
- Counteroffer

Acceptance (Mutual Consent)
- By offeree
- Communicated to the offeror
- In specified manner
- Doesn't vary terms

tells the buyer that the foundation is completely sound is committing actual fraud. A promise that's made without any intention of keeping it can also be considered actual fraud.

- **Constructive fraud** occurs when a person who occupies a position of confidence and trust, or who has superior knowledge of the subject matter, makes a false statement with no intent to deceive. For example, if a seller innocently points out incorrect lot boundaries, that may be considered constructive fraud.

Undue influence is using one's influence to pressure a person into making a contract, or taking advantage of another's distress or weakness of mind to induce him to enter into a contract.

Duress is compelling a person to do something—such as enter into a contract—against her will, with the use of force or constraint or the threat of force or constraint.

Lawful Objective

The third requirement for a valid contract is a lawful objective. Both the purpose of the contract and the consideration for the contract (discussed below) must be lawful. Examples of contracts with unlawful objectives are a contract requiring payment of an interest rate in excess of the state's usury limit, or a contract relating to unlawful gambling. If a contract doesn't have a lawful objective, it's void.

Sometimes contracts contain some lawful provisions and some unlawful provisions. In these situations, it may be possible to sever the unlawful portions of the contract and enforce the lawful portions.

Example: Callahan and Baker enter into a contract for the sale of an apartment house. A clause in the contract prohibits the buyer from renting the apartments to persons of a certain race. The contract concerning the sale of the property would probably be enforceable, but the racially restrictive clause would be void because it's unlawful.

Consideration

The fourth element of a valid contract is **consideration**. Consideration is something of value exchanged by the contracting parties. It might be money, goods, or services, or a promise to provide money, goods, or services. Whatever form it takes, the consideration must be either a benefit to the party receiving it or a detriment to the party offering it. The typical real estate purchase agreement involves a promise by the buyer to pay a certain amount of money to the seller at a certain time, and a promise by the seller to convey title to the buyer when the price has been paid. Both parties have given and received consideration.

While consideration is usually the promise to do a particular act, it can also be a promise to not do a particular act. For example, Aunt Martha might promise to pay her nephew Charles $1,000 if he promises to stop smoking.

As a general rule, a contract is enforceable as long as the consideration has value, even though the value of the consideration exchanged is unequal. A contract to sell a piece of property worth $220,000 for $190,000 is enforceable. However, in cases where the disparity in value is quite large (for example, a contract to sell a piece of property worth $300,000 for $95,000), a court may refuse to enforce the contract. This is particularly likely to happen if the parties have unequal bargaining power (for example, if the buyer is a real estate developer and the seller is elderly, uneducated, and inexperienced in business).

The Writing Requirement

The requirements we've covered so far—capacity, mutual consent, a lawful objective, and consideration—apply to any kind of contract. For most contracts used in real estate transactions, there is a fifth requirement: they must be put into writing, as required by the statute of frauds.

The **statute of frauds** is a state law that requires certain types of contracts to be in writing and signed. Only the types of contracts covered by the statute of frauds have to be in writing; other contracts may be oral.

Each state has its own statute of frauds, and the requirements vary slightly from state to state. As a general rule, however, almost all of the contracts typically used in a real estate transaction are covered by the statute of frauds. In California, the statute of frauds applies to:

1. an agreement that will not be performed within a year of its making, or not during the lifetime of the promisor;
2. any agreement for the sale or exchange of real property or an interest in real property;
3. a lease of real property that will expire more than one year after it was agreed to;
4. an agency agreement authorizing an agent to purchase or sell real property, or lease it for more than one year;

Fig. 6.3 Real estate contract requirements

A Valid Real Estate Contract

- Capacity
- Mutual consent
- Lawful objective
- Consideration
- In writing

5. an agency agreement authorizing an agent to find a buyer or seller for real property, if the agent will receive compensation; and
6. an assumption of a mortgage or deed of trust.

The "writing" required by the statute of frauds does not have to be in any particular form, nor does it have to be contained entirely in one document. A note or memorandum about the agreement or a series of letters will suffice, as long as the writing:

1. identifies the subject matter of the contract,
2. indicates an agreement between the parties and its essential terms, and
3. is signed by the party or parties to be bound.

If the parties fail to put a contract that falls under the statute of frauds in writing, the contract is usually unenforceable. However, occasionally a court will enforce such an unwritten agreement. This might occur if there is both evidence that the contract exists and evidence of its terms, and if the party trying to enforce it has completely or substantially performed her contractual obligations. This is rare; the safest course is to put a contract in writing.

If a contract is partly printed and partly handwritten (like a filled-out contract form) and there's a conflict between the handwritten and printed portions, the handwritten portion takes precedence. It's presumed to be a more reliable indication of the parties' intent than the printed portion.

In California, when certain types of contracts are negotiated in Spanish, Chinese, Korean, Tagalog, or Vietnamese between a business and a consumer, the consumer must be given a translated copy of the contract before signing the English version. This requirement applies to many consumer contracts, including loans for personal, family, or household purposes; "Article VII" loans (see Chapter 10); reverse mortgages; and residential rental agreements for a period longer than one month. (It doesn't apply to listing agreements, buyer representation agreements, or purchase agreements, however.) Also, when a financial institution negotiates a loan secured by residential real property in one of the five languages listed, the borrower must be given either a translated copy of the contract or a translated summary of its terms within three business days after applying for the loan.

Legal Status of Contracts

Four terms are used to describe the legal status of a contract: void, voidable, unenforceable, or valid. These terms have already been used in our discussion, and now we'll look more closely at what each one means.

Void

A void contract is no contract at all; it has no legal effect. This most often occurs because one of the essential elements, such as mutual consent or consideration, is completely lacking.

Example: Talbot signed a contract promising to deed some property to Worth, but Worth did not offer any consideration in exchange for Talbot's promise. Since the contract is not supported by consideration, it is void.

A void contract may be disregarded. Neither party is required to take legal action to withdraw from the agreement.

Voidable

A voidable contract appears to be valid, but has some defect giving one or both of the parties the power to withdraw from the agreement. For instance, a contract entered into as a result of fraud is voidable by the defrauded party.

Unlike a contract that is void from the outset, a voidable contract can't simply be ignored. Failure to take legal action to rescind a contract within a reasonable time may result in a court declaring that the contract was ratified. (In some cases, the injured party may want to continue with the agreement; if so, she may expressly ratify it.)

Unenforceable

An unenforceable contract is one that can't be enforced in court for one of the following reasons:

1. its contents cannot be proved,
2. it is voidable by the other party, or
3. the statute of limitations has expired.

Contents Cannot Be Proved. This problem is usually associated with oral agreements. Even if the law doesn't require a certain kind of contract to be written, it's a good idea to put it in writing. A written contract helps avoid confusion and misunderstanding, and also makes it easier to prove the terms of the agreement in court, if necessary.

A contract that is in writing must clearly state all of its terms. Vaguely worded contracts are considered illusory and unenforceable.

Contract Voidable by Other Party. If a contract is voidable by one of the parties, it is unenforceable by the other party. (Note that the party who has the option of voiding the contract can choose instead to enforce the contract against the other party.)

Fig. 6.4 Legal status of contracts

Type of Contract	Legal Effect	Example
Void	No contract at all	An agreement for which there is no consideration
Voidable	Valid until rescinded by one party	A contract entered into as a result of fraud
Unenforceable	One or both parties cannot sue to enforce	A contract after the limitations period expires
Valid	Binding and enforceable	An agreement that fulfills all of the legal requirements

Statute of Limitations Expired. A statute of limitations is a law that sets a deadline for filing a lawsuit. Unless an injured party files suit before the deadline set by the applicable statute of limitations, his legal claim is lost forever. The purpose of a statute of limitations is to prevent one person from suing another too many years after an event, when memories have faded and evidence has been lost.

Every state has a statute of limitations for contracts. If one of the parties to a contract fails to perform her obligations (breaches the contract), the other party must sue within a certain number of years after the breach. Otherwise, the limitations period will run out and the contract will become unenforceable.

In California, the statute of limitations generally requires lawsuits concerning written contracts to be filed within four years after their breach, and lawsuits concerning many oral contracts to be filed within two years after their breach.

The doctrine of **laches** is related to the concept of statutes of limitations. Laches is an equitable principle that courts can use to prevent someone from asserting a claim after an unreasonable delay. For instance, suppose a property owner knowingly stands by while a neighbor builds a house that encroaches a few feet onto his property. He then sues, demanding that it be torn down. Because the property owner's unreasonable delay caused the neighbor harm, the court may use the doctrine of laches to deny the requested remedy.

Valid

If an agreement has all of the essential elements, can be proved in court, and is free of negative influences, it's a valid contract that can be enforced in a court of law.

Discharging a Contract

Once there is a valid, enforceable contract, it may be discharged by:

1. full performance, or
2. agreement between the parties.

Full Performance

Full performance means that the parties have performed all of their obligations; the contract is executed. For example, once the deed to a property has been delivered to the buyer and the seller has received the purchase price, their purchase agreement has been discharged by full performance.

Agreement Between the Parties

The parties to a contract can agree to discharge the contract in any of the following ways:

- rescission,
- cancellation,
- assignment, or
- novation.

Rescission. Sometimes the parties to a contract agree that they would be better off if the contract had never been signed. In such a case, they may decide to rescind the contract. A rescission is sometimes described as "a contract to destroy a contract."

To rescind a purchase agreement, the buyer and the seller sign an agreement that terminates their original agreement and puts them as nearly as possible back in the positions they were in before they entered into it. If any money or other consideration has changed hands, it will be returned.

In certain circumstances, a contract can be rescinded by court order (rather than by agreement between the parties). Court-ordered rescission is discussed later in this chapter.

Cancellation. A cancellation does not go as far as a rescission. The parties agree to terminate the contract, but previous acts are unaffected. For example, money that was paid prior to the cancellation is not returned.

When entering into a purchase agreement, a buyer generally gives the seller a deposit to show that she's acting in good faith and intends to fulfill the terms of their agreement. This is called a **good faith deposit**, and the seller is entitled to keep it if the buyer defaults on the contract. If the buyer and seller agree to terminate the contract and the seller refunds the good faith deposit to the buyer, the contract has been rescinded. If the parties agree that the seller will keep the deposit, the contract has been canceled.

Assignment. Sometimes one of the parties to a contract wants to withdraw by assigning his interest in the contract to another person. As a general rule, a contract can be assigned to another unless a clause in the contract prohibits assignment. Technically, assignment doesn't actually discharge the contract. The new party (the assignee) assumes primary liability for the contractual obligations, but the withdrawing party (the assignor) is still secondarily liable.

Example: A buyer is purchasing a home under a 15-year land contract. In the absence of any prohibitive language, she can sell the home, accept a cash downpayment, and assign her contract rights and liabilities to the new buyer. The new buyer would assume primary liability for the contract debt, but the original buyer would retain secondary liability.

One exception to the rule that a contract can be assigned unless otherwise agreed: a personal services contract can't be assigned without the other party's consent.

Example: A nightclub has a contract with a singer for several performances. The singer can't assign her contract to another singer, because it's a personal services contract. The nightclub management has a right to choose who will be singing in their establishment.

Novation. The term "novation" has two generally accepted meanings. One type of novation is the substitution of a new party into an existing obligation. If a seller releases the original buyer from a purchase agreement in favor of a new buyer under the same contract, there has been a novation. The first buyer is relieved of all liability connected with the contract.

Novation may also be the substitution of a new obligation for an old one. If a landlord and a tenant agree to tear up a three-year lease in favor of a new ten-year lease, that's a novation.

Assignment vs. Novation. The difference between assignment and novation concerns the withdrawing party's liability. When a contract is assigned, there is continuing liability for the assignor. In a novation, on the other hand, the withdrawing party is released from liability, because she was replaced with another person who was approved by the other party. Novation, unlike assignment, always requires the other party's consent.

Breach of Contract

A breach of contract occurs when one of the parties fails, without legal excuse, to perform any of the promises contained in the agreement. The injured party can seek a remedy in court only if the breach is a **material breach**. A breach is material when the promise that has not been fulfilled is an important part of the contract.

Many standard contract forms state that **"time is of the essence."** That phrase is used to warn the parties that timely performance is crucial and failure to meet a deadline would be a material breach. If one party misses a deadline, the other party may choose whether to proceed with the contract or use the time is of the essence clause as the basis for ending it.

Remedies for Breach of Contract

There are four possible legal remedies for a breach of contract:

- rescission,
- compensatory damages,
- liquidated damages, or
- specific performance.

Rescission. As was previously explained, a rescission is a termination of the contract that returns the parties to their original positions. In the case of a purchase agreement, the seller refunds the buyer's good faith deposit and the buyer gives up her equitable interest in the property. The rescission can be by agreement, or it can be ordered by a court at the request of one party when the other party has breached the contract.

Compensatory Damages. Financial losses that a party suffers as a result of a breach of contract are referred to as **damages**.

Example: Able, a manufacturer, contracts to buy 50,000 hinges from Baker for $12,000, and Baker promises to deliver the hinges by April 22.

As it turns out, Baker fails to deliver the hinges on time, and Able (in order to fulfill commitments to her customers) must quickly purchase the hinges from another supplier. This other supplier charges Able $17,000—$5,000 more than Baker was charging. Able has suffered $5,000 in damages as a result of Baker's breach of contract.

The most common remedy for a breach of contract is an award of **compensatory damages**. This is a sum of money that a court orders the breaching party to pay to the other party, to compensate the other party for losses suffered as a result of the breach of contract. Compensatory damages are generally intended to put the nonbreaching party in the financial position she would have been in if the breaching party had fulfilled the terms of the contract.

Example: Continuing with the previous example, suppose Able sues Baker for breach of contract. The court orders Baker to pay Able $5,000 in damages. When Baker pays Able the $5,000, that puts Able in the financial position she would have been in if Baker had delivered the hinges on time.

Liquidated Damages. The parties to a contract sometimes agree in advance to an amount that will serve as full compensation to be paid in the event that one of the parties breaches the contract. This sum is called **liquidated damages**.

Example: Let's return to the previous example. Now suppose that Able and Baker included a liquidated damages provision in their contract. The provision states that if Baker breaches the agreement, he will pay Able $3,000, and that will serve as full compensation for the breach.

Baker fails to deliver the hinges to Able on time, Able must purchase them from another supplier, and that costs her an extra $5,000. But because of the liquidated damages provision in the contract, Able is only entitled to receive $3,000 from Baker. She can't sue for any additional amount, even though her actual damages were greater than $3,000.

Although a liquidated damages provision limits the amount of compensation the nonbreaching party will receive, it benefits both parties by making it easier to settle their dispute without going to court. It's sometimes difficult for the nonbreaching party to prove the extent of the actual damages she suffered; a liquidated damages provision makes that unnecessary.

In a real estate transaction, the buyer's good faith deposit is often treated as liquidated damages. If the buyer breaches the purchase agreement, the seller is entitled to keep the deposit as liquidated damages. The seller usually can't sue the buyer for an additional amount. (Note that California has special rules that govern liquidated damages clauses in purchase agreements. See Chapter 7.)

On the other hand, a typical purchase agreement doesn't have a liquidated damages provision that applies if it's the seller who breaches instead of the buyer. If the seller breaches the contract, the buyer can sue for compensatory damages.

Fig. 6.5 Breach of contract

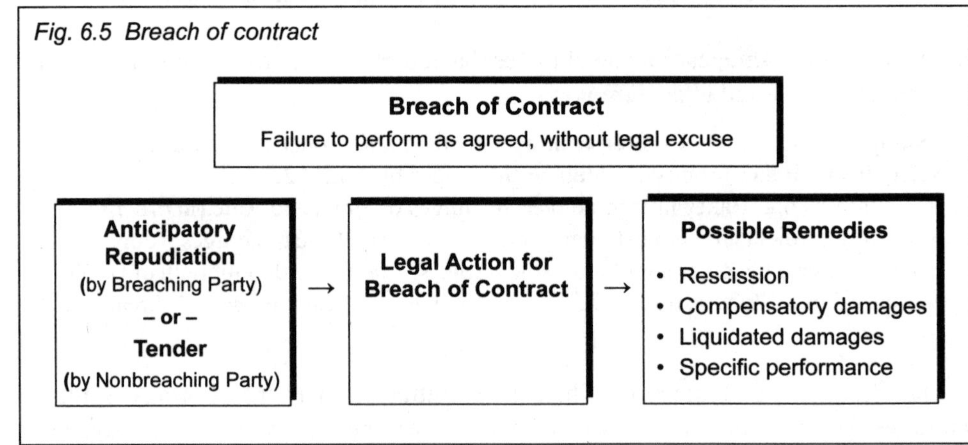

Specific Performance. Specific performance is a legal action designed to compel a breaching party to perform the contract as agreed. For example, if a seller breaches a purchase agreement, a court could issue an order of specific performance, requiring the seller to sign and deliver a deed to the buyer, fulfilling the terms of their contract.

Specific performance is usually available as a remedy only when monetary damages would not be sufficient compensation. For instance, in our example involving failure to deliver hinges as agreed, the court wouldn't order Baker to deliver the hinges to Able, because hinges could be obtained from another supplier and financial compensation was really all Able needed. In contrast, specific performance may be an appropriate remedy for a seller's breach of a purchase agreement, because a piece of real estate is unique; there's no other property that's exactly like the one the seller agreed to sell. Payment of damages would not enable the buyer to purchase another property just like it.

Tender

A tender is an unconditional offer by one of the contract parties to perform his part of the agreement. It is frequently referred to as "an offer to make an offer good." A tender is usually made when it appears that the other party is going to default; it is necessary before legal action can be taken to remedy the breach of contract.

> **Example:** A seller suspects that the buyer doesn't plan to complete the purchase, and he intends to sue the buyer if this happens. Before he can sue, the seller must attempt to deliver the deed to the buyer as promised in the purchase agreement. When the tender is made, if the buyer refuses to pay the agreed price and accept the deed, the buyer is placed in default and the seller may then file a lawsuit.

If a buyer has reason to believe the seller doesn't plan to complete the sale, the buyer tenders by attempting to deliver to the seller the full payment promised in the purchase agreement. When the seller refuses to accept the money and deliver the deed, the seller is in default.

Sometimes there is an **anticipatory repudiation** by one of the parties. An anticipatory repudiation is a positive statement by the defaulting party indicating that he will not or cannot fulfill the terms of the agreement. When this happens, no tender is necessary as a basis for a legal action.

Chapter Summary

1. A contract is an agreement between two or more competent persons to do or not do certain things in exchange for consideration. Every contract is either express or implied, either unilateral or bilateral, and either executory or executed.
2. For a contract to be valid and binding, the parties must have the legal capacity to contract, and there must be mutual consent (offer and acceptance), a lawful objective, and consideration. The statute of frauds requires nearly all real estate contracts to be in writing.
3. A contract may be void, voidable, unenforceable, or valid.
4. An existing contract can be discharged by full performance or by agreement between the parties. The parties can agree to terminate the contract by rescission or cancellation, or there can be an assignment or a novation.
5. A breach of contract occurs when a party fails, without legal excuse, to perform any material promise contained in the agreement. When a breach occurs, the four possible remedies are rescission, compensatory damages, liquidated damages, or specific performance.

Key Terms

Contract—An agreement between two or more competent persons to do or not do certain things in exchange for consideration.

Capacity—The ability to enter into a legally binding contract. A person must be mentally competent and at least 18 years of age to have the capacity to contract.

Mutual consent—The agreement of both parties to the terms of the contract, effected by offer and acceptance.

Offer—A communication that shows the willingness of the person making it (the offeror) to enter into a contract, and that has definite and certain terms.

Acceptance—A communication showing the willingness of the offeree to be bound by the terms of the offer.

Counteroffer—A qualified acceptance. Technically, it is a rejection of the offer, with a new offer made on slightly different terms.

Fraud—The misrepresentation of a material fact to someone who relies on the misrepresentation as the truth in deciding whether to enter into a contract.

Undue influence—Pressuring someone or taking advantage of his distress to induce him to enter into a contract.

Duress—Compelling someone to enter into a contract with the use or threat of force or constraint.

Consideration—Something of value exchanged by the parties to a contract; either a benefit to the party receiving it or a detriment to the party offering it.

Statute of frauds—A state law that requires certain types of contracts (including most contracts related to real estate transactions) to be in writing and signed.

Valid—When a contract has all of the required elements and is enforceable in court.

Void—When a contract lacks an essential element, so that it has no legal force or effect.

Voidable—When one of the parties can choose to rescind the contract, because of lack of capacity, fraud, undue influence, or distress.

Unenforceable—When a contract cannot be enforced in a court of law because its contents cannot be proved, or it is voidable by the other party, or the statute of limitations has expired.

Rescission—When a contract is terminated and any consideration given is returned, putting the parties as nearly as possible back into the position they were in prior to entering into the contract.

Cancellation—When a contract is terminated but previous contractual acts are unaffected.

Assignment—When one party transfers her rights and obligations under the contract to another party, but remains secondarily liable.

Novation—When one party is completely replaced with another, or one contract is completely replaced with another, and all liability under the original contract ends.

Damages—Losses that a person suffers because someone else has breached a contract or otherwise failed to fulfill a legal obligation.

Compensatory damages—An amount that a court orders the party who breached a contract to pay the other party, to compensate her for losses suffered as a result of the breach and put her in the position she would have been in if the breaching party had fulfilled the terms of their contract.

Liquidated damages—An amount that the parties agree in advance will serve as full compensation if one of them defaults.

Specific performance—A remedy for breach of contract in which the court orders the defaulting party to perform as agreed in the contract.

Tender—An unconditional offer by one of the parties to perform his part of the agreement, made when it appears that the other party is going to default.

Chapter Quiz

1. A contract can be valid and binding even though:
   a) it is not supported by consideration
   b) it does not have a lawful objective
   c) it is not put into writing
   d) there was no offer and acceptance

2. To have legal capacity to contract, a person must have:
   a) reached the age of majority
   b) been declared competent by a court
   c) a high school diploma or general equivalency certificate
   d) All of the above

3. An offer to purchase property would be terminated by any of the following, except:
   a) failure to communicate acceptance of the offer within the prescribed period
   b) revocation after acceptance has been communicated
   c) a qualified acceptance by the offeree
   d) death or insanity of the offeror

4. A counteroffer:
   a) terminates the original offer
   b) will result in a valid contract if accepted by the other party
   c) Both of the above
   d) Neither of the above

5. Tucker sends Johnson a letter offering to buy his property for $400,000 in cash, with the transaction to close in 60 days. Johnson sends Tucker a letter that says, "I accept your offer; however, the closing will take place in 90 days." Which of the following is true?
   a) Johnson's statement isn't a valid acceptance
   b) Johnson's statement is a counteroffer
   c) There's no contract unless Tucker accepts the counteroffer
   d) All of the above

6. Which of these could be consideration for a contract?
   a) $163,000
   b) A promise to convey title
   c) A promise to not sell the property during the next 30 days
   d) All of the above

7. An executory contract is one that:
   a) is made by the executor of an estate for the sale of probate property
   b) has not yet been performed
   c) has been completely performed
   d) has been proposed but not accepted by either party

8. A void contract is one that:
   a) lacks an essential contract element
   b) needs to be rescinded by the injured party
   c) can be rescinded by agreement
   d) can no longer be enforced because the deadline set by the statute of limitations has passed

9. A voidable contract is:
   a) not enforceable by either party
   b) enforceable by the injured party
   c) void unless action is taken to rescind it
   d) None of the above

10. The statute of frauds is a law that requires:
    a) all contracts to be supported by consideration
    b) unlawful provisions to be severed from a contract
    c) certain contracts to be unilateral
    d) certain contracts to be in writing and signed

11. A contract can be discharged by all of the following except:
    a) novation
    b) performance
    c) cancellation
    d) breach

12. Brown and Murdock have a five-year contract. After two years, they agree to tear up that contract and replace it with a new ten-year contract. This is an example of:
    a) novation
    b) rescission
    c) duress
    d) specific performance

13. Graves and Chung are parties to a contract that doesn't prohibit assignment. If Chung assigns his interest in the contract to Stewart:
    a) Graves isn't required to fulfill the contract
    b) Graves can sue for anticipatory repudiation
    c) Chung remains secondarily liable to Graves
    d) Chung is relieved of all further liability under the contract

14. A clause in the contract provides that if one party breaches, the other will be entitled to $3,500 and cannot sue for more than that. This is a:
    a) just compensation provision
    b) compensation cap
    c) satisfaction clause
    d) liquidated damages provision

15. The McClures agreed to sell their house to Jacobsen, but then they breached the contract by refusing to go through with the sale. If Jacobsen wants a court order requiring the McClures to convey the house to her as agreed, she should sue for:
    a) damages
    b) specific performance
    c) liquidated damages
    d) rescission

Answer Key

1. c) Only certain types of contracts are required to be in writing, but all contracts require consideration, a lawful objective, and offer and acceptance.

2. a) A person has capacity to contract if he has reached the age of majority (in California, age 18) and is mentally competent. It isn't necessary to be declared competent by a court, however.

3. b) If the offeree accepts the offer before the offeror revokes it, a binding contract is formed.

4. c) A counteroffer terminates the original offer (operating as a rejection), but if the counteroffer is then accepted, a valid contract is formed.

5. d) All of the options are true statements.

6. d) Consideration can be anything of value: money, goods, services, or a promise to do or not do something.

7. b) An executory contract has not yet been performed; an executed contract is one that has been fully performed.

8. a) A contract that lacks an essential element (such as consideration) is void. It has no legal force or effect, so there is nothing to rescind.

9. b) A voidable contract can be rescinded by the injured party.

10. d) The statute of frauds requires certain contracts to be in writing and signed by the party or parties to be bound.

11. d) Performance, cancellation, and novation are all ways of discharging a contract. Breach does not discharge the contract; the breaching party is liable to the other party.

12. a) Novation is the replacement of an existing contract with a new contract, or the replacement of a party to a contract with a new party.

13. c) A contract can be assigned unless otherwise agreed, but the assignor remains secondarily liable to the other party.

14. d) Liquidated damages is an amount the contracting parties agree in advance will be paid as full compensation if one of them breaches the contract.

15. b) If the court granted Jacobsen specific performance, the McClures would be ordered to convey the house as agreed in the contract (not merely to pay Jacobsen damages as compensation).

Chapter 7

Types of Real Estate Contracts

I. Listing Agreements
   A. Earning a commission
      1. Ready, willing, and able buyer
      2. Types of listing agreements
   B. Elements of a listing agreement
II. Buyer Representation Agreements
   A. Provisions in a buyer representation agreement
   B. Broker's compensation
III. Purchase Agreements
   A. Requirements for a valid purchase agreement
   B. Provisions in a purchase agreement
   C. Amendments
IV. Land Contracts
   A. Rights and responsibilities of vendor and vendee
   B. Remedies for default
   C. Use of land contracts
V. Option Agreements
   A. Requirements for a valid option
   B. Option rights
   C. Recording an option
   D. Contrasted with a right of first refusal
VI. Leases
   A. Requirements for a valid lease
   B. Rights and responsibilities of landlord and tenant
   C. Transferring leased property
   D. Termination of a lease
   E. Types of leases

Chapter Overview

In addition to understanding the basic principles of contract law, real estate agents must be familiar with the specific types of contracts used in real estate transactions. This chapter describes the types of contracts that agents are most likely to encounter in their work, including listing agreements, buyer representation agreements, purchase agreements, land contracts, options, and leases.

Listing Agreements

A **listing agreement** is a written contract between a property seller and a real estate broker. (As an example, a CAR Residential Listing Agreement form is shown in Figure 7.1.) The seller hires the broker to find a buyer who is ready, willing, and able to buy the property on the seller's terms. A listing agreement does not give the broker the authority to accept offers on behalf of the seller, or to transfer title to the seller's property.

Even though the listing agreement form is frequently filled out and signed by a salesperson working for the listing broker, the contract is between the seller and the broker (not the salesperson). Only a broker may directly contract with members of the public for brokerage services.

A listing agreement creates an agency relationship between the broker and the seller. As we'll discuss in Chapter 8, agency carries with it a high level of responsibility. The broker is required to act in the best interests of the seller when acting as the seller's agent pursuant to their contract.

The standard form of payment for a real estate broker is a **commission**, also called a **brokerage fee**. The commission is usually computed as a percentage of the purchase price (the price that the property is sold for), as opposed to the listing price.

In California, a broker can't sue a seller to collect a commission unless they had a written listing agreement. (Note that an oral agreement between brokers to split a commission is enforceable, even though an oral listing agreement is not.) The broker must also have been properly licensed at the time the brokerage services were provided. In addition, the broker must have fulfilled the terms of the listing agreement that establish under what circumstances the seller is obligated to pay the broker a commission.

Earning a Commission

A listing agreement can make payment of the broker's commission dependent on any lawful conditions that are mutually acceptable to the broker and the seller. For example, the seller might ask to include a "no sale, no commission" provision in the agreement. This would make the broker's commission payable only if the transaction actually closes and the seller receives full payment from the buyer. If this condition isn't met due to circumstances beyond the seller's control (for example, because the buyer couldn't obtain financing), the commission doesn't have to be paid. But if the condition isn't met because of the bad faith or fraud of the seller, the broker is still entitled to the commission.

Fig. 7.1 Listing agreement

CALIFORNIA ASSOCIATION OF REALTORS®

RESIDENTIAL LISTING AGREEMENT
(Exclusive Authorization and Right to Sell)
(C.A.R. Form RLA, Revised 11/13)

1. **EXCLUSIVE RIGHT TO SELL:** ______ ("Seller") hereby employs and grants ______ ("Broker") beginning (date) ______ and ending at 11:59 P.M. on (date) ______ ("Listing Period") the exclusive and irrevocable right to sell or exchange the real property in the City of ______, County of ______, Assessor's Parcel No. ______, California, described as: ______ ("Property").
2. **ITEMS EXCLUDED AND INCLUDED:** Unless otherwise specified in a real estate purchase agreement, all fixtures and fittings that are attached to the Property are included, and personal property items are excluded, from the purchase price.
ADDITIONAL ITEMS EXCLUDED: ______.
ADDITIONAL ITEMS INCLUDED: ______.
Seller intends that the above items be excluded or included in offering the Property for sale, but understands that: (i) the purchase agreement supersedes any intention expressed above and will ultimately determine which items are excluded and included in the sale; and (ii) Broker is not responsible for and does not guarantee that the above exclusions and/or inclusions will be in the purchase agreement.
3. **LISTING PRICE AND TERMS:**
   A. The listing price shall be: ______ Dollars ($ ______).
   B. Additional Terms: ______.
4. **COMPENSATION TO BROKER:**
Notice: The amount or rate of real estate commissions is not fixed by law. They are set by each Broker individually and may be negotiable between Seller and Broker (real estate commissions include all compensation and fees to Broker).
   A. Seller agrees to pay to Broker as compensation for services irrespective of agency relationship(s), either ☐ ______ percent of the listing price (or if a purchase agreement is entered into, of the purchase price), or ☐ $ ______, AND ______, as follows:
   (1) If during the Listing Period, or any extension, Broker, cooperating broker, Seller or any other person procures a ready, willing, and able buyer(s) whose offer to purchase the Property on any price and terms is accepted by Seller, provided the Buyer completes the transaction or is prevented from doing so by Seller. (Broker is entitled to compensation whether any escrow resulting from such offer closes during or after the expiration of the Listing Period, or any extension.)
   OR (2) If within ______ calendar days (a) after the end of the Listing Period or any extension; or (b) after any cancellation of this Agreement, unless otherwise agreed, Seller enters into a contract to sell, convey, lease or otherwise transfer the Property to anyone ("Prospective Buyer") or that person's related entity: (i) who physically entered and was shown the Property during the Listing Period or any extension by Broker or a cooperating broker; or (ii) for whom Broker or any cooperating broker submitted to Seller a signed, written offer to acquire, lease, exchange or obtain an option on the Property. Seller, however, shall have no obligation to Broker under paragraph 4A(2) unless, not later than 3 calendar days after the end of the Listing Period or any extension or cancellation, Broker has given Seller a written notice of the names of such Prospective Buyers.
   OR (3) If, without Broker's prior written consent, the Property is withdrawn from sale, conveyed, leased, rented, otherwise transferred, or made unmarketable by a voluntary act of Seller during the Listing Period, or any extension.
   B. If completion of the sale is prevented by a party to the transaction other than Seller, then compensation due under paragraph 4A shall be payable only if and when Seller collects damages by suit, arbitration, settlement or otherwise, and then in an amount equal to the lesser of one-half of the damages recovered or the above compensation, after first deducting title and escrow expenses and the expenses of collection, if any.
   C. In addition, Seller agrees to pay Broker: ______.
   D. Seller has been advised of Broker's policy regarding cooperation with, and the amount of compensation offered to, other brokers.
   (1) Broker is authorized to cooperate with and compensate brokers participating through the multiple listing service(s) ("MLS") by offering to MLS brokers out of Broker's compensation specified in 4A, either ☐ ______ percent of the purchase price, or ☐ $ ______.
   (2) Broker is authorized to cooperate with and compensate brokers operating outside the MLS as per Broker's policy.
   E. Seller hereby irrevocably assigns to Broker the above compensation from Seller's funds and proceeds in escrow. Broker may submit this Agreement, as instructions to compensate Broker pursuant to paragraph 4A, to any escrow regarding the Property involving Seller and a buyer, Prospective Buyer or other transferee.
   F. **(1)** Seller represents that Seller has not previously entered into a listing agreement with another broker regarding the Property, unless specified as follows: ______.
   (2) Seller warrants that Seller has no obligation to pay compensation to any other broker regarding the Property unless the Property is transferred to any of the following individuals or entities: ______.
   (3) If the Property is sold to anyone listed above during the time Seller is obligated to compensate another broker: (i) Broker is

Seller's Initials (______)(______)

RLA REVISED 11/13 (PAGE 1 OF 5) Print Date

Reviewed by ______ Date ______

EQUAL HOUSING OPPORTUNITY

Property Address:____ Date:____________

not entitled to compensation under this Agreement; and (ii) Broker is not obligated to represent Seller in such transaction.

5. MULTIPLE LISTING SERVICE:

A. Broker is a participant/subscriber to ____________________ Multiple Listing Service (MLS) and possibly others. Unless otherwise instructed in writing the Property will be listed with the MLS(s) specified above. That MLS is (or if checked ☐ is not) the primary MLS for the geographic area of the Property. All terms of the transaction, including sales price and financing, if applicable, (i) will be provided to the MLS in which the property is listed for publication, dissemination and use by persons and entities on terms approved by the MLS and (ii) may be provided to the MLS even if the Property is not listed with the MLS.

BENEFITS OF USING THE MLS; IMPACT OF OPTING OUT OF THE MLS; PRESENTING ALL OFFERS

WHAT IS AN MLS? The MLS is a database of properties for sale that is available and disseminated to and accessible by all other real estate agents who are participants or subscribers to the MLS. Property information submitted to the MLS describes the price, terms and conditions under which the Seller's property is offered for sale (including but not limited to the listing broker's offer of compensation to other brokers). It is likely that a significant number of real estate practitioners in any given area are participants or subscribers to the MLS. The MLS may also be part of a reciprocal agreement to which other multiple listing services belong. Real estate agents belonging to other multiple listing services that have reciprocal agreements with the MLS also have access to the information submitted to the MLS. The MLS may further transmit the MLS database to Internet sites that post property listings online.

EXPOSURE TO BUYERS THROUGH MLS: Listing property with an MLS exposes a seller's property to all real estate agents and brokers (and their potential buyer clients) who are participants or subscribers to the MLS or a reciprocating MLS.

CLOSED/PRIVATE LISTING CLUBS OR GROUPS: Closed or private listing clubs or groups are not the same as the MLS. The MLS referred to above is accessible to all eligible real estate licensees and provides broad exposure for a listed property. Private or closed listing clubs or groups of licensees may have been formed outside the MLS. Private or closed listing clubs or groups are accessible to a more limited number of licensees and generally offer less exposure for listed property. Whether listing property through a closed, private network - and excluding it from the MLS - is advantageous or disadvantageous to a seller, and why, should be discussed with the agent taking the Seller's listing.

NOT LISTING PROPERTY IN A LOCAL MLS: If the Property is listed in an MLS which does not cover the geographic area where the Property is located then real estate agents and brokers working that territory, and Buyers they represent looking for property in the neighborhood, may not be aware the Property is for sale.

OPTING OUT OF MLS: If Seller elects to exclude the Property from the MLS, Seller understands and acknowledges that: (a) real estate agents and brokers from other real estate offices, and their buyer clients, who have access to that MLS may not be aware that Seller's Property is offered for sale; (b) Information about Seller's Property will not be transmitted to various real estate Internet sites that are used by the public to search for property listings; (c) real estate agents, brokers and members of the public may be unaware of the terms and conditions under which Seller is marketing the Property.

REDUCTION IN EXPOSURE: Any reduction in exposure of the Property may lower the number of offers and negatively impact the sales price.

PRESENTING ALL OFFERS: Seller understands that Broker must present all offers received for Seller's Property unless Seller gives Broker written instructions to the contrary.

Seller's Initials (__________ **)(** __________ **)** **Broker's Initials (** __________ **)(** __________ **)**

B. MLS rules generally provide that residential real property and vacant lot listings be submitted to the MLS within 2 days or some other period of time after all necessary signatures have been obtained on the listing agreement. Broker will not have to submit this listing to the MLS if, within that time, Broker submits to the MLS a form signed by Seller (C.A.R. Form SELM or the local equivalent form).

C. MLS rules allow MLS data to be made available by the MLS to additional Internet sites unless Broker gives the MLS instructions to the contrary. Seller acknowledges that for any of the below opt-out instructions to be effective, Seller must make them on a separate instruction to Broker signed by Seller (C.A.R. Form SELI or the local equivalent form). Specific information that can be excluded from the Internet as permitted by (or in accordance with) the MLS is as follows:
(1) Property Availability: Seller can instruct Broker to have the MLS not display the Property on the Internet.
(2) Property Address: Seller can instruct Broker to have the MLS not display the Property address on the Internet.
Seller understands that the above opt-outs would mean consumers searching for listings on the Internet may not see the Property or Property's address in response to their search.
(3) Feature Opt-Outs: Seller can instruct Broker to advise the MLS that Seller does not want visitors to MLS Participant or Subscriber Websites or Electronic Displays that display the Property listing to have the features below. Seller understands (i) that these opt-outs apply only to Websites or Electronic Displays of MLS Participants and Subscribers who are real estate broker and agent members of the MLS; (ii) that other Internet sites may or may not have the features set forth herein; and (iii) that neither Broker nor the MLS may have the ability to control or block such features on other Internet sites.
(a) Comments And Reviews: The ability to write comments or reviews about the Property on those sites; or the ability to link to another site containing such comments or reviews if the link is in immediate conjunction with the Property.

Seller's Initials (__________)(__________)

RLA REVISED 11/13 (PAGE 2 OF 5) Reviewed by _______ Date _______

RESIDENTIAL LISTING AGREEMENT - EXCLUSIVE (RLA PAGE 2 OF 5)

Property Address:____ Date:_______________

(b) Automated Estimate Of Value: The ability to create an automated estimate of value or to link to another site containing such an estimate of value if the link is in immediate conjunction with the Property.

6. **SELLER REPRESENTATIONS:** Seller represents that, unless otherwise specified in writing, Seller is unaware of: (i) any Notice of Default recorded against the Property; (ii) any delinquent amounts due under any loan secured by, or other obligation affecting, the Property; (iii) any bankruptcy, insolvency or similar proceeding affecting the Property; (iv) any litigation, arbitration, administrative action, government investigation or other pending or threatened action that affects or may affect the Property or Seller's ability to transfer it; and (v) any current, pending or proposed special assessments affecting the Property. Seller shall promptly notify Broker in writing if Seller becomes aware of any of these items during the Listing Period or any extension thereof.

7. **BROKER'S AND SELLER'S DUTIES:** (a) Broker agrees to exercise reasonable effort and due diligence to achieve the purposes of this Agreement. Unless Seller gives Broker written instructions to the contrary, Broker is authorized to (i) order reports and disclosures as necessary, (ii) advertise and market the Property by any method and in any medium selected by Broker, including MLS and the Internet, and, to the extent permitted by these media, control the dissemination of the information submitted to any medium; and (iii) disclose to any real estate licensee making an inquiry the receipt of any offers on the Property and the offering price of such offers. (b) Seller agrees to consider offers presented by Broker, and to act in good faith to accomplish the sale of the Property by, among other things, making the Property available for showing at reasonable times and, subject to paragraph 4F, referring to Broker all inquiries of any party interested in the Property. Seller is responsible for determining at what price to list and sell the Property. Seller further agrees to indemnify, defend and hold Broker harmless from all claims, disputes, litigation, judgments attorney fees and costs arising from any incorrect information supplied by Seller, or from any material facts that Seller knows but fails to disclose.

8. **DEPOSIT:** Broker is authorized to accept and hold on Seller's behalf any deposits to be applied toward the purchase price.

9. **AGENCY RELATIONSHIPS:**
   - **A.** Disclosure: If the Property includes residential property with one-to-four dwelling units, Seller shall receive a "Disclosure Regarding Agency Relationships" (C.A.R. Form AD) prior to entering into this Agreement.
   - **B.** Seller Representation: Broker shall represent Seller in any resulting transaction, except as specified in paragraph 4F.
   - **C.** Possible Dual Agency With Buyer: Depending upon the circumstances, it may be necessary or appropriate for Broker to act as an agent for both Seller and buyer, exchange party, or one or more additional parties ("Buyer"). Broker shall, as soon as practicable, disclose to Seller any election to act as a dual agent representing both Seller and Buyer. If a Buyer is procured directly by Broker or an associate-licensee in Broker's firm, Seller hereby consents to Broker acting as a dual agent for Seller and Buyer. In the event of an exchange, Seller hereby consents to Broker collecting compensation from additional parties for services rendered, provided there is disclosure to all parties of such agency and compensation. Seller understands and agrees that: (i) Broker, without the prior written consent of Seller, will not disclose to Buyer that Seller is willing to sell the Property at a price less than the listing price; (ii) Broker, without the prior written consent of Buyer, will not disclose to Seller that Buyer is willing to pay a price greater than the offered price; and (iii) except for (i) and (ii) above, a dual agent is obligated to disclose known facts materially affecting the value or desirability of the Property to both parties.
   - **D.** Other Sellers: Seller understands that Broker may have or obtain listings on other properties, and that potential buyers may consider, make offers on, or purchase through Broker, property the same as or similar to Seller's Property. Seller consents to Broker's representation of sellers and buyers of other properties before, during and after the end of this Agreement.
   - **E.** Confirmation: If the Property includes residential property with one-to-four dwelling units, Broker shall confirm the agency relationship described above, or as modified, in writing, prior to or concurrent with Seller's execution of a purchase agreement.

10. **SECURITY AND INSURANCE:** Broker is not responsible for loss of or damage to personal or real property, or person, whether attributable to use of a keysafe/lockbox, a showing of the Property, or otherwise. Third parties, including, but not limited to, appraisers, inspectors, brokers and prospective buyers, may have access to, and take videos and photographs of, the interior of the Property. Seller agrees: (i) to take reasonable precautions to safeguard and protect valuables that might be accessible during showings of the Property; and (ii) to obtain insurance to protect against these risks. Broker does not maintain insurance to protect Seller.

11. **PHOTOGRAPHS AND INTERNET ADVERTISING:**
   - **A.** In order to effectively market the Property for sale it is often necessary to provide photographs, virtual tours and other media to buyers. Seller agrees (or ☐ if checked, does not agree) that Broker may photograph or otherwise electronically capture images of the exterior and interior of the Property ("Images") for static and/or virtual tours of the Property by buyers and others on Broker's website, the MLS, and other marketing sites. Seller acknowledges that once Images are placed on the Internet neither Broker nor Seller has control over who can view such Images and what use viewers may make of the Images, or how long such Images may remain available on the Internet. Seller further agrees that such Images are the property of Broker and that Broker may use such Images for advertisement of Broker's business in the future.
   - **B.** Seller acknowledges that prospective buyers and/or other persons coming onto the property may take photographs, videos or other images of the property. Seller understands that Broker does not have the ability to control or block the taking and use of Images by any such persons. (If checked) ☐ Seller instructs Broker to publish in the MLS that taking of Images is limited to those persons preparing Appraisal or Inspection reports. Seller acknowledges that unauthorized persons may take images who do not have access to or have not read any limiting instruction in the MLS or who take images regardless of any limiting instruction in the MLS. Once Images are taken and/or put into electronic display on the Internet or otherwise, neither Broker nor Seller has control over who views such Images nor what use viewers may make of the Images.

12. **KEYSAFE/LOCKBOX:** A keysafe/lockbox is designed to hold a key to the Property to permit access to the Property by Broker, cooperating brokers, MLS participants, their authorized licensees and representatives, authorized inspectors, and accompanied prospective buyers. Broker, cooperating brokers, MLS and Associations/Boards of REALTORS® are not insurers against injury, theft, loss, vandalism or damage attributed to the use of a keysafe/lockbox. Seller does (or if checked ☐ does not) authorize Broker to install a keysafe/lockbox. If Seller does not occupy the Property, Seller shall be responsible for obtaining occupant(s)' written permission for use of a keysafe/lockbox (C.A.R. Form KLA).

RLA REVISED 11/13 (PAGE 3 OF 5)

Seller's Initials (__________)(__________)

Reviewed by _______ Date _______

RESIDENTIAL LISTING AGREEMENT - EXCLUSIVE (RLA PAGE 3 OF 5)

Property Address: ______________________________ Date: ______________

13. SIGN: Seller does (or if checked ☐ does not) authorize Broker to install a FOR SALE/SOLD sign on the Property.

14. EQUAL HOUSING OPPORTUNITY: The Property is offered in compliance with federal, state and local anti-discrimination laws.

15. ATTORNEY FEES: In any action, proceeding or arbitration between Seller and Broker regarding the obligation to pay compensation under this Agreement, the prevailing Seller or Broker shall be entitled to reasonable attorney fees and costs from the non-prevailing Seller or Broker, except as provided in paragraph 19A.

16. ADDITIONAL TERMS: ☐ REO Advisory Listing (C.A.R. Form REOL) ☐ Short Sale Information and Advisory (C.A.R. Form SSIA)

____

____

____

____

____

____

17. MANAGEMENT APPROVAL: If an associate-licensee in Broker's office (salesperson or broker-associate) enters into this Agreement on Broker's behalf, and Broker or Manager does not approve of its terms, Broker or Manager has the right to cancel this Agreement, in writing, within **5 Days** After its execution.

18. SUCCESSORS AND ASSIGNS: This Agreement shall be binding upon Seller and Seller's successors and assigns.

19. DISPUTE RESOLUTION:

A. MEDIATION: Seller and Broker agree to mediate any dispute or claim arising between them regarding the obligation to pay compensation under this Agreement, before resorting to arbitration or court action. Mediation fees, if any, shall be divided equally among the parties involved. If, for any dispute or claim to which this paragraph applies, any party (i) commences an action without first attempting to resolve the matter through mediation, or (ii) before commencement of an action, refuses to mediate after a request has been made, then that party shall not be entitled to recover attorney fees, even if they would otherwise be available to that party in any such action. THIS MEDIATION PROVISION APPLIES WHETHER OR NOT THE ARBITRATION PROVISION IS INITIALED. **Exclusions from this mediation agreement are specified in paragraph 19C.**

B. ARBITRATION OF DISPUTES:

Seller and Broker agree that any dispute or claim in Law or equity arising between them regarding the obligation to pay compensation under this Agreement, which is not settled through mediation, shall be decided by neutral, binding arbitration. The arbitrator shall be a retired judge or justice, or an attorney with at least 5 years of residential real estate Law experience, unless the parties mutually agree to a different arbitrator. The parties shall have the right to discovery in accordance with Code of Civil Procedure §1283.05. In all other respects, the arbitration shall be conducted in accordance with Title 9 of Part 3 of the Code of Civil Procedure. Judgment upon the award of the arbitrator(s) may be entered into any court having jurisdiction. Enforcement of this agreement to arbitrate shall be governed by the Federal Arbitration Act. Exclusions from this arbitration agreement are specified in paragraph 19C.

"NOTICE: BY INITIALING IN THE SPACE BELOW YOU ARE AGREEING TO HAVE ANY DISPUTE ARISING OUT OF THE MATTERS INCLUDED IN THE 'ARBITRATION OF DISPUTES' PROVISION DECIDED BY NEUTRAL ARBITRATION AS PROVIDED BY CALIFORNIA LAW AND YOU ARE GIVING UP ANY RIGHTS YOU MIGHT POSSESS TO HAVE THE DISPUTE LITIGATED IN A COURT OR JURY TRIAL. BY INITIALING IN THE SPACE BELOW YOU ARE GIVING UP YOUR JUDICIAL RIGHTS TO DISCOVERY AND APPEAL, UNLESS THOSE RIGHTS ARE SPECIFICALLY INCLUDED IN THE 'ARBITRATION OF DISPUTES' PROVISION. IF YOU REFUSE TO SUBMIT TO ARBITRATION AFTER AGREEING TO THIS PROVISION, YOU MAY BE COMPELLED TO ARBITRATE UNDER THE AUTHORITY OF THE CALIFORNIA CODE OF CIVIL PROCEDURE. YOUR AGREEMENT TO THIS ARBITRATION PROVISION IS VOLUNTARY."

"WE HAVE READ AND UNDERSTAND THE FOREGOING AND AGREE TO SUBMIT DISPUTES ARISING OUT OF THE MATTERS INCLUDED IN THE 'ARBITRATION OF DISPUTES' PROVISION TO NEUTRAL ARBITRATION."

Seller's Initials ______ / ______ **Broker's Initials** ______ / ______

C. ADDITIONAL MEDIATION AND ARBITRATION TERMS: The following matters shall be excluded from mediation and arbitration: (i) a judicial or non-judicial foreclosure or other action or proceeding to enforce a deed of trust, mortgage or installment land sale contract as defined in Civil Code §2985; (ii) an unlawful detainer action; (iii) the filing or enforcement of a mechanic's lien; and (iv) any matter that is within the jurisdiction of a probate, small claims or bankruptcy court. The filing of a court action to enable the recording of a notice of pending action, for order of attachment, receivership, injunction, or other provisional remedies, shall not constitute a waiver or violation of the mediation and arbitration provisions.

RLA REVISED 11/13 (PAGE 4 OF 5)

Seller's Initials (________)(________)

Reviewed by ______ Date ______

RESIDENTIAL LISTING AGREEMENT - EXCLUSIVE (RLA PAGE 4 OF 5)

Property Address:______________________________ Date:____________

20. ENTIRE AGREEMENT: All prior discussions, negotiations and agreements between the parties concerning the subject matter of this Agreement are superseded by this Agreement, which constitutes the entire contract and a complete and exclusive expression of their agreement, and may not be contradicted by evidence of any prior agreement or contemporaneous oral agreement. If any provision of this Agreement is held to be ineffective or invalid, the remaining provisions will nevertheless be given full force and effect. This Agreement and any supplement, addendum or modification, including any photocopy or facsimile, may be executed in counterparts.

21. OWNERSHIP, TITLE AND AUTHORITY: Seller warrants that: (i) Seller is the owner of the Property; (ii) no other persons or entities have title to the Property; and (iii) Seller has the authority to both execute this Agreement and sell the Property. Exceptions to ownership, title and authority are as follows: ______________________________
______________________________.

By signing below, Seller acknowledges that Seller has read, understands, received a copy of and agrees to the terms of this Agreement.

Seller______________________________ Date ____________
Address ______________________ City ____________ State _____ Zip ________
Telephone ______________ Fax ______________ Email ______________

Seller ______________________________ Date ____________
Address ______________________ City ____________ State _____ Zip ________
Telephone ______________ Fax ______________ Email ______________

Real Estate Broker (Firm) ______________________ Cal BRE Lic.# ____________
By (Agent) ______________________ Cal BRE Lic.# ____________ Date ____________
Address ______________________ City ____________ State _____ Zip ________
Telephone ______________ Fax ______________ Email ______________

Published and Distributed by:
REAL ESTATE BUSINESS SERVICES, INC.
a subsidiary of the California Association of REALTORS®

Reviewed by ______ Date ______

RLA REVISED 11/13 (PAGE 5 OF 5)

RESIDENTIAL LISTING AGREEMENT - EXCLUSIVE (RLA PAGE 5 OF 5)

Unless otherwise agreed, however, certain standard rules are followed regarding payment of the broker's commission. These include the rules concerning a ready, willing, and able buyer, and those concerning the three types of listings.

Ready, Willing, and Able Buyer. As a general rule, a listing agreement obligates the seller to pay the listing broker a commission only if a **ready, willing, and able** buyer is found during the listing period.

Acceptable Offer. A buyer is considered "ready and willing" if he makes an offer that meets the seller's stated terms. In the listing agreement, the seller sets forth the terms on which she wants to sell the property: price, closing date, financing arrangements, etc. If a buyer makes an offer that matches those terms, the broker is usually entitled to the commission—even if the seller decides not to accept that offer after all.

When a buyer makes an offer on terms other than those set forth in the listing agreement, the seller can turn down the offer without becoming liable for the broker's commission. But if the seller accepts an offer, she generally is required to pay the broker's commission even if the offer did not match the terms set forth in the listing agreement.

Able to Buy. A ready and willing buyer is considered "able" if he has the capacity to contract and the financial ability to complete the purchase. The buyer must have enough cash to buy the property on the agreed terms, or else be eligible for the necessary financing.

Commission Without Closing. Generally, once a ready, willing, and able buyer has been found, the broker has earned the commission, whether or not the sale is ever completed. When failure to close is the seller's fault, the broker is still entitled to the commission (although the broker might decide not to demand payment). For example, once the seller accepts an offer, she still owes the broker a commission if the sale fails to close for any of these reasons:

- the seller has a change of heart and decides not to sell,
- the seller doesn't have marketable title,
- the seller is unable to deliver possession of the property to the buyer, or
- the seller and the buyer mutually agree to terminate their contract.

Unless specifically required by the listing agreement, it isn't even necessary for the buyer and the seller to execute a written purchase agreement in order for the broker to be entitled to a commission. It is enough if the buyer and the seller have reached an agreement as to the essential terms of the sale: the price, downpayment, loan term, interest rate, and amortization. If the seller backs out before the agreement is put into writing, the broker could still claim the commission.

Sometimes the seller and the broker disagree as to whether the buyer located by the broker was in fact ready, willing, and able. In California, a court will presume that the buyer was ready, willing, and able if a written purchase agreement was signed. Since the seller accepted the buyer by entering into the contract, the seller has waived the right to claim that the buyer was unacceptable. This rule can be applied even if the buyer immediately defaulted because of financial inability to go through with the purchase.

On the other hand, if no contract has been signed and the agreement between the buyer and the seller is still at the unwritten stage when it falls through, the broker is not entitled to a commission unless she can prove that the buyer was financially able to perform the contract.

Types of Listing Agreements. When a seller is required to pay a broker's commission also depends on the type of listing agreement they have. The three basic types of listing agreements in current use are:

- the open listing,
- the exclusive agency listing, and
- the exclusive right to sell listing.

Open Listing. Under an open listing agreement, the seller is obligated to pay the broker a commission only if the broker was the **procuring cause** of the sale. The procuring cause is the person who was primarily responsible for bringing about the agreement between the parties. To be the procuring cause, a broker (or one of his salespersons) must have personally negotiated the offer from the ready, willing, and able buyer and communicated the offer to the seller.

An open listing is also called a nonexclusive listing, because a seller is free to give open listings to any number of brokers. If a seller signs two open listing agreements with two different brokers, and one of the brokers sells the property, only the broker who made the sale is entitled to a commission. The other broker isn't compensated for his efforts. Or if the seller sells the property directly, without the help of either broker, then the seller doesn't have to pay any commission at all. The sale of the property terminates all outstanding listings.

The open listing arrangement has obvious disadvantages. If two competing brokers both negotiate with the person who ends up buying the property, there may be a dispute over which broker was the procuring cause of the sale. Also, because a broker with an open listing agreement is not assured of a commission when the property sells, he may not put as much effort into marketing the property, so it may take longer to sell. For the most part, open listing agreements are used only when a seller is unwilling to execute an exclusive listing agreement. Multiple listing services generally do not accept open listings.

Exclusive Agency Listing. In an exclusive agency listing, the seller agrees to list with only one broker, but retains the right to sell the property herself without being obligated to pay the broker a commission. The broker is entitled to a commission if anyone other than the seller finds a buyer for the property, but not if the seller finds the buyer without the help of an agent.

In California, an exclusive agency listing must have a definite termination date; otherwise, the broker may be subject to disciplinary action (see Chapter 16).

Exclusive Right to Sell Listing. Under an exclusive right to sell listing, the seller agrees to list with only one broker, and that broker is entitled to a commission if the property sells during the listing term, regardless of who finds the buyer. Even if the seller makes the sale directly, the broker is still entitled to the commission.

In spite of the designation "exclusive right to sell," remember that this type of listing agreement doesn't actually authorize the broker to sell the property. As with the other types of listings, the broker is authorized only to submit offers to purchase to the seller.

The exclusive right to sell listing is preferred by most brokers, because it provides the most protection for the broker. It's the type of listing that's most commonly used.

Like an exclusive agency listing, an exclusive right to sell listing requires a definite termination date.

Due Diligence. There's a distinction between open and exclusive listings concerning the broker's contractual obligations. An open listing is usually a unilateral contract: the seller promises to pay the broker a commission if the broker finds a buyer, but the broker doesn't promise to make any effort to find one. If the broker does nothing at all, it isn't a breach of contract.

On the other hand, an exclusive listing is usually a bilateral contract. In most exclusive listings, in exchange for the seller's promise to pay a commission no matter who finds a buyer (or if any agent finds a buyer), the broker promises to exercise due diligence and make a reasonable effort to find a buyer. If the seller can prove that the listing broker and salesperson did nothing to help sell the property, a court might not require the seller to pay the broker's commission.

Elements of a Listing Agreement

A listing agreement must have all of the essential elements of a valid contract that were discussed in the previous chapter, including competent parties, offer and acceptance, consideration, and a lawful purpose. Also, under the statute of frauds, a listing agreement must be in writing and must be signed by the seller. (If the property has more than one owner, only one of them has to sign the listing.) The broker usually also signs the listing agreement, although her signature is not strictly required. The broker gives implied consent to the terms of the agreement by starting to market the property.

If there is no written listing agreement, the broker can't sue the seller for a commission, even though an oral agreement may have established an agency relationship between the broker and the seller (see Chapter 8).

At a minimum, a listing agreement should include provisions that:

- identify the property,
- set acceptable terms of sale,
- grant the broker authority,
- determine the broker's compensation, and
- state when the agreement will expire.

Property Description. A listing agreement must identify the seller's property. The street address is useful, but it may not be enough to identify the property with certainty. It's a good idea to attach a legal description of the property to the listing agreement as an exhibit. Any pages attached to a contract should be dated and initialed by the parties, to show that the attachments are intended to be part of the agreement.

Terms of Sale. A listing agreement should specify what the seller wants in the way of an offer. This includes how much money the seller wants for the property (the listing price) and any other terms of sale that matter to the seller. Any items that the seller wants to exclude from or include in the sale that wouldn't otherwise be excluded or included should also be noted in the listing agreement.

As we explained earlier, the seller can reject any offer that doesn't meet the terms of sale described in the listing agreement without becoming liable for a commission.

However, if an offer is made that does meet those terms, and the seller rejects the offer, the broker may be entitled to a commission. Thus, it is very important for all of the essential terms of sale to be set forth clearly and fully in the listing agreement.

Broker's Authority. The listing agreement sets forth the broker's authority to find a buyer for the property. The broker is usually also given the authority to accept and hold good faith deposits on the seller's behalf. In the rare case where a broker is not given authority to accept deposits for the seller, if the prospective buyer gives the broker a deposit, then the broker is acting as an agent for the buyer in regard to the deposit. In this situation, the seller wouldn't be liable to the buyer if the broker were to lose or misappropriate the deposit.

Commission. A provision stating the rate or amount of the broker's commission is another key part of every listing agreement. The commission is usually computed as a percentage of the purchase price. The commission rate or amount must be negotiable between the seller and the broker. In fact, it's a violation of state and federal antitrust laws for brokers to set uniform commission rates. Any discussion of commission rates among members of competing firms could give rise to a charge of price fixing (see Chapter 16).

A special law applies to listing agreements for one- to four-unit residential properties and mobile homes. If the broker uses a preprinted form for the listing agreement, it must state in boldface type that the amount or rate of the commission is not fixed by law and may be negotiated. The commission rate or amount can't be printed in the form—it must be filled in for each transaction.

Sometimes the amount of the broker's commission is determined in an unusual way. Under a **net listing**, the seller stipulates the net amount of money he requires from the sale of the property. The broker then tries to sell the property for more than that net amount. When the property is sold, the seller receives the required net and the broker keeps any money in excess of that amount as the commission.

Example: The seller insists on getting $645,000 from the sale of her property. The broker sells the property for $678,000. $678,000 less the required $645,000 net equals $33,000. Thus, the broker's commission is $33,000. If the broker had sold the property for more, his commission would have been more. Likewise, if the broker had sold the property for less, his commission would have been less.

Net listings can be open, exclusive agency, or exclusive right to sell listings. Whatever the type, net listings carry the potential for abuse; an unscrupulous broker could easily use a net listing to take advantage of a seller. In California, a broker who uses a net listing must reveal the amount of his commission to the seller before the seller becomes committed to the transaction. Failure to do so may result in disciplinary action.

Payment. A broker's commission is typically paid with a check, but if the seller and the broker agree, the commission payment can take the form of a new promissory note, an assignment of an existing note, or an assignment of funds from the buyer to the seller.

Ordinarily, the commission is the only compensation the broker receives. The broker doesn't present the seller with a bill for expenses incurred in selling the property, unless the seller specifically agreed to this arrangement in the listing agreement.

It should be noted that a salesperson may only receive a commission from the broker she is licensed under. The salesperson can't accept any compensation from any other broker or agent, or directly from the seller. If the seller fails to pay the broker his commission, it's the broker who must sue the seller. The salesperson can't sue the seller, even though she's entitled to a portion of the broker's commission.

Commission Splits. At least in urban and suburban areas, most brokers belong to a **multiple listing service** (MLS), an organization of brokers who share information about their listings. In the listing agreement forms used by multiple listing services, the seller authorizes the listing broker to share the commission paid by the seller with other brokers. This is called a **commission split**. The standard MLS arrangement is for the listing broker to pay half of her commission to the selling broker. The selling broker is the broker who finds the buyer, or whose salesperson finds the buyer.

Safety Clauses. A safety clause (also called a protection clause, protection period clause, or extender clause) is found in most listing agreements. Under this type of provision, the broker is entitled to a commission if the seller sells the property after the listing term expires to any person the broker negotiated with during the listing term. This protects the broker from parties who conspire to deprive the broker of a commission by waiting until the listing has expired before they sign a purchase agreement. The broker usually has to provide the seller with a list of the parties he negotiated with, and the list must be delivered to the seller on or before the listing's termination date. This lets the seller know whether she'll become liable for a commission if she sells the property to a particular buyer.

Termination Date. A listing agreement should include a termination date: the date on which the listing will expire and the broker's authority to act on the seller's behalf will end. This is especially important for an exclusive listing, because the seller isn't really free to work with a different broker until the listing expires. As was mentioned earlier, in California every exclusive agency or exclusive right to sell listing agreement must have a definite termination date. This is a requirement of the Real Estate Law (see Chapter 16). Note that the law does not set either a minimum or a maximum limit on the length of the listing period.

Buyer Representation Agreements

A **buyer representation agreement** is a written agreement between a real estate buyer and a broker. (As an example, a CAR buyer representation agreement form is shown in Figure 7.2.) With this type of contract, a prospective buyer employs a broker to help her find and purchase a suitable property. As with a listing agreement, even though the buyer representation agreement form is likely to be filled out by a salesperson, the contract is between the buyer and the broker, not the salesperson, and it creates an agency relationship between the broker and the buyer (see Chapter 8).

Like a listing agreement, a buyer representation agreement can be exclusive or nonexclusive. Under the terms of an exclusive agreement, the broker may be entitled to compensation if the buyer purchases property during the term of the agreement, whether or not it's the broker who finds the property or negotiates with the seller.

Fig. 7.2 Buyer representation agreement

CALIFORNIA ASSOCIATION OF REALTORS®

BUYER REPRESENTATION AGREEMENT - EXCLUSIVE

(C.A.R. Form BRE, Revised 4/13)

1. **EXCLUSIVE RIGHT TO REPRESENT:** ____________________ ("Buyer") grants ____________________ ("Broker") beginning on (date) __________ and ending at: **(i)** 11:59 P.M. on (date) __________, or **(ii)** completion of a resulting transaction, whichever occurs first ("Representation Period"), the exclusive and irrevocable right, on the terms specified in this Agreement, to represent Buyer in acquiring real property or a manufactured home as follows:
   - A. **PROPERTY TO BE ACQUIRED:**
     (1) Any purchase, lease or other acquisition of any real property or manufactured home described as Location: ____________________
     Other: ____________________
     Price range: $ __________ to $ __________
     OR ☐ **(2)** The following specified properties only: ____________________
     OR ☐ **(3)** Only the properties identified on the attached list.
   - B. Broker agrees to exercise due diligence and reasonable efforts to fulfill the following authorizations and obligations.
   - C. Broker will perform its obligations under this Agreement through the individual signing for Broker below or another real estate licensee assigned by Broker, who is either Broker individually or an associate-licensee (an individual licensed as a real estate salesperson or Broker who works under Broker's real estate license). Buyer agrees that Broker's duties are limited by the terms of this Agreement, including those limitations set forth in paragraphs 5 and 6.
2. **AGENCY RELATIONSHIPS:**
   - A. **DISCLOSURE:** If the property described in paragraph 4 includes residential property with one to four dwelling units, Buyer acknowledges receipt of the "Disclosure Regarding Real Estate Agency Relationships" (C.A.R. Form AD) prior to entering into this Agreement.
   - B. **BUYER REPRESENTATION:** Broker will represent, as described in this Agreement, Buyer in any resulting transaction.
   - C. **(1) POSSIBLE DUAL AGENCY WITH SELLER:** (C(1) APPLIES UNLESS C(2)(i) or (ii) is checked below.) Depending on the circumstances, it may be necessary or appropriate for Broker to act as an agent for both Buyer and a seller, exchange party, or one or more additional parties ("Seller"). Broker shall, as soon as practicable, disclose to Buyer any election to act as a dual agent representing both Buyer and Seller. If Buyer is shown property listed with Broker, Buyer consents to Broker becoming a dual agent representing both Buyer and Seller with respect to those properties. In event of dual agency, Buyer agrees that: **(a)** Broker, without the prior written consent of Buyer, will not disclose to Seller that the Buyer is willing to pay a price greater than the price offered; **(b)** Broker, without the prior written consent of Seller, will not disclose to Buyer that Seller is willing to sell Property at a price less than the listing price; and **(c)** other than as set forth in (a) and (b) above, a dual agent is obligated to disclose known facts materially affecting the value or desirability of the property to both parties.
     OR (2) SINGLE AGENCY ONLY: (APPLIES ONLY IF (i) or (ii) is checked below.)
     ☐ **(i) Broker's firm lists properties for sale:** Buyer understands that this election will prevent Broker from showing Buyer those properties that are listed with Broker's firm or from representing Buyer in connection with those properties. Buyer's acquisition of a property listed with Broker's firm shall not affect Broker's right to be compensated under paragraph 3. In any resulting transaction in which Seller's property is not listed with Broker's firm, Broker will be the exclusive agent of Buyer and not a dual agent also representing Seller.
     OR ☐ **(ii) Broker's firm DOES NOT list property:** Entire brokerage firm only represents buyers and does not list property. In any resulting transaction, Broker will be the exclusive agent of Buyer and not a dual agent also representing Seller.
   - D. **OTHER POTENTIAL BUYERS:** Buyer understands that other potential buyers may, through Broker, consider, make offers on or acquire the same or similar properties as those Buyer is seeking to acquire. Buyer consents to Broker's representation of such other potential buyers before, during and after the Representation Period, or any extension thereof.
   - E. **NON CONFIDENTIALITY OF OFFERS:** Buyer is advised that Seller or Listing Agent may disclose the existence, terms, or conditions of Buyer's offer unless all parties and their agent have signed a written confidentiality agreement. Whether any such information is actually disclosed depends on many factors, such as current market conditions, the prevailing practice in the real estate community, the Listing Agent's marketing strategy and the instructions of the Seller.
   - F. **CONFIRMATION:** If the Property (as defined below) includes residential property with one to four dwelling units, Broker shall confirm the agency relationship described above, or as modified, in writing, prior to or coincident with Buyer's execution of a Property Contract (as defined below).
3. **COMPENSATION TO BROKER:**
   NOTICE: The amount or rate of real estate commissions is not fixed by law. They are set by each Broker individually and may be negotiable between Buyer and Broker (real estate commissions include all compensation and fees to Broker).
   Buyer agrees to pay to Broker, irrespective of agency relationship(s), as follows:
   - A. **AMOUNT OF COMPENSATION: (Check (1), (2) or (3). Check only one.)**
     ☐ **(1)** ______ percent of the acquisition price AND (if checked ☐) $ ____________________,
     OR ☐ **(2)** $ ____________________,
     OR ☐ **(3)** Pursuant to the compensation schedule attached as an addendum ____________________.

SAMPLE

Buyer's Initials (________)(________)

BRE REVISED 4/13 (PAGE 1 OF 4) Print Date

Reviewed by ______ Date ______

EQUAL HOUSING OPPORTUNITY

BUYER REPRESENTATION AGREEMENT – EXCLUSIVE (BRE PAGE 1 OF 4)

Buyer: ______________________________ Date: ______________

B. **COMPENSATION PAYMENTS AND CREDITS:** Buyer is responsible for payment of compensation provided for in this Agreement. **However, if anyone other than Buyer compensates Broker for services covered by this Agreement, that amount shall be credited toward Buyer's obligation to pay compensation.** If the amount of compensation Broker receives from anyone other than Buyer exceeds Buyer's obligation, the excess amount shall be disclosed to Buyer and if allowed by law paid to Broker, or (if checked) ☐ credited to Buyer, or ☐ other ______________________________.

C. **BROKER RIGHT TO COMPENSATION:** Broker shall be entitled to the compensation provided for in paragraph 3A:
(1) If during the Representation Period, or any extension thereof, Buyer enters into an agreement to acquire property described in paragraph **1A**, on terms acceptable to Buyer provided Seller completes the transaction or is prevented from doing so by Buyer. (Broker shall be entitled to compensation whether any escrow resulting from such agreement closes during or after the expiration of the Representation Period.)
(2) If, within ___ **calendar days** after expiration of the Representation Period or any extension thereof, Buyer enters into an agreement to acquire property described in paragraph 1, which property Broker introduced to Buyer, or for which Broker acted on Buyer's behalf. The obligation to pay compensation pursuant to this paragraph shall arise only if, prior to or within **3 (or ☐ _____) calendar days** after expiration of this Agreement or any extension thereof, Broker gives Buyer a written notice of those properties which Broker introduced to Buyer, or for which Broker acted on Buyer's behalf.

D. **TIMING OF COMPENSATION:** Compensation is payable:
(1) Upon completion of any resulting transaction, and if an escrow is used, through escrow.
(2) If acquisition is prevented by default of Buyer, upon Buyer's default.
(3) If acquisition is prevented by a party to the transaction other than Buyer, when Buyer collects damages by suit, settlement or otherwise. Compensation shall equal one-half of the damages recovered, not to exceed the compensation provided for in paragraph 3A, after first deducting the unreimbursed payments, credits and expenses of collection, if any.

E. Buyer hereby irrevocably assigns to Broker the compensation provided for in paragraph 3A from Buyer's funds and proceeds in escrow. Buyer agrees to submit to escrow any funds needed to compensate Broker under this Agreement. Broker may submit this Agreement, as instructions to compensate Broker, to any escrow regarding property involving Buyer and a seller or other transferor.

F. **"BUYER"** includes any person or entity, other than Broker, related to Buyer or who in any manner acts on Buyer's behalf to acquire property described in paragraph **1A**

G. **(1)** Buyer has not previously entered into a representation agreement with another broker regarding property described in paragraph **1A**, unless specified as follows (name other broker here): ______________________________
(2) Buyer warrants that Buyer has no obligation to pay compensation to any other broker regarding property described in paragraph **1A**, unless Buyer acquires the following property(ies): ______________________________
(3) If Buyer acquires a property specified in G(2) above during the time Buyer is obligated to compensate another broker, Broker is neither: **(i)** entitled to compensation under this Agreement, nor **(ii)** obligated to represent Buyer in such transaction.

4. **INTERNET ADVERTISING; INTERNET BLOGS; SOCIAL MEDIA:** Buyer acknowledges and agrees that: (i) properties presented to them may have been marketed through a "virtual tour" on the Internet, permitting potential buyers to view properties over the Internet, or that the properties may have been the subject of comments or opinions of value by others on Internet blogs or other social media sites; (ii) neither the service provider(s) nor Broker has control over who will obtain access to such services or what action such persons might take; and (iii) Broker has no control over how long the information concerning the properties will be available on the Internet or social media sites.

5. **BROKER AUTHORIZATIONS AND OBLIGATIONS:**

A. Buyer authorizes Broker to: **(i)** locate and present selected properties to Buyer, present offers authorized by Buyer, and assist Buyer in negotiating for acceptance of such offers; **(ii)** assist Buyer with the financing process, including obtaining loan pre-qualification; **(iii)** upon request, provide Buyer with a list of professionals or vendors who perform the services described in the attached Buyer's Inspection Advisory; **(iv)** order reports, and schedule and attend meetings and appointments with professionals chosen by Buyer; **(v)** provide guidance to help Buyer with the acquisition of property; and **(vi)** obtain a credit report on Buyer.

B. For property transactions of which Broker is aware and not precluded from participating in by Buyer, Broker shall provide and review forms to create a property contract ("Property Contract") for the acquisition of a specific property ("Property"). With respect to such Property, Broker shall: **(i)** if the Property contains residential property with one to four dwelling units, conduct a reasonably competent and diligent on-site visual inspection of the accessible areas of the Property (excluding any common areas), and disclose to Buyer all facts materially affecting the value or desirability of such Property that are revealed by this inspection; **(ii)** deliver or communicate to Buyer any disclosures, materials or information received by, in the personal possession of or personally known to the individual signing for Broker below during the Representation Period; and **(iii)** facilitate the escrow process, including assisting Buyer in negotiating with Seller. Unless otherwise specified in writing, any information provided through Broker in the course of representing Buyer has not been and will not be verified by Broker. Broker's services are

Buyer's Initials (__________)(__________)

Reviewed by _______ Date _______

BRE REVISED 4/13 (PAGE 2 OF 4)

BUYER REPRESENTATION AGREEMENT – EXCLUSIVE (BRE PAGE 2 OF 4)

Buyer: ______________________________ Date: ______________

performed in compliance with federal, state and local anti-discrimination laws.

6. **SCOPE OF BROKER DUTY:**

A. While Broker will perform the duties described in paragraph 6B, Broker recommends that Buyer select other professionals, as described in the attached Buyer's Inspection Advisory, to investigate the Property through inspections, investigations, tests, surveys, reports, studies and other available information ("Inspections") during the transaction. Buyer agrees that these Inspections, to the extent they exceed the obligations described in paragraph 6B, are not within the scope of Broker's agency duties. Broker informs Buyer that it is in Buyer's best interest to obtain such Inspections.

B. Buyer acknowledges and agrees that Broker: **(i)** does not decide what price Buyer should pay or Seller should accept; **(ii)** does not guarantee the condition of the Property; **(iii)** does not guarantee the performance, adequacy or completeness of inspections, services, products or repairs provided or made by Seller or others; **(iv)** does not have an obligation to conduct an inspection of common areas or offsite areas of the Property; **(v)** shall not be responsible for identifying defects on the Property, in common areas or offsite unless such defects are visually observable by an inspection of reasonably accessible areas of the Property or are known to Broker; **(vi)** shall not be responsible for inspecting public records or permits concerning the title or use of the Property; **(vii)** shall not be responsible for identifying the location of boundary lines or other items affecting title; **(viii)** shall not be responsible for verifying square footage, representations of others or information contained in Investigation reports, Multiple Listing Service, advertisements, flyers or other promotional material; **(ix)** shall not be responsible for providing legal or tax advice regarding any aspect of a transaction entered into by Buyer or Seller; and **(x)** shall not be responsible for providing other advice or information that exceeds the knowledge, education and experience required to perform real estate licensed activity. Buyer agrees to seek legal, tax, insurance, title and other desired assistance from appropriate professionals.

C. Broker owes no duty to inspect for common environmental hazards, earthquake weaknesses, or geologic and seismic hazards. If Buyer receives the booklets titled "Environmental Hazards: A Guide for Homeowners, Buyers, Landlords and Tenants," "The Homeowner's Guide to Earthquake Safety," or "The Commercial Property Owner's Guide to Earthquake Safety," the booklets are deemed adequate to inform Buyer regarding the information contained in the booklets and, other than as specified in 6B above, Broker is not required to provide Buyer with additional information about the matters described in the booklets.

7. **BUYER OBLIGATIONS:**

A. Buyer agrees to timely view and consider properties selected by Broker and to negotiate in good faith to acquire a property. Buyer further agrees to act in good faith toward the completion of any Property Contract entered into in furtherance of this Agreement. Within **5 (or ☐ ______) calendar days** from the execution of this Agreement, Buyer shall provide relevant personal and financial information to Broker to assure Buyer's ability to acquire property described in paragraph 4. If Buyer fails to provide such information, or if Buyer does not qualify financially to acquire property described in paragraph 4, then Broker may cancel this Agreement in writing. Buyer has an affirmative duty to take steps to protect him/herself, including discovery of the legal, practical and technical implications of discovered or disclosed facts, and investigation of information and facts which are known to Buyer or are within the diligent attention and observation of Buyer. Buyer is obligated, and agrees, to read all documents provided to Buyer. Buyer agrees to seek desired assistance from appropriate professionals, selected by Buyer, such as those referenced in the attached Buyer's Inspection Advisory.

B. Buyer shall notify Broker in writing (C.A.R. Form BMI) of any material issue to Buyer, such as, but not limited to, Buyer requests for information on, or concerns regarding, any particular area of interest or importance to Buyer ("Material Issues").

C. **Buyer agrees to: (i) indemnify, defend and hold Broker harmless from all claims, disputes, litigation, judgments, costs and attorney fees arising from any incorrect information supplied by Buyer, or from any Material Issues that Buyer fails to disclose in writing to Broker; and (ii) pay for reports, Inspections and meetings arranged by Broker on Buyer's behalf.**

D. Buyer is advised to read the attached Buyer's Inspection Advisory for a list of items and other concerns that typically warrant Inspections or investigation by Buyer or other professionals.

8. **OTHER TERMS AND CONDITIONS:** The following disclosures or addenda are attached:

A. ☑ Buyer's Inspection Advisory (C.A.R. Form BIA-B)

B. ☐ Statewide Buyer and Seller Advisory (C.A.R. Form SBSA)

C. ☐ ______________________________

D. ☐ ______________________________

9. **ATTORNEY FEES:** In any action, proceeding or arbitration between Buyer and Broker regarding the obligation to pay compensation under this Agreement, the prevailing Buyer or Broker shall be entitled to reasonable attorney fees and costs, except as provided in paragraph 11A.

10. **ENTIRE AGREEMENT:** All understandings between the parties are incorporated in this Agreement. Its terms are intended by the parties as a final, complete and exclusive expression of their agreement with respect to its subject matter, and may not be contradicted by evidence of any prior agreement or contemporaneous oral agreement. This Agreement may not be extended, amended, modified, altered or changed, except in writing signed by Buyer and Broker. In the event that any provision of this Agreement is held to be ineffective or invalid, the remaining provisions will nevertheless be given full force and effect. This Agreement and any supplement, addendum or modification, including any copy, whether by copier, facsimile, NCR or electronic, may

Buyer's Initials (_________)(_________)

BRE REVISED 4/13 (PAGE 3 OF 4)

Reviewed by ______ Date ______

EQUAL HOUSING OPPORTUNITY

BUYER REPRESENTATION AGREEMENT – EXCLUSIVE (BRE PAGE 3 OF 4)

Buyer: ______________________________ Date: __________

be signed in two or more counterparts, all of which shall constitute one and the same writing.

11. DISPUTE RESOLUTION:

A. MEDIATION: Buyer and Broker agree to mediate any dispute or claim arising between them out of this Agreement, or any resulting transaction, before resorting to arbitration or court action, subject to paragraph 11B(2) below. Paragraph 11B(2) below applies whether or not the arbitration provision is initialed. Mediation fees, if any, shall be divided equally among the parties involved. If, for any dispute or claim to which this paragraph applies, any party commences an action without first attempting to resolve the matter through mediation, or refuses to mediate after a request has been made, then that party shall not be entitled to recover attorney's fees, even if they would otherwise be available to that party in any such action. THIS MEDIATION PROVISION APPLIES WHETHER OR NOT THE ARBITRATION PROVISION IS INITIALED.

B. ARBITRATION OF DISPUTES: (1) Buyer and Broker agree that any dispute or claim in Law or equity arising between them regarding the obligation to pay compensation under this Agreement, which is not settled through mediation, shall be decided by neutral, binding arbitration, including and subject to paragraph 11B(2) below. The arbitrator shall be a retired judge or justice, or an attorney with at least five years of residential real estate law experience, unless the parties mutually agree to a different arbitrator, who shall render an award in accordance with substantive California law. The parties shall have the right to discovery in accordance with California Code of Civil Procedure §1283.05. In all other respects, the arbitration shall be conducted in accordance with Title 9 of Part III, of the California Code of Civil Procedure. Judgment upon the award of the arbitrator(s) may be entered in any court having jurisdiction. Interpretation of this Agreement to arbitrate shall be governed by the Federal Arbitration Act.

(2) EXCLUSIONS FROM MEDIATION AND ARBITRATION: The following matters are excluded from mediation and arbitration: (i) a judicial or non-judicial foreclosure or other action or proceeding to enforce a deed of trust, mortgage or installment land sale contract as defined in California Civil Code §2985; (ii) an unlawful detainer action; (iii) the filing or enforcement of a mechanic's lien; and (iv) any matter that is within the jurisdiction of a probate, small claims or bankruptcy court. The filing of a court action to enable the recording of a notice of pending action, for order of attachment, receivership, injunction, or other provisional remedies, shall not constitute a waiver of the mediation and arbitration provisions.

"NOTICE: BY INITIALING IN THE SPACE BELOW YOU ARE AGREEING TO HAVE ANY DISPUTE ARISING OUT OF THE MATTERS INCLUDED IN THE 'ARBITRATION OF DISPUTES' PROVISION DECIDED BY NEUTRAL ARBITRATION AS PROVIDED BY CALIFORNIA LAW. YOU ARE GIVING UP ANY RIGHTS YOU MIGHT POSSESS TO HAVE THE DISPUTE LITIGATED IN A COURT OR JURY TRIAL. BY INITIALING IN THE SPACE BELOW YOU ARE GIVING UP YOUR JUDICIAL RIGHTS TO DISCOVERY AND APPEAL, UNLESS THOSE RIGHTS ARE SPECIFICALLY INCLUDED IN THE 'ARBITRATION OF DISPUTES' PROVISION. IF YOU REFUSE TO SUBMIT TO ARBITRATION AFTER AGREEING TO THIS PROVISION, YOU MAY BE COMPELLED TO ARBITRATE UNDER THE AUTHORITY OF THE CALIFORNIA CODE OF CIVIL PROCEDURE. YOUR AGREEMENT TO THIS ARBITRATION PROVISION IS VOLUNTARY."

"WE HAVE READ AND UNDERSTAND THE FOREGOING AND AGREE TO SUBMIT DISPUTES ARISING OUT OF THE MATTERS INCLUDED IN THE 'ARBITRATION OF DISPUTES' PROVISION TO NEUTRAL ARBITRATION."

Buyer's Initials ____/____ Broker's Initials ____/____

Buyer acknowledges that Buyer has read, understands, received a copy of and agrees to the terms of this Agreement.

Buyer ______________________________ Date __________

Address ____________________ City __________ State ______ Zip ______

Telephone ______________ Fax ______________ E-mail ______________

Buyer ______________________________ Date __________

Address ____________________ City __________ State ______ Zip ______

Telephone ______________ Fax ______________ E-mail ______________

Real Estate Broker (Firm) ______________________________ DRE License # __________

By (Agent) ______________ DRE License # ______________ Date __________

Address ____________________ City __________ State ______ Zip ______

Telephone ______________ Fax ______________ E-mail ______________

Published and Distributed by:
REAL ESTATE BUSINESS SERVICES, INC.
a subsidiary of the California Association of REALTORS®
525 South Virgil Avenue, Los Angeles, California 90020

BRE REVISED 4/13 (PAGE 4 OF 4)

Reviewed by ______ Date ______

BUYER REPRESENTATION AGREEMENT – EXCLUSIVE (BRE PAGE 4 OF 4)

To comply with the statute of frauds, a buyer representation agreement must be in writing and signed by the buyer to be enforceable.

The term of the broker's relationship with the seller should be established in the contract. The Real Estate Law requires an exclusive buyer representation agreement, like an exclusive listing agreement, to specify a termination date.

Provisions in a Buyer Representation Agreement

A buyer representation agreement usually has provisions concerning the general characteristics of the property the buyer wants, the acceptable price range, the broker's duties, and the broker's compensation.

The type of property that the buyer wants should be described in enough detail so that the contract accurately states the buyer's requirements. The buyer could become liable for the broker's compensation if the broker finds property within the stated price range that fits the description provided, even if the buyer doesn't want to purchase it.

Sometimes a buyer hires a broker not to find property but to negotiate the purchase of a particular property that the buyer has already found. In that case, the buyer representation agreement should include a legal description of the property.

The broker's duties listed in the contract may include locating properties, preparing offers on the buyer's behalf and presenting them to sellers, negotiating with sellers, helping the buyer obtain financing, and providing other guidance. In an exclusive representation agreement, the broker usually agrees to make a reasonably diligent effort on the buyer's behalf.

The representation agreement is also likely to make it clear that the broker isn't prevented from working with other buyers during the term of the contract, or from showing other buyers the same properties she's showing this buyer. When the broker negotiates for the purchase of a property on behalf of this buyer, it won't be a breach of contract or a violation of the broker's duties if she also negotiates for the same property on behalf of another buyer at the same time.

Broker's Compensation

Of course, a buyer representation agreement includes a promise to compensate the broker. The compensation must be negotiable, and if the buyer is seeking to purchase residential property with up to four units, the agreement must include a notice explaining that the compensation is negotiable.

The agreement should specify the conditions under which the broker's compensation will be earned and how the compensation will be determined. There are a variety of ways in which a broker representing a buyer may be compensated.

Most buyer representation agreements provide for payment by means of a commission split when the buyer purchases a home that's listed through a multiple listing service. As we said earlier, MLS listing agreements authorize the listing broker to share the commission with other brokers. Typically, the listing broker will pay half of his commission to the broker who finds a buyer, regardless of which party that other broker is representing.

Example: Helman lists her property with Broker Thurston and agrees to pay him a commission of 6% of the sales price. The listing agreement provides that Thurston will pay half of his commission to the broker who finds a buyer.

Broker Adams has a buyer representation agreement with Gray. Gray offers $650,000 for Helman's house and Helman accepts the offer.

When the transaction closes, Helman pays a $39,000 commission; $19,500 goes to Broker Thurston and $19,500 goes to Broker Adams.

When a broker representing a buyer accepts a commission split, she's effectively being paid by the seller rather than by her own client, the buyer. Under California law, a broker's duties to her client aren't affected by which party pays her fee. (See Chapter 8.)

However, a buyer representation agreement may provide for a **buyer-paid fee** instead of a commission split. The buyer-paid fee might be based on an hourly rate, in which case the broker is essentially a consultant. Alternatively, the broker may charge a percentage fee, so that the commission is a percentage of the purchase price. A third possibility is a flat fee—a specified sum that's payable if the buyer purchases a property during the term of the representation agreement.

Many buyer representation agreements provide that the broker will accept a commission split if one is available, but the buyer will pay the broker a fee if the purchased property was unlisted (for example, if the property was for sale by owner).

Some brokers collect a **retainer** when they enter into a buyer representation agreement, to ensure that their services won't go entirely uncompensated. A retainer is a sum of money paid up front, before services are provided. A retainer is usually nonrefundable, but it will be credited against any fee or commission that the broker becomes entitled to.

Purchase Agreements

When a real estate seller accepts a buyer's offer to purchase the property, they enter into a **purchase agreement**. A purchase agreement is a written contract between a buyer and a seller that establishes all of the terms of the sale.

In a residential transaction, the buyer's offer is usually prepared by filling out a standard purchase agreement form. (As an example, a CAR Residential Purchase Agreement form is shown in Figure 7.3.) The buyer signs the form, which is then presented to the seller along with a good faith deposit. If the seller decides to accept the offer, she also signs the form, and the form then becomes the binding contract of sale. If the agent holds the good faith deposit on the seller's behalf instead of passing it on to an escrow agent, the form serves as the buyer's receipt for the good faith deposit; this is why you may hear the purchase agreement also referred to as a **deposit receipt**.

After a purchase agreement has been signed, there are still many details to be taken care of before the transaction can close: financing arrangements, inspections, a title search, and so on. As a legally binding contract, the purchase agreement keeps the buyer and the seller committed to the transaction while all of those tasks are performed. It protects both parties by providing legal recourse if either of them backs out of the transaction.

Once both the buyer and the seller have signed the purchase agreement, the buyer is considered to have **equitable title** to the property. This essentially means that, as a matter of fairness, a court would recognize that the buyer has an interest in the property, even though the seller still has legal title to it. If the seller breaches the contract, the court could issue an order of specific performance requiring the seller to deed the property to the buyer (see Chapter 6).

Fig. 7.3 Residential purchase agreement

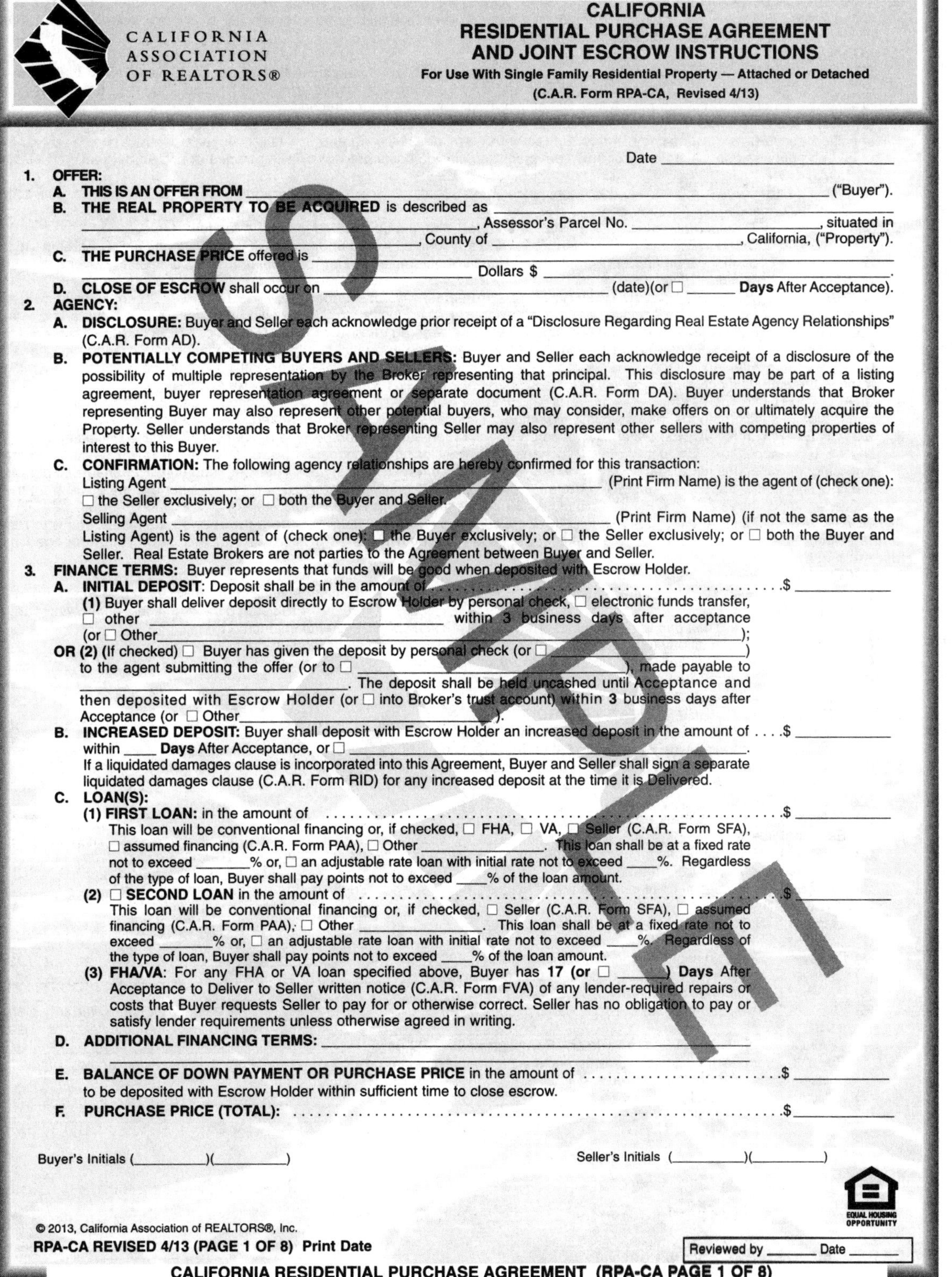

CALIFORNIA ASSOCIATION OF REALTORS®

CALIFORNIA RESIDENTIAL PURCHASE AGREEMENT AND JOINT ESCROW INSTRUCTIONS

For Use With Single Family Residential Property — Attached or Detached

(C.A.R. Form RPA-CA, Revised 4/13)

Date ____________________

1. **OFFER:**
   A. **THIS IS AN OFFER FROM** ____________________ ("Buyer").
   B. **THE REAL PROPERTY TO BE ACQUIRED** is described as ____________________, Assessor's Parcel No. __________, situated in __________, County of __________, California, ("Property").
   C. **THE PURCHASE PRICE** offered is ____________________ Dollars $ __________.
   D. **CLOSE OF ESCROW** shall occur on __________ (date)(or ☐ ______ **Days** After Acceptance).
2. **AGENCY:**
   A. **DISCLOSURE:** Buyer and Seller each acknowledge prior receipt of a "Disclosure Regarding Real Estate Agency Relationships" (C.A.R. Form AD).
   B. **POTENTIALLY COMPETING BUYERS AND SELLERS:** Buyer and Seller each acknowledge receipt of a disclosure of the possibility of multiple representation by the Broker representing that principal. This disclosure may be part of a listing agreement, buyer representation agreement or separate document (C.A.R. Form DA). Buyer understands that Broker representing Buyer may also represent other potential buyers, who may consider, make offers on or ultimately acquire the Property. Seller understands that Broker representing Seller may also represent other sellers with competing properties of interest to this Buyer.
   C. **CONFIRMATION:** The following agency relationships are hereby confirmed for this transaction:
   Listing Agent ____________________ (Print Firm Name) is the agent of (check one): ☐ the Seller exclusively; or ☐ both the Buyer and Seller.
   Selling Agent ____________________ (Print Firm Name) (if not the same as the Listing Agent) is the agent of (check one): ☐ the Buyer exclusively; or ☐ the Seller exclusively; or ☐ both the Buyer and Seller. Real Estate Brokers are not parties to the Agreement between Buyer and Seller.
3. **FINANCE TERMS:** Buyer represents that funds will be good when deposited with Escrow Holder.
   A. **INITIAL DEPOSIT**: Deposit shall be in the amount of .... $ __________
   (1) Buyer shall deliver deposit directly to Escrow Holder by personal check, ☐ electronic funds transfer, ☐ other __________ within 3 business days after acceptance (or ☐ Other __________);
   OR (2) (If checked) ☐ Buyer has given the deposit by personal check (or ☐ __________) to the agent submitting the offer (or to ☐ __________), made payable to __________. The deposit shall be held uncashed until Acceptance and then deposited with Escrow Holder (or ☐ into Broker's trust account) within 3 business days after Acceptance (or ☐ Other __________).
   B. **INCREASED DEPOSIT:** Buyer shall deposit with Escrow Holder an increased deposit in the amount of .... $ __________ within ____ **Days** After Acceptance, or ☐ __________.
   If a liquidated damages clause is incorporated into this Agreement, Buyer and Seller shall sign a separate liquidated damages clause (C.A.R. Form RID) for any increased deposit at the time it is Delivered.
   C. **LOAN(S):**
   (1) FIRST LOAN: in the amount of .... $ __________
   This loan will be conventional financing or, if checked, ☐ FHA, ☐ VA, ☐ Seller (C.A.R. Form SFA), ☐ assumed financing (C.A.R. Form PAA), ☐ Other __________. This loan shall be at a fixed rate not to exceed ______% or, ☐ an adjustable rate loan with initial rate not to exceed ____%. Regardless of the type of loan, Buyer shall pay points not to exceed ____% of the loan amount.
   (2) ☐ **SECOND LOAN** in the amount of .... $ __________
   This loan will be conventional financing or, if checked, ☐ Seller (C.A.R. Form SFA), ☐ assumed financing (C.A.R. Form PAA), ☐ Other __________. This loan shall be at a fixed rate not to exceed ______% or, ☐ an adjustable rate loan with initial rate not to exceed ____%. Regardless of the type of loan, Buyer shall pay points not to exceed ____% of the loan amount.
   (3) FHA/VA: For any FHA or VA loan specified above, Buyer has **17** (or ☐ ______) **Days** After Acceptance to Deliver to Seller written notice (C.A.R. Form FVA) of any lender-required repairs or costs that Buyer requests Seller to pay for or otherwise correct. Seller has no obligation to pay or satisfy lender requirements unless otherwise agreed in writing.
   D. **ADDITIONAL FINANCING TERMS:** ____________________
   E. **BALANCE OF DOWN PAYMENT OR PURCHASE PRICE** in the amount of .... $ __________ to be deposited with Escrow Holder within sufficient time to close escrow.
   F. **PURCHASE PRICE (TOTAL):** .... $ __________

Buyer's Initials (________)(________) Seller's Initials (________)(________)

EQUAL HOUSING OPPORTUNITY

RPA-CA REVISED 4/13 (PAGE 1 OF 8) Print Date

Reviewed by ______ Date ______

CALIFORNIA RESIDENTIAL PURCHASE AGREEMENT (RPA-CA PAGE 1 OF 8)

Property Address: ______________________ Date: ____________

G. **VERIFICATION OF DOWN PAYMENT AND CLOSING COSTS:** Buyer (or Buyer's lender or loan broker pursuant to 3H(1) shall, within **7 (or ☐ ________) Days** After Acceptance, Deliver to Seller written verification of Buyer's down payment and closing costs. (If checked, ☐ verification attached.)

H. **LOAN TERMS:**

(1) LOAN APPLICATIONS: Within **7 (or ☐ ______) Days** After Acceptance, Buyer shall Deliver to Seller a letter from lender or loan broker stating that, based on a review of Buyer's written application and credit report, Buyer is prequalified or preapproved for any NEW loan specified in 3C above. (If checked, ☐ letter attached.)

(2) LOAN CONTINGENCY: Buyer shall act diligently and in good faith to obtain the designated loan(s). Obtaining the loan(s) specified above **is a contingency** of this Agreement unless otherwise agreed in writing. Buyer's contractual obligations to obtain and provide deposit, balance of down payment and closing costs **are not contingencies** of this Agreement.

(3) LOAN CONTINGENCY REMOVAL:

(i) Within **17 (or ☐ ______) Days** After Acceptance, Buyer shall, as specified in paragraph 14, in writing remove the loan contingency or cancel this Agreement;

OR (ii) (If checked) ☐ the loan contingency shall remain in effect until the designated loans are funded.

(4) ☐ NO LOAN CONTINGENCY (If checked): Obtaining any loan specified above is NOT a contingency of this Agreement. If Buyer does not obtain the loan and as a result Buyer does not purchase the Property, Seller may be entitled to Buyer's deposit or other legal remedies.

I. **APPRAISAL CONTINGENCY AND REMOVAL:** This Agreement is (**or**, if checked, ☐ is NOT) contingent upon a written appraisal of the Property by a licensed or certified appraiser at no less than the specified purchase price. If there is a loan contingency, Buyer's removal of the loan contingency shall be deemed removal of this appraisal contingency (**or,** ☐ if checked, Buyer shall, as specified in paragraph 14B(3), in writing remove the appraisal contingency or cancel this Agreement within **17 (or ____) Days** After Acceptance). If there is no loan contingency, Buyer shall, as specified in paragraph 14B(3), in writing remove the appraisal contingency or cancel this Agreement within **17 (or ☐ ____) Days** After Acceptance.

J. ☐ **ALL CASH OFFER** (If checked): Buyer shall, within **7 (or ☐ ______) Days** After Acceptance, Deliver to Seller written verification of sufficient funds to close this transaction. (If checked, ☐ verification attached.)

K. **BUYER STATED FINANCING:** Seller has relied on Buyer's representation of the type of financing specified (including but not limited to, as applicable, amount of down payment, contingent or non contingent loan, or all cash). If Buyer seeks alternate financing, (i) Seller has no obligation to cooperate with Buyer's efforts to obtain such financing, and (ii) Buyer shall also pursue the financing method specified in this Agreement. Buyer's failure to secure alternate financing does not excuse Buyer from the obligation to purchase the Property and close escrow as specified in this Agreement.

4. **ALLOCATION OF COSTS** (If checked): Unless otherwise specified here, in writing, **this paragraph** only determines who is to pay for the inspection, test or service ("Report") mentioned; it **does not determine who is to pay for any work recommended or identified in the Report.**

A. **INSPECTIONS AND REPORTS:**

(1) ☐ Buyer ☐ Seller shall pay for an inspection and report for wood destroying pests and organisms ("Wood Pest Report") prepared by ______________________ a registered structural pest control company.
(2) ☐ Buyer ☐ Seller shall pay to have septic or private sewage disposal systems inspected ____________.
(3) ☐ Buyer ☐ Seller shall pay to have domestic wells tested for water potability and productivity ____________.
(4) ☐ Buyer ☐ Seller shall pay for a natural hazard zone disclosure report prepared by ____________.
(5) ☐ Buyer ☐ Seller shall pay for the following inspection or report ____________.
(6) ☐ Buyer ☐ Seller shall pay for the following inspection or report ____________.

B. **GOVERNMENT REQUIREMENTS AND RETROFIT:**

(1) ☐ Buyer ☐ Seller shall pay for smoke detector installation and/or water heater bracing, if required by Law. Prior to Close Of Escrow, Seller shall provide Buyer written statement(s) of compliance in accordance with state and local Law, unless exempt.
(2) ☐ Buyer ☐ Seller shall pay the cost of compliance with any other minimum mandatory government retrofit standards, inspections and reports if required as a condition of closing escrow under any Law. ____________.

C. **ESCROW AND TITLE:**

(1) ☐ Buyer ☐ Seller shall pay escrow fee ____________.
Escrow Holder shall be ____________.
(2) ☐ Buyer ☐ Seller shall pay for **owner's** title insurance policy specified in paragraph 12E ____________.
Owner's title policy to be issued by ____________.
(Buyer shall pay for any title insurance policy insuring Buyer's **lender**, unless otherwise agreed in writing.)

D. **OTHER COSTS:**

(1) ☐ Buyer ☐ Seller shall pay County transfer tax or fee ____________.
(2) ☐ Buyer ☐ Seller shall pay City transfer tax or fee ____________.
(3) ☐ Buyer ☐ Seller shall pay Homeowner's Association ("HOA") transfer fee ____________.
(4) ☐ Buyer ☐ Seller shall pay HOA document preparation fees ____________.
(5) ☐ Buyer ☐ Seller shall pay for any private transfer fee ____________.
(6) ☐ Buyer ☐ Seller shall pay for the cost, not to exceed $ ____________, of a one-year home warranty plan, issued by ____________, with the following optional coverages:
☐ Air Conditioner ☐ Pool/Spa ☐ Code and Permit upgrade ☐ Other: ____________.
Buyer is informed that home warranty plans have many optional coverages in addition to those listed above. Buyer is advised to investigate these coverages to determine those that may be suitable for Buyer.
(7) ☐ Buyer ☐ Seller shall pay for ____________.
(8) ☐ Buyer ☐ Seller shall pay for ____________.

Buyer's Initials (________)(________) Seller's Initials (________)(________)

Reviewed by ______ Date ______

EQUAL HOUSING OPPORTUNITY

Property Address: ____ Date: ________________

5. CLOSING AND POSSESSION:

A. Buyer intends (or □ does not intend) to occupy the Property as Buyer's primary residence.

B. Seller-occupied or vacant property: Possession shall be delivered to Buyer at 5 PM or (□ _____ □ AM/□ PM) on the date of Close Of Escrow; □ on ______________________________; or □ no later than _______ **Days** After Close Of Escrow. If transfer of title and possession do not occur at the same time, Buyer and Seller are advised to: **(i)** enter into a written occupancy agreement (C.A.R. Form PAA, paragraph 2.); and **(ii)** consult with their insurance and legal advisors.

C. Tenant-occupied property: (i) Property shall be vacant at least **5** (**or** □ ______) **Days** Prior to Close Of Escrow, unless otherwise agreed in writing. **Note to Seller: If you are unable to deliver Property vacant in accordance with rent control and other applicable Law, you may be in breach of this Agreement.**

OR (ii) (if checked) □ **Tenant to remain in possession.** (C.A.R. Form PAA, paragraph 3.)

D. At Close Of Escrow, **(i)** Seller assigns to Buyer any assignable warranty rights for items included in the sale, and **(ii)** Seller shall Deliver to Buyer available Copies of warranties. Brokers cannot and will not determine the assignability of any warranties.

E. At Close Of Escrow, unless otherwise agreed in writing, Seller shall provide keys and/or means to operate all locks, mailboxes, security systems, alarms and garage door openers. If Property is a condominium or located in a common interest subdivision, Buyer may be required to pay a deposit to the Homeowners' Association ("HOA") to obtain keys to accessible HOA facilities.

6. STATUTORY DISCLOSURES (INCLUDING LEAD-BASED PAINT HAZARD DISCLOSURES) AND CANCELLATION RIGHTS:

A. (1) Seller shall, within the time specified in paragraph 14A, Deliver to Buyer, if required by Law: **(i)** Federal Lead-Based Paint Disclosures (C.A.R. Form FLD) and pamphlet ("Lead Disclosures"); and **(ii)** disclosures or notices required by sections 1102 et. seq. and 1103 et. seq. of the Civil Code ("Statutory Disclosures"). Statutory Disclosures include, but are not limited to, a Real Estate Transfer Disclosure Statement ("TDS"), Natural Hazard Disclosure Statement ("NHD"), notice or actual knowledge of release of illegal controlled substance, notice of special tax and/or assessments (or, if allowed, substantially equivalent notice regarding the Mello-Roos Community Facilities Act and Improvement Bond Act of 1915) and, if Seller has actual knowledge, of industrial use and military ordnance location (C.A.R. Form SPQ or SSD).

(2) Buyer shall, within the time specified in paragraph 14B(1), return Signed Copies of the Statutory and Lead Disclosures to Seller.

(3) In the event Seller, prior to Close Of Escrow, becomes aware of adverse conditions materially affecting the Property, or any material inaccuracy in disclosures, information or representations previously provided to Buyer, Seller shall promptly provide a subsequent or amended disclosure or notice, in writing, covering those items. **However, a subsequent or amended disclosure shall not be required for conditions and material inaccuracies** of which Buyer is otherwise aware, or which are **disclosed in reports provided to or obtained by Buyer or ordered and paid for by Buyer.**

(4) If any disclosure or notice specified in 6A(1), or subsequent or amended disclosure or notice is Delivered to Buyer after the offer is Signed, Buyer shall have the right to cancel this Agreement within **3 Days** After Delivery in person, or **5 Days** After Delivery by deposit in the mail, by giving written notice of cancellation to Seller or Seller's agent.

(5) Note to Buyer and Seller: Waiver of Statutory and Lead Disclosures is prohibited by Law.

B. NATURAL AND ENVIRONMENTAL HAZARDS: Within the time specified in paragraph 14A, Seller shall, if required by Law: **(i)** Deliver to Buyer earthquake guides (and questionnaire) and environmental hazards booklet; **(ii)** even if exempt from the obligation to provide a NHD, disclose if the Property is located in a Special Flood Hazard Area; Potential Flooding (Inundation) Area; Very High Fire Hazard Zone; State Fire Responsibility Area; Earthquake Fault Zone; Seismic Hazard Zone; and **(iii)** disclose any other zone as required by Law and provide any other information required for those zones.

C. WITHHOLDING TAXES: Within the time specified in paragraph 14A, to avoid required witholding, Seller shall Deliver to Buyer or qualified substitute, an affidavit sufficient to comply with federal (FIRPTA) and California withholding Law (C.A.R. Form AS or QS).

D. MEGAN'S LAW DATABASE DISCLOSURE: Notice: Pursuant to Section 290.46 of the Penal Code, information about specified registered sex offenders is made available to the public via an Internet Web site maintained by the Department of Justice at www.meganslaw.ca.gov. Depending on an offender's criminal history, this information will include either the address at which the offender resides or the community of residence and ZIP Code in which he or she resides. (Neither Seller nor Brokers are required to check this website. If Buyer wants further information, Broker recommends that Buyer obtain information from this website during Buyer's inspection contingency period. Brokers do not have expertise in this area.)

E. NOTICE REGARDING GAS AND HAZARDOUS LIQUID TRANSMISSION PIPELINES: This notice is being provided simply to inform you that information about the general location of gas and hazardous liquid transmission pipelines is available to the public via the National Pipeline Mapping System (NPMS) Internet Web site maintained by the United States Department of Transportation at http://www.npms.phmsa.dot.gov/. To seek further information about possible transmission pipelines near the Property, you may contact your local gas utility or other pipeline operators in the area. Contact information for pipeline operators is searchable by ZIP Code and county on the NPMS Internet Web site.

7. CONDOMINIUM/PLANNED DEVELOPMENT DISCLOSURES:

A. SELLER HAS: 7 (or □ ______) Days After Acceptance to disclose to Buyer whether the Property is a condominium, or is located in a planned development or other common interest subdivision (C.A.R. Form SPQ or SSD).

B. If the Property is a condominium or is located in a planned development or other common interest subdivision, Seller has **3** (**or** □ ______) **Days** After Acceptance to request from the HOA (C.A.R. Form HOA): **(i)** Copies of any documents required by Law; **(ii)** disclosure of any pending or anticipated claim or litigation by or against the HOA; **(iii)** a statement containing the location and number of designated parking and storage spaces; **(iv)** Copies of the most recent 12 months of HOA minutes for regular and special meetings; and **(v)** the names and contact information of all HOAs governing the Property (collectively, "CI Disclosures"). Seller shall itemize and Deliver to Buyer all CI Disclosures received from the HOA and any CI Disclosures in Seller's possession. Buyer's approval of CI Disclosures is a contingency of this Agreement as specified in paragraph 14B(3).

8. ITEMS INCLUDED IN AND EXCLUDED FROM PURCHASE PRICE:

A. NOTE TO BUYER AND SELLER: Items listed as included or excluded in the MLS, flyers or marketing materials are **not** included in the purchase price or excluded from the sale unless specified in 8B or C.

B. ITEMS INCLUDED IN SALE:

(1) All EXISTING fixtures and fittings that are attached to the Property;

(2) EXISTING electrical, mechanical, lighting, plumbing and heating fixtures, ceiling fans, fireplace inserts, gas logs and grates, solar systems, built-in appliances, window and door screens, awnings, shutters, window coverings, attached floor coverings, television antennas, satellite dishes, private integrated telephone systems, air coolers/conditioners, pool/spa equipment, garage door openers/remote controls, mailbox, in-ground landscaping, trees/shrubs, water softeners, water purifiers, security systems/alarms; (If checked) □ stove(s), □ refrigerator(s);

Buyer's Initials (__________)(__________) Seller's Initials (__________)(__________)

RPA-CA REVISED 4/13 (PAGE 3 OF 8) Print Date

Reviewed by _______ Date _______

EQUAL HOUSING OPPORTUNITY

CALIFORNIA RESIDENTIAL PURCHASE AGREEMENT (RPA-CA PAGE 3 OF 8)

Property Address: ______________________________ Date: ______________

(3) The following additional items:____.
(4) Seller represents that all items included in the purchase price, unless otherwise specified, are owned by Seller.
(5) All items included shall be transferred free of liens and without Seller warranty.

C. **ITEMS EXCLUDED FROM SALE:** Unless otherwise specified, audio and video components (such as flat screen TVs and speakers) are excluded if any such item is not itself attached to the Property, even if a bracket or other mechanism attached to the component is attached to the Property; and ________________________________.

9. **CONDITION OF PROPERTY:** Unless otherwise agreed: **(i) the Property is sold (a) in its PRESENT physical ("as-is") condition as of the date of Acceptance and (b) subject to Buyer's Investigation rights; (ii)** the Property, including pool, spa, landscaping and grounds, is to be maintained in substantially the same condition as on the date of Acceptance; and **(iii)** all debris and personal property not included in the sale shall be removed by Close Of Escrow.

A. Seller shall, within the time specified in paragraph 14A, DISCLOSE KNOWN MATERIAL FACTS AND DEFECTS affecting the Property, including known insurance claims within the past five years, and make any and all other disclosures required by law.

B. Buyer has the right to inspect the Property and, as specified in paragraph 14B, based upon information discovered in those inspections: (i) cancel this Agreement; or (ii) request that Seller make Repairs or take other action.

C. **Buyer is strongly advised to conduct investigations of the entire Property in order to determine its present condition. Seller may not be aware of all defects affecting the Property or other factors that Buyer considers important. Property improvements may not be built according to code, in compliance with current Law, or have had permits issued.**

10. **BUYER'S INVESTIGATION OF PROPERTY AND MATTERS AFFECTING PROPERTY:**

A. Buyer's acceptance of the condition of, and any other matter affecting the Property, is a contingency of this Agreement as specified in this paragraph and paragraph 14B. Within the time specified in paragraph 14B(1), Buyer shall have the right, at Buyer's expense unless otherwise agreed, to conduct inspections, investigations, tests, surveys and other studies ("Buyer Investigations"), including, but not limited to, the right to: **(i)** inspect for lead-based paint and other lead-based paint hazards; **(ii)** inspect for wood destroying pests and organisms; **(iii)** review the registered sex offender database; **(iv)** confirm the insurability of Buyer and the Property; and **(v)** satisfy Buyer as to any matter specified in the attached Buyer's Inspection Advisory (C.A.R. Form BIA). Without Seller's prior written consent, Buyer shall neither make nor cause to be made: **(i)** invasive or destructive Buyer Investigations; or **(ii)** inspections by any governmental building or zoning inspector or government employee, unless required by Law.

B. Seller shall make the Property available for all Buyer Investigations. Buyer shall **(i)** as specified in paragraph 14B, complete Buyer Investigations and, either remove the contingency or cancel this Agreement, and **(ii)** give Seller, at no cost, complete Copies of all Investigation reports obtained by Buyer, which obligation shall survive the termination of this Agreement.

C. Seller shall have water, gas, electricity and all operable pilot lights on for Buyer's Investigations and through the date possession is made available to Buyer.

D. **Buyer indemnity and seller protection for entry upon property:** Buyer shall: **(i)** keep the Property free and clear of liens; **(ii)** repair all damage arising from Buyer Investigations; and **(iii)** indemnify and hold Seller harmless from all resulting liability, claims, demands, damages and costs. Buyer shall carry, or Buyer shall require anyone acting on Buyer's behalf to carry, policies of liability, workers' compensation and other applicable insurance, defending and protecting Seller from liability for any injuries to persons or property occurring during any Buyer Investigations or work done on the Property at Buyer's direction prior to Close Of Escrow. Seller is advised that certain protections may be afforded Seller by recording a "Notice of Non-responsibility" (C.A.R. Form NNR) for Buyer Investigations and work done on the Property at Buyer's direction. Buyer's obligations under this paragraph shall survive the termination of this Agreement.

11. **SELLER DISCLOSURES; ADDENDA; ADVISORIES; OTHER TERMS:**

A. **Seller Disclosures (if checked):** Seller shall, within the time sepcified in paragraph 14A, complete and provide Buyer with a:
☐Seller Property Questionnaire (C.A.R. Form SPQ) **OR** ☐Supplemental Contractual and Statutory Disclosure (C.A.R. Form SSD)

B. **Addenda (if checked):** ☐Addendum # (C.A.R. Form ADM)
☐Wood Destroying Pest Inspection and Allocation of Cost Addendum (C.A.R. Form WPA)
☐Purchase Agreement Addendum (C.A.R. Form PAA) ☐Septic, Well and Property Monument Addendum (C.A.R. Form SWPI)
☐Short Sale Addendum (C.A.R. Form SSA) ☐Other

C. **Advisories (If checked):** ☐Buyer's Inspection advisory (C.A.R. Form BIA)
☐Probate Advisory (C.A.R. Form PAK) ☐Statewide Buyer and Seller Advisory (C.A.R.Form SBSA)
☐Trust Advisory (C.A.R. Form TA) ☐REO Advisory (C.A.R. Form REO)

D. **Other Terms:**

12. **TITLE AND VESTING:**

A. Within the time specified in paragraph 14, Buyer shall be provided a current preliminary title report, which shall include a search of the General Index, Seller shall within 7 Days After Acceptance, give Escrow Holder a completed Statement of Information. The preliminary report is only an offer by the title insurer to issue a policy of title insurance and may not contain every item affecting title. Buyer's review of the preliminary report and any other matters which may affect title are a contingency of this Agreement as specified in paragraph 14B.

B. Title is taken in its present condition subject to all encumbrances, easements, covenants, conditions, restrictions, rights and other matters, whether of record or not, as of the date of Acceptance except: **(i)** monetary liens of record unless Buyer is assuming those obligations or taking the Property subject to those obligations; and **(ii)** those matters which Seller has agreed to remove in writing.

C. Within the time specified in paragraph 14A, Seller has a duty to disclose to Buyer all matters known to Seller affecting title, whether of record or not.

D. At Close Of Escrow, Buyer shall receive a grant deed conveying title (or, for stock cooperative or long-term lease, an assignment of stock certificate or of Seller's leasehold interest), including oil, mineral and water rights if currently owned by Seller. Title shall vest as designated in Buyer's supplemental escrow instructions. THE MANNER OF TAKING TITLE MAY HAVE SIGNIFICANT LEGAL AND TAX CONSEQUENCES. CONSULT AN APPROPRIATE PROFESSIONAL.

E. Buyer shall receive a CLTA/ALTA Homeowner's Policy of Title Insurance. A title company, at Buyer's request, can provide information about the availability, desirability, coverage, and cost of various title insurance coverages and endorsements. If Buyer desires title coverage other than that required by this paragraph, Buyer shall instruct Escrow Holder in writing and pay any increase in cost.

Buyer's Initials (________)(________) Seller's Initials (________)(________)

RPA-CA REVISED 4/13 (PAGE 4 OF 8) Print Date

Reviewed by ______ Date ______

EQUAL HOUSING OPPORTUNITY

CALIFORNIA RESIDENTIAL PURCHASE AGREEMENT (RPA-CA PAGE 4 OF 8)

Property Address: ____ Date: ______________

13. SALE OF BUYER'S PROPERTY:

A. This Agreement is NOT contingent upon the sale of any property owned by Buyer.

OR B. ☐ (If checked): The attached addendum (C.A.R. Form COP) regarding the contingency for the sale of property owned by Buyer is incorporated into this Agreement.

14. TIME PERIODS; REMOVAL OF CONTINGENCIES; CANCELLATION RIGHTS: The following time periods may only be extended, altered, modified or changed by mutual written agreement. Any removal of contingencies or cancellation under this paragraph by either Buyer or Seller must be exercised in good faith and in writing (C.A.R. Form CR or CC).

A. SELLER HAS: 7 (or ☐ ______) Days After Acceptance to Deliver to Buyer all Reports, disclosures and information for which Seller is responsible under paragraphs 4, 6A, B and C, 7A, 9A, 11A and B and 12A. Buyer may give Seller a Notice to Seller to Perform (C.A.R. Form NSP) if Seller has not Delivered the items within the time specified.

B. (1) BUYER HAS: 17 (or ☐ ______) Days After Acceptance, unless otherwise agreed in writing, to:
(i) complete all Buyer Investigations; approve all disclosures, reports and other applicable information, which Buyer receives from Seller; and approve all matters affecting the Property; and
(ii) Deliver to Seller Signed Copies of Statutory and Lead Disclosures Delivered by Seller in accordance with paragraph 6A.

(2) Within the time specified in 14B(1), Buyer may request that Seller make repairs or take any other action regarding the Property (C.A.R. Form RR). Seller has no obligation to agree to or respond to Buyer's requests.

(3) By the end of the time specified in 14B(1) (or as otherwise specified in this Agreement), Buyer shall, Deliver to Seller a removal of the applicable contingency or cancellation (C.A.R. Form CR or CC) of this Agreement. However, if any report, disclosure or information for which Seller is responsible is not Delivered within the time specified in 14A, then Buyer has **5 (or ☐ ______) Days** After Delivery of any such items, or the time specified in 14B(1), whichever is later, to Deliver to Seller a removal of the applicable contingency or cancellation of this Agreement.

(4) Continuation of Contingency: Even after the end of the time specified in 14B(1) and before Seller cancels, if at all, pursuant to 14C, Buyer retains the right to either (i) in writing remove remaining contingencies, or (ii) cancel this Agreement based on a remaining contingency. Once Buyer's written removal of all contingencies is Delivered to Seller, Seller may not cancel this Agreement pursuant to 14C(1).

C. SELLER RIGHT TO CANCEL:

(1) Seller right to Cancel; Buyer Contingencies: If, by the time specified in this Agreement, Buyer does not Deliver to Seller a removal of the applicable contingency or cancellation of this Agreement then Seller, after first Delivering to Buyer a Notice to Buyer to Perform (C.A.R. Form NBP) may cancel this Agreement. In such event, Seller shall authorize return of Buyer's deposit.

(2) Seller right to Cancel; Buyer Contract Obligations: Seller, after first Delivering to Buyer a NBP may cancel this Agreement for any of the following reasons: **(i)** if Buyer fails to deposit funds as required by 3A or 3B; **(ii)** if the funds deposited pursuant to 3A or 3B are not good when deposited; **(iii)** if Buyer fails to Deliver a notice of FHA or VA costs or terms as required by 3C(3) (C.A.R. Form FVA); **(iv)** if Buyer fails to Deliver a letter as required by 3H; **(v) if Buyer fails to** Deliver verification as required by 3G or 3J; **(vi)** if Seller reasonably disapproves of the verification provided by 3G or 3J; **(vii)** if Buyer fails to return Statutory and Lead Disclosures as required by paragraph 6A(2); or **(viii)** if Buyer fails to sign or initial a separate liquidated damages form for an increased deposit as required by paragraphs 3B and 25. **In such event,** Seller shall authorize return of Buyer's deposit.

(3) Notice To Buyer To Perform: The NBP shall: **(i)** be in writing; **(ii)** be signed by Seller; and **(iii)** give Buyer at least **2** (or ☐ _____) Days After Delivery (or until the time specified in the applicable paragraph, whichever occurs last) to take the applicable action. A NBP may not be Delivered any earlier than **2 Days** Prior to the expiration of the applicable time for Buyer to remove a contingency or cancel this Agreement or meet an obligation specified in 14C (2).

D. EFFECT OF BUYER'S REMOVAL OF CONTINGENCIES: If Buyer removes, in writing, any contingency or cancellation rights, unless otherwise specified in a separate written agreement between Buyer and Seller, Buyer shall conclusively be deemed to have: **(i)** completed all Buyer Investigations, and review of reports and other applicable information and disclosures pertaining to that contingency or cancellation right; **(ii)** elected to proceed with the transaction; and **(iii)** assumed all liability, responsibility and expense for Repairs or corrections pertaining to that contingency or cancellation right, or for inability to obtain financing.

E. CLOSE OF ESCROW: Before Seller or Buyer may cancel this Agreement for failure of the other party to close escrow pursuant to this Agreement, Seller or Buyer must first Deliver to the other a demand to close escrow (C.A.R. Form DCE).

F. EFFECT OF CANCELLATION ON DEPOSITS: If Buyer or Seller gives written notice of cancellation pursuant to rights duly exercised under the terms of this Agreement, Buyer and Seller agree to Sign mutual instructions to cancel the sale and escrow and release deposits, if any, to the party entitled to the funds, less fees and costs incurred by that party. Fees and costs may be payable to service providers and vendors for services and products provided during escrow. **Release of funds will require mutual Signed release instructions from Buyer and Seller, judicial decision or arbitration award. A Buyer or Seller may be subject to a civil penalty of up to $1,000 for refusal to sign such instructions if no good faith dispute exists as to who is entitled to the deposited funds (Civil Code §1057.3).**

15. REPAIRS: Repairs shall be completed prior to final verification of condition unless otherwise agreed in writing. Repairs to be performed at Seller's expense may be performed by Seller or through others, provided that the work complies with applicable Law, including governmental permit, inspection and approval requirements. Repairs shall be performed in a good, skillful manner with materials of quality and appearance comparable to existing materials. It is understood that exact restoration of appearance or cosmetic items following all Repairs may not be possible. Seller shall: **(i)** obtain receipts for Repairs performed by others; **(ii)** prepare a written statement indicating the Repairs performed by Seller and the date of such Repairs; and **(iii)** provide Copies of receipts and statements to Buyer prior to final verification of condition.

16. FINAL VERIFICATION OF CONDITION: Buyer shall have the right to make a final inspection of the Property within **5 (or ____________) Days** Prior to Close Of Escrow, NOT AS A CONTINGENCY OF THE SALE, but solely to confirm: **(i)** the Property is maintained pursuant to paragraph 9; **(ii)** Repairs have been completed as agreed; and **(iii)** Seller has complied with Seller's other obligations under this Agreement (C.A.R. Form VP).

17. PRORATIONS OF PROPERTY TAXES AND OTHER ITEMS: Unless otherwise agreed in writing, the following items shall be PAID CURRENT and prorated between Buyer and Seller as of Close Of Escrow: real property taxes and assessments, interest, rents, HOA regular, special, and emergency dues and assessments imposed prior to Close Of Escrow, premiums on insurance assumed by Buyer, payments on bonds and assessments assumed by Buyer, and payments on Mello-Roos and other Special Assessment District bonds and assessments that are now a lien. The following items shall be assumed by Buyer WITHOUT CREDIT toward the purchase price: prorated payments on Mello-Roos and other Special Assessment District bonds and assessments and HOA special assessments that are now a lien but not yet due. Property will be reassessed upon change of ownership. Any supplemental tax bills shall be paid as follows: **(i)** for periods after Close Of Escrow, by Buyer; and **(ii)** for periods prior to Close Of Escrow, by Seller (see C.A.R. Form SPT or SBSA for further information). TAX BILLS ISSUED AFTER CLOSE OF ESCROW SHALL BE HANDLED DIRECTLY BETWEEN BUYER AND SELLER. Prorations shall be made based on a 30-day month.

Buyer's Initials (__________)(__________) Seller's Initials (__________)(__________)

RPA-CA REVISED 4/13 (PAGE 5 OF 8) Print Date

Reviewed by ______ Date ______

EQUAL HOUSING OPPORTUNITY

CALIFORNIA RESIDENTIAL PURCHASE AGREEMENT (RPA-CA PAGE 5 OF 8)

Property Address: ________________________________ Date: ____________

18. SELECTION OF SERVICE PROVIDERS: Brokers do not guarantee the performance of any vendors, service or product providers ("Providers"), whether referred by Broker or selected by Buyer, Seller or other person. Buyer and Seller may select ANY Providers of their own choosing.

19. MULTIPLE LISTING SERVICE ("MLS"): Brokers are authorized to report to the MLS a pending sale and, upon Close Of Escrow, the sales price and other terms of this transaction shall be provided to the MLS to be published and disseminated to persons and entities authorized to use the information on terms approved by the MLS.

20. EQUAL HOUSING OPPORTUNITY: The Property is sold in compliance with federal, state and local anti-discrimination Laws.

21. ATTORNEY FEES: In any action, proceeding, or arbitration between Buyer and Seller arising out of this Agreement, the prevailing Buyer or Seller shall be entitled to reasonable attorney fees and costs from the non-prevailing Buyer or Seller, except as provided in paragraph 26A.

22. DEFINITIONS: As used in this Agreement:

- **A. "Acceptance"** means the time the offer or final counter offer is accepted in writing by a party and is delivered to and personally received by the other party or that party's authorized agent in accordance with the terms of this offer or a final counter offer.
- **B. "C.A.R. Form"** means the specific form referenced or another comparable form agreed to by the parties.
- **C. "Close Of Escrow"** means the date the grant deed, or other evidence of transfer of title, is recorded.
- **D. "Copy"** means copy by any means including photocopy, NCR, facsimile and electronic.
- **E. "Days"** means calendar days. However, after Acceptance, the last **Day** for performance of any act required by this Agreement (including Close Of Escrow) shall not include any Saturday, Sunday, or legal holiday and shall instead be the next Day.
- **F. "Days After"** means the specified number of calendar days after the occurrence of the event specified, not counting the calendar date on which the specified event occurs, and ending at 11:59PM on the final day.
- **G. "Days Prior"** means the specified number of calendar days before the occurrence of the event specified, not counting the calendar date on which the specified event is scheduled to occur.
- **H. "Deliver", "Delivered" or "Delivery"** means and shall be effective upon (i) personal receipt by Buyer or Seller or the individual Real Estate Licensee for that principal as specified in paragraph D of the section titled Real Estate Brokers on page 8, regardless of the method used (i.e. messanger, maill, email, fax, other); OR (ii) if checked, ☐ per the attached addendum (C.A.R. Form RDN).
- **I. "Electronic Copy" or "Electronic Signature"** means, as applicable, an electronic copy or signature complying with California Law. Buyer and Seller agree that electronic means will not be used by either party to modify or alter the content or integrity of this Agreement without the knowledge and consent of the other.
- **J. "Law"** means any law, code, statute, ordinance, regulation, rule or order, which is adopted by a controlling city, county, state or federal legislative, judicial or executive body or agency.
- **K. "Repairs"** means any repairs (including pest control), alterations, replacements, modifications or retrofitting of the Property provided for under this Agreement.
- **L. "Signed"** means either a handwritten or electronic signature on an original document, Copy or any counterpart.

23. BROKER COMPENSATION: Seller or Buyer, or both, as applicable, agrees to pay compensation to Broker as specified in a separate written agreement between Broker and that Seller or Buyer. Compensation is payable upon Close Of Escrow, or if escrow does not close, as otherwise specified in the agreement between Broker and that Seller or Buyer.

24. JOINT ESCROW INSTRUCTIONS TO ESCROW HOLDER:

- **A. The following paragraphs, or applicable portions thereof, of this Agreement constitute the joint escrow instructions of Buyer and Seller to Escrow Holder,** which Escrow Holder is to use along with any related counter offers and addenda, and any additional mutual instructions to close the escrow: 1, 3, 4, 6C, 11B and D, 12, 13B, 14F, 17, 22, 23, 24, 28, 30 and paragraph D of the section titled Real Estate Brokers on page 8. If a Copy of the separate compensation agreement(s) provided for in paragraph 23, or paragraph D of the section titled Real Estate Brokers on page 8 is deposited with Escrow Holder by Broker, Escrow Holder shall accept such agreement(s) and pay out from Buyer's or Seller's funds, or both, as applicable, the Broker's compensation provided for in such agreement(s). The terms and conditions of this Agreement not set forth in the specified paragraphs are additional matters for the information of Escrow Holder, but about which Escrow Holder need not be concerned. Buyer and Seller will receive Escrow Holder's general provisions directly from Escrow Holder and will execute such provisions upon Escrow Holder's request. To the extent the general provisions are inconsistent or conflict with this Agreement, the general provisions will control as to the duties and obligations of Escrow Holder only. Buyer and Seller will execute additional instructions, documents and forms provided by Escrow Holder that are reasonably necessary to close the escrow.
- **B.** A Copy of this Agreement shall be delivered to Escrow Holder within **3** business days after Acceptance (or ☐ ________________________). Escrow Holder shall provide Seller's Statement of Information to Title company when received from Seller. Buyer and Seller authorize Escrow Holder to accept and rely on Copies and Signatures as defined in this Agreement as originals, to open escrow and for other purposes of escrow. The validity of this Agreement as between Buyer and Seller is not affected by whether or when Escrow Holder Signs this Agreement.
- **C.** Brokers are a party to the escrow for the sole purpose of compensation pursuant to paragraph 23 and paragraph D of the section titled Real Estate Brokers on page 8. Buyer and Seller irrevocably assign to Brokers compensation specified in paragraph 23, respectively, and irrevocably instruct Escrow Holder to disburse those funds to Brokers at Close Of Escrow or pursuant to any other mutually executed cancellation agreement. Compensation instructions can be amended or revoked only with the written consent of Brokers. Buyer and Seller shall release and hold harmless Escrow Holder from any liability resulting from Escrow Holder's payment to Broker(s) of compensation pursuant to this Agreement. Escrow Holder shall immediately notify Brokers: **(i)** if Buyer's initial or any additional deposit is not made pursuant to this Agreement, or is not good at time of deposit with Escrow Holder; or **(ii)** if Buyer and Seller instruct Escrow Holder to cancel escrow.
- **D.** A Copy of any amendment that affects any paragraph of this Agreement for which Escrow Holder is responsible shall be delivered to Escrow Holder within **2** business days after mutual execution of the amendment.

Buyer's Initials (______)(______) Seller's Initials (______)(______)

RPA-CA REVISED 4/13 (PAGE 6 OF 8) Print Date

Reviewed by _____ Date _____

EQUAL HOUSING OPPORTUNITY

CALIFORNIA RESIDENTIAL PURCHASE AGREEMENT (RPA-CA PAGE 6 OF 8)

Property Address: ______________________________ Date: ______________

25. LIQUIDATED DAMAGES: If Buyer fails to complete this purchase because of Buyer's default, Seller shall retain, as liquidated damages, the deposit actually paid. If the Property is a dwelling with no more than four units, one of which Buyer intends to occupy, then the amount retained shall be no more than 3% of the purchase price. Any excess shall be returned to Buyer. Release of funds will require mutual, Signed release instructions from both Buyer and Seller, judicial decision or arbitration award. AT TIME OF THE INCREASED DEPOSIT BUYER AND SELLER SHALL SIGN A SEPARATE LIQUIDATED DAMAGES PROVISION FOR ANY INCREASED DEPOSIT (C.A.R. FORM RID)

Buyer's Initials _____/_____ Seller's Initials _____/_____

26. DISPUTE RESOLUTION:

A. **MEDIATION:** Buyer and Seller agree to mediate any dispute or claim arising between them out of this Agreement, or any resulting transaction, before resorting to arbitration or court action. **Buyer and Seller also agree to mediate any disputes or claims with Broker(s), who, in writing, agree to such mediation prior to, or within a reasonable time after, the dispute or claim is presented to the Broker.** Mediation fees, if any, shall be divided equally among the parties involved. If, for any dispute or claim to which this paragraph applies, any party (i) commences an action without first attempting to resolve the matter through mediation, or (ii) before commencement of an action, refuses to mediate after a request has been made, then that party shall not be entitled to recover attorney fees, even if they would otherwise be available to that party in any such action. THIS MEDIATION PROVISION APPLIES WHETHER OR NOT THE ARBITRATION PROVISION IS INITIALED. **Exclusions from this mediation agreement are specified in paragraph 26C.**

B. **ARBITRATION OF DISPUTES:**
Buyer and Seller agree that any dispute or claim in Law or equity arising between them out of this Agreement or any resulting transaction, which is not settled through mediation, shall be decided by neutral, binding arbitration. Buyer and Seller also agree to arbitrate any disputes or claims with Broker(s), who, in writing, agree to such arbitration prior to, or within a reasonable time after, the dispute or claim is presented to the Broker. The arbitrator shall be a retired judge or justice, or an attorney with at least 5 years of residential real estate Law experience, unless the parties mutually agree to a different arbitrator. The parties shall have the right to discovery in accordance with Code of Civil Procedure §1283.05. In all other respects, the arbitration shall be conducted in accordance with Title 9 of Part 3 of the Code of Civil Procedure. Judgment upon the award of the arbitrator(s) may be entered into any court having jurisdiction. Enforcement of this agreement to arbitrate shall be governed by the Federal Arbitration Act. Exclusions from this arbitration agreement are specified in paragraph 26C.

"NOTICE: BY INITIALING IN THE SPACE BELOW YOU ARE AGREEING TO HAVE ANY DISPUTE ARISING OUT OF THE MATTERS INCLUDED IN THE 'ARBITRATION OF DISPUTES' PROVISION DECIDED BY NEUTRAL ARBITRATION AS PROVIDED BY CALIFORNIA LAW AND YOU ARE GIVING UP ANY RIGHTS YOU MIGHT POSSESS TO HAVE THE DISPUTE LITIGATED IN A COURT OR JURY TRIAL. BY INITIALING IN THE SPACE BELOW YOU ARE GIVING UP YOUR JUDICIAL RIGHTS TO DISCOVERY AND APPEAL, UNLESS THOSE RIGHTS ARE SPECIFICALLY INCLUDED IN THE 'ARBITRATION OF DISPUTES' PROVISION. IF YOU REFUSE TO SUBMIT TO ARBITRATION AFTER AGREEING TO THIS PROVISION, YOU MAY BE COMPELLED TO ARBITRATE UNDER THE AUTHORITY OF THE CALIFORNIA CODE OF CIVIL PROCEDURE. YOUR AGREEMENT TO THIS ARBITRATION PROVISION IS VOLUNTARY."

"WE HAVE READ AND UNDERSTAND THE FOREGOING AND AGREE TO SUBMIT DISPUTES ARISING OUT OF THE MATTERS INCLUDED IN THE 'ARBITRATION OF DISPUTES' PROVISION TO NEUTRAL ARBITRATION."

Buyer's Initials _____/_____ Seller's Initials _____/_____

C. **ADDITIONAL MEDIATION AND ARBITRATION TERMS:**

(1) EXCLUSIONS: The following matters are excluded from mediation and arbitration: (i) a judicial or non-judicial foreclosure or other action or proceeding to enforce a deed of trust, mortgage or installment land sale contract as defined in Civil Code §2985; (ii) an unlawful detainer action; (iii) the filing or enforcement of a mechanic's lien; and (iv) any matter that is within the jurisdiction of a probate, small claims or bankruptcy court. The filing of a court action to enable the recording of a notice of pending action, for order of attachment, receivership, injunction, or other provisional remedies, shall not constitute a waiver nor violation of the mediation and arbitration provisions.

(2) BROKERS: Brokers shall not be obligated nor compelled to mediate or arbitrate unless they agree to do so in writing. Any Broker(s) participating in mediation or arbitration shall not be deemed a party to the Agreement.

27. TERMS AND CONDITIONS OF OFFER:
This is an offer to purchase the Property on the above terms and conditions. The liquidated damages paragraph or the arbitration of disputes paragraph is incorporated in this Agreement if initialed by all parties or if incorporated by mutual agreement in a counter offer or addendum. If at least one but not all parties initial, a counter offer is required until agreement is reached. Seller has the right to continue to offer the Property for sale and to accept any other offer at any time prior to notification of Acceptance. Buyer has read and acknowledges receipt of a Copy of the offer and agrees to the above confirmation of agency relationships. If this offer is accepted and Buyer subsequently defaults, Buyer may be responsible for payment of Brokers' compensation. This Agreement and any supplement, addendum or modification, including any Copy, may be Signed in two or more counterparts, all of which shall constitute one and the same writing.

28. TIME OF ESSENCE; ENTIRE CONTRACT; CHANGES: Time is of the essence. All understandings between the parties are incorporated in this Agreement. Its terms are intended by the parties as a final, complete and exclusive expression of their Agreement with respect to its subject matter, and may not be contradicted by evidence of any prior agreement or contemporaneous oral agreement. If any provision of this Agreement is held to be ineffective or invalid, the remaining provisions will nevertheless be given full force and effect. Except as otherwise specified, this Agreement shall be interpreted and disputes shall be resolved in accordance wth the laws of the State of California. **Neither this Agreement nor any provision in it may be extended, amended, modified, altered or changed, except in writing Signed by Buyer and Seller.**

Buyer's Initials (__________)(__________) Seller's Initials (__________)(__________)

RPA-CA REVISED 4/13 (PAGE 7 OF 8) Print Date

Reviewed by _______ Date _______

CALIFORNIA RESIDENTIAL PURCHASE AGREEMENT (RPA-CA PAGE 7 OF 8)

Property Address: ________________________ Date: ____________

29. EXPIRATION OF OFFER: This offer shall be deemed revoked and the deposit shall be returned unless the offer is Signed by Seller and a Copy of the Signed offer is personally received by Buyer, or by ________________________, who is authorized to receive it, by 5:00 PM on the third Day after this offer is signed by Buyer (or, if checked, ☐ by ________________________ ☐AM/☐PM, on ____________(date))

Date ____________ Date ____________

BUYER ____________ BUYER ____________

(Print name) **(Print name)**

(Address)

30. ACCEPTANCE OF OFFER: Seller warrants that Seller is the owner of the Property, or has the authority to execute this Agreement. Seller accepts the above offer, agrees to sell the Property on the above terms and conditions, and agrees to the above confirmation of agency relationships. Seller has read and acknowledges receipt of a Copy of this Agreement, and authorizes Broker to Deliver a Signed Copy to Buyer.

☐ (If checked) **SUBJECT TO ATTACHED COUNTER OFFER (C.A.R. Form CO) DATED:** ____________.

Date ____________ Date ____________

SELLER ____________ SELLER ____________

(Print name) **(Print name)**

(Address)

(____/____) (Initials) **CONFIRMATION OF ACCEPTANCE:** A Copy of Signed Acceptance was personally received by Buyer or Buyer's authorized agent on (date) ____________ at ________ ☐AM/☐PM. **A binding Agreement is created when a Copy of Signed Acceptance is personally received by Buyer or Buyer's authorized agent whether or not confirmed in this document. Completion of this confirmation is not legally required in order to create a binding Agreement; it is solely intended to evidence the date that Confirmation of Acceptance has occurred.**

REAL ESTATE BROKERS:

A. Real Estate Brokers are not parties to the Agreement between Buyer and Seller.

B. Agency relationships are confirmed as stated in paragraph 2.

C. If specified in paragraph 3A, Agent who submitted the offer for Buyer acknowledges receipt of deposit.

D. COOPERATING BROKER COMPENSATION: Listing Broker agrees to pay Cooperating Broker **(Selling Firm)** and Cooperating Broker agrees to accept, out of Listing Broker's proceeds in escrow: **(i)** the amount specified in the MLS, provided Cooperating Broker is a Participant of the MLS in which the Property is offered for sale or a reciprocal MLS; or **(ii)** ☐ (if checked) the amount specified in a separate written agreement (C.A.R. Form CBC) between Listing Broker and Cooperating Broker. Declaration of License and Tax (C.A.R. Form DLT) may be used to document that tax reporting will be required or that an exemption exists.

Real Estate Broker (Selling Firm) ____________ DRE Lic. # ____________
By ____________ DRE Lic. # ____________ Date ____________
Address ____________ City ____________ State ________ Zip ________
Telephone ____________ Fax ____________ E-mail ____________
Real Estate Broker (Listing Firm) ____________ DRE Lic. # ____________
By ____________ DRE Lic. # ____________ Date ____________
Address ____________ City ____________ State ________ Zip ________
Telephone ____________ Fax ____________ E-mail ____________

ESCROW HOLDER ACKNOWLEDGMENT:

Escrow Holder acknowledges receipt of a Copy of this Agreement, (if checked, ☐ a deposit in the amount of $ ____________), counter offer numbers ____________ ☐ Seller's Statement of Information and ____________, and agrees to act as Escrow Holder subject to paragraph 24 of this Agreement, any supplemental escrow instructions and the terms of Escrow Holder's general provisions.

Escrow Holder is advised that the date of Confirmation of Acceptance of the Agreement as between Buyer and Seller is ____________

Escrow Holder ____________ Escrow # ____________
By ____________ Date ____________
Address ____________
Phone/Fax/E-mail ____________
Escrow Holder is licensed by the California Department of ☐ Corporations, ☐ Insurance, ☐ Real Estate. License # ____________

PRESENTATION OF OFFER: (____________) Listing Broker presented this offer to Seller on ____________(date).
Broker or Designee Initials

REJECTION OF OFFER: (________)(________) No counter offer is being made. This offer was rejected by Seller on ____________(date).
Seller's Initials

Published and Distributed by:
REAL ESTATE BUSINESS SERVICES, INC.
a subsidiary of the CALIFORNIA ASSOCIATION OF REALTORS®
525 South Virgil Avenue, Los Angeles, California 90020

Reviewed by
Broker or Designee ________ Date ________

EQUAL HOUSING OPPORTUNITY

REVISION DATE 4/13 Print Date

CALIFORNIA RESIDENTIAL PURCHASE AGREEMENT (RPA-CA PAGE 8 OF 8)

Requirements for a Valid Purchase Agreement

The statute of frauds requires an agreement to buy and sell real property to be in writing and signed by both the buyer(s) and the seller(s). The basic requirements for a valid purchase agreement are fairly simple. Essentially, the contract must:

- identify the parties,
- describe the property,
- indicate the price and the method of payment, and
- set a closing date, when title and possession are to be transferred.

However, most purchase agreement forms go into considerably more detail than that. It's important for the contract to clearly and accurately state everything that the parties have agreed to. In a real estate transaction, who is required to do what, and when they're required to do it, depends on the terms of the purchase agreement.

Provisions in a Purchase Agreement

In addition to provisions identifying the parties, describing the property, and establishing the terms of sale, a purchase agreement usually includes contingency clauses, warranties, disclosures, and provisions concerning title, escrow, closing, deadlines, the buyer's deposit, and the broker's compensation.

Identification of the Parties. The buyers and the sellers must be properly identified in the agreement. Everyone who has an ownership interest in the property must sign the contract as sellers, and all parties (sellers and buyers) must have the capacity to enter into a contract. If the property being sold is owned as community property, both spouses must sign as sellers. If it's being acquired as community property, both spouses must sign as buyers.

Property Description. The purchase agreement must describe the property with certainty. As with the listing agreement, a full legal description of the property isn't required. Even so, it's a good practice to always include the legal description. If it's too long to fit in the blanks on the form, a copy of the legal description should be initialed by the parties and attached to the purchase agreement as an exhibit.

Terms of Sale. The purchase agreement should set forth as clearly as possible all of the terms of the sale, such as the total purchase price, the amount of the downpayment, the method of payment, and what items are included in or excluded from the sale.

Many purchase agreement forms include a preprinted checklist of the most common types of financing arrangements. But regardless of the form used, the financing arrangements should be fully described, including the type of loan the buyer intends to obtain, the principal amount, the interest rate, how the loan is amortized, and the term of the loan. (Types of financing programs are discussed in Chapter 10.)

Contingency Clauses. Most purchase agreements are conditional, or contingent. For example, it's common to condition a sale on the buyer's ability to obtain the necessary financing. If the buyer isn't able to obtain the financing after making a good faith effort to do so, she doesn't have to go through with the purchase; she can withdraw without forfeiting the deposit.

Any and all conditions must be clearly stated in the purchase agreement. A provision setting forth a condition is called a **contingency clause**. A contingency clause should state exactly what must occur to fulfill the condition, and it should explain how one party is to notify the other when the condition has been either fulfilled or waived. There should also be a time limit placed on the condition (for example, if the condition isn't fulfilled or waived by January 15, the contract is void). Finally, the contingency clause should explain the parties' rights in the event that the condition isn't fulfilled or waived.

If a real estate licensee believes that a condition imposed in a purchase agreement may affect the date of closing or the date the buyer can take possession of the property, the licensee is required to explain that to the parties. Failure to do so is a violation of the California Real Estate Law and may lead to disciplinary action (see Chapter 16).

Condition of the Property. A purchase agreement may include a variety of provisions concerning the condition of the property. The seller may warrant the condition of certain elements (such as the roof, plumbing, or appliances) in the purchase agreement, or the agreement may state that the property is being sold "as is." (Note that even if the property is sold "as is," there's a legal obligation to disclose all known material defects to the buyer. See Chapter 8.) The contract is also likely to address the buyer's right to inspect the property.

Disclosures. In California, a residential purchase agreement often has a provision concerning the transfer disclosure statement and other specific disclosures the seller may be required by law to provide (see Chapter 8). And certain required disclosures must be included in the contract itself. One example is a provision that explains how to access the "Megan's Law" database on the Internet. The database lists areas where registered sex offenders are residing.

Conveyance and Title. The purchase agreement should specify the type of deed that will be used to convey title to the buyer (ordinarily a grant deed). The contract usually also states that the title is free from undisclosed liens and encumbrances, and that the seller will pay for a title insurance policy protecting the buyer.

Escrow and Closing. It's a good idea for a purchase agreement to include the arrangements for escrow. At the very least, the agreement should set the closing date for the transaction. Both parties must agree to the identity of the escrow agent; one party can't choose the escrow agent without the other's consent.

Possession. Possession of the property is usually transferred to the buyer on the closing date, but other arrangements can be made in the purchase agreement. If possession will be transferred either before or after closing, the parties should execute a separate rental agreement called an **interim occupancy agreement**.

The Uniform Vendor and Purchaser Risk Act is a law that determines who suffers the loss when property subject to a purchase agreement is damaged or destroyed before closing. Under the terms of the act, until either possession or legal title is transferred to the buyer, the risk of loss is the seller's. For example, suppose a home buyer is planning to move in a week before the closing date—a week before title is to be transferred. If the house is destroyed by an earthquake the day before the buyer moves in (takes possession), the seller bears the loss. The buyer can withdraw from the contract, and her deposit must be returned. But if the earthquake occurs after the buyer takes possession, then the buyer bears the loss; she still must complete the purchase.

The parties may choose to apportion the risk of loss differently by including a **risk clause** in the purchase agreement.

Time is of the Essence. Nearly all purchase agreements contain a "time is of the essence" clause (see Chapter 6). Thus, failure to meet any of the deadlines set in the agreement is a breach of contract.

Good Faith Deposit. The purchase agreement should not only acknowledge receipt of the buyer's good faith deposit, it should also explain the circumstances in which the deposit will be refunded to the buyer or forfeited to the seller. In many cases, the deposit is treated as liquidated damages (see Chapter 6). To be enforceable in California, a liquidated damages provision in a real estate purchase agreement must be in boldface or red type and must be initialed by the parties. In a transaction involving residential property with up to four units when the buyer intended to reside on the property, the amount that the seller can retain as liquidated damages generally may not exceed 3% of the purchase price.

If the buyer defaults and the seller keeps the deposit as liquidated damages, the broker is often entitled to half of the amount retained by the seller (but not more than the broker would have collected if the transaction had closed). Listing agreements commonly provide that liquidated damages will be shared with the broker in this way.

The form of the deposit should be stated in the contract. A check is usual, but another form of payment—such as a promissory note—may be used. The form of the deposit must be disclosed to the seller before he accepts the offer.

Broker's Compensation. Many purchase agreements also provide for the payment of the broker's commission. In most cases, this provision is merely a reaffirmation of the commission agreement set forth in the listing agreement. Such a provision wouldn't do anything to protect the interest of a broker who agrees to work under an oral listing agreement, though.

License Identification Number. Whenever a purchase agreement is used in a transaction that a real estate licensee is involved in as an agent, his license identification number must be disclosed in the purchase agreement. If he has a mortgage loan originator endorsement (see Chapter 16), his identification number from the Nationwide Mortgage Licensing System and Registry must also be disclosed in the agreement.

Amendments

After the buyer and seller have signed the purchase agreement, the terms of the contract can only be modified in writing. All parties who signed the original agreement must sign the amendment, or it will be unenforceable. An amendment may also be referred to as a **rider**.

Don't confuse an amendment with an addendum. An amendment is a written modification that occurs after the parties have signed the purchase agreement. An addendum, by contrast, is an attachment added to the agreement prior to signature.

Land Contracts

What we'll refer to as a **land contract** is also known by several other names: real property sales contract, real estate contract, conditional sales contract, installment sales contract, or contract for deed. Under a land contract, a buyer purchases property on an installment basis, rather than paying the seller the full purchase price all at once. The buyer takes possession of the property immediately, but the seller doesn't convey title to the buyer until the full price has been paid.

The California statute concerning land contracts provides this definition:

> "...an agreement in which one party agrees to convey title to real property to another party upon the satisfaction of specified conditions set forth in the contract and that does not require conveyance of title within one year from the date of formation of the contract."

The parties to a land contract are usually referred to as the **vendor** (the seller) and the **vendee** (the buyer). The following example illustrates how a land contract works.

> **Example:** Bender agrees to buy Jones's farm for $500,000, to be paid at the rate of $50,000 per year, plus 7% interest, for ten years. Jones (the vendor) allows Bender (the vendee) to take possession of the farm, and she promises to convey title to Bender when he has paid the full purchase price. Bender and Jones have entered into a land contract.

During the period in which the vendee is making payments on the contract, the vendor retains legal title to the property. The vendor doesn't deliver the deed to the vendee until the full purchase price has been paid. In the meantime, the vendee has equitable title to the property.

Rights and Responsibilities of Vendor and Vendee

While the vendee is paying off the contract, the vendor has the right to transfer or encumber the property without the vendee's consent. However, if legal title is transferred, the new owner takes title subject to the rights of the vendee under the land contract.

If the vendor creates any liens against the property, the law requires the vendor to apply the vendee's contract payments to amounts due on the liens. This protects the vendee from the possibility that the vendor will default on the liens and lose the property through foreclosure.

> **Example:** Under the terms of a land contract, the vendee is paying the vendor $2,000 a month. The vendor takes out a loan secured by his equity in the property, and the monthly payment on that loan is $1,400. The vendor must apply the first $1,400 of the vendee's $2,000 monthly payment to that debt, instead of using the money for some other purpose.

The vendor must pay off any liens before delivering the deed to the vendee. The vendor is required to deliver clear, marketable title when the vendee pays off the contract.

A land contract can't be recorded unless the vendor's signature has been acknowledged. The vendor can't prevent or prohibit the vendee from recording the contract.

If, for some reason, a land contract isn't recorded, there are some additional statutory restrictions on the vendor's right to create liens. Unless the vendee consents to the liens, the vendor can't encumber the property with liens that add up to more than the unpaid contract balance. And the monthly payments on those liens can't total more than the vendee's monthly payment on the land contract.

The vendee's main responsibility is to make the required installment payments to the vendor. The vendee is generally also responsible for keeping the property insured and paying the property taxes.

In a land contract for residential property with up to four units, the vendor can prohibit prepayment only during the first 12 months following the sale. (Prepayment refers to paying all or part of the amount owed before it's due. See Chapter 9.) After that point, the vendee has the legal right to prepay any or all of the contract price. So if the vendee wants to pay off the entire balance of the contract price a year after entering into the contract, the vendor can't refuse to accept the payment.

The vendee has the right to encumber the property, although few lenders are willing to make loans with a vendee's equitable interest as the only security. The vendee may sell her interest in the property by assigning the right to receive the deed when the contract price has been paid in full. (However, the vendee will remain responsible for making the contract payments unless the vendor releases the vendee from liability.) The vendee also has the right to devise (will) her interest.

Remedies for Default

If the vendee pays the purchase price in full, but the vendor fails to transfer legal title to the property, the vendee can sue for specific performance of the contract (see Chapter 6).

If the vendee defaults (for example, by failing to make the installment payments), the vendor can terminate the contract by sending the vendee the proper notice. The vendor must reimburse the vendee for the amount paid to the vendor under the contract. However, the vendee's reimbursement can be reduced by any damages that the vendor incurred, and by the fair market rental value of the property for the period the vendee was in possession.

Example: Under a land contract, Porter paid Rollins $22,800 over a ten-month period. The rental value of the property for that period was $2,000 per month, or $20,000. Porter would be entitled to a reimbursement of only $2,800 ($22,800 – $20,000 = $2,800).

The vendee has the right to cure the default and reinstate the contract. And once the vendee has paid a substantial portion of the contract price, he gains a right of redemption (see Chapter 9).

If the vendee doesn't cure the default or redeem the property, then the vendor is entitled to retake possession. However, a recorded land contract is a cloud on the property's title; the vendor may need to obtain a quitclaim deed from the vendee or file a quiet title action to make the title marketable again.

Use of Land Contracts

A land contract is used as an alternative to a mortgage or deed of trust in a seller-financed real estate transaction. The seller extends credit to the buyer and holds legal title to the property as security for the repayment of the debt, instead of having a lien as security.

At one time, many sellers who offered financing to their buyers preferred to use a land contract instead of a mortgage or a deed of trust, because it was easier to reclaim the property if the buyer defaulted. However, because of changes in California law, vendees under a land contract now have rights of reinstatement, reimbursement, and redemption. As a result, land contracts have fallen out of favor; most sellers prefer to use a deed of trust for seller financing. One exception is the Cal-Vet program, which regularly uses land contracts to finance home purchases by veterans. (See Chapter 9 for more information about deeds of trust, and Chapter 10 for more information about the Cal-Vet program.)

Option Agreements

An **option agreement** is essentially a contract to make a contract. It is sometimes called a contract to keep an offer open. An option agreement creates a right to buy or lease a specified property for a fixed price within a set period of time. The parties to an option agreement are called the **optionor** (the one who grants the option right) and the **optionee** (the one who is granted the option right). In an option to purchase, the optionor is the seller and the optionee is the buyer.

> **Example:** Alvarez is offering to sell his property for $620,000. Conners isn't yet sure that she wants to buy the property, but she doesn't want to lose the opportunity to do so. She asks Alvarez to give her a three-week option to purchase, and Alvarez agrees. They execute a written option agreement, and Conners pays Alvarez $1,000 as consideration for the option. The option gives Conners the right to buy the property at the stated price ($620,000) during the next three weeks, but it doesn't obligate her to buy it at all.

The optionor is bound to keep the offer open for the period specified in the option agreement. He isn't allowed to sell or lease the property to anyone other than the optionee until the option expires.

If the optionee decides to exercise the option (that is, to buy or lease the property on the stated terms), she must give written notice of acceptance to the optionor. If the optionee fails to exercise the option within the specified time limit, the option expires automatically.

Requirements for a Valid Option

Because an option is a contract, it must have all of the elements required for a valid contract, including consideration. The consideration may be a nominal amount—there's no set minimum. But some consideration must, in fact, pass from the optionee to the optionor; a mere statement of consideration in the agreement isn't sufficient. (There is an exception to this rule for lease/option agreements, where the provisions of the lease are treated as sufficient consideration to support the option.)

An option agreement must be in writing; oral options are unenforceable. And since an option to purchase anticipates that a sale may take place, the underlying terms of the sale (price, financing, and so on) should be spelled out in the option agreement.

Option Rights

The executed option gives the optionee a contract right, but it doesn't create an interest in real property. An option is not a lien, and also cannot be used as security for a mortgage or a deed of trust.

If the optionor dies during the option period, that won't affect the rights of the optionee, who may still exercise the right to purchase or lease. The option contract is binding on the heirs and assignees of the optionor.

An option can be assigned, unless the agreement includes a provision prohibiting assignment. There's an exception to this rule when the consideration provided by the optionee is in the form of an unsecured promissory note. In that case, the optionee must obtain the optionor's written permission before the option may be assigned.

Occasionally, when a real estate licensee takes a listing on a property, she also takes an option on the property. Before a licensee can exercise an option on a property that she has listed, the licensee must reveal to the seller, in writing, the full amount of the licensee's anticipated profit and get the seller's written consent to that profit.

Recording an Option

An option agreement may be recorded to give third parties constructive notice of the option. In that case, if the optionee exercises the option, his interest in the property will relate back to the date the option was recorded, taking priority over the rights of intervening third parties.

A recorded option that is never exercised creates a cloud on the optionor's title. The optionor should obtain a release from the optionee and record the release to remove the cloud.

Right of First Refusal

An option shouldn't be confused with a **right of first refusal**, which gives a person the first opportunity to purchase or lease real property if and when it becomes available. For instance, a lease might give the tenant a right of first refusal to purchase the property if the landlord decides to sell it.

Once the property owner offers the property for sale or receives an offer to buy from a third party, the holder of the right of first refusal must be given a chance to match the offer. If she doesn't want the property or is unwilling to match the offer, the property may be sold to someone else.

Leases

A lease is both a method of conveyance and a contract. A lease conveys a less-than-freehold (leasehold) estate from the **landlord** (the property owner) to a **tenant**. The conveyance of an interest in real property through the terms of a lease is called a **demise**. The holder of a leasehold estate—the tenant—doesn't own the property, but rather has a right to exclusive possession of the property for a specified period of time. Sometimes the landlord (also called the lessor) and the tenant (also called the lessee) are said to be "in privity," which means they have a mutual interest in one property.

A lease contract is sometimes called a **rental agreement**. It sets out the rights and responsibilities of the two contracting parties, the landlord and the tenant. Note, however, that certain covenants and terms are implied by law in all leases, whether or not they're written in the agreement. These implied covenants will be discussed shortly.

A lease usually creates either a term tenancy (for example, a one-year lease) or a periodic tenancy (for example, a month-to-month lease). A term tenancy terminates automatically at the end of the specified term, unless the landlord and the tenant agree to renew it. A periodic tenancy automatically renews itself at the end of each period, unless one of the parties gives the other notice of termination. (We'll explain the rules for notice of termination later in the chapter.) See Chapter 2 for more information about the different types of leasehold estates.

Requirements for a Valid Lease

As with any contract, the parties to a lease must be competent and must mutually consent to its terms. Consideration (typically the rental payment) is also required. The amount of the rent and when it is due should be specified.

Under the statute of frauds, a lease must be in writing if it's for longer than one year, or if it won't be fully performed within one year after the contract is made. Any lease that should be in writing but is not creates a periodic tenancy.

A written lease must be signed by the landlord. Usually the tenant also signs the lease, but that isn't required. A tenant who takes possession of the property and pays rent is considered to have accepted the terms of the lease. Even so, it's best to have both parties sign. Also, since a lease is a contract pertaining to real property, an accurate legal description of the property should be included.

Rights and Responsibilities of Landlord and Tenant

The rights and responsibilities of the parties during a tenancy are determined partly by the terms of their lease agreement and partly by the body of legal rules known as landlord-tenant law. The rules we'll discuss in this chapter are from state law. Note that some California cities have local laws that provide greater protection to tenants.

Use of the Premises. A tenant's use of the leased property is restricted by law to legal uses. Many landlords place additional restrictions on the use of the property—for example, restricting commercial space to retail use. The restricting language in the lease must be clear, or the restrictions will be unenforceable. At a minimum, the lease should state that the premises are to be used only for the specified purpose and for no other. If there is no limitation in the lease, or if the language isn't clearly restrictive, the tenant may use the premises for any legal purpose.

Payment of Rent. Most leases require the rent to be paid at the beginning of the rental period. However, if the lease doesn't specify when the rent is to be paid, it isn't due until the end of the rental period.

A landlord can't require a tenant to pay rent in cash unless the tenant's rent check has been returned, either because there were insufficient funds in the tenant's account or because the tenant stopped payment. In this situation, the landlord may give the tenant written notice that cash payments will be required for up to three months.

A month-to-month tenant generally must be given 30 days' notice before a rent increase (or other change in lease terms) can take effect. For residential property with up to four units, if the rent increases more than 10% in a 12-month period, 60 days' notice is required.

Security Deposit. California law defines a security deposit as any payment, fee, deposit, or charge (including an advance payment of rent) paid by the tenant to secure the performance of the lease agreement. Such a payment is considered a security deposit no matter what the landlord and tenant call it.

The total security deposit for a residential lease generally can't exceed twice the monthly rental payment for unfurnished units, or three times the monthly payment for furnished units. However, if the lease term is six months or longer, the landlord can require a deposit of six times the monthly payment or more, as long as it is designated as an advance payment of rent.

Within 21 calendar days after a residential tenant vacates the leased property, the landlord must return the security deposit to the tenant, or send a letter explaining the reason for not returning any portion of the deposit. If the deposit or a written explanation isn't given to the tenant within the 21-day period, the landlord could be liable for a penalty of up to twice the amount of the security deposit, in addition to actual damages. Labeling a deposit "nonrefundable" (for example, "nonrefundable cleaning deposit") has no bearing on this requirement; the landlord must still return the payment or give a written explanation within 21 days. In fact, it's illegal to describe a deposit as nonrefundable in a residential lease.

All or a portion of a tenant's security deposit may be withheld to cover unpaid rent, or to pay for cleaning the rental unit or repairing damage caused by the tenant. The tenant can't be charged for normal wear and tear, however.

Entry and Inspection. Most leases give the landlord the right to enter and inspect the leased premises during the lease term. California law provides that a residential landlord may enter the premises in an emergency, or in order to make repairs or improvements, perform other services, or show the premises to prospective buyers or tenants. Except in an emergency, the landlord is generally required to give the tenant at least 24 hours' notice. The entry must be during normal business hours unless the tenant consents to a different time or has abandoned the property.

Repairs and Improvements. A tenant isn't ordinarily required to make any repairs to the leased property. However, the tenant must return the property to the landlord in the same condition as it was in at the beginning of the lease term, with allowances for normal wear and tear. The landlord is typically responsible for making necessary repairs to the common areas, such as stairs, hallways, or elevators. A residential landlord is required to maintain the property in habitable condition, as we'll discuss shortly.

Neither the tenant nor the landlord is obligated to improve the property. The tenant may make improvements, which often can be removed by the tenant when the lease expires. (See the discussion of trade fixtures in Chapter 1.)

Renewal. A lease that creates a term tenancy may contain a provision that gives the tenant an option to renew the lease at the end of the term. Most renewal options require the tenant to give notice of his intention to exercise the option on or before a specific date.

To renew a lease, the parties often sign a renewal agreement. But a lease may be renewed by implication rather than express agreement. When the tenant makes a lease payment after the lease has expired, and the landlord accepts the payment, that can be considered an implied renewal of the lease. In this situation, the renewal term is the same as the term of the original lease. However, there are two significant limitations on that rule. One is that the renewal term may not exceed one year (because the renewal is not in writing). The other is that when rent is payable monthly, renewal by implication creates only a month-to-month lease.

> **Example:** A tenant had a three-year lease with rent payable on a quarterly basis. After the three-year term ends, the tenant offers the landlord another quarter's rent, and the landlord accepts it. This acceptance renews the lease by implication. But the lease is renewed for only one year, not for three years, because a lease for more than one year must be in writing.
>
> Now suppose instead that the tenant had a three-year lease with rent payable monthly. After the three-year term ends, the tenant offers the landlord another month's rent, and the landlord accepts it. Because the rental payments are monthly, this establishes a month-to-month tenancy, not a one-year lease.

Contact Information. A residential lease must include the name, telephone number, and address of: the owner or an agent of the owner; the property manager, if there is one; and the person or entity who will receive the tenant's rental payments. If there's no written lease, this information must be provided to the tenant in writing within 15 days after the rental agreement is made. Alternatively, the information may be posted in the building's elevators and in one other conspicuous place (or in two conspicuous places if there are no elevators).

Transferring Leased Property

A landlord can sell the leased property during the term of the lease, but the buyer takes title subject to the lease. This means the buyer must honor the lease for the remainder of its term. (There's an exception if the property is sold involuntarily. As we'll discuss shortly, the buyer at a foreclosure sale doesn't necessarily have to honor an existing lease.)

The tenant can also transfer her leasehold estate to another party, through assignment, subleasing, or novation. The tenant has the right to assign or sublease without the landlord's consent, unless the lease provides otherwise. A novation always requires the landlord's consent.

Fig. 7.4 Transferring leased property

Assignment	Tenant transfers the entire remainder of the leasehold estate
Sublease	Tenant transfers less than the entire remainder of the leasehold estate
Novation	Lease is replaced with a new one, or one party is replaced by another party

In an **assignment**, the tenant transfers the entire remainder of her leasehold estate.

> **Example:** Landlord leases the premises to Tenant for a period starting January 1, 2014 and ending June 30, 2017. On July 1, 2014, Tenant leases the premises to the XYZ Corporation for a term starting July 1, 2014 and ending June 30, 2017. The agreement between Tenant and XYZ is an assignment, because it transfers the entire remainder of the unexpired term—in other words, Tenant's entire interest.

The assignee becomes liable for paying the rent to the landlord (the original lessor) and the assignor (the original tenant) becomes secondarily liable for the rent. This means that the assignee has the primary responsibility for paying the rent, but the original tenant still has the duty to pay the landlord if the assignee doesn't.

In a **sublease**, the original tenant transfers only part of his remaining interest. He may be giving the subtenant (the new tenant) the right to share possession with him, or the right to possess only part of the leased property. Or he may be giving the subtenant the right to possess the whole property, but for only part of the unexpired term.

> **Example:** Landlord leases the premises to Tenant for a period starting January 1, 2014 and ending June 30, 2017. On July 1, 2014, Tenant leases the premises to the XYZ Corporation for a period from July 1, 2014 through June 30, 2016, reserving the last year for himself. This agreement is a sublease because the tenant has transferred less than the unexpired balance of the lease term.

The subtenant is liable for the rent to the original tenant, rather than to the landlord, and the original tenant is still liable to the landlord. This situation is sometimes referred to as a **sandwich lease**, because the original tenant is in the middle, sandwiched between the landlord and the subtenant.

In some cases, the terms of an assignment or a sublease may conflict with those of the original lease. If so, the terms of the original lease will take precedence.

A **novation** occurs when a new contract is created and the old contract is extinguished. When an existing lease is replaced either with a new lease between the same parties, or with a new lease between different parties, it has been novated. The purpose of a novation is to terminate the liability of the tenant under the original lease.

Termination of a Lease

A lease may be terminated by expiration; notice of termination; surrender; the landlord's breach of an implied promise; the tenant's failure to pay rent or unauthorized use of the premises; foreclosure; destruction of the premises; or condemnation.

Expiration. A lease for a specified term (a term tenancy) expires automatically at the end of the term. No notice of termination is required.

Notice of Termination. With a periodic tenancy, either the landlord or the tenant may terminate the lease at any point by giving the other party proper notice of termination. The notice must be in writing. The required notice period is usually the same as the lease period. That means seven days' notice is required to end a week-to-week tenancy, and 30 days' notice is required to end a month-to-month tenancy. There's an exception to that rule: residential landlords generally must give 60 days' notice of termination to tenants who have lived on the property for a year or more.

Surrender. A landlord and tenant may mutually agree to terminate a lease at any time. This is called surrender.

Breach of Implied Covenant of Quiet Enjoyment. In every lease there is an implied covenant of quiet enjoyment. This is the landlord's implied promise that she will refrain from unlawfully interfering with the tenant's possession of the leased property, and that no third party will lawfully claim a right to possess the property. The tenant is guaranteed the exclusive possession and quiet enjoyment of the property.

The covenant of quiet enjoyment is breached when a tenant is wrongfully evicted from the leased property. There are two types of eviction: actual and constructive.

Actual eviction occurs when the landlord actually expels the tenant from the property. **Constructive eviction** occurs when the landlord causes or permits a substantial interference with the tenant's possession of the property. For example, failure to provide heat in the wintertime has been found to result in constructive eviction.

If the landlord breaches the covenant of quiet enjoyment by wrongful eviction or in some other way, the tenant is relieved of her obligations under the lease and may treat it as terminated.

Breach of Implied Warranty of Habitability. In all residential leases, the landlord gives an implied guarantee that the premises meet all building and housing code regulations that affect health and safety on the premises. This is called the implied warranty of habitability. If the premises don't meet the code requirements and the tenant notifies the landlord of the defective condition, then the landlord must correct the problem within certain time limits prescribed by statute. If the landlord fails to make the required repairs, the tenant can terminate the lease. Or if the landlord takes legal action to evict the tenant for nonpayment of rent, the tenant can use the uninhabitable condition of the premises as a defense.

Failure to Pay Rent. The tenant has a duty to pay rent as required by the terms of the lease. However, if the tenant fails to pay the rent, the leasehold estate is not automatically terminated. The landlord is required by statute to give notice of nonpayment to the tenant. If the tenant still fails to pay after receiving notice, the landlord may bring a court action for **unlawful detainer** to evict the tenant.

If the court finds the tenant in default, it may issue a **writ of possession**, which requires the tenant to move out peaceably or else be forcibly removed by the sheriff.

Although unlawful detainer actions are given priority on the court's docket, the process of legal eviction is often slow. However, landlords should be warned against taking matters into their own hands. A landlord who tries a "self-help" eviction (forcing the tenant out with threats, or by cutting off the utilities) instead of the legal process may end up defending a costly lawsuit.

Illegal or Unauthorized Use. If the tenant uses the premises in an illegal manner (in violation of the zoning code, for example), the landlord may demand that the tenant cease the illegal activity or leave the premises. Also, if the tenant uses the premises in a manner not authorized by the lease, the tenant has violated the agreement and the landlord may terminate the lease.

Foreclosure. If a lien against the leased property is foreclosed on because the landlord has defaulted on a loan or other obligation, the foreclosure may terminate the lease. As a general rule, a foreclosure sale purchaser has to honor an existing lease only if it has higher priority than the foreclosed lien.

However, under a federal law passed in 2009, someone who buys leased residential property at a foreclosure sale is required to honor the lease for the remainder of its term, unless the buyer herself intends to occupy the property as a personal residence. In that case, the buyer must give the tenant 90 days' notice before terminating the tenancy. A residential tenant who doesn't have a lease for a specific term (for example, if it's a month-to-month tenancy) is also entitled to 90 days' notice, whether or not the buyer is planning to move into the home herself. Although this federal law is scheduled to expire at the end of 2014, it's possible that Congress will extend it temporarily or permanently.

Destruction of the Premises. Unless there is a provision to the contrary, if the lease is for the use of the land and any buildings or other improvements on the land, or for the use of an entire building, the destruction of the building(s) won't necessarily terminate the lease. The destruction of a building doesn't prevent the use and enjoyment of the land, and therefore the purpose of the lease isn't frustrated. The tenant isn't relieved from the duty to pay the rent to the end of the lease period. If, however, the lease is only for a part of a building, such as an office, apartment, or commercial space, the destruction of the building frustrates the entire purpose of the lease, so the tenant will be released from the duty to pay rent.

Condemnation. Condemnation of property can also result in premature termination of a lease. (See Chapter 5 for a discussion of condemnation and the power of eminent domain.)

Types of Leases

There are five major types of leases: the fixed lease, the graduated lease, the percentage lease, the net lease, and the ground lease.

Sometimes called a "flat," "straight," or "gross" lease, a **fixed lease** provides for a fixed rental amount. The tenant is obligated to pay a fixed sum of money, and the landlord is obligated to pay all of the property's operating expenses: utilities, maintenance costs, taxes, and insurance. This type of lease is most commonly used for residential apartment rentals.

A **net lease** requires the tenant to pay the landlord a fixed rent, plus some or all of the operating expenses.

A **graduated lease** is similar to a fixed lease, but it provides for periodic increases in the rent, usually set at specific future dates. The increases are often based on the Consumer Price Index or a similar cost-of-living index, which is an indicator of changes in a dollar's purchasing power. These increases are made possible by the inclusion of an **escalation clause**. This type of lease is also called a "step-up lease."

A **percentage lease** is common in the commercial setting, especially for properties located in shopping centers. The rent is based on a percentage of the gross or net income from the tenant's business. Typically, the lease provides for a minimum rent plus a percentage of the tenant's business income above a stated minimum.

When a tenant leases land and agrees to construct a building on that land, it is called a **ground lease**. Ground leases are common in metropolitan areas; they are usually long-term, in order to make the construction of buildings worth the tenant's while.

Section 8 Rent Vouchers

A significant problem, especially in urban areas, is the lack of affordable housing for low-income households. Section 8 (also called the Housing Choice Voucher program) is a rent subsidy program funded by the U.S. Department of Housing and Urban Development and administered by local public housing agencies. The program helps create a larger pool of affordable housing for low-income families, the elderly, and the disabled.

Section 8 tenants aren't required to live in government housing projects; instead, they can rent apartments or houses from private landlords, as long as the housing meets minimum standards. A tenant enrolled in the program pays part of the rent that the landlord is charging, and a voucher issued by the public housing agency covers the rest of the rent. The tenant's share of the rent is based on her income.

Chapter Summary

1. With a listing agreement, a property owner hires a real estate broker to find a buyer who is ready, willing, and able to buy the owner's property on the owner's terms. There are three main types of listing agreements: open listings, exclusive agency listings, and exclusive right to sell listings. The exclusive right to sell listing is the type most commonly used.

2. Listing agreements must include a property description, the terms of sale the property owner is willing to accept, the amount or rate of the commission, and the conditions under which the commission is earned. Most listing agreements also include a safety clause, which entitles the broker to a commission if the property is sold after the listing expires to anyone the broker negotiated with during the listing term.

3. A buyer representation agreement is a contract between a buyer and a real estate broker. The buyer usually hires the broker to help him locate suitable property and negotiate for its purchase. The agreement may be exclusive or nonexclusive.

4. A purchase agreement form serves as the buyer's offer to purchase, as the receipt for the buyer's good faith deposit, and, when it's signed by the seller, as the binding contract between the buyer and the seller. The purchase agreement must identify the parties, describe the property, and set forth the price, the method of payment, and the closing date.

5. Under a land contract, the buyer (vendee) purchases the property on an installment basis. The seller (vendor) retains legal title to the property while the contract is being paid off, but the vendee has the right to possess the property during that period. When the vendee has paid the full purchase price, the vendor delivers the deed to the vendee.

6. In an option to purchase, the optionee has a right to buy the property at a specified price (but is under no obligation to buy), and the optionor isn't allowed to sell the property to anyone other than the optionee during the option period.

7. A landlord-tenant relationship is created with a lease. A lease must be in writing if it will not be fully performed within a year after the contract is made. A valid lease also requires consideration (usually the rental payment), the signature of the landlord, and a description of the property. Most leases include a security deposit requirement, a limitation on the use of the premises, and a clause allowing entry and inspection by the landlord.

Key Terms

Listing agreement—An agreement between a property owner and a real estate broker, in which the owner hires the broker to find a buyer who is ready, willing, and able to buy the owner's property on the owner's terms.

Open listing—A type of listing that requires the property owner to pay a broker's commission only if the broker is the procuring cause of the sale.

Procuring cause—The real estate agent who is primarily responsible for bringing about a sale; the one who actually negotiates an agreement with the ready, willing, and able buyer.

Exclusive agency listing—A type of listing that requires the property owner to pay the broker a commission when the property is sold during the listing term by anyone other than the seller. If the seller finds the buyer, the broker is not entitled to a commission.

Exclusive right to sell listing—A type of listing that requires the property owner to pay the broker a commission if the property is sold during the listing term, no matter who sells the property.

Net listing—A type of listing in which the commission is any amount received from the sale over and above the "net" required by the seller.

Safety clause—A provision in a listing agreement that obligates the seller to pay a commission if the property is sold within a certain period after the listing expires to someone the broker negotiated with during the listing period. Also called a protection clause, a protection period clause, or an extender clause.

Buyer representation agreement—An agreement between a prospective property buyer and a real estate broker, in which the buyer hires the broker to find suitable property to purchase.

Purchase agreement—A contract between a buyer and a seller of real property. Also called a purchase and sale agreement, a contract of sale, or a deposit receipt.

Contingency clause—A contract clause which provides that unless some specified event occurs, the contract is null and void.

Land contract—A contract for the sale of real property in which the buyer (vendee) pays the purchase price in installments. The vendee takes possession of the property, but the seller (vendor) retains legal title until the full price has been paid.

Option agreement—An agreement that gives one party the right to buy or lease the other party's property at a set price for a certain period of time.

Lease—A contract in which one party (the tenant or lessee) pays the other (the landlord or lessor) rent in exchange for the possession of real estate. Also called a rental agreement.

Demise—A conveyance of an interest in real property through the terms of a lease.

Unlawful detainer—A court action brought by a landlord to evict a tenant.

Chapter Quiz

1. The type of listing that provides for payment of a commission to the listing broker regardless of who sells the property is a/an:
   a) open listing
   b) exclusive agency listing
   c) exclusive right to sell listing
   d) net listing

2. The type of listing that provides for the payment of a commission to the listing broker only if she was the procuring cause of the sale is a/an:
   a) open listing
   b) exclusive agency listing
   c) exclusive right to sell listing
   d) net listing

3. The type of listing that provides for the payment of a commission that consists of any proceeds from the sale over a specified amount is a/an:
   a) open listing
   b) exclusive agency listing
   c) exclusive right to sell listing
   d) net listing

4. The listing broker has negotiated an offer from a ready, willing, and able buyer that matches the seller's terms of sale set forth in the listing agreement. Which of the following is true?
   a) The seller is required to accept the offer and pay the listing broker a commission
   b) The seller is required to accept the offer, but not required to pay the listing broker a commission
   c) The listing broker has earned the commission, whether or not the seller accepts the offer
   d) The listing broker hasn't earned the commission unless this is an exclusive agency listing

5. A safety clause provides that:
   a) the broker is entitled to a commission whether or not he is the procuring cause
   b) the buyer must share the cost of the broker's commission
   c) the seller warrants the safety of the premises
   d) the broker is entitled to a commission if the property is sold after the listing expires to someone the broker previously showed the property to

6. All of the following are required for a buyer representation agreement except:
   a) the buyer's signature
   b) a legal description of the property
   c) consideration
   d) a termination date

7. A purchase agreement serves as:
   a) the buyer's receipt for the good faith deposit
   b) the buyer's offer to purchase
   c) a binding contract between the buyer and the seller
   d) All of the above

8. A purchase agreement should state:
   a) only the purchase price, leaving the other terms to be worked out in the final contract
   b) the listing price as well as the purchase price
   c) the total purchase price, the method of payment, and the basic financing terms
   d) the seller's reasons for selling the property

9. A provision in the purchase agreement states that it won't be a binding contract unless the buyer can obtain financing. This provision is called:
   a) a contingency clause
   b) a defeasibility clause
   c) a bump clause
   d) an escrow clause

10. Under a land contract, the vendee initially gets:
    a) possession but not title
    b) title but not possession
    c) possession and title, but not the right to transfer ownership
    d) the right to novate the contract without the vendor's permission

11. An option:
    a) can be assigned, unless otherwise agreed
    b) is a type of lien
    c) creates an interest in real property
    d) should not be recorded

12. To be binding, a lease must be signed by the:
    a) broker
    b) beneficiary
    c) landlord
    d) tenant

13. When leased property is sold voluntarily, the lease:
    a) automatically terminates
    b) is breached by constructive eviction
    c) must be renegotiated by the tenant and the new owner
    d) is binding on the new owner

14. An oral lease may be valid if it is for:
    a) one year or less
    b) two years or less
    c) three years or less
    d) four years or less

15. When a tenant assigns a lease, the assignee (the new tenant) becomes:
    a) secondarily responsible for payment of the rent
    b) the subtenant
    c) primarily responsible for payment of the rent
    d) None of the above

Answer Key

1. c) An exclusive right to sell listing obligates the seller to pay the listing broker a commission if the property sells during the listing period, regardless of who brings about the sale.

2. a) An open listing obligates the seller to pay a commission to the listing broker only if the broker was the procuring cause of the sale.

3. d) A net listing is a way of determining the amount of the commission, rather than the circumstances under which a commission is owed.

4. c) When the broker presents an offer from a ready, willing, and able buyer that matches the seller's terms of sale, the broker has earned the commission, whether or not the seller accepts the offer. The seller is under no obligation to accept the offer.

5. d) A safety clause entitles the broker to a commission if the property is sold within a certain time after the listing expires to someone the broker introduced to the property or negotiated with during the listing period.

6. b) A legal description isn't required in a buyer representation agreement, because the buyer usually hasn't located the property she wants to purchase yet. Consideration and the buyer's signature are required for any buyer representation agreement, and an exclusive agreement must have a termination date.

7. d) The purchase agreement is used to set forth the buyer's offer, and it also serves as the receipt for the good faith deposit. If the seller signs the form, it becomes a binding contract.

8. c) A purchase agreement should state all of the terms of sale, including the total purchase price, the method of payment, and the terms on which the buyer will finance the purchase. It is the parties' final contract, not a preliminary agreement.

9. a) A provision that makes a purchase agreement contingent on the occurrence of a certain event is called a contingency clause.

10. a) Under a land contract, the vendee (buyer) gets possession of the land right away, but does not acquire title until the purchase price is paid in full.

11. a) Unless otherwise agreed, an option can be assigned. It is not a type of lien and doesn't create an interest in the property.

12. c) Though it is wise to have both the landlord and the tenant sign the lease, only the landlord needs to sign in order for it to be valid. By taking possession of the leased property and paying the rent, a tenant is presumed to have accepted the lease terms.

13. d) The buyer takes title to the leased property subject to the existing lease, and must abide by its terms.

14. a) Leases need not be in writing if they will be fully performed within one year after the agreement is made.

15. c) An assignee has primary liability for paying the rent to the landlord. The original tenant retains secondary liability for the rent.

Chapter 8

Real Estate Agency Law

I. Introduction to Agency
   A. Agency relationships
   B. Agency law
II. Creating an Agency Relationship
III. Legal Effects of Agency
   A. Scope of authority
   B. Actual vs. apparent authority
   C. Vicarious liability
   D. Imputed knowledge
IV. Duties in an Agency Relationship
   A. Agent's duties to the principal
      1. Utmost care
      2. Integrity and honesty
      3. Loyalty
      4. Disclosure of material facts to the principal
   B. Agent's duties to third parties
      1. Reasonable care and skill
      2. Good faith and fair dealing
      3. Duty to inspect
      4. Transfer disclosure statement
      5. Other state property disclosure requirements
      6. Lead-based paint disclosures
   C. Breach of duty
V. Terminating an Agency Relationship
VI. Real Estate Agency Relationships
   A. Historical background
   B. Types of agency relationships
      1. Seller agency
      2. Buyer agency
      3. Dual agency
VII. Agency Disclosure Requirements
VIII. Broker/Salesperson Relationship

Chapter Overview

Agency is a special legal relationship that involves certain duties and liabilities. The law of agency governs many aspects of a real estate agent's relationships with clients and customers. The first part of this chapter explains what an agency relationship is and how one is created, and then discusses agency duties and liabilities. The second part of this chapter describes the various types of agency relationships that are possible in real estate transactions. California's agency disclosure requirements and the broker/salesperson relationship are also covered.

Introduction to Agency

We'll begin our discussion of real estate agency with some basic definitions and some information about the framework of agency law.

Agency Relationships

An agency relationship arises when one person authorizes another to represent him, subject to his control, in dealings with third parties. The parties in an agency relationship are the **agent**, the person who's authorized to represent another, and the **principal**, the party who authorizes and controls the actions of the agent. Persons outside the agency relationship who seek to deal with the principal through the agent are called **third parties**.

There is an agency relationship between a property seller and the real estate broker that the seller has listed the property with. The seller is the principal, who hires the broker to act as her agent. The broker/agent represents the seller/principal's interests in negotiations with potential buyers/third parties. The seller/principal is referred to as the broker's client.

A real estate broker may also have an agency relationship with a buyer. The buyer hires the broker to locate a particular kind of property and negotiate its purchase. The broker is the buyer's agent, and the buyer is that broker's principal (or client).

There is also an agency relationship between a real estate broker and the salespersons who work for the broker. In other words, a real estate salesperson is her broker's agent.

A real estate salesperson isn't licensed to represent sellers or buyers directly, without a broker. (See Chapter 16.) So, strictly speaking, in the eyes of the law it's the broker, not the salesperson, who has an agency relationship with a seller or buyer. Of course, in common parlance salespersons as well as brokers are called real estate agents. Also, as agents of their brokers, salespersons owe essentially the same duties to clients and third parties as their brokers do.

Although our discussion of agency will focus on brokers and salespersons working with sellers and buyers, note that brokers involved in property management may have agency relationships with landlords or tenants. Brokers working with landlords and tenants have essentially the same agency duties as brokers working with sellers and buyers.

Agency Law

An agency relationship has significant legal implications. For a third party, dealing with the agent can be the legal equivalent of dealing with the principal. For instance, when an agent who is authorized to do so signs a document or makes a promise, it's as if the principal signed or promised. And in some cases, if the agent does something wrong, the principal may be held liable to third parties for harm resulting from the agent's actions.

Those rules are part of general agency law, a body of law that applies to agency relationships in nearly any context. For example, it governs the relationship between lawyer and client, or between trustee and beneficiary. It also applies to the relationship between a real estate agent and her client, whether the client is a seller, a buyer, a landlord, or a tenant.

Creating an Agency Relationship

No particular formalities are required to create an agency relationship; the only requirement is the consent of both parties. Under general agency law, an agency relationship may be formed in four ways: by express agreement, by ratification, by estoppel, or by implication.

Express Agreement

Most agencies are created by express agreement: the principal appoints someone to act as his agent, and the agent accepts the appointment. The agreement doesn't have to be in writing in order to create a valid agency relationship.

The agency agreement also doesn't have to be supported by consideration. Agency rights, responsibilities, and liabilities arise even when the principal has no contractual obligation to compensate the agent for the services rendered.

For example, if a broker doesn't have a written listing agreement with a seller, the broker can't sue the seller for compensation. Yet even without a written agreement, the broker still may be the seller's agent, with all of the duties and liabilities that agency entails.

Ratification

An agency is created by ratification when the principal gives approval after the fact to acts performed by:

- a person who had no authority to act for the principal, or
- an agent whose actions exceeded the authority granted by the principal.

The principal may ratify unauthorized acts expressly, or by accepting the benefits of the acts. For example, if the principal accepts a contract offer negotiated by someone who wasn't authorized to negotiate on her behalf, the principal has ratified the agency.

Estoppel

Under the legal doctrine of estoppel, a party isn't allowed to take a position that contradicts her previous conduct if someone else has reasonably relied on the previous conduct. For example, a court may rule that an agency relationship was created by estoppel, even if the principal denies that someone was acting as her agent.

Example: Carl has the mistaken impression that Alan is acting as Pam's agent. Pam deliberately doesn't correct the misunderstanding. Acting in reliance on his belief that Alan speaks for Pam, Carl decides to buy Pam's property based on information Alan gave him. The information turns out to be false, and Carl suffers a financial loss. He sues Pam, whose main defense is that Alan wasn't her agent. The court considers the circumstances and rules that an agency relationship between Pam and Alan was created by estoppel. Because of her previous conduct, Pam is estopped from denying that Alan was her agent.

Implication

An agency may be created by implication when one person behaves toward another in a way that suggests or implies that she is acting as that other person's agent. If the other person reasonably believes there is an agency relationship, and the supposed agent fails to correct that mistake, she may owe the other person agency duties.

Although agency by implication resembles agency by estoppel, there's a significant difference between them. An agency by estoppel requires the principal to acknowledge that an agency relationship exists, to protect the interests of a third party. An agency by implication requires the agent to acknowledge that an agency relationship exists, to protect the principal's interests.

The Legal Effects of Agency

Once an agency relationship has been established, the principal is bound by acts of the agent that are within the scope of the agent's actual or apparent authority. Under general agency law, the principal may be held liable for harm caused by the agent's negligent or wrongful acts. In addition, the principal may be held to know information that is known to the agent. We'll examine each of these legal effects of agency in turn.

Scope of Authority

The extent to which the principal can be bound by the agent's actions depends first of all on the scope of authority granted to the agent. In California, there are two basic types of agents:

- general agents, and
- special agents.

A **general agent** is authorized to handle all of the principal's affairs in one or more specified areas. He has the authority to conduct a wide range of activities on an ongoing basis on behalf of the principal. For example, a business manager who has the authority to handle personnel matters, enter into contracts, and manage the day-to-day operations of the business is considered to be a general agent.

A **special agent** has limited authority to do a specific thing or conduct a specific transaction. For instance, an attorney who is hired to litigate a specific legal matter, such as a person's divorce, is a special agent.

In most cases, a real estate broker representing a seller or a buyer is a special agent, because the broker has only limited authority. A seller hires a broker to find a buyer for a particular piece of property, and the broker is only authorized to negotiate with third parties, not to sign a contract on the seller's behalf. Similarly, a broker representing a buyer is hired for a particular transaction and is authorized to negotiate for the buyer but not to sign a contract. A seller or a buyer can grant a real estate broker broader powers, but doesn't ordinarily do so.

On the other hand, a real estate broker providing property management services to a property owner on an ongoing basis might be considered the owner's general agent, depending on the scope of authority she grants the broker.

Actual vs. Apparent Authority

An agent may have actual authority to perform an action on the principal's behalf, or else may have only apparent authority.

Actual authority is authority granted to the agent by the principal, either expressly or by implication. Express actual authority is communicated to the agent in express terms, either orally or in writing. Implied actual authority is the authority to do what is necessary to carry out actions that were expressly authorized.

Example: When a seller lists property with a broker, the broker is given express actual authority to find a buyer for the property. Based on custom in the real estate industry, the broker also has the implied actual authority to delegate certain tasks to a licensed salesperson. In contrast, the authority granted to the broker doesn't imply the power to enter into a contract or execute a deed on the seller's behalf.

A person has **apparent authority** when she has no actual authority to act, but the principal negligently or deliberately allows it to appear that the person's actions are authorized. In other words, the principal's words or conduct lead a third party to believe that this person (the **apparent agent** or **ostensible agent**) has authority to act on behalf of the principal. This type of authority corresponds to an agency created by estoppel, which was explained earlier.

Fig. 8.1 Types of agency authority

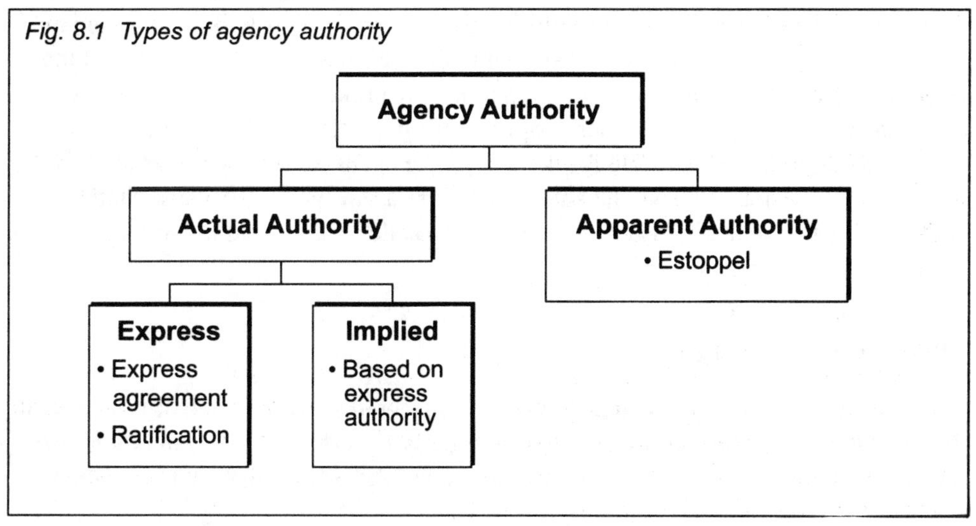

A principal is bound by acts performed within the scope of an ostensible agent's apparent authority. However, declarations of the agent alone can't establish apparent authority; the principal must be aware of the declarations or acts and make no effort to deny that they are authorized.

A third party has a duty, when dealing with an agent, to make a reasonable effort to discover the scope of the agent's authority. The third party won't be able to hold the principal liable when an agent acts beyond the scope of his actual authority and the principal's conduct doesn't indicate approval of those acts. When a contract between the principal and a third party limits the agent's authority to make representations, the third party is on notice that any representations made by the agent beyond the written terms of the agreement are unauthorized and not binding on the principal.

Here's an example of what can happen when an agent exceeds the authority granted by the principal.

> **Example:** Before signing the listing agreement, the seller crossed out the provision that authorized the broker to "receipt for deposits"—that is, to accept good faith deposits from prospective buyers on the seller's behalf. If the broker exceeds her authority and accepts a deposit check from a buyer, then she's acting as the buyer's agent, not as the seller's agent, in regard to the deposit. If the broker misappropriated the buyer's deposit, it would be the buyer's loss. (If the broker had specific written authorization from the seller to accept deposits, the seller would have to bear the loss.)

Vicarious Liability

A **tort** is a negligent or intentional wrongful act involving breach of a duty imposed by law (as opposed to breach of a contractual duty). It's a mistake, accident, or misconduct that results in an injury or financial harm to another person. For example, negligent driving that results in an accident and injures another driver is a tort. Someone who commits a tort may be sued by the injured party and required to compensate him.

Under general agency law, a principal may be held liable for her agent's negligent or wrongful acts. This is referred to as **vicarious liability**. Thus, a real estate broker can be held liable for the acts of a salesperson who works for him. And a buyer or a seller can be held liable for the acts of her real estate broker.

Under the doctrine of vicarious liability, a buyer or seller may also be held liable for the acts of a salesperson who's working for his broker. This liability is based on the theory that the broker is vicariously liable for the salesperson's actions, and the principal is in turn vicariously liable for actions the broker is liable for. Unless an agent has no authority to hire other people to fulfill the terms of the agency, the principal may be legally responsible for the acts of the agent's agent. A real estate broker is generally presumed to have the authority to hire a salesperson, because that's the standard practice in the industry. So a buyer or a seller can be held liable for a real estate salesperson's acts.

Imputed Knowledge

Under general agency law, a principal is considered to have notice of information that the agent has, even if the agent never actually tells the principal. In other words, the agent's knowledge is automatically imputed to the principal. As a result, the principal could be held liable for failing to disclose a problem to a third party, even if the agent never informed the principal of the problem. This is referred to as the **imputed knowledge** rule.

Duties in an Agency Relationship

An agent owes certain duties to her principal, and both the agent and the principal have certain responsibilities to third parties.

The Agent's Duties to the Principal

An agency relationship is a **fiduciary** relationship. A fiduciary is a person who stands in a special position of trust and confidence in relation to someone else. The other party has a legal right to rely on the fiduciary, and the law holds the fiduciary to high standards of conduct.

As a fiduciary, an agent must serve the best interests of the principal. He owes the principal the fiduciary duties of **utmost care, integrity, honesty, and loyalty**.

The agent owes these fiduciary duties to the principal from the time the agency relationship begins, and the agent must continue to fulfill them until the relationship ends. Certain obligations, such as the obligation to protect the principal's confidential information (discussed below), continue even after an agency relationship ends.

Utmost Care. An agent must carry out his duties with utmost care and skill. If an agent claims to possess certain skills or abilities, the agent must act as a competent person having those skills and abilities would act. For example, a person who holds himself out as a real estate broker must exercise the care and skill that a competent broker would bring to the agency. If the broker (or the broker's salesperson) causes the principal harm due to carelessness or incompetence, the broker will be liable to the principal.

A real estate agent isn't required to be an expert on every aspect of a real estate transaction. However, an agent must be able to recognize when it's necessary or appropriate for the principal to consult an expert for advice about taxes, legal issues, the condition of the property, or other matters.

Integrity and Honesty. An agent must meet the highest standards of integrity and honesty in all of her dealings with the principal. She must act ethically and take responsibility for her actions, and she must not withhold information from the principal that could affect his decisions in the transaction (see below).

The agent must account for any funds or other valuable items she receives on behalf of her principal. She's required to report to the principal on the status of those funds, known as **trust funds**, and avoid mixing (**commingling**) them with her own money. In California, a real estate broker is required to deposit all trust funds in a special trust or escrow account to prevent improper use of the funds. California's trust fund requirements are discussed in Chapter 16.

Loyalty. The agency relationship is based on confidence, so loyalty is essential. The agent must place the principal's interests above the interests of a third party, and also above the agent's own interests.

Because of the duty of loyalty, an agent can't reveal the principal's **confidential information** to other parties or take advantage of it himself.

Example: In negotiations with a prospective buyer, a seller's real estate agent shouldn't reveal the seller's financial condition or willingness to accept less than the listing price, unless the seller has authorized such a disclosure.

Confidential information learned in the course of an agency relationship must be protected even after the agency has ended.

Loyalty to the principal also means that the agent mustn't make any **secret profits** from the agency. Any financial gain must be disclosed to the principal. For example, it would be a breach of fiduciary duty for a broker to list a property for less than it's worth, secretly buy it through an intermediary, and then sell it for a profit. The California Real Estate Law also specifically prohibits a real estate agent from buying an interest in property from the principal (through a relative or friend, for example) without the principal's full knowledge and consent.

Another aspect of the duty of loyalty is **obedience**. The agent must obey the instructions of the principal and carry them out in good faith. The agent's acts must conform to the purpose and intent of the instructions. A broker can be held liable for any loss caused by failure to obey the principal's instructions.

Disclosure of Material Facts to the Principal. To fulfill her fiduciary duties, an agent must inform the principal of any **material facts** that come to the agent's attention. Any fact that could influence the principal's judgment in the transaction is a material fact that must be disclosed. For instance, if a seller's real estate agent discovers that a potential buyer is in a shaky financial situation, the agent must inform the seller, even if it means losing a sale and a commission.

It's important for an agent to remember that communication to the agent is deemed to be communication to the principal (this is the imputed knowledge rule we explained earlier). If a third party provides information to the agent, in the eyes of the law the information has been provided to the principal, regardless of whether the agent actually told the principal. Thus, the principal may be held liable for failure to perform some required task the agent knew about but never communicated to the principal. However, the agent will in turn be liable to the principal for any loss caused by the failure to communicate information or disclose material facts.

A real estate agent representing a seller must be especially careful to avoid these disclosure problems:

- failure to present all offers,
- failure to inform the principal of the property's true value,
- failure to disclose any relationship between the agent and the buyer, and
- failure to reveal a dual agency.

A real estate agent representing a seller must **present all offers** to the seller, regardless of how unacceptable a particular offer may appear to be. The principal, not the agent, decides whether or not to accept a particular offer. The agent should never hesitate to inform the principal of an offer, even if its acceptance would mean a smaller commission for the agent; the agent's first loyalty must be to the principal. Furthermore, a seller's agent should present an offer even if the prospective buyer did not submit a good faith deposit along with the offer.

An agent is also required to inform the principal of the **property's true value**. It isn't improper for a seller's agent to buy the principal's property with the principal's knowledge and consent, and then resell the property for a profit. But the agent must provide the principal with her estimate of the real value of the property before the property is sold. (An ordinary buyer—an unlicensed person who isn't acting as the seller's agent—is under no obligation to tell the seller that he plans to resell at a profit.) Note that if a real estate agent knowingly or intentionally misrepresents the value of real property to anyone (not just the principal), it's a violation of the Real Estate Law. (See Chapter 16.)

The seller's agent must inform the principal if the agent has any **relationship with a buyer**—before the principal decides whether to accept the buyer's offer. If the buyer is a friend, relative, or business associate of the agent, or a company in which the agent has an interest, there may be a conflict of interest. The principal has a right to have this information when making his decision. The agent must also inform the principal if the agent plans to split the commission payment with the buyer.

In addition, the agent is required to reveal a **dual agency**. There is a dual agency when a real estate broker is employed by both the seller and the buyer in the same transaction. In California, dual agency is legal in a real estate transaction as long as the broker has fully informed and obtained the consent of both parties. However, a conflict of interest is inherent in a dual agency. A seller wants to get the highest possible price for the property, while the buyer wants to pay the lowest possible price. It's difficult, if not impossible, to adequately represent these two opposing interests simultaneously. We'll discuss dual agency and agency disclosure requirements in more detail later in the chapter.

The Agent's Duties to Third Parties

While agents owe utmost care, integrity, honesty, and loyalty to their principals, this doesn't mean they can treat third parties with reckless disregard. In recent years, courts have held real estate agents to increasingly higher standards in their interactions with third parties.

A real estate agent owes a third party a duty of reasonable care and skill and a duty of good faith and fair dealing. In addition, in residential transactions there is a duty to inspect the property.

Reasonable Care and Skill. An agent must use reasonable care and skill in providing services to third parties as well as to the principal. If the agent's negligence or incompetence harms a third party, the agent may be liable.

Good Faith and Fair Dealing. Real estate agents are legally as well as ethically required to treat third parties fairly. When representing a seller, an agent must disclose all material facts about the property to prospective buyers. The agent also must avoid inaccuracies in statements to prospective buyers. Any intentional material misrepresentation may constitute **actual fraud**, and even an unintentional misrepresentation could be considered negligence or **constructive fraud**. Whether the misrepresentation was intentional or not, the buyer might have the right to rescind the transaction and/or sue for damages. (Note that these requirements apply to sellers as well as their real estate agents; sellers also have a duty to disclose material facts about the property to buyers and avoid misrepresentations.)

A distinction is often drawn between misrepresentations, on the one hand, and opinions, predictions, or "puffing" on the other. These are nonfactual or exaggerated statements that a buyer should realize she can't rely on. Since it isn't reasonable to rely on them, opinions, predictions, and puffing generally can't be the basis for a lawsuit.

Examples:

Opinion: *"I think this is the best buy on the market."*

Prediction: *"The properties in this neighborhood could double in value over the next five years."*

Puffing: *"This is a dream house, luxurious in every detail."*

Although statements such as these may not be actionable, it's unethical for a real estate agent to make any statement to a buyer concerning the property that the agent doesn't believe. Also, something an agent regards as harmless "sales talk" could be understood as a statement of fact by an unsophisticated buyer, and a court might decide it is actionable. For instance, an agent who made the prediction about a dramatic increase in property values given in our example could be on dangerous ground.

Aside from avoiding misrepresentation, both a seller and a seller's agent have a duty to disclose any known **latent defects** in the property to buyers. A latent defect is a hidden defect, one that isn't discoverable by ordinary inspection.

Example: The seller tells his real estate agent that the roof leaks in heavy rains. This is a latent defect; buyers who are shown the property on sunny days won't be able to see it for themselves. The seller and the agent are legally required to disclose this problem.

Stigmatized Properties. There are some facts that don't have to be disclosed to a prospective buyer (or tenant), because the information could unfairly stigmatize the property. California law specifically provides that property owners and real estate agents do not have to disclose that property was occupied by someone who had or died from AIDS or was HIV-positive. In fact, if a prospective buyer asks an agent whether anyone with AIDS or HIV lived on the property, the agent should decline to answer the question. Answering could violate fair housing laws that prohibit discrimination based on disability (see Chapter 14).

California law also provides that owners and agents aren't required to disclose that someone died on the property more than three years earlier, no matter what the cause of death was. However, if a prospective buyer asked about deaths on the property and the seller or his agent intentionally gave a false answer, that would be a fraudulent misrepresentation.

Duty to Inspect. At one time, agents representing the seller were required only to pass on the seller's information about the property to prospective buyers; the law didn't require them to inspect the property and look for problems. Today, however, California law specifically imposes a duty of inspection on any agent who represents the seller of a one- to four-unit residential property, unless it's a new home in a subdivision offered for sale for the first time. The duty also applies to agents who cooperate with a seller's agent in finding a buyer for such a property. The duty to inspect was first created by a California appellate court in the 1984 case of *Easton v. Strassburger*, and it was later codified in the Civil Code.

To fulfill this duty, an agent must conduct a reasonably competent and diligent visual inspection of the property and disclose to prospective buyers any material information the inspection reveals. Stating that the property is for sale "as is" doesn't negate the agent's duty to inspect it and disclose material facts about its condition.

The agent isn't required to inspect areas of the property that aren't reasonably accessible to visual inspection. In the case of a condominium or cooperative unit, the agent is only required to inspect the unit being sold, not the common areas.

If an agent fails to inspect residential property and make disclosures as required, and the buyer is harmed as a result, the buyer can sue the agent and her broker. A lawsuit based on the duty to inspect must be filed within two years after the buyer takes possession of the property.

It should be noted that the agent's duty to inspect the property doesn't relieve buyers of the duty to use reasonable care to protect themselves.

Transfer Disclosure Statement. Any disclosures required as a result of an agent's property inspection are usually made in the appropriate section of the real estate transfer disclosure statement, a form that must be presented to the prospective buyer in any transaction involving one- to four-unit residential property. The transfer disclosure statement is used to list the seller's disclosures concerning:

- what's included in the sale;
- any known defects in the property; and
- any other problems with the property, such as environmental hazards, structural changes made without appropriate permits, or neighborhood nuisances.

In addition, the form has separate sections to be filled out by the listing agent and the selling agent (the agent who obtained the buyer's offer). Each agent is required to make note of any material facts discovered in his or her own visual inspection of the property; the listing agent is also required to disclose material facts about the condition of the property learned from the seller. The selling agent is responsible for providing the completed disclosure statement to a prospective buyer.

It's important to remember that an agent should fill out only her own section of the form, not the seller's sections. Filling out those sections is the seller's responsibility. An example of a real estate transfer disclosure statement is shown in Figure 8.2.

The transfer disclosure statement should be delivered to buyers as soon as possible. The law gives buyers three days from the time the disclosure statement is delivered (or five days from the time it is mailed) to rescind the purchase agreement, if they decide they don't want to purchase the property after all.

Some transactions involving one- to four-unit residential property don't require a transfer disclosure statement. These include transfers that occur as a result of a mortgage or deed of trust foreclosure, probate proceedings, divorce settlements, or other court orders. Sales of property in new subdivisions are also exempt.

In some cities and counties, local laws require sellers to give buyers a local option transfer disclosure statement in addition to the state-required transfer disclosure statement. A local option statement provides information about the neighborhood or community.

Other State Property Disclosure Requirements. In addition to a transfer disclosure statement, a number of other disclosures may be required by California law in a particular transaction. Some concern the property's physical condition, others are required because of the property's location. Like the transfer disclosure statement, these other disclosures are generally required in sales of residential property with up to four units.

Fig. 8.2 Transfer disclosure statement

CALIFORNIA ASSOCIATION OF REALTORS®

REAL ESTATE TRANSFER DISCLOSURE STATEMENT
(CALIFORNIA CIVIL CODE §1102, ET SEQ.)
(C.A.R. Form TDS, Revised 4/14)

THIS DISCLOSURE STATEMENT CONCERNS THE REAL PROPERTY SITUATED IN THE CITY OF ______________, COUNTY OF ______________, STATE OF CALIFORNIA, DESCRIBED AS ______________.

THIS STATEMENT IS A DISCLOSURE OF THE CONDITION OF THE ABOVE DESCRIBED PROPERTY IN COMPLIANCE WITH SECTION 1102 OF THE CIVIL CODE AS OF (date) ______________. IT IS NOT A WARRANTY OF ANY KIND BY THE SELLER(S) OR ANY AGENT(S) REPRESENTING ANY PRINCIPAL(S) IN THIS TRANSACTION, AND IS NOT A SUBSTITUTE FOR ANY INSPECTIONS OR WARRANTIES THE PRINCIPAL(S) MAY WISH TO OBTAIN.

I. COORDINATION WITH OTHER DISCLOSURE FORMS

This Real Estate Transfer Disclosure Statement is made pursuant to Section 1102 of the Civil Code. Other statutes require disclosures, depending upon the details of the particular real estate transaction (for example: special study zone and purchase-money liens on residential property).

Substituted Disclosures: The following disclosures and other disclosures required by law, including the Natural Hazard Disclosure Report/Statement that may include airport annoyances, earthquake, fire, flood, or special assessment information, have or will be made in connection with this real estate transfer, and are intended to satisfy the disclosure obligations on this form, where the subject matter is the same:

☐ Inspection reports completed pursuant to the contract of sale or receipt for deposit.
☐ Additional inspection reports or disclosures: ______________

II. SELLER'S INFORMATION

The Seller discloses the following information with the knowledge that even though this is not a warranty, prospective Buyers may rely on this information in deciding whether and on what terms to purchase the subject property. Seller hereby authorizes any agent(s) representing any principal(s) in this transaction to provide a copy of this statement to any person or entity in connection with any actual or anticipated sale of the property.

THE FOLLOWING ARE REPRESENTATIONS MADE BY THE SELLER(S) AND ARE NOT THE REPRESENTATIONS OF THE AGENT(S), IF ANY. THIS INFORMATION IS A DISCLOSURE AND IS NOT INTENDED TO BE PART OF ANY CONTRACT BETWEEN THE BUYER AND SELLER.

Seller ☐ is ☐ is not occupying the property.

A. The subject property has the items checked below:*

☐ Range
☐ Oven
☐ Microwave
☐ Dishwasher
☐ Trash Compactor
☐ Garbage Disposal
☐ Washer/Dryer Hookups
☐ Rain Gutters
☐ Burglar Alarms
☐ Carbon Monoxide Device(s)
☐ Smoke Detector(s)
☐ Fire Alarm
☐ TV Antenna
☐ Satellite Dish
☐ Intercom
☐ Central Heating
☐ Central Air Conditioning
☐ Evaporator Cooler(s)

☐ Wall/Window Air Conditioning
☐ Sprinklers
☐ Public Sewer System
☐ Septic Tank
☐ Sump Pump
☐ Water Softener
☐ Patio/Decking
☐ Built-in Barbecue
☐ Gazebo
☐ Security Gate(s)
☐ Garage:
☐ Attached ☐ Not Attached
☐ Carport
☐ Automatic Garage Door Opener(s)
☐ Number Remote Controls ____
☐ Sauna
☐ Hot Tub/Spa:
☐ Locking Safety Cover

☐ Pool:
☐ Child Resistant Barrier
☐ Pool/Spa Heater:
☐ Gas ☐ Solar ☐ Electric
☐ Water Heater:
☐ Gas ☐ Solar ☐ Electric
☐ Water Supply:
☐ City ☐ Well
☐ Private Utility or Other ______________
☐ Gas Supply:
☐ Utility ☐ Bottled (Tank)
☐ Window Screens
☐ Window Security Bars
☐ Quick Release Mechanism on Bedroom Windows
☐ Water-Conserving Plumbing Fixtures

Exhaust Fan(s) in ______________ 220 Volt Wiring in ______________ Fireplace(s) in ______________
☐ Gas Starter ________ ☐ Roof(s): Type: ______________ Age: ________ (approx.)
☐ Other: ______________

Are there, to the best of your (Seller's) knowledge, any of the above that are not in operating condition? ☐ Yes ☐ No. If yes, then describe. (Attach additional sheets if necessary): ______________

(*see note on page 2)

Buyer's Initials (________)(________) Seller's Initials (________)(________)

TDS REVISED 4/14 (PAGE 1 OF 3) Print Date

Reviewed by ______ Date ______

EQUAL HOUSING OPPORTUNITY

REAL ESTATE TRANSFER DISCLOSURE STATEMENT (TDS PAGE 1 OF 3)

Reprinted with permission, California Association of REALTORS®. Endorsement not implied.

Property Address: ______________________________ Date:__________

B. Are you (Seller) aware of any significant defects/malfunctions in any of the following? ☐ Yes ☐ No. If yes, check appropriate space(s) below.

☐ Interior Walls ☐ Ceilings ☐ Floors ☐ Exterior Walls ☐ Insulation ☐ Roof(s) ☐ Windows ☐ Doors ☐ Foundation ☐ Slab(s)
☐ Driveways ☐ Sidewalks ☐ Walls/Fences ☐ Electrical Systems ☐ Plumbing/Sewers/Septics ☐ Other Structural Components

(Describe: ______________________________

______________________________)

If any of the above is checked, explain. (Attach additional sheets if necessary.): ______________________________

____

____

*Installation of a listed appliance, device, or amenity is not a precondition of sale or transfer of the dwelling. The carbon monoxide device, garage door opener, or child-resistant pool barrier may not be in compliance with the safety standards relating to, respectively, carbon monoxide device standards of Chapter 8 (commencing with Section 13260) of Part 2 of Division 12 of, automatic reversing device standards of Chapter 12.5 (commencing with Section 19890) of Part 3 of Division 13 of, or the pool safety standards of Article 2.5 (commencing with Section 115920) of Chapter 5 of Part 10 of Division 104 of, the Health and Safety Code. Window security bars may not have quick-release mechanisms in compliance with the 1995 edition of the California Building Standards Code. Section 1101.4 of the Civil Code requires all single-family residences built on or before January 1, 1994, to be equipped with water-conserving plumbing fixtures after January 1, 2017. Additionally, on and after January 1, 2014, a single-family residence built on or before January 1, 1994, that is altered or improved is required to be equipped with water-conserving plumbing fixtures as a condition of final approval. Fixtures in this dwelling may not comply with section 1101.4 of the Civil Code.

C. Are you (Seller) aware of any of the following:

1. Substances, materials, or products which may be an environmental hazard such as, but not limited to, asbestos, formaldehyde, radon gas, lead-based paint, mold, fuel or chemical storage tanks, and contaminated soil or water on the subject property .... ☐ Yes ☐ No
2. Features of the property shared in common with adjoining landowners, such as walls, fences, and driveways, whose use or responsibility for maintenance may have an effect on the subject property .... ☐ Yes ☐ No
3. Any encroachments, easements or similar matters that may affect your interest in the subject property .... ☐ Yes ☐ No
4. Room additions, structural modifications, or other alterations or repairs made without necessary permits .... ☐ Yes ☐ No
5. Room additions, structural modifications, or other alterations or repairs not in compliance with building codes .... ☐ Yes ☐ No
6. Fill (compacted or otherwise) on the property or any portion thereof .... ☐ Yes ☐ No
7. Any settling from any cause, or slippage, sliding, or other soil problems .... ☐ Yes ☐ No
8. Flooding, drainage or grading problems .... ☐ Yes ☐ No
9. Major damage to the property or any of the structures from fire, earthquake, floods, or landslides .... ☐ Yes ☐ No
10. Any zoning violations, nonconforming uses, violations of "setback" requirements .... ☐ Yes ☐ No
11. Neighborhood noise problems or other nuisances .... ☐ Yes ☐ No
12. CC&R's or other deed restrictions or obligations .... ☐ Yes ☐ No
13. Homeowners' Association which has any authority over the subject property .... ☐ Yes ☐ No
14. Any "common area" (facilities such as pools, tennis courts, walkways, or other areas co-owned in undivided interest with others) .... ☐ Yes ☐ No
15. Any notices of abatement or citations against the property .... ☐ Yes ☐ No
16. Any lawsuits by or against the Seller threatening to or affecting this real property, claims for damages by the Seller pursuant to Section 910 or 914 threatening to or affecting this real property, claims for breach of warranty pursuant to Section 900 threatening to or affecting this real property, or claims for breach of an enhanced protection agreement pursuant to Section 903 threatening to or affecting this real property, including any lawsuits or claims for damages pursuant to Section 910 or 914 alleging a defect or deficiency in this real property or "common areas" (facilities such as pools, tennis courts, walkways, or other areas co-owned in undivided interest with others) .... ☐ Yes ☐ No

If the answer to any of these is yes, explain. (Attach additional sheets if necessary.): ______________________________

____

____

____

D. 1. The Seller certifies that the property, as of the close of escrow, will be in compliance with Section 13113.8 of the Health and Safety Code by having operable smoke detector(s) which are approved, listed, and installed in accordance with the State Fire Marshal's regulations and applicable local standards.

2. The Seller certifies that the property, as of the close of escrow, will be in compliance with Section 19211 of the Health and Safety Code by having the water heater tank(s) braced, anchored, or strapped in place in accordance with applicable law.

Buyer's Initials (__________)(__________)

TDS REVISED 4/14 (PAGE 2 OF 3)

Reviewed by ______ Date ______

EQUAL HOUSING OPPORTUNITY

REAL ESTATE TRANSFER DISCLOSURE STATEMENT (TDS PAGE 2 OF 3)

Property Address: ______________________________ Date:____________

Seller certifies that the information herein is true and correct to the best of the Seller's knowledge as of the date signed by the Seller.

Seller______________________________ Date ____________

Seller______________________________ Date ____________

III. AGENT'S INSPECTION DISCLOSURE

(To be completed only if the Seller is represented by an agent in this transaction.)

THE UNDERSIGNED, BASED ON THE ABOVE INQUIRY OF THE SELLER(S) AS TO THE CONDITION OF THE PROPERTY AND BASED ON A REASONABLY COMPETENT AND DILIGENT VISUAL INSPECTION OF THE ACCESSIBLE AREAS OF THE PROPERTY IN CONJUNCTION WITH THAT INQUIRY, STATES THE FOLLOWING:

☐ See attached Agent Visual Inspection Disclosure (AVID Form)

☐ Agent notes no items for disclosure.

☐ Agent notes the following items: ______________________________

Agent (Broker Representing Seller) ____________ By ______________________ Date__________
(Please Print) (Associate Licensee or Broker Signature)

IV. AGENT'S INSPECTION DISCLOSURE

(To be completed only if the agent who has obtained the offer is other than the agent above.)

THE UNDERSIGNED, BASED ON A REASONABLY COMPETENT AND DILIGENT VISUAL INSPECTION OF THE ACCESSIBLE AREAS OF THE PROPERTY, STATES THE FOLLOWING:

☐ See attached Agent Visual Inspection Disclosure (AVID Form)

☐ Agent notes no items for disclosure.

☐ Agent notes the following items: ______________________________

Agent (Broker Obtaining the Offer) ____________ By ______________________ Date__________
(Please Print) (Associate Licensee or Broker Signature)

V. BUYER(S) AND SELLER(S) MAY WISH TO OBTAIN PROFESSIONAL ADVICE AND/OR INSPECTIONS OF THE PROPERTY AND TO PROVIDE FOR APPROPRIATE PROVISIONS IN A CONTRACT BETWEEN BUYER AND SELLER(S) WITH RESPECT TO ANY ADVICE/INSPECTIONS/DEFECTS.

I/WE ACKNOWLEDGE RECEIPT OF A COPY OF THIS STATEMENT.

Seller ______________ Date ________ Buyer ______________ Date________

Seller ______________ Date ________ Buyer ______________ Date________

Agent (Broker Representing Seller) ____________ By ______________ Date________
(Please Print) (Associate Licensee or Broker Signature)

Agent (Broker Obtaining the Offer) ____________ By ______________ Date________
(Please Print) (Associate Licensee or Broker Signature)

SECTION 1102.3 OF THE CIVIL CODE PROVIDES A BUYER WITH THE RIGHT TO RESCIND A PURCHASE CONTRACT FOR AT LEAST THREE DAYS AFTER THE DELIVERY OF THIS DISCLOSURE IF DELIVERY OCCURS AFTER THE SIGNING OF AN OFFER TO PURCHASE. IF YOU WISH TO RESCIND THE CONTRACT, YOU MUST ACT WITHIN THE PRESCRIBED PERIOD.

A REAL ESTATE BROKER IS QUALIFIED TO ADVISE ON REAL ESTATE. IF YOU DESIRE LEGAL ADVICE, CONSULT YOUR ATTORNEY.

Published and Distributed by:
REAL ESTATE BUSINESS SERVICES, INC.
a subsidiary of the California Association of REALTORS®
525 South Virgil Avenue, Los Angeles, California 90020

TDS REVISED 4/14 (PAGE 3 OF 3)

Reviewed by ________ Date ________

EQUAL HOUSING OPPORTUNITY

REAL ESTATE TRANSFER DISCLOSURE STATEMENT (TDS PAGE 3 OF 3)

Natural Hazards Disclosure. A natural hazards disclosure statement is used to disclose whether a home is in an area or zone designated as especially subject to flooding, wildfires, or earthquakes; in the vicinity of an airport; or within one mile of a farm or mining operation.

The disclosure form can be completed by the seller or the seller's agent, or by a consultant hired for that purpose. No matter who fills out the form, the information provided must be based on maps drawn by state or federal authorities (not just the seller's or agent's own knowledge).

Earthquake Guide. Whether or not the property is in an earthquake fault zone, buyers purchasing a home built before 1960 using light-frame construction must be given a booklet called *A Homeowner's Guide to Earthquake Safety*. If improvements suggested in the booklet haven't been made, that must be disclosed to the buyers.

Taxes and Assessments. If residential property is subject to special taxes under the Mello-Roos Community Facilities Act or subject to assessments for bonds issued under the Improvement Bond Act of 1915, the seller must make a good faith effort to obtain a disclosure concerning the lien from the taxing district and give it to buyers.

Sellers also have to disclose that buyers may receive a supplemental property tax bill (see Chapter 5).

Transfer Fees. Sometimes a subdivision's CC&Rs provide that when property in the subdivision is sold, the buyer will be charged a **transfer fee** to fund maintenance of subdivision amenities, improvements, or open space. If so, the seller must disclose the amount and other information about the fee to prospective buyers.

Sex Offender Information Website. A residential purchase agreement must contain a notice that the California Department of Justice has made information about registered sex offenders available to the public on a website. This is often referred to as the Megan's Law disclosure.

Drug Labs. After determining that property has been contaminated by methamphetamine activity, the local health department will issue an order prohibiting use or habitation of the property. If it is put up for sale before the department declares that it is clean and needs no further action, the seller must give buyers a copy of this order.

Miscellaneous. Sellers are also required to inform buyers if the property is within one mile of an ordnance location (an area that was once used for military training, and which may contain live ammunition); if there are window security bars, and how the safety release mechanisms work; and if the property is adjacent to an industrial use, zoned for industrial use, or affected by an industrial nuisance.

Lead-based Paint Disclosures. Transactions that involve housing built before 1978 are subject to a federal law concerning lead-based paint, a health hazard to children. The law requires a seller or landlord to disclose the location of any lead-based paint he is aware of in the home or common areas; provide a copy of any report concerning lead-based paint in the home, if it has been inspected; and give buyers or tenants a pamphlet on lead-based paint prepared by the U.S. Environmental Protection Agency.

In addition, buyers (though not tenants) must be offered at least a ten-day period in which to have the home tested for lead-based paint.

The purchase agreement or lease must include specific warnings and signed statements from the parties acknowledging that the requirements of this law were fulfilled. The acknowledgments must be kept for at least three years.

Breach of Duty

If a licensee breaches any duties owed to either a principal or a third party, it's considered a tort. (A tort, as we explained earlier, is a wrongful act resulting from a breach of a duty imposed by law.) The party injured by the tort, whether it's the principal or a third party, is then entitled to sue for redress.

The most common remedy in a tort suit is compensatory damages. A court will order the licensee to compensate the injured party for the financial loss he suffered. This might include repaying any commission collected in a transaction. The injured party may also be allowed to rescind the transaction.

If a licensee misrepresents property to a buyer, the buyer can sue the licensee and her broker in a tort action. In addition, the buyer can sue the broker's principal, the seller. That's because, according to the doctrine of vicarious liability, a principal is liable for torts committed by the agent within the scope of her agency. So the seller could be held liable to the buyer even if the seller wasn't aware of the licensee's misrepresentations. An innocent seller who has been held liable for his agent's misconduct could, in turn, sue the licensee and her broker.

Most breaches of duty by licensees are also violations of the California Real Estate Law. The Bureau of Real Estate may take disciplinary action against a licensee and her broker even if the injured party doesn't pursue a lawsuit. Disciplinary action may include fines as well as license suspension or revocation (see Chapter 16).

Terminating an Agency Relationship

Once an agency relationship has terminated, the agent is no longer authorized to represent the principal. Under general agency law, an agency may be terminated either by acts of the parties or by operation of law.

Termination by Acts of the Parties

The ways in which the parties can terminate an agency relationship include:

- mutual agreement,
- revocation by the principal, and
- renunciation by the agent.

Mutual Agreement. The parties may terminate the agency by mutual agreement at any time. If the original agreement was in writing, the termination agreement should also be in writing.

Principal Revokes. The principal may revoke the agency by firing the agent whenever he wishes. (Remember that an agency relationship requires the consent of both parties.) However, in some cases revoking an agency breaches a contractual agreement, and the principal may be liable for any damages suffered by the agent because of the breach.

An **agency coupled with an interest** can't be revoked. An agency is coupled with an interest if the agent has a financial interest in the subject matter of the agency. For instance, if a real estate licensee co-owns a property with other people, and they've authorized him to represent them in selling the property, it's an agency coupled with an interest. The co-owners can't revoke it.

Fig. 8.3 *Termination of agency relationships*

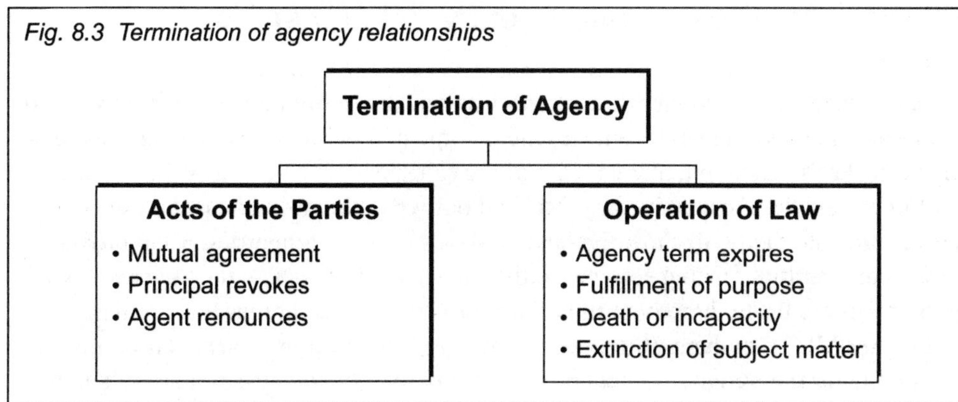

Agent Renounces. An agent can renounce the agency at any time. Like revocation, renunciation may be a breach of contract, in which case the agent could be liable for the principal's damages resulting from the breach. But since an agency contract is a personal services contract (the agent agreed to provide personal services to the principal), the principal couldn't demand specific performance as a remedy. The courts won't force a person to perform personal services, because that would violate the constitutional prohibition against involuntary servitude.

Termination by Operation of Law

Several events terminate an agency relationship automatically, without action by either party. These events include:

- expiration of the agency term,
- fulfillment of the purpose of the agency,
- the death or incapacity of either party, and
- extinction of the subject matter.

Expiration of Agency Term. An agency terminates automatically when its term expires. If an agency agreement didn't include an expiration date, it will be deemed to expire within a reasonable time. (How much time a court would consider reasonable will vary, depending on the type of agency in question.) If there's no expiration date, either party may terminate the agency without liability for damages, although the other party might be able to demand reimbursement for expenses incurred before the termination.

Fulfillment of Purpose. An agency relationship terminates when its purpose has been fulfilled. For example, if a broker is hired to sell the principal's property and the broker does so, the agency is terminated by fulfillment.

Death or Incapacity. An agency is terminated before it expires if either the agent or the principal dies. An agency also terminates if either party becomes mentally incompetent. Generally, the agent has no authority to act after the death or incapacity of the principal, even if the agent is unaware of the principal's death or incapacity.

Extinction of Subject Matter. The subject matter of a real estate agency is the property in question. If the property is in any way extinguished (for example, sold or destroyed), the agency automatically terminates.

Real Estate Agency Relationships

A typical residential real estate transaction is likely to involve more than one real estate agent. Someone who wants to find a home in a particular area contacts a real estate broker's office in that area. One of the salespersons who works for that broker will interview the prospective buyer to find out what kind of a home she wants and can afford, and then will show the buyer various suitable properties. Most brokers belong to a multiple listing service, so the salesperson will show the buyer not only homes that are listed directly with his own broker, but also homes that are listed with other MLS members. If the buyer becomes interested in a particular home, negotiations for the purchase of that home will involve the listing agent as well as the salesperson who has been showing properties to the buyer.

Meanwhile, other real estate agents may be showing the same house to other prospective buyers. By the time the transaction closes, it may involve a listing broker, a listing salesperson, a selling broker, and a selling salesperson, in addition to other cooperating agents who showed the home to buyers who didn't want it or didn't offer enough for it.

Understanding the agency relationships in this transaction means understanding which party each of these real estate licensees is representing. As a first step, you should be familiar with all of the following terms.

- **Real estate agent:** Real estate agent is the generic term used to refer to real estate licensees. Real estate brokers are the only real estate agents who are authorized to represent a buyer or a seller directly; real estate salespersons act on behalf of their real estate brokers.
- **Client:** A client is a person who has engaged the services of a real estate agent. A client may be a seller, a buyer, a landlord, or a tenant.
- **Customer:** A real estate agent who is representing a seller or a landlord will sometimes refer to a potential buyer or tenant as a customer.
- **Listing agent:** Either the listing salesperson or the listing broker may be referred to as the listing agent. The listing salesperson is the salesperson who takes the listing on a home. (She may or may not be the one who eventually procures a buyer for the listed home.) The listing broker is the broker that the listing salesperson works for.
- **Selling agent:** Either the selling salesperson or the selling broker may be referred to as the selling agent. The selling salesperson is the salesperson who procures a buyer for a property. (He may or may not have taken the listing for the property sold.) The selling broker is the broker that the selling salesperson works for.
- **Cooperating agent:** A cooperating agent is a licensee other than the listing agent who attempts to find a buyer for the property. (The cooperating agent who succeeds in procuring a buyer is then the selling agent.)
- **In-house sale:** A sale in which the buyer and the seller are brought together by salespersons working for the same broker. This may also be called a designated, assigned, or appointed agency, because one agent in the brokerage is assigned or appointed to represent one party, while another agent within the same firm represents the other party (with the firm's broker representing both parties).
- **Cooperative sale:** A sale in which the listing agent and the selling agent work for different brokers.

Agency Relationships: A Historical Perspective

In the 1980s, various organizations, including the Federal Trade Commission, the National Association of Realtors®, and the Association of Real Estate License Law Officials, conducted studies of agency representation in real estate transactions. They concluded that many real estate buyers and sellers were confused about which party a real estate agent represented. Buyers, in particular, appeared bewildered by the rules of real estate agency. They often thought the real estate agent that they were working with was representing them, when in fact the agent was almost always representing the seller.

Unilateral Offer of Subagency. This confusion was based on a standard provision found in MLS listing agreements at that time. This provision essentially stated that any member of the multiple listing service who found a buyer for a listed property would automatically be a **subagent** of the seller. (A subagent is an agent of an agent.) This meant that the selling agent as well as the listing agent represented the seller. This listing provision was referred to as a "unilateral offer of subagency."

As long as this provision remained in listing agreements, it was quite inconvenient to enter into a buyer agency relationship. In order to represent a buyer in a particular MLS transaction, a licensee had to reject the offer of subagency in a timely fashion and then enter into a separate written agreement with the buyer. This was rarely done; so in nearly all transactions, all of the licensees involved represented the seller.

Inadvertent Dual Agency. However, even though the subagency arrangement was well established, it was easy for a buyer to mistakenly believe that the selling agent was acting as the buyer's agent, not the seller's. After all, the selling agent was working with the buyer on a continuous and usually friendly basis. The agent would often encourage the buyer's loyalty by going out of his way to meet the buyer's needs. As a result, the buyer often told the selling agent confidential information. Yet because the selling agent was representing the seller, he had a duty to pass along that confidential information to the seller. If the agent fulfilled that responsibility, the buyer might well be surprised and dismayed. But in many cases, the selling agent would let his natural desire to help the buyer interfere with the fiduciary duties owed to the seller. This confusion caused trouble for everyone, and sometimes resulted in the creation of an inadvertent dual agency.

Example: Martinez was a salesperson working for Baker Realty. Over the course of several weeks, she showed the Greens many homes. Martinez liked the Greens and worked very hard to find them a good house. She gave them advice about purchasing a home and discussed their financial situation with them. Understandably, the Greens believed that Martinez was their agent. But Martinez didn't have an agency agreement with the Greens, and that meant (under the traditional presumption) that she was acting in the capacity of a seller's agent.

The Greens decided to make an offer on a house listed by Broker Rush. They were very excited about the house, and they told Martinez that they were willing to pay full price for it. Nevertheless, they wanted to start out with an offer that was $10,000 less than the listing price.

If Martinez failed to disclose to the seller that the Greens were willing to pay the full listing price, it would be a breach of her duty of loyalty to the seller. However, her conduct had caused the Greens to believe that she was representing them, creating an agency by implication. Thus, if Martinez did disclose this information to the seller, the Greens could claim that she had breached her duty of loyalty to them. And because she was inadvertently acting as agent for both parties, both could claim that she acted as a dual agent without their consent.

Cooperation and Compensation. In the 1990s, as new legal requirements and various other considerations made real estate transactions more complex, buyers became more interested in having their own agents to represent them. In response to the growing popularity of buyer agency, many multiple listing services replaced the unilateral offer of subagency in their listing agreements with a "cooperation and compensation" provision. Under the terms of this provision, other members of the MLS act only as cooperating agents, not as subagents. A cooperating agent is simply any member of the MLS who attempts to find a buyer; the listing agreement doesn't set any type of agency relationship for a cooperating agent. It becomes up to each individual cooperating agent to decide whether she will represent the seller or the buyer in a given transaction.

Disclosure Laws. In an effort to reduce confusion over agency representation, California and many other states passed agency disclosure laws—laws that require real estate agents to disclose to both the buyer and the seller which party they are representing in a transaction. (California's disclosure requirements are explained at the end of this chapter.) But even agency disclosures don't always prevent problems. Real estate agents must understand the consequences of the different types of agency relationships and learn to avoid the pitfalls that certain situations present.

Types of Agency Relationships

In California, real estate agents can have the following types of agency relationships with their clients:

- seller agency,
- buyer agency, or
- dual agency.

Seller Agency. A seller agency relationship is ordinarily created with a written listing agreement (discussed in Chapter 7). Under the terms of the listing agreement, the primary task of a seller's agent is to find a buyer for the seller's property at a price that's acceptable to the seller. To accomplish this, the seller's agent advises the seller about preparing the property for sale, helps the seller decide on the listing price, markets the property, and negotiates on the seller's behalf with buyers and with other real estate agents.

A seller agency relationship can be created even in the absence of a written listing agreement, by the words or conduct of the parties. (See the discussion of implied agency earlier in this chapter.) However, without a written agreement, the broker will not be entitled to sue the seller for a commission if the seller refuses to pay.

Seller's Agents and Buyers. Throughout a transaction, a seller's agent must use his best efforts to promote the interests of the seller. Yet the seller's agent may also provide some services to a prospective buyer. For example, the seller's agent may help a buyer who doesn't have her own agent fill out a purchase offer form. Assisting the buyer in this way is considered to be in the best interests of the seller, and therefore doesn't violate the agent's duties to the seller. Of course, the seller's agent must disclose to the buyer that he is acting as the seller's agent.

Fig. 8.4 Types of real estate agency relationships

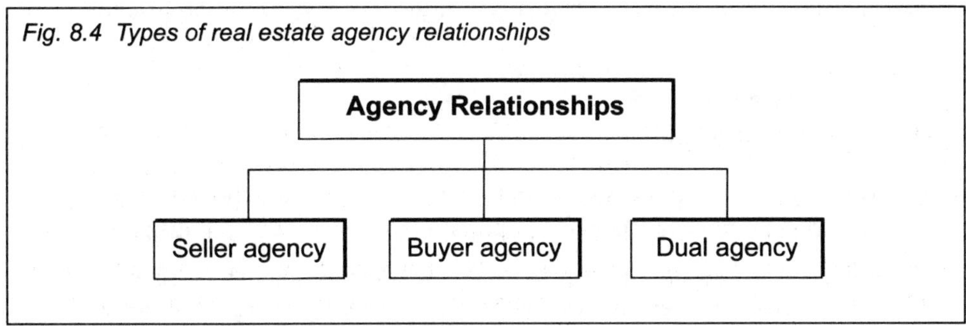

A seller's agent must be very careful to treat the buyer fairly, but the agent must not act as if he is representing the buyer. In other words, the agent must fully disclose all known material facts and answer the buyer's questions honestly. However, the agent shouldn't give the buyer advice, such as suggesting how much to offer for the listed property.

Example: Harrison, who works for Broker Yates, recently listed Taylor's house. The listing price is $515,000, but Harrison has reason to believe that Taylor would accept an offer of $500,000. Harrison shows the listed house to Markham, who asks Harrison, "How low do you think the seller will go?" Harrison should make it clear to Markham that she's representing Taylor and can't divulge confidential information to Markham. If she did, Taylor could sue Harrison and her broker for breach of agency duties.

The situation in which the problem of inadvertent dual agency is most likely to come up is when the listing agent (who always represents the seller) is the one who finds a buyer for the property. This is especially true if the listing agent has had a previous agency relationship with the buyer. It may be difficult for the agent to represent the seller's interests without feeling some loyalty to the buyer as well.

Example: After Harrison finds a buyer for Taylor's house, Taylor asks Harrison to help him find another home. Harrison shows Taylor one of her own listings, a house owned by a seller named Woods.

Under these circumstances, it would be easy for Taylor to think that Harrison is acting as his agent. However, because of the listing agreement with Woods, Harrison is the seller's agent, and she should emphasize this fact to Taylor. Taylor should be reminded that Harrison is obligated to disclose material information that Taylor tells her to the seller, and that in all negotiations Harrison will be representing the seller's best interests. However, a real estate agent is not permitted to disclose confidential information about a principal even after the termination of the agency relationship. Thus, Harrison cannot disclose to the seller any confidential information about Taylor that she learned during her agency relationship with Taylor.

Buyer Agency. The traditional seller agency arrangement (in which the real estate licensee who helps buyers look for a home is a seller's agent, and the buyers don't have an agent of their own) can work well for buyers. A seller's agent gives buyers access to multiple listing inventory, is legally required to provide complete and honest information about properties, and will present their offers to sellers. However, a buyer's agent can offer clients some services and advantages that a seller's agent can't provide to customers; and many buyers now prefer to work with a real estate licensee who's representing them, not the seller.

Advantages of Buyer Agency. The chief advantages of buyer agency include:

- loyalty and confidentiality,
- objective advice, and
- help with negotiations.

A buyer's agent owes fiduciary duties to the buyer. For many buyers, the duty of loyalty and confidentiality is the most important advantage of buyer agency.

Example: Broker Mendoza is helping Buyer Jackson find a home. He shows Jackson many houses, and there are two that interest her. One is a large fixer-upper selling for $445,000. The other is a small, newer house in mint condition selling for $420,000. Because Mendoza must put Jackson's interests before his own, he advises her to purchase the smaller house because it better suits her needs and is more likely to appreciate. He does so even though he would earn a bigger commission if she bought the more expensive house.

Mendoza advises Jackson to offer $412,000 for the $420,000 house. Jackson agrees to start with $412,000, although she tells Mendoza that she's willing to pay the full listing price. Because Mendoza is Jackson's agent, he's obligated to keep that information confidential. If he were the seller's agent, he would be required to disclose it to the seller.

A buyer's agent can be relied upon to give the buyer objective advice about the pros and cons of purchasing a particular home. He will point out various issues the buyer should be aware of, such as energy costs, the need for future repairs, and property value trends. By contrast, a seller's agent will present the property in the most positive light and may use expert sales techniques to convince the buyer to sign on the dotted line.

Buyers often feel uncomfortable negotiating for a property, especially one they really want to buy. They may be afraid to make a mistake through ignorance, or they may feel pressured to make a high offer quickly before someone else snaps up the property. A buyer's agent can use her negotiating skills and intimate knowledge of the real estate market to help the buyer get the property on the best possible terms.

Another potential advantage of buyer agency is access to more homes. A buyer's agent may arrange to be compensated if the buyer purchases any property, whether or not it's listed with a multiple listing service. So a buyer's agent may pursue less traditional means of searching for properties, and may be more willing to show the buyer homes that are for sale by owner, have open listings, or are in foreclosure or probate proceedings.

Compensation Doesn't Affect Agency. When a buyer purchases listed property, the buyer's agent is usually paid through a commission split with the listing agent (see Chapter 7). This means that the buyer's agent is being paid by the seller, at least indirectly. A state statute specifically provides that a seller or buyer's payment of compensation to a real estate licensee doesn't determine their agency relationship. Thus, a commission split arrangement doesn't create an agency relationship between the buyer's agent and the seller, and it doesn't involve any violation of the fiduciary duties that the buyer's agent owes the buyer.

Dual Agency. As was explained earlier, a dual agency relationship exists when an agent represents both the seller and the buyer in the same transaction. (In contrast, if an agent is representing only one of the parties, it's sometimes called single agency.) A dual agent owes fiduciary duties to both principals. Because the interests of the buyer and the seller usually conflict, it's difficult to represent both without being disloyal to one or both of them.

> **Example:** Broker Kogawa represents both the buyer and the seller in a transaction. The seller informs Kogawa that she's in a big hurry to sell and will accept any reasonable offer. The buyer tells Kogawa that he's very interested in the house, and willing to pay the full listing price. Should Kogawa tell the buyer of the seller's eagerness to sell? Should Kogawa tell the seller about the buyer's willingness to pay the full price?

Because it's impossible to fully represent the interests of both parties at the same time, dual agency is sometimes referred to as **limited dual agency**.

Disclosed Dual Agency. Dual agency is legal in California. However, before acting as a dual agent, a broker must have the informed written consent of both parties to the transaction. Acting as a dual agent without full disclosure to one or both parties is a violation of the Real Estate Law and grounds for disciplinary action (see Chapter 16). In that situation, it's possible that neither party would have to pay the brokerage commission and either could rescind the transaction.

Each party to a dual agency should be informed that he or she won't receive full representation. Certain facts must necessarily be withheld from each party; the dual agent can't reveal confidential information about one party to the other party. Returning to the previous example, as a dual agent Kogawa must not tell the buyer the seller's bottom line price, nor tell the seller how much the buyer is willing to pay.

Statutory agency disclosure requirements are discussed in the next section of this chapter. Real estate agents should be particularly careful with their disclosures in the context of dual agency. Buyers and sellers, eager to get on with the business of buying and selling a home, may agree to a dual agency without really understanding what it means. They may accept the agent's explanation at face value and sign a disclosure form without question. Later, one party might feel that the agent breached his fiduciary duties. That kind of disappointment may lead to legal action.

Inadvertent Dual Agency. As we've discussed, a dual agency may be created unintentionally. In fact, many dual agency lawsuits involve an accidental or unintended dual agency in which the conduct of the seller's agent, or the personal relationship between the agent and the buyer, is such that an implied agency is created with the buyer. An agent's best protection against inadvertent dual agency is to comply carefully with the agency disclosure requirements and then act in accordance with the disclosure, never forgetting which party she's representing.

Agency Disclosure Requirements

To avoid some of the confusion about who is representing whom, California law requires real estate agents in residential transactions to make agency disclosures to their clients and customers. This requirement applies to transactions that involve property with one to four dwelling units.

The first step in the disclosure process is providing an **agency disclosure form** (see Figure 8.5). This form gives a clear explanation of the duties of a seller's agent, a buyer's agent, and a dual agent. An agent must give the parties the disclosure form and also have them sign a copy to acknowledge that they received it.

The listing agent must give a copy of the agency disclosure form to the seller before the seller signs the listing agreement. The selling agent must give a copy to each party as soon as practicable, but in any event to the buyer before the buyer signs the offer to purchase, and to the seller before the offer is presented. (If the selling agent isn't dealing with the seller directly, the selling agent's disclosure form may be delivered to the seller by the listing agent or by certified mail.)

In addition to giving the parties the general disclosure form explaining the different types of real estate agency relationships, each agent is required to disclose whether he or she is representing only the seller, only the buyer, or both the seller and the buyer in this particular transaction. The agents must make their disclosures to the parties as soon as practicable. Each agent's disclosures must be confirmed in writing by having the parties sign an **agency confirmation statement** before or at the same time that they enter into a contract. An agency confirmation statement doesn't have to be a separate document; in most cases, a confirmation statement is included in the purchase agreement (see Chapter 7).

The Broker/Salesperson Relationship

To end the chapter, let's discuss the legal relationship between a real estate salesperson and the broker she works for. Under the California Real Estate Law (see Chapter 16), a real estate salesperson can't act directly as the agent of a principal in a real estate transaction. Rather, the salesperson acts as the agent of her broker, and it's the broker who acts as the principal's agent. (State law expressly provides that a real estate salesperson is never a subagent of her broker's principal. However, this rule does not prevent the vicarious liability we discussed earlier from applying between a buyer or seller and a salesperson.)

Independent Contractor vs. Employee

For certain purposes, when one person hires another to work for him, the worker is classified either as the hirer's employee or as an independent contractor. An **independent contractor** is hired to perform a particular task and generally uses his own judgment to decide how the task should be completed. An **employee**, on the other hand, is hired to perform whatever tasks the employer requires and is usually told how to accomplish each task. An employee is supervised and controlled much more closely than an independent contractor. Various employment and tax laws apply only to employees and not to independent contractors.

A real estate broker is virtually always an independent contractor in relation to her principal (the buyer or the seller). When it comes to the relationship between a broker and a salesperson, however, the distinction between employee and independent contractor has been more of an issue.

If a broker closely monitored and directed the activities of a salesperson, controlling how he carried out his work, the salesperson could be considered an employee in the eyes of the law. For example, if the broker required the salesperson to work on a set schedule, told the salesperson when to go where, and decided what steps the salesperson should take in marketing each property, a court might very well rule that the salesperson was the broker's employee.

Fig. 8.5 Agency disclosure statement

DISCLOSURE REGARDING REAL ESTATE AGENCY RELATIONSHIP

(As required by the Civil Code)
(C.A.R. Form AD, Revised 11/12)

❑ (If checked) This form is being provided in connection with a transaction for a leasehold interest in a dwelling exceeding one year as per Civil Code section 2079.13(j) and (l).

When you enter into a discussion with a real estate agent regarding a real estate transaction, you should from the outset understand what type of agency relationship or representation you wish to have with the agent in the transaction.

SELLER'S AGENT

A Seller's agent under a listing agreement with the Seller acts as the agent for the Seller only. A Seller's agent or a subagent of that agent has the following affirmative obligations:

To the Seller: A Fiduciary duty of utmost care, integrity, honesty and loyalty in dealings with the Seller.

To the Buyer and the Seller:

(a) Diligent exercise of reasonable skill and care in performance of the agent's duties.
(b) A duty of honest and fair dealing and good faith.
(c) A duty to disclose all facts known to the agent materially affecting the value or desirability of the property that are not known to, or within the diligent attention and observation of, the parties. An agent is not obligated to reveal to either party any confidential information obtained from the other party that does not involve the affirmative duties set forth above.

BUYER'S AGENT

A selling agent can, with a Buyer's consent, agree to act as agent for the Buyer only. In these situations, the agent is not the Seller's agent, even if by agreement the agent may receive compensation for services rendered, either in full or in part from the Seller. An agent acting only for a Buyer has the following affirmative obligations:

To the Buyer: A fiduciary duty of utmost care, integrity, honesty and loyalty in dealings with the Buyer.

To the Buyer and the Seller:

(a) Diligent exercise of reasonable skill and care in performance of the agent's duties.
(b) A duty of honest and fair dealing and good faith.
(c) A duty to disclose all facts known to the agent materially affecting the value or desirability of the property that are not known to, or within the diligent attention and observation of, the parties.

An agent is not obligated to reveal to either party any confidential information obtained from the other party that does not involve the affirmative duties set forth above.

AGENT REPRESENTING BOTH SELLER AND BUYER

A real estate agent, either acting directly or through one or more associate licensees, can legally be the agent of both the Seller and the Buyer in a transaction, but only with the knowledge and consent of both the Seller and the Buyer.

In a dual agency situation, the agent has the following affirmative obligations to both the Seller and the Buyer:

(a) A fiduciary duty of utmost care, integrity, honesty and loyalty in the dealings with either the Seller or the Buyer.
(b) Other duties to the Seller and the Buyer as stated above in their respective sections.

In representing both Seller and Buyer, the agent may not, without the express permission of the respective party, disclose to the other party that the
Seller will accept a price less than the listing price or that the Buyer will pay a price greater than the price offered.

The above duties of the agent in a real estate transaction do not relieve a Seller or Buyer from the responsibility to protect his or her own interests. You should carefully read all agreements to assure that they adequately express your understanding of the transaction. A real estate agent is a person qualified to advise about real estate. If legal or tax advice is desired, consult a competent professional.

Throughout your real property transaction you may receive more than one disclosure form, depending upon the number of agents assisting in the transaction. The law requires each agent with whom you have more than a casual relationship to present you with this disclosure form. You should read its contents each time it is presented to you, considering the relationship between you and the real estate agent in your specific transaction. **This disclosure form includes the provisions of Sections 2079.13 to 2079.24, inclusive, of the Civil Code set forth on page 2. Read it carefully. I/WE ACKNOWLEDGE RECEIPT OF A COPY OF THIS DISCLOSURE AND THE PORTIONS OF THE CIVIL CODE PRINTED ON THE BACK (OR A SEPARATE PAGE).**

Buyer/Seller/Landlord/Tenant ______________________ Date __________

Buyer/Seller/Landlord/Tenant ______________________ Date __________

Agent ______________________ DRE Lic. # __________
Real Estate Broker (Firm)

By ______________________ DRE Lic. # __________ Date __________
(Salesperson or Broker-Associate)

Agency Disclosure Compliance (Civil Code §2079.14):

• When the listing brokerage company also represents Buyer/Tenant: The Listing Agent shall have one AD form signed by Seller/Landlord and a different AD form signed by Buyer/Tenant.

• When Seller/Landlord and Buyer/Tenant are represented by different brokerage companies: (i) the Listing Agent shall have one AD form signed by Seller/Landlord and (ii) the Buyer's/Tenant's Agent shall have one AD form signed by Buyer/Tenant and either that same or a different AD form presented to Seller/Landlord for signature prior to presentation of the offer. If the same form is used, Seller may sign here:

______________________ ______________________
Seller/Landlord Date Seller/Landlord Date

Reviewed by ______ Date ______

AD REVISED 11/12 (PAGE 1 OF 2) Print Date

DISCLOSURE REGARDING REAL ESTATE AGENCY RELATIONSHIP (AD PAGE 1 OF 2)

Reprinted with permission, California Association of REALTORS®. Endorsement not implied.

CIVIL CODE SECTIONS 2079.24 (2079.16 APPEARS ON THE FRONT)

2079.13 As used in Sections 2079.14 to 2079.24, inclusive, the following terms have the following meanings: **(a)** "Agent" means a person acting under provisions of title 9 (commencing with Section 2295) in a real property transaction, and includes a person who is licensed as a real estate broker under Chapter 3 (commencing with Section 10130) of Part 1 of Division 4 of the Business and Professions Code, and under whose license a listing is executed or an offer to purchase is obtained. **(b)** "Associate licensee" means a person who is licensed as a real estate broker or salesperson under Chapter 3 (commencing with Section 10130) of Part 1 of Division 4 of the Business and Professions Code and who is either licensed under a broker or has entered into a written contract with a broker to act as the broker's agent in connection with acts requiring a real estate license and to function under the broker's supervision in the capacity of an associate licensee. The agent in the real property transaction bears responsibility for his or her associate licensees who perform as agents of the agent. When an associate licensee owes a duty to any principal, or to any buyer or seller who is not a principal, in a real property transaction, that duty is equivalent to the duty owed to that party by the broker for whom the associate licensee functions. **(c)** "Buyer" means a transferee in a real property transaction, and includes a person who executes an offer to purchase real property from a seller through an agent, or who seeks the services of an agent in more than a casual, transitory, or preliminary manner, with the object of entering into a real property transaction. "Buyer" includes vendee or lessee. **(d)** "Dual agent" means an agent acting, either directly or through an associate licensee, as agent for both the seller and the buyer in a real property transaction. **(e)** "Listing agreement" means a contract between an owner of real property and an agent, by which the agent has been authorized to sell the real property or to find or obtain a buyer. **(f)** "Listing agent" means a person who has obtained a listing of real property to act as an agent for compensation. **(g)** "Listing price" is the amount expressed in dollars specified in the listing for which the seller is willing to sell the real property through the listing agent. **(h)** "Offering price" is the amount expressed in dollars specified in an offer to purchase for which the buyer is willing to buy the real property. **(i)** "Offer to purchase" means a written contract executed by a buyer acting through a selling agent which becomes the contract for the sale of the real property upon acceptance by the seller. **(j)** "Real property" means any estate specified by subdivision (1) or (2) of Section 761 in property which constitutes or is improved with one to four dwelling units, any leasehold in this type of property exceeding one year's duration, and mobile homes, when offered for sale or sold through an agent pursuant to the authority contained in Section 10131.6 of the Business and Professions Code. **(k)** "Real property transaction" means a transaction for the sale of real property in which an agent is employed by one or more of the principals to act in that transaction, and includes a listing or an offer to purchase. **(l)** "Sell," "sale," or "sold" refers to a transaction for the transfer of real property from the seller to the buyer, and includes exchanges of real property between the seller and buyer, transactions for the creation of a real property sales contract within the meaning of Section 2985, and transactions for the creation of a leasehold exceeding one year's duration. **(m)** "Seller" means the transferor in a real property transaction, and includes an owner who lists real property with an agent, whether or not a transfer results, or who receives an offer to purchase real property of which he or she is the owner from an agent on behalf of another. "Seller" includes both a vendor and a lessor. **(n)** "Selling agent" means a listing agent who acts alone, or an agent who acts in cooperation with a listing agent, and who sells or finds and obtains a buyer for the real property, or an agent who locates property for a buyer or who finds a buyer for a property for which no listing exists and presents an offer to purchase to the seller. **(o)** "Subagent" means a person to whom an agent delegates agency powers as provided in Article 5 (commencing with Section 2349) of Chapter 1 of Title 9. However, "subagent" does not include an associate licensee who is acting under the supervision of an agent in a real property transaction

2079.14 Listing agents and selling agents shall provide the seller and buyer in a real property transaction with a copy of the disclosure form specified in Section 2079.16, and, except as provided in subdivision (c), shall obtain a signed acknowledgement of receipt from that seller or buyer, except as provided in this section or Section 2079.15, as follows: **(a)** The listing agent, if any, shall provide the disclosure form to the seller prior to entering into the listing agreement. **(b)** The selling agent shall provide the disclosure form to the seller as soon as practicable prior to presenting the seller with an offer to purchase, unless the selling agent previously provided the seller with a copy of the disclosure form pursuant to subdivision (a). **(c)** Where the selling agent does not deal on a face-to-face basis with the seller, the disclosure form prepared by the selling agent may be furnished to the seller (and acknowledgement of receipt obtained for the selling agent from the seller) by the listing agent, or the selling agent may deliver the disclosure form by certified mail addressed to the seller at his or her last known address, in which case no signed acknowledgement of receipt is required. **(d)** The selling agent shall provide the disclosure form to the buyer as soon as practicable prior to execution of the buyer's offer to purchase, except that if the offer to purchase is not prepared by the selling agent, the selling agent shall present the disclosure form to the buyer not later than the next business day after the selling agent receives the offer to purchase from the buyer.

2079.15 In any circumstance in which the seller or buyer refuses to sign an acknowledgement of receipt pursuant to Section 2079.14, the agent, or an associate licensee acting for an agent, shall set forth, sign, and date a written declaration of the facts of the refusal.

2079.16 Reproduced on Page 1 of this AD form.

2079.17(a) As soon as practicable, the selling agent shall disclose to the buyer and seller whether the selling agent is acting in the real property transaction exclusively as the buyer's agent, exclusively as the seller's agent, or as a dual agent representing both the buyer and the seller. This relationship shall be confirmed in the contract to purchase and sell real property or in a separate writing executed or acknowledged by the seller, the buyer, and the selling agent prior to or coincident with execution of that contract by the buyer and the seller, respectively. **(b)** As soon as practicable, the listing agent shall disclose to the seller whether the listing agent is acting in the real property transaction exclusively as the seller's agent, or as a dual agent representing both the buyer and seller. This relationship shall be confirmed in the contract to purchase and sell real property or in a separate writing executed or acknowledged by the seller and the listing agent prior to or coincident with the execution of that contract by the seller.

(c) The confirmation required by subdivisions (a) and (b) shall be in the following form.

____(DO NOT COMPLETE. SAMPLE ONLY)____ is the agent of (check one): ❑ the seller exclusively; or ❑ both the buyer and seller.
(Name of Listing Agent)

____(DO NOT COMPLETE. SAMPLE ONLY)____ is the agent of (check one): ❑ the buyer exclusively; or ❑ the seller exclusively; or ❑ both the buyer and seller.
(Name of Selling Agent if not the same as the Listing Agent)

(d) The disclosures and confirmation required by this section shall be in addition to the disclosure required by Section 2079.14.

2079.18 No selling agent in a real property transaction may act as an agent for the buyer only, when the selling agent is also acting as the listing agent in the transaction.

2079.19 The payment of compensation or the obligation to pay compensation to an agent by the seller or buyer is not necessarily determinative of a particular agency relationship between an agent and the seller or buyer. A listing agent and a selling agent may agree to share any compensation or commission paid, or any right to any compensation or commission for which an obligation arises as the result of a real estate transaction, and the terms of any such agreement shall not necessarily be determinative of a particular relationship.

2079.20 Nothing in this article prevents an agent from selecting, as a condition of the agent's employment, a specific form of agency relationship not specifically prohibited by this article if the requirements of Section 2079.14 and Section 2079.17 are complied with.

2079.21 A dual agent shall not disclose to the buyer that the seller is willing to sell the property at a price less than the listing price, without the express written consent of the seller. A dual agent shall not disclose to the seller that the buyer is willing to pay a price greater than the offering price, without the express written consent of the buyer. This section does not alter in any way the duty or responsibility of a dual agent to any principal with respect to confidential information other than price.

2079.22 Nothing in this article precludes a listing agent from also being a selling agent, and the combination of these functions in one agent does not, of itself, make that agent a dual agent.

2079.23 A contract between the principal and agent may be modified or altered to change the agency relationship at any time before the performance of the act which is the object of the agency with the written consent of the parties to the agency relationship.

2079.24 Nothing in this article shall be construed to either diminish the duty of disclosure owed buyers and sellers by agents and their associate licensees, subagents, and employees or to relieve agents and their associate licensees, subagents, and employees from liability for their conduct in connection with acts governed by this article or for any breach of a fiduciary duty or a duty of disclosure.

REBS INC
Published and Distributed by:
REAL ESTATE BUSINESS SERVICES, INC.
a subsidiary of the California Association of REALTORS®
525 South Virgil Avenue, Los Angeles, California 90020

Reviewed by ______ Date ______

EQUAL HOUSING OPPORTUNITY

AD REVISED 11/12 (PAGE 2 OF 2)

DISCLOSURE REGARDING REAL ESTATE AGENCY RELATIONSHIP (AD PAGE 2 OF 2)

However, most brokers exercise much less control over a salesperson's work than that. They generally focus on the end results—listings, closings, and satisfied clients—and not on the details of how the salesperson accomplishes those results. A broker usually isn't concerned with where the salesperson is or what she's doing at any given time. The salesperson is paid on the basis of results (by commission) rather than hours spent on the job. Thus, in most cases, a salesperson is considered to be an independent contractor, not the broker's employee.

If a salesperson were an employee, the broker would be required to withhold money from the salesperson's compensation for income tax, social security, and unemployment insurance. An independent contractor, on the other hand, is responsible for paying his own social security and income taxes, and doesn't have unemployment insurance.

The Internal Revenue Code provides that a real estate salesperson will be considered an independent contractor for income tax purposes if three conditions are met:

1. the individual is a licensed real estate salesperson;
2. substantially all of his or her compensation is based on commission rather than hours worked; and
3. the services are performed under a written contract providing that the individual won't be treated as an employee for federal tax purposes.

Note that classification as an independent contractor for income tax purposes doesn't affect worker's compensation requirements in California. Real estate brokers are required to provide worker's compensation coverage for their commissioned sales staff as well as for salaried employees.

Supervision and Liability

The California Real Estate Law states that while a salesperson may be treated either as an independent contractor or as an employee for tax purposes, that distinction won't affect the requirements or liabilities established in the Real Estate Law. Thus, regardless of whether a salesperson is an independent contractor or an employee, the broker is responsible for supervising the salesperson's actions, and the broker may be held liable for the salesperson's misconduct. (See Chapter 16.)

Broker/Salesperson Contracts

California law requires a broker to have a written agreement with each licensee who works for her. (As an example, the CAR Independent Contractor Agreement form is shown in Figure 8.6.) The agreement must be signed by both parties.

The agreement should include all the basic terms of the relationship, such as the duties of the parties, the amount and type of supervision to be exercised by the broker, the basis for the licensee's compensation, and the grounds for terminating the relationship. As mentioned above, if the salesperson is going to be treated as an independent contractor, the written contract must specifically provide that the salesperson won't be treated as an employee for tax purposes.

Fig. 8.6 Broker/salesperson contract

CALIFORNIA ASSOCIATION OF REALTORS®

INDEPENDENT CONTRACTOR AGREEMENT
(Between Broker and Associate-Licensee)
(C.A.R. Form ICA, Revised 11/13)

This Agreement, dated ____________________, is made between ____________________ ("Broker") and ____________________ ("Associate-Licensee").

In consideration of the covenants and representations contained in this Agreement, Broker and Associate-Licensee agree as follows:

1. **BROKER:** Broker represents that Broker is duly licensed as a real estate broker by the State of California, □ doing business as ____________________ (firm name), □ a sole proprietorship, □ a partnership, or □ a corporation. Broker is a member of the ____________________ Association(s) of REALTORS®, and a subscriber to the ____________________ Multiple Listing Service(s). Broker shall keep Broker's license current during the term of this Agreement.
2. **ASSOCIATE-LICENSEE:** Associate-Licensee represents that: **(i)** he/she is duly licensed by the State of California as a □ real estate broker, □ real estate salesperson, and **(ii)** he/she has not used any other names within the past five years, except ____________________. Associate-Licensee shall keep his/her license current during the term of this Agreement, including satisfying all applicable continuing education and provisional license requirements.
3. **INDEPENDENT CONTRACTOR RELATIONSHIP:**
   A. Broker and Associate-Licensee intend that, to the maximum extent permissible by law: **(i)** This Agreement does not constitute an employment agreement by either party; **(ii)** Broker and Associate-Licensee are independent contracting parties with respect to all services rendered under this Agreement; and **(iii)** This Agreement shall not be construed as a partnership.
   B. Broker shall not: **(i)** restrict Associate-Licensee's activities to particular geographical areas, or **(ii)** dictate Associate-Licensee's activities with regard to hours, leads, open houses, opportunity or floor time, production, prospects, sales meetings, schedule, inventory, time off, vacation, or similar activities, except to the extent required by law.
   C. Associate-Licensee shall not be required to accept an assignment by Broker to service any particular current or prospective listing or parties.
   D. Except as required by law: **(i)** Associate-Licensee retains sole and absolute discretion and judgment in the methods, techniques, and procedures to be used in soliciting and obtaining listings, sales, exchanges, leases, rentals, or other transactions, and in carrying out Associate-Licensee's selling and soliciting activities; **(ii)** Associate-Licensee is under the control of Broker as to the results of Associate-Licensee's work only, and not as to the means by which those results are accomplished; **(iii)** Associate-Licensee has no authority to bind Broker by any promise or representation; and **(iv)** Broker shall not be liable for any obligation or liability incurred by Associate-Licensee.
   E. Associate-Licensee's only remuneration shall be the compensation specified in paragraph 8.
   F. Associate-Licensee who only performs as a real estate sales agent, shall not be treated as an employee for state and federal tax purposes. However, an Associate-Licensee who performs loan activity shall be treated as an employee for state and federal tax purposes unless the activity satisfies the legal requirements to establish an independent contractor relationship.
   G. The fact the Broker may carry workers' compensation insurance for Broker's own benefit and for the mutual benefit of Broker and licensees associated with Broker, including Associate-Licensee, shall not create an inference of employment. (Workers' Compensation Advisory: Even though a Real Estate sales person may be treated as independent contractors for tax and other purposes, the California Labor and Workforce Development Agency considers them to be employees for workers' compensation purposes. According to that Agency: **(i)** Broker must obtain workers' compensation insurance for a Real Estate sales person and **(ii)** Broker, not a Real Estate sales person, must bear the cost of workers'compensation insurance. Penalties for failure to carry workers' compensation include, among others, the issuance of stop-work orders and fines of up to $1,000 per agent, not to exceed $100,000 per company.)
4. **LICENSED ACTIVITY:**
   A. All listings of property, and all agreements, acts or actions for performance of licensed acts, which are taken or performed in connection with this Agreement, shall be taken and performed in the name of Broker. Associate-Licensee agrees to and does hereby contribute all right and title to such listings to Broker for the benefit and use of Broker, Associate-Licensee, and other licensees associated with Broker.
   B. Broker shall make available to Associate-Licensee, equally with other licensees associated with Broker, all current listings in Broker's office, except any listing which Broker may choose to place in the exclusive servicing of Associate-Licensee or one or more other specific licensees associated with Broker.

Broker's Initials (________)(________) Associate-Licensee's Initials (________)(________)

ICA REVISED 11/13 (PAGE 1 OF 4)

Reviewed by ______ Date ______

EQUAL HOUSING OPPORTUNITY

INDEPENDENT CONTRACTOR AGREEMENT (ICA PAGE 1 OF 4)

Reprinted with permission, California Association of REALTORS®. Endorsement not implied.

C. Associate-Licensee shall provide and pay for all professional licenses, supplies, services, and other items required in connection with Associate-Licensee's activities under this Agreement, or any listing or transaction, without reimbursement from Broker except as required by law.

D. Associate-Licensee shall work diligently and with his/her best efforts to: **(i)** sell, exchange, lease, or rent properties listed with Broker or other cooperating Brokers; **(ii)** solicit additional listings, clients, and customers; and **(iii)** otherwise promote the business of serving the public in real estate transactions to the end that Broker and Associate-Licensee may derive the greatest benefit possible, in accordance with law.

E. Associate-Licensee shall not commit any unlawful act under federal, state or local law or regulation while conducting licensed activity. Associate-Licensee shall at all times be familiar, and comply, with all applicable federal, state and local laws, including, but not limited to, anti-discrimination laws and restrictions against the giving or accepting a fee, or other thing of value, for the referral of business to title companies, escrow companies, home inspection companies, pest control companies and other settlement service providers pursuant to the California Business and Professions Code and the Real Estate Settlement Procedures Acts (RESPA).

F. Broker shall make available for Associate-Licensee's use, along with other licensees associated with Broker, the facilities of the real estate office operated by Broker at ____________________ and the facilities of any other office locations made available by Broker pursuant to this Agreement.

G. **PROHIBITED ACTIVITIES:** Associate-Licensee agrees not to engage in any of the following Real Estate licensed activities without the express written consent of Broker:
☐ Property Management; ☐ Loan Brokerage ☐ Business Brokerage; ☐ ____________________
☐ ____________________

However, if Associate-Licensee has a Real Estate Broker's License, Associate-Licensee may nonetheless engage in the following prohibited activity(ies) only: ____________________ provided that (1) such prohibited activities are not done under the Broker's License, (2) no facilities of Broker (including but not limited to phones, fax, computers, and office space) are used for any such prohibited activities, (3) Associate-Licensee shall not use any marketing, solicitation or contact information that include Broker's name (including business cards) for such prohibited activities, (4) Associate-Licensee informs any actual or intended Principal for whom Associate-Licensee performs or intends to perform such prohibited activities the name of the broker under whose license the prohibited activities are performed, and (5) if Associate-Licensee is performing other permitted licensed activity for that Principal under Broker's license, then Associate-Licensee shall inform any actual or intended Principal for whom the prohibited activities are performed that the prohibited activities are not performed under Broker's license.

5. **PROPRIETARY INFORMATION AND FILES:**

A. All files and documents pertaining to listings, leads and transactions are the property of Broker and shall be delivered to Broker by Associate-Licensee immediately upon request or termination of this Agreement.

B. Associate-Licensee acknowledges that Broker's method of conducting business is a protected trade secret.

C. Associate-Licensee shall not use to his/her own advantage, or the advantage of any other person, business, or entity, except as specifically agreed in writing, either during Associate-Licensee's association with Broker, or thereafter, any information gained for or from the business, or files of Broker.

6. **SUPERVISION:** Associate-Licensee, within 24 hours (or ☐ ____________________) after preparing,signing, or receiving same, shall submit to Broker, or Broker's designated licensee: **(i)** all documents which may have a material effect upon the rights and duties of principals in a transaction; **(ii)** any documents or other items connected with a transaction pursuant to this Agreement in the possession of or available to Associate Licensee; and **(iii)** all documents associated with any real estate transaction in which Associate-Licensee is a principal.

7. **TRUST FUNDS:** All trust funds shall be handled in compliance with the Business and Professions Code, and other applicable laws.

8. **COMPENSATION:**

A. **TO BROKER:** Compensation shall be charged to parties who enter into listing or other agreements for services requiring a real estate license:
☐ as shown in "Exhibit A" attached, which is incorporated as a part of this Agreement by reference, or
☐ as follows: ____________________
____

Any deviation which is not approved in writing in advance by Broker, shall be: (1) deducted from Associate-Licensee's compensation, if lower than the amount or rate approved above; and, (2) subject to Broker approval, if higher than the amount approved above. Any permanent change in commission schedule shall be disseminated by Broker to Associate-Licensee.

B. **TO ASSOCIATE-LICENSEE:** Associate-Licensee shall receive a share of compensation actually collected by Broker, on listings or other agreements for services requiring a real estate license, which are solicited and obtained by Associate-Licensee, and on transactions of which Associate-Licensee's activities are the procuring cause, as follows:
☐ as shown in "Exhibit B" attached, which is incorporated as a part of this Agreement by reference, or
☐ other: ____________________
____

Broker's Initials (__________)(__________) Associate-Licensee's Initials (__________)(__________)

ICA REVISED 11/13 (PAGE 2 OF 4)

Reviewed by ______ Date ______

EQUAL HOUSING OPPORTUNITY

INDEPENDENT CONTRACTOR AGREEMENT (ICA PAGE 2 OF 4)

C. **PARTNERS, TEAMS, AND AGREEMENTS WITH OTHER ASSOCIATE-LICENSEES IN OFFICE:** If Associate-Licensee and one or more other Associate-Licensees affiliated with Broker participate on the same side (either listing or selling) of a transaction, the commission allocated to their combined activities shall be divided by Broker and paid to them according to their written agreement. Broker shall have the right to withhold total compensation if there is a dispute between associate-licensees, or if there is no written agreement, or if no written agreement has been provided to Broker.

D. **EXPENSES AND OFFSETS:** If Broker elects to advance funds to pay expenses or liabilities of Associate-Licensee, or for an advance payment of, or draw upon, future compensation, Broker may deduct the full amount advanced from compensation payable to Associate-Licensee on any transaction without notice. If Associate-Licensee's compensation is subject to a lien, garnishment or other restriction on payment, Broker shall charge Associate-Licensee a fee for complying with such restriction.

E. **PAYMENT: (i)** All compensation collected by Broker and due to Associate-Licensee shall be paid to Associate-Licensee, after deduction of expenses and offsets, immediately or as soon thereafter as practicable, except as otherwise provided in this Agreement, or a separate written agreement between Broker and Associate-Licensee. **(ii)** Compensation shall not be paid to Associate-Licensee until both the transaction and file are complete. **(iii)** Broker is under no obligation to pursue collection of compensation from any person or entity responsible for payment. Associate-Licensee does not have the independent right to pursue collection of compensation for activities which require a real estate license which were done in the name of Broker. **(iv)** Expenses which are incurred in the attempt to collect compensation shall be paid by Broker and Associate-Licensee in the same proportion as set forth for the division of compensation (paragraph 8(B)). **(v)** If there is a known or pending claim against Broker or Associate-Licensee on transactions for which Associate-Licensee has not yet been paid, Broker may withhold from compensation due Associate-Licensee on that transaction amounts for which Associate-Licensee could be responsible under paragraph 14, until such claim is resolved. **(vi)** Associate-Licensee shall not be entitled to any advance payment from Broker upon future compensation.

F. **UPON OR AFTER TERMINATION:** If this Agreement is terminated while Associate-Licensee has listings or pending transactions that require further work normally rendered by Associate-Licensee, Broker shall make arrangements with another associate-licensee to perform the required work, or Broker shall perform the work him/herself. The licensee performing the work shall be reasonably compensated for completing work on those listings or transactions, and such reasonable compensation shall be deducted from Associate-Licensee's share of compensation. Except for such offset, Associate-Licensee shall receive the compensation due as specified above.

9. **TERMINATION OF RELATIONSHIP:** Broker or Associate-Licensee may terminate their relationship under this Agreement at any time, with or without cause. After termination, Associate-Licensee shall not solicit: **(i)** prospective or existing clients or customers based upon company- generated leads obtained during the time Associate-Licensee was affiliated with Broker; **(ii)** any principal with existing contractual obligations to Broker; or **(iii)** any principal with a contractual transactional obligation for which Broker is entitled to be compensated. Even after termination, this Agreement shall govern all disputes and claims between Broker and Associate-Licensee connected with their relationship under this Agreement, including obligations and liabilities arising from existing and completed listings, transactions, and services.

10. **DISPUTE RESOLUTION:**
Broker and Associate-Licensee agree to mediate all disputes and claims between them arising from or connected in any way with this Agreement before resorting to court action. If any dispute or claim is not resolved through mediation, or otherwise, instead of resolving the matter in court, Broker and Associate-Licensee may mutually agree to submit the dispute to arbitration at, and pursuant to the rules and bylaws of, the Association of REALTORS® to which both parties belong.

11. **AUTOMOBILE:** Associate-Licensee shall maintain automobile insurance coverage for liability and property damage in the following amounts $______________/$______________. Broker shall be named as an additional insured party on Associate-Licensee's policies. A copy of the endorsement showing Broker as an additional insured shall be provided to Broker.

12. **PERSONAL ASSISTANTS:** Associate-Licensee may make use of a personal assistant, provided the following requirements are satisfied. Associate-Licensee shall have a written agreement with the personal assistant which establishes the terms and responsibilities of the parties to the employment agreement, including, but not limited to, compensation, supervision and compliance with applicable law. The agreement shall be subject to Broker's review and approval. Unless otherwise agreed, if the personal assistant has a real estate license, that license must be provided to the Broker. Both Associate-Licensee and personal assistant must sign any agreement that Broker has established for such purposes.

13. **OFFICE POLICY MANUAL:** If Broker's office policy manual, now or as modified in the future, conflicts with or differs from the terms of this Agreement, the terms of the office policy manual shall govern the relationship between Broker and Associate-Licensee.

Broker's Initials (________)(________) Associate-Licensee's Initials (________)(________)

ICA REVISED 11/13 (PAGE 3 OF 4)

Reviewed by ______ Date ______

EQUAL HOUSING OPPORTUNITY

INDEPENDENT CONTRACTOR AGREEMENT (ICA PAGE 3 OF 4)

14. INDEMNITY AND HOLD HARMLESS; NOTICE OF CLAIMS:

A. Regarding any action taken or omitted by Associate-Licensee, or others working through, or on behalf of Associate-Licensee in connection with services rendered or to be rendered pursuant to this Agreement or Real Estate licensed activity prohibited by this agreement: **(i)** Associate-Licensee agrees to indemnify, defend and hold Broker harmless from all claims, disputes, litigation, judgments, awards, costs and attorney's fees, arising therefrom and **(ii)** Associate-Licensee shall immediately notify Broker if Associate-Licensee is served with or becomes aware of a lawsuit or claim regarding any such action.

B. Any such claims or costs payable pursuant to this Agreement, are due as follows:

☐ Paid in full by Associate-Licensee, who hereby agrees to indemnify and hold harmless Broker for all such sums, or

☐ In the same ratio as the compensation split as it existed at the time the compensation was earned by Associate-Licensee ☐ Other: ____

Payment from Associate-Licensee is due at the time Broker makes such payment and can be offset from any compensation due Associate-Licensee as above. Broker retains the authority to settle claims or disputes, whether or not Associate-Licensee consents to such settlement.

15. ADDITIONAL PROVISIONS: ____

____

16. DEFINITIONS: As used in this Agreement, the following terms have the meanings indicated:

A. "Listing" means an agreement with a property owner or other party to locate a buyer, exchange party, lessee, or other party to a transaction involving real property, a mobile home, or other property or transaction which may be brokered by a real estate licensee, or an agreement with a party to locate or negotiate for any such property or transaction.

B. "Compensation" means compensation for acts requiring a real estate license, regardless of whether calculated as a percentage of transaction price, flat fee, hourly rate, or in any other manner.

C. "Transaction" means a sale, exchange, lease, or rental of real property, a business opportunity, or a manufactured home, which may lawfully be brokered by a real estate licensee.

17. ATTORNEY FEES: In any action, proceeding, or arbitration between Broker and Associate-Licensee arising from or related to this Agreement, the prevailing Broker or Associate-Licensee shall be entitled to reasonable attorney fees and costs.

18. ENTIRE AGREEMENT: All prior agreements between the parties concerning their relationship as Broker and Associate-Licensee are incorporated in this Agreement, which constitutes the entire contract. Its terms are intended by the parties as a final and complete expression of their agreement with respect to its subject matter, and may not be contradicted by evidence of any prior agreement or contemporaneous oral agreement. This Agreement may not be amended, modified, altered, or changed except by a further agreement in writing executed by Broker and Associate-Licensee.

Broker:

____
(Brokerage firm name)

By ______________________________________
Its Broker/Office manager (circle one)

____
(Print name)

____
(Address)

____
(City, State, Zip)

____
(Telephone) (Fax)

Associate-Licensee:

____
(Signature)

____
(Print name)

____
(Address)

____
(City, State, Zip)

____
(Telephone) (Fax)

Published and Distributed by:
REAL ESTATE BUSINESS SERVICES, INC.
a subsidiary of the California Association of REALTORS®
525 South Virgil Avenue, Los Angeles, California 90020

ICA REVISED 11/13 (PAGE 4 OF 4)

Reviewed by ______ Date ______

EQUAL HOUSING OPPORTUNITY

INDEPENDENT CONTRACTOR AGREEMENT (ICA PAGE 4 OF 4)

Chapter Summary

1. In an agency relationship, the agent represents the principal in dealings with third parties. An agent may be a general agent or a special agent, depending on the scope of authority granted.

2. Most agency relationships are created by express agreement (oral or written), but they can also be created by ratification, estoppel, or implication. Acts performed by an agent or an ostensible agent are binding on the principal if they fall within the scope of the agent's actual or apparent authority.

3. An agent owes the principal fiduciary duties, including utmost care, integrity, honesty, and loyalty. The agent must obey the principal's instructions, avoid conflicts of interest, and disclose material facts to the principal. A seller's agent must inform the principal of all offers, the property's true value, any relationship between the agent and the buyer, and a dual agency.

4. An agent owes third parties the duties of reasonable care and skill and good faith and fair dealing. Neither the seller nor the seller's agent may misrepresent the property, and they must reveal any known latent defects to prospective buyers. In a residential transaction, an agent has the duty to visually inspect the property and reveal the results of that inspection to prospective buyers.

5. An agency relationship may be terminated by mutual agreement, revocation, renunciation, expiration, fulfillment of purpose, the death or incapacity of either party, or extinction of the subject matter.

6. A seller agency is usually created with a listing agreement. A seller's agent may provide services to a buyer (a customer) without violating her fiduciary duties to the seller, but she must be careful to avoid any actions that might give rise to an inadvertent agency relationship with the buyer.

7. A buyer's agent can offer a buyer services that a seller's agent cannot, including loyalty and confidentiality, objective advice, and help with negotiations. A buyer's agent may be paid by the seller without establishing an agency with the seller.

8. Dual agency occurs when an agent represents both the seller and the buyer in the same transaction. Dual agencies are unlawful without the informed written consent of both parties. Dual agencies may arise inadvertently, through the agent's actions.

9. California law requires real estate agents to disclose to the buyer and the seller which party they represent. An agent must give the buyer and the seller an agency disclosure form and have them sign an agency confirmation statement.

10. For the purposes of certain tax and employment laws, a real estate salesperson may be classified as either an employee or an independent contractor. In most cases, a salesperson is considered to be an independent contractor, even though the broker has legal responsibility for the salesperson's conduct. In California, a broker must have a written contract with each of the licensees who work for her.

Key Terms

Principal—The person who authorizes an agent to act on her behalf.

Agent—A person authorized to represent another in dealings with third parties.

Third party—A person seeking to deal with the principal through the agent.

Fiduciary—Someone who holds a special position of trust and confidence in relation to another.

Ratification—When the principal gives approval to unauthorized actions after they are performed, creating an agency relationship after the fact.

Estoppel—When the principal allows a third party to believe an agency relationship exists, so that the principal is estopped (legally precluded) from denying the agency.

Actual authority—Authority the principal grants to the agent either expressly or by implication.

Apparent authority—Where no actual authority has been granted, but the principal allows it to appear that the agent is authorized, and therefore is estopped from denying the agency. Also called ostensible authority.

Material facts—Information that could affect a party's decisions in a transaction, such as information that has a substantial negative impact on the value of the property, or that indicates one of the parties may not be able to perform as agreed.

Secret profit—Any profit an agent receives as a result of the agency relationship and doesn't disclose to the principal.

Listing agent—The agent who takes the listing on a property, and who may or may not be the agent who procures a buyer.

Selling agent—The agent who procures a buyer for a property, and who may or may not have taken the listing.

Cooperating agent—Any agent other than the listing agent who attempts to find a buyer for a property.

In-house transaction—A sale in which the buyer and the seller are brought together by salespersons working for the same broker.

Cooperative transaction—A sale in which the buyer and the seller are brought together by salespersons who work for two different brokers.

Employee—Someone who works under the direction and control of the employer.

Independent contractor—A person who contracts to do a job for another, but retains control over how he will carry out the task, instead of having to follow detailed instructions.

Chapter Quiz

1. An agency relationship can be created in any of the following ways, except:
   a) written agreement
   b) oral agreement
   c) ratification
   d) verification

2. An agency relationship requires:
   a) consideration
   b) the consent of both parties
   c) an enforceable contract
   d) None of the above

3. Garcia acted on behalf of Hilton without her authorization. At a later date, Hilton gave her approval to Garcia's actions. This is an example of:
   a) express agreement
   b) ratification
   c) estoppel
   d) assumption of authority

4. A seller lists his home with a broker at $390,000; he asks for a quick sale. When the listing broker shows the home to a buyer, he says the seller is financially insolvent and will take $375,000. The buyer offers $375,000 and the seller accepts. The broker:
   a) didn't violate his duties to the seller, because the seller accepted the offer
   b) didn't violate his duties to the seller, since he fulfilled the purpose of his agency
   c) violated his duties to the seller by disclosing confidential information to the buyer
   d) was unethical, but didn't violate his duties to the seller, since he didn't receive a secret profit

5. Stark lists his property with Bell, a licensed broker. Bell shows the property to her cousin, who decides he would like to buy it. Which of the following is true?
   a) Bell can present her cousin's offer to Stark, as long as she tells Stark that the prospective buyer is one of her relatives
   b) Bell violated her fiduciary duties to Stark by showing the property to one of her relatives
   c) It wasn't unethical for Bell to show the property to a relative, but it would be a violation of her duties if she presented her cousin's offer to Stark
   d) It isn't necessary for Bell to tell Stark that the buyer is related to her, as long as he is offering the full listing price for the property

6. An agency relationship can be terminated by:
   a) renunciation without the principal's consent
   b) incapacity of either party
   c) extinction of the subject matter
   d) All of the above

7. A real estate agent tells potential buyers: "This is a great old house. They just don't make them like they used to." In fact, the house isn't especially superior to most modern houses. This statement would probably be considered:
   a) a misrepresentation
   b) actual fraud
   c) constructive fraud
   d) puffing

8. In most cases, a listing broker:
   a) is authorized to enter into contracts on behalf of the seller
   b) is considered a special agent
   c) Both of the above
   d) Neither of the above

9. Dual agency is:
   a) no longer legal in California
   b) legal as long as both principals consent to the arrangement in writing
   c) legal as long as the agent receives equal compensation from both principals
   d) encouraged by many professional associations as the best way of representing a client's interests

10. Able listed Glover's property. Able:
    a) can't give a buyer any information about Glover's property without being considered a dual agent
    b) may give a buyer information about Glover's property without owing agency duties to the buyer
    c) must sign a disclaimer of liability if he presents a buyer's offer to purchase to Glover
    d) is an inadvertent dual agent

11. A principal may be held liable for:
    a) the actions of his broker
    b) the actions of his broker's salesperson
    c) his own actions
    d) All of the above

12. Which of the following is not a benefit of buyer agency?
    a) The agent owes fiduciary duties to the buyer
    b) The buyer gets the benefit of objective advice
    c) Since the agent represents both parties, the buyer has access to information about the seller's bottom-line sales price
    d) The buyer gets help deciding how much to offer for a property

13. A buyer's agent accepted compensation from the seller. This arrangement:
    a) violated the agent's fiduciary duties to the buyer
    b) didn't affect her agency relationship with the buyer
    c) is legal only if the compensation wasn't based on the property's purchase price
    d) would be legal in other states, but isn't in California

14. Disclosure of and consent to a dual agency:
    a) must be in writing
    b) is required only in an in-house transaction
    c) should come after the parties sign the purchase agreement
    d) must be given to the buyer only after presenting the written offer to purchase

15. A dual agent must:
    a) keep each party's negotiating position confidential
    b) disclose all information to both parties, no matter how confidential
    c) act only as a facilitator, with no agency duties to either party
    d) refer all conflicts of interest to the Board of Equalization

Answer Key

1. d) An agency relationship may be created by express agreement (written or oral), ratification, estoppel, or implication.

2. b) The consent of both parties is necessary to the creation of an agency relationship, but consideration is not. There doesn't have to be an enforceable contract between the principal and the agent.

3. b) An agency relationship is created by ratification when the principal gives approval to unauthorized actions after the fact.

4. c) The broker was disloyal to his principal and violated his fiduciary duties by disclosing confidential information to a third party.

5. a) A seller's real estate agent is required to tell the seller if the prospective buyer is related to the agent.

6. d) Any of the choices listed can terminate an agency relationship.

7. d) This is an example of puffing, an exaggerated statement that the buyers should realize they can't depend on.

8. b) A listing broker is usually a special agent, with limited authority to represent the principal in a particular transaction. A listing broker is ordinarily not authorized to sign contracts on behalf of the principal.

9. b) Dual agency is legal, but only if both the seller and the buyer are informed that the agent is representing both of them, and they both give their written consent to the arrangement.

10. b) A seller's agent can give a buyer information about the seller's property without becoming a dual agent.

11. d) A principal may be liable for his own actions, the actions of his broker, and the actions of his broker's salesperson.

12. c) A buyer who retains her own agent doesn't get information about the seller's negotiating position. Also, a buyer's agent isn't representing both parties; and if he were (that is, if he were acting as a dual agent) he would be required to keep the seller's price information confidential.

13. b) Buyer's agents often accept a share of the commission that the listing broker receives from the seller. Under California law, a real estate licensee's agency relationships aren't affected by which party pays her compensation.

14. a) Disclosure of a dual agency must be in writing, and the parties' consent must also be in writing.

15. a) A dual agent must not disclose confidential information about one party to the other party. This includes information on each party's negotiating position.

Chapter 9

Principles of Real Estate Financing

I. Economics of Real Estate Finance
   A. Real estate cycles
   B. Interest rates and federal policy
      1. Fiscal policy
      2. Monetary policy
      3. Other federal influences on finance

II. Real Estate Finance Markets
   A. Primary market
   B. Secondary market
      1. Buying and selling loans
      2. Secondary market entities

III. Real Estate Finance Documents
   A. Promissory notes
      1. Basic provisions
      2. Types of notes
      3. Signing and endorsing a note
   B. Security instruments
      1. Relationship between note and security instrument
      2. Title theory vs. lien theory
      3. Mortgage vs. deed of trust
      4. Borrower's signature
      5. Recording
      6. Instruments as personal property
      7. Assignment
   C. Provisions in finance documents
   D. Foreclosure
      1. Judicial foreclosure
      2. Nonjudicial foreclosure
      3. Comparison of judicial and nonjudicial foreclosure
      4. Alternatives to foreclosure
      5. Foreclosure vs. bankruptcy

IV. Types of Mortgage Loans

V. Land Contracts

Chapter Overview

Financing—lending and borrowing money—is essential to the real estate industry. If financing weren't available, buyers would have to pay cash for their property, and very few people could afford to do so. Whether they're working with buyers or sellers, real estate agents need a thorough understanding of real estate finance to get transactions closed. This chapter starts with background information about real estate cycles, how the government influences real estate finance, and the secondary market. The chapter then goes on to explain how mortgages and other financing instruments work, the foreclosure process, and the various types of mortgage loans. The process of applying for a mortgage loan is covered in Chapter 10.

The Economics of Real Estate Finance

Nearly every buyer needs to borrow money in order to purchase real estate. Whether a particular buyer will be able to obtain a loan depends in part on her personal financial circumstances, and in part on national and local economic conditions. To help you understand the economic factors that affect real estate lending, we're going to discuss real estate cycles and the government's role in the economy.

Real Estate Cycles

From a lender's point of view, a loan is an investment. A lender loans money in the expectation of a return on the investment. The borrower will repay the money borrowed, plus interest; the interest is the lender's return.

As a general rule, investors demand a higher return on risky investments than they do on comparatively safe ones. That holds true for loan transactions. The greater the risk that the borrower won't repay the loan, the higher the interest rate charged. But the interest rate a lender charges on a particular loan also depends on market forces and real estate cycles.

The real estate market is cyclical: it goes through active periods followed by slumps. These periodic shifts in the level of activity in the real estate market are called **real estate cycles**. Residential real estate cycles can be dramatic or moderate, and they can be local or regional. At any given time and place, there may be a buyer's market, where few people are buying and homes sit on the market for a long time, or there may be a seller's market, where many people are buying and homes sell rapidly.

These cycles obey the law of supply and demand. When demand for a product exceeds the supply (a seller's market), the price charged for the product tends to rise, and the price increase stimulates more production. As production increases, more of the demand is satisfied, until eventually the supply outstrips demand and a buyer's market is created. At that point, prices fall and production tapers off until demand catches up with supply, and the cycle begins again.

Real estate cycles are caused in part by changes in the supply of and demand for mortgage loan funds. The supply of mortgage funds depends on how much money investors have available and choose to invest in real estate loans. The demand for mortgage funds depends on how many people want to purchase real estate and can afford to borrow enough money to do so.

Interest rates represent the price of mortgage funds. They affect supply and demand, and they also fluctuate in response to changes in supply and demand. Interest is sometimes called the cost of money.

Generally, when mortgage funds are plentiful, interest rates are low. When funds become scarce, interest rates increase; this is called a **tight money market**. While changes in interest rates do not usually have an immediate impact on property values, in a tight market, sellers may have to resort to offering to finance part of the purchase price in order to close a sale.

In a healthy economy, supply and demand are more or less in balance. This is the ideal; in reality, the forces affecting supply and demand are constantly changing, and so is the balance between them. But as long as supply and demand are reasonably close, the economy functions well. When supply far exceeds demand, or vice versa, the economy suffers.

Real estate cycles can be moderated, though not eliminated, by factors that either help keep interest rates under control or directly affect the supply of mortgage funds. Federal economic policy plays a key role in moderating real estate cycles.

Interest Rates and Federal Policy

Economic stability is directly tied to the supply of and demand for money. If money is plentiful and can be borrowed cheaply (that is, interest rates are low), increased economic activity is often the result. On the other hand, if funds are scarce and/or expensive to borrow, an economic slowdown will probably result.

Thus, manipulation of the availability and cost of money can help achieve economic balance. The federal government influences real estate finance, as well as the rest of the U.S. economy, through its **fiscal policy** and its **monetary policy**.

Fiscal Policy. Fiscal policy refers to the way in which the federal government manages its money. Congress and the president determine fiscal policy through tax legislation and the federal budget. The U.S. Treasury implements fiscal policy by managing tax revenues, expenditures, and the national debt.

When the federal government spends more money than it takes in, a shortfall called the **federal deficit** results. It is the Treasury's responsibility to borrow enough money to cover the deficit. It does this by issuing interest-bearing securities that are backed by the U.S. government and purchased by private investors. The securities include Treasury bills, notes, and bonds. Some investors prefer to invest in these government securities instead of other investments, because they are comparatively low-risk.

When the government borrows money, it competes with private industry for available investment funds. Economists and politicians debate what impact this has on the economy. According to some, by draining the number of dollars in circulation, heavy government borrowing may lead to an economic slowdown. The greater the federal deficit, the more money the government has to borrow, and the greater the effect on the economy. Other economists argue that the federal deficit has little effect on interest rates.

The government's taxation policies also affect the supply of and demand for money. As with the deficit, the effect of taxation on the economy is controversial.

Basically, when taxes are low, taxpayers have more money to lend and invest. When taxes are high, taxpayers not only have less money to lend or invest, they also may be more likely to invest what money they do have in tax-exempt securities instead of taxable investments. Since real estate and real estate mortgages are taxable investments, this may have a significant impact on real estate financing.

Monetary Policy. Monetary policy refers to the direct control the federal government exerts over the money supply and interest rates. The main goal of monetary policy is to keep the U.S. economy healthy.

Monetary policy is determined by the Federal Reserve, commonly called "the Fed." The Federal Reserve System, established in 1913, is the nation's central banking system. It is governed by the Federal Reserve Board and the board's chairman. It has twelve districts nationwide, with a Federal Reserve Bank in each district. Thousands of commercial banks across the country are members of the Federal Reserve. Although the Fed is responsible for regulating commercial banks, setting and implementing the government's monetary policy is perhaps the Fed's most important function.

The major objectives of monetary policy are high employment, economic growth, price stability, interest rate stability, and stability in financial and foreign exchange markets. Although these goals are interrelated, we are most concerned with the Federal Reserve policies that affect the availability and cost of borrowed money (interest rates), since those have the most direct impact on the real estate industry.

One of the Fed's main goals is to limit inflation. **Inflation** is a general rise in the price of goods and services over time, which reduces each dollar's purchasing power. Consumer price indexes, which track changes in the price of certain commodities from year to year, are used to measure the rate of inflation.

Inflation tends to occur in periods of rapid economic growth. While economic growth is ideal, too much growth too fast can push prices too high, which may cause a sudden reduction in demand and an economic recession. By raising interest rates, the Fed can put a brake on inflation.

The Fed uses three tools to implement its monetary policy and influence the economy:

- key interest rates,
- reserve requirements, and
- open market operations.

Key Interest Rates. The Fed has control over two interest rates, the federal funds rate and the discount rate. These are the interest rates charged when a bank borrows money, either from another bank or from a Federal Reserve Bank. When the Fed takes action to raise or lower the interest rates that its member banks have to pay, the banks will typically raise or lower the interest rates they charge their customers. Lower interest rates tend to stimulate the economy, and higher rates tend to slow it down. The Fed may increase rates if it decides that a slower pace is desirable to keep price inflation in check.

Reserve Requirements. Commercial banks are required to keep certain percentages of their customers' funds on deposit at the Federal Reserve Bank. These reserve requirements help prevent financial panics (a "run on the bank") by assuring depositors that their funds are safe and accessible; their bank will always have enough money available to meet unusual customer demand.

Reserve requirements also give the Fed some control over the growth of credit. By increasing reserve requirements, the Fed can reduce the amount of money banks have available to lend. On the other hand, a reduction in reserve requirements frees more money for investment or lending. So an increase in reserve requirements tends to decrease available loan funds and increase interest rates. Conversely, a decrease in reserve requirements tends to increase available loan funds and decrease interest rates.

Open Market Operations. The Fed also buys and sells government securities; these transactions are called open market operations. They are the Fed's chief method of controlling the money supply, and with the money supply, inflation and interest rates. Only money in circulation is considered part of the money supply, so actions by the Fed that put money into circulation increase the money supply, and actions that take money out of circulation decrease it.

When the Fed buys government securities from an investor, it increases the money supply, because the money that the Fed uses to pay for the securities goes into circulation. When the Fed sells government securities, the money that the buyer uses to pay for the securities is taken out of circulation, decreasing the money supply. Interest rates tend to fall with increases in the money supply, and to rise with decreases in the money supply.

Other Federal Influences on Finance. Aside from the Federal Reserve, there are a number of other federal agencies and programs that have an impact on real estate finance.

Federal Home Loan Bank System. The Federal Home Loan Bank System (FHLB) is made up of twelve regional, privately owned wholesale banks. The banks loan funds to FHLB members—local community lenders—and accept their mortgages and other loans as collateral. The FHLB, which is headed by the Federal Housing Finance Board, is active in promoting affordable housing.

Federal Deposit Insurance Corporation. The FDIC was created in 1933 to insure bank deposits against bank insolvency. If a bank or other lending institution fails, the FDIC will step in to protect the institution's customers against the loss of their deposited funds, up to specified limits.

HUD. The Department of Housing and Urban Development (HUD) is a federal cabinet department. Among many other things, HUD's responsibilities include urban renewal projects, public housing, FHA-insured loan programs, and enforcement of the Federal Fair Housing Act (see Chapter 14). Ginnie Mae (discussed later in this chapter) and the Federal Housing Administration (discussed in Chapter 10) are both part of HUD.

Rural Housing Service. Formerly known as the Farmers Home Administration or FmHA, the Rural Housing Service is an agency within the Department of Agriculture. To help people living in rural areas purchase and improve their homes, the Rural Housing Service makes loans and grants and also guarantees loans made by lending institutions. In addition, it finances the construction of affordable housing in rural areas.

Farm Credit System. Originally developed by the federal government, the Farm Credit System is now a privately owned cooperative. It provides financial assistance to farmers, ranchers, and others in rural areas.

Real Estate Finance Markets

There are two "markets" that supply the funds available for real estate loans: the primary market and the secondary market. In addition to using monetary policy to control the money supply and interest rates, another way in which the federal government has helped moderate the severity and duration of real estate cycles is by establishing a strong, nationwide secondary market. The secondary market limits the adverse effects of local economic circumstances on real estate lending. We'll look first at the primary market, then at the secondary market.

Primary Market

The primary market is the market in which mortgage lenders make loans to home buyers. When buyers apply for a loan to finance their purchase, they're seeking a loan in the primary market.

Originally, the primary market was entirely local. It was made up of the various lending institutions in a community—the local banks and savings and loan associations. (Today the primary market is considerably more complicated, since there are interstate lenders, online lenders, nationwide mortgage companies, and so on.) The traditional source of funds for the primary market was the savings of individuals and businesses in the local area. A bank or savings and loan would use the savings deposits of members of the local community to make mortgage loans to members of that same community.

The local economy has a significant effect on the amount of deposited funds available to a lender, and on the local demand for them. When employment is high, consumers are more likely to borrow money for cars, vacations, or homes. Businesses expand and borrow to finance their growth. At the same time, fewer people are saving. This decrease in deposits means that less local money is available for lending, making it difficult to meet the increased demand for loans. On the other hand, when an area is in an economic slump, consumers are more inclined to save than to borrow. Businesses suspend plans for growth. The result is a drop in the demand for money, and the local lending institutions' deposits grow.

From a lender's point of view, either too little or too much money on deposit is cause for concern. In the first case, with little money to lend, a lender's primary source of income is affected. In the second case, the lender is paying interest to its depositors, and if it is unable to reinvest the deposited funds quickly, it will lose money.

The solution to these problems has been for lenders to look beyond their local area. When local savings deposits are low, a lender needs to get funds from other parts of the country to lend locally. When local demand for loans is low, a lender needs to send funds to other parts of the country where demand is higher. This is where the secondary market comes in. The secondary market makes it easy for lenders to obtain funds from around the country.

Secondary Market

The secondary market is a national market. In the secondary market, private investors, government entities, and government-sponsored enterprises buy and sell mortgages secured by real estate in all parts of the United States.

Fig. 9.1 By selling mortgages on the secondary market, lenders obtain funds to make more loans.

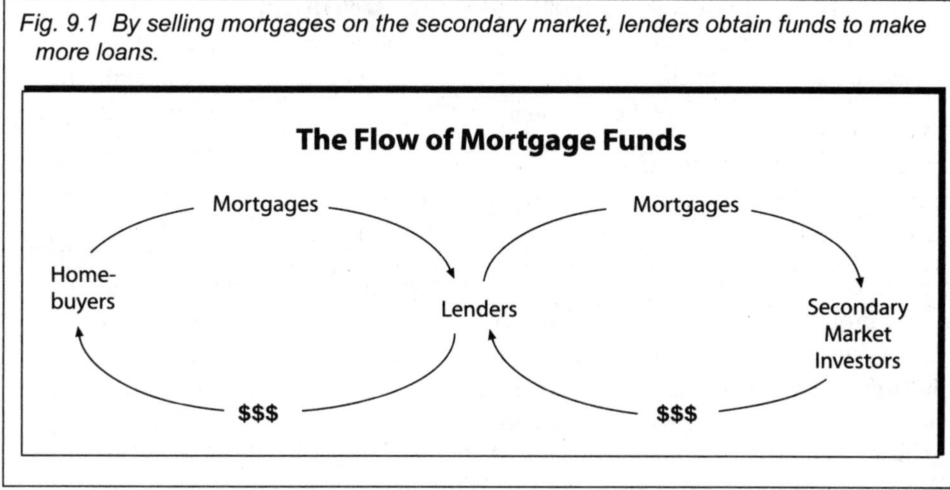

Buying and Selling Loans. Mortgage loans can be bought and sold just like other investments—stocks or bonds, for example. The value of a loan is influenced by the rate of return on the loan compared to the market rate of return, as well as the degree of risk associated with the loan (the likelihood of default). For instance, a **seasoned loan**—one with a history of several years of timely payments by the borrower—is less risky than a new, untested loan. As a result, a seasoned loan is worth more to an investor than a new loan for the same amount.

Investors generally buy mortgage loans at a discount, for less than their face value. However, if a borrower defaults on a loan purchased at a discount, the investor can still foreclose (force the sale of the property to recoup the amount of the debt) for the full face amount of the mortgage. For example, if an investor bought a $200,000 mortgage for $180,000 and the borrower immediately defaulted on the loan, the investor could foreclose for the full $200,000.

The availability of funds in the primary market depends a great deal on the existence of the national secondary market. As explained above, a particular lender may have either too much or too little money to lend, depending on conditions in the local economy. It is the secondary market that provides balance by transferring funds from areas where there is an excess to areas where there is a shortage. When local demand for funds is high, lenders can sell loans they've already made on the secondary market and use the proceeds of those sales to make more loans. When local demand for loan funds is low, lenders can use their excess funds to purchase loans on the secondary market.

The secondary market has a stabilizing effect on local mortgage markets. Lenders are willing to commit themselves to long-term real estate loans even when local funds are scarce, because they can raise more funds by liquidating their loans on the secondary market.

Secondary Market Entities. The federal government has played a central role in developing the secondary market for mortgage loans, primarily by establishing three secondary market entities: Fannie Mae, Freddie Mac, and Ginnie Mae. We'll describe each of these entities shortly, after a general description of what they do.

A secondary market entity buys large numbers of mortgage loans from primary market lenders, and then issues securities using the loans as collateral ("securitizes" the loans). The entity sells these **mortgage-backed securities** to private investors. As the underlying loans are repaid by the borrowers, the secondary market entity passes the payments through to the investors, providing a return on their investment. The securities are guaranteed by the secondary market entity, so the investors will receive their payments from the entity even if borrowers default on some of the underlying loans.

Of course, the secondary market entities don't want to buy loans that carry a high risk of default. To prevent that, the entities have established their own **underwriting standards**. Underwriting standards are the criteria used to evaluate a loan applicant and the property offered as security, to determine if the loan would be a good investment or would involve too much risk. Lenders may apply their own underwriting standards when they make loans, but they generally won't be able to sell the loans to a secondary market entity unless the loans conform to the entity's underwriting standards. Because most lenders want to have the option of selling their loans on the secondary market, the majority of conventional mortgage loans in the U.S. are now made in accordance with the entities' standards. (Underwriting standards are discussed in more detail in Chapter 10.)

Fannie Mae. The most prominent of the secondary market entities is the Federal National Mortgage Association (FNMA), often referred to as "Fannie Mae." Fannie Mae started out as a federal agency in 1938. Its original purpose was to provide a secondary market for FHA-insured loans.

Fannie Mae was eventually reorganized as a private corporation, but it is still chartered by the federal government. It's sometimes referred to as a **government-sponsored enterprise**, or GSE. Fannie Mae purchases conventional, FHA, and VA loans to use as the collateral for its mortgage-backed securities. (These different types of loans are discussed in Chapter 10.)

Freddie Mac. Congress created the Federal Home Loan Mortgage Corporation (FHLMC), nicknamed "Freddie Mac," in 1970. Its original purpose was to assist savings and loan associations (which had been hit particularly hard by a recession) by buying their conventional loans. Freddie Mac is now authorized to purchase and securitize conventional, FHA, and VA loans from any type of lender. Like Fannie Mae, Freddie Mac is a government-sponsored enterprise.

Ginnie Mae. The Government National Mortgage Association (GNMA) is one of the federal agencies that make up HUD. Among many other things, Ginnie Mae guarantees securities backed by loans made through the FHA and VA loan programs. Note that Ginnie Mae is a government agency, not a government-sponsored enterprise like Fannie Mae and Freddie Mac.

Current Status of Secondary Market Entities. Because of severe financial problems brought on by the recession that began in 2007, the federal government was forced to place both Fannie Mae and Freddie Mac into conservatorship in late 2008. This was essentially a government takeover of both entities, and it will continue until their solvency is restored.

As part of the takeover, Congress also created a new government regulator for the two entities, the Federal Housing Finance Agency (FHFA). Previously, Fannie Mae and Freddie Mac had been supervised by HUD; now Ginnie Mae is the only secondary market entity that HUD has authority over.

Real Estate Finance Documents

Now let's turn to the legal aspects of real estate financing. Once a buyer has found a lender willing to finance his purchase on acceptable terms, the buyer is required to sign the finance documents. The legal documents used in conjunction with most real estate loans are a promissory note and a security instrument, which is either a mortgage or a deed of trust. We'll look first at promissory notes, and then at security instruments and foreclosure procedures.

Promissory Notes

A promissory note is a written promise to repay a debt. One person loans another money, and the other signs a promissory note, promising to repay the loan (plus interest, in most cases). The borrower who signs the note is called the **maker**, and the lender is called the **payee**.

Basic Provisions. A promissory note states the loan amount (the **principal**), the amount of the payments, when and how the payments are to be made, and the maturity date—when the loan is to be repaid in full.

The note also states the interest rate, and whether the rate is fixed or variable. For certain loans, the state **usury law** prohibits the interest rate charged from exceeding a specified maximum. In California, most loans secured by real property are exempt from the usury law, but it can apply to a mortgage loan made by a private individual without the help of a mortgage broker or a real estate agent.

Naturally, the names of the borrowers will be listed on the promissory note. If each of the borrowers is to be individually liable for the entire loan amount, then the note will state that the borrowers are "jointly and severally" liable for the debt.

A promissory note used in a real estate transaction doesn't need to contain a legal description of the property, because the note concerns only the debt, not the property.

Fig. 9.2 Promissory note

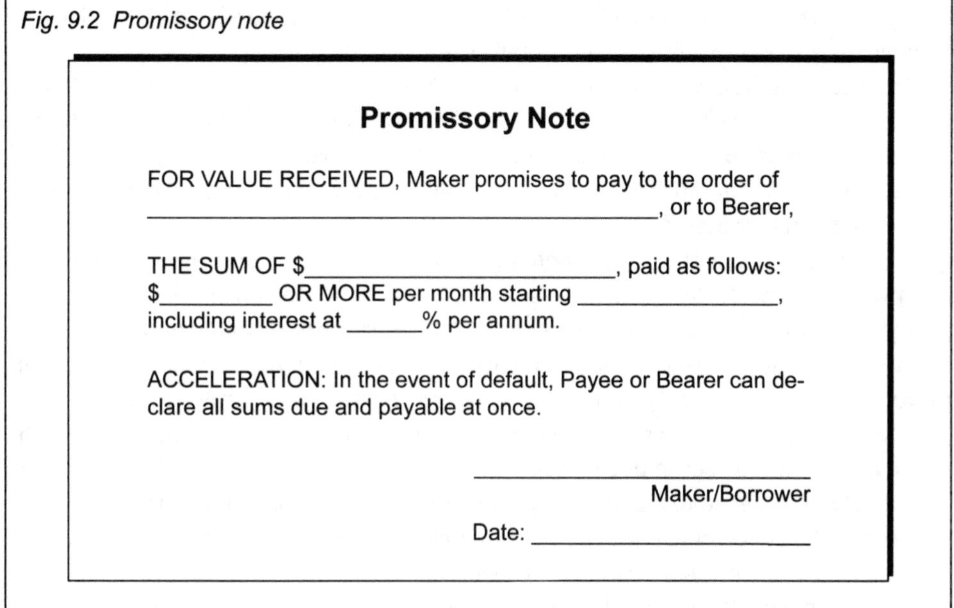

Promissory Note

FOR VALUE RECEIVED, Maker promises to pay to the order of
_______________________________________, or to Bearer,

THE SUM OF $_______________________, paid as follows:
$_________ OR MORE per month starting _______________,
including interest at ______% per annum.

ACCELERATION: In the event of default, Payee or Bearer can declare all sums due and payable at once.

____
Maker/Borrower

Date: ___________________

The legal description is instead included in the security instrument. Because the promissory note doesn't concern the property, it ordinarily isn't recorded.

The note usually explains the consequences of a failure to repay the loan as agreed. Real estate lenders often protect themselves with late charges, acceleration clauses, and similar provisions; these will be discussed later in this chapter.

Sometimes a promissory note will provide that the borrower must keep a certain amount of money on deposit with the lender as a condition of the loan. The amount of money required to be on deposit is referred to as a compensating balance.

Types of Notes. There are various types of promissory notes, classified according to the way the principal and interest are paid off. With a **straight note** (also called a **term note**), the regular periodic payments during the loan term are **interest-only payments**: they cover the interest that's accruing, but pay back none of the principal. The full amount of the principal is due in a lump sum (called a **balloon payment**) when the loan term ends. With an **installment note**, the periodic payments include part of the principal as well as interest. If the installment note is **fully amortized**, the periodic payments are enough to pay off the entire loan, both principal and interest, by the end of the term.

Whether the payments are interest-only or amortized, the interest paid on a real estate loan is **simple interest**. This means it is computed annually on the remaining principal balance. (This is in contrast to compound interest, which is computed on the principal amount plus the accrued interest.)

Because the interest due on a real estate loan is computed on the remaining principal balance, a straight note will cost the borrower more in interest over the life of the loan than an amortized loan. This is because the balance of an amortized loan is continually getting smaller; the amount of interest paid on the amortized loan is reduced with each payment. (Amortization is discussed in more detail in Chapter 10.)

Signing and Endorsing a Note. In most cases, a promissory note is a **negotiable instrument**, which means that the payee—the lender—has the option of assigning the debt to someone else by endorsing the note. Endorsing a promissory note transfers the right to payment to another party, in the same way that endorsing a check does. (A check is another example of a negotiable instrument.)

Because the payee can assign the note to a third party, only one copy of the note is signed by the maker. This is for the maker's protection, to prevent the payee from assigning the note more than once, which would mean that more than one party could demand payment from the maker. When the debt is paid off, the signed copy is returned to the maker marked "Paid."

To be negotiable, a promissory note must state that it is payable either "to the order of" someone or "to bearer." To sell a note (at the secondary market level), the payee endorses it to a third party purchaser. If the purchaser buys the note for value, in good faith, and without notice of defenses against it, then the purchaser is a **holder in due course**. If the holder in due course later sues the maker for nonpayment, certain defenses that the maker might have been able to raise against the payee can't be raised against the holder in due course.

If a note is endorsed to a particular person, that's called a special endorsement. Otherwise, the endorsement is said to be "in blank." A payee may also specify that the endorsement is **without recourse** (or without warranty). This means that the matter of future payments is strictly between the maker and the third party purchaser; the original payee won't be liable to the holder in due course if the maker fails to pay as agreed. An endorsement without recourse is sometimes called a qualified endorsement.

Security Instruments

When someone borrows money to buy real estate, in addition to signing a promissory note in favor of the lender, she's also required to sign a security instrument. As we said earlier, the security instrument is either a mortgage or a deed of trust.

Relationship Between Note and Security Instrument. It's important to understand the relationship between the promissory note and the security instrument. The promissory note is the borrower's binding promise to repay the loan. The security instrument is a contract that makes the real property collateral for the loan; it secures the loan by creating a lien on the property. If the borrower doesn't repay the loan as agreed, the security instrument gives the lender the right to foreclose on the property.

A promissory note can be enforced even if it isn't accompanied by a security instrument. If the borrower doesn't repay as agreed, then the lender can file a lawsuit and obtain a judgment against the defaulting borrower. But without a security instrument, the lender might have no way of collecting the judgment. For example, the borrower may have already sold all of his property, leaving nothing for the lender (now the judgment creditor) to obtain a lien against.

Title Theory vs. Lien Theory. To understand how security instruments work, it's useful to know how they developed. Historically, to protect the lender against default, a real estate borrower was required to transfer title to the property to the lender for the term of the loan. The borrower remained in possession of the property and had the full use of it, but the lender held title until the loan was paid off. If it wasn't paid off as agreed, the lender could take possession of the property.

This arrangement—in which title to property is given as collateral, but the borrower retains possession—is called **hypothecation**. When title is transferred only as collateral, unaccompanied by possessory rights, it is called bare title, naked title, or **legal title**. The property rights the borrower retains (without legal title) are referred to as equitable rights or **equitable title**.

In the United States today, the execution of a mortgage or a deed of trust is still regarded as a transfer of legal title to the lender or trustee in a handful of states. Those states are called "title theory" states. However, most states now follow "lien theory." According to lien theory, execution of a mortgage or a deed of trust only creates a lien against the property; it doesn't transfer title. The borrower retains full title to the property throughout the term of the loan, and the lender simply has the right to foreclose on the lien if the borrower defaults.

California has a mixed approach. It is a lien theory state in regard to mortgages, but can be considered a title theory state in regard to deeds of trust. We'll explain this in more detail shortly.

There actually aren't many differences between lending and foreclosure procedures in title theory and lien theory states now; the distinction is more theoretical than practical. Under either theory, the borrower will lose the property if the loan isn't repaid.

Of course, personal property as well as real property may be used as collateral for a loan. When a borrower transfers possession of an item of personal property to a lender pending repayment of the loan, it's called a **pledge**. Alternatively, the borrower may retain possession of the personal property and give the lender a security interest in it. In that case, the borrower signs a document called a **security agreement**. A security agreement is the equivalent of a mortgage or deed of trust for personal property.

Mortgage vs. Deed of Trust. Now let's consider the two types of real property security instruments: mortgages and deeds of trust. Both are contracts in which a real property owner gives someone else a security interest in the property, usually as collateral for a loan. The most important difference between a mortgage and a deed of trust concerns the procedures for foreclosure in the event that the borrower defaults. We will discuss the foreclosure process later in this chapter.

There are two parties to a mortgage: the **mortgagor** and the **mortgagee**. The mortgagor is the property owner and borrower. The mortgagee is the lender.

A deed of trust (sometimes called a trust deed) has three parties: the **trustor** or **grantor** (the borrower), the **beneficiary** (the lender), and the **trustee**. The trustee is a neutral third party who will handle the foreclosure process, if that proves necessary.

Foreclosure can be considerably easier with a deed of trust than with a mortgage, which makes deeds of trust popular with lenders. In California and a number of other states, deeds of trust are now much more widely used than mortgages.

The terminology used in a deed of trust has its roots in title theory. The document is called a "deed," and it conveys legal title to the trustee; the trustor has equitable title during the loan term. The trustee holds the deed "in trust" pending repayment of the debt. The trustee's title is inactive unless a default occurs. When the loan has been repaid, the trustee "reconveys" title to the trustor.

Note that the terms "mortgage" and "mortgage loan" are often used to refer to any type of loan secured by real property, whether the security instrument actually used in the transaction is a mortgage or a deed of trust.

Borrower's Signature. A mortgage or a deed of trust is valid only if it's in writing and signed by the borrower (the property owner).

Recording. Whether it's a mortgage or a deed of trust, the lender should record the security instrument immediately, at the time the loan is made. The security instrument doesn't have to be recorded to create a valid lien on the property, but without recording only the lender and the borrower would know the lien exists. Other parties who acquired an interest in the property without notice of the lender's security interest wouldn't be subject to it, and subsequent liens would have priority over the lender's.

A real estate licensee who acts as a mortgage loan broker in a transaction is responsible for recording the security instrument. It generally must be recorded before the loan funds are disbursed, but can be recorded within ten days afterward with the written authorization of the lender.

Instruments as Personal Property. Note that even though it creates a lien against real property, a mortgage or deed of trust is itself classified as personal property. A promissory note is also personal property.

Assignment. When a lender sells a mortgage or deed of trust to an investor, in addition to endorsing the promissory note, the lender executes a document called an assignment of mortgage (or deed of trust).

The investor may request an **offset statement** from the borrower. In an offset statement, the borrower confirms the status of the loan (the interest rate, principal balance, etc.) and describes any claims that could affect the investor's interest. The investor may also obtain a similar statement concerning the loan's status from the lender; this is called a **beneficiary's statement**.

Provisions in Finance Documents

Next, let's look at key provisions in the legal documents for a real estate loan. Some of these are essential, while others are optional, or used only in certain situations. Some of them may appear in the promissory note as well as, or instead of, the security instrument. And in a few cases (noted below), there's a distinction between the type of provision found in a mortgage and the type found in a deed of trust.

Mortgaging or Granting Clause. A security instrument must include a statement expressing what the instrument is designed to do, indicating that the property is being promised as security for the loan. In a mortgage, this is called the mortgaging clause. In a deed of trust, it's called the granting clause, and it typically states that the borrower "grants and conveys" title to the property to the trustee.

Once a property has been promised as security for a loan, the borrower must get permission from the lender before making any changes that will affect either the value of the property (such as changing the boundaries of the lot) or the priority of the lien (such as entering into a debt consolidation agreement). Furthermore, the lender's lien will extend to any after-acquired title the borrower obtains in the property; for example, if the borrower improves the property, the lender's lien attaches to the improvements.

Property Description. Like a deed or any other document that transfers an interest in real estate, the security instrument must contain a complete and unambiguous description of the collateral property.

Taxes and Insurance. Security instruments invariably require the borrower to pay general real estate taxes, special assessments, and hazard insurance premiums when due. If the borrower were to allow the taxes to become delinquent or the insurance to lapse, the value of the lender's security interest could be severely diminished—by tax lien foreclosure or by a fire, for example.

Acceleration Clause. An acceleration clause states that if the borrower defaults, the lender has the option of declaring the entire loan balance—all of the principal still owed—due and payable immediately. This is referred to as **accelerating** the loan or "calling the note." (You may also hear an acceleration clause referred to as a **call provision**.) If the borrower fails to pay the balance as demanded, the lender can sue on the note or foreclose on the property.

An acceleration clause usually appears in both the promissory note and the security instrument. Acceleration can be triggered by failure to make loan payments as agreed in the note, or by breach of a provision in the security instrument, such as failure to keep the property insured.

An acceleration clause in a promissory note doesn't have any effect on the negotiability of the note, although it may make the note more attractive to investors.

Alienation Clause. An alienation clause is also called a **due-on-sale clause**. This provision gives the lender the right to accelerate the loan—demanding immediate payment of the entire loan balance, as described above—if the borrower sells the property or otherwise alienates an interest in it. (Alienation refers to any transfer of an interest in real estate; see Chapter 3.) An alienation clause doesn't prohibit the sale of the property, but it allows the lender to force the borrower to pay off the loan if the property is sold without the lender's approval.

Whether or not there is an alienation clause in the mortgage or deed of trust, sale of the property doesn't extinguish the lender's lien. If the loan isn't paid off at closing, the buyer will take title subject to the lien. The buyer may also arrange to assume the loan.

In an **assumption**, the borrower sells the security property to a buyer who agrees to accept legal responsibility for the loan and pay it off according to its terms. The buyer takes on primary liability to the lender for repayment of the loan, but the seller (the original borrower) retains secondary liability in case the buyer defaults.

By contrast, when a buyer takes title subject to an existing mortgage or deed of trust without assuming it, the seller remains fully liable for the debt. The buyer isn't personally liable to the lender, although in case of default the lender can still foreclose on the property.

Even though the sale of the property doesn't extinguish the mortgage or deed of trust lien, lenders prefer to have the opportunity to approve or reject a prospective buyer. Thus, most mortgages and deeds of trust include an alienation clause. After evaluating a proposed buyer and concluding that he's creditworthy, the lender may agree to an assumption of the loan. The lender will charge an assumption fee and may also raise the interest rate on the loan. In most cases, the lender will release the original borrower from any further liability; this is called a novation.

Late Payment Penalty. If a lender wants to impose a penalty for late payments, the penalty must be clearly defined in the finance documents. California law generally restricts these penalties to 6% of the overdue payment on an owner-occupied dwelling, while federal law limits the penalties on federally insured and high-cost mortgages to 4% of the overdue payment, with certain exceptions. California law requires that a payment be at least 10 days late before any penalty can be assessed, while the federal law concerning high-cost mortgage requires a 15-day period.

Note that late payment penalties aren't considered to be interest on the loan, so they aren't deductible on the borrower's income tax return.

Lock-in Clause. A lock-in clause prohibits the borrower from **prepaying** the loan—paying the lender before payment is due. The borrower is "locked in" to the loan for a specified number of months or years (or even for the full term), in order to protect the lender's expected yield on its investment. In California, the finance documents for a loan on residential property with four units or less cannot contain a lock-in clause; the borrower must be allowed to prepay at any time. However, a prepayment penalty is not prohibited for such a loan, subject to the restrictions described below.

Prepayment Penalty. Under the terms of some loans, the lender may impose a penalty if the borrower prepays all or part of the loan balance. For example, a promissory note might state, "The borrower may prepay up to 15% of the original loan amount during any twelve-month period without penalty. If the borrower prepays more than 15%, a prepayment fee equal to six months' interest on the excess will be charged."

A prepayment penalty is intended to compensate the lender for interest that it expected to collect, but won't be collecting because the borrower is paying the loan off early. The prepayment of a loan without a penalty does not in itself cause a direct loss to the lender, but the lender's profit on the loan will be less than expected.

A lender may be willing to waive a prepayment penalty if market interest rates are high. Under those circumstances, when borrowers prepay their loans, the lender can turn around and lend the same money at a higher rate.

California law places restrictions on prepayment penalties for loans secured by owner-occupied residential property with up to four units. For these loans, the lender can charge prepayment penalties only during the first five years of the loan term. The borrower is allowed to prepay up to 20% of the original principal amount in any twelve-month period without penalty.

Federal law also limits prepayment penalties; for example, they are prohibited in adjustable-rate mortgages and certain high-cost loans. In addition, loans that will be insured or guaranteed by the federal government (FHA or VA loans, for example) cannot include a prepayment penalty provision, and loans that are going to be sold to Fannie Mae or Freddie Mac also do not ordinarily include one. As a result, institutional lenders generally don't charge prepayment penalties on home loans.

A loan without a prepayment penalty is sometimes referred to as an **open mortgage**. When prepayment is allowed without penalty, the promissory note usually states that the borrower can make the required payment "or more" on the specified payment date.

Subordination Clause. Occasionally a security instrument includes a subordination clause, which states that the instrument will have lower lien priority than another mortgage or deed of trust to be executed in the future. The clause makes it possible for a later security instrument to assume a higher priority position—usually first lien position—even though this earlier security instrument was executed and recorded first.

Subordination clauses are common in mortgages and deeds of trust that secure purchase loans for unimproved land, when the borrower is planning to get a construction loan later on. The construction lender will demand first lien position for its loan. Lien priority is ordinarily determined by recording date ("first in time is first in right"), but the subordination clause in the earlier land loan allows the later construction loan to have first lien position.

A subordination clause benefits the borrower, because it makes it easier for the borrower to obtain additional financing on the security property.

Defeasance Clause. A defeasance clause states that when the debt has been paid, the borrower will regain title and the security instrument will be canceled.

If the security instrument is a deed of trust, when the trustor has repaid the loan, the lien is removed by means of a **deed of reconveyance**, also called a reconveyance deed. Within 30 days after the loan payoff, the beneficiary (lender) must submit a request for reconveyance to the trustee. Within 21 days after receiving the request, the trustee must execute and record a deed of reconveyance. If these requirements aren't fulfilled, the responsible parties can be fined and ordered to pay damages to cover any loss resulting from the failure to record the lien release document promptly.

When a debt secured by a mortgage has been paid in full, a document called a **certificate of discharge** (or sometimes a "satisfaction of mortgage") is used to release the mortgage lien. The mortgagee must record the certificate of discharge within 30 days, or be subject to the penalties listed above.

Either a certificate of discharge or a deed of reconveyance may be referred to as a **lien release**. After a mortgage or deed of trust lien has been released, upon the written request of the borrower, the mortgagee or trustee is required to return the original note and security instrument to the borrower.

Foreclosure

If a borrower doesn't repay a secured loan as agreed, the lender may foreclose and collect the debt from the proceeds of a forced sale. A lender may also declare a default and foreclose if some other violation of the loan agreement occurs, such as an illegal use of the property, or a failure to maintain the property or keep it insured. Establishing the lender's right to foreclose is the basic purpose of a security instrument.

There are two main forms of foreclosure: judicial and nonjudicial. As a general rule, mortgages are foreclosed judicially, and deeds of trust are foreclosed nonjudicially. We'll give an overview of each form, then discuss alternatives to foreclosure and steps lenders may be required to take before starting the foreclosure process.

Judicial Foreclosure. As the term suggests, a judicial foreclosure is carried out through the court system. When a mortgage borrower defaults, the lender files a lawsuit against the borrower in the county where the collateral property is located. If there are any junior lienholders (lienholders whose liens have lower priority than the mortgage being foreclosed on), they are also included in the foreclosure action, so that they can take steps to protect their interests. (A junior lienholder may be adversely affected by foreclosure of a senior lien if the sale proceeds aren't sufficient to pay off all of the liens against the property.)

The lender records a **lis pendens**, which is a notice of a pending legal action (in this case, the foreclosure action) that could affect specified real property. A lis pendens makes the final court judgment binding on anyone who might acquire an interest in the property while the foreclosure action is pending.

When the complaint is heard in court, in the absence of unusual circumstances, the judge will issue a **decree of foreclosure**, ordering the property to be sold to satisfy the debt. The judge appoints a receiver to conduct the sale. The sale, which takes the form of a public auction, is sometimes referred to as a **sheriff's sale**.

Reinstatement. While the foreclosure action is pending, the borrower can "cure" the loan default by paying all the past due amounts, plus the costs and fees of the lawsuit. This is called **reinstatement**. When the loan is reinstated, all foreclosure proceedings are terminated, and the mortgage continues in full force and effect. Once the decree of foreclosure is issued, this right of reinstatement no longer exists.

Redemption. Sometimes the borrower has one more chance to reclaim the property. After the sheriff's sale, the borrower may have the right to **redeem** the property by paying off the entire debt, including interest, costs, and fees. The time period during which this **statutory right of redemption** exists varies. The redemption period continues for three months after the sale if the sale proceeds were enough to pay off the debt, plus interest, costs, and fees. The redemption period continues for one year after the sale date if the proceeds weren't enough to pay off the full debt. However, if the lender waives its right to a deficiency judgment (discussed below) or is prohibited from obtaining a deficiency judgment, there's no statutory right of redemption at all.

Certificate of Sale. If the property is sold subject to the statutory right of redemption, the successful bidder at the sheriff's sale receives a **certificate of sale** instead of a deed. The borrower is entitled to keep possession of the property during the redemption period, provided she pays a reasonable rent to the holder of the certificate of sale. Only at the end of the redemption period is the certificate holder given a **sheriff's deed**, which transfers title and the right of possession.

The redemption period makes bidding at a sheriff's sale unappealing to many investors, who would generally prefer to take title to a purchased property without delay. For this reason, there are often no outside bidders at a judicial foreclosure sale, and the lender acquires the property by bidding the amount the borrower owes. This is called **credit bidding**.

If there are outside bidders at the auction and the proceeds from the sale exceed the amount necessary to satisfy all valid liens against the property, the surplus belongs to the borrower.

Deficiency Judgments. If the proceeds of the foreclosure sale are insufficient to satisfy the debt, the lender can obtain a **deficiency judgment** against the borrower, unless the transaction is exempted by the antideficiency rules. A deficiency judgment is a personal judgment against the borrower for the difference between the amount owing on the debt and the net proceeds from the foreclosure sale.

The antideficiency rules prohibit deficiency judgments under the following circumstances:

1. when the fair market value of the property exceeds the amount of the debt;
2. when the security instrument is a purchase money mortgage given to the seller for all or part of the purchase price (seller financing);
3. when the security instrument is a mortgage given to a third-party lender to finance the purchase of an owner-occupied dwelling with four or fewer units; or
4. after a residential short sale has been completed with the lender's consent. (In a short sale, the mortgagor sells the property for less than the remaining amount of indebtedness due at the time of sale.)

As you can see, a deficiency judgment would be prohibited after foreclosure of a typical home purchase loan.

Nonjudicial Foreclosure. Deeds of trust have a special provision that mortgages generally lack: a **power of sale** clause. If the borrower defaults, this provision authorizes the trustee to sell the property, through a process known as nonjudicial foreclosure. To foreclose nonjudicially, it's not necessary to file a lawsuit or get a decree of foreclosure from a judge. Instead, the trustee can sell the property at an auction called a **trustee's sale**, then use the sale proceeds to pay off the debt owed to the lender (beneficiary). At a trustee's sale, as at a sheriff's sale, the lender may credit bid, acquiring the property for the amount owed, if no one else bids more. And if a trustee's sale results in a surplus, the excess amount belongs to the borrower.

Notices of Default and Sale. A nonjudicial foreclosure must be conducted in accordance with the procedures prescribed by statute. First, the trustee must record a **notice of default** in the county where the property is located, and also send a copy of the notice to the borrower and all lienholders. The trustee must wait at least three months before taking the next step: issuing a **notice of sale**. The three-month wait-

Fig. 9.3 Comparison of mortgages and deeds of trust

Security Instruments	
Mortgage	**Deed of Trust**
• Mortgagor and mortgagee • Judicial foreclosure • Reinstatement before decree of foreclosure • Redemption after sheriff's sale • Deficiency judgment allowed (subject to limitations)	• Trustor, beneficiary, and trustee • Nonjudicial foreclosure • Reinstatement before trustee's sale • No post-sale redemption • No deficiency judgment

ing period is mandatory, but the notice of sale can be filed up to five days before the end of the three-month period. The date set for the sale may be no earlier than three months plus 20 days from the filing of the notice of default. The notice of sale must be recorded, posted on the security property, and sent to everyone who received a notice of default. In addition, the notice of sale must be published in a newspaper of general circulation at least once a week for three weeks.

Reinstatement and Redemption. As with a mortgage foreclosure, the borrower under a deed of trust has a period in which he can reinstate the loan and stop the foreclosure proceedings. The borrower may reinstate the loan at any time from the notice of default up until five business days before the sale. This means the reinstatement period is at least three months and 15 days. The loan is reinstated by paying all past-due installments, plus costs and fees. If the loan is reinstated, the trustee can't sell the property.

Alternatively, the borrower can redeem the property by paying off the full balance of the loan plus costs at any time prior to the actual sale. The borrower also has the right to retain possession of the property until the sale takes place.

Trustee's Deed. The successful bidder at the trustee's sale receives a **trustee's deed**, which terminates all of the borrower's rights in the property. There's no post-sale redemption period or right of possession for the borrower, as there may be in a judicial foreclosure.

Deficiency Judgments. After the nonjudicial foreclosure of a deed of trust, the lender's recovery is limited to the proceeds of the trustee's sale. The lender can't bring any further action against the borrower, even if the sale proceeds don't cover the amount owed on the loan. A suit to recover the deficiency is barred by the anti-deficiency rules discussed above. However, if a deed of trust is foreclosed judicially, a deficiency judgment may be possible.

Protection of Junior Lienholders. A trustee's sale under a deed of trust extinguishes not only the borrower's interest in the property, but also the interests of any junior lienholders (those with liens subordinate to the deed of trust). A junior lienholder gets a share of the sale proceeds only if there's money left over after senior liens have been paid off.

To provide junior lienholders with some protection, the law requires the senior lienholder to send notices of default and sale to everyone who has a recorded interest in the property that's junior to the lien being foreclosed on. If the notices aren't sent to a lienholder of record, that lienholder isn't bound by the trustee's sale.

A junior lienholder who receives a notice of default can protect her interest by paying the delinquencies on the senior lien (curing the default) and adding the amount of these payments to the balance due under the junior lien. The junior lienholder may then foreclose on her own lien. A purchaser at a junior lienholder's sale takes title to the property subject to the senior liens.

Comparison of Judicial and Nonjudicial Foreclosure. From a lender's point of view, nonjudicial foreclosure has two main advantages over judicial foreclosure. First, it's often faster, since court proceedings can be very slow. Second, the trustee's sale is final; there's no statutory redemption period afterward. The disadvantage of nonjudicial foreclosure for the lender is that there's no right to a deficiency judgment after the trustee's sale. If the proceeds of the trustee's sale aren't enough to satisfy the debt, the lender takes a loss. The lender isn't allowed to sue the borrower to make up the deficiency.

Alternatives to Foreclosure. There are three alternatives to foreclosure for defaulting homeowners: loan workouts, deeds in lieu of foreclosure, and short sales. A lender might agree to one of these alternatives to save time, money, and aggravation.

Loan Workouts. In some situations, arranging a loan workout with the lender is the simplest way to avoid foreclosure. Some workouts involve an adjustment in the repayment schedule, often referred to as a **forbearance**. The borrower gets extra time to make up a missed payment, or is allowed to stop making payments altogether for a limited time. (The skipped payments are added on to the repayment schedule.) If a forbearance wouldn't solve the problem—for instance, if the payment amount is about to increase dramatically, far beyond the borrower's means—the lender may agree to modify the terms of the loan. A **loan modification** might involve changing an adjustable-rate mortgage into a fixed-rate mortgage (to prevent it from resetting to a higher interest rate), reducing the interest rate, or reducing the amount of principal owed, for example.

Homeowners facing foreclosure may turn to a business or an individual (often a real estate agent) who offers loan modification or forbearance services, negotiating workouts with lenders in exchange for a fee. To help prevent fraud, if a loan is secured by residential property with up to four units, it's illegal to collect an advance fee for these services. Compensation can be accepted only after the services have been fully performed. (See Chapter 16 for more information about advance fees.) Also, before entering into a fee agreement, borrowers must be given a notice explaining that it isn't necessary to pay for loan modification or forbearance services; they can negotiate with their lender directly, or obtain the same services for free from a federally approved housing counseling agency.

Fig. 9.4 Preventing foreclosure

Alternatives to Foreclosure

- Loan workout
  - forbearance
  - loan modification
- Deed in lieu of foreclosure
- Short sale

Illegal to collect advance fees for loan modification or foreclosure consulting services

Deed in Lieu of Foreclosure. A defaulting borrower who can't negotiate a loan workout may opt to give the lender a deed in lieu of foreclosure, often just called a deed in lieu. The deed in lieu transfers title from the borrower to the lender; this satisfies the debt and stops foreclosure proceedings. The borrower will want to make sure that the lender doesn't have the right to sue for a deficiency following the sale.

The lender takes title subject to any other liens that encumber the property. Thus, before accepting a deed in lieu, the lender will determine what other liens have attached to the property since the original loan was made.

Short Sales. Another alternative to foreclosure is a short sale, sometimes referred to as a debt forgiveness sale. In a short sale, the owner sells the house for whatever it will bring (something "short" of the amount owed, because the home's market value has decreased). The lender receives the sale proceeds and, in return, releases the borrower from the debt. Under California law, a lender who holds first lien position on residential property and agrees to a short sale cannot seek a deficiency judgment against the borrower.

The existence of junior liens won't necessarily prevent a lender from approving a short sale. With a short sale—in contrast to a deed in lieu—the lender isn't taking responsibility for the property or its liens. However, junior liens will complicate matters, since all of the lienholders must consent to the sale. Junior lienholders aren't likely to get much, if anything, from a short sale, so they may well be unwilling to approve the transaction. In this situation, foreclosure may be inevitable.

A real estate agent who provides an opinion of value in connection with a residential short sale may be subject to disciplinary action (license suspension or revocation) if it's determined that the opinion was intended to manipulate the lender into rejecting the proposed sale, or to obtain a listing or some other financial advantage for the agent.

Foreclosure Consultants. Once the foreclosure process has begun, defaulting borrowers might decide to hire a foreclosure consultant. Foreclosure consultants offer to help borrowers get their loans reinstated, stop or postpone the foreclosure proceedings, obtain surplus proceeds after a foreclosure sale, and so on. The business has been rife with fraudulent practices, such as charging high fees while providing worthless services or no services at all. As a result, the Federal Trade Commission recently introduced new rules governing for-profit companies that offer paid services to homeowners seeking assistance with modifications or foreclosure. Among other things, these rules prohibit such companies from making false or misleading claims, and require them to disclose certain information about their services.

Additionally, state law requires residential foreclosure consultants to have a written contract with their clients that gives the clients a right of rescission if they want to back out of the contract within five days after signing it. As with loan modification services, advance fees are not allowed. There are also limits on the amount of compensation foreclosure consultants can charge, and they're prohibited from acquiring an interest in a client's home through foreclosure.

Homeowner Bill of Rights. Another issue for defaulting borrowers has been lender and mortgage servicer misconduct in the loan modification or foreclosure process. Many lenders and loan servicers have been accused of failing to negotiate modifications in good faith, using fraudulent documents, and other abusive practices. California's Homeowner Bill of Rights, which became effective in 2013, is intended to protect borrowers facing foreclosure from such practices. Under this law, once a loan modification application has been submitted, the lender (or loan servicer) can't proceed with a foreclosure until it makes a decision on the modification application.

In addition, the borrower must be given a "single point of contact": one person representing the lender or servicer who will work through the modification process with the borrower. The law also prohibits lenders and servicers from "robo-signing," or signing foreclosure documents without reviewing or verifying them.

If a lender or servicer violates this law, a borrower may sue for injunctive relief or damages. And a violation of this law by a real estate licensee will be considered a violation of the license law.

Real Estate Agents Providing Loan Services. Real estate agents are generally exempt from the rules concerning foreclosure consultants, but they can lose that exemption under certain circumstances. Also, real estate agents who offer to provide either foreclosure consulting services or loan modification services are required to have a mortgage loan originator's endorsement for their license.

Foreclosure vs. Bankruptcy. Although they can both happen to a person at the same time, foreclosure and bankruptcy are entirely separate legal procedures. A real property owner who is facing foreclosure is not necessarily also facing bankruptcy. And a property owner can declare bankruptcy without necessarily having his property foreclosed on.

Bankruptcy is a federal court procedure that enables a debtor to reduce, modify, or eliminate debts that have become unmanageable. If a mortgage or deed of trust borrower who is facing foreclosure files for bankruptcy, the foreclosure proceedings are temporarily stayed (put on hold). Any other actions by creditors are also stayed.

There are two types of consumer bankruptcy: Chapter 7 and Chapter 13. (A third type of bankruptcy, Chapter 11, applies only to businesses.) In Chapter 13, the debtor enters into a repayment plan to partially repay the creditors over time. The debtor is ordinarily allowed to keep her property.

In a Chapter 7 bankruptcy, most of the debtor's obligations are completely discharged. However, certain debts are nondischargeable. These include child support, alimony, student loans, and federal income taxes for the three years previous to filing bankruptcy.

In exchange for the discharge, the Chapter 7 debtor is required to surrender all nonexempt property. Household goods and cars are exempt (with certain limits); life insurance, pensions, and public benefits are also exempt.

If the debtor owns a home, the homestead exemption will protect at least some of the debtor's equity. In California, the exemption amount is $75,000 for an individual, $100,000 for a member of a family unit, and $175,000 for someone who's over 65 or disabled. If the debtor's equity is less than the applicable exemption amount and the mortgage payments are current, the debtor will be allowed to keep the home. If the debtor's equity is greater than the exemption amount, the home will be sold. (See Chapter 4 for more information about the homestead exemption.)

Types of Mortgage Loans

There are many types of mortgage loans, loans secured by real property that are used in various circumstances or designed to serve particular functions. In this section, we'll explain some of the types you're most likely to encounter or hear mentioned. Even though we'll generally be referring to these as mortgages or mortgage loans, remember that in California the security instrument used for these loans would usually be a deed of trust instead of a mortgage.

First Mortgage. A first mortgage is simply any security instrument that holds first lien position; it has the highest lien priority. A second mortgage is one that holds second lien position, and so on.

Senior and Junior Mortgages. Any mortgage that has a higher lien position than another is called a senior mortgage in relation to the other one, which is called a junior mortgage. A first mortgage is senior to a second mortgage; a second mortgage is junior to a first mortgage, but senior to a third.

As explained in Chapter 4, lien priority matters in the event of a foreclosure, since the sale proceeds are used to pay off the first lien first. If any money remains, the second lien is paid, then the third, and so on, until the money is exhausted. Obviously, it is much better to be in first lien position than in third.

Purchase Money Mortgage. This term is used in two ways. Sometimes it means any mortgage loan used to finance the purchase of the property that's the collateral for the loan: a buyer borrows money to buy property and gives the lender a mortgage on that same property to secure the loan.

In other cases, "purchase money mortgage" is used more narrowly, to mean a mortgage that a buyer gives to a seller in a seller-financed transaction. Instead of paying the full price in cash at closing, the buyer gives the seller a mortgage on the property and pays the price off in installments. In such a situation, the seller is said to "take back" or "carry back" the mortgage.

> **Example:** The sales price is $240,000. The buyer makes a $24,000 downpayment and signs a purchase money mortgage and a promissory note in favor of the seller for $216,000. The buyer will pay the seller in monthly installments at 7% interest over 15 years.

In this narrower sense, a purchase money mortgage is sometimes called a **soft money mortgage**, because the borrower receives credit instead of actual cash. If a borrower gives a lender a mortgage and receives cash in return (as with a bank loan), it's called a **hard money mortgage**.

Swing Loan. It often happens that buyers are ready to purchase a new home before they've succeeded in selling their current home. They need funds for their downpayment and closing costs right away, without waiting for the proceeds from the eventual sale of the current home. In this situation, the buyers may be able to obtain a swing loan. A swing loan is usually secured by equity in the property that's for sale, and it will be paid off when that sale closes. A swing loan may also be called a **gap loan** or a **bridge loan**.

Budget Mortgage. With a budget mortgage, the borrower's monthly payment includes not just principal and interest on the loan, but one-twelfth of the year's property taxes and hazard insurance premiums as well. The lender holds the tax and insurance payments in an impound account (reserve account) until they're due. Many residential loans are secured by budget mortgages. It's a practical way for lenders to make sure the property taxes and insurance premiums are paid on time.

Package Mortgage. When personal property is sold together with real estate, both the personal property and the real estate may be financed with a single loan. This is called a package mortgage. For example, if a buyer bought ovens, freezers, and other equipment along with a restaurant building, the purchase might be financed with a package mortgage.

Construction Loan. A construction loan (sometimes called an **interim loan**) is a temporary loan used to finance the construction of improvements on the land. When the construction is completed, the construction loan is replaced by permanent financing, which is called a **take-out loan**. A lender's promise to make a take-out loan at a later time when the borrower needs it is called a **standby loan commitment**.

If a construction loan has no specific maturity date (for example, if the loan is due "in five years"), the period of repayment begins to run on the date stated in the promissory note. For instance, if the loan term is five years and the note is dated January 10, but the loan funds aren't disbursed until March 15, the five-year period begins running on January 10.

Construction loans can be profitable, but they're considered quite risky. Accordingly, lenders charge high interest rates and loan fees on construction loans, then supervise the progress of the construction. There's always a danger that the borrower will overspend on a construction project and exhaust the loan proceeds before construction is completed. If the borrower can't afford to finish, the lender is left with a security interest in a partially completed project.

Lenders have devised a variety of plans for disbursement of construction loan proceeds that guard against overspending by the borrower. Perhaps the most common is the **fixed disbursement plan**. This calls for a series of predetermined disbursements, called **obligatory advances**, at various stages of construction. Interest begins to accrue with the first disbursement.

> **Example:** A construction loan agreement stipulates that the lender will release 10% of the proceeds when the project is 20% complete, and thereafter 20% draws will be available whenever construction has progressed another 20% toward completion.

The lender will often hold back 10% or more of the loan proceeds until the period for claiming mechanic's liens has expired, to protect against unpaid liens that could affect the marketability of the property. The construction loan agreement usually states that if a valid mechanic's lien is recorded, the lender may use the undisbursed portion of the loan to pay it off.

Blanket Mortgage. When a borrower mortgages more than one piece of real property as security for a single loan, it's called a blanket mortgage. For example, if one property doesn't provide sufficient collateral for a loan, another property that the borrower owns may be offered as additional collateral. The borrower will give the lender a blanket mortgage covering both properties.

Blanket mortgages are also used in subdivision development. For instance, a ten-acre parcel subdivided into twenty lots might be used to secure one loan made to the subdivider.

Blanket mortgages usually have a **partial release clause** (also called a partial satisfaction clause, or in a blanket deed of trust, a partial reconveyance clause). This provision requires the lender to release some of the security property from the blanket lien when specified portions of the overall debt have been paid off.

Example: A ten-acre parcel subdivided into twenty lots secures a $1,500,000 loan. After selling one lot for $175,000, the subdivider pays the lender $150,000 and receives a release for the lot that is being sold. The blanket mortgage is no longer a lien against that lot, so the subdivider can convey clear title to the lot buyer.

A release schedule determines how much of the loan must be paid off in order to have a lot released from the blanket lien. The borrower typically has to pay off a larger share of the loan to release the first lots sold than to release the last lots sold. This arrangement helps protect the lender's security interest, since the best lots in a development often sell first.

Note that a mortgage isn't the only type of lien that can be a blanket encumbrance. A contractor who provides labor or materials on more than one property owned by the same person can obtain a blanket mechanic's lien.

Participation Mortgage. A participation mortgage allows the lender to participate in the earnings generated by the mortgaged property, usually in addition to collecting interest payments on the principal. In some cases the lender participates by becoming a part-owner of the property. Participation loans are most common on large commercial projects where the lender is an insurance company or other large investor.

Shared Appreciation Mortgage. Real property generally appreciates (increases in value) over time. Appreciation ordinarily benefits only the property owner, by adding to his equity. (The equity is the difference between the market value of the property and the liens against it.) With a shared appreciation mortgage, however, the lender is entitled to a specified share of the increase in the property's value. This is sometimes called an **equity sharing** arrangement.

Wraparound Mortgage. A wraparound mortgage is a new mortgage that includes or "wraps around" an existing first mortgage on the property. Wraparounds are generally used only in seller-financed transactions.

Example: A home is being sold for $200,000; there is an existing $80,000 mortgage on the property. Instead of assuming that mortgage, the buyer merely takes title subject to it. The buyer gives the seller a $40,000 downpayment and a second mortgage for the remaining $160,000 of the purchase price. The $160,000 second mortgage is a wraparound mortgage. Each month, the buyer makes a payment on the wraparound to the seller, and the seller uses part of that payment to make the monthly payment on the underlying $80,000 mortgage.

Wraparound financing works only if the underlying loan does not contain an alienation clause (see the discussion earlier in this chapter). Otherwise the lender would require the seller to pay off the underlying loan at the time of sale. A wraparound arrangement should always be designed so that the underlying loan will be paid off before the wraparound, to ensure that the buyer's title will not still be encumbered with the seller's debt after the buyer has paid the full purchase price.

If the security instrument used for this type of financing arrangement is a deed of trust rather than a mortgage, it's called an **all-inclusive deed of trust**.

Open-end Mortgage. An open-end mortgage sets a borrowing limit, but allows the borrower to reborrow, when needed, any part of the debt that has been repaid, without having to negotiate a new mortgage. The interest rate on the loan is usually a variable rate that rises and falls with market interest rates. An open-end mortgage is often used as a business tool by builders and farmers.

Graduated Payment Mortgage. A graduated payment mortgage allows the borrower to make smaller payments at first and gradually step up to larger payments. For example, the payments might increase annually for the first three to five years of the loan, and then remain level for the rest of the loan term. This arrangement can benefit borrowers who expect their earnings to increase during the next few years.

Growing Equity Mortgage. A growing equity mortgage, sometimes called a rapid payoff mortgage, is also beneficial to borrowers whose income is expected to increase. This type of mortgage uses a fixed interest rate throughout its term, but payments will increase according to an index or preset schedule. The amount of the increase is applied directly to the principal balance, thus allowing the borrower to pay off the loan more quickly.

Subprime Mortgage. A subprime mortgage is a loan made to a borrower who wouldn't qualify for an ordinary mortgage loan, perhaps because her credit history or debt-to-income ratio doesn't meet the usual standards, or because she's unable or unwilling to provide the documentation usually required. A subprime lender typically charges higher interest rates and fees to offset the extra risk the loan entails. Subprime lending is discussed in more detail in Chapter 10.

Home Equity Loan. A borrower can obtain a mortgage loan using the equity in property that he already owns as collateral. This is called an equity loan. When the property is the borrower's residence, it's called a home equity loan.

Equity, as we said earlier, is the difference between a property's market value and the liens against it. In other words, it's the portion of the property's current value that the owner owns free and clear, which is therefore available to serve as collateral for another loan. A home equity loan is typically a second mortgage; the existing first mortgage is the loan the owner used to purchase the property.

Sometimes a home equity loan is used to finance remodeling or other improvements to the property. In other cases, it's used for expenses unrelated to the property, such as a major purchase, college tuition, or medical bills, or to pay off credit cards. The interest rate on the home equity loan is often much lower than the rate on the credit cards, and the interest on the loan is usually tax-deductible, whereas the credit card interest is not. (Mortgage interest is currently the only type of interest on consumer debt that is deductible. See Chapter 15.)

Instead of having to apply for a home equity loan when they need money for a particular purpose, some homeowners have a **home equity line of credit** (or **HELOC**) that they can draw on when the need arises. This works in much the same way as a credit card—with a credit limit and minimum monthly payments—except that the debt is automatically secured by the borrower's home. A HELOC is a revolving credit account, in contrast to a home equity loan, which is an installment loan with regular payments made over a certain term.

Reverse Mortgage. A reverse mortgage (sometimes called a reverse equity or reverse annuity mortgage) is designed to provide income to older homeowners. An owner borrows against his home's equity but will receive a monthly check from the lender, rather than making monthly payments to the lender. Typically, a reverse mortgage borrower must be over a certain age (for example, 62 or 65) and must own the home with little or no outstanding mortgage balance. The home usually must be sold when the owner dies in order to pay off the reverse mortgage.

Refinancing. Borrowers who refinance their mortgage are actually obtaining an entirely new mortgage loan to replace the existing one. The funds from the refinance loan are used to pay off the existing loan.

Refinancing may be obtained from the same lender that made the existing loan, or from a different lender. Borrowers often choose to refinance when market interest rates drop; refinancing at a lower interest rate can result in substantial savings over the long run. Another situation in which borrowers are likely to refinance is when the payoff date of the existing mortgage is approaching and a large balloon payment will be required.

In some cases, borrowers get a refinance loan for more than the amount needed to pay off their existing loan, so that they also receive cash from the transaction. This is called **cash-out refinancing**. Depending on the terms of the refinance loan, the additional funds might be used for property improvements, debt consolidation, or other purposes.

Land Contracts

Most real estate buyers finance their purchases with loans from an institutional lender. But as we've discussed, some transactions are financed by the seller; the seller extends credit to the buyer, accepting a downpayment and arranging to be paid over time, instead of requiring full payment at closing. In certain cases, a seller offers more favorable terms than institutional lenders (such as an exceptionally low interest rate), in order to attract a wider range of potential buyers and obtain a higher price for the property.

In a seller-financed transaction, the seller may have the buyer execute a mortgage or a deed of trust, just as an institutional lender would. (As explained earlier, this is often called a purchase money mortgage.) Sellers also have the option of using a third type of security instrument: the **land contract**, also called a contract for deed, installment sales contract, real estate contract, or contract of sale.

The parties to a land contract are the **vendor** (the seller) and the **vendee** (the buyer). The vendee agrees to pay the purchase price (plus interest) in installments over a specified number of years. The vendee takes possession of the property right away, but the vendor retains legal title until the full price has been paid. In the meantime, the vendee has equitable title to the property. When the contract is finally paid off, the vendor delivers the deed to the vendee.

The rights and responsibilities of the vendor and vendee under a land contract are discussed in more detail in Chapter 7.

Chapter Summary

1. The federal government influences real estate finance directly and indirectly through its fiscal and monetary policy. The federal deficit may affect the availability of investment funds. The Federal Reserve Board uses key interest rates, reserve requirements, and open market operations to implement monetary policy, influencing the pace of economic growth and market interest rates.

2. In the primary market, lenders make mortgage loans to borrowers. In the secondary market, mortgages are bought and sold by investors. The federal government created the major secondary market entities (Fannie Mae, Freddie Mac, and Ginnie Mae) to help moderate local real estate cycles.

3. A promissory note is a written promise to repay a debt. For a real estate loan, the borrower is required to sign a negotiable promissory note. The borrower is also required to sign a security instrument, to make the borrower's property collateral for the loan.

4. The two main types of security instruments are mortgages and deeds of trust. The central difference between the two is that a deed of trust includes a power of sale clause, which allows the trustee to foreclose nonjudicially in the event of default.

5. The provisions that may be found in a security instrument include a mortgaging or granting clause, a description of the property serving as collateral for the loan, a provision concerning taxes and insurance, an acceleration clause, an alienation clause, a late payment penalty provision, a lock-in clause, a prepayment penalty provision, and/or a subordination clause. If the security instrument doesn't include an alienation clause, the loan may be assumed without the lender's permission.

6. In a judicial foreclosure, the lender files a lawsuit and the court issues a decree of foreclosure. The borrower has the right to cure the default and reinstate the loan before the sheriff's sale, and a statutory right of redemption for a certain period afterwards. The lender may be entitled to a deficiency judgment. Mortgages are typically foreclosed judicially.

7. A deed of trust includes a power of sale clause, so it can be foreclosed nonjudicially, by the trustee. Nonjudicial foreclosure is generally faster and less expensive than judicial foreclosure. Until shortly before the trustee's sale, the borrower has the right to cure the default and reinstate the loan. After the sale, the borrower has no right of redemption. The lender can't obtain a deficiency judgment.

8. There are many types of mortgage loans, including purchase money, swing, budget, package, construction, blanket, participation, shared appreciation, wraparound, open-end, graduated payment, growing equity, subprime, home equity, and reverse mortgage loans. In a refinancing, a new mortgage loan is used to pay off an existing mortgage.

Key Terms

Federal Reserve Board—The body that regulates commercial banks and sets and implements the federal government's monetary policy; commonly called "the Fed."

Discount rate and federal funds rate—Two interest rates controlled by the Fed that have an effect on market interest rates.

Reserve requirements—The percentage of customer deposits that a commercial bank must keep on reserve with a Federal Reserve Bank.

Open market operations—The Fed's activities in buying and selling government securities.

Primary market—The finance market in which individuals obtain loans from banks, savings and loans, and other lenders.

Secondary market—The finance market in which mortgage loans are bought and sold as investments.

Promissory note—A written promise to repay a debt.

Mortgage—A two-party security instrument that gives the lender (mortgagee) the right to foreclose on the security property by judicial process if the borrower (mortgagor) defaults.

Deed of trust—A three-party security instrument that includes a power of sale clause, allowing the trustee to foreclose nonjudicially if the borrower (trustor) fails to pay the lender (beneficiary) or otherwise defaults.

Acceleration clause—A provision in loan documents that gives the lender the right to demand immediate payment in full if the borrower defaults.

Alienation clause—A provision in a security instrument that gives the lender the right to accelerate the loan if the borrower transfers the property. Also called a due-on-sale clause.

Assumption—When a borrower sells the security property to a buyer who agrees to take on personal liability for repayment of the existing mortgage or deed of trust.

Defeasance clause—A provision giving the borrower the right to regain title to the security property when the debt is repaid.

Certificate of discharge—The document a mortgagee gives to the mortgagor when the mortgage debt is paid off, releasing the property from the lien. Also called a satisfaction of mortgage.

Deed of reconveyance—The document a trustee gives the trustor when the debt secured by a deed of trust is paid off, releasing the property from the lien.

Land contract—A contract between a real estate seller (vendor) and a buyer (vendee), in which the seller retains legal title to the property while the buyer pays off the purchase price in installments.

Chapter Quiz

1. In a tight money market, when business is slow, a reduction in interest rates would be expected to cause:
   a) an increase in real estate sales
   b) more bank lending activity
   c) increased business activity
   d) All of the above

2. Which of the following actions by the Federal Reserve Board would tend to increase the money supply?
   a) Selling government securities on the open market
   b) Buying government securities on the open market
   c) Increasing the federal discount rate
   d) Increasing reserve requirements

3. Funds for single-family mortgage loans are supplied by:
   a) Fannie Mae
   b) savings and loan associations
   c) Both a) and b)
   d) Neither a) nor b)

4. With an installment note, the periodic payments:
   a) include both principal and interest
   b) are interest only
   c) are principal only
   d) are called balloon payments

5. A mortgage loan provision that permits the lender to declare the entire loan balance due upon default by the borrower is a/an:
   a) acceleration clause
   b) escalator clause
   c) forfeiture clause
   d) subordination clause

6. A mortgage loan provision that permits the lender to declare the entire loan balance due if the property is sold is a/an:
   a) escalator clause
   b) subordination clause
   c) alienation clause
   d) prepayment provision

7. After a sheriff's sale, the mortgagor has a specified period in which to redeem the property. This period is called the:
   a) lien period
   b) equitable redemption period
   c) statutory redemption period
   d) reinstatement period

8. After a trustee's sale, if there are any sale proceeds left over after paying off liens and foreclosure expenses, the money belongs to the:
   a) sheriff
   b) beneficiary
   c) trustee
   d) foreclosed owner

9. The document that a mortgagee gives a mortgagor after the debt has been completely paid off is called a:
   a) partial release
   b) certificate of discharge
   c) deed of reconveyance
   d) sheriff's deed

10. In a nonjudicial foreclosure, the borrower is entitled to:
    a) a statutory redemption period following the sheriff's sale
    b) a deficiency judgment
    c) a deed in lieu of foreclosure
    d) cure the default and reinstate the loan before the trustee's sale

11. When a buyer gives a mortgage to the seller rather than an institutional lender, it may be referred to as a:
    a) purchase money mortgage
    b) land contract
    c) shared appreciation mortgage
    d) reverse equity mortgage

12. A budget mortgage:
    a) is a loan made to a low-income borrower
    b) is a construction loan with a fixed disbursement plan
    c) is secured by personal property as well as real property
    d) has monthly payments that include taxes and insurance as well as principal and interest

13. The owner of five parcels of real property wants a loan. She offers all five parcels as security. She will be required to execute a:
    a) soft money mortgage
    b) participation mortgage
    c) package mortgage
    d) blanket mortgage

14. Victor is borrowing money to buy some land, and he plans to build a home on the property later on. To ensure that he will be able to get a construction loan when the time comes, Victor should make sure the mortgage he executes for the land loan includes a/an:
    a) lien waiver
    b) subordination clause
    c) acceleration clause
    d) wraparound clause

15. Under a fixed disbursement plan for a construction loan, the contractor is usually entitled to his final draw when:
    a) the project has been satisfactorily completed
    b) 80% of the work has been completed
    c) the building department issues a certificate of occupancy
    d) the period for claiming mechanic's liens expires

Answer Key

1. d) The Fed lowers interest rates during an economic downturn in an attempt to stimulate the economy.

2. b) When the Fed buys government securities, it puts more money into circulation, which increases the money supply.

3. c) Mortgage funds come from primary market lenders (such as a savings and loan) and from the secondary market (where investors like Fannie Mae buy mortgages).

4. a) An installment note involves periodic payments that include some of the principal as well as interest.

5. a) An acceleration clause gives the lender the right to declare the entire debt immediately due and payable if the borrower defaults.

6. c) An alienation clause allows the lender to accelerate the loan if the borrower transfers the security property without the lender's approval.

7. c) The statutory redemption period is the period of time after the sheriff's sale in which the borrower has the right to redeem the property by paying off the entire debt, plus costs.

8. d) Any excess proceeds from a foreclosure sale belong to the borrower—that is, to the foreclosed owner.

9. b) When the debt has been fully paid off, a mortgagee gives the mortgagor a certificate of discharge, releasing the property from the lien.

10. d) In the nonjudicial foreclosure of a deed of trust, the trustor is permitted to cure the default and reinstate the loan before the trustee's sale is held.

11. a) A mortgage given by a buyer to a seller is sometimes called a purchase money mortgage.

12. d) A budget mortgage payment includes a share of the property taxes and hazard insurance as well as principal and interest.

13. d) A blanket mortgage has more than one parcel of property as collateral.

14. b) A subordination clause in the mortgage for the land loan would give it lower priority than a mortgage executed later on for a construction loan. Lenders generally require first lien position for construction loans, because they are considered especially risky.

15. d) Construction lenders usually delay the final disbursement until no more mechanic's liens can be filed.

Chapter 10

Applying for a Residential Loan

I. Choosing a Lender
   A. Types of mortgage lenders
   B. Loan costs
      1. Origination fees
      2. Discount points
      3. Interest rate lock-ins
   C. Truth in Lending Act
   D. California finance disclosure requirements
      1. Mortgage Loan Broker Law
      2. Seller Financing Disclosure Law
II. The Loan Application Process
   A. Preapproval
   B. Loan application form
   C. Underwriting the loan
   D. Subprime lending
III. Basic Loan Features
   A. Loan term
   B. Amortization
   C. Loan-to-value ratios
   D. Secondary financing
   E. Fixed and adjustable interest rates
IV. Residential Financing Programs
   A. Conventional loans
   B. FHA-insured loans
   C. Rural Housing Service loans
   D. VA-guaranteed loans
   E. Cal-Vet loans
V. Predatory Lending
VI. Mortgage Fraud

Chapter Overview

When it's time to arrange financing, a home buyer must shop for a loan, choose a lender, and fill out a loan application. Then the lender will evaluate the application and decide whether or not to approve the loan. The first part of this chapter describes the different types of lenders, explains loan fees, and discusses the Truth in Lending Act and state loan disclosure laws. The next sections cover the application form, the underwriting process, and the basic features of a home purchase loan, followed by an overview of residential financing programs. The chapter ends with a discussion of predatory lending and mortgage fraud.

Choosing a Lender

Many home buyers look to their real estate agent for guidance in choosing a lender. Agents should be familiar with the lenders in their area and know how to help buyers compare the loans that different lenders are offering. We're going to discuss the various types of lenders that make home purchase loans, the fees that lenders charge, the Truth in Lending Act, and state finance disclosure laws.

Types of Mortgage Lenders

Most home buyers finance their purchase with a loan from one of these sources of residential financing:

- commercial banks,
- thrift institutions,
- credit unions, and
- mortgage companies.

At one time, financial institutions in the United States were quite specialized. Each type of institution served a different function; each had its own types of services and its own types of loans. In recent decades, federal deregulation of depository institutions removed many of the restrictions that differentiated them. To a great extent, all depository institutions can now be regarded as "financial supermarkets," offering a wide range of services and loans—including residential mortgage loans.

There still are differences between the various types of mortgage lenders, in terms of lending practices and government regulations. Those differences don't necessarily affect a loan applicant who wants to finance the purchase of a home, however. A home buyer decides between two lenders because of the types of loans they're offering, the interest rates and fees they're charging, and the quality of service they provide, not because one is a savings and loan and the other is a mortgage company. Even so, it's worthwhile to have a general understanding of the different types of mortgage lenders.

Commercial Banks. A commercial bank is either a national bank, chartered (authorized to do business) by the federal government, or a state bank, chartered by a state government. Commercial banks are the largest source of investment funds in the

United States. As their name implies, they were traditionally oriented toward commercial lending activities, supplying short-term loans for business ventures and construction activities.

In the past, residential mortgages weren't a major part of commercial banks' business. That was partly because most of their customer deposits were demand deposits, subject to withdrawal on short notice or without notice, like the money in checking accounts. So the government limited the amount of long-term investments commercial banks could make. But eventually banks began accepting more and more long-term deposits; demand deposits now represent a considerably smaller share of banks' total deposits than they did at one time.

While banks have continued to emphasize commercial loans, they have also diversified their lending, with a substantial increase in personal loans and home mortgages, especially to already-existing customers. They now have a significant share of the residential finance market.

Thrift Institutions. Savings and loan associations and savings banks are often grouped together and referred to as thrift institutions, or thrifts. Like commercial banks, thrifts are chartered by either the federal government or a state government.

Savings and Loans. Savings and loans (S&Ls) started out in the nineteenth century strictly as residential real estate lenders. Over the years they carried on their original function, investing the majority of their assets in purchase loans for single-family homes. By the mid-1950s, they dominated local residential mortgage markets, becoming the nation's largest single source of funds for financing homes.

Many factors contributed to the dominance of savings and loans. One of the most important was that home purchase loans had become long-term loans (often with 30-year terms). S&Ls used the savings deposits of their customers as their main source of loan funds. Since most of the funds held by S&Ls were long-term deposits, S&Ls were comfortable making long-term home loans.

While savings and loans are involved in other types of lending, home mortgage loans remain their main focus. However, due to the increasing involvement of other types of lenders, S&Ls no longer dominate the residential finance market.

Savings Banks. Like S&Ls, savings banks also got their start in the nineteenth century. They offered financial services to small depositors, especially immigrants and members of the working class. They were called mutual savings banks (MSBs) because they were organized as mutual companies, owned by and operated for the benefit of their depositors (as opposed to stockholders).

Traditionally, MSBs were similar to savings and loans. They served their local communities. Their customers were individuals rather than businesses, and most of their deposits were savings deposits. Although the MSBs made many residential mortgage loans, they didn't concentrate on them to the extent that S&Ls did. The MSBs were also involved in other types of lending, such as personal loans.

Today savings banks can be organized as mutual companies or stock companies. Residential mortgages continue to be an important part of their business.

Credit Unions. Credit unions are depository institutions, like banks and thrifts. But unlike banks and thrifts, credit unions often serve only members of a particular group, such as the members of a union or a professional association, or the employees of a large company.

Credit unions traditionally provided small personal loans to their members. In recent years, many credit unions have emphasized home equity loans. (A home equity loan is a mortgage on the borrower's equity in the home she already owns. See Chapter 9.) Now many credit unions also make home purchase loans.

Mortgage Companies. Unlike banks, thrifts, and credit unions, mortgage companies aren't depository institutions, so they don't lend out depositors' funds. Instead, they often act as **loan correspondents**, intermediaries between large investors and home buyers applying for financing.

A loan correspondent lends an investor's money to buyers and then **services** the loans (collecting and processing the loan payments on behalf of the investor) in exchange for servicing fees. Banks and thrifts sometimes act as loan correspondents, but mortgage companies have specialized in this role.

Mortgage companies frequently act on behalf of large investors such as life insurance companies and pension funds. These investors control vast amounts of capital in the form of insurance premiums and employer contributions to employee pensions. This money generally isn't subject to sudden withdrawal, so it's well suited to investment in long-term mortgages. Since these large investors typically operate on a national scale, they have neither the time nor the resources to understand the particular risks of local real estate markets or to deal with the day-to-day management of their loans. So instead of making loans directly to borrowers, insurance companies, pension plans, and other large investors often hire local loan correspondents. They generally prefer large, long-term commercial loans and stay away from high-risk, short-term construction loans.

Mortgage companies also borrow money from banks on a short-term basis and use the money to make (or **originate**) loans, which they then package and sell to the secondary market entities and other private investors. Using short-term financing to make loans before selling them to permanent investors is referred to as **warehousing**.

Banks and thrifts generally keep some of the loans they make "in portfolio," instead of selling them to investors. In contrast, mortgage companies don't keep any of the loans they make. The loans are either made on behalf of an investor or else sold to an investor. In many cases, insurance companies, pension funds, and other large investors now simply buy loans from mortgage companies instead of using them as loan correspondents.

The number of mortgage companies increased rapidly during the 1990s, and they eventually came to dominate the residential finance market as savings and loans once had. Mortgage companies played a major role in the subprime lending boom, and recent problems in the subprime market have had a greater impact on mortgage companies than on other types of residential lenders, diminishing their market share. (Subprime lending is discussed later in this chapter.)

Mortgage companies are sometimes called **mortgage bankers**. Traditionally, a distinction was made between mortgage bankers and mortgage brokers. A **mortgage broker** simply negotiated loans, bringing borrowers together with lenders in exchange for a commission. Once a loan had been arranged, the mortgage broker's involvement ended. In contrast, a mortgage banker actually made loans (using an investor's funds or borrowed funds), sold or delivered the loans to an investor, and then (in many cases) serviced the loans to the end of their terms, in exchange for servicing fees. As a result of changes in the mortgage industry, there is no longer a clear-cut distinction between these two roles, and the more general term "mortgage company" is typically used instead of "mortgage banker" in most contexts.

Mortgage Loan Originators. Whether home buyers seeking financing apply to a bank, a thrift, a credit union, or a mortgage company, they're likely to receive assistance from a **mortgage loan originator**, or MLO. This might be a loan officer at a bank, a mortgage broker who works for a mortgage company, or a real estate agent acting as an independent mortgage broker, for example. The MLO typically discusses financing options with the buyers, helps them fill out a loan application form, gathers the necessary documentation, and submits the completed application package for processing and underwriting.

Under the definition established in the Secure and Fair Enforcement for Mortgage Licensing Act of 2008, known as the **SAFE Act**, a mortgage loan originator is any individual who, for compensation or gain, takes a residential mortgage loan application or offers or negotiates the terms of a residential mortgage loan. The SAFE Act requires MLOs to be licensed and/or registered through the Nationwide Mortgage Licensing System and Registry. Mortgage loan originators who work for a federally insured depository institution or a subsidiary have to register, but do not have to be licensed; most other MLOs must be registered and state-licensed. See Chapter 16 for information about the MLO endorsement for California real estate licensees.

A real estate licensee who provides only real estate brokerage services generally is not considered to be an MLO and therefore is exempt from the requirements of the SAFE Act. However, a real estate licensee who receives any compensation from a lender, a mortgage broker, or another mortgage loan originator is not exempt.

Private Lenders. Real estate limited partnerships, real estate investment trusts (see Chapter 2), and other types of private investment groups put a great deal of money into real estate. They often finance large residential developments and commercial ventures such as shopping centers and office buildings. They don't offer loans to individual home buyers, however.

From the home buyer's point of view, the most important type of private lender is the home seller. Sometimes sellers provide all of the financing for the purchase of their homes, and it's quite common for sellers to supplement the financing their buyers obtain from an institutional lender. In fact, sellers are the most common source of second (or junior) mortgages for home purchases. Sellers are an especially important source of financing when institutional loans are hard to come by or market interest rates are high.

Loan Costs

For the majority of buyers, the primary consideration in choosing a lender is how much the loan they need is going to cost. While the interest rate has the greatest impact, lenders impose other charges that can greatly affect the cost of a loan. Two of the most significant are origination fees and discount points. These are often lumped together and referred to simply as "points." The term "point" is short for "percentage point." A point is one percentage point (one percent) of the loan amount. For example, on a $100,000 loan, one point would be $1,000; six points would be $6,000.

Origination Fees. Processing loan applications and making loans is called loan origination. A loan origination fee is designed to pay for the administrative costs the lender incurs in processing a loan; it is sometimes called a service fee, an administrative charge, or just a loan fee. Institutional lenders charge an origination fee in almost every mortgage loan transaction. It's ordinarily paid by the buyer.

> **Example:** The buyer is borrowing $200,000, and the lender is charging 1.5 points (1.5% of the loan amount, or $3,000) as an origination fee. The buyer will pay this $3,000 fee to the lender in order to obtain the loan.

Discount Points. Lenders charge discount points to increase their upfront yield on a loan. (The yield is the return or profit on the investment.) By charging discount points, a lender not only gets interest throughout the loan term, but also collects an additional sum of money up front, when the loan is funded. As a result, the lender is willing to make the loan at a lower interest rate than it would have without the discount points. In effect, the lender is paid a lump sum at closing so the borrower can avoid paying more interest later. A lower interest rate also translates into a lower monthly payment.

Discount points aren't charged in all residential loan transactions, but they're quite common. The number of discount points charged depends partly on how the loan's interest rate compares to market interest rates. Typically, a lender offering an especially low rate charges more points to make up for it.

> **Example:** A lender analyzes market conditions and determines that it would currently take approximately six discount points to increase the lender's yield on a 30-year loan by 1%. Based on that estimate, the lender offers borrowers an interest rate 1% below market but charges six discount points to make up the difference. The lender would charge borrowers three points if they want a rate that's 0.5% below market, or nine points for a rate that's 1.5% below market.

As the example suggests, the number of discount points required to increase a lender's yield on a loan by one percentage point varies depending on market conditions, the length of the loan term, and other factors. To find out exactly how many points a particular lender will charge for a specified interest rate reduction in the current market, it's necessary to ask the lender.

In some cases, the seller is willing to pay the discount points on the buyer's loan in order to help the buyer qualify for financing. Even when the lender isn't charging discount points, the seller may offer to pay points to make the loan more affordable. This type of arrangement is called a **buydown**: the seller pays the lender points to "buy down" the interest rate on the buyer's loan.

Rate Lock-ins. A prospective borrower may want to have the interest rate quoted by the lender "locked in" for a specified period. Unless the interest rate is locked in, the lender can change it at any time until the transaction closes. If market interest rates are rising, the lender is likely to increase the interest rate on the loan. That could cost the borrower a lot of money over the long term, or else actually price the borrower out of the transaction altogether.

On the other hand, locking in the interest rate is generally not desirable when market interest rates are expected to go down. A lender will typically charge the borrower the locked-in rate even if market rates drop in the period before closing.

Most lenders charge the borrower a fee to lock in the interest rate. The fee is typically applied to the borrower's closing costs if the transaction closes. If the lender rejects the borrower's application, the fee is refunded; it will be forfeited to the lender, though, if the borrower withdraws from the transaction.

Truth in Lending Act

An origination fee, discount points, and other charges may increase the cost of a mortgage loan significantly. They also make it more difficult to compare the cost of loans offered by different lenders. For example, suppose one lender charges 7% interest, a 1% origination fee, and no discount points, while another charges 6.75% interest, a 1% origination fee, and two discount points. It isn't easy to tell at a glance which of these loans will cost the borrower more in the long term. (The second loan is just slightly less expensive.)

The **Truth in Lending Act** (TILA) is a federal consumer protection law that addresses this problem of comparing loan costs. It requires lenders to disclose the complete cost of credit to consumer loan applicants, and it also regulates how consumer loans are advertised. The Truth in Lending Act is implemented by **Regulation Z**, a regulation issued by the Federal Reserve Board. The requirements of TILA and Regulation Z are enforced by the Consumer Financial Protection Bureau.

Loans Covered by TILA. A loan is a **consumer loan** if it's used for personal, family, or household purposes. A consumer loan is covered by the Truth in Lending Act if it is to be repaid in more than four installments, or is subject to finance charges, and is either:

- for $53,500 or less (as of 2014; the dollar figure is adjusted annually, based on the Consumer Price Index), or
- secured by real property.

Thus, any mortgage loan is covered by the Truth in Lending Act as long as the proceeds are used for personal, family, or household purposes (such as buying a home or sending children to college).

Loans Exempt from TILA. The Truth in Lending Act applies only to loans made to natural persons, so loans made to corporations or organizations aren't covered. Loans for business, commercial, or agricultural purposes are also exempt. So are loans in excess of the dollar amount shown above, unless the loan is secured by real property. (Real estate loans for personal, family, or household purposes are covered regardless of the loan amount.) Most seller financing is exempt, because extending credit isn't in the seller's ordinary course of business.

Disclosure Requirements. In transactions that are subject to TILA, lenders are required to give prospective borrowers a disclosure statement. (An example of a TILA disclosure form is shown in Figure 10.1.) Two especially important figures that must appear on the statement are the total finance charge and the annual percentage rate.

The **total finance charge** is the sum of all fees and charges the borrower will pay in connection with the loan. In addition to the interest on the loan, any of the following that are going to be paid by the borrower would be included in the total finance charge: origination fee, discount points, finder's fee, service fees, mortgage insurance premiums, and mortgage broker's compensation.

In real estate loan transactions, appraisal fees, credit report charges, inspection fees, and title fees aren't included in the total finance charge. Also, any charges that will be paid by someone other than the borrower—points paid by the seller, for example—aren't included.

Fig. 10.1 TILA disclosure form

TRUTH IN LENDING DISCLOSURE STATEMENT

Creditor	Applicant(s)
Mailing Address	Property Address
Loan Number	Preparation Date

ANNUAL PERCENTAGE RATE	FINANCE CHARGE	Amount Financed	Total of Payments
The cost of your credit as a yearly rate.	The dollar amount the credit will cost you.	The amount of credit provided to you or on your behalf.	The amount you will have paid after you have made all payments as scheduled.
E %	E$	E$	E$

PAYMENT SCHEDULE:

NUMBER OF PAYMENTS	* AMOUNT OF PAYMENTS	MONTHLY PAYMENTS ARE DUE BEGINNING	NUMBER OF PAYMENTS	* AMOUNT OF PAYMENTS	MONTHLY PAYMENTS ARE DUE BEGINNING

* Includes mortgage insurance premiums, excludes taxes, hazard insurance or flood insurance.

DEMAND FEATURE: ☐ This loan does not have a Demand Feature ☐ This loan has a Demand Feature.

ITEMIZATION: You have a right at this time to an ITEMIZATION OF AMOUNT FINANCED.
I/We ☐ do ☐ do not want an itemization.

REQUIRED DEPOSIT:
☐ The annual percentage rate does not take into account your required deposit.

VARIABLE RATE FEATURE:
☐ This Loan has a Variable Rate Feature. Variable Rate Disclosures have been provided to you earlier.

SECURITY: You are giving a security interest in:

ASSUMPTION: Someone buying this property
☐ cannot assume the remaining balance due under original mortgage terms.
☐ may assume, subject to lender's conditions, the remaining balance due under original mortgage terms.

FILING / RECORDING FEES: $

PROPERTY INSURANCE:
☐ Property / hazard insurance is a required condition of this loan. Borrower may purchase this insurance from any insurance company acceptable to the lender.
Hazard insurance ☐ is ☐ is not available through the lender at an estimated cost of for a month term.

LATE CHARGES: If your payment is more than days late, you will be charged a late charge of % of the overdue payment.

PREPAYMENT: If you prepay this loan in full or in part, you
☐ may ☐ will not have to pay a penalty.
☐ may ☐ will not be entitled to a refund of part of the finance charge.

See your contract documents for any additional information regarding non-payment, default, required repayment in full before scheduled date, and payment refunds and penalties.
E means estimate.

I/We hereby acknowledge reading and receiving a complete copy of this disclosure. I/We understand there is no commitment for the creditor to make this loan and there is no obligation for me/us to accept this loan upon delivery or signing of this disclosure.

__________ Date __________ Date

__________ Date __________ Date

GENESIS 2000, INC. * V9.3/W11.0 * (818) 223-3260 Form RegZD (03/95)

The **annual percentage rate** (APR) expresses the total cost of the loan as an annual percentage of the amount borrowed. This key figure enables a prospective borrower to compare loans more accurately than the interest rate alone. The APR is sometimes referred to as the effective rate of interest, as opposed to the nominal rate (the interest rate stated on the face of the promissory note).

In addition to the total finance charge and the APR, the disclosure statement must list the amount financed, the total of all payments, the number of payments, and the payment amount(s). It must also provide other information, such as whether the borrower will be charged a prepayment penalty if the loan is paid off early.

Timing of Disclosures. When a lender receives a written application for a consumer loan that would be secured by the borrower's dwelling—whether it would be a purchase loan, a home equity loan, or refinancing—the lender must give the applicant a TILA disclosure statement at the time of application, or deliver or mail it to her within three business days. The disclosure statement must contain a good faith estimate of the loan costs. Until this requirement has been fulfilled, the lender is not allowed to charge the applicant any fees, except a fee for obtaining her credit report.

Mortgage loan applicants must receive the TILA disclosure statement at least seven business days before closing, so that they have time to consider the information provided. And if any of the original estimates turn out to be inaccurate, the lender must provide corrected information at least three business days before closing.

Right of Rescission. The Truth in Lending Act provides for a right of rescission in connection with certain types of mortgage loans. When the security property is the borrower's current principal residence, the borrower may rescind the loan agreement up until three days after signing it, receiving the disclosure statement, or receiving notice of the right of rescission, whichever comes latest. If the borrower never receives the disclosure statement or the notice, the right of rescission doesn't expire for three years.

The right of rescission generally applies only to home equity loans and to refinancing with a new lender. There's no right of rescission for a loan financing the purchase or construction of the borrower's residence. And there's no right of rescission for refinancing from the same lender that made the loan it's replacing, unless the lender is advancing additional funds ("cash out" refinancing). In that case, the right of rescission applies only to the additional amount.

Advertising Under TILA. The Truth in Lending Act strictly controls advertising of credit terms. Its advertising rules apply to anyone who advertises consumer credit, not just lenders. For example, a real estate agent advertising financing terms for a listed home has to comply with TILA and Regulation Z.

It's always legal to state the cash price or the annual percentage rate in an ad. If the APR is stated, the interest rate can also be included. But if the ad mentions other loan terms known as **triggering terms** (the downpayment amount or percentage, the repayment period or number of payments, the amount of any payment, or the amount of any finance charge), then the rest of the terms of repayment must also be disclosed. For example, if an ad says, "Buyer can assume seller's loan—monthly payment only $1,525," it will violate the Truth in Lending Act if it doesn't go on to reveal the APR, any required downpayment, and the repayment schedule (with the number and timing of the payments and all payment amounts, including any balloon payment). However, general statements such as "low downpayment," "easy terms," or "affordable interest rate" don't trigger the full disclosure requirement.

California Finance Disclosure Requirements

In addition to the Truth in Lending Act (a federal law), there are some state laws that help ensure that California home buyers get the information they need to make an informed decision about financing. These laws include the Mortgage Loan Broker Law and the Seller Financing Disclosure Law.

Mortgage Loan Broker Law. As we've discussed, real estate agents sometimes help buyers obtain financing. Under California law, a real estate agent who arranges or negotiates a loan for compensation is considered to be acting as a mortgage loan broker. The agent must comply with the Mortgage Loan Broker Law, also known as the Real Property Loan Law, or Article VII of the Real Estate Law.

The Mortgage Loan Broker Law requires real estate agents acting as loan brokers to give borrowers a disclosure statement. And for loans secured by residential property with up to four units, the law restricts the size of the fees and commissions that may be paid by the borrower or received by the loan broker. The following is only an overview of some of the law's main provisions.

Disclosure Statement. The disclosure statement required by the Mortgage Loan Broker Law must be on a form approved by the Real Estate Commissioner. The California Bureau of Real Estate's version of the disclosure form for traditional mortgage products is shown in Figure 10.2. A different form is required for nontraditional mortgage products, loans that allow negative amortization or allow the borrower to defer repayment of principal or interest.

The statement discloses all of the costs involved in obtaining the loan, and the actual amount the borrower will receive after all of the costs and fees are deducted from the loan. The borrower must receive the statement before signing the note and security instrument, or within three days of the lender's receipt of the borrower's loan application, whichever is earlier.

A disclosure statement is required whenever a real estate agent negotiates a loan or performs services for borrowers or lenders in connection with a loan. It's required for loans secured by commercial property as well as for residential loans. The disclosure statement must be kept on file by the real estate agent for at least three years.

In a loan transaction that's subject to the Real Estate Settlement Procedures Act (covered in Chapter 12), the good faith estimate required by RESPA may also satisfy the Mortgage Loan Broker Law's disclosure statement requirement.

Commissions, Costs, and Terms. The Mortgage Loan Broker Law limits the commissions and costs that a real estate agent may charge borrowers for arranging an "Article VII loan" secured by residential property with one to four units. An Article VII loan is either:

- a first deed of trust for less than $30,000, or
- a junior deed of trust for less than $20,000.

Fig. 10.2 Mortgage loan disclosure statement

Page 1 of 3

STATE OF CALIFORNIA
DEPARTMENT OF REAL ESTATE
Providing Service, Protecting You

MORTGAGE LOAN DISCLOSURE STATEMENT (TRADITIONAL)

RE 882 (Rev. 10/10)

BORROWER'S NAME(S)

REAL PROPERTY COLLATERAL: THE INTENDED SECURITY FOR THIS PROPOSED LOAN WILL BE A DEED OF TRUST OR MORTGAGE ON (STREET ADDRESS OR LEGAL DESCRIPTION)

THIS MORTGAGE LOAN DISCLOSURE STATEMENT IS BEING PROVIDED BY THE FOLLOWING CALIFORNIA REAL ESTATE BROKER ACTING AS A MORTGAGE BROKER

INTENDED LENDER TO WHOM YOUR LOAN APPLICATION WILL BE DELIVERED (IF KNOWN) ☐ Unknown

- For any federally related mortgage loans, HUD/RESPA laws require that a Good Faith Estimate (GFE) be provided. A RE 882 Mortgage Loan Disclosure Statement (MLDS) is required by California law and must also be provided.
- The information provided below reflects estimates of the charges you are likely to incur at the settlement of your loan. The fees, commissions, costs and expenses listed are estimates; the actual charges may be more or less. Your transaction may not involve a charge for every item listed and any additional items charged will be listed.

Item	Paid to Others		Paid to Broker
Items Payable in Connection with Loan			
Mortgage Broker Commission/Fee			$
Lender's Loan Origination Fee	$		
Lender's Loan Discount Fee	$		
Appraisal Fee	$		$
Credit Report	$		$
Lender's Inspection Fee	$		$
Tax Service Fee	$		$
Processing Fee	$		$
Underwriting Fee	$		$
Wire Transfer Fee	$		$
Items Required by Lender to be Paid in Advance			
Interest for ________ days at $____________ per day	$		$
Hazard Insurance Premiums	$		$
County Property Taxes	$		$
Mortgage Insurance Premiums	$		$
VA Funding Fee/FHA MIP/PMI	$		$
Other:________________	$		$
Reserves Deposited with Lender			
Hazard Insurance: _____ months at $____________/mo.	$		$
Co. Property Taxes: _____ months at $____________/mo.	$		$
Mortgage Insurance: _____ months at $____________/mo.	$		$
Other:________________	$		$
Title Charges			
Settlement or Closing/Escrow Fee	$		$
Document Preparation Fee	$		$
Notary Fee	$		$
Title Insurance	$		$
Other:________________	$		$
Government Recording and Transfer Charges			
Recording Fees	$		$
City/County Tax/Stamps	$		$
Other:________________	$		$
Additional Settlement Charges			
Pest Inspection	$		$
Credit Life, and/or Disabilty Insurance (See Note below)✱	$		$
Subtotals of Initial Fees, Commissions, Costs and Expenses	$		$
Total of Initial Fees, Commissions, Costs and Expenses		$	

Compensation to Broker (Not Paid Out of Loan Proceeds)

Yield Spread Premium, Service Release Premium or Other Rebate Received from Lender $____________

Yield Spread Premium, Service Release Premium or Other Rebate Credited to Borrower $____________

Total Amount of Compensation Retained by Broker $____________

✱ **Note: The purchase of Credit Life and/or Disability Insurance is NOT required as a condition of making this proposed loan.**

RE 882 – Page 2 of 3

ADDITIONAL REQUIRED CALIFORNIA DISCLOSURES

Proposed Loan Amount		$________
Initial Commissions, Fees, Costs, and Expenses Summarized on Page 1	$________	
Down Payment or Loan Payoffs/Creditors (List):	$________	
	$________	
________________	$________	
________________	$________	
________________		
Subtotal of All Deductions	$________	
Estimated Cash at Closing ☐ **To You** ☐ **That You Must Pay**		$________

GENERAL INFORMATION ABOUT LOAN

PROPOSED INTEREST RATE: ________% ☐ FIXED RATE ☐ INITIAL VARIABLE RATE	Proposed Monthly Loan Payments: $________ Principal & Interest (P&I) If the loan is a variable interest rate loan, the payment will vary. See loan documents for details. Total Number of Installments: ________ Loan Term: ________ Years ________ Months

BALLOON PAYMENT INFORMATION

IS THIS LOAN SUBJECT TO A BALLOON PAYMENT?	DUE DATE OF FINAL BALLOON PAYMENT (ESTIMATED MONTH/DAY/YEAR)	AMOUNT OF BALLOON PAYMENT
☐ Yes ☐ No		$

IF YES, THE FOLLOWING PARAGRAPH APPLIES:

NOTICE TO BORROWER: IF YOU DO NOT HAVE THE FUNDS TO PAY THE BALLOON PAYMENT WHEN IT COMES DUE, YOU MAY HAVE TO OBTAIN A NEW LOAN AGAINST YOUR PROPERTY TO MAKE THE BALLOON PAYMENT. IN THAT CASE, YOU MAY AGAIN HAVE TO PAY COMMISSIONS, FEES, AND EXPENSES FOR THE ARRANGING OF THE NEW LOAN. IN ADDITION, IF YOU ARE UNABLE TO MAKE THE MONTHLY PAYMENTS OR THE BALLOON PAYMENT, YOU MAY LOSE THE PROPERTY AND ALL OF YOUR EQUITY THROUGH FORECLOSURE. KEEP THIS IN MIND IN DECIDING UPON THE AMOUNT AND TERMS OF THIS LOAN.

PREPAYMENT INFORMATION

PREPAYMENT PENALTY?	# OF YEARS THAT PREPAYMENT PENALTY IS IN EFFECT	MAXIMUM DOLLAR AMOUNT OF PENALTY
☐ Yes ☐ No		

IS THERE A PREPAYMENT PENALTY FOR PAYING IN EXCESS OF 20% OF THE ORIGINAL OR UNPAID LOAN BALANCE?

☐ Yes ☐ No If Yes, see loan documents for details.

TAXES AND INSURANCE

IMPOUND ACCOUNT?	IMPOUND ACCOUNT WILL INCLUDE				
☐ Yes ☐ No	County Property Taxes	Mortgage Insurance	Hazard Insurance	Flood Insurance	Other: ________
APPROXIMATE AMOUNT THAT WILL BE COLLECTED MONTHLY $	☐ Yes ☐ No	☐ Yes ☐ No	☐ Yes ☐ No	☐ Yes ☐ No	☐ Yes ☐ No
IF NO, PLAN FOR THESE PAYMENTS ACCORDINGLY	BORROWER MUST PLAN FOR PAYMENTS OF THE FOLLOWING ITEMS				
→	County Property Taxes	Mortgage Insurance	Hazard Insurance	Flood Insurance	Other: ________
	☐ Yes ☐ No	☐ Yes ☐ No	☐ Yes ☐ No	☐ Yes ☐ No	☐ Yes ☐ No

Note: In a purchase transaction, county property taxes are calculated based on the sales price of the property and may require the payment of an additional (supplemental) tax bill issued by the county tax authority. The payment of county property taxes (including supplemental bills) may be paid by your lender if an impound/escrow account has been established.

If an impound/escrow account has not been established, the payment of all tax bills including any and all supplemental tax bills will be the responsibility of the borrower(s).

OTHER LIENS

LIENS CURRENTLY ON THIS PROPERTY FOR WHICH THE BORROWER IS OBLIGATED

Lienholder's Name	*Amount Owing*	*Priority*

LIST LIENS THAT WILL REMAIN OR ARE ANTICIPATED TO REMAIN ON THIS PROPERTY AFTER THE PROPOSED LOAN FOR WHICH YOU ARE APPLYING IS MADE OR ARRANGED (INCLUDING THE PROPOSED LOAN FOR WHICH YOU ARE APPLYING):

Lienholder's Name	*Amount Owing*	*Priority*

NOTICE TO BORROWER: BE SURE THAT YOU STATE THE AMOUNT OF ALL LIENS AS ACCURATELY AS POSSIBLE. IF YOU CONTRACT WITH THE BROKER TO ARRANGE THIS LOAN, BUT IT CANNOT BE ARRANGED BECAUSE YOU DID NOT STATE THESE LIENS CORRECTLY, YOU MAY BE LIABLE TO PAY COMMISSIONS, COSTS, FEES, AND EXPENSES EVEN THOUGH YOU DO NOT OBTAIN THE LOAN.

RE 882 – Page 3 of 3

ARTICLE 7 COMPLIANCE

If this proposed loan is secured by a first deed of trust in a principal amount of less than $30,000 or secured by a junior lien in a principal amount of less than $20,000, the undersigned broker certifies that the loan will be made in compliance with Article 7 of Chapter 3 of the Real Estate Law.

WILL THIS LOAN BE MADE WHOLLY OR IN PART FROM BROKER CONTROLLED FUNDS AS DEFINED IN SECTION 10241(J) OF THE BUSINESS AND PROFESSIONS CODE?

☐ May ☐ Will ☐ Will Not

Note: If the broker indicates in the above statement that the loan "may" be made out of broker-controlled funds, the broker must inform the borrower prior to the close of escrow if the funds to be received by the borrower are in fact broker-controlled funds.

STATED INCOME

IS THIS LOAN BASED ON LIMITED OR NO DOCUMENTATION OF YOUR INCOME AND/OR ASSETS?

☐ Yes ☐ No If Yes, be aware that this loan may have a higher interest rate or more points or fees than other products requiring documentation.

NOTICE TO BORROWER: THIS IS NOT A LOAN COMMITMENT

Do not sign this statement until you have read and understood all of the information in it. All parts of this form must be completed before you sign it. Borrower hereby acknowledges the receipt of a copy of this statement.

NAME OF BROKER	LICENSE ID NUMBER	BROKER'S REPRESENTATIVE	LICENSE ID NUMBER
	NMLS ID NUMBER		NMLS ID NUMBER
BROKER'S ADDRESS			
BROKER'S SIGNATURE	DATE	OR SIGNATURE OF REPRESENTATIVE	DATE
BORROWER'S SIGNATURE	DATE	BORROWER'S SIGNATURE	DATE

Department of Real Estate license information telephone number: 877-373-4542, or check license status at www.dre.ca.gov

NMLS - http://mortgage.nationwidelicensingsystem.org/about/pages/nmlsconsumeraccess.aspx

The Real Estate Broker negotiating the loan shall retain on file for a period of three years a true and correct copy of this disclosure signed and dated by the borrower(s).

THE RE 885 MORTGAGE LOAN DISCLOSURE STATEMENT, NON-TRADITIONAL MORTGAGE MUST BE USED FOR NON-TRADITIONAL MORTGAGE LOANS OF RESIDENTIAL PROPERTY (1-4 UNITS).

Non-Traditional Mortgage Loans are loan products that allow the borrower to defer payments of principal or interest. If any of the payments are not full principal and interest payments, then it is considered a Non-Traditional Mortgage Loan.

For these loans, the maximum commission the loan broker can charge is:

- for a first deed of trust:
  - 5% of the principal if the loan term is less than three years, or
  - 10% of the principal if the loan term is three years or more.
- for a junior deed of trust:
  - 5% of the principal if the term is less than two years,
  - 10% of the principal if the term is at least two years, but less than three years, or
  - 15% of the principal if the term is three years or more.

The costs of making these loans (such as the appraisal and escrow fees) can't exceed 5% of the loan amount, or $390, whichever is greater. But the costs charged to the borrower must never exceed $700 (not counting the loan broker's commission) and must not exceed the actual costs.

Balloon Payments. The Mortgage Loan Broker Law also prohibits balloon payments in Article VII loans that are to be paid off in less than three years. And when the property is an owner-occupied home, a balloon payment is prohibited if the loan term is less than six years. (These rules don't apply to seller financing, however.) For the purposes of this law, a balloon payment is one that is more than twice as large as the smallest payment required by the loan agreement.

Penalties for Violation. If a real estate agent negotiates a loan in violation of the Mortgage Loan Broker Law, she must refund any compensation she received. The refund must be made within 20 days after a written demand from the borrower is delivered or mailed to the agent (the loan broker). If the 20-day deadline isn't met, the borrower can sue the loan broker for actual damages or for twice the amount of the broker's compensation, whichever is more, plus costs and attorney's fees.

Seller Financing Disclosure Law. The Seller Financing Disclosure Law is also called the Residential Purchase Money Loan Disclosure Law. When a seller carries back a purchase money loan on residential property, this state law requires certain disclosures to be made to both the buyer and the seller if an "arranger of credit" is involved. An arranger of credit, for the purposes of this law, is anyone (other than the buyer or seller) who:

- is involved in negotiating the credit agreement,
- participates in preparing the documents, or
- is directly or indirectly compensated for arranging for the financing or the property sale that is facilitated by the financing.

There's an exception for escrow agents and for attorneys representing either party—these aren't considered arrangers of credit. But if an attorney or a real estate agent is a party to the transaction, he is considered an arranger of credit if neither party is represented by a real estate agent.

Coverage of the Law. The disclosure law applies when the seller gives the buyer credit for all or part of the purchase price, if:

1. the transaction concerns residential property with up to four units,
2. the credit arrangements involve a finance charge or provide for more than four payments (not including the downpayment), and
3. an arranger of credit is involved.

Fig. 10.3 Seller financing disclosure statement

CALIFORNIA ASSOCIATION OF REALTORS®

SELLER FINANCING ADDENDUM AND DISCLOSURE (SEE IMPORTANT DISCLOSURE ON PAGE 4)
(California Civil Code §§2956-2967)
(C.A.R. Form SFA, Revised 11/13)

This is an addendum to the ☐ Residential Purchase Agreement, ☐ Counter Offer, or ☐ Other ____________ , ("Agreement"), dated ______,
On property known as ____________ ("Property"),
between ____________ ("Buyer"),
and ____________ ("Seller").
Seller agrees to extend credit to Buyer as follows:

1. **PRINCIPAL; INTEREST; PAYMENT; MATURITY TERMS:** ☐ Principal amount $ ________, interest at ______% per annum, payable at approximately $ ________ per ☐ month, ☐ year, or ☐ other ________, remaining principal balance due in _____ years.
2. **LOAN APPLICATION; CREDIT REPORT:** Within **5 (or ☐ ______) Days** After Acceptance: (a) Buyer shall provide Seller a completed loan application on a form acceptable to Seller (such as a FNMA/FHLMC Uniform Residential Loan Application for residential one to four unit properties); and (b) Buyer authorizes Seller and/or Agent to obtain, at Buyer's expense, a copy of Buyer's credit report. Buyer shall provide any supporting documentation reasonably requested by Seller. Seller, after first giving Buyer a Notice to Buyer to Perform, may cancel this Agreement in writing and authorize return of Buyer's deposit if Buyer fails to provide such documents within that time, or if Seller disapproves any above item within **5 (or ☐ ______) Days** After receipt of each item.
3. **CREDIT DOCUMENTS:** This extension of credit by Seller will be evidenced by: ☐ Note and deed of trust; ☐ All-inclusive note and deed of trust; ☐ Installment land sale contract; ☐ Lease/option (when parties intend transfer of equitable title); OR ☐ Other (specify) ____________

THE FOLLOWING TERMS APPLY ONLY IF CHECKED. SELLER IS ADVISED TO READ ALL TERMS, EVEN THOSE NOT CHECKED, TO UNDERSTAND WHAT IS OR IS NOT INCLUDED, AND, IF NOT INCLUDED, THE CONSEQUENCES THEREOF.

4. ☐ **LATE CHARGE:** If any payment is not made within ____ **Days** After it is due, a late charge of either $ ________, or ____% of the installment due, may be charged to Buyer. **NOTE:** On single family residences that Buyer intends to occupy, California Civil Code §2954.4(a) limits the late charge to no more than 6% of the total installment payment due and requires a grace period of no less than 10 days.
5. ☐ **BALLOON PAYMENT:** The extension of credit will provide for a balloon payment, in the amount of $ ________, plus any accrued interest, which is due on ____________ (date).
6. ☐ **PREPAYMENT:** If all or part of this extension of credit is paid early, Seller may charge a prepayment penalty as follows (if applicable): ____________. Caution: California Civil Code §2954.9 contains limitations on prepayment penalties for residential one-to-four unit properties.
7. ☐ **DUE ON SALE:** If any interest in the Property is sold or otherwise transferred, Seller has the option to require immediate payment of the entire unpaid principal balance, plus any accrued interest.

8.* ☐ **REQUEST FOR COPY OF NOTICE OF DEFAULT:** A request for a copy of Notice of Default as defined in California Civil Code §2924b will be recorded. If Not, Seller is advised to consider recording a Request for Notice of Default.

9.* ☐ **REQUEST FOR NOTICE OF DELINQUENCY:** A request for Notice of Delinquency, as defined in California Civil Code §2924e, to be signed and paid for by Buyer, will be made to senior lienholders. **If not,** Seller is advised to consider making a Request for Notice of Delinquency. Seller is advised to check with senior lienholders to verify whether they will honor this request.

10.* ☐ **TAX SERVICE:**
   A. If property taxes on the Property become delinquent, tax service will be arranged to report to Seller. **If not,** Seller is advised to consider retaining a tax service, or to otherwise determine that property taxes are paid.
   B. ☐ Buyer, ☐ Seller, shall be responsible for the initial and continued retention of, and payment for, such tax service.

11. ☐ **TITLE INSURANCE:** Title insurance coverage will be provided to **both** Seller and Buyer, insuring their respective interests in the Property. **If not,** Buyer and Seller are advised to consider securing such title insurance coverage.
12. ☐ **HAZARD INSURANCE:**
    A. The parties' escrow holder or insurance carrier will be directed to include a loss payee endorsement, adding Seller to the Property insurance policy. If not, Seller is advised to secure such an endorsement, or acquire a separate insurance policy.
    B. Property insurance **does not** include earthquake or flood insurance coverage, unless checked:
    ☐ Earthquake insurance will be obtained; ☐ Flood insurance will be obtained.
13. ☐ **PROCEEDS TO BUYER:** Buyer will receive cash proceeds at the close of the sale transaction. The amount received will be approximately $________, from ________ (indicate source of proceeds). Buyer represents that the purpose of such disbursement is as follows: ________.
14. ☐ **NEGATIVE AMORTIZATION; DEFERRED INTEREST:** Negative amortization results when Buyer's periodic payments are less than the amount of interest earned on the obligation. Deferred interest also results when the obligation does not require periodic payments for a period of time. In either case, interest is not payable as it accrues. This accrued interest will have to be paid by Buyer at a later time, and may result in Buyer owing more on the obligation than at its origination. The credit being extended to Buyer by Seller will provide for negative amortization or deferred interest as indicated below. (Check A, B, or C. CHECK ONE ONLY.)
    ☐ **A.** All negative amortization or deferred interest shall be added to the principal ________ (e.g., annually, monthly, etc.), and thereafter shall bear interest at the rate specified in the credit documents (compound interest);
    OR ☐ **B.** All deferred interest shall be due and payable, along with principal, at maturity;
    OR ☐ **C.** Other ____________.

*(For Paragraphs 8-10) In order to receive timely and continued notification, Seller is advised to record appropriate notices and/or to notify appropriate parties of any change in Seller's address.

Buyer's Initials (________)(________) Seller's Initials (________)(________)

SFA REVISED 11/13 (PAGE 1 OF 3) Print Date

Reviewed by ______ Date ______

EQUAL HOUSING OPPORTUNITY

SELLER FINANCING ADDENDUM AND DISCLOSURE (SFA PAGE 1 OF 4)

Reprinted with permission, California Association of REALTORS®. Endorsement not implied.

Property Address: ______________________ Date: __________

15. ☐ **ALL-INCLUSIVE DEED OF TRUST; INSTALLMENT LAND SALE CONTRACT:** This transaction involves the use of an all-inclusive (or wraparound) deed of trust or an installment land sale contract. That deed of trust or contract shall provide as follows:

A. In the event of an acceleration of any senior encumbrance, the party responsibile for payment, or for legal defense is: ☐ Buyer ☐ Seller ; OR ☐ **Is not** specified in the credit or security documents.

B. In the event of the prepayment of a senior encumbrance, the responsibilities and rights of Buyer and Seller regarding refinancing, prepayment penalties, and any prepayment discounts are: ______________________; OR ☐ **Are not** specified in the documents evidencing credit.

C. Buyer will make periodic payments to ______________________ (Seller, collection agent, or any neutral third party), who will be responsible for disbursing payments to the payee(s) on the senior encumbrance(s) and to Seller. NOTE: The Parties are advised to designate a neutral third party for these purposes.

16. ☐ **TAX IDENTIFICATION NUMBERS:** Buyer and Seller shall each provide to each other their Social Security Numbers or Taxpayer Identification Numbers.

17. ☐ **OTHER CREDIT TERMS** ______________________

18. ☐ **RECORDING:** The documents evidencing credit (paragraph 3) will be recorded with the county recorder where the Property is located. If not, Buyer and Seller are advised that their respective interests in the Property may be jeopardized by intervening liens, judgments, encumbrances, or subsequent transfers.

19. ☐ **JUNIOR FINANCING:** There will be additional financing, secured by the Property, junior to this Seller financing. Explain: ______________________

20. SENIOR LOANS AND ENCUMBRANCES: The following information is provided on loans and/or encumbrances that will be senior to Seller financing. NOTE: The following are estimates, unless otherwise marked with an asterisk (*). If checked: ☐ A separate sheet with information on additional senior loans/encumbrances is attached

	1st	2nd
A. Original Balance	$ ________	$ ________
B. Current Balance	$ ________	$ ________
C. Periodic Payment (e.g. $100/month):	$ ________	$ ____ / ____
Including Impounds of:	$ ________	$ ____ / ____
D. Interest Rate (per annum)	________ %	________ %
E. Fixed or Variable Rate:	________	________
If Variable Rate: Lifetime Cap (Ceiling)	________	________
Indicator (Underlying Index)	________	________
Margins	________	________
F. Maturity Date	________	________
G. Amount of Balloon Payment	$ ________	$ ________
H. Date Balloon Payment Due	________	________
I. Potential for Negative Amortization? (Yes, No, or Unknown)	________	________
J. Due on Sale? (Yes, No, or Unknown)	________	________
K. Pre-payment penalty? (Yes, No, or Unknown)	________	________
L. Are payments current? (Yes, No, or Unknown)	________	________

21. BUYER'S CREDITWORTHINESS: (CHECK EITHER A OR B. Do not check both.) In addition to the loan application, credit report and other information requested under paragraph 2:

A. ☐ No other disclosure concerning Buyer's creditworthiness has been made to Seller;

OR B. ☐ The following representations concerning Buyer's creditworthiness are made by Buyer(s) to Seller:

Borrower	**Co-Borrower**
1. Occupation ________	1. Occupation ________
2. Employer ________	2. Employer ________
3. Length of Employment ________	3. Length of Employment ________
4. Monthly Gross Income ________	4. Monthly Gross Income ________
5. Other ________	5. Other ________

22. ADDED, DELETED OR SUBSTITUTED BUYERS: The addition, deletion or substitution of any person or entity under this Agreement or to title prior to close of escrow shall require Seller's written consent. Seller may grant or withhold consent in Seller's sole discretion. Any additional or substituted person or entity shall, if requested by Seller, submit to Seller the same documentation as required for the original named Buyer. Seller and/or Brokers may obtain a credit report, at Buyer's expense, on any such person or entity.

Buyer's Initials (________)(________) Seller's Initials (________)(________)

SFA REVISED 11/13 (PAGE 2 OF 4)

Reviewed by ______ Date ______

EQUAL HOUSING OPPORTUNITY

SELLER FINANCING ADDENDUM AND DISCLOSURE (SFA PAGE 2 OF 4)

Property Address: ______________________ Date: __________

23. CAUTION:

A. If the Seller financing requires a balloon payment, Seller shall give Buyer written notice, according to the terms of Civil Code §2966, at least 90 and not more than 150 days before the balloon payment is due if the transaction is for the purchase of a dwelling for not more than four families.

B. If **any** obligation secured by the Property calls for a balloon payment, Seller and Buyer are aware that refinancing of the balloon payment at maturity may be difficult or impossible, depending on conditions in the conventional mortgage marketplace at that time. There are no assurances that new financing or a loan extension will be available when the balloon prepayment, or any prepayment, is due.

C. If **any** of the existing or proposed loans or extensions of credit would require refinancing as a result of a lack of full amortization, such refinancing might be difficult or impossible in the conventional mortgage marketplace.

D. In the event of default by Buyer: (1) Seller may have to reinstate and/or make monthly payments on any and all senior encumbrances (including real property taxes) in order to protect Seller's secured interest; (2) Seller's rights are generally limited to foreclosure on the Property, pursuant to California Code of Civil Procedure §580b; and (3) the Property may lack sufficient equity to protect Seller's interests if the Property decreases in value.

If this three-page Addendum and Disclosure is used in a transaction for the purchase of a dwelling for not more than four families, it shall be prepared by an Arranger of Credit as defined in California Civil Code §2957(a). (The Arranger of Credit is usually the agent who obtained the offer.)

____

Arranger of Credit - (Print Firm Name) By Date

Address ______________________ City __________ State ______ Zip ______

Phone ______________________ Fax ______________________

BUYER AND SELLER ACKNOWLEDGE AND AGREE THAT BROKERS: (A) WILL NOT PROVIDE LEGAL OR TAX ADVICE; (B) WILL NOT PROVIDE OTHER ADVICE OR INFORMATION THAT EXCEEDS THE KNOWLEDGE, EDUCATION AND EXPERIENCE REQUIRED TO OBTAIN A REAL ESTATE LICENSE; OR (C) HAVE NOT AND WILL NOT VERIFY ANY INFORMATION PROVIDED BY EITHER BUYER OR SELLER. BUYER AND SELLER AGREE THAT THEY WILL SEEK LEGAL, TAX AND OTHER DESIRED ASSISTANCE FROM APPROPRIATE PROFESSIONALS. BUYER AND SELLER ACKNOWLEDGE THAT THE INFORMATION EACH HAS PROVIDED TO THE ARRANGER OF CREDIT FOR INCLUSION IN THIS DISCLOSURE FORM IS ACCURATE. BUYER AND SELLER FURTHER ACKNOWLEDGE THAT EACH HAS RECEIVED A COMPLETED COPY OF THIS DISCLOSURE FORM.

Buyer ______________________________________ Date ______
(signature)

Address ______________________ City __________ State ______ Zip ______

Phone ______________ Fax ______________ E-mail ______________

Buyer ______________________________________ Date ______
(signature)

Address ______________________ City __________ State ______ Zip ______

Phone ______________ Fax ______________ E-mail ______________

Seller ______________________________________ Date ______
(signature)

Address ______________________ City __________ State ______ Zip ______

Phone ______________ Fax ______________ E-mail ______________

Seller ______________________________________ Date ______
(signature)

Address ______________________ City __________ State ______ Zip ______

Phone ______________ Fax ______________ E-mail ______________

REBSINC
Published and Distributed by:
REAL ESTATE BUSINESS SERVICES, INC.
a subsidiary of the California Association of REALTORS®
525 South Virgil Avenue, Los Angeles, California 90020

Reviewed by ______ Date ______

EQUAL HOUSING OPPORTUNITY

SFA REVISED 11/13 (PAGE 3 OF 4)

SELLER FINANCING ADDENDUM AND DISCLOSURE (SFA PAGE 3 OF 4)

Property Address: ______________________ Date: __________

IMPORTANT SELLER FINANCING DISCLOSURE - PLEASE READ CAREFULLY

The Dodd-Frank Wall Street Reform and Consumer Protection Act (Dodd-Frank) has made significant and important changes affecting seller financing on residential properties. Effective January 10, 2014, sellers who finance the purchase of residential property containing 1-4 units may be considered "loan originators" required to comply with certain Truth In Lending Act ("TILA") requirements. Even under Dodd-Frank however, the following two exemptions exist:

1. The seller finances only **ONE** property in any 12 month period and:
   a. The seller is a natural person, a trust or an estate, and
   b. The seller did not construct the property, and
   c. The financing has a fixed rate or does not adjust for the first 5 years, and
   d. The financing does not result in negative amortization.

OR

2. The seller finances no more than **THREE** properties in any 12 month period and:
   a. The seller is a natural person or organization (corporation, LLC, partnership, trust, estate, association, etc.), and
   b. The seller did not construct the property, and
   c. The loan is fully amortized, i.e., no balloon payment, and
   d. The financing has a fixed rate or does not adjust for the first 5 years, and
   e. The borrow has the reasonable ability to repay the loan.

Sellers who finance the purchase of residential property containing 1-4 units meeting either of the two exemptions are not subject to the TILA requirements above may continue to, and are required by California Law to, use the Seller Financing Addendum.

Sellers who finance the purchase of residential property containing 1-4 units who do not meet either of the two tests above should still complete the Seller Finance Addendum and speak to a lawyer about other TILA disclosures that may be required.

Sellers who finance the purchase of residential property containing 5 or more units, vacant land, or commercial properties are not subject to the TILA disclosures nor are they required to use the Seller Financing Addendum.

A seller who originates a single extension of credit through a mortgage broker and additionally meets the definition of a "high-cost" mortgage under Dodd-Frank may be subject to the Truth in Lending Act's requirement to verify the borrower's ability to repay.

Buyer's Initials (________)(________) Seller's Initials (________)(________)

SFA REVISED 11/13 (PAGE 4 OF 4)

Reviewed by ______ Date ______

EQUAL HOUSING OPPORTUNITY

SELLER FINANCING ADDENDUM AND DISCLOSURE (SFA PAGE 4 OF 4)

A transaction is exempt if it's already covered by another disclosure law, such as the Truth in Lending Act, the Real Estate Settlement Procedures Act, or the Mortgage Loan Broker Law.

Disclosure Requirements. When the Seller Financing Disclosure Law applies to a transaction, the required disclosures must be made before the buyer signs the note or the security instrument. The seller must make disclosures to the buyer, and the buyer must make disclosures to the seller. The arranger of credit is responsible for ensuring that each party discloses all required information to the other.

The statute contains a long list of required disclosures. Here are some of them:

1. the terms of the note and the security instrument;
2. a description of the terms and conditions of senior encumbrances (such as a first deed of trust that the buyer will be assuming);
3. whether the financing will result in a balloon payment (if so, the buyer must be warned that it may be difficult to obtain refinancing to cover the balloon payment); and
4. employment, income, and credit information about the buyer, or else a statement that the arranger of credit has made no representations regarding the buyer's creditworthiness.

As an example of a form that could be used to comply with this law, a CAR Seller Financing Addendum and Disclosure form is shown in Figure 10.3.

The Loan Application Process

Once a buyer has compared loan costs and selected a lender, the next step is applying for the loan. The buyer fills out a loan application form and provides the lender with supporting documentation (usually with the help of a mortgage loan originator, such as a loan officer or a mortgage broker). The application is then submitted to the lender's underwriting department, which evaluates the application and ultimately approves or rejects the proposed loan.

Preapproval

Traditionally, buyers would first find the house that they wanted and then apply for a loan. Now, however, getting **preapproved** for a mortgage loan is considered the standard practice in many areas. To get preapproved, prospective buyers submit a loan application to a lender before starting to house-hunt. If the lender approves the application, the buyers are preapproved for a specified maximum loan amount.

Preapproval lets the buyers know in advance, before shopping, just how expensive a house they can afford. If a house meets the lender's standards and is in the established price range, the buyers will be able to buy it. This spares the buyers the disappointment of initially choosing a house that turns out to be too expensive and having the loan request turned down. Preapproval also helps streamline the closing process once the buyers have found the right house.

The Application Form

A mortgage loan application form asks the prospective borrower for detailed information about her finances. The lender requires this information because it wants its loans to be profitable investments. A loan is unlikely to be profitable if the borrower doesn't have the financial resources to make the payments reliably, or if the borrower has a habit of defaulting on debts. The application helps the lender identify and turn down potential borrowers who are likely to create collection problems.

Most mortgage lenders use the Uniform Residential Loan Application form developed by Fannie Mae and Freddie Mac. The form requires all of the following information:

1. Personal information, such as the applicant's social security number, age, education, marital status, and number of dependents.
2. Current housing expense (monthly rent or house payment, including principal and interest, property taxes, hazard insurance, any mortgage insurance, and any homeowners or condominium association dues).
3. Employment information (such as job title, type of business, and duration of employment) concerning the applicant's current position and, if he's been with the current employer for less than two years, concerning previous jobs.
4. Income from all sources, including employment (salary, wages, bonuses, and/or commissions), investments (dividends and interest), and pensions.
5. Assets, which may include money in bank accounts, stocks and bonds, real estate, life insurance, retirement funds, cars, jewelry, and other personal property.
6. Liabilities, including credit card debts, car loans, real estate loans, spousal maintenance or child support payments, and unpaid taxes.

The lender will verify the applicant's information concerning income, assets, and liabilities (for example, by contacting his employer and his bank).

Underwriting the Loan

Once a loan application has been submitted and the information has been verified, the loan is ready for underwriting. **Loan underwriting** is the process of evaluating both the applicant and the property she wants to buy to determine whether they meet the lender's minimum standards. The person who conducts the evaluation is called a loan underwriter or credit underwriter. The guidelines that the underwriter uses to decide whether a proposed loan would be an acceptable risk (in other words, whether the applicant qualifies for the loan) are called **underwriting standards** or **qualifying standards.**

A lender is generally free to set its own underwriting standards. In practice, though, most lenders apply underwriting standards set by the major secondary market entities, Fannie Mae and Freddie Mac. And for FHA and VA loans, standards set by HUD or the VA must be used.

Qualifying the Buyer. In evaluating a loan applicant's financial situation, an underwriter must consider many factors. These factors fall into three main groups: credit history, income, and net worth.

Credit History. The first major component of creditworthiness is credit history, or credit reputation. An underwriter typically requests credit reports on the loan applicant from more than one credit reporting agency. The reports indicate how reliably the applicant has paid bills and other debts, and whether there have been any serious problems such as bankruptcy or foreclosure.

In addition to reviewing credit reports, underwriters also use **credit scores** to help assess how likely it is that a loan applicant will default on the proposed loan. A credit reporting agency calculates an individual's credit score using the credit report and a statistical model that correlates different types of negative credit information with actual loan defaults.

Credit problems can be an indication of financial irresponsibility, but sometimes they result from a personal crisis such as loss of a job, divorce, or hospitalization. A loan applicant with a poor credit history should explain any extenuating circumstances to the lender.

The activities of credit reporting agencies are regulated under the federal Fair Credit Reporting Act and the California Consumer Credit Reporting Agencies Act. Under the California law, a credit reporting agency must give consumers a copy of their credit information upon request. If an agency fails to comply, a consumer may sue the agency for actual damages, punitive damages of up to $5,000, attorney's fees, and court costs. Consumers have the right to dispute information in their credit reports. The agencies must investigate and make corrections where necessary.

Income. Another primary consideration for the underwriter is whether the loan applicant's monthly income is enough to cover the proposed monthly mortgage payment in addition to all of the applicant's other expenses. So the underwriter needs to determine how much income the applicant has.

Not all income is equal in an underwriter's eyes, however. To be taken into account in deciding whether the applicant qualifies for the loan, income must meet standards of quality and durability. In other words, it must be from a dependable source, such as an established business, and it must be likely to continue for some time. Income that meets the tests of quality and durability is generally referred to as the loan applicant's **stable monthly income**.

For example, a regular salary from permanent employment would count as stable monthly income, and so would Social Security retirement benefits. On the other hand, neither occasional overtime pay from a permanent job nor wages from a temporary job would be considered stable monthly income, because they couldn't be relied upon to continue.

Once the underwriter has calculated the loan applicant's stable monthly income, the next step is to measure its adequacy: Is the stable monthly income enough so that the applicant can afford the proposed monthly mortgage payment? To answer this question, underwriters use **income ratios**. The rationale behind the ratios is that if a borrower's expenses exceed a certain percentage of his monthly income, he may have a difficult time making the payments on the loan.

There are two main types of income ratios:

- A **housing expense to income ratio** measures the proposed monthly mortgage payment against the applicant's stable monthly income.
- A **debt to income ratio** measures all of the applicant's monthly obligations (the proposed mortgage payment, plus car payments, child support payments, etc.) against the stable monthly income.

For these calculations, the monthly mortgage payment includes principal, interest, property taxes, and hazard insurance (often abbreviated PITI). When applicable, it also includes mortgage insurance and homeowners or condominium association dues. Each income ratio is expressed as a percentage; for example, a loan applicant's housing expense to income ratio would be 29% if her proposed mortgage payment represented 29% of her stable monthly income. Whether that ratio would be considered too high would depend on the lender and on the type of loan applied for. Each of the major residential financing programs (conventional, FHA, and VA) has its own income ratio limits.

Net Worth. The third prong of the underwriting process is evaluating the applicant's net worth. An individual's net worth is determined by subtracting her total personal liabilities from her total personal assets. If a loan applicant has built up a significant net worth from earnings, savings, and other investments, that's an indication of creditworthiness. The applicant apparently knows how to manage her financial affairs.

Getting an idea of the loan applicant's financial skills isn't the only reason for investigating her net worth, however. The underwriter needs to make sure that the applicant has sufficient funds to cover the downpayment, the closing costs, and other expenses incidental to the purchase of the property.

In addition, it's desirable for a loan applicant to have cash reserves left over after closing. Reserves provide some assurance that she would be able to a handle financial emergency, such as unexpected bills or a temporary interruption of income, without defaulting on the mortgage. Some lenders require an applicant to have sufficient reserves to cover a certain number of mortgage payments. Even when reserves aren't required, they strengthen the loan application.

Qualifying the Property. In addition to deciding whether the buyer is a good risk, the underwriter also has to consider whether the property that the buyer wants to purchase is a good risk. Is the property worth enough to serve as collateral for the loan amount in question? In other words, if foreclosure became necessary, would the property sell for enough money to pay off the loan? To answer these questions, the underwriter relies on an appraisal report ordered by the lender. The appraisal report provides an expert's estimate of the property's value. (Appraisal is covered in Chapter 11.)

Automated Underwriting. Within the limits set by the underwriting standards they apply, underwriters draw on their own experience and judgment in deciding whether to recommend that a particular loan be approved or denied. For this reason, underwriting is often described as an art, not a science. However, automated underwriting (AU) has moved the underwriting process at least somewhat closer to the scientific end of the spectrum. In automated underwriting, a computer program performs a preliminary analysis of the loan application and the applicant's credit report and makes a recommendation for or against approval. A human underwriter then evaluates the application in light of the AU recommendation.

AU systems are based on statistics regarding the performance of millions of loans—whether the borrowers made the payments on time or defaulted. Analysis of these statistics provides strong evidence of which factors in a loan application make default more or less likely.

AU can streamline the underwriting process, as it often requires significantly less paperwork. This enables lenders to make approval decisions more quickly.

Loan Commitment. Once the underwriting analysis has been completed, a report summarizing the characteristics of the prospective borrower, the property, and the proposed loan is prepared. This summary, sometimes called a **mortgage evaluation,**

is submitted to a loan committee, which will make the final decision on whether to approve the loan. If the committee's decision is favorable, the lender issues a **loan commitment**, agreeing to make the loan on specified terms.

Subprime Lending

What happens to home buyers whose credit history doesn't meet standard underwriting requirements? Some of them may be able to obtain a loan by applying to a **subprime** lender. Subprime lending involves making riskier loans than prime (or standard) lending.

Although many of the buyers who get subprime mortgages have blemished credit histories and mediocre credit scores, that's not always the case. For example, subprime financing may also be necessary for buyers who:

- can't (or would rather not have to) meet the income and asset documentation requirements of prime lenders;
- have good credit but carry more debt than prime lenders allow; or
- want to purchase nonstandard properties that prime lenders don't regard as acceptable collateral.

Subprime lenders apply more flexible underwriting standards and, in exchange, typically charge much higher interest rates and fees than prime lenders. In addition to having high interest rates and fees, subprime loans are more likely than prime loans to have features such as prepayment penalties, balloon payments, and negative amortization. These features help subprime lenders counterbalance some of the extra risks involved in their loans, although they can also cause trouble for the borrowers. (See the discussion of predatory lending later in this chapter.)

A boom in subprime lending began in the late 1990s and continued into the new century. However, a significant number of the subprime loans made during the boom turned out to be poor risks. Many of them called for monthly payments that were initially low but increased sharply a few years into the loan term, and the borrowers couldn't handle the sudden increases (a problem known as "payment shock"). The resulting foreclosure epidemic that began in 2008 has affected not just the mortgage industry but the economy as a whole.

The secondary market entities and various government agencies have responded to the crisis by taking steps to discourage high-risk subprime lending. Among other things, the Conference of State Bank Supervisors and the American Association of Residential Mortgage Regulators issued two publications, one called the Statement on Subprime Lending, the other called Guidance on Nontraditional Mortgage Products. California law now requires state-licensed lenders and mortgage brokers to adopt policies and procedures intended to achieve the objectives set forth in those publications.

Basic Loan Features

In this section, we'll look at the basic features of a home mortgage loan. These include the loan term, the amortization, the loan-to-value ratio, a secondary financing arrangement (in some cases), and a fixed or adjustable interest rate. A lender is likely

Fig. 10.4 A 15-year loan offers substantial savings over a 30-year loan.

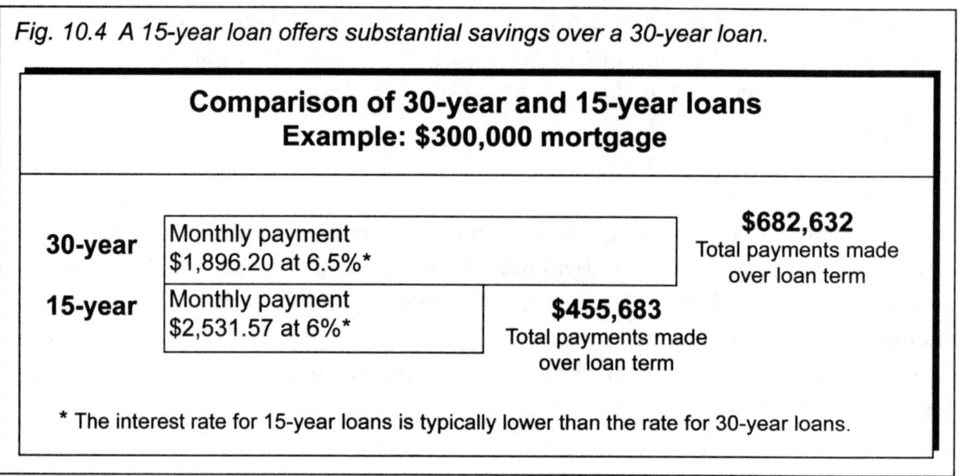

to present a home buyer with a number of options concerning these various loan features. Each of them has an impact on how large a loan the buyer will qualify for, and ultimately on how expensive a home the buyer can purchase.

Loan Term

A mortgage loan's **term** (also known as the **repayment period**) has a significant impact on both the monthly mortgage payment and the total amount of interest paid over the life of the loan. The longer the term, the lower the monthly payment, and the more interest paid.

Since the 1930s, the standard term for a mortgage loan has been 30 years. This long repayment period makes the monthly payments affordable, which reduces the risk of default.

Although 30-year loans continue to predominate, 15-year loans are also popular. A 15-year loan has higher monthly payments than a comparable 30-year loan, but the 15-year loan offers substantial savings for the borrower in the long run. Lenders frequently offer lower interest rates on 15-year loans, because the shorter term means less risk for the lender. And the borrower will save thousands of dollars in total interest charges over the life of the loan (see Figure 10.4). A 15-year loan also offers free and clear ownership of the property in half the time.

However, for many borrowers, the higher monthly payments for a 15-year loan mean that they'd have to buy a much less expensive property than a 30-year loan would allow them to afford.

> **Example:** Bob has a choice between a 30-year loan at 6.5% and a 15-year loan at 6%. Based on his stable monthly income, he can afford to make monthly principal and interest payments of $3,000. This is enough to amortize a $475,000 loan at 6.5% over 30 years, but it will amortize only about $355,500 at 6% over 15 years. In other words, Bob could qualify for a $475,000 loan under the 30-year plan, but will be able to borrow only $355,500 if he chooses the 15-year option.

There are alternatives to 15- and 30-year loans. For some borrowers, a 20-year loan is a good compromise between the two, with some of the advantages of each. And while 30 years is the maximum repayment period in many loan programs, some programs allow borrowers to choose a 40-year term, in order to maximize their purchasing power.

Amortization

Most mortgage loans are **fully amortized**. A fully amortized loan is repaid within a certain period of time by means of regular payments that include a portion for principal and a portion for interest. As each payment is made, the appropriate amount of principal is deducted from the debt and the remainder of the payment, which represents the interest, is retained by the lender as earnings or profit. With each payment, the amount of the debt is reduced and the interest due with the next payment is recalculated based on the lower principal balance. The total payment remains the same throughout the term of the loan, but every month the interest portion of the payment is reduced and the principal portion is increased. (See Figure 10.5.) The final payment pays off the loan completely; the principal balance is zero and no further interest is owed.

Example: A $500,000 loan at 5.75% interest can be fully amortized over a 30-year term with monthly principal and interest payments of $2,917.86. If the borrower pays $2,917.86 each month, then the loan will be fully repaid (with interest) after 30 years.

There are two alternatives to fully amortized loans: partially amortized loans and interest-only loans. A **partially amortized** loan requires regular payments of both principal and interest, but those payments aren't enough to repay all of the principal; the borrower is required to make a large balloon payment (the remaining principal balance) at the end of the loan term.

Example: A $500,000 partially amortized mortgage at 5.75% interest calls for regular monthly payments of $2,917.86 for principal and interest, with a loan term of five years. Because the monthly payments are more than enough to cover the

Fig. 10.5 Payments for a fully amortized loan

Example: $500,000 loan @ 5.75%, 30-year term, monthly payments

Payment No.	Beginning Balance	Total Payment	Interest Portion	Principal Portion	Ending Balance
1	$500,000.00	$2,917.86	$2,395.83	$522.03	$499,477.97
2	$499,477.97	$2,917.86	$2,393.33	$524.53	$498,953.44
3	$498,953.44	$2,917.86	$2,390.82	$527.04	$498,426.40
4	$498,426.40	$2,917.86	$2,388.29	$529.57	$497,896.83
5	$497,896.83	$2,917.86	$2,385.76	$532.10	$497,364.73

interest accruing on the loan, some of the principal will be repaid during the five-year term. But since it would take 30 years to fully repay the loan at this rate, most of the principal (roughly $464,000) will still be unpaid after five years. This amount will be due as a balloon payment. To pay it, the borrower will have to refinance the property or come up with the funds from some other source.

With an **interest-only** loan, the borrower's regular payments during the loan term cover the interest accruing on the loan, without paying any of the principal off. The entire principal amount—the amount originally borrowed—is due at the end of the term.

Example: A five-year, $500,000, interest-only loan at 5.75% interest requires monthly payments of $2,395.83, the amount needed to cover the monthly interest accruing on the loan. At the end of the five-year term, the borrower owes the lender the full amount of the principal ($500,000).

The term "interest-only loan" is also used to refer to a loan that's structured to allow interest-only payments during a specified period at the beginning of the loan term. At the end of the initial period, the borrower must begin making amortized payments that will pay off all of the principal and interest by the end of the term. This type of interest-only loan was very popular during the subprime boom, since the low initial payments enabled buyers to purchase a more expensive home than they otherwise could have. For many buyers, however, these loans eventually backfire. When the interest-only period ends, they can't afford the amortized payments, and the payment shock ultimately results in foreclosure.

Loan-to-Value Ratios

The loan-to-value ratio (LTV) for a particular transaction expresses the relationship between the loan amount and the value of the property. The lower the LTV, the smaller the loan amount and the bigger the downpayment.

Example: If a lender makes an $80,000 loan secured by a home appraised at $100,000, the loan-to-value ratio is 80%. The loan amount is 80% of the property's value, and the buyer makes a 20% downpayment. If the lender loaned $75,000 secured by the same property, the LTV would be 75% and the downpayment 25%.

The downpayment represents the borrower's initial investment or equity in the property. (A property owner's equity is the difference between the property's market value and the amount of the liens against it.) The lower the loan-to-value ratio, the greater the borrower's equity. Appreciation of the property benefits the borrower, since any increase in the property's value increases the borrower's equity interest.

The loan-to-value ratio affects the degree of risk involved in the loan—both the risk of default and the risk of loss in the event of default. A borrower who has a substantial investment in the property—a significant amount of equity—will try harder to avoid foreclosure. And when foreclosure is necessary, the lender is more likely to recover the entire debt if the LTV is relatively low. If a lender makes a loan with a 100% LTV, it will recover the outstanding loan balance and all of its costs in a foreclosure sale only if property values have appreciated and the property sells for significantly more than its original purchase price. This is because the foreclosure process itself costs the lender a considerable amount of money.

The higher the LTV, the greater the lender's risk. (In fact, lenders may apply special rules to high-LTV loans because of the extra risk they pose.) So lenders use loan-to-value ratios to set maximum loan amounts.

Example: If a lender's maximum LTV for a certain type of loan is 75%, and the property's appraised value is $100,000, then $75,000 would be the maximum loan amount.

Lenders actually base the maximum loan amount on the sales price or the appraised value, whichever is less. Thus, if the $100,000 property in the example above were selling for $95,000, the maximum loan amount would be $71,250 (75% of $95,000).

Secondary Financing

Sometimes a buyer obtains two mortgage loans at once: a primary loan to pay for most of the purchase price, and a second loan to pay part of the downpayment or closing costs required for the first loan. This supplementary second loan is called **secondary financing**. Secondary financing may come from an institutional lender, the seller, or a private third party.

In most cases, the primary lender will allow secondary financing only if it complies with certain requirements. For example, the borrower must be able to qualify for the combined payment on the first and second loans. The borrower usually has to make a minimum downpayment out of her own funds. And the second loan must be payable at any time, without a prepayment penalty.

Fixed and Adjustable Interest Rates

A fixed-rate loan is repaid over its term at an unchanging rate of interest. For example, the interest rate is set at 6% when the loan is made, and the borrower pays 6% interest on the unpaid principal balance throughout the loan term.

When market interest rates are relatively low and stable, fixed-rate loans work well for borrowers and lenders. But in periods when market rates are high and volatile, neither borrowers nor lenders are comfortable with fixed-rate loans. High interest rates price many borrowers out of the market. And if market rates are fluctuating rapidly, lenders prefer not to tie up their funds for long periods at a set interest rate.

A type of loan that addresses both of these issues is the **adjustable-rate mortgage** (ARM), sometimes called a variable-rate loan. An ARM permits the lender to periodically adjust the loan's interest rate so that it accurately reflects changes in the cost of money. If market rates climb, the borrower's interest rate and monthly payment go up; if market rates decline, the borrower's interest rate and payment go down.

Depending on economic conditions and other factors, lenders may offer ARMs at a lower initial interest rate than the rate they're charging for fixed-rate loans. For example, a lender might offer fixed-rate loans at 6% and ARMs at 5.25%.

How an ARM Works. With an ARM, the borrower's interest rate is determined initially by the cost of money at the time the loan is made. Once the rate has been set, it's tied to one of several widely recognized indexes, and future interest adjustments are based on the upward and downward movements of the index.

Index and Margin. An **index** is a published statistical rate that is a reliable indicator of changes in the cost of money. Examples include the one-year Treasury bill index and the Eleventh District cost of funds index. At the time a loan is made, the lender selects the index it prefers, and thereafter the loan's interest rate will rise and fall with the rates reported for the index.

Since the index is a reflection of the lender's cost of money, it's necessary to add a **margin** to the index to ensure sufficient income for administrative expenses and profit. The lender's margin might be 2% or 3%, or somewhere in between. The index plus the margin equals the interest rate charged to the borrower.

Example:

3.5%	Current index value
+ 2.25%	Margin
5.75%	Borrower's interest rate

It's the index that fluctuates during the loan term and causes the borrower's interest rate to increase and decrease; the lender's margin remains constant.

Adjustment Periods. The borrower's interest rate isn't adjusted every time the index changes. Each ARM has a **rate adjustment period**, which determines how often its interest rate is adjusted. A rate adjustment period of one year is the most common.

An ARM also has a **payment adjustment period**, which determines how often the borrower's monthly mortgage payment is increased or decreased (reflecting changes in the interest rate). For most ARMs, payment adjustments are made at the same intervals as rate adjustments.

Caps. If market interest rates rise rapidly, so will an ARM's index, which could lead to a sharp increase in the interest rate the lender charges the borrower. Of course, a higher interest rate translates into a higher monthly payment. This creates the potential for **payment shock**. In other words, the monthly payments on an ARM might increase so dramatically that the borrower can't afford them.

To help protect borrowers from payment shock and lenders from default, ARMs have interest rate and payment caps. An **interest rate cap** limits how much the lender can raise the interest rate on the loan, even if the index goes way up. A **mortgage payment cap** limits how much the lender can increase the monthly payment.

Negative Amortization. If an ARM has certain features, payment increases may not keep up with increases in the loan's interest rate, so that the monthly payments don't cover all of the interest owed. The lender usually handles this by adding the unpaid interest to the loan's principal balance; this is called **negative amortization**. Ordinarily, a loan's principal balance declines steadily, although gradually. But negative amortization causes the principal balance to go up instead of down. The borrower may owe the lender more money than he originally borrowed. Today, most lenders structure their ARMs to avoid negative amortization and lessen the chance of default and foreclosure.

Hybrid ARMs. With a hybrid ARM, the interest rate is fixed for a specified number of years at the start of the loan term, and then the rate becomes adjustable. For example, a 3/1 hybrid ARM has a fixed rate during the first three years, with annual rate adjustments after that. A 5/1 ARM has a five-year fixed-rate period, and so on. As a general rule, the longer the initial fixed-rate period, the higher the initial interest rate.

Residential Financing Programs

Residential financing programs can be divided into two main groups: conventional loans and government-sponsored loans. In this section, we'll look first at conventional loans, and then at four government-sponsored loan programs: the FHA-insured loan program, the Rural Housing Service loan program, the VA-guaranteed loan program, and the Cal-Vet loan program. As you'll see, each of these has its own qualifying standards and its own rules concerning the downpayment and other aspects of the loan.

Conventional Loans

A conventional loan is simply any institutional loan that isn't insured or guaranteed by a government agency. For example, FHA-insured loans are not conventional loans, because they are backed by a government agency, the Federal Housing Administration.

The rules for conventional loans presented here reflect the criteria established by the secondary market entities that purchase conventional loans, Fannie Mae and Freddie Mac (see Chapter 9). When a loan doesn't meet secondary market criteria, it's considered **nonconforming** and usually can't be sold to the secondary market entities. Most lenders want to be able to sell their loans on the secondary market, so they tailor their standards for conventional loans to match those set by Fannie Mae or Freddie Mac.

Conforming Loan Limits. A loan generally won't be eligible for purchase by Fannie Mae or Freddie Mac if the loan amount exceeds the applicable conforming loan limit. (There are different maximums for properties with one, two, three, or four dwelling units.) The conforming loan limits are based on median housing prices nationwide, and they may be adjusted annually to reflect changes in median prices.

Conventional loans that exceed the conforming loan limits are known as **jumbo loans**. Lenders typically charge higher interest rates and apply stricter underwriting standards when making jumbo loans.

Conventional LTVs. Traditionally, the standard loan-to-value ratio for a conventional loan has been 80% of the appraised value or sales price of the home, whichever is less. Lenders feel confident that a borrower who makes a 20% downpayment with his own funds is unlikely to default; the borrower has too much to lose. And even if the borrower were to default, a foreclosure sale would be likely to generate at least 80% of the purchase price.

While an 80% LTV may still be regarded as the traditional standard, today many conventional loans have much higher loan-to-value ratios. Many lenders allow LTVs up to 95%; and loans with a 97% LTV may be available through special programs (although conventional loans with LTVs that high are increasingly rare).

Because the lender's risk is greater when the borrower's downpayment is smaller, lenders require borrowers to obtain private mortgage insurance for any conventional loan with an LTV over 80%. (Private mortgage insurance is discussed below.) Some lenders also charge higher interest rates and larger loan fees for conventional loans with higher LTVs. The rules for loans with LTVs over 90% tend to be especially strict.

Owner-Occupancy. Residential lenders make a distinction between owner-occupied homes and investment properties. An owner-occupied home, as the term suggests, is one that the owner (the borrower) plans to live in himself, either as his principal residence or as a second home. An investment property is a house that the owner/investor intends to rent out to tenants. Owner-occupants are considered less likely to default than non-occupant borrowers.

Owner-occupancy isn't a requirement for conventional loans, except for loans made through certain special programs (affordable housing programs, for example). In some cases, however, a lender will apply stricter rules to investors than to owner-occupants. For instance, a lender might set 95% as its maximum LTV for owner-occupants, but limit investors to a 90% LTV.

Private Mortgage Insurance. Private mortgage insurance (PMI) is issued by private insurance companies, as opposed to the government's FHA mortgage insurance program. PMI is designed to protect lenders from the greater risk of high-LTV loans. The insurance makes up for the reduced borrower equity. PMI is usually required on all conventional loans that have an LTV over 80%—in other words, whenever the borrower's downpayment is less than 20%.

When insuring a loan, the mortgage insurance company actually assumes only a portion of the risk of default. It typically covers the upper 20% or 25% of the loan amount, not the entire loan amount. The higher the LTV, the higher the coverage requirements and the premiums, since the risk of default is greater. For example, a loan with a 95% LTV will have a higher coverage requirement than a 90% loan.

If the borrower eventually defaults and foreclosure results in losses for the lender, the lender (at the insurer's option) will either sell the property or relinquish it to the insurer, then make a claim for reimbursement of losses up to the policy limit. Losses may take the form of unpaid principal and interest, property taxes, attorney's fees, the costs of maintaining the property during foreclosure and resale, and the expense of selling the property.

As a borrower pays off a loan, the loan-to-value ratio decreases. With a lower LTV, the lender's risk of loss is reduced, and eventually the private mortgage insurance has fulfilled its purpose. Under the federal Homeowners Protection Act, lenders must cancel PMI once a loan has been paid down to 80% of the property's original value, if the borrower requests cancellation. When the loan balance reaches 78%, cancellation is required whether or not it's requested.

Conventional Qualifying Standards. Fannie Mae and Freddie Mac have detailed guidelines for evaluating a conventional loan applicant's credit history, income, and net worth. The entities set minimum credit scores for the loans they buy. Also, a borrower whose credit score is above the minimum, but still comparatively low, is usually charged a risk-based loan fee called a delivery fee or loan-level price adjustment (LLPA). This fee can be substantial. Additional LLPAs may be charged based on other special risk factors in a transaction; for example, an LLPA might be charged because the loan has an adjustable interest rate. (The risk of default is greater with an ARM, because of the potential for payment shock.)

To determine if an applicant's stable monthly income is sufficient, an underwriter may consider both the housing expense to income ratio and the debt to income ratio.

Example: Suppose a lender's maximum housing expense to income ratio is 28% and maximum debt to income ratio is 36%. If an applicant's housing expense to income ratio is 26% (under the lender's limit), but her debt to income ratio is 40% (over the lender's limit), then the lender probably won't approve the loan unless there are special considerations.

In some cases, the underwriter will consider only the debt to income ratio. Because the debt to income ratio takes all of the applicant's monthly obligations into account, it's considered a more reliable indicator of creditworthiness than the housing expense to income ratio.

Some lenders require an applicant for a conventional loan to have the equivalent of two months of mortgage payments in reserve after making the downpayment and paying all their closing costs. For loans with LTVs over 90%, a lender might require three months of mortgage payments in reserve.

Assumption. The security instruments used for most conventional loans include an alienation clause, which means the borrower can't sell the property and arrange for the buyer to assume the loan without the lender's permission. Typically, the lender will evaluate the buyer with the same qualifying standards that it applies in a new loan transaction. If the lender approves the assumption, it will charge an assumption fee, and it may also adjust the interest rate to the prevailing rates at that time.

FHA-Insured Loans

The Federal Housing Administration (FHA) was created by Congress in 1934 in the National Housing Act. The purpose of the act, and of the FHA, was to generate new jobs through increased construction activity, to exert a stabilizing influence on the mortgage market, and to promote the financing, repair, improvement, and sale of real estate nationwide. An additional by-product of the FHA housing program was the establishment of minimum housing construction standards.

Today the FHA is part of the Department of Housing and Urban Development (HUD). Its primary function is insuring mortgage loans; the FHA compensates lenders who make loans through its programs for losses that result from borrower default. The FHA does not build homes or make loans.

In effect, the FHA serves as a giant mortgage insurance agency. Its insurance program, sometimes referred to as the **Mutual Mortgage Insurance Plan**, is funded with premiums paid by FHA borrowers.

Lenders who have been approved by the FHA to make insured loans either submit applications from prospective borrowers to the local FHA office for approval or, if authorized by the FHA to do so, perform the underwriting functions themselves. Lenders who are authorized to underwrite their own FHA loan applications are called "direct endorsement lenders."

Lenders who don't underwrite their own FHA loans forward applications to the local FHA office for underwriting and approval. Note that the FHA doesn't accept applications directly from prospective borrowers. Borrowers must begin by applying to a lender such as a bank or a mortgage company for an initial loan commitment.

As the insurer, the FHA is liable to the lender for the full amount of any losses resulting from the borrower's default and a subsequent foreclosure. In exchange for insuring a loan, the FHA regulates many of the terms and conditions on which the loan is made.

Characteristics of FHA Loans. The typical FHA-insured loan has a 30-year term, although the borrower may have the option of a shorter term. The property purchased with an FHA loan may have up to four dwelling units, and it must be the borrower's primary residence. All FHA loans must have first lien position.

The downpayment required for an FHA loan is often considerably less than it would be for a conventional loan financing the same purchase (see below). Regardless of the size of the downpayment, mortgage insurance is required on all FHA loans.

Prepayment penalties aren't allowed. An FHA loan can be paid off at any time without penalty.

FHA Loan Amounts. FHA programs are primarily intended to help low- and middle-income home buyers. So HUD sets maximum loan amounts, limiting the size of loans that can be insured under its programs. FHA maximum loan amounts vary from one place to another because they are based on median housing costs in each area. An area where housing is expensive has a higher maximum loan amount than a low-cost area does.

However, there's also a "ceiling" for FHA loan amounts that applies nationwide; no matter how high prices are in a particular area, FHA loans can't exceed that ceiling. As a result, FHA financing tends to be less useful in areas where housing is exceptionally expensive. The FHA ceiling is tied to the conforming loan limits for conventional loans, and it is subject to annual adjustment.

Loan-to-Value Ratios. The loan amount for a particular transaction is determined not just by the FHA loan ceiling for the local area, but also by the FHA's rules concerning loan-to-value ratios.

The maximum loan-to-value ratio for an FHA loan depends on the borrower's credit score. If the borrower's credit score is 580 or above, the maximum LTV is 96.5%. If his score is 500 to 579, the maximum LTV is 90%. Someone with a score below 500 isn't eligible for an FHA loan.

The difference between the maximum loan amount for a transaction and the appraised value or sales price (whichever is less) is called the borrower's **minimum cash investment**. In a transaction with maximum financing (a 96.5% LTV), the borrower must make a minimum cash investment of 3.5%.

FHA Qualifying Standards. As with any institutional mortgage loan, the underwriting for an FHA-insured loan involves the analysis of the applicant's credit history, income, and net worth. But the FHA's underwriting standards aren't as strict as the Fannie Mae/Freddie Mac standards used for conventional loans. The FHA standards make it easier for low- and middle-income home buyers to qualify for a mortgage.

Income. An underwriter evaluating an application for an FHA loan will apply two ratios to determine the adequacy of the applicant's income, a housing expense to income ratio and a debt to income ratio. The FHA's maximum income ratios are higher than the ones typically set for conventional loans. This means that an FHA borrower's mortgage payment and other monthly obligations can be a larger percentage of his income than a conventional borrower's.

Although FHA programs are targeted at low- and middle-income buyers, there's no maximum income limit. A person with a high income could qualify for an FHA loan, as long as the requested loan didn't exceed the maximum loan amount for the area.

Funds for Closing. At closing an FHA borrower must have sufficient funds to cover the minimum cash investment, any discount points she has agreed to pay, and certain other closing costs. (Note that secondary financing generally can't be used for the minimum cash investment, unless the source of the second loan is a family member or government agency.) An FHA borrower usually isn't required to have reserves after closing.

FHA Insurance Premiums. Mortgage insurance premiums for FHA loans are commonly referred to as the **MIP**. For most FHA loans, the borrower pays both a one-time premium and annual premiums. The one-time premium may be paid at closing, or else financed along with the loan amount and paid off over the loan term.

Previously, the FHA's annual MIP could be canceled once the loan's principal balance reached a certain percentage of the property's original value. However, the FHA changed this cancellation policy in 2013. Under the new rules, for loans with an original loan-to-value ratio over 90%, the annual MIP must be paid for the entire loan term. For loans with an original LTV of 90% or less, the annual MIP will be canceled after 11 years.

Assumption of FHA Loans. FHA loans made before 1990 can be assumed without the lender's approval, if the seller doesn't need a release of liability. Loans made since then can be assumed only by a buyer who meets FHA underwriting standards. The buyer must intend to occupy the home as his primary residence.

Rural Housing Service Loans

The Rural Housing Service (RHS) is a federal agency within the U.S. Department of Agriculture (USDA) that makes and guarantees loans used to purchase, build, or rehabilitate homes in rural areas. These are often referred to as **rural development loans**, or RD loans; they're also called USDA loans or Section 502 loans.

A rural area is generally defined as open country or a town with a rural character and a population of 10,000 or less. (Under special circumstances, a town with a population of up to 20,000 may be considered rural.)

To qualify for an RHS program, a borrower must currently be without adequate housing. The borrower must also be able to afford the proposed mortgage payments and have a reasonable credit history. A home purchased, built, or improved with a Rural Housing Service loan must be modest in size, design, and cost.

Direct Loans. Low-income borrowers (whose income is no more than 80% of the area median income) may obtain financing from RHS for 100% of the purchase price. The loan term may be as long as 38 years, depending on the borrower's income level. The interest rate is set by RHS, and the loan is serviced by RHS.

Guaranteed Loans. The Rural Housing Service also guarantees loans made by approved lenders to borrowers whose income is no more than 115% of the area median income. Approved lenders include any state housing agency, FHA- and VA-approved lenders, and lenders participating in other RHS-guaranteed loan programs. The loan amount may be 100% of the purchase price. The loan term is 30 years, and the interest rate is set by the lender.

VA-Guaranteed Loans

The VA-guaranteed home loan program was established to help veterans finance the purchase of their homes with affordable loans. VA financing offers several advantages over conventional financing. The program is administered by the U.S. Department of Veterans Affairs (the VA).

Eligibility for VA Loans. Eligibility for a VA home loan is based on length of active duty service in the U.S. armed forces. The minimum requirement varies from **90 days** to **24 months**, depending on when the veteran served. (Longer periods are required for peacetime service than for wartime service.) Eligibility may also be based on longtime service in the National Guard or reserves. Military personnel who receive a dishonorable discharge aren't eligible for a VA loan.

A veteran's surviving spouse may be eligible for a VA loan if he or she has not remarried and the veteran was killed in action or died of service-related injuries. A veteran's spouse may also be eligible if the veteran is listed as missing in action or is a prisoner of war.

Application Process. To get a VA-guaranteed loan, a veteran must apply to an institutional lender and provide a **Certificate of Eligibility** issued by the VA. The lender will process the veteran's loan application and forward it to the VA. Note that the Certificate of Eligibility isn't a guarantee that the veteran will qualify for a loan.

The property that the veteran wants to purchase must be appraised in accordance with VA guidelines. The appraised value is set forth in a document called a **Notice of Value**, or NOV (also referred to as a Certificate of Reasonable Value, or CRV).

When a VA loan has been approved, the loan is guaranteed by the federal government. If the borrower defaults, the VA will reimburse the lender for all or part of any resulting loss. The loan guaranty works essentially like mortgage insurance; it protects the lender against a large loss if the borrower fails to repay the loan.

Characteristics of VA Loans. A VA loan can be used to finance the purchase or construction of a single-family residence or a multifamily residence with up to four units. The veteran must intend to occupy the home, or one of the units.

VA-guaranteed loans are attractive to borrowers for several reasons, including the following:

- Unlike most loans, a VA loan typically doesn't require a downpayment. The loan amount can be as large as the sales price or the appraised value, whichever is less. In other words, the loan-to-value ratio can be 100%.
- The VA doesn't set a maximum loan amount or impose any income restrictions. VA loans aren't limited to low- or middle-income buyers.
- VA underwriting standards are significantly less stringent than conventional underwriting standards.
- VA loans don't require the extra expense of mortgage insurance.

A VA borrower is required to pay a funding fee (currently 2.15% of the loan amount for most first-time VA borrowers). The fee is reduced if the borrower is going to make a downpayment of 5% or more.

VA Guaranty. Like private mortgage insurance, the VA guaranty covers only part of the loan amount, up to a maximum set by the government. The maximum guaranty amount is increased periodically. The amount of the guaranty available to a particular veteran is sometimes called the vet's "entitlement."

Because the guaranty amount is limited, a large loan amount presents some extra risk for the lender. Many lenders require the VA borrower to make at least a small downpayment if the loan amount exceeds a certain limit (typically four times the guaranty amount). This is a limit set by the lender, however, not by the VA.

Restoration of Entitlement. If a veteran sells property that was financed with a VA loan and repays the loan in full from the proceeds of the sale, he's entitled to a full restoration of guaranty rights for future use. However, because of the owner-occupancy requirement, the veteran must demonstrate a need for new housing in order to obtain a new VA loan. (Restoration is also known as reinstatement of entitlement.)

Substitution of Entitlement. If a home purchased with a VA loan is sold and the loan is assumed instead of repaid, the veteran's entitlement can be restored under certain circumstances. The buyer who assumes the loan must be an eligible veteran and must agree to substitute her entitlement for the seller's. The loan payments must be current, and the buyer must be an acceptable credit risk. If these conditions are met, the veteran can formally request a substitution of entitlement from the VA.

Note that a VA loan can be assumed by a non-veteran who meets the VA's standards of creditworthiness. But the entitlement of the veteran seller will not be restored if the buyer assuming the loan isn't a veteran.

Liability. Despite the VA guaranty, a borrower still has personal liability for a VA loan. If a foreclosure sale results in a loss and it's determined that the borrower was guilty of fraud or bad faith in connection with the loan, the borrower may be liable to the VA for the amount it paid to cover the lender's loss. Even if there was no bad faith, the borrower's guaranty entitlement won't be restored until he reimburses the VA for the full amount paid on his behalf.

Qualifying Standards. Instead of using both a housing expense to income ratio and a debt to income ratio, the VA uses only a debt to income ratio. The VA's maximum debt to income ratio is considerably higher than the maximum generally allowed for a conventional loan.

In addition to the debt to income ratio, the underwriter will also consider the veteran's **residual income**. This is calculated by subtracting the proposed mortgage payment, all other recurring obligations, and certain taxes from the veteran's gross monthly income. The veteran's residual income must meet the VA's minimum requirements, which vary based on the region of the country where the veteran lives, family size, and the size of the proposed loan.

At least for some loan applicants, it can be much easier to qualify for a VA loan than for a conventional loan. Home buyers who are eligible veterans should keep the option of VA financing in mind.

Cal-Vet Loans

The state of California also offers attractive loans to eligible veterans. Its program is called the California Veterans Farm and Home Purchase Program. The loans are commonly called Cal-Vet loans. A Cal-Vet loan may be used to purchase either a farm or a home (including a single-family home, a mobile home, a condominium unit, or a residence with two to four units that meets certain requirements). The California Department of Veterans Affairs processes, originates, and services the loans until they are paid in full.

The Cal-Vet program works very differently from the federal VA guaranty program. Under the Cal-Vet program, the state actually purchases and takes title to the home chosen by a veteran applicant. The state then sells the property to the applicant under a land contract. The state retains title to the property throughout the contract term. During this period the veteran has an equitable interest in the property. When the contract price has been paid, the state gives the veteran a grant deed, transferring legal title.

Eligibility. To be eligible for a Cal-Vet loan, veterans generally must have been honorably discharged and have served at least 90 days of active duty. (At one time, wartime service was required, but that's no longer true.) Veterans discharged before 90 days because of a service-connected disability are also eligible.

In addition, current service members are eligible for a Cal-Vet loan after 90 days of active duty. Members of the California National Guard or the U.S. Reserves are eligible if they've served at least one year of a six-year obligation.

A veteran's surviving spouse may obtain a Cal-Vet loan if the veteran died as a result of injuries sustained in the line of duty, is designated as missing or as a prisoner of war, or died after applying for a Cal-Vet loan.

Restrictions. Some Cal-Vet loans are subject to the following restrictions:

- the borrower must either be a first-time home buyer or purchasing a home in an area targeted as economically distressed;
- the purchase price of the property can't exceed a specified limit that's based on average prices in the area; and
- the borrower's family income can't exceed a specified limit that varies depending on family size and the county where the property is located.

Keep in mind that these restrictions don't apply to all applicants. Someone interested in a Cal-Vet loan should check with the California Department of Veterans Affairs to determine whether they apply in his case.

Applying for a Cal-Vet Loan. An application for a Cal-Vet loan can be submitted directly to the Department of Veterans Affairs or to a mortgage broker expressly authorized to handle Cal-Vet loans.

Cal-Vet Rules and Requirements. Cal-Vet loans are generally subject to the following rules and requirements.

Occupancy. The borrower or her immediate family must occupy the property within 60 days after closing. Transferring, encumbering, or leasing the property is prohibited without permission.

Loan Term and Prepayment. The standard contract term for a Cal-Vet loan is 30 years, although the borrower may choose to pay the loan off sooner than that. Cal-Vet loans can be prepaid at any time without penalty. They cannot be assumed by a buyer, however.

Guaranty or PMI. Although the state sells the property to the veteran under a land contract, the state obtains either a federal VA guaranty or private mortgage insurance to protect its interest, unless there's a downpayment of 20% or more.

To pay for the VA guaranty or the PMI coverage, the borrower is charged a percentage of the loan amount as a funding fee. The percentage varies depending on the program and the size of the borrower's downpayment.

Loan Amount, Downpayment, and LTV. A Cal-Vet loan can't exceed the maximum loan amount set by the state. If the loan has a VA guaranty, no downpayment is required. Otherwise, a downpayment of at least 3% is usually required, so that the maximum loan-to-value ratio is 97%. Secondary financing is allowed, but the total amount borrowed can't exceed the appraised value.

Interest Rate. The state sets a below-market interest rate for Cal-Vet loans. The rate may vary over the loan term, but can't increase more than 0.5%.

Other Fees and Points. Cal-Vet borrowers must pay an application fee, an appraisal fee, and a 1% origination fee. Discount points are not charged in connection with Cal-Vet loans.

Life Insurance. A new Cal-Vet borrower under age 62 has the option of purchasing life insurance through the Cal-Vet program. If the borrower dies, the insurance pays from one to five years of principal and interest installments on the loan. After the insurance proceeds have been applied, the borrower's heirs can continue with the loan payments if they choose to, instead of having to sell the property in order to pay off the loan.

Predatory Lending

Predatory lending refers to practices that unscrupulous mortgage lenders and mortgage brokers use to take advantage of (prey upon) unsophisticated borrowers for their own profit. Real estate agents, appraisers, and home improvement contractors sometimes participate in predatory lending schemes, and in some cases a buyer or a seller may play a role in deceiving the other party.

Predatory lending is especially likely to occur in the subprime market. It tends to be more common in refinancing and home equity lending, but home purchase loans are also affected.

Here are some examples of predatory lending practices:

- **Predatory steering:** Steering a buyer toward a more expensive loan when the buyer could qualify for a less expensive one.
- **Fee packing:** Charging interest rates, points, or processing fees that far exceed the norm and aren't justified by the cost of the services provided.
- **Loan flipping:** Encouraging a homeowner to refinance repeatedly in a short period, when there's no real benefit to doing so.

- **Predatory property flipping:** Buying property at a discount (because the seller needs a quick sale) and then rapidly reselling it to an unsophisticated buyer for an inflated price. This is illegal when a real estate agent, an appraiser, a mortgage broker, and/or a lender commit fraud to deceive the seller and/or buyer about the true value of the property.
- **Disregarding borrower's ability to pay:** Making a loan based only on the property's value, without using appropriate underwriting standards to determine whether the borrower can afford the loan payments. In this situation, the predator is likely to be someone who won't be affected when the borrower eventually defaults, such as a mortgage broker.
- **Fraud:** Misrepresenting or concealing unfavorable loan terms or excessive fees, falsifying documents, or using other fraudulent means to induce a prospective buyer to enter into a loan agreement.
- **Balloon payment abuses:** Making a partially amortized or interest-only loan with low monthly payments, without disclosing to the borrower that a large balloon payment will be required after a short period.
- **Excessive or unfair prepayment penalties:** Imposing an unusually large penalty, failing to limit the penalty period to the first few years of the loan term, and/or charging the penalty even if the loan is prepaid because the property is being sold.

Predatory lenders and mortgage brokers deliberately target potential borrowers who aren't able to understand the transaction they're entering into, or don't know that better alternatives are available to them. Borrowers are especially likely to be targeted if they are elderly, have a limited income, are less educated, or speak limited English. Elderly victims who are cognitively impaired and who have a lot of equity in their homes are the most frequent victims of refinancing schemes.

There are federal and state laws intended to curb predatory lending. The federal Home Ownership and Equity Protection Act (HOEPA), passed in 1994, added special restrictions on "high-cost" mortgage loans to the Truth in Lending Act. It was quite limited in scope, however, applying only to very high-cost home equity loans and refinancing, not to home purchase loans. Between 2008 and 2010, as part of their response to the subprime crisis and the foreclosure epidemic, Congress and the Federal Reserve made changes to the Truth in Lending Act and Regulation Z that made many more loans—including high-cost home purchase loans—subject to special restrictions. Lenders who charge high rates and fees on loans secured by the borrower's principal residence must make additional disclosures, aren't allowed to engage in certain practices, and can't include certain provisions in their loan agreements.

California has its own predatory lending law, which also requires special disclosures and prohibits certain practices and provisions for high-cost loans. Like the current federal law, the state law applies to purchase loans, home equity loans, and refinancing secured by the borrower's principal residence.

Mortgage Fraud

Mortgage fraud refers to using deception to obtain a mortgage loan by defrauding the lender. It may be perpetrated by borrowers, or by professionals in the mortgage industry or the real estate industry. In some cases, borrowers and professionals conspire to carry out a fraudulent scheme. Borrowers generally commit mortgage fraud by providing false information on a loan application, in order to obtain a loan they're not qualified for. A real estate agent, appraiser, or mortgage broker usually commits mortgage fraud to make a profit, often by manipulating innocent borrowers or property sellers.

Both federal and state law prohibit mortgage fraud. In 2009, in response to the mortgage crisis, Congress passed the Fraud Enforcement and Recovery Act, which toughened existing federal antifraud provisions and took particular aim at mortgage fraud. Mortgage fraud is a felony in California, punishable by imprisonment for one year. Under the relevant provision in the Penal Code, a person commits mortgage fraud if she does any of the following during the mortgage lending process or in connection with a mortgage loan with the intent to defraud:

- deliberately makes a misrepresentation or omits information;
- deliberately uses or facilitates the use of a misrepresentation or omission, knowing that it is deceptive;
- receives any funds in connection with a closing that she knows resulted from a deliberate misrepresentation or omission; or
- records a document she knows contains a deliberate misrepresentation or omission.

Chapter Summary

1. Real estate lenders in the primary market include commercial banks, thrift institutions, credit unions, mortgage companies, and private lenders.

2. Lenders charge an origination fee to cover their administrative costs, and sometimes charge discount points to increase the upfront yield on the loan. One point is 1% of the loan amount.

3. The Truth in Lending Act applies to any consumer loan that's secured by real property. It requires lenders to give loan applicants a disclosure statement about loan costs. It also regulates how financing information is presented in advertising. California's finance disclosure laws include the Mortgage Loan Broker Law and the Seller Financing Disclosure Law.

4. In qualifying a buyer for a real estate loan, an underwriter examines the buyer's income, net worth, and credit history to determine if he can be expected to make the proposed monthly mortgage payments. Income ratios measure the adequacy of the buyer's stable monthly income.

5. The traditional loan term for a mortgage loan is 30 years, but 15-year, 20-year, and 40-year loans are also available. A 15-year loan requires much higher payments than a comparable 30-year loan, but it saves the borrower thousands of dollars in interest in the long run.

6. A fully amortized loan has level payments that pay off all of the principal and interest by the end of the loan term. Most mortgage loans are fully amortized, but there are also partially amortized and interest-only mortgage loans.

7. The loan-to-value ratio for a particular transaction expresses the relationship between the loan amount and the property's appraised value or sales price, whichever is less. The higher the loan-to-value ratio, the greater the lender's risk.

8. Secondary financing may be used to cover part of the downpayment and closing costs required for the primary loan. A secondary financing arrangement must comply with rules set by the primary lender.

9. The interest rate on a mortgage loan may be either fixed or adjustable. With an adjustable-rate mortgage, the interest rate is tied to an index, and it's adjusted at specified intervals to reflect changes in the index.

10. A conventional loan is an institutional loan that isn't insured or guaranteed by the government. Conventional loans are often classified by loan-to-value ratio (as 80% loans, 90% loans, 95% loans, and so on). Private mortgage insurance is required for loans with LTVs over 80%.

11. FHA-insured loans are distinguished from conventional loans by less stringent qualifying standards, lower downpayments, and less cash needed for closing. The maximum loan amount available for an FHA loan depends on housing costs in the area where the property is located.

12. The federal Rural Housing Service makes and guarantees loans for homes in rural areas. Low- or moderate-income borrowers who lack adequate housing may qualify if they can afford the mortgage payments and have reasonable credit histories.

13. Eligible veterans may apply for a VA-guaranteed home loan. No downpayment is required for a VA loan. The VA sets a maximum guaranty amount, but does not set a maximum loan amount. The qualifying standards for VA loans are less stringent than the standards for conventional loans.

14. In the Cal-Vet loan program, the state will purchase a home that an eligible veteran wants and sell it to the veteran using a land contract. Advantages of the Cal-Vet program include low downpayment requirements, minimal loan fees, and low interest rates.

15. Unscrupulous lenders and mortgage brokers use predatory lending practices to take advantage of unsophisticated borrowers. Appraisers and real estate agents sometimes participate in predatory lending schemes. The elderly and other vulnerable groups are especially likely to be targeted.

16. Mortgage fraud refers to obtaining a mortgage loan by defrauding the lender. It may be perpetrated by borrowers, real estate agents, or mortgage professionals.

Key Terms

Mortgage company—A type of lender that isn't a depository institution and that makes loans for sale on the secondary market or on behalf of large investors.

Mortgage loan originator—An individual who, for compensation or gain, takes a residential mortgage application or negotiates the terms of a residential mortgage loan.

Point—One percent of the principal amount of a loan.

Origination fee—A fee that a lender charges to compensate for the administrative costs of processing a loan.

Discount points—A fee that a lender may charge to increase the upfront yield on the loan.

Annual percentage rate (APR)—Under the Truth in Lending Act, the relationship between the total cost of the loan and the amount borrowed, expressed as an annual percentage.

Loan underwriting—Evaluating the creditworthiness of the buyer and the value of the property to determine if a loan should be approved.

Credit score—A number that is calculated by applying a statistical model to a loan applicant's credit report, used as an indication of how likely the applicant is to default on the proposed loan.

Automated underwriting (AU)—Analysis of a loan application with a computer program that makes a preliminary recommendation for or against approval.

Stable monthly income—Income that satisfies the lender's standards of quality and durability.

Income ratios—Percentages used to determine whether a loan applicant's stable monthly income is sufficient.

Housing expense to income ratio—A percentage that measures a loan applicant's proposed monthly mortgage payment against her stable monthly income.

Debt to income ratio—A percentage that measures all of a loan applicant's monthly obligations (including the proposed mortgage payment) against stable monthly income.

Net worth—An individual's total personal assets minus his total personal liabilities.

Fully amortized loan—A loan that is fully paid off by the end of its term by means of regular principal and interest payments.

Loan-to-value ratio (LTV)—The relationship between the loan amount and the property's appraised value or sales price, whichever is less.

Secondary financing—A second loan to help pay the downpayment or closing costs associated with the primary loan.

Fixed-rate loan—A loan repaid over its term at an unchanging rate of interest.

Adjustable-rate mortgage (ARM)—A loan that allows the lender to periodically adjust the loan's interest rate to reflect changes in market interest rates.

Index—A published rate used as a reliable indicator of the current cost of money.

Margin—The difference between the index value on an ARM and the interest rate the borrower is charged.

Negative amortization—When unpaid interest is added to a loan's principal balance.

Conventional loan—Any institutional loan that isn't insured or guaranteed by a government agency.

Nonconforming loan—A loan that doesn't meet the underwriting standards of the major secondary market entities.

PMI—Private mortgage insurance; insurance designed to protect lenders from the greater risks of high-LTV conventional loans.

MIP—The mortgage insurance premiums required for FHA-insured loans.

Certificate of Eligibility—The document that establishes a veteran's eligibility to apply for a VA home loan.

Notice of Value—The document issued when a home is appraised in connection with the underwriting of a VA loan.

Residual income—The amount of monthly income a VA borrower has left over after deducting monthly expenses and taxes.

Predatory lending—Lending practices used by unscrupulous lenders and mortgage brokers to take advantage of unsophisticated borrowers.

Mortgage fraud—Using deception to obtain a mortgage loan by defrauding the lender.

Chapter Quiz

1. A mortgage company:
   a) arranges loans but doesn't service them
   b) services loans but doesn't make them
   c) is the same as a mortgage broker
   d) is sometimes called a mortgage banker

2. To increase its upfront yield on a loan, the lender is charging 2% of the loan amount, to be paid at closing. This charge is called:
   a) the origination fee
   b) PMI
   c) the index
   d) discount points

3. The Truth in Lending Act and Regulation Z:
   a) place restrictions on how much a lender can charge for a consumer loan
   b) require lenders to give loan applicants a disclosure statement concerning loan costs
   c) prohibit lenders from advertising specific financing terms
   d) All of the above

4. A loan's APR expresses the relationship between the:
   a) total finance charge and the loan amount
   b) interest rate on the loan and the discount rate
   c) downpayment and the total finance charge
   d) monthly payment and the interest rate

5. After determining the quantity of the loan applicant's stable monthly income, the underwriter measures the adequacy of the income using:
   a) the consumer price index
   b) income ratios
   c) credit scoring
   d) federal income tax tables

6. In comparison to a 30-year loan, a 15-year loan:
   a) typically has a lower interest rate
   b) typically has a lower monthly payment
   c) requires the borrower to pay much more total interest
   d) All of the above

7. A house was appraised for $403,000 and its sales price is $400,000. If the loan-to-value ratio is 90%, how much is the loan amount?
   a) $322,400
   b) $360,000
   c) $362,700
   d) $393,000

8. With an adjustable-rate mortgage, the interest rate:
   a) is adjusted at specified intervals, and so is the payment amount
   b) is adjusted monthly, and so is the payment amount
   c) increases and decreases, but the payment amount remains the same
   d) may increase periodically, but won't decrease

9. Unpaid interest added to the loan balance is referred to as:
   a) payment shock
   b) partial amortization
   c) negative amortization
   d) participation interest

10. For conventional loans, private mortgage insurance is required when the loan-to-value ratio is:
    a) 75% or higher
    b) 90% or higher
    c) over 95%
    d) over 80%

11. The FHA:
    a) makes loans
    b) insures loans
    c) buys and sells loans
    d) All of the above

12. All of the following statements about FHA loans are true, except:
    a) no downpayment is required
    b) the borrower usually isn't required to have reserves after closing
    c) mortgage insurance is required on all loans
    d) the borrower must occupy the property as her primary residence

13. A VA loan can be assumed:
    a) only by an eligible veteran
    b) only by an eligible veteran who agrees to a substitution of entitlement
    c) by any buyer who passes the credit check
    d) by any buyer, without regard to creditworthiness

14. All of the following statements about Cal-Vet loans are true, except:
    a) the veteran purchases the property from the state under a land contract
    b) a surviving spouse may obtain a loan
    c) the loan can be paid off early without penalty
    d) the veteran must apply within five years after discharge from the military

15. Which of the following statements about predatory lending is true?
    a) Most subprime lenders engage in predatory practices
    b) Predatory lending doesn't occur in connection with home purchase loans
    c) Predatory lenders are especially likely to target the elderly and people who speak only limited English
    d) All of the above

Answer Key

1. d) A mortgage company is sometimes called a mortgage banker. Mortgage companies make loans and also service loans on behalf of investors.

2. d) Discount points are a percentage of the loan amount paid at closing to increase the lender's upfront yield on the loan.

3. b) TILA and Regulation Z require lenders to disclose loan costs to loan applicants, but they don't restrict how much a lender can charge in connection with a loan. And while these laws regulate how financing terms are presented in advertising, they don't prohibit advertisement of financing terms.

4. a) The APR is the annual percentage rate, which indicates the relationship between the total finance charge and the loan amount.

5. b) Income ratios are used to measure the adequacy or sufficiency of a loan applicant's stable monthly income.

6. a) Fifteen-year mortgages usually have lower interest rates than 30-year mortgages. The monthly payment amount is higher, and the total interest paid over the life of the loan is much less.

7. b) The loan amount is $360,000, because the loan-to-value ratio is based on the appraised value or the sales price, whichever is less. $400,000 × 90% = $360,000.

8. a) Both the interest rate and the payment amount for an ARM are adjusted at specified intervals. The rate and the payment amount may increase or decrease to reflect changes in the index.

9. c) Negative amortization is unpaid interest that is added to the loan balance.

10. d) When the LTV of a conventional loan is over 80%, PMI is required.

11. b) The FHA only insures loans made by institutional lenders. It doesn't make loans itself, nor does it buy and sell loans on the secondary market.

12. a) A downpayment is required for an FHA loan.

13. c) A VA loan can be assumed by any buyer, whether or not the buyer is an eligible veteran. The buyer is required to pass a credit check, however.

14. d) Applying for a Cal-Vet loan within five years after discharge isn't a requirement of the program.

15. c) Predatory lenders are especially likely to target elderly people and other vulnerable groups. Predatory lending is a problem in connection with home purchase loans as well as home equity loans and refinancing. It's especially likely to occur in the subprime market, but it's not true that most subprime lenders engage in predatory practices.

Chapter 11

Real Estate Appraisal

I. Introduction to Appraisal
   A. Purpose and use of an appraisal
   B. Appraiser-client relationship
   C. Licensing and certification of appraisers
II. Value
   A. Elements of value
   B. Types of value
   C. Principles of value
III. The Appraisal Process
IV. Gathering Data
   A. General data
      1. Economic trends
      2. Neighborhood analysis
   B. Specific data
      1. Site analysis
      2. Building analysis
V. Methods of Appraisal
   A. Sales comparison approach to value
      1. Elements of comparison
      2. Comparing properties and making adjustments
      3. Use of listings
   B. Cost approach to value
      1. Replacement cost vs. reproduction cost
      2. Estimating replacement cost
      3. Estimating depreciation
      4. Adding land value
   C. Income approach to value
      1. Gross income
      2. Operating expenses
      3. Capitalization
      4. Gross income multipliers
   D. Site valuation
VI. Reconciliation and Final Estimate of Value

Chapter Overview

The foundation of every real estate transaction is the value placed on the property in question. The value of a home affects its selling price, financing terms, rental rate, property tax assessment, and insurance coverage, and the income tax consequences of owning it. The parties to a transaction need to know what the property is worth aside from any emotional or subjective considerations, and for this they rely on an appraisal. This chapter examines the concept of value and explains the various methods appraisers use to estimate value.

Introduction to Appraisal

An **appraisal** is an estimate or an opinion of value. It usually takes the form of a written statement, called an **appraisal report**, setting forth the appraiser's opinion of the value of a piece of property as of a given date. An appraisal is sometimes called a **valuation**.

Purpose and Use of an Appraisal

In appraisal terminology, a distinction is made between the purpose and the use of an appraisal. The basic **purpose** of an appraisal is to estimate value; in most cases the appraiser is estimating the property's market value (defined later in this chapter). The **use** of an appraisal refers to the reason the appraisal is being made. For example, an appraisal's use may be to help a seller decide on a fair listing price, or to help a buyer determine how much to pay for a property. Most often, the use of an appraisal is to help a lender decide whether the property a buyer has chosen is suitable security for a loan, and if so, what the maximum loan amount should be.

In addition to helping to determine a fair price or a maximum loan amount, an appraiser's services are regularly required in order to:

- identify raw land's highest and best use;
- estimate a property's value for purposes of taxation (assessment);
- establish rental rates;
- estimate the relative values of properties being exchanged;
- determine the amount of hazard insurance coverage necessary;
- estimate remodeling costs or their contribution to value;
- help establish just compensation in a condemnation proceeding; or
- estimate the value of properties involved in the liquidation of estates, corporate mergers and acquisitions, or bankruptcies.

The Appraiser-Client Relationship

An appraiser may work for a financial institution, a private corporation with an active real estate department, a government agency, or an appraisal company. Or an appraiser may work as a **fee appraiser**, an independent appraiser hired to appraise a particular property in exchange for a fee. Most appraisers are fee appraisers, either self-employed or employed through an appraisal firm.

The person who hires the appraiser is the client. The appraiser is the client's agent. A principal/agent relationship exists and the laws of agency apply (see Chapter 8). Because of the fiduciary relationship that exists between the appraiser and his client, an appraiser has a duty of confidentiality and should discuss the results of the appraisal process only with the client, unless given permission to discuss them with a third party. Duties imposed by the agency relationship also require an appraiser to disclose in the appraisal report any interest he has in the property being appraised; in fact, in many transactions, federal law prohibits an appraiser from having any interest in the subject property. And if the appraiser is uncertain about any aspect of the appraisal—whether to classify a particular item as real or personal property, for example—that information should also be included in the appraisal report.

An appraiser's fee is determined in advance, using a rate customary to the local market, based on the expected difficulty of the appraisal and the amount of time it's likely to take. The fee can't be calculated as a percentage of the appraised value of the property, nor can it be based on the client's satisfaction with the appraiser's findings.

To help ensure their independence and impartiality, appraisers in home loan transactions are subject to special rules. For example, if a loan will be secured by the borrower's home, it is illegal for the appraiser to have any financial interest in the property. If a loan will be sold to Fannie Mae or Freddie Mac, the appraiser is not permitted to have any substantive communication with the mortgage loan originator; the appraisal must be arranged either through an independent appraisal management company, or through a separate department within the lender's organization. In addition, the appraiser can't be selected or compensated by a real estate agent.

Under both federal and California law, it's illegal for someone with an interest in a transaction to attempt to improperly influence the appraisal through coercion, extortion, or bribery. It is permissible to ask the appraiser to consider additional property information, explain the basis for her value estimate more fully, or correct errors in the appraisal report.

By law, only an appraiser may formally offer an opinion of a property's value. A real estate agent may help a client price a property, but this is done through the less rigorous process of competitive market analysis. Similarly, a home inspector may issue a detailed report on a property's condition, but may not estimate the property's value.

Licensing and Certification of Appraisers

The state of California licenses and certifies appraisers. Although the state doesn't require all appraisers to be licensed or certified, under federal law only appraisals prepared by state-licensed or certified appraisers in accordance with the Uniform Standards of Professional Appraisal Practice (USPAP) can be used in "federally related" loan transactions. USPAP is a set of guidelines adopted by the Appraisal Foundation, a nonprofit organization. (An appraiser who fails to abide by these standards in order to defraud a federally insured lender could be found guilty of a felony.) The majority of real estate loans are federally related, since the category includes loans made by any bank or savings and loan association that's regulated or insured by the federal government. Transactions for $250,000 or less are exempt from this requirement, however.

Note that for the purposes of the California appraisal licensing law, the definition of an appraisal doesn't include opinions of value given by real estate licensees in the ordinary course of their real estate activities. Thus, a competitive market analysis prepared by a real estate agent for a listing presentation wouldn't be considered an appraisal.

In California, the Bureau of Real Estate Appraisers examines appraisers and issues licenses. There are four levels of appraisal licenses.

1. **Certified General Real Estate Appraisers** may appraise any type of real property.
2. **Certified Residential Real Estate Appraisers** may appraise any one- to four-unit residential property, and any nonresidential property with a value up to $250,000.
3. An appraiser with a **Residential License** may appraise any one- to four-unit residential property with a transaction value up to $1 million, and any nonresidential property with a value up to $250,000.
4. An appraiser with a **Trainee License** must work under the technical supervision of a licensed appraiser and may assist on any appraisal that falls within the scope of the supervising appraiser's license.

An appraisal license is valid for two years. To renew a license, the appraiser must have completed a seven-hour National USPAP Update course during the license term and must pay a renewal fee. An additional 14 hours of continuing education are required each calendar year; documentation of continuing education must be submitted every four years.

Value

Value is a term with many meanings. One common definition is "the present worth of future benefits." Value may also be defined as the ability of an item or service to command other items or services in exchange, or as the relationship between a desired thing and the person who desires it. Value is usually measured in terms of money.

Elements of Value

For a product to have value, it must have four basic attributes, called the elements of value: utility, scarcity, demand, and transferability.

A product must render a service or fill a need in order to have value; this is called utility. But utility must exist in conjunction with the other elements of value or the product has no economic value. For example, air has great utility, but it's universally available; because it lacks scarcity, it has no economic value.

Generally, the scarcer an item is, the greater its value. For instance, if diamonds were to become much more plentiful, their value would decline.

Demand is also an essential part of value. There is demand for an item if it produces a desire to own. And there is **effective demand** when that desire is coupled with purchasing power.

Of course, if an item can't be transferred from one party to another, it won't have any economic value. Transferability refers to the ability to transfer possession and control of the rights that constitute ownership of property.

Types of Value

For appraisal purposes, value falls into two general classifications: **value in use** and **value in exchange**. Value in use is the subjective value that a particular person places on a property, while value in exchange is the objective value of a property as viewed by the average person. A property's value in use and value in exchange may be quite different, depending on the circumstances.

> **Example:** A large, expensive, one-bedroom home, designed, built, and occupied by its owner, would undoubtedly be worth more to the owner than to the average buyer. Most buyers would look at the property objectively and expect more than one bedroom for the price.

Value in exchange is the more significant of the two types of value. Value in exchange is better known as **market value**. Estimating a property's market value is the purpose of most appraisals.

Market Value. Here's the most widely accepted definition of market value, the one used by the federal financial institution regulatory agencies:

> *The most probable price which a property should bring in a competitive and open market under all conditions requisite to a fair sale, the buyer and seller each acting prudently and knowledgeably, and assuming the price is not affected by undue stimulus.*

Notice that according to this definition, market value is the *most probable* price (not "the highest price") that the property *should bring* (not "will bring"). Appraisal is a matter of estimation and likelihood, not certainty.

Notice, too, that market value is the most probable price that should be paid if the property is purchased under normal conditions. A sale can generally be considered to have taken place under normal conditions if:

- it was an arm's length transaction (a sale between unrelated parties);
- the property was offered on the open market for a reasonable length of time;
- the buyer and the seller both acted prudently and knowledgeably; and
- neither party was subject to undue stimulus or unusual pressure.

The Federal Housing Administration offers this succinct explanation of market value: "The price which typical buyers would be warranted in paying for the property for long-term use or investment, if they were well informed and acted intelligently, voluntarily, and without necessity."

Market Value vs. Market Price. It's important to distinguish between market value and market price. Market price is the price that was actually paid for a property, regardless of what kind of conditions the sale took place under (whether the parties to the transaction were well informed, subject to unusual pressure, and so on). Market value is the price that should be paid if a property is purchased under normal conditions, as described above.

Principles of Value

Of the major forces that influence our attitudes and behavior, four interact to create, support, or erode property values:

- social ideals and standards,
- economic fluctuations,
- government regulations, and
- physical and environmental factors.

A change in attitudes regarding family size and the emergence of the two-car family are examples of social forces that affect the value of homes (in this case, homes with too many bedrooms or one-car garages). Economic forces include employment levels, interest rates, and any other factors that affect the community's purchasing power. Government regulations, such as zoning ordinances, serve to promote, stabilize, or discourage the demand for property. Physical and environmental factors, such as climate, earthquakes, and flood control measures, can also have an impact on property values.

All four of these forces affect value independently of the owner's efforts. For instance, an economic force such as inflation will cause a property's value to increase, even though the owner has done nothing at all to improve the property. When the value of a property increases due to outside forces, the increase is referred to as an **unearned increment**.

Over the years, appraisers have developed a reliable body of principles, referred to as the **principles of value**, that take these forces into account and guide appraisers in making decisions in the valuation process. Note that these principles are valid no matter which appraisal method is used to arrive at an estimate of value.

Principle of Highest and Best Use. A property's **highest and best use** is the most profitable use it can be put to, the use that will provide the greatest net return to the owner over a period of time. **Net return** usually refers to net income, but it can't always be measured in terms of money. With residential properties, for example, net return might manifest itself in the form of amenities—the pleasure and satisfaction derived from living on the property.

Determining the highest and best use may be a simple matter of confirming that deed restrictions or an existing zoning ordinance limit the property to its present use. Often the present use of a property is its highest and best use. But change is constant, and a warehouse site that was once profitable might now generate a greater net return as a gas station.

Principle of Change. The principle of change holds that real estate values are constantly in flux, moving up and down in response to changes in the various social, economic, governmental, and environmental forces that affect value. A property's value also changes as the property itself improves or deteriorates. A property that was worth $500,000 last year might be worth $525,000 today; or it might be worth only $475,000. Its value is likely to change in the coming year as well. Because value is

Fig. 11.1 Principle of highest and best use

Highest and Best Use (Alternative Use Considerations)		
	Annual Income	**Estimated Value**
Present Use: Warehouse	$77,120 (actual)	$701,000
Alternative Use 1: Parking lot	$67,200 (estimated)	$611,000
Alternative Use 2: Gas station	$82,000 (estimated)	$745,500
Alternative Use 3: Triplex	$57,200 (estimated)	$520,000

always subject to change, an estimate of value must be tied to a given date, called the **effective date** of the appraisal.

Related to the principle of change is the idea that property has a four-phase life cycle: **integration**, **equilibrium**, **disintegration**, and **rejuvenation**. Integration (also called growth or development) is the early stage, when the property is being developed. Equilibrium is a period of stability, when the property undergoes little, if any, change. Disintegration is a period of decline, when the property's economic usefulness is near an end and constant upkeep is necessary. And rejuvenation (also known as revitalization) is a period of renewal, when the property is reborn, perhaps with a different highest and best use.

Rejuvenation or revitalization of a property can take different forms. If a building is restored to good condition without being changed, it's called **rehabilitation**. If the floor plan or style is altered, it's called **remodeling**. And an entire neighborhood can be rejuvenated by **redevelopment**, as when rundown buildings are demolished and replaced in an urban renewal project.

Every property has both a physical life cycle and an economic life cycle. A property's **economic life** (also called its useful life) is the period when the land and its improvements are profitable. The economic life almost always ends before the physical life. The appraiser must take these life cycle stages into account when estimating a property's present worth.

Principle of Anticipation. It's the future, not the past, that's important to appraisers. Knowing that property values change, an appraiser asks: What is happening to this property? What is its future? How do prospective buyers view its potential? The appraiser must be aware of the social, economic, governmental, and environmental factors that will affect the future value of the property.

Value is created by the anticipated future benefits of owning a property. It is future benefits, not past benefits, that arouse a desire to own.

Anticipation can help or hurt value, depending on what informed buyers and sellers expect to happen to the property in the future. They usually expect property values to increase, but in certain situations they anticipate that values will decline, as when the community is experiencing a severe recession.

Principle of Supply and Demand. The principle of supply and demand affects almost every commodity, including real estate. Values tend to rise as demand increases and supply decreases, and to diminish when the reverse is true. It's not so much the demand for or supply of real estate in general that affects values, but the demand for or supply of a particular type of property. For instance, a generally depressed community may have one or two very attractive, sought-after neighborhoods. The value of homes in those neighborhoods remains high, no matter what the general trend is for the rest of the community.

Principle of Substitution. The principle of substitution states that no one will pay more for a property than they would have to pay for an equally desirable substitute property, provided there would be no unreasonable delay in acquiring that substitute. Explained another way, the principle of substitution holds that if two properties for sale are equally desirable (whether in terms of their use, their design, or the income they generate), the least expensive will be in greater demand. The principle of substitution is the basis of all three methods of appraisal (discussed below).

Principle of Conformity. The maximum value of land is achieved when there's an acceptable degree of social and economic conformity (similarity) in the area. Conformity should be reasonable, not carried to an extreme.

In a residential appraisal, aspects of conformity that the appraiser considers are similarities in the age, size, style, and quality of the homes in the neighborhood. Nonconformity can work to the benefit or to the detriment of the nonconforming home. The value of a home of much lower quality than those around it is increased by its association with the higher quality homes; this is the principle of **progression.**

> **Example:** A small, unkempt home surrounded by large, attractive homes will be worth more in this neighborhood than it would be if it were situated in a neighborhood of other small homes in poor condition.

Conversely, the value of a large, expensive home in a neighborhood of small, inexpensive homes will suffer because of its surroundings; this is the principle of **regression**.

Principle of Contribution. The principle of contribution concerns the value that an improvement contributes to the overall value of the property. Some improvements contribute more to value than they cost to make; others cost more than they contribute to value.

For example, a remodeled basement can increase the value of a home, but usually doesn't increase it by as much as the remodeling cost to carry out. On the other hand, the addition of a second bathroom may increase a home's value by more than the cost of installing it.

Principle of Competition. Competition can have a dramatic impact on the value of property, especially income property. For example, if one convenience store in a neighborhood is extremely profitable, its success is very likely to bring a competing convenience store into the area. This competition will probably mean lower profits for the first store (as some of its customers begin doing business with the second store), and lower profits will reduce the property's value.

Principle of Balance. This principle maintains that the maximum value of real estate is achieved when the **agents in production—labor**, **coordination**, **capital**, and **land**—are in proper balance with each other.

To see whether the agents in production are in proper balance, the appraiser deducts a dollar figure that can be attributed to each agent from the property's gross earnings. First, the appraiser deducts the wages (labor) that are paid as a part of the property's operating costs. Next, the appraiser deducts the cost of the management (coordination). The third item deducted is the expense of principal and interest (capital), which represents the funds invested in the building and equipment. The **surplus productivity**—whatever earnings remain after the first three productive agents have been deducted—is credited to the land for its part in the production of the gross income.

The amount credited to the land will reflect the land's value under its present use. If an imbalance exists and too much of the gross earnings are attributed to the land, the buildings are probably an underimprovement and the land is not serving its highest and best use. If too little income is credited to the land, the buildings are probably an overimprovement and, again, the land is not serving its highest and best use.

The Appraisal Process

Properly done, the appraisal process is orderly and systematic. While there's no official procedure, appraisers generally carry out the appraisal process in the following manner.

1. **Define the problem.** Each client wants an appraiser to solve a specific problem: to estimate the value of a particular property as of a particular date and for a particular purpose. The first step in the appraisal process is to define the problem to be solved. This involves identifying the subject property—what property and which aspect(s) of it are to be appraised. Typically, the appraiser considers all of the elements of real property: the land and its improvements, all of the rights that go along with land ownership, and the utility of the property. (The value of land and its improvements together is called the **improved value.**) The appraiser must also establish the purpose of the appraisal and how the client intends to use it. Unless instructed to do otherwise, the appraiser will estimate the property's value as of the date the appraisal is performed.
2. **Determine the scope of work.** This refers to figuring out what's involved in solving the problem. The scope of work includes both the type and quantity of information needed, as well the type of analysis that will be used in the appraisal assignment. Determining the scope of work also includes planning the tasks involved in completing the appraisal; complex assignments may require consulting additional experts, for example.
3. **Collect and verify the data.** Appraisal data can be divided into two categories: general and specific. **General data** concerns matters outside the subject property that affect its value. It includes population trends, prevailing economic circumstances, zoning, and proximity to shopping, schools, and transportation, as well as the condition and quality of the neighborhood. **Specific data** concerns the subject property itself. The

Fig. 11.2 The appraisal process

Steps in the Appraisal Process

1. Define the problem
2. Determine scope of work
3. Collect and verify data
4. Analyze data
5. Determine site value
6. Apply appropriate valuation methods
7. Reconcile value indicators
8. Issue appraisal report

appraiser will gather information about the title, the buildings, and the site. (General and specific data will be discussed in more detail in the next section of the chapter.)

4. **Analyze data.** To analyze the data, the appraiser must judge the relevance of each piece of information that has been collected. For instance, the appraiser will consider what market trend data says about the subject property's value.
5. **Determine site value.** A site valuation is an estimate of a property's value excluding the value of any existing or proposed improvements. For vacant land, site valuation is no different than appraising the property. For improved property (such as property with a house on it), site valuation involves appraising the property as if vacant. A separate site valuation may be necessary depending on which method of appraisal the appraiser is applying (for example, the cost approach to value requires this; see below).
6. **Apply the appropriate methods of appraisal.** In some cases, the appraiser will approach the problem of estimating value three different ways: with the sales comparison approach, the cost approach, and the income approach. In other cases, she will use only the method that seems most appropriate for the problem to be solved. Whether one, two, or three approaches are used is a matter of judgment.

   Sometimes a particular method cannot be used. Raw land, for example, cannot be appraised using the cost approach. A public library, on the other hand, must be appraised by the cost approach because it does not generate income and no market exists for it.
7. **Reconcile value indicators for the final value estimate.** The figures yielded by each of the three approaches are called value indicators; each gives an indication of what the property is worth, but the appraiser must reconcile the differences between them and decide on a final value estimate. In the reconciliation process, the appraiser takes into consideration the purpose of the appraisal, the type of property being appraised, and the reliability of the data gathered for each approach.

8. **Issue appraisal report.** The appraiser's last step is to prepare an appraisal report, presenting the value estimate and summarizing the underlying data for the client. When property is appraised to determine its value as collateral for a loan, the appraiser's client is the lender.

Gathering Data

Once the appraiser knows what property she is to appraise and what the purpose of the appraisal is, she begins to gather the necessary data. As mentioned above, data is broken down into general data (about the neighborhood and other external influences) and specific data (about the subject property itself).

General Data

General data includes both general economic data about the community and information about the subject property's neighborhood.

Economic Trends. The appraiser examines economic trends for hints as to the direction the property's value might take in the future. A trend is a series of related developments that form a pattern. Economic trends can take shape at the local, regional, national, or international level, although local trends have the most significant impact on a property's value. Generally, prosperous conditions tend to have a positive effect on property values; economic declines have the opposite effect.

Economic forces include population growth shifts, employment and wage levels (purchasing power), price levels, building cycles, personal tax and property tax rates, building costs, and interest rates.

Neighborhood Analysis. A property's value is inevitably tied to its surrounding neighborhood. A neighborhood is a residential, commercial, industrial, or agricultural area that contains similar types of properties. Its boundaries are determined by physical barriers (such as highways and bodies of water), land use patterns, the age or value of homes or other buildings, and the economic status of the residents.

Neighborhoods are continually changing and, like the individual properties that make them up, they have a four-phase life cycle of integration, equilibrium, disintegration, and rejuvenation. When evaluating the future of a neighborhood, the appraiser must consider its physical, social, and economic characteristics, and also governmental influences.

Here are some of the specific factors appraisers look at when gathering data about a residential neighborhood:

1. **Percentage of home ownership.** Is there a high degree of owner-occupancy, or do rental properties predominate? Owner-occupied neighborhoods are generally better maintained and less susceptible to deterioration.
2. **Vacant homes and lots.** An unusual number of vacant homes or lots suggests a low level of interest in the area, which has a negative effect on property values. On the other hand, significant construction activity in a neighborhood signals strong interest in the area.

Fig. 11.3 Neighborhood data form

NEIGHBORHOOD DATA FORM

Property adjacent to:
NORTH *Plum Boulevard, garden apartments*
SOUTH *Cherry Boulevard, single-family residences*
EAST *14th Avenue, single-family residences*
WEST *12th Avenue, single-family residences*

Population: ☐ increasing ☐ decreasing ☑ stable

Stage of Life Cycle: ☐ integration ☑ equilibrium ☐ disintegration ☐ rebirth

Tax Rate: ☐ higher ☐ lower ☑ same as competing areas

Services: ☑ police ☑ fire ☑ garbage ☐ other

Average family size: *3.5*
Predominant occupations: *white collar, skilled tradesman*

Distance from:
Commercial areas *3 miles*
Primary schools *6 blocks*
Secondary schools *1 mile*
Recreational areas *2 miles*
Cultural areas *3 miles*
Places of worship *Methodist, Catholic, Baptist*
Public transportation *Bus stops nearby, excellent service*
Freeways/highways *10 blocks*

Typical Properties	%	Age	Price Range	% Owner-Occupied
vacant lots	0			
single-family residences	80%	10 years	$380,000-395,000	93%
2- to 4-unit apartments	15%	15 years		
over 4-unit apartments	5%	5 years		
non-residential	0			

Nuisances in neighborhood (odors, noise, etc.) *none*
Hazards in neighborhood (chemical storage, pollution, etc.) *none*

3. **Conformity.** The homes in a neighborhood should be reasonably similar to one another in style, age, size, and quality. Strictly enforced zoning and private restrictions promote conformity and protect property values.
4. **Changing land use.** Is the neighborhood in the midst of a transition from residential use to some other type of use? If so, the properties may be losing their value.
5. **Contour of the land.** Mildly rolling topography is preferred to terrain that's either monotonously flat or excessively hilly.

6. **Streets.** Wide, gently curving streets and cul-de-sacs (short dead-end streets) are more appealing than narrow or straight streets. Streets should be hard-surfaced and well maintained.
7. **Utilities.** Does the neighborhood have adequate utility services, including electricity, water, gas, sewers, telephones, and cable TV? A site without sewer service needs a septic system. For a newly developed site, a **percolation test** might be required to measure how quickly water dissipates through the soil. The results of the test will determine whether a septic system can be added to the property.
8. **Nuisances.** Nuisances in or near a neighborhood (odors, eyesores, industrial noises or pollutants, or exposure to unusual winds, smog, or fog) hurt property values.
9. **Prestige.** Is the neighborhood considered prestigious, in comparison to others in the community? If so, that will increase property values.
10. **Proximity.** How far is it to traffic arterials and to important points such as downtown, employment centers, and shopping centers?
11. **Schools.** What schools serve the neighborhood? Are they highly regarded? Are they within walking distance? The quality of a school or school district can make a major difference in property values in a residential neighborhood.
12. **Public services.** Is the neighborhood properly served by public transportation, police, and fire units?
13. **Government influences.** Does zoning in and around the neighborhood promote residential use and insulate the property owner from nuisances? How do property tax rates compare with those of other neighborhoods nearby? High property taxes may discourage new construction.

Specific Data

Specific data has to do with the property itself. Often the appraiser will evaluate the site (the land and utilities) and the improvements to the site (the buildings) separately. This is standard in certain contexts; for example, a property tax assessment shows the distribution of value between the land and the improvements. One reason for appraising the land separately is to see if it's worth too much or too little compared to the value of the improvements. When an imbalance exists, the land isn't serving its highest and best use. The primary purpose of site analysis is to determine highest and best use.

Site Analysis. A thorough site analysis calls for accumulation of a good deal of data concerning the property's physical characteristics, as well as factors that affect its use or the title. A site's physical characteristics include all of the following:

1. **Width.** This refers to the lot's measurements from one side boundary to the other. Width can vary from front to back, as in the case of a pie-shaped lot on a cul-de-sac.
2. **Frontage.** Frontage is the length of the front boundary of the lot, the boundary that abuts a street or a body of water. The amount of frontage is often a more important consideration than width because it measures the property's accessibility, or its access to something desirable.

3. **Area.** Area is the size of the site, usually measured in square feet or acres. Comparisons between lots often focus on the features of frontage and area.

   Commercial land (especially retail property) is usually valued in terms of frontage; that is, it's worth a certain number of dollars per front foot. Industrial land, on the other hand, tends to be valued in terms of square feet or acreage. Residential lots are measured both ways: by square feet or acreage in most instances, but by front foot when the property abuts a lake or river, or some other desirable feature.

   Occasionally, newly subdivided land is measured in "commercial acres." A **commercial acre** is the buildable portion of an acre that remains after part of the land has been dedicated for streets, sidewalks, and parks.
4. **Depth.** Depth is the distance between a site's front boundary and its rear boundary. Greater depth (more than the norm) can mean greater value, but it doesn't always. For example, suppose Lot 1 and Lot 2 have the same amount of frontage along a lake, but Lot 2 is deeper; Lot 2 isn't necessarily more valuable than Lot 1. The additional square footage of Lot 2 might simply be considered **excess land.**

   Each situation must be analyzed individually. Even when greater depth or less depth affects value, the increase or decrease in value usually isn't proportional to the increase or decrease in depth.

   There are various rules of thumb concerning the relationship between depth and value. One of the most common is the 4-3-2-1 rule, which states that the front quarter of a lot holds 40% of its overall value; the second quarter holds 30%; the next quarter holds 20%; and the back quarter holds only 10% of the value. Because it's less accessible, the rear portion of a lot is less useful.

   In some situations a **depth table** is used to evaluate how a lot's depth affects its value. This is a table of mathematical factors that can be

Fig. 11.4 Site data form

SITE DATA FORM

Address: *10157 - 13th Avenue*
Legal Description: *see attached description*

Size *50′ x 200′* Shape *Rectangular*
Square Feet *10,000* Street Paving *Asphalt*
Landscaping *professional* Topsoil *good*
Drainage *good* Frontage *good*
☐ corner lot ☑ inside lot

Utilities: ☑ water ☑ telephone ☑ gas ☑ sewers ☑ electricity ☑ storm drains

Improvements: ☑ sidewalks ☑ curb ☑ alleys ☑ driveway

multiplied by the front foot value of a standard lot to estimate the value of a lot with a specified depth. Depth tables aren't considered accurate enough for most appraisal purposes. However, tax assessors sometimes use depth tables when valuing commercial property for tax purposes.

Under certain circumstances, combining two or more adjoining lots to achieve greater width, depth, or area will make the larger parcel more valuable than the sum of the values of its component parcels. The increment of value that results when two or more lots are combined to produce greater value is called **plottage**. The process of assembling lots to increase their total value is most frequently part of industrial or commercial land development.

5. **Shape.** Lots with uniform width and depth (such as rectangular lots) are almost always more useful than irregularly shaped lots. This is true for any kind of lot—residential, commercial, or industrial.
6. **Topography.** A site is generally more valuable if it's aesthetically appealing. Rolling terrain is preferable to flat, monotonous land. On the other hand, if the site would be costly to develop because it sits well above or below the street or is excessively hilly, then that lessens its value.
7. **Utilities.** Site analysis includes an investigation into the availability and cost of utility connections. Remote parcels lose value because the cost of bringing utility lines to the site is high or even prohibitive.
8. **Site in relation to area.** How a lot is situated in relation to the surrounding area influences its value. For instance, a retail store is often worth more if it's located on a corner, because it enjoys more exposure and its customers have access from two different streets. The effect the corner location has on the value of a business site is called **corner influence**.

   By contrast, a corner location has a negative effect on the value of a residential property. That's because a corner lot is more exposed to through traffic than a lot in the middle of the block. Similarly, the lots inside a subdivision are considered more desirable than the ones on the perimeter, next to the arterial streets.

Building Analysis. The improvements to the site must also be analyzed, along with any special amenities. (**Amenities** are attractive features such as a nice view or beautiful landscaping.) Of course, the functional utility of a home depends on the needs and desires of its occupants, but there are some primary considerations that apply to most homes. These include:

1. **Construction quality.** Is the quality of the materials and workmanship good, average, or poor?
2. **Age/condition.** How old is the home? Is its overall condition good, average, or poor? If the foundation shows signs of cracking, or doors and windows don't close properly, an appraiser may recommend a soil engineer's report to check the soil stability.
3. **Size of house (square footage).** The outside dimensions of a home are used to calculate its square footage. The square footage includes the improved living area, but not the garage, basement, and porches. (Note that an appraiser will exclude the square footage of any addition that was built without a permit.) Commercial buildings, including warehouses, are also measured in terms of square feet.

Fig. 11.5 Building data form

BUILDING DATA FORM

Address: *10157 - 13th Avenue*
Age: *7 yrs.* Square feet: *1,350*
Number of rooms: *7* Quality of construction: *excellent*
Style: *ranch*

	Good	Bad	Fair
Exterior (general condition)	✓		
Foundation(slab/bsmt./crawl sp.)	✓		
Exterior (brick/frame/veneer/stucco/aluminum)	✓		
Garage(attached/detached/single/double)	✓		
Patio/porch/shed/other	✓		
Interior (general condition)	✓		
Walls (drywall/wood/plaster)	✓		
Ceilings	✓		
Floor (wood/tile/carpet/concrete)	✓		
Electrical wiring	✓		
Heating (electrical/gas/oil/other)	✓		
Air conditioning	✓		
Fireplace(s) *one*	✓		
Kitchen	✓		
Bathroom(s) *two*	✓		
Bedroom(s) *three*	✓		

Additional amenities *none*
Design advantages *convenient, sunny kitchen*
Design flaws *none*
Energy efficiency *insulation, weather-stripping, storm windows, heat pump*

	Living Rm.	Dining Rm.	Ktchn.	Bdrm.	Bath	Family Rm.
Basement						
1st Floor	✓	✓	✓	✓	✓	
2nd Floor						
Attic						

Depreciation:
Deferred Maintenance *normal wear*
Functional Obsolescence *none*
External Obsolescence *none*

4. **Orientation.** Orientation refers to how a building is positioned on the property in relation to views, privacy, and exposure to wind, sunlight, and noise.
5. **Basement.** A functional basement, especially a finished basement, contributes to value. (As we mentioned earlier, however, the amount a finished basement contributes to value often isn't enough to recover the cost of the finish work.)

6. **Interior layout.** Is the floor plan functional and convenient? It shouldn't be necessary to pass through a public room (such as the living room) to reach other rooms, or to pass through one of the bedrooms to reach another.
7. **Number of rooms.** The appraiser will add up the total number of rooms in the house, excluding the bathrooms and (usually) any basement rooms.
8. **Number of bedrooms.** The number of bedrooms has a major impact on value. For instance, if all else is equal, a two-bedroom home is worth considerably less than a three-bedroom home.
9. **Number of bathrooms.** A full bath is a lavatory (wash basin), toilet, bathtub, and shower; a three-quarters bath is a lavatory, toilet, and either a bathtub or a shower (not both); a half bath is a lavatory and toilet only. The number of bathrooms can have a noticeable effect on value.
10. **Air conditioning.** The presence or absence of an air conditioning system is important in hot regions.
11. **Energy efficiency.** With spiraling energy costs, an energy-efficient home is more valuable than a comparable one that isn't. Energy-efficient features such as double-paned windows, good insulation, and weather stripping increase value.
12. **Garage/carport.** As a general rule, an enclosed garage is considered better than a carport. How many cars can the garage accommodate? Is there work or storage space in addition to parking space? Is it possible to enter the home directly from the garage or carport, protected from the weather?

Methods of Appraisal

Once the appraiser has accumulated the necessary general and specific data, he will begin applying one or more of the three methods of appraising property:

- the sales comparison approach,
- the cost approach, and
- the income approach.

Different types of properties lend themselves to different appraisal methods. For example, appraisers rely most on the sales comparison method in valuing older residential properties and vacant land. Churches and public buildings, such as libraries or courthouses, aren't sold on the open market, nor do they generate income, so the cost approach is invariably used. On the other hand, the income approach is usually the most reliable method for appraising an apartment complex.

Sales Comparison Approach to Value

The sales comparison approach (also known as the market data approach) is the best method for appraising residential property, and the most reliable method for appraising raw land. It involves comparing the subject property to similar properties that have recently sold, which are referred to as **comparable sales** or **comparables**. The appraiser gathers pertinent information about comparables and makes feature-by-feature comparisons with the subject property. The appraiser then translates her findings into an estimate of the market value of the subject property. Appraisers use this method whenever possible because the sales prices of comparables—which reflect the actions of informed buyers and sellers in the marketplace—are excellent indicators of market value.

For residential property, an appraiser needs at least three reliable comparable sales to have enough data for the sales comparison approach. It's usually possible to find three good comparables, but when it isn't (for instance, if the market is inactive), the appraiser will turn to the alternative appraisal methods—the cost approach and the income approach.

Elements of Comparison. To determine whether a particular sale can legitimately be used as a comparable, the appraiser will check the following aspects of the transaction, which are known as the primary elements of comparison.

Date of Comparable Sale. A comparable sale should be recent, within the past six months if possible. Recent sales give a more accurate indication of what's currently happening in the marketplace. If the market has been inactive and there aren't three legitimate comparable sales from the past six months, then the appraiser can go back further. (Comparable sales over one year old generally aren't acceptable, however.) When the market is going through a major shift, such as a rapid downswing during a recession, comparable sales should be no more than three months old.

When using a comparable more than six months old (or more than three months old in a rapidly declining market), it's necessary to make adjustments for the time factor, allowing for inflationary or deflationary trends or any other forces that have affected prices in the area.

Example: A comparable residential property sold ten months ago for $680,000. Local property values have risen by 5% over the past ten months. The comparable property, then, should be worth approximately 5% more than it was worth ten months ago.

$680,000	Value ten months ago
× 105%	Inflation factor
$714,000	Approximate present value

Location of Comparable Sale. Whenever possible, comparables should be selected from the neighborhood where the subject property is located. In the absence of any legitimate comparables in the neighborhood, the appraiser can look elsewhere, but the properties selected should at least come from comparable neighborhoods.

If a comparable selected from an inferior neighborhood is structurally identical to the subject property, it's probably less valuable; conversely, a structurally identical comparable in a superior neighborhood is probably more valuable than the subject property. It's generally conceded that location contributes more to the value of real estate than any other characteristic. A high-quality property can't overcome the adverse effects on value that a low-quality neighborhood causes. On the other hand, the value of a relatively weak property is enhanced by a stable and desirable neighborhood.

Physical Characteristics. To qualify as a comparable, a property should have physical characteristics (construction quality, design, amenities, etc.) that are similar to those of the subject property. When a comparable has a feature that the subject property lacks, or lacks a feature that the subject property has, the appraiser will adjust the comparable's price.

Example: One of the comparables the appraiser is using is quite similar to the subject property overall, but there are several significant differences. The subject property has a two-car garage, while the comparable has only a one-car garage. Based on experience, the appraiser estimates that space for a second car adds approximately $25,000 to the value of a home in this area. The comparable actually sold for $720,500. The appraiser will add $25,000 to that price, to estimate what the comparable would have been worth with a two-car garage.

On the other hand, the comparable has a fireplace and the subject property does not. The appraiser estimates that a fireplace adds approximately $1,800 to the value of a home. She will subtract $1,800 from the comparable's price, to estimate what the comparable would have sold for without a fireplace.

After adjusting the comparable's price up or down for each difference in this way, the appraiser can identify what the comparable would have sold for if it had been identical to the subject property. When the appraiser repeats this process for each comparable, the value of the subject property becomes evident.

Terms of Sale. The terms of sale can affect the price a buyer will pay for a property. Attractive financing concessions (such as seller-paid discount points or seller financing with an especially low interest rate) can make a buyer willing to pay a higher price than she would otherwise be willing to pay.

An appraiser has to take into account the influence the terms of sale may have had on the price paid for a comparable property. If the seller offered the property on very favorable terms, there's a good chance the sales price didn't represent the true market value of the comparable.

Under the Uniform Standards of Professional Appraisal Practice, an appraiser giving an estimate of market value must state whether it's the most probable price:

1. in terms of cash;
2. in terms of financial arrangements equivalent to cash; or
3. in other precisely defined terms.

If the estimate is based on financing with special conditions or incentives, those terms must be clearly set forth, and the appraiser must estimate their effect on the property's value. Market data supporting the value estimate (comparable sales) must be explained in the same way.

Conditions of Sale. Last but not least, a comparable sale can be relied on as an indication of what the subject property is worth only if it took place under normal conditions. In other words, it was a sale between unrelated parties (an arm's length transaction), both the buyer and the seller were informed of the property's attributes and deficiencies, both were acting free of unusual pressure, and the property was offered for sale on the open market for a reasonable length of time.

So the appraiser must investigate the circumstances of each comparable sale to determine whether the price paid was influenced by conditions that would render it unreliable as an indication of value. For example, if the property sold only days before a scheduled foreclosure sale, the sales price probably reflected the pressure that the seller was acting under. Or if it wasn't an arm's length transaction—if the buyer and seller were relatives or friends—it's possible that the price was less than it would have been between two strangers. Or if the home sold the same day it was listed, it may have been underpriced. In each of these cases, there's reason to suspect that the sales price didn't reflect the property's true value, so the appraiser would not use the transaction as a comparable sale.

Fig. 11.6 Comparable sales comparison chart

Comparable Sales Comparison Chart					
	Subject Property	Comparables			
		1	2	3	4
Sales price		*$391,750*	*$396,500*	*$387,000*	*$388,500*
Location	*quiet street*				
Age	*7 yrs.*				
Lot size	*50'x200'*				
Construction	*frame*			*+6,000*	
Style	*ranch*				
Number of Rooms	*7*		*–5,000*		
Number of Bedrooms	*3*				
Number of Baths	*2*	*+3,500*			*+3,500*
Square feet	*1,350*				
Exterior	*good*				
Interior	*good*				
Garage	*1 car attached*				
Other improvements		*–4,000*			
Financing					
Date of sale		*–3,000*	*–3,000*		
Net Adjustments		*–3,500*	*–8,000*	*+6,000*	*+3,500*
Adjusted Price		*$388,250*	*$388,500*	*$393,000*	*$392,000*

Comparing Properties and Making Adjustments. A proper comparison between the subject property and each comparable is essential to an accurate estimate of value. The more similar the properties, the easier the comparison. A comparable property that's the same design and in the same condition as the subject property, on a very similar site in the same neighborhood, which sold under typical financing terms the previous month, will give an excellent indication of the market value of the subject property.

However, except perhaps in a new subdivision where the houses are nearly identical, the appraiser usually can't find such ideal comparables. There are likely to be at least some significant differences between the comparables and the subject property. So, as you've seen, the appraiser has to make adjustments, taking into account differences in time, location, physical characteristics, and terms of sale, in order to arrive at an **adjusted selling price** for each comparable.

It stands to reason that the more adjustments an appraiser has to make, the less reliable the resulting estimate of value will be. These adjustments are an inevitable part of the sales comparison approach, but appraisers try to keep them to a minimum by selecting the best comparables available.

The appraiser bases his estimate of the subject property's value on the adjusted prices of the comparables, but the value estimate is never merely an average of those prices; careful analysis is required. Also note that the original cost of the subject property (how much the current owners paid for it) is irrelevant to the appraisal process.

Use of Listings. When comparable sales are scarce (for example, when the market is just emerging from a dormant period), the appraiser may compare the subject property to properties that are presently listed for sale. The appraiser must keep in mind, however, that listing prices tend to be high and often represent the ceiling of the market value range. The appraiser might also use prices offered by buyers (but not accepted by the sellers), though these can be difficult to confirm, since records of offers aren't always kept. Offers are usually at the low end of the value range. Actual market value is typically somewhere between offers and listing prices.

Note that assessed values set for tax purposes are never used in place of comparable sales.

Cost Approach to Value

The second method of appraisal, the cost approach, is based on the premise that the value of a property is limited by the cost of replacing it. (This follows from the principle of substitution: If the asking price for a home were more than it would cost to build a new one just like it, no one would buy it.) The estimate of value arrived at through the cost approach usually represents the upper limits of the property's value.

The cost approach involves estimating how much it would cost to replace the subject property's existing buildings, then adding to that the estimated value of the site. Because the cost approach involves estimating the value of land and buildings separately, then adding the estimates together, it's sometimes called the **summation method**.

There are three steps to the cost approach:

1. Estimate the cost of replacing the improvements.
2. Estimate and deduct any accrued depreciation.
3. Add the value of the lot to the depreciated value of the improvements.

We'll look at each of these steps. First, however, it's important to distinguish between replacement cost and reproduction cost. **Reproduction cost** is the cost of constructing an exact duplicate—a replica—of the subject building, at current prices. **Replacement cost**, on the other hand, is the current cost of constructing a building with a utility equivalent to the subject's—that is, a building that can be used in the same way as the subject. Reproduction cost and replacement cost may be the same if the subject property is a new home. But if the structure is older and was built with the detailed workmanship and expensive materials of earlier times, then the reproduction cost and the replacement cost will be quite different. So the appraiser must base her estimate of value on the replacement cost. The reproduction cost would be prohibitive, and it wouldn't represent the current market value of the improvements.

Estimating Replacement Cost. The replacement cost of a building can be estimated in three different ways:

1. the square foot method,
2. the unit-in-place method, and
3. the quantity survey method.

Square Foot. The simplest way to estimate replacement cost is the square foot method (also known as the **comparative cost** method or comparative unit method). By analyzing the average cost per square foot of construction for recently built comparable homes, the appraiser can calculate the square-foot cost of replacing the subject home. The number of square feet in a home is determined by measuring the outside dimensions of each floor of the structure.

To calculate the cost of replacing the subject property's improvements, the appraiser multiplies the estimated cost per square foot by the number of square feet in the subject.

Example: The subject property is a two-story house with a wooden exterior, containing 2,600 square feet. Based on an analysis of the construction costs of three recently built homes of comparable size and quality, the appraiser estimates that it would cost $202.35 per square foot to replace the home.

$202.35	Cost per square foot
× 2,600	Square feet
$526,110	Estimated cost of replacing improvements

Of course, a comparable structure (or "benchmark" building) is unlikely to be exactly the same as the subject property. Variations in design, shape, and grade of construction will affect the square-foot cost, either moderately or substantially. When recently built comparable homes aren't available, then the appraiser relies on current cost manuals to estimate the basic construction costs.

Unit-in-Place. The unit-in-place method involves estimating the cost of replacing specific components of the building, such as the floors, roof, plumbing, and foundation. For example, one of the estimates might be a certain number of dollars per one hundred square feet of roofing. Another component estimate would be a certain amount per cubic yard of concrete for an installed foundation. Then the appraiser adds all of the estimates together to determine the replacement cost of the structure itself.

Quantity Survey. The quantity survey method involves a detailed estimate of the quantities and prices of construction materials and labor, which are added to the indirect costs (building permit, survey, etc.) for what is generally regarded as the most accurate replacement cost estimate. Because it's complex and time consuming, this method is generally used only by experienced contractors and price estimators.

Fig. 11.7 Calculating value using the cost approach

Cost Approach

Replacement cost of improvements
– Depreciation of improvements
+ Value of land

Value of subject property

Fig. 11.8 A house with four bedrooms and just one bath loses value due to functional obsolescence.

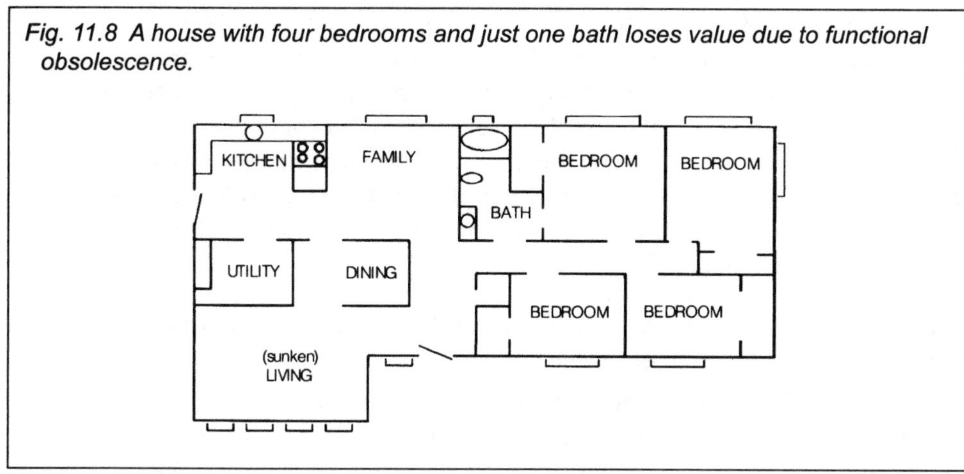

Estimating Depreciation. When the property being appraised is a used home, the presumption is that it is not as valuable as a comparable new home; it has depreciated in value. So after estimating replacement cost—which indicates what the improvements would be worth if they were new—the appraiser's next step is to estimate depreciation. **Depreciation** is a loss in value due to any cause.

Don't confuse an appraiser's approach to depreciation with an accountant's. While an accountant is concerned with book depreciation for tax purposes, appraisers are concerned with actual losses in the value of real property.

Always remember that it's only the property improvements that depreciate, not the land. An appraiser regards land as indestructible; it doesn't lose value.

Types of Depreciation. Value can be lost as a result of physical deterioration, functional obsolescence, or external obsolescence.

- **Physical deterioration** is a loss in value due to wear and tear, damage, or structural defects. It's easier to spot this type of depreciation than the other types, and it's also easier to estimate its impact on value.

  Physical deterioration may be either curable or incurable. Depreciation is considered **curable** if the cost of correcting it could be recovered in the sales price when the property is sold. Depreciation is considered **incurable** if it's impossible to correct, or if it would cost so much to correct that it would be impractical to do so. Curable physical deterioration is frequently referred to as **deferred maintenance**.
- **Functional obsolescence** is a loss in value due to functional inadequacies, often caused by age or by poor design. Examples include an inconvenient floor plan (a bedroom opens directly off the living room), an unappealing design (massive cornices on the outside of the building), outdated fixtures (an old stove and no dishwasher), or too few bathrooms in relation to the number of bedrooms. Like physical deterioration, functional obsolescence may be curable or incurable.

  Functional obsolescence results whenever a building lacks functional utility. A building's **functional utility** is its ability to fulfill the desires of its occupants or users; it includes attractiveness as well as actual usefulness.

- **External obsolescence** (also referred to as economic obsolescence) is caused by conditions outside the property itself, such as zoning changes, neighborhood deterioration, traffic problems, poor access to important areas like downtown or employment centers, or exposure to nuisances, like noise from airport flight patterns. Identifying external obsolescence is the primary purpose of an appraiser's neighborhood analysis. External obsolescence is beyond a property owner's control, so it's virtually always incurable.

Note that more value is typically lost due to functional and external obsolescence than to physical deterioration.

Methods of Estimating Depreciation. Accurately estimating how much depreciation has accrued is the most difficult phase of the replacement cost approach. Depreciation estimates are often highly subjective, and they're never any more reliable than the judgment and skill of the appraiser who is making them.

The various methods of estimating depreciation are divided into indirect methods and direct methods. **Indirect methods** include the capitalization method and the market data method, and **direct methods** include the straight-line method and the engineering method.

When applying the **capitalization method** to estimate depreciation, the appraiser uses the income approach to value (discussed later in the chapter) to estimate the current value of the building. This figure, which is called the capitalized value, should be lower than the appraiser's replacement cost estimate, since the replacement cost indicates what the building would be worth if it were new. The difference between the replacement cost and the capitalized value is the amount of depreciation that has accrued.

Example:

$700,000	Replacement cost
– 610,000	Capitalized value
$90,000	Depreciation

With the **market data method**, the appraiser uses the market data (sales comparison) approach to estimate the current value of the building. Again, the appraiser subtracts this value estimate from the replacement cost estimate, and the difference is the depreciation.

The **straight-line method** of estimating depreciation is the easiest method to apply. The appraiser estimates what the useful life (economic life) of the building would be if it were new. She then divides the estimated useful life into the building's replacement cost to determine how much depreciation would occur each year, assuming the improvements lose value evenly over the years. The amount of annual depreciation is then multiplied by the age of the building.

It should be noted that when an appraiser considers the age of a property, he's concerned with its **effective age**, rather than its actual chronological age. The effective age depends on how long the appraiser believes the structure will remain productive in its present use. If, in the appraiser's opinion, a 75-year-old building has 33 productive years ahead of it, and similar buildings typically have a 40-year useful life, then the building's effective age would be seven years old, rather than 75 years old. (Remember that a building's physical life is typically longer than its useful life. That's why the axiom "More buildings are torn down than fall down" is true.)

The following example shows how the straight-line method of estimating depreciation works.

Example: After estimating that a building's replacement cost is $800,000, the appraiser uses the straight-line method to estimate how much the building has depreciated. Based on her knowledge of similar structures, she concludes that the building's useful life is 40 years. By dividing the replacement cost by the useful life, the appraiser determines that the value of the building decreases by $20,000 each year because of depreciation ($800,000 ÷ 40 years = $20,000 per year).

Suppose the appraiser decides that the building has a remaining useful life of 33 years. Its effective age is therefore seven years. The appraiser multiplies $20,000 (the annual depreciation figure) by seven (the building's effective age) to arrive at the estimated amount of depreciation. $20,000 × 7 = $140,000. Therefore, the depreciated value of the building is $660,000 ($800,000 – $140,000 = $660,000).

Straight-line depreciation can also be expressed as a percentage of the building's useful life. The appraiser can divide the useful life (40 years) into the building's replacement cost new (100% of its value) to determine the percentage of its original value it will lose each year (100% ÷ 40 = 2.5% per year).

The straight-line method is sometimes called the **age-life method** because the depreciation estimate is based on a building's effective age in relation to a typical economic life.

The **engineering method** of estimating depreciation, sometimes called the **observed condition method**, calls for the appraiser to inspect the structure, making observations about actual depreciation. The conclusions are entirely a matter of the appraiser's judgment and skill. Generally, the observed condition method of estimating depreciation is considered the most reliable.

Adding Land Value. The last step in the replacement cost process is to add the value of the land to the depreciated value of the improvements. The value of the land is estimated by the sales comparison method. Prices recently paid for lots similar to the subject lot are compared and used as indications of what the subject lot is worth. (Site valuation is discussed later in this chapter.)

Income Approach to Value

The third major method of appraisal, the income approach, is also known as the capitalization method. It's based on the idea that there's a relationship between the income a property generates (its productivity) and its market value to an investor. In effect, the income approach seeks to determine the present value of a property's future income.

Gross Income. When using the income approach, the appraiser first finds the property's gross income. He does this by estimating the rent the property would command if it were presently available for lease on the open market. What it would earn on the open market is called the **economic rent**, as distinguished from what it is actually earning now, which is called the **contract rent** or **historical rent**. Contract rent can be used to gauge the property's earnings potential. A pattern of rent increases or decreases is a strong indication of whether the contract rent is above or below the economic rent.

The property's economic rent is also called its **potential gross income** or **gross scheduled income**. This is what it could earn if it were fully occupied and all rents owed were collected. But it's unrealistic to expect a rental property to be fully occupied throughout its productive life; vacancies must be expected. Also, there are going to be tenants who don't pay their rent. So the appraiser must make a deduction from potential gross income to allow for occasional vacancies and unpaid rents. Called a **vacancy factor**, this deduction is expressed as a percentage of the potential gross income. For example, the appraiser might deduct 5% from potential gross income as a vacancy factor. Once the vacancy factor is deducted, the appraiser is left with a more reliable income figure, called **effective gross income**.

Operating Expenses. From the effective gross income, the appraiser deducts the expenses connected with operating the building. They fall into three classifications: fixed expenses, maintenance expenses, and reserves for replacement.

- **Fixed expenses:** Property taxes and hazard insurance.
- **Maintenance expenses:** Services for tenants, utilities, supplies, cleaning, repairs, administrative expenses, management fees, and building employee wages.
- **Reserves for replacement:** Regular allowances set aside to replace structures and equipment that are expected to wear out, such as roofs, heating equipment, air conditioners, and (in a residential building) kitchen ranges and refrigerators.

The income that is left when operating expenses are deducted from effective gross income is called **net income**. It's net income that is capitalized to determine the property's value (see the next section).

Some expenses, such as the owner's income taxes, the depreciation reserves, and the mortgage payments (called **debt service**) aren't deducted from the effective gross income to arrive at the net income. These aren't considered operating expenses from an appraisal standpoint.

Capitalization. The process of converting net income into a meaningful value is called capitalization. The mathematical procedure is expressed in this formula:

Annual Net Income ÷ Capitalization Rate = Value

Example: The property's net income is $45,700 and the capitalization rate is 11%. According to the capitalization formula, the property's value is $415,455.

$45,700 ÷ 0.11 = $415,455

The capitalization rate is the rate of return an investor (a potential purchaser) would want to receive on the money she invests in the property (the purchase price). When the investor chooses the rate of return, it's plugged into the formula shown above. By dividing the net income by the desired rate of return, the investor can determine how much she can pay for the property and still realize that desired return.

Example: The property's annual net income is $160,000 and the investor's desired return is 9.5%.

$$\$160,000 \div 9.5\% = \$1,684,211$$

The investor can pay up to $1,684,211 for a property earning $160,000 in net income and realize her desired yield of 9.5%.

Recapture. As general rule, a capitalization rate must take into consideration both the investor's desired rate of return on the investment and the return of the investment. Interest is a **return on** an investment. This is the investor's profit on the amount of money he has invested in the purchase of the property. The **return of** an investment is the investor's ability to recoup the purchase price of the property at the end of his term of ownership. This return of the investment is also called **recapture**.

The portion of the purchase price attributable to the land doesn't have to be recaptured during the investment period, because land is indestructible and its value can be recovered when the property is sold. The improvements, however, are assets that will wear out. Because the purchase price of the improvements won't be recovered when the property is sold, most investors insist on including in their capitalization rate a provision for recapturing their original investment. In other words, a recapture provision is included in anticipation of future depreciation accrual. A capitalization rate that provides for both interest and recapture is called an **overall rate**.

Example: Ted bought a small apartment building for $1,250,000. The land is worth $500,000 and the building is worth $750,000. The building has a remaining economic life of 30 years. Ted expects a 10% return on his investment. He also wants the value of the building ($750,000) to be repaid over the 30-year economic life. That works out to $25,000 a year, or 2% of the purchase price annually. This 2% return *of* his investment, added to his 10% return *on* the investment, results in an overall rate of 12%.

Selecting a Capitalization Rate. To appraise property using the income approach, the appraiser must be familiar with the rate of return that investors generally demand for similar properties.

There are a number of methods an appraiser may use to determine an appropriate capitalization rate for a property. For instance, the appraiser could analyze recent sales of comparable income properties and assume that the subject property would have a capitalization rate similar to theirs. This is known as the **direct comparison method**.

Another method of selecting a capitalization rate is the **band of investment method**, which takes into account prevailing mortgage interest rates that would apply to the investor's loan, in addition to the rate of return required on the investor's equity investment.

The third method used to select a rate is the **summation method**. With this method, the appraiser builds a capitalization rate for the subject property by considering the four component parts of a capitalization rate, assigning an appropriate percentage to each component, and then adding them together to reach the total rate. Here are the four components:

1. **Safe rate**—the rate paid on secure investments such as savings accounts or long-term government bonds.
2. **Risk rate**—the portion of the rate designed to compensate the investor for the hazards that are peculiar to the investment; this component increases or decreases according to the degree of risk involved.

3. **Nonliquidity rate**—the extra return an investor will expect from a nonliquid investment such as real estate.
4. **Management rate**—the part of the rate that compensates the owner/investor for managing the investment and reinvesting the money the investment yields.

Regardless of the method used for selecting the capitalization rate, two very important considerations are the quality and the durability of the investment property's income. **Quality** (how reliable the tenants are) and **durability** (how long the income can be expected to last) influence the risk factor. The greater the risk, the higher the capitalization rate and the lower the property's value. On the other hand, the smaller the risk, the lower the capitalization rate and the higher the value.

Capitalization Methods. After the appraiser has calculated the subject property's net income and chosen a capitalization rate, the final step in the income approach is capitalizing the property's income to arrive at an estimate of value. At this point, the appraiser may simply divide the property's income by the appropriate capitalization rate to find its value, as we discussed earlier.

Alternatively, the appraiser may use a method that values the land and building separately. These are the building residual technique and the land residual technique. These methods are called residual techniques because they involve capitalizing a **residual**, which means something that's left over.

The first step in the **building residual technique** is to value the land separately from the building. The appraiser then deducts from the property's annual net income the portion of the income that must be attributable to the land to justify its value. What remains (what's left over) is the income to be credited to the building. The final step is to divide the net income attributable to the building by an appropriate overall capitalization rate to find the value of the building.

The building residual method is most reliable when land values are relatively stable and can be determined easily (because of an abundance of comparable sales and market data). It's also used when appraising older buildings where depreciation is difficult to measure.

In the **land residual technique**, the building is appraised separately. Then the net income that must be attributable to the building is deducted to arrive at the net income to be credited to the land. The land's earnings are then capitalized to determine the land's value. (Note that the capitalization rate used in this step is only an interest rate, with no recapture provision, because land doesn't depreciate.)

The land residual technique is used when the land value can't be estimated by the sales comparison method because of an absence of comparable sales. It's also used when the building the land supports is new and represents its highest and best use.

You may also hear reference to the **property residual technique**, which treats the land and building as one. This is no different from the basic capitalization procedure (Value = Income ÷ Capitalization Rate) that you're already familiar with, though; no residual is involved.

Gross Income Multipliers. Residences generally aren't thought of as income-producing properties, so traditional income analysis techniques don't apply. If a residential appraiser uses the income approach at all, he will use a simplified version called the **gross income multiplier method**. As a rule, this method is applied only when appraising rental homes. It's sometimes called the **gross rent multiplier method**, since rents are typically the only form of income generated by rental homes.

In the gross income multiplier method, the appraiser looks at the relationship between a rental property's income and the price paid for the property.

Example:

Sales price:	$275,000
Monthly rent:	$1,815
Conclusion:	The monthly rent is equal to 0.66% of the sales price; the sales price is approximately 150 times the monthly rent

Monthly rents may run about 1% of selling prices in one market, and more or less in another. A market exists where specific rental properties compete with each other for tenants. For competitive reasons, rents charged for similar properties tend to be much alike within the same market. As a result, if one rental property has a monthly income that is 1% of its sales price, comparable properties will have similar income-to-price ratios.

A monthly multiplier is established by dividing the sales price by the monthly rental income. An annual multiplier is calculated by dividing the sales price by the annual rental income.

Example:

Sales Price		Monthly Rent		Monthly Multiplier
$275,000	÷	$1,815	=	151.52

Sales Price		Annual Rent		Annual Multiplier
$275,000	÷	$21,780	=	12.63

After locating at least four comparable residential rental properties, the appraiser can determine their monthly or annual gross income multipliers (either is acceptable—it's a matter of the appraiser's preference) by dividing the rents into their respective selling prices.

Example:

Comp No.	Sales Price	Monthly Rent	Monthly Multiplier
1	$264,500	$1,800	146.94
2	$276,525	$1,825	151.52
3	$268,300	$1,850	145.03
4	$280,750	$1,895	148.15

The appraiser uses the multipliers of the comparables to determine an appropriate multiplier for the subject property, taking into account the similarities and differences between the properties. Then the appraiser multiplies the rent that the subject property is generating by the chosen multiplier for a rough estimate of its value as income-producing property.

The principal weakness of the gross income multiplier method is that it's based on gross income figures and doesn't take into account vacancies or operating expenses. If two rental homes have the same rental income, the gross income multiplier method would indicate that they're worth the same amount; but if one is older and has higher maintenance costs, the net return to the owner would be less, and so would the value of the property.

If possible, the appraiser should use the subject property's economic rent as opposed to the contract rent (the rent the owner is actually receiving) in calculating the gross income multiplier.

> **Example:** The owner leased the home two years ago for $1,850 a month, and the lease contract has another year to go. Market rents have risen sharply over the past two years, so that the property could now command a much higher rent—probably about $2,200 a month. If the appraiser were to use the $1,850 contract rent in the gross income multiplier method instead of the $2,200 economic rent, it would distort the estimate of value.

Site Valuation

There are a number of situations in which an appraiser values a site apart from any improvements. A client may ask an appraiser to value unimproved property, also referred to as vacant land or raw land. Or when appraising improved property, an appraiser may be called upon to appraise the site and the buildings separately (for example, when property is being assessed for tax purposes). Occasionally, an appraiser is asked to appraise a property on which there is a building that needs to be torn down. In that case, the appraiser will need to appraise the site at its highest and best use, and then deduct the cost of removing the structure.

There are four main ways to appraise a site:

1. the sales comparison method,
2. the land residual technique,
3. the distribution method, and
4. the development method.

Sales Comparison Method. The sales comparison approach is the method of site valuation preferred by most appraisers, because it reflects the actions of informed buyers and sellers in the marketplace. With this method, the appraiser uses the sales prices of vacant sites that have recently sold and that are similar to the subject property's site to arrive at an estimate of its value.

Land Residual Technique. The land residual technique, which we discussed earlier, is site valuation by the income approach. It's used for improved property. The appraiser determines the income attributable to the land, then calculates the value of the land by capitalizing its income.

Distribution Method. In the distribution method—also called allocation or abstraction—the appraiser analyzes recent sales of improved properties to determine what percentage of their sales prices involved land costs. If the lots typically account for 18% to 20% of the cost of the properties, the appraiser might conclude that the portion of the subject property's overall value attributable to the land is about 18% to 20%.

The distribution method isn't as reliable as the sales comparison method. Its principal weakness is that in many cases there are no consistent land-to-property value ratios on which the appraiser can rely.

Development Method. Also called the anticipated use method, this valuation technique is applied fairly often. It's used to value vacant land when the highest and best use of the land is for subdivision and development. In this method, the appraiser estimates the future value of the developed lots, and then subtracts the costs of development to arrive at the current value of the land.

Reconciliation and Final Estimate of Value

Throughout the appraisal process, the appraiser is gathering facts on which he will base the ultimate conclusion, the final estimate of the property's value. In many cases, the facts require nothing beyond simple verification; their meaning is self-evident. In other cases, they require expert interpretation. Appraisers refer to the assembly and interpretation of all the facts that influence a property's value as **reconciliation**. Nowhere in the appraisal process do the appraiser's experience and judgment play a more critical role.

The final value estimate isn't simply the average of the results yielded by the three appraisal methods—sales comparison, cost, and income. Rather, it's the figure that represents the appraiser's expert opinion of the subject property's value after all the data have been assembled and analyzed.

After determining the final estimate of value, the appraiser presents it to the client in an appraisal report. The two most common types of reports are the narrative report and the form report. A **narrative report** is a thorough, detailed, written presentation of the facts and reasoning behind the appraiser's estimate of value. The property value is usually stated in the section of the narrative report that discusses the purpose of the appraisal. A **form report** is a brief, standard form used by lending institutions and government agencies (for example, the FHA and the VA), presenting only the key data and the appraiser's conclusions. This is the most common type of appraisal report. The Uniform Residential Appraisal Report form, used in most residential transactions, is shown in Figure 11.9.

Fig. 11.9 Uniform Residential Appraisal Report form

Uniform Residential Appraisal Report

File #

The purpose of this summary appraisal report is to provide the lender/client with an accurate, and adequately supported, opinion of the market value of the subject property.

SUBJECT

Property Address | City | State | Zip Code
Borrower | Owner of Public Record | County
Legal Description
Assessor's Parcel # | Tax Year | R.E. Taxes $
Neighborhood Name | Map Reference | Census Tract
Occupant ☐ Owner ☐ Tenant ☐ Vacant | Special Assessments $ | ☐ PUD | HOA $ | ☐ per year ☐ per month
Property Rights Appraised ☐ Fee Simple ☐ Leasehold ☐ Other (describe)
Assignment Type ☐ Purchase Transaction ☐ Refinance Transaction ☐ Other (describe)
Lender/Client | Address
Is the subject property currently offered for sale or has it been offered for sale in the twelve months prior to the effective date of this appraisal? ☐ Yes ☐ No
Report data source(s) used, offering price(s), and date(s).

CONTRACT

I ☐ did ☐ did not analyze the contract for sale for the subject purchase transaction. Explain the results of the analysis of the contract for sale or why the analysis was not performed.
Contract Price $ | Date of Contract | Is the property seller the owner of public record? ☐Yes ☐No | Data Source(s)
Is there any financial assistance (loan charges, sale concessions, gift or downpayment assistance, etc.) to be paid by any party on behalf of the borrower? ☐ Yes ☐ No
If Yes, report the total dollar amount and describe the items to be paid.

NEIGHBORHOOD

Note: Race and the racial composition of the neighborhood are not appraisal factors.

Neighborhood Characteristics	One-Unit Housing Trends	One-Unit Housing		Present Land Use %
Location ☐ Urban ☐ Suburban ☐ Rural	Property Values ☐ Increasing ☐ Stable ☐ Declining	PRICE	AGE	One-Unit %
Built-Up ☐ Over 75% ☐ 25–75% ☐ Under 25%	Demand/Supply ☐ Shortage ☐ In Balance ☐ Over Supply	$ (000)	(yrs)	2-4 Unit %
Growth ☐ Rapid ☐ Stable ☐ Slow	Marketing Time ☐ Under 3 mths ☐ 3–6 mths ☐ Over 6 mths	Low		Multi-Family %
Neighborhood Boundaries		High		Commercial %
		Pred.		Other %

Neighborhood Description
Market Conditions (including support for the above conclusions)

SITE

Dimensions | Area | Shape | View
Specific Zoning Classification | Zoning Description
Zoning Compliance ☐ Legal ☐ Legal Nonconforming (Grandfathered Use) ☐ No Zoning ☐ Illegal (describe)
Is the highest and best use of the subject property as improved (or as proposed per plans and specifications) the present use? ☐ Yes ☐ No If No, describe

Utilities	Public	Other (describe)		Public	Other (describe)	Off-site Improvements—Type	Public	Private
Electricity	☐	☐	Water	☐	☐	Street	☐	☐
Gas	☐	☐	Sanitary Sewer	☐	☐	Alley	☐	☐

FEMA Special Flood Hazard Area ☐ Yes ☐ No | FEMA Flood Zone | FEMA Map # | FEMA Map Date
Are the utilities and off-site improvements typical for the market area? ☐ Yes ☐ No If No, describe
Are there any adverse site conditions or external factors (easements, encroachments, environmental conditions, land uses, etc.)? ☐ Yes ☐ No If Yes, describe

IMPROVEMENTS

General Description		Foundation		Exterior Description materials/condition		Interior materials/condition
Units ☐ One ☐ One with Accessory Unit		☐ Concrete Slab ☐ Crawl Space		Foundation Walls		Floors
# of Stories		☐ Full Basement ☐ Partial Basement		Exterior Walls		Walls
Type ☐ Det. ☐ Att. ☐ S-Det./End Unit		Basement Area sq. ft.		Roof Surface		Trim/Finish
☐ Existing ☐ Proposed ☐ Under Const.		Basement Finish %		Gutters & Downspouts		Bath Floor
Design (Style)		☐ Outside Entry/Exit ☐ Sump Pump		Window Type		Bath Wainscot
Year Built		Evidence of ☐ Infestation		Storm Sash/Insulated		Car Storage ☐ None
Effective Age (Yrs)		☐ Dampness ☐ Settlement		Screens		☐ Driveway # of Cars
Attic	☐ None	Heating ☐ FWA ☐ HWBB ☐ Radiant		Amenities	☐ Woodstove(s) #	Driveway Surface
☐ Drop Stair	☐ Stairs	☐ Other	Fuel	☐ Fireplace(s) #	☐ Fence	☐ Garage # of Cars
☐ Floor	☐ Scuttle	Cooling ☐ Central Air Conditioning		☐ Patio/Deck	☐ Porch	☐ Carport # of Cars
☐ Finished	☐ Heated	☐ Individual	☐ Other	☐ Pool	☐ Other	☐ Att. ☐ Det. ☐ Built-in

Appliances ☐Refrigerator ☐Range/Oven ☐Dishwasher ☐Disposal ☐Microwave ☐Washer/Dryer ☐Other (describe)
Finished area **above** grade contains: | Rooms | Bedrooms | Bath(s) | Square Feet of Gross Living Area Above Grade
Additional features (special energy efficient items, etc.)
Describe the condition of the property (including needed repairs, deterioration, renovations, remodeling, etc.).
Are there any physical deficiencies or adverse conditions that affect the livability, soundness, or structural integrity of the property? ☐ Yes ☐ No If Yes, describe
Does the property generally conform to the neighborhood (functional utility, style, condition, use, construction, etc.)? ☐ Yes ☐ No If No, describe

Freddie Mac Form 70 March 2005 | Page 1 of 6 | Fannie Mae Form 1004 March 2005

Uniform Residential Appraisal Report

File #

There are comparable properties currently offered for sale in the subject neighborhood ranging in price from $ to $.

There are comparable sales in the subject neighborhood within the past twelve months ranging in sale price from $ to $.

SALES COMPARISON APPROACH

FEATURE	SUBJECT	COMPARABLE SALE # 1		COMPARABLE SALE # 2		COMPARABLE SALE # 3	
Address							
Proximity to Subject							
Sale Price	$		$		$		$
Sale Price/Gross Liv. Area	$ sq. ft.	$ sq. ft.		$ sq. ft.		$ sq. ft.	
Data Source(s)							
Verification Source(s)							
VALUE ADJUSTMENTS	DESCRIPTION	DESCRIPTION	+(-) $ Adjustment	DESCRIPTION	+(-) $ Adjustment	DESCRIPTION	+(-) $ Adjustment
Sale or Financing Concessions							
Date of Sale/Time							
Location							
Leasehold/Fee Simple							
Site							
View							
Design (Style)							
Quality of Construction							
Actual Age							
Condition							
Above Grade	Total / Bdrms. / Baths	Total / Bdrms. / Baths		Total / Bdrms. / Baths		Total / Bdrms. / Baths	
Room Count							
Gross Living Area	sq. ft.	sq. ft.		sq. ft.		sq. ft.	
Basement & Finished Rooms Below Grade							
Functional Utility							
Heating/Cooling							
Energy Efficient Items							
Garage/Carport							
Porch/Patio/Deck							
Net Adjustment (Total)		☐ + ☐ -	$	☐ + ☐ -	$	☐ + ☐ -	$
Adjusted Sale Price of Comparables		Net Adj. % Gross Adj. %	$	Net Adj. % Gross Adj. %	$	Net Adj. % Gross Adj. %	$

I ☐ did ☐ did not research the sale or transfer history of the subject property and comparable sales. If not, explain

My research ☐ did ☐ did not reveal any prior sales or transfers of the subject property for the three years prior to the effective date of this appraisal.

Data source(s)

My research ☐ did ☐ did not reveal any prior sales or transfers of the comparable sales for the year prior to the date of sale of the comparable sale.

Data source(s)

Report the results of the research and analysis of the prior sale or transfer history of the subject property and comparable sales (report additional prior sales on page 3).

ITEM	SUBJECT	COMPARABLE SALE # 1	COMPARABLE SALE # 2	COMPARABLE SALE # 3
Date of Prior Sale/Transfer				
Price of Prior Sale/Transfer				
Data Source(s)				
Effective Date of Data Source(s)				

Analysis of prior sale or transfer history of the subject property and comparable sales

Summary of Sales Comparison Approach

Indicated Value by Sales Comparison Approach $

RECONCILIATION

Indicated Value by: Sales Comparison Approach $ Cost Approach (if developed) $ Income Approach (if developed) $

This appraisal is made ☐ "as is", ☐ subject to completion per plans and specifications on the basis of a hypothetical condition that the improvements have been completed, ☐ subject to the following repairs or alterations on the basis of a hypothetical condition that the repairs or alterations have been completed, or ☐ subject to the following required inspection based on the extraordinary assumption that the condition or deficiency does not require alteration or repair:

Based on a complete visual inspection of the interior and exterior areas of the subject property, defined scope of work, statement of assumptions and limiting conditions, and appraiser's certification, my (our) opinion of the market value, as defined, of the real property that is the subject of this report is $, as of , which is the date of inspection and the effective date of this appraisal.

Freddie Mac Form 70 March 2005 Page 2 of 6 Fannie Mae Form 1004 March 2005

Uniform Residential Appraisal Report

File #

ADDITIONAL COMMENTS

COST APPROACH TO VALUE (not required by Fannie Mae)

Provide adequate information for the lender/client to replicate the below cost figures and calculations.

Support for the opinion of site value (summary of comparable land sales or other methods for estimating site value)

ESTIMATED ☐ REPRODUCTION OR ☐ REPLACEMENT COST NEW	OPINION OF SITE VALUE .... = $			
Source of cost data	Dwelling Sq. Ft. @ $ .... =$			
Quality rating from cost service Effective date of cost data	Sq. Ft. @ $ .... =$			
Comments on Cost Approach (gross living area calculations, depreciation, etc.)				
	Garage/Carport Sq. Ft. @ $ .... =$			
	Total Estimate of Cost-New .... = $			
	Less Physical	Functional	External	
	Depreciation			=$( )
	Depreciated Cost of Improvements......... =$			
	"As-is" Value of Site Improvements......... =$			
Estimated Remaining Economic Life (HUD and VA only) Years	Indicated Value By Cost Approach .... =$			

INCOME APPROACH TO VALUE (not required by Fannie Mae)

Estimated Monthly Market Rent $ X Gross Rent Multiplier = $ Indicated Value by Income Approach

Summary of Income Approach (including support for market rent and GRM)

PROJECT INFORMATION FOR PUDs (if applicable)

Is the developer/builder in control of the Homeowners' Association (HOA)? ☐ Yes ☐ No Unit type(s) ☐ Detached ☐ Attached

Provide the following information for PUDs ONLY if the developer/builder is in control of the HOA and the subject property is an attached dwelling unit.

Legal name of project

Total number of phases Total number of units Total number of units sold

Total number of units rented Total number of units for sale Data source(s)

Was the project created by the conversion of an existing building(s) into a PUD? ☐ Yes ☐ No If Yes, date of conversion

Does the project contain any multi-dwelling units? ☐ Yes ☐ No Data source(s)

Are the units, common elements, and recreation facilities complete? ☐ Yes ☐ No If No, describe the status of completion.

Are the common elements leased to or by the Homeowners' Association? ☐ Yes ☐ No If Yes, describe the rental terms and options.

Describe common elements and recreational facilities

Freddie Mac Form 70 March 2005 Page 3 of 6 Fannie Mae Form 1004 March 2005

Uniform Residential Appraisal Report

File #

This report form is designed to report an appraisal of a one-unit property or a one-unit property with an accessory unit; including a unit in a planned unit development (PUD). This report form is not designed to report an appraisal of a manufactured home or a unit in a condominium or cooperative project.

This appraisal report is subject to the following scope of work, intended use, intended user, definition of market value, statement of assumptions and limiting conditions, and certifications. Modifications, additions, or deletions to the intended use, intended user, definition of market value, or assumptions and limiting conditions are not permitted. The appraiser may expand the scope of work to include any additional research or analysis necessary based on the complexity of this appraisal assignment. Modifications or deletions to the certifications are also not permitted. However, additional certifications that do not constitute material alterations to this appraisal report, such as those required by law or those related to the appraiser's continuing education or membership in an appraisal organization, are permitted.

SCOPE OF WORK: The scope of work for this appraisal is defined by the complexity of this appraisal assignment and the reporting requirements of this appraisal report form, including the following definition of market value, statement of assumptions and limiting conditions, and certifications. The appraiser must, at a minimum: (1) perform a complete visual inspection of the interior and exterior areas of the subject property, (2) inspect the neighborhood, (3) inspect each of the comparable sales from at least the street, (4) research, verify, and analyze data from reliable public and/or private sources, and (5) report his or her analysis, opinions, and conclusions in this appraisal report.

INTENDED USE: The intended use of this appraisal report is for the lender/client to evaluate the property that is the subject of this appraisal for a mortgage finance transaction.

INTENDED USER: The intended user of this appraisal report is the lender/client.

DEFINITION OF MARKET VALUE: The most probable price which a property should bring in a competitive and open market under all conditions requisite to a fair sale, the buyer and seller, each acting prudently, knowledgeably and assuming the price is not affected by undue stimulus. Implicit in this definition is the consummation of a sale as of a specified date and the passing of title from seller to buyer under conditions whereby: (1) buyer and seller are typically motivated; (2) both parties are well informed or well advised, and each acting in what he or she considers his or her own best interest; (3) a reasonable time is allowed for exposure in the open market; (4) payment is made in terms of cash in U. S. dollars or in terms of financial arrangements comparable thereto; and (5) the price represents the normal consideration for the property sold unaffected by special or creative financing or sales concessions* granted by anyone associated with the sale.

*Adjustments to the comparables must be made for special or creative financing or sales concessions. No adjustments are necessary for those costs which are normally paid by sellers as a result of tradition or law in a market area; these costs are readily identifiable since the seller pays these costs in virtually all sales transactions. Special or creative financing adjustments can be made to the comparable property by comparisons to financing terms offered by a third party institutional lender that is not already involved in the property or transaction. Any adjustment should not be calculated on a mechanical dollar for dollar cost of the financing or concession but the dollar amount of any adjustment should approximate the market's reaction to the financing or concessions based on the appraiser's judgment.

STATEMENT OF ASSUMPTIONS AND LIMITING CONDITIONS: The appraiser's certification in this report is subject to the following assumptions and limiting conditions:

1. The appraiser will not be responsible for matters of a legal nature that affect either the property being appraised or the title to it, except for information that he or she became aware of during the research involved in performing this appraisal. The appraiser assumes that the title is good and marketable and will not render any opinions about the title.

2. The appraiser has provided a sketch in this appraisal report to show the approximate dimensions of the improvements. The sketch is included only to assist the reader in visualizing the property and understanding the appraiser's determination of its size.

3. The appraiser has examined the available flood maps that are provided by the Federal Emergency Management Agency (or other data sources) and has noted in this appraisal report whether any portion of the subject site is located in an identified Special Flood Hazard Area. Because the appraiser is not a surveyor, he or she makes no guarantees, express or implied, regarding this determination.

4. The appraiser will not give testimony or appear in court because he or she made an appraisal of the property in question, unless specific arrangements to do so have been made beforehand, or as otherwise required by law.

5. The appraiser has noted in this appraisal report any adverse conditions (such as needed repairs, deterioration, the presence of hazardous wastes, toxic substances, etc.) observed during the inspection of the subject property or that he or she became aware of during the research involved in performing this appraisal. Unless otherwise stated in this appraisal report, the appraiser has no knowledge of any hidden or unapparent physical deficiencies or adverse conditions of the property (such as, but not limited to, needed repairs, deterioration, the presence of hazardous wastes, toxic substances, adverse environmental conditions, etc.) that would make the property less valuable, and has assumed that there are no such conditions and makes no guarantees or warranties, express or implied. The appraiser will not be responsible for any such conditions that do exist or for any engineering or testing that might be required to discover whether such conditions exist. Because the appraiser is not an expert in the field of environmental hazards, this appraisal report must not be considered as an environmental assessment of the property.

6. The appraiser has based his or her appraisal report and valuation conclusion for an appraisal that is subject to satisfactory completion, repairs, or alterations on the assumption that the completion, repairs, or alterations of the subject property will be performed in a professional manner.

Uniform Residential Appraisal Report

File #

APPRAISER'S CERTIFICATION: The Appraiser certifies and agrees that:

1. I have, at a minimum, developed and reported this appraisal in accordance with the scope of work requirements stated in this appraisal report.

2. I performed a complete visual inspection of the interior and exterior areas of the subject property. I reported the condition of the improvements in factual, specific terms. I identified and reported the physical deficiencies that could affect the livability, soundness, or structural integrity of the property.

3. I performed this appraisal in accordance with the requirements of the Uniform Standards of Professional Appraisal Practice that were adopted and promulgated by the Appraisal Standards Board of The Appraisal Foundation and that were in place at the time this appraisal report was prepared.

4. I developed my opinion of the market value of the real property that is the subject of this report based on the sales comparison approach to value. I have adequate comparable market data to develop a reliable sales comparison approach for this appraisal assignment. I further certify that I considered the cost and income approaches to value but did not develop them, unless otherwise indicated in this report.

5. I researched, verified, analyzed, and reported on any current agreement for sale for the subject property, any offering for sale of the subject property in the twelve months prior to the effective date of this appraisal, and the prior sales of the subject property for a minimum of three years prior to the effective date of this appraisal, unless otherwise indicated in this report.

6. I researched, verified, analyzed, and reported on the prior sales of the comparable sales for a minimum of one year prior to the date of sale of the comparable sale, unless otherwise indicated in this report.

7. I selected and used comparable sales that are locationally, physically, and functionally the most similar to the subject property.

8. I have not used comparable sales that were the result of combining a land sale with the contract purchase price of a home that has been built or will be built on the land.

9. I have reported adjustments to the comparable sales that reflect the market's reaction to the differences between the subject property and the comparable sales.

10. I verified, from a disinterested source, all information in this report that was provided by parties who have a financial interest in the sale or financing of the subject property.

11. I have knowledge and experience in appraising this type of property in this market area.

12. I am aware of, and have access to, the necessary and appropriate public and private data sources, such as multiple listing services, tax assessment records, public land records and other such data sources for the area in which the property is located.

13. I obtained the information, estimates, and opinions furnished by other parties and expressed in this appraisal report from reliable sources that I believe to be true and correct.

14. I have taken into consideration the factors that have an impact on value with respect to the subject neighborhood, subject property, and the proximity of the subject property to adverse influences in the development of my opinion of market value. I have noted in this appraisal report any adverse conditions (such as, but not limited to, needed repairs, deterioration, the presence of hazardous wastes, toxic substances, adverse environmental conditions, etc.) observed during the inspection of the subject property or that I became aware of during the research involved in performing this appraisal. I have considered these adverse conditions in my analysis of the property value, and have reported on the effect of the conditions on the value and marketability of the subject property.

15. I have not knowingly withheld any significant information from this appraisal report and, to the best of my knowledge, all statements and information in this appraisal report are true and correct.

16. I stated in this appraisal report my own personal, unbiased, and professional analysis, opinions, and conclusions, which are subject only to the assumptions and limiting conditions in this appraisal report.

17. I have no present or prospective interest in the property that is the subject of this report, and I have no present or prospective personal interest or bias with respect to the participants in the transaction. I did not base, either partially or completely, my analysis and/or opinion of market value in this appraisal report on the race, color, religion, sex, age, marital status, handicap, familial status, or national origin of either the prospective owners or occupants of the subject property or of the present owners or occupants of the properties in the vicinity of the subject property or on any other basis prohibited by law.

18. My employment and/or compensation for performing this appraisal or any future or anticipated appraisals was not conditioned on any agreement or understanding, written or otherwise, that I would report (or present analysis supporting) a predetermined specific value, a predetermined minimum value, a range or direction in value, a value that favors the cause of any party, or the attainment of a specific result or occurrence of a specific subsequent event (such as approval of a pending mortgage loan application).

19. I personally prepared all conclusions and opinions about the real estate that were set forth in this appraisal report. If I relied on significant real property appraisal assistance from any individual or individuals in the performance of this appraisal or the preparation of this appraisal report, I have named such individual(s) and disclosed the specific tasks performed in this appraisal report. I certify that any individual so named is qualified to perform the tasks. I have not authorized anyone to make a change to any item in this appraisal report; therefore, any change made to this appraisal is unauthorized and I will take no responsibility for it.

20. I identified the lender/client in this appraisal report who is the individual, organization, or agent for the organization that ordered and will receive this appraisal report.

Freddie Mac Form 70 March 2005 | Page 5 of 6 | Fannie Mae Form 1004 March 2005

Uniform Residential Appraisal Report

File #

21. The lender/client may disclose or distribute this appraisal report to: the borrower; another lender at the request of the borrower; the mortgagee or its successors and assigns; mortgage insurers; government sponsored enterprises; other secondary market participants; data collection or reporting services; professional appraisal organizations; any department, agency, or instrumentality of the United States; and any state, the District of Columbia, or other jurisdictions; without having to obtain the appraiser's or supervisory appraiser's (if applicable) consent. Such consent must be obtained before this appraisal report may be disclosed or distributed to any other party (including, but not limited to, the public through advertising, public relations, news, sales, or other media).

22. I am aware that any disclosure or distribution of this appraisal report by me or the lender/client may be subject to certain laws and regulations. Further, I am also subject to the provisions of the Uniform Standards of Professional Appraisal Practice that pertain to disclosure or distribution by me.

23. The borrower, another lender at the request of the borrower, the mortgagee or its successors and assigns, mortgage insurers, government sponsored enterprises, and other secondary market participants may rely on this appraisal report as part of any mortgage finance transaction that involves any one or more of these parties.

24. If this appraisal report was transmitted as an "electronic record" containing my "electronic signature," as those terms are defined in applicable federal and/or state laws (excluding audio and video recordings), or a facsimile transmission of this appraisal report containing a copy or representation of my signature, the appraisal report shall be as effective, enforceable and valid as if a paper version of this appraisal report were delivered containing my original hand written signature.

25. Any intentional or negligent misrepresentation(s) contained in this appraisal report may result in civil liability and/or criminal penalties including, but not limited to, fine or imprisonment or both under the provisions of Title 18, United States Code, Section 1001, et seq., or similar state laws.

SUPERVISORY APPRAISER'S CERTIFICATION: The Supervisory Appraiser certifies and agrees that:

1. I directly supervised the appraiser for this appraisal assignment, have read the appraisal report, and agree with the appraiser's analysis, opinions, statements, conclusions, and the appraiser's certification.

2. I accept full responsibility for the contents of this appraisal report including, but not limited to, the appraiser's analysis, opinions, statements, conclusions, and the appraiser's certification.

3. The appraiser identified in this appraisal report is either a sub-contractor or an employee of the supervisory appraiser (or the appraisal firm), is qualified to perform this appraisal, and is acceptable to perform this appraisal under the applicable state law.

4. This appraisal report complies with the Uniform Standards of Professional Appraisal Practice that were adopted and promulgated by the Appraisal Standards Board of The Appraisal Foundation and that were in place at the time this appraisal report was prepared.

5. If this appraisal report was transmitted as an "electronic record" containing my "electronic signature," as those terms are defined in applicable federal and/or state laws (excluding audio and video recordings), or a facsimile transmission of this appraisal report containing a copy or representation of my signature, the appraisal report shall be as effective, enforceable and valid as if a paper version of this appraisal report were delivered containing my original hand written signature.

APPRAISER

Signature ____________________

Name ____________________

Company Name ____________________

Company Address ____________________

____

Telephone Number ____________________

Email Address ____________________

Date of Signature and Report ____________________

Effective Date of Appraisal ____________________

State Certification # ____________________

or State License # ____________________

or Other (describe) ____________ State # ____________

State ____________________

Expiration Date of Certification or License ____________________

ADDRESS OF PROPERTY APPRAISED

____

____

APPRAISED VALUE OF SUBJECT PROPERTY $ ____________

LENDER/CLIENT

Name ____________________

Company Name ____________________

Company Address ____________________

____

Email Address ____________________

SUPERVISORY APPRAISER (ONLY IF REQUIRED)

Signature ____________________

Name ____________________

Company Name ____________________

Company Address ____________________

____

Telephone Number ____________________

Email Address ____________________

Date of Signature ____________________

State Certification # ____________________

or State License # ____________________

State ____________________

Expiration Date of Certification or License ____________

SUBJECT PROPERTY

☐ Did not inspect subject property

☐ Did inspect exterior of subject property from street

Date of Inspection ____________________

☐ Did inspect interior and exterior of subject property

Date of Inspection ____________________

COMPARABLE SALES

☐ Did not inspect exterior of comparable sales from street

☐ Did inspect exterior of comparable sales from street

Date of Inspection ____________________

Chapter Summary

1. An appraisal is an estimate or an opinion of value. Most real estate appraisals concern the property's market value, the price it is likely to be purchased for if sold under normal conditions: in an arm's length transaction, with the property offered on the open market for a reasonable length of time, when the parties are both acting prudently and knowledgeably, and when neither of them is subject to undue stimulus or unusual pressure.

2. Appraisers have developed many "principles of value" that guide them in the valuation process. These include the principles of highest and best use, change, anticipation, supply and demand, substitution, conformity, contribution, competition, and balance.

3. The steps in the appraisal process include defining the problem, determining what data is needed and where it can be found, gathering and verifying general and specific data, selecting and applying the valuation methods, reconciling the value indicators, and issuing the appraisal report.

4. General data concerns factors outside the subject property itself that influence the property's value. The appraiser gathers general data by evaluating economic and social trends and by performing a neighborhood analysis. Specific data (about the subject property itself) is gathered through site analysis and building analysis.

5. In the sales comparison approach to value (which is the most important method of appraisal for residential properties), the appraiser compares the subject property to comparable properties that were sold recently, and uses the adjusted selling prices of the comparables to estimate the value of the subject property.

6. In the cost approach to value, the appraiser estimates the cost of replacing the improvements, deducts any depreciation, and adds the estimated value of the land to arrive at an estimate of the value of the whole property. The three types of depreciation are physical deterioration, functional obsolescence, and external obsolescence. Depreciation is curable if the cost of correcting it could be recovered when the property is sold. Land doesn't depreciate.

7. In the income approach to value, the appraiser divides the property's net income by a capitalization rate to estimate its value to an investor. The appraiser first estimates the property's potential gross income (economic rent), then deducts a vacancy factor to determine the effective gross income, then deducts operating expenses to determine net income. The gross income multiplier method is a simplified version of the income approach that's sometimes used in appraising rental homes.

8. The methods used for site valuation (appraising raw land, or appraising a site separately from its improvements) are the sales comparison method, the land residual technique, the distribution method, and the development method.

Key Terms

Market value—The most probable price that a property should bring in a competitive and open market under all conditions requisite to a fair sale, the buyer and seller each acting prudently and knowledgeably, and assuming the price isn't affected by undue stimulus.

Arm's length transaction—A sale in which there is no pre-existing family or business relationship between the parties.

Highest and best use—The most profitable use of the property; the one that provides the greatest net return over time.

Principle of change—Real property is in a constant state of change. It goes through a four-phase life cycle of integration, equilibrium, disintegration, and rejuvenation.

Principle of substitution—No one will pay more for a piece of property than they would have to pay for an equally desirable substitute.

Sales comparison approach—The method of appraisal in which the appraiser compares the subject property to recently sold comparable properties.

Cost approach—The method of appraisal in which the appraiser estimates the replacement cost of the building, deducts depreciation, and adds the value of the site.

Depreciation—Loss in value due to any cause. Depreciation is curable if the cost of correcting it could be recovered in the sales price when the property is sold.

Physical deterioration—Depreciation caused by wear and tear, damage, or structural defects. Curable physical deterioration is called deferred maintenance.

Functional obsolescence—Depreciation caused by functional inadequacies or outmoded design.

External obsolescence—Depreciation caused by forces outside the property, such as neighborhood decline or proximity to nuisances. Also called economic obsolescence.

Income approach—The method of appraising property in which net income is converted into value using a capitalization rate.

Effective gross income—A property's potential gross income, minus a vacancy factor.

Net income—A property's effective gross income, minus operating expenses.

Capitalization rate—The rate of return an investor wants on her investment in the property.

Economic rent—The rent that a property would earn on the open market if it were currently available for rent, as distinguished from the rent it's actually earning now (the contract rent).

Chapter Quiz

1. An appraisal is:
   a) a scientific determination of a property's value
   b) a property's average value, as indicated by general and specific data
   c) an estimate of a property's value as of a specific date
   d) a mathematical analysis of a property's value

2. The focus of most appraisals is the subject property's:
   a) market value
   b) market price
   c) sales price
   d) value in use

3. A property's highest and best use is:
   a) the use that will generate the greatest net return
   b) the best use it could be put to if there were no zoning or other restrictions
   c) the use that best promotes the public health, safety, and welfare
   d) the use that is best suited to the present owner's plans

4. The earliest phase of a property's life cycle, when it is being developed, is called:
   a) substitution
   b) regression
   c) integration
   d) disintegration

5. Developers have announced plans to build a multimillion dollar shopping center next door to a vacant commercial lot you own. Property values in the area will tend to increase as a result of this announcement. This is an example of the principle of:
   a) highest and best use
   b) supply and demand
   c) substitution
   d) anticipation

6. The owner of an apartment building has asked an appraiser to determine if it would make financial sense to put in a swimming pool for the tenants' use. The appraiser will be most concerned with the principle of:
   a) regression
   b) substitution
   c) conformity
   d) contribution

7. If someone were to build a high-quality home costing $550,000 in a neighborhood where all of the other homes were valued at around $275,000, the more expensive home would suffer a loss in value. This illustrates the principle of:
   a) regression
   b) supply and demand
   c) progression
   d) aversion

8. An appraiser gathers general data in a:
   a) site analysis
   b) building analysis
   c) neighborhood analysis
   d) None of the above

9. The sales comparison approach would almost certainly be much more important than the other two methods (the cost approach and the income approach) in the appraisal of:
   a) a six-unit apartment building
   b) an industrial building
   c) a shopping center
   d) a single-family home

10. A residential appraiser looking for good comparables is most likely to consider homes that:
    a) have not changed hands within the past three years
    b) are currently listed for sale
    c) were sold within the past three to six months
    d) were listed for less than they eventually sold for

11. In which of the following situations would the sales comparison method of appraisal be least reliable?
    a) When all of the comparables are in the same price range
    b) When the real estate market has been inactive for quite a while
    c) When some of the comparables are located in another neighborhood
    d) When the subject property is in better condition than the comparables

12. When applying the sales comparison method to appraise a single-family home, an appraiser would never use as a comparable a similar home that:
    a) sold over six months ago
    b) sold recently but is located in another neighborhood
    c) was sold by owners who were forced to sell because of financial difficulties
    d) is situated on a corner lot

13. When using the replacement cost approach, which of the following would be least important?
    a) Current construction cost per square foot
    b) Rental cost per square foot
    c) Depreciation
    d) Estimated land value

14. An appraiser is applying the cost approach in valuing an elegant building that was built in 1894. Which of the following is most likely to be true?
    a) The building's replacement cost is the same as its reproduction cost
    b) The building's replacement cost is a better indicator of its market value than its reproduction cost
    c) The building's reproduction cost is a better indicator of its market value than its replacement cost
    d) The building's replacement cost is much greater than its reproduction cost

15. In the income approach to value, which of the following isn't considered to be one of the property's operating expenses?
    a) General real estate taxes
    b) Maintenance expenses
    c) Reserves for replacement
    d) Mortgage payments

Answer Key

1. c) An appraisal is only an estimate or opinion of value, and it is valid only in regard to a specified date.

2. a) An appraiser is usually asked to determine the subject property's market value (value in exchange).

3. a) The highest and best use is the use that would produce the greatest net return over time, given the current zoning and other restrictions on use.

4. c) Integration is the period during which the property is being developed.

5. d) This is an example of the principle of anticipation, which holds that value is created by the expectation of future benefits to be derived from owning a property.

6. d) The appraiser will be concerned with the principle of contribution. Will the proposed improvement—the swimming pool—contribute enough to the property's value (in the form of higher rents from tenants, and, ultimately, net income to the owner) to justify the expense of installing it?

7. a) The principle of regression holds that association with properties of much lower quality reduces a property's value.

8. c) General data is data concerning factors outside the subject property itself that affect the property's value. A neighborhood analysis involves collection of general data, whereas the site analysis and building analysis involve collection of specific data about the subject property itself.

9. d) In the appraisal of single-family homes, the sales comparison approach is given the most weight.

10. c) A sales comparison appraisal of residential property is usually based on the sales prices of homes that sold within the past three to six months.

11. b) There's little data available in an inactive market. (However, the appraiser can use comparable sales that took place up to one year earlier, if he determines the rate of appreciation or depreciation and adjusts the prices accordingly.)

12. c) Forced sales are never used as comparables for appraisal purposes. Comparable sales must have occurred under normal conditions, where neither party was acting under unusual pressure.

13. b) The cost approach involves estimating the current cost of construction, subtracting the amount of accrued depreciation, then adding back in the estimated value of the land. How much the property rents for is irrelevant in the cost approach.

14. b) The cost of producing a replica of an old building at current prices (reproduction cost) is invariably much higher than the cost of constructing a building with the equivalent utility using modern materials (replacement cost). Reproduction cost isn't a good indicator of an old building's market value.

15. d) The mortgage payments—referred to as the property's debt service—aren't considered operating expenses for the purposes of the income approach.

Chapter 12

Closing Real Estate Transactions

I. Escrow
   A. Escrow services
   B. Termination of escrow
   C. Escrow agents
II. Closing Costs and Settlement Statements
   A. Preparing a settlement statement
   B. Guide to settlement statements
      1. Settlement charges
      2. Prorations
      3. Cash at closing
III. Income Tax Aspects of Closing
   A. Form 1099-S reporting
   B. Form 8300 reporting
   C. FIRPTA
   D. California withholding law
IV. Real Estate Settlement Procedures Act
   A. Transactions covered by RESPA
   B. RESPA requirements

Chapter Overview

The real estate agent's job doesn't end when the parties sign the purchase agreement. Many matters must be taken care of before the sale can be finalized, and the service provided by the real estate agent during the closing process is just as important as the agent's marketing efforts before the sale. Guiding the parties through closing prevents unnecessary delays and earns the agent a reputation for professionalism. This chapter explains the purpose of escrow and the steps involved in closing. It also discusses how settlement statements work, how closing costs are allocated and prorated, income tax aspects of closing, and the requirements of the federal Real Estate Settlement Procedures Act.

Introduction

Once a buyer and a seller have signed a purchase agreement, the parties and their agents begin making preparations to finalize the transaction. Finalizing a real estate transaction is called **closing** or **settlement**.

The closing process varies considerably from one state to another. In some states, all of the parties involved in the transaction get together in person to sign and exchange legal documents and transfer funds. In many other states, including California, the closing process is handled by a third party, through the creation of an escrow.

Escrow

Escrow is an arrangement in which money and documents are held by a third party (the **escrow agent**) on behalf of the buyer and the seller until the transaction is ready to close. The escrow agent is a dual agent, representing both the buyer and the seller, with fiduciary duties to both parties (see the discussion of dual agency in Chapter 8).

The parties usually give the escrow agent written **escrow instructions**, which determine under what conditions and at what time the agent will distribute the money and documents to the proper parties. The escrow instructions are a bilateral contract between the buyer and the seller. Neither party may choose the escrow agent or set the terms and conditions of escrow without the consent of the other party.

The escrow instructions ordinarily reflect the requirements for the transaction that were set forth in the purchase agreement. If there's a conflict between the terms of the purchase agreement and the escrow instructions, the escrow agent is generally supposed to comply with the later of the two contracts—the escrow instructions. To avoid this type of conflict, the escrow instructions can be incorporated into the purchase agreement, as in the CAR purchase agreement form shown in Chapter 7 (Figure 7.3).

The purpose of escrow is to ensure that the seller receives the purchase price, the buyer receives clear title to the property, and the lender's security interest in the property is perfected. Escrow protects each party from the other's change of mind. For example, if the seller suddenly doesn't want to sell the property as agreed, she can't just refuse to deliver the deed to the buyer. Once a deed has been given to an escrow agent, if the buyer fulfills all of the conditions specified in the escrow instructions and deposits the purchase price into escrow, the escrow agent is required to deliver the deed to the buyer. An added advantage of escrow is convenience: the parties don't have to be present to close the transaction.

Escrow Services

Escrow agents perform a wide variety of services to prepare a transaction for closing. Escrow closings may involve all of the following steps:

- ordering a title report from the title insurance company;
- ordering inspections;
- paying off existing loans secured by the property;
- preparing the deed and other documents;
- depositing funds from the buyer (and seller if necessary);
- requesting the funding of the buyer's loan;
- prorating expenses and allocating closing costs;
- preparing settlement statements;
- obtaining title insurance policies;
- arranging to have documents recorded; and
- disbursing funds and delivering documents.

However, the escrow agent's services are usually quite limited in nature. For example, while an escrow agent will order a title report in accordance with the escrow instructions, the escrow agent won't go over the report with the parties and discuss any unexpected problems that the report might reveal. Reviewing the report and deciding whether to proceed with the transaction is up to the parties.

Termination of Escrow

Escrow terminates when the transaction closes. Alternatively, it will terminate if the terms of the escrow instructions haven't been fulfilled by the scheduled closing date (or if no closing date has been set, within a reasonable time). As a general rule, escrow can be terminated earlier only if the buyer and the seller mutually consent to the termination. Neither party can terminate the escrow unilaterally, without the other's consent. Nor does the death or incapacity of either party terminate the escrow.

Example: The seller deposits a properly executed deed into escrow and dies shortly afterward. If the buyer fulfills the terms of the escrow instructions, the transaction will still close, in spite of the death of the seller.

When a transaction fails to close, there may be a dispute between the buyer and the seller over which of them is entitled to funds or other items that were placed into escrow. If the parties are unable to resolve the dispute, the escrow agent should file an **interpleader** action, turning the matter over to a court. The court will decide which party is the rightful owner of the items in escrow. It isn't the escrow agent's role to arbitrate a dispute between the parties.

Escrow Agents

Title companies are the most common escrow agents in northern California. In the southern part of the state, independent escrow companies also close a large number of transactions. Many institutional lenders have their own escrow departments, to close their own loan transactions.

California's Escrow Law requires all escrow companies to be licensed by the state Department of Business Oversight. Only corporations may be licensed as escrow companies; individuals aren't eligible. Banks, savings and loans, insurance companies, title companies, attorneys, and real estate brokers are exempt from this licensing requirement, because they're regulated by other agencies.

Note that the exemption from the escrow licensing requirement for real estate brokers doesn't cover every situation a broker could be involved in. The exemption is limited to activities that require a real estate license and that occur in the course of a real estate transaction in which the broker is either representing one of the parties or is herself one of the parties. This exemption allows brokers to provide escrow services to their clients, and they may charge a fee for these services. The exemption doesn't permit real estate brokers to operate as escrow agents for transactions in which they have no bona fide interest other than that of providing escrow services.

A real estate broker who engages in escrow activities in five or more transactions during a calendar year, or whose escrow activities total $1 million or more in a year, is required to file an annual report with the Bureau of Real Estate.

Closing Costs and Settlement Statements

Most real estate transactions involve a wide variety of costs in addition to the purchase price: inspection fees, title insurance charges, loan fees, and so on. These are known as **closing costs**. Some of these closing costs are paid by the buyer, and some are paid by the seller. Some are paid by one party to the other; for example, the buyer may have to reimburse the seller for property taxes the seller already paid. Other closing costs are paid by one of the parties to a third party; the seller may be required to pay a pest inspector's fee, for instance.

There are also other payments to be made in connection with closing. For example, the seller often has to pay off an existing mortgage or other liens. Determining who is required to pay how much to whom at closing can be a complicated matter.

So for each transaction, the escrow agent prepares a **settlement statement**. A settlement statement (also known as a closing statement) sets forth all of the financial aspects of the transaction in detail. It shows exactly how much the buyer will have to pay at closing, and exactly how much the seller will take away from closing. A simplified example of a settlement statement is shown in Figure 12.1.

Preparing a Settlement Statement

The items listed on the settlement statement are either **debits** or **credits**. A debit is a charge payable *by* a particular party; the purchase price is a debit for the buyer, for example, and the sales commission is a debit for the seller. Credits are items payable *to* a party; the buyer is credited for her new loan, and the seller for the purchase price.

Fig. 12.1 Simplified settlement statement

	Buyer		**Seller**	
	Debits	**Credits**	**Debits**	**Credits**
Purchase price	695,000.00			695,000.00
Deposit		15,000.00		
Documentary transfer tax			764.50	
Sales commission			41,700.00	
Payoff of seller's loan			486,500.00	
Assumption of seller's loan				
New loan		625,500.00		
Seller financing				
Owner's title insurance			1,738.00	
Lender's title insurance	673.00			
Origination/assumption fee	9,382.50			
Discount points				
Mortgage insurance	813.16			
Property taxes				
In arrears				
Paid in advance	2,956.00			2,956.00
Hazard insurance				
Assumption of policy				
New policy	1,452.00			
Interest				
Payoff of seller's loan			582.86	
Assumption				
New loan (prepaid)	1,028.20			
Impound account				
Payoff of seller's loan				786.05
Assumption				
Credit report	45.00			
Appraisal	415.00			
Survey				
Pest inspection and repairs			230.00	
Personal property				
Recording fees	50.00		25.00	
Escrow fee	250.00		250.00	
Balance due from buyer		71,564.86		
Balance due to seller			166,951.69	
TOTALS	712,064.86	712,064.86	698,742.05	698,742.05

Preparing a settlement statement involves little more than determining what charges and credits apply to a given transaction and making sure each one is allocated to the right party. When allocating expenses, an escrow agent is generally guided by the terms of the purchase agreement or the escrow instructions. The allocation can also be determined by custom (local or general), provided the custom doesn't conflict with the terms of the parties' contract. For example, in most places the buyer usually pays the cost of an appraisal, so that cost would ordinarily be charged to the buyer. But if the seller agreed in the purchase agreement to pay the appraisal fee, the agreement would take precedence over custom and the expense would be a debit for the seller on the settlement statement.

Of course, neither custom nor the agreement between the parties will be honored if they are contrary to local, state, or federal law.

Although a real estate agent typically won't ever be called upon to prepare a formal settlement statement, agents should know what closing costs are likely to be involved in a transaction and how they're customarily allocated. The buyer and the seller may want to negotiate the allocation of particular costs, and in any case they should have a good idea of their costs before signing a contract. A real estate agent should be able to prepare a preliminary estimate of closing costs for each party.

Guide to Settlement Statements

The simplified settlement statement in Figure 12.1 uses the double entry accounting method, so each party has a credit column and a debit column. The sum of the buyer's credits must equal the sum of the buyer's debits. The sum of the seller's credits must equal the sum of the seller's debits. Think of the settlement statement as a check register for a bank account. Debits are like checks written against the account, and credits are the equivalent of deposits into the account. When the transaction closes, the balance in each party's account should be zero.

When an item is payable by one party to the other, it will appear on the settlement statement as a debit for the paying party and as a credit for the party paid. An obvious example is the purchase price, which is a debit for the buyer and a credit for the seller.

If an item is paid by one of the parties to a third party, it appears on the settlement statement in the paying party's debit column, and it doesn't appear in the other party's columns at all. For example, the seller is customarily charged for the documentary transfer tax, which is paid to the county treasurer. The tax is a debit for the seller, but it isn't a credit for the buyer.

Similarly, certain items are shown as a credit for one party, but not as a debit for the other. The impound account for the seller's loan is an example. If the sale calls for the payoff of the seller's existing mortgage, any property tax, insurance, or other reserves held by the seller's lender are refunded. They are a credit for the seller, but not a debit for the buyer.

Settlement Charges. Here is a list of items that will or may appear on the settlement statement for a typical residential transaction.

Purchase Price. Paid by the buyer to the seller, the purchase price is listed as a debit for the buyer and a credit for the seller.

Good Faith Deposit. In most transactions, the buyer provides a good faith deposit when the purchase agreement is signed. If the transaction closes, the deposit is applied to the purchase price. Since the buyer has already paid the deposit, it appears on the settlement statement as a credit for the buyer. And since the full purchase price is already a debit for the buyer and a credit for the seller, no entry is made on the seller's side of the statement.

Sales Commission. The real estate broker's commission is normally paid by the seller, so it's entered as a debit for the seller.

New Loan. If the buyer secures a new loan to finance part or all of the sale, the loan amount is listed as a credit for the buyer. Like the deposit, the buyer's loan is part of the purchase price already credited to the seller, so no entry is made on the seller's side of the statement.

Assumed Loan. If the buyer assumes the seller's existing loan, it's part of the money used to finance the transaction, so (like a new loan) it's credited to the buyer. The assumed loan balance is a debit for the seller.

Seller Financing. If the seller accepts a mortgage or deed of trust from the buyer for part of the purchase price, that shows up in the buyer's credit column, just like an institutional loan. At the same time, a seller financing arrangement reduces the amount of cash the seller will receive at closing, so it's listed as a debit for the seller.

If the property is sold under a land contract, the contract price (less the downpayment) is credit extended by the seller. It reduces the seller's net at closing and is used by the buyer to finance the purchase, so it's a debit for the seller and a credit for the buyer.

Payoff of Seller's Loan. If the seller has a loan to pay off, the escrow agent requests a **beneficiary's statement** from the seller's lender. This document states the loan's remaining principal balance. The loan payoff is a debit for the seller. No entry is made on the buyer's side of the settlement statement.

Prepayment Penalty. A prepayment penalty is a charge the seller's lender may impose on the seller for paying the loan off before the end of its term. It would be a debit for the seller on the settlement statement.

Seller's Impound Account. As was mentioned earlier, the seller often has reserves or impounds on deposit with the lender to cover certain expenses connected with the property. These expenses, sometimes referred to as the **recurring costs**, include property taxes and insurance, and in some cases assessments, homeowners or condominium association fees, or other periodic charges. (The principal and interest payments on the mortgage aren't considered part of the recurring costs, however.) During the loan term, the lender may require the borrower to make regular payments toward the recurring costs, and these payments are kept in an **impound account** (also called a reserve account or an escrow account). The lender uses the funds in the impound account to pay the taxes, insurance, and other charges when they come due.

When the seller's loan is paid off, the unused balance in the impound account is refunded to the seller. It appears as a credit on the seller's side of the settlement statement. If the buyer is assuming the loan and the impound account, the reserves would appear as a credit for the seller and a debit for the buyer.

Appraisal Fee. The appraisal is usually required by the buyer's lender, so the fee is ordinarily a debit for the buyer.

Credit Report. The buyer's lender charges the buyer for the credit investigation, so this is also a debit for the buyer.

Survey. Sometimes a lender requires a survey as a condition for making the loan. Unless otherwise agreed, the cost of the survey is a debit for the buyer.

Origination Fee. This is the lender's one-time charge to the borrower for setting up the loan (see Chapter 10). It's a debit for the buyer.

Discount Points. The discount points are a debit for the buyer, unless the seller has agreed to pay for a buydown (again, see Chapter 10). In that case, the points are a debit for the seller.

Assumption Fee. A lender charges an assumption fee when the buyer is assuming the seller's existing loan. The assumption fee is a debit for the buyer.

Mortgage Insurance Premiums. In transactions involving mortgage insurance, the lender may require a certain number of monthly premiums to be paid in advance. These are a debit for the buyer.

Owner's Title Insurance Premium. In northern California, the buyer usually pays the premium for the owner's title insurance policy (which protects the buyer). In southern California, the seller usually pays it.

Lender's Title Insurance Premium. The lender requires the buyer to provide an extended coverage policy to protect the lender's lien priority. The premium for this policy is a debit for the buyer, unless otherwise agreed.

Sale of Personal Property. If the seller is selling the buyer some personal property along with the real property, the price of these items should be a credit for the seller and a debit for the buyer. (The seller should sign a bill of sale to be delivered to the buyer at closing along with the deed.)

Inspection Fees. The cost of an inspection is allocated by agreement between the parties. For example, the buyer might agree to pay for the cost of a pest inspection, while the seller agrees to pay for repairs if the inspection shows that any are necessary.

Hazard Insurance Policy. The lender generally requires the buyer to pay for one to three years of hazard insurance coverage in advance. This is a debit for the buyer.

Documentary Transfer Tax. This is a tax imposed on every sale of real property in California (see Chapter 5). It's also called the **excise tax**. It's customarily paid by the seller, so it would usually be listed in the seller's debit column.

Attorney's Fees. A buyer or seller who is represented by an attorney in the transaction is responsible for his own attorney's fees. On the settlement statement, the fees will show up as a debit for the appropriate party.

Recording Fees. The fees for recording the various documents involved in the transaction are usually charged to the party who benefits from the recording. For example, the fees for recording the deed and the new mortgage or deed of trust are debits for the buyer; the fee for recording a satisfaction of the old mortgage is a debit for the seller.

Escrow Fee. Also called a settlement fee or closing fee, the escrow fee is the escrow agent's charge for her services. The buyer and the seller commonly agree to split the escrow fee; in that case, half the fee will appear in each party's debit column.

Prorations. There are, of course, various recurring expenses connected with ownership of real estate, including property taxes, hazard insurance premiums, and mortgage interest payments. As a general rule, the seller is responsible for these expenses during his period of ownership, but not beyond. In preparing a settlement statement, the escrow agent checks to see whether the seller will be current, in arrears (late), or paid in advance with respect to these expenses on the closing date.

The escrow agent then **prorates** the expenses, determining what portion the seller is responsible for. To prorate an expense is to divide and allocate it proportionately, according to time, interest, or benefit.

If, in regard to a particular expense, the seller will be in arrears on the closing date, the amount that he owes is entered as a debit on the settlement statement. If the seller has paid in advance, he's entitled to a partial refund, which appears as a credit on the statement. If the expense is one that will continue after closing (as in the case of property taxes), the buyer is responsible for it once her period of ownership begins. That will show up on the buyer's side of the settlement statement as a credit (if the seller is in arrears) or as a debit (if the seller has paid in advance).

The first step in prorating an expense is to divide it by the number of days it covers to determine the **per diem** (daily) rate. So an annual expense would be divided by 365 days (366 in a leap year); the per diem rate would be **1/365th** of the annual amount. A monthly expense would be divided by the number of days in the month in question (28, 29, 30, or 31).*

The next step is to determine the number of days during which a particular party is responsible for the expense. The final step is to multiply that number of days by the per diem rate, to arrive at the share of the expense that party is responsible for. Examples appear below. (See Chapter 17 for further discussion of proration calculations.)

Property Taxes. If the seller has already paid the property taxes for the year, she's entitled to a prorated refund at closing. On the settlement statement, this will appear as a credit for the seller and a debit for the buyer. (Note: In California, the property tax year runs from July 1 to June 30. See Chapter 5.)

Example: Sharon is selling her house to Ben, with closing set for January 2. This year's property taxes are $4,380. The escrow agent calculates the per diem rate by dividing the property tax figure by 365, the number of days in the year.

$$\$4{,}380 \div 365 = \$12.00 \text{ per diem}$$

Sharon, the seller, is responsible for the property taxes through January 1—in other words, for the first 185 days of the year. The buyer, Ben, is responsible for the taxes from January 2 forward—the remaining 180 days in the year.

Sharon has already paid the full year's taxes, so at closing she'll be entitled to a credit for the share that is Ben's responsibility. The escrow agent multiplies the number of days for which Ben is responsible by the per diem rate to determine the amount Ben will owe Sharon at closing.

$$\$12.00 \times 180 = \$2{,}160$$

This $2,160 will appear as a credit on the seller's side of the settlement statement, and as a debit on the buyer's side of the statement.

---

* It was once a common practice to simplify proration calculations by using a 360-day year and 30-day months (regardless of how many days there actually were in a particular month or year). But now that calculators and computers are everywhere, most closing agents use the exact number of days in the year or month in question. Also, note that in order for the result of a proration to be completely accurate, the per diem rate must be calculated to an accuracy of at least four decimal places for monthly amounts, and five decimal places for annual amounts. Here again, calculators make this a painless process.

If the taxes are in arrears, the amount the seller should have paid for the period before closing will be a debit for the seller on the settlement statement.

Hazard Insurance. The premiums for hazard insurance (homeowner's insurance) are paid in advance. At closing, the seller is entitled to a refund for the unused portion of the policy. For example, if the seller has paid the premium for the year, and there are three months left in the year, the seller is entitled to a refund of one-fourth of the premium. This would show up as a credit for the seller on the settlement statement. If the buyer is going to assume the policy, the seller will be credited and the buyer will be debited for the appropriate amount.

Interest on Seller's Loan. Interest on a real estate loan is paid in arrears. In other words, the interest accruing during a given month is paid as part of the next month's payment. For instance, a loan payment due on September 1 includes the interest that accrued during August. If a transaction closes in the middle of the payment period, the seller owes the lender some interest.

> **Example:** The closing date is August 15. Although the seller made a payment on her loan on August 1, that payment didn't include any of the interest that's accruing during August. At closing, the seller will owe the lender interest for the period from August 1 through August 15. The escrow agent prorates the interest, charging the seller only for those days, rather than the whole month's interest. The prorated amount is entered on the settlement statement as a debit for the seller.
>
> If the buyer assumes the loan, his first payment will be due September 1, and it will pay all of the interest for August. The seller will be debited for the interest owed up to August 15, and the buyer will be credited for the same amount.

Prepaid Interest on Buyer's Loan. Another expense the escrow agent prorates (one that doesn't concern the seller) is the interest on the buyer's new mortgage loan. Just as the interest on the seller's loan does not affect the buyer, the prepaid interest on the buyer's loan does not affect the seller. As a general rule, the first payment date of a new loan isn't the first day of the month immediately following closing, but rather the first day of the next month after that.

> **Example:** The buyer is financing the purchase with a new institutional loan. Closing takes place on January 23. The buyer isn't required to make a payment on the new loan on February 1. Instead, the first payment isn't due until March 1.

Even though the first payment isn't due for an extra month, interest begins accruing on the loan on the closing date. As was explained above, the first regular payment will cover the interest for the preceding month. So if the transaction closes on January 23, the first payment will be due on March 1, and that payment will cover the interest that accrued in February. However, it won't cover the interest accrued between January 23 and January 31. Instead, the lender requires the buyer to pay the interest for those nine days in January at closing. This is called **prepaid interest** or **interim interest**. It will appear as a debit for the buyer on the settlement statement.

> **Example:** The buyer is borrowing $430,000 at 7% interest to finance the purchase. The annual interest on the loan during the first year will be $30,100 ($430,000 × 7% = $30,100). The escrow agent divides that annual figure by 365 to determine the per diem interest rate.
>
> $$\$30{,}100 \div 365 = \$82.47 \text{ per diem}$$

There are nine days between the closing date (January 23) and the first day of the following month, so the lender will expect the buyer to prepay nine days' worth of interest at closing.

$$\$82.47 \times 9 \text{ days} = \$742.23 \text{ prepaid interest}$$

$742.23 will be entered as a debit for the buyer on the settlement statement.

The buyer and seller will both be responsible for interest on the closing date (unless the loan is being assumed). That is because there are two entirely different loans at issue, one of which ends on the closing date, and the other of which begins on the closing date. If the loan is being assumed, the parties will need to agree on which party is responsible for interest on the closing date; in the same way, the parties must also agree on (or rely on local custom for) which party is responsible for property taxes on the closing date.

Rent. So far we've only discussed prorated expenses. In some transactions, there is also income to be prorated at closing. If the property generates rental income and the tenants have paid for some period beyond the closing date, the seller is debited and the buyer credited for the rent paid in advance. If the rent is paid in arrears, the seller will be credited for the amount due up to closing, and the buyer will be debited for the same amount.

Note that tenants' security deposits aren't prorated. The seller must transfer all of the deposits to the buyer, since the leases will continue after closing.

Cash at Closing. As we said earlier, on a settlement statement the sum of one party's credits should equal the sum of that party's debits, so that the final balance in each party's "account" is zero. In order for the statement to work this way, it must list the amount of cash that the buyer will have to bring to closing, and also the amount of cash the seller will take away from closing.

Balance Due from Buyer. Add up all of the buyer's credits, then add up all of the buyer's debits. Subtract the buyer's credits from the buyer's debits to find the balance due, which is the amount of cash the buyer will have to pay at closing. Enter this amount as a credit for the buyer. Now the buyer's credits column should add up to exactly the same amount as the buyer's debits column.

Balance Due to Seller. Add up all of the seller's credits, then add up all of the seller's debits. Subtract the seller's debits from the seller's credits. The result is the amount of cash the seller will receive at closing (if any). Enter this amount as a debit if credits exceed debits, but as a credit if debits exceed credits. Now the seller's credits column should add up to exactly the same amount as the seller's debits column.

Note that the buyer's two column totals must match each other, and the seller's two column totals must match each other. However, the buyer's column totals don't have to match the seller's column totals. Although there's a remote possibility that the buyer's totals could match the seller's totals in a particular transaction, they ordinarily do not.

Income Tax Aspects of Closing

Nearly all real estate transactions have tax implications (see Chapter 13), and it's up to each party to fulfill her own tax obligations. However, there are certain requirements related to income taxes that must be taken care of when a transaction closes.

Form 1099-S Reporting

The Internal Revenue Service generally requires an escrow agent to report real property sales on Form 1099-S. The form is used to report the seller's name and social security number and the gross proceeds from the sale.

However, the form doesn't have to be filed for the sale of a principal residence if: 1) the seller certifies in writing that none of the gain is taxable; and 2) the sale is for $250,000 or less ($500,000 or less if the seller is married). Certain other types of transactions are also exempt from this requirement.

The escrow agent is not allowed to charge an extra fee for complying with 1099-S reporting requirements.

Form 8300 Reporting

The IRS requires an escrow agent who receives more than $10,000 in cash to report the cash payment on Form 8300. This rule applies whether the cash was received in a single transaction or in a series of related transactions.

Example: ABC Escrow is handling the closing for buyer Sam. As part of the process, Sam will bring $12,000 cash to closing. He gives ABC Escrow $8,000 on Thursday, and the remaining $4,000 on Friday. Although the individual amounts are less than $10,000, ABC Escrow will need to submit Form 8300 to the IRS because the transactions are related.

The escrow agent must file Form 8300 within 15 days of receiving the cash. A copy of the form should be kept on file for five years.

FIRPTA

The Foreign Investment in Real Property Tax Act (FIRPTA) helps prevent foreign investors from evading their tax liability on income generated from the sale of real estate. It requires a property buyer to determine whether the seller is a "foreign person," defined as someone who is not a U.S. citizen and not a resident alien. If the seller is a foreign person, the buyer must withhold 10% of the amount realized and forward that amount to the IRS. (In most cases, the amount realized is simply the sales price.) Payment must be made within 20 days after the transfer date. The escrow agent usually handles these requirements on behalf of the buyer. Note that many residential transactions are exempt from FIRPTA.

California Withholding Law

California also has a state law that requires buyers to withhold funds for tax purposes. To comply with this law, a buyer (or the escrow agent) must withhold 3.33% of the total sales price from the seller and send the funds to the Franchise Tax Board. Alternatively, the seller may choose to have a specified percentage of the gain on the sale withheld. (The percentage is the maximum tax rate that would apply.)

For an individual seller, the state withholding requirement applies if the seller's last known address is outside of California (even if the seller is a U.S. citizen). However, the transaction is exempt if the property sold was the seller's principal residence or was last used as a principal residence, or if the sales price was $100,000 or less. If the seller is a company or organization rather than an individual, the withholding requirement may apply even if the seller has a California address, unless the seller qualifies for a specific exemption from the withholding law.

Real Estate Settlement Procedures Act

The Real Estate Settlement Procedures Act (**RESPA**), a federal law, was passed in 1974. It affects how closing is handled in most residential transactions financed with institutional loans. The law has two main goals:

- to provide borrowers with information about their closing costs, to help them become better shoppers for settlement services; and
- to eliminate kickbacks and referral fees that unnecessarily increase the costs of settlement.

Transactions Covered by RESPA

RESPA applies to "federally related" loan transactions. A loan is federally related if:

1. it will be secured by a mortgage or deed of trust against:
   - property on which there is (or on which the loan proceeds will be used to build) a dwelling with four or fewer units;
   - a condominium unit or a cooperative apartment;
   - a lot with (or on which the loan proceeds will be used to place) a mobile home; and
2. the lender is federally regulated, has federally insured accounts, is assisted by the federal government, makes loans in connection with a federal program, sells loans to Fannie Mae, Ginnie Mae, or Freddie Mac, or makes real estate loans totaling more than $1,000,000 per year.

In short, the act applies to most institutional lenders and to most residential loans.

Exemptions. RESPA does not apply to the following loan transactions:

- a loan used to purchase 25 acres or more;
- a loan used primarily for a business, commercial, or agricultural purpose;
- a loan used to purchase vacant land, unless there will be a one- to four-unit dwelling built on it or a mobile home placed on it;
- temporary financing, such as a construction loan; or
- an assumption for which the lender's approval is neither required nor obtained.

Note that RESPA also does not apply to seller-financed transactions, since those are not federally regulated.

Fig. 12.2 Good faith estimate of closing costs

OMB Approval No. 2502-0265

Good Faith Estimate (GFE)

Name of Originator	Borrower
Originator Address	Property Address
Originator Phone Number	
Originator Email	Date of GFE

Purpose

This GFE gives you an estimate of your settlement charges and loan terms if you are approved for this loan. For more information, see HUD's *Special Information Booklet* on settlement charges, your *Truth-in-Lending Disclosures,* and other consumer information at www.hud.gov/respa. If you decide you would like to proceed with this loan, contact us.

Shopping for your loan

Only you can shop for the best loan for you. Compare this GFE with other loan offers, so you can find the best loan. Use the shopping chart on page 3 to compare all the offers you receive.

Important dates

1. The interest rate for this GFE is available through ☐. After this time, the interest rate, some of your loan Origination Charges, and the monthly payment shown below can change until you lock your interest rate.
2. This estimate for all other settlement charges is available through ☐.
3. After you lock your interest rate, you must go to settlement within ☐ days (your rate lock period) to receive the locked interest rate.
4. You must lock the interest rate at least ☐ days before settlement.

Summary of your loan

Your initial loan amount is	$
Your loan term is	years
Your initial interest rate is	%
Your initial monthly amount owed for principal, interest, and any mortgage insurance is	$ per month
Can your interest rate rise?	☐ No ☐ Yes, it can rise to a maximum of %. The first change will be in .
Even if you make payments on time, can your loan balance rise?	☐ No ☐ Yes, it can rise to a maximum of $
Even if you make payments on time, can your monthly amount owed for principal, interest, and any mortgage insurance rise?	☐ No ☐ Yes, the first increase can be in and the monthly amount owed can rise to $. The maximum it can ever rise to is $.
Does your loan have a prepayment penalty?	☐ No ☐ Yes, your maximum prepayment penalty is $.
Does your loan have a balloon payment?	☐ No ☐ Yes, you have a balloon payment of $ due in years.

Escrow account information

Some lenders require an escrow account to hold funds for paying property taxes or other property-related charges in addition to your monthly amount owed of $☐.
Do we require you to have an escrow account for your loan?
☐ No, you do not have an escrow account. You must pay these charges directly when due.
☐ Yes, you have an escrow account. It may or may not cover all of these charges. Ask us.

Summary of your settlement charges

A	Your Adjusted Origination Charges *(See page 2.)*	$
B	Your Charges for All Other Settlement Services *(See page 2.)*	$
A+B	Total Estimated Settlement Charges	$

Understanding your estimated settlement charges

Your Adjusted Origination Charges	
1. **Our origination charge** This charge is for getting this loan for you.	
2. **Your credit or charge (points) for the specific interest rate chosen** ☐ The credit or charge for the interest rate of [ ] % is included in "Our origination charge." (See item 1 above.) ☐ You receive a credit of $ [ ] for this interest rate of [ ] %. This credit **reduces** your settlement charges. ☐ You pay a charge of $ [ ] for this interest rate of [ ] %. This charge (points) **increases** your total settlement charges. The tradeoff table on page 3 shows that you can change your total settlement charges by choosing a different interest rate for this loan.	
A Your Adjusted Origination Charges	$

Some of these charges can change at settlement. See the top of page 3 for more information.

Your Charges for All Other Settlement Services	
3. **Required services that we select** These charges are for services we require to complete your settlement. We will choose the providers of these services. *Service* / *Charge*	
4. **Title services and lender's title insurance** This charge includes the services of a title or settlement agent, for example, and title insurance to protect the lender, if required.	
5. **Owner's title insurance** You may purchase an owner's title insurance policy to protect your interest in the property.	
6. **Required services that you can shop for** These charges are for other services that are required to complete your settlement. We can identify providers of these services or you can shop for them yourself. Our estimates for providing these services are below. *Service* / *Charge*	
7. **Government recording charges** These charges are for state and local fees to record your loan and title documents.	
8. **Transfer taxes** These charges are for state and local fees on mortgages and home sales.	
9. **Initial deposit for your escrow account** This charge is held in an escrow account to pay future recurring charges on your property and includes ☐ all property taxes, ☐ all insurance, and ☐ other [ ].	
10. **Daily interest charges** This charge is for the daily interest on your loan from the day of your settlement until the first day of the next month or the first day of your normal mortgage payment cycle. This amount is $[ ] per day for [ ] days (if your settlement is [ ]).	
11. **Homeowner's insurance** This charge is for the insurance you must buy for the property to protect from a loss, such as fire. *Policy* / *Charge*	
B Your Charges for All Other Settlement Services	$
A + B Total Estimated Settlement Charges	$

Good Faith Estimate (HUD-GFE) 2

Instructions

Understanding which charges can change at settlement

This GFE estimates your settlement charges. At your settlement, you will receive a HUD-1, a form that lists your actual costs. Compare the charges on the HUD-1 with the charges on this GFE. Charges can change if you select your own provider and do not use the companies we identify. (See below for details.)

These charges **cannot increase** at settlement:	The total of these charges **can increase up to 10%** at settlement:	These charges **can change** at settlement:
▪ Our origination charge ▪ Your credit or charge (points) for the specific interest rate chosen *(after you lock in your interest rate)* ▪ Your adjusted origination charges *(after you lock in your interest rate)* ▪ Transfer taxes	▪ Required services that we select ▪ Title services and lender's title insurance *(if we select them or you use companies we identify)* ▪ Owner's title insurance *(if you use companies we identify)* ▪ Required services that you can shop for *(if you use companies we identify)* ▪ Government recording charges	▪ Required services that you can shop for *(if you do not use companies we identify)* ▪ Title services and lender's title insurance *(if you do not use companies we identify)* ▪ Owner's title insurance *(if you do not use companies we identify)* ▪ Initial deposit for your escrow account ▪ Daily interest charges ▪ Homeowner's insurance

Using the tradeoff table

In this GFE, we offered you this loan with a particular interest rate and estimated settlement charges. However:

- If you want to choose this same loan with **lower settlement charges,** then you will have a **higher interest rate.**
- If you want to choose this same loan with a **lower interest rate,** then you will have **higher settlement charges.**

If you would like to choose an available option, you must ask us for a new GFE.

Loan originators have the option to complete this table. Please ask for additional information if the table is not completed.

	The loan in this GFE	The same loan with lower settlement charges	The same loan with a lower interest rate
Your initial loan amount	$	$	$
Your initial interest rate[1]	%	%	%
Your initial monthly amount owed	$	$	$
Change in the monthly amount owed from this GFE	No change	You will pay $ **more** every month	You will pay $ **less** every month
Change in the amount you will pay at settlement with this interest rate	No change	Your settlement charges will be **reduced** by $	Your settlement charges will **increase** by $
How much your total estimated settlement charges will be	$	$	$

[1] *For an adjustable rate loan, the comparisons above are for the initial interest rate before adjustments are made.*

Using the shopping chart

Use this chart to compare GFEs from different loan originators. Fill in the information by using a different column for each GFE you receive. By comparing loan offers, you can shop for the best loan.

	This loan	Loan 2	Loan 3	Loan 4
Loan originator name				
Initial loan amount				
Loan term				
Initial interest rate				
Initial monthly amount owed				
Rate lock period				
Can interest rate rise?				
Can loan balance rise?				
Can monthly amount owed rise?				
Prepayment penalty?				
Balloon payment?				
Total Estimated Settlement Charges				

If your loan is sold in the future

Some lenders may sell your loan after settlement. Any fees lenders receive in the future cannot change the loan you receive or the charges you paid at settlement.

RESPA Requirements

RESPA has these requirements for federally related loan transactions:

1. Within three days after receiving a written loan application, the lender or loan originator (for example, a mortgage broker) must give all applicants:
   - a **booklet about settlement procedures**, prepared by HUD, that explains RESPA, closing costs, and the settlement statement;
   - a **mortgage servicing disclosure statement**, which discloses whether the lender intends to service the loan or transfer it to another lender; and
   - a **good faith estimate of closing costs** (see Figure 12.2), disclosing the costs that the borrower (the buyer) will be expected to pay in the transaction.

   A lender or loan originator may not charge a loan applicant any fees other than a credit report fee until the lender has provided the good faith estimate (GFE) and the applicant has expressed an intent to continue with the loan transaction.
2. If the lender or any settlement service provider requires the borrower to use a particular appraiser, title company, or other service provider, that requirement must be disclosed to the borrower when the loan application or service agreement is signed.
3. If any settlement service provider refers a borrower to an affiliated provider, that joint business relationship must be fully disclosed, as well as the fact that the referral is optional. Fee estimates for the services in question must also be given.
4. The closing agent (whoever handles closing, whether it's an escrow agent, a loan originator, a real estate broker, a lawyer, etc.) must itemize all loan settlement charges on a **uniform settlement statement** form (discussed below).
5. If the borrower will have to make deposits into an impound account (a reserve or escrow account) to cover taxes, insurance, and other recurring costs, the lender cannot require excessive deposits (more than necessary to cover the expenses when they come due, plus a two-month cushion).
6. A lender or other settlement service provider (such as a title company) may not:
   - pay or receive a kickback or referral fee (a payment from one settlement service provider to another provider for referring customers);
   - pay or receive an unearned fee (a charge that one settlement service provider shares with another provider who hasn't actually performed any services in exchange for the payment); or
   - charge a fee for the preparation of the uniform settlement statement, an impound account statement, or the disclosure statement required by the Truth in Lending Act.
7. The seller may not require the buyer to use a particular title company.

Note that RESPA's prohibition against kickbacks does not apply to referral fees that one real estate licensee or firm pays to another for referring potential brokerage customers or clients (see Chapter 16).

Fig. 12.3 Uniform settlement statement

OMB Approval No. 2502-0265

U.S. Department of Housing and Urban Development

A. Settlement Statement (HUD-1)

B. Type of Loan

1. [ ] FHA 2. [ ] RHS 3. [ ] Conv. Unins. 4. [ ] VA 5. [ ] Conv. Ins.	6. File Number:	7. Loan Number:	8. Mortgage Insurance Case Number:

C. Note: This form is furnished to give you a statement of actual settlement costs. Amounts paid to and by the settlement agent are shown. Items marked "(p.o.c.)" were paid outside the closing; they are shown here for informational purposes and are not included in the totals.

D. Name & Address of Borrower:	E. Name & Address of Seller:	F. Name & Address of Lender:
G. Property Location:	H. Settlement Agent:	I. Settlement Date:
	Place of Settlement:	

J. Summary of Borrower's Transaction		K. Summary of Seller's Transaction	
100. Gross Amount Due from Borrower		**400. Gross Amount Due to Seller**	
101. Contract sales price		401. Contract sales price	
102. Personal property		402. Personal property	
103. Settlement charges to borrower (line 1400)		403.	
104.		404.	
105.		405.	
Adjustment for items paid by seller in advance		**Adjustments for items paid by seller in advance**	
106. City/town taxes to		406. City/town taxes to	
107. County taxes to		407. County taxes to	
108. Assessments to		408. Assessments to	
109.		409.	
110.		410.	
111.		411.	
112.		412.	
120. Gross Amount Due from Borrower		**420. Gross Amount Due to Seller**	
200. Amounts Paid by or in Behalf of Borrower		**500. Reductions In Amount Due to Seller**	
201. Deposit or earnest money		501. Excess deposit (see instructions)	
202. Principal amount of new loan(s)		502. Settlement charges to seller (line 1400)	
203. Existing loan(s) taken subject to		503. Existing loan(s) taken subject to	
204.		504. Payoff of first mortgage loan	
205.		505. Payoff of second mortgage loan	
206.		506.	
207.		507.	
208.		508.	
209.		509.	
Adjustments for items unpaid by seller		**Adjustments for items unpaid by seller**	
210. City/town taxes to		510. City/town taxes to	
211. County taxes to		511. County taxes to	
212. Assessments to		512. Assessments to	
213.		513.	
214.		514.	
215.		515.	
216.		516.	
217.		517.	
218.		518.	
219.		519.	
220. Total Paid by/for Seller		**520. Total Reduction Amount Due Seller**	
300. Cash at Settlement from/to Borrower		**600. Cash at Settlement to/from Seller**	
301. Gross amount due from borrower (line 120)		601. Gross amount due to seller (line 420)	
302. Less amounts paid by/for borrower (line 220)	( )	602. Less reductions in amount due seller (line 520)	( )
303. Cash [ ] **From** [ ] **To Borrower**		**603. Cash** [ ] **To** [ ] **From Seller**	

The Public Reporting Burden for this collection of information is estimated at 35 minutes per response for collecting, reviewing, and reporting the data. This agency may not collect this information, and you are not required to complete this form, unless it displays a currently valid OMB control number. No confidentiality is assured; this disclosure is mandatory. This is designed to provide the parties to a RESPA covered transaction with information during the settlement process.

Previous editions are obsolete Page 1 of 3 HUD-1

L. Settlement Charges		
700. Total Real Estate Broker Fees	Paid From Borrower's Funds at Settlement	Paid From Seller's Funds at Settlement
Division of commission (line 700) as follows:		
701. $ to		
702. $ to		
703. Commission paid at settlement		
704.		
800. Items Payable in Connection with Loan		
801. Our origination charge $ (from GFE #1)		
802. Your credit or charge (points) for the specific interest rate chosen $ (from GFE #2)		
803. Your adjusted origination charges (from GFE A)		
804. Appraisal fee to (from GFE #3)		
805. Credit report to (from GFE #3)		
806. Tax service to (from GFE #3)		
807. Flood certification (from GFE #3)		
808.		
900. Items Required by Lender to Be Paid in Advance		
901. Daily interest charges from to @$ /day (from GFE #10)		
902. Mortgage insurance premium for months to (from GFE #3)		
903. Homeowner's insurance for years to (from GFE #11)		
904.		
1000. Reserves Deposited with Lender		
1001. Initial deposit for your escrow account (from GFE #9)		
1002. Homeowner's insurance months @ $ per month $		
1003. Mortgage insurance months @ $ per month $		
1004. Property taxes months @ $ per month $		
1005. months @ $ per month $		
1006. months @ $ per month $		
1007. Aggregate Adjustment –$		
1100. Title Charges		
1101. Title services and lender's title insurance (from GFE #4)		
1102. Settlement or closing fee $		
1103. Owner's title insurance (from GFE #5)		
1104. Lender's title insurance $		
1105. Lender's title policy limit $		
1106. Owner's title policy limit $		
1107. Agent's portion of the total title insurance premium $		
1108. Underwriter's portion of the total title insurance premium $		
1200. Government Recording and Transfer Charges		
1201. Government recording charges (from GFE #7)		
1202. Deed $ Mortgage $ Releases $		
1203. Transfer taxes (from GFE #8)		
1204. City/County tax/stamps Deed $ Mortgage $		
1205. State tax/stamps Deed $ Mortgage $		
1206.		
1300. Additional Settlement Charges		
1301. Required services that you can shop for (from GFE #6)		
1302. $		
1303. $		
1304.		
1305.		
1400. Total Settlement Charges (enter on lines 103, Section J and 502, Section K)		

Previous editions are obsolete Page 2 of 3 HUD-1

Comparison of Good Faith Estimate (GFE) and HUD-1 Charges		Good Faith Estimate	HUD-1
Charges That Cannot Increase	**HUD-1 Line Number**		
Our origination charge	# 801		
Your credit or charge (points) for the specific interest rate chosen	# 802		
Your adjusted origination charges	# 803		
Transfer taxes	#1203		

Charges That in Total Cannot Increase More Than 10%		Good Faith Estimate	HUD-1
Government recording charges	# 1201		
	#		
	#		
	#		
	#		
	#		
	#		
	#		
	Total		
	Increase between GFE and HUD-1 Charges	$ or	%

Charges That Can Change		Good Faith Estimate	HUD-1
Initial deposit for your escrow account	#1001		
Daily interest charges	# 901 $ /day		
Homeowner's insurance	# 903		
	#		
	#		
	#		

Loan Terms

Your initial loan amount is	$
Your loan term is	years
Your initial interest rate is	%
Your initial monthly amount owed for principal, interest, and and any mortgage insurance is	$ includes ☐ Principal ☐ Interest ☐ Mortgage Insurance
Can your interest rate rise?	☐ No. ☐ Yes, it can rise to a maximum of %. The first change will be on and can change again every after . Every change date, your interest rate can increase or decrease by %. Over the life of the loan, your interest rate is guaranteed to never be **lower** than % or **higher** than %.
Even if you make payments on time, can your loan balance rise?	☐ No. ☐ Yes, it can rise to a maximum of $.
Even if you make payments on time, can your monthly amount owed for principal, interest, and mortgage insurance rise?	☐ No. ☐ Yes, the first increase can be on and the monthly amount owed can rise to $. The maximum it can ever rise to is $.
Does your loan have a prepayment penalty?	☐ No. ☐ Yes, your maximum prepayment penalty is $.
Does your loan have a balloon payment?	☐ No. ☐ Yes, you have a balloon payment of $ due in years on .
Total monthly amount owed including escrow account payments	☐ You do not have a monthly escrow payment for items, such as property taxes and homeowner's insurance. You must pay these items directly yourself. ☐ You have an additional monthly escrow payment of $ that results in a total initial monthly amount owed of $. This includes principal, interest, any mortgage insurance and any items checked below: ☐ Property taxes ☐ Homeowner's insurance ☐ Flood insurance ☐ ☐ ☐

Note: If you have any questions about the Settlement Charges and Loan Terms listed on this form, please contact your lender.

Previous editions are obsolete Page 3 of 3 HUD-1

Uniform Settlement Statement. The escrow agent (or other closing agent) must provide completed uniform settlement statement forms to the borrower, the seller, and the lender on or before the closing date. (The borrower may sign a written waiver of the right to receive the statement by closing, in which case the forms must be provided to the parties as soon as practicable after closing.) If the borrower requests it, the escrow agent must allow the borrower to inspect the statement one business day before closing.

A copy of the uniform settlement statement form, often called a HUD-1 form, is shown in Figure 12.3. It doesn't have the same format as the simplified settlement statement shown earlier in this chapter (with buyer's credit and debit columns and seller's credit and debit columns side by side), but it presents the same information.

On the uniform settlement statement, each party's closing costs are itemized on the second page of the form, with the buyer's costs in the left column and the seller's costs in the right column. (See Figure 12.3.) Each party's costs are added up, and the total is transferred to the first page of the form. The buyer's total costs are entered on line 103, and the seller's total costs are entered on line 502.

On the first page of the uniform settlement statement, lines 101 through 120 correspond to the "Buyer's Debits" column on our simplified version. Lines 201 through 220 correspond to the "Buyer's Credits" column. Lines 401 through 420 are the equivalent of the "Seller's Credits" column, and 501 through 520 represent the "Seller's Debits" column. The amount of cash the buyer must bring to closing is shown on line 303, and the amount of cash the seller will receive at closing is shown on line 603.

Estimates vs. Actual Charges. Some of the charges listed on the good faith estimate form given to the buyer at the beginning of the loan application process are in fact only estimates, so they won't necessarily match the buyer's actual charges at closing. However, RESPA doesn't allow certain charges on the GFE to be increased, and it limits how much certain others may be increased. There are three categories:

1. Charges that cannot increase at closing. This includes all of the lender's or loan originator's points and fees, and also the transfer taxes.
2. Charges for required services, such as the appraisal and title insurance, if the service provider was chosen or recommended by the lender. The total amount of these charges can increase no more than 10%.
3. Charges that can change any amount, because they're difficult to predict at the outset, such as hazard insurance.

The categories are explained in more detail on the third page of the good faith estimate form itself (see Figure 12.2). The third page of the uniform settlement statement (Figure 12.3) provides a side-by-side comparison of the estimated and actual charges.

Chapter Summary

1. After a purchase agreement has been signed, the next stage of the transaction is the closing process. Closing is usually handled through escrow, an arrangement in which money and documents are held by a third party (the escrow agent) on behalf of the buyer and the seller, and distributed when all of the conditions set forth in the escrow instructions have been fulfilled.

2. In California, a real estate broker may act as the closing agent in a transaction in which she is also providing brokerage services.

3. The escrow agent prepares a settlement statement, detailing all of the charges payable by (debits) and payable to (credits) each of the parties at closing. Who pays which closing costs may be determined by agreement or by local custom. Some expenses must be prorated as of the closing date.

4. Certain requirements related to income taxes must be fulfilled when a real estate transaction closes. These include Form 1099-S reporting, Form 8300 reporting, and the requirements of FIRPTA and the California withholding law.

5. RESPA applies to most residential loan transactions involving institutional lenders. It requires lenders or loan originators to give loan applicants a good faith estimate of closing costs within three days after a written loan application is submitted. RESPA also requires the closing agent to complete a uniform settlement statement and make it available to the buyer one day before closing, if the buyer asks to see it in advance.

Key Terms

Closing—The final stage of a real estate transaction, in which documents are signed and delivered and funds are transferred. Also called settlement.

Escrow—An arrangement in which money and documents are held by a third party on behalf of a buyer and a seller until their transaction is ready to close.

Escrow agent—A third party who holds money and documents in trust and carries out the closing process. Also called a closing agent.

Escrow instructions—A bilateral contract between the buyer and the seller that tells the escrow agent how to proceed and states the conditions each party must fulfill before the transaction can close.

Settlement statement—A statement that sets forth all of the financial aspects of a real estate transaction in detail and indicates how much cash each party will be required to pay or will receive at closing. Also called a closing statement.

Debit—A charge payable by a party, either to the other party or to a third party.

Credit—A charge payable to a party, either by the other party or by a third party.

Impound account—Funds on deposit with a lender to pay the property taxes, insurance premiums, and other recurring costs when due. Also called a reserve account or an escrow account.

Prorate—To divide and allocate an expense proportionately, according to time, interest, or benefit, determining what share of it a particular party is responsible for.

Prepaid interest—Interest on the buyer's new mortgage loan that the lender requires to be paid at closing, covering the period from the closing date through the last day of the month.

Good faith estimate (GFE)—A disclosure of closing costs that lenders and loan originators are required to give loan applicants within three days after receiving a written application, in transactions covered by the Real Estate Settlement Procedures Act (RESPA).

Uniform settlement statement—The settlement statement form that closing agents are required to use in transactions covered by RESPA. Also called a HUD-1 form.

Chapter Quiz

1. Which of the following wouldn't be prorated at closing in the sale of a rental property?
   a) Prepaid property taxes
   b) Interest on seller's existing loan
   c) Security deposit
   d) Interest on buyer's new loan

2. Every debit on the buyer's side of the settlement statement is a charge that:
   a) will be paid to the buyer at closing
   b) must be paid by the buyer at closing
   c) the buyer must pay to the seller at closing
   d) the seller must pay to the buyer at closing

3. On a settlement statement, the purchase price will be listed as:
   a) a debit for the buyer
   b) a debit for the seller
   c) Both of the above
   d) Neither of the above

4. The transaction is closing on September 16. The seller has already paid the annual premium for hazard insurance, and the buyer won't be assuming the policy. On the settlement statement, part of the insurance premium will be listed as:
   a) a debit for the buyer and a credit for the seller
   b) a debit for the seller and a credit for the buyer
   c) a credit for the buyer
   d) a credit for the seller

5. How does the buyer's good faith deposit show up on a settlement statement?
   a) It's listed as a debit on the buyer's side of the statement, and as a credit on the seller's side
   b) It's listed as a credit on the buyer's side of the statement, but it isn't listed on the seller's side because it's included in the purchase price
   c) It's listed as a credit on the seller's side of the statement, but it isn't listed on the buyer's side because it will be refunded at closing
   d) It's listed as a debit on both the buyer's side and the seller's side of the statement

6. When a buyer assumes a mortgage, how does the mortgage balance appear on the settlement statement?
   a) Only as a credit for the seller
   b) Only as a debit on the seller's side of the statement
   c) As a credit for the buyer and a debit for the seller
   d) As a credit for the seller and a debit for the buyer

7. Which of the following is ordinarily one of the seller's closing costs?
   a) Sales commission
   b) Credit report fee
   c) Appraisal fee
   d) Origination fee

8. Which of the following is ordinarily one of the buyer's closing costs?
   a) Sales commission
   b) Lender's title insurance premium
   c) Documentary transfer tax
   d) None of the above

9. On a settlement statement, prepaid interest would usually appear as a:
   a) seller's debit
   b) buyer's credit
   c) seller's credit
   d) buyer's debit

10. The Matsons are selling their home. They are current on their mortgage payments, having made their most recent payment on May 1. They will be paying off their mortgage when the sale closes on May 17. At closing, the Matsons will probably be:
    a) entitled to a refund of the mortgage interest accruing in May
    b) required to pay the mortgage interest accruing in May
    c) entitled to a refund of the prepayment penalty
    d) required to pay part of the mortgage interest that accrued in April

11. A settlement statement:
    a) is given to the buyer but not the seller
    b) sets out the charges to be paid by each party
    c) is given only to the buyer's lender
    d) is required only in transactions closed by independent escrow companies

12. When an item is prorated it means that:
    a) it's deleted from the cost of the sale
    b) it's calculated on the basis of a particular time period
    c) it isn't paid until closing
    d) the escrow agent must pay the fee

13. Under RESPA, a loan is considered federally related if:
    a) it will be used to finance the purchase of real property
    b) the property has up to four dwelling units
    c) the lender is federally regulated
    d) All of the above

14. Under FIRPTA:
    a) a foreign investor can never buy or sell property without special authorization
    b) if a seller isn't a U.S. citizen or a resident alien, the escrow agent will have to deduct 10% of the net sale proceeds and send it to the IRS
    c) escrow agents must notify the real estate broker if the buyer is a foreign investor
    d) a foreign investor purchasing property in the U.S. must pay an additional 10% over and above the purchase price and submit it to the IRS

15. For an additional $200, the seller has agreed to include her riding lawn mower in the real property transaction. In addition to the deed, the seller should sign a/an:
    a) bill of sale
    b) uniform settlement statement
    c) appraisal report
    d) voucher

Answer Key

1. c) Security deposits aren't prorated at closing; they are simply transferred to the buyer of the rental property.

2. b) A debit on the buyer's side of the statement is a charge that the buyer must pay. In some cases, it's a charge that the buyer must pay to the seller (a refund for taxes paid in advance, for example), but in other cases the buyer owes it to a third party (the loan fee paid to the lender, for example).

3. a) The purchase price is a debit for the buyer and a credit for the seller.

4. d) The seller is entitled to a refund for the insurance he paid in advance, and this will show up as a credit on the seller's side of the settlement statement. Since the buyer isn't assuming the policy, the seller's insurance isn't listed on the buyer's side of the statement.

5. b) The good faith deposit is a credit for the buyer, since it has already been paid. It doesn't appear on the seller's side of the statement, because the full purchase price is listed as a credit for the seller, and the deposit is included in the price.

6. c) A loan the buyer uses to finance the transaction is listed as a credit for the buyer, whatever its source. When the financing comes through the seller—either through an assumption of the seller's loan, or through seller financing—it's a debit for the seller as well as a credit for the buyer.

7. a) The seller almost always pays the real estate broker's commission. The other expenses listed relate to the buyer's loan, and they're ordinarily paid by the buyer.

8. b) The buyer is usually required to pay the premium for the lender's extended coverage title insurance policy.

9. d) Prepaid interest—interest on a new loan to cover the period from the closing date through the last day of the month—is one of the buyer's debits.

10. b) Because mortgage interest is paid in arrears (the month after it accrues), at closing the sellers will be required to pay the interest that has accrued during May. Their May 1 mortgage payment included the interest that accrued in April.

11. b) A settlement statement sets forth the items that must be paid by each party, and also the items that must be paid to each party.

12. b) Prorating an expense is allocating it on the basis of a particular time period, such as a certain number of days.

13. d) All of these are elements of a federally related loan under RESPA.

14. b) In a transaction subject to FIRPTA, if the seller isn't a U.S. citizen or a resident alien, the escrow agent is required to deduct 10% of the net sale proceeds and send it to the IRS.

15. a) A bill of sale is used to transfer title to personal property.

Chapter 13

Income Taxation and Real Estate

I. Basic Taxation Concepts
  A. Progressive tax
  B. Income
  C. Deductions and tax credits
  D. Gains and losses
    1. Capital gains and losses
    2. Business and rental property
  E. Basis
    1. Initial basis
    2. Adjusted basis
  F. Realization
  G. Recognition and deferral
  H. Classifications of real property
II. Nonrecognition Transactions
  A. Installment sales
  B. Involuntary conversions
  C. "Tax-free" exchanges
III. Exclusion of Gain from the Sale of a Principal Residence
IV. Deductions Available to Property Owners
  A. Depreciation deductions
  B. Uninsured casualty or theft loss deductions
  C. Repair deductions
  D. Property tax deductions
  E. Mortgage interest deductions
  F. Deductibility of points and other loan costs
  G. Deducting operational losses from rental property
  H. Rental payment deductions
V. California Income Tax

Chapter Overview

Almost every business transaction has tax consequences, and real estate transactions are no exception. Not only are there taxes that arise at the time of sale (such as the documentary transfer tax discussed in Chapter 5), there are also income tax ramifications for the parties involved. This chapter provides an overview of how federal income taxation affects the transfer and ownership of real estate. It explains some income tax terminology, discusses certain types of transactions that receive special treatment, and also covers tax deductions available to real estate owners.

Basic Taxation Concepts

As you no doubt know, in the United States the federal government taxes the income of individuals and businesses on an annual basis. Before discussing how the transfer or acquisition of real estate can affect the federal income taxes a seller or a buyer is required to pay, we need to explain some basic terms and concepts.

Progressive Tax

A tax may be "proportional," "regressive," or "progressive," depending on how its burden is distributed among taxpayers. A tax is proportional if the same tax rate is applied to all levels of income. A tax is regressive if the rate applied to higher levels of income is lower than the rate applied to lower levels. Our federal income tax is a **progressive** tax. This means that the more a taxpayer earns in a given tax year, the higher her tax rate will be. In other words, someone who earns a large income is generally required not just to pay more taxes than someone who earns a small income, but to pay a greater percentage of her income in taxes.

Tax rates increase in uneven steps called **tax brackets**. An additional dollar earned by a given taxpayer may be taxed at a higher rate than the dollar earned just before it, because it crosses the line into a higher bracket. But the additional dollar earned won't increase the tax the taxpayer is required to pay on dollars previously earned. The term **marginal tax rate** refers to the rate that will apply to the last dollar that a taxpayer earns.

Income

When asked about their income, many people tend to think only in terms of the wages or salary they earn at a job. The Internal Revenue Service (IRS) takes a much broader view of income, however. It regards any economic benefit realized by a taxpayer as part of his income, unless it's a type of benefit specifically excluded from income by the tax code. (The concept of realization is discussed below.)

Deductions and Tax Credits

The tax code authorizes certain expenses to be deducted from income. For example, if a business loses money in a particular tax year, the owner may be allowed to deduct the loss. A taxpayer who's entitled to a **deduction** can subtract a specified amount from her income before it's taxed. By reducing the amount of income that's taxed, the deduction also reduces the amount of tax the taxpayer owes.

In contrast to deductions, **tax credits** are subtracted directly from the amount of tax owed. The taxpayer's income is added up, the tax rate is applied, and then any applicable tax credits are subtracted to determine how much the taxpayer will actually have to pay.

The government often uses deductions and tax credits to implement social and economic policy. For example, allowing homeowners to deduct mortgage interest from their taxable income helps make homeownership more affordable. (The mortgage interest deduction is explained later in this chapter.)

Gains and Losses

The sale or exchange of an asset (such as real estate) nearly always results in either a **gain** or a **loss**. Gains are treated as income, so any gain is taxable unless the tax code specifically says otherwise. On the other hand, a loss may be deducted from income only if the deduction is specifically authorized by the tax code.

Most deductible losses are losses incurred in a trade or business or in transactions entered into for profit. A business entity (such as a corporation) can deduct all of its losses. An individual taxpayer can deduct a loss only if it was incurred in connection with:

1. the taxpayer's trade or business,
2. a transaction entered into for profit, or
3. a casualty loss or theft of the taxpayer's property.

No deduction is allowed for a loss suffered on the sale of the taxpayer's principal residence or other real property owned for personal use.

Capital Gains and Losses. A gain or loss on the sale of an asset held for personal use or as an investment is considered a **capital gain** or a **capital loss**. Capital gains and capital losses are netted against each other. If there's a net gain, it's taxed as a capital gain. Capital gains receive favorable tax treatment: the maximum tax rate applied to most capital gains is considerably lower than the rate for ordinary income.

On the other hand, there is an annual limit on the deductibility of capital losses. No more than $3,000 in net capital losses can be deducted in a single tax year. Capital losses in excess of the limit may be carried forward and deducted in future years.

Remember that losses on personal use property aren't deductible, so they aren't netted against capital gains.

Business and Rental Property. Gains and losses on the sale of real property used in a business or held for the production of income (rental property) are treated somewhat differently from gains and losses on the sale of personal use and investment property. If business property or rental property is owned for more than one year and then sold, a gain on the sale is treated as a capital gain. But a loss on the sale is deductible as an ordinary loss rather than a capital loss. This is an advantage, because the $3,000 annual limit on the deduction of capital losses doesn't apply. The full amount of the loss can be deducted in the year it's incurred.

Basis

For income tax purposes, a property owner's **basis** in the property is his investment in it. If a taxpayer sells an asset, the basis is the maximum amount that he can receive in payment for the asset without realizing a gain. To determine gains and losses, it's necessary to know the taxpayer's basis in the property in question.

Initial Basis. In most cases, a taxpayer's **initial basis** (also called cost basis or unadjusted basis) is equal to the original cost of acquisition—how much it cost to acquire the property. If she paid $480,000 for a rental house plus $14,000 in closing costs, she has an initial basis of $494,000 in the property. She could turn around and sell the house for $494,000 without having realized a gain.

Adjusted Basis. A property's initial basis may be increased or decreased to arrive at an **adjusted basis**, which reflects capital expenditures and any allowable depreciation deductions.

Capital expenditures are expenditures made to improve the property, such as money a homeowner spends on adding a new room or remodeling the kitchen. Capital expenditures increase the value of the property or significantly extend its useful life. They're added to the initial basis in calculating the adjusted basis.

> **Example:** Greene buys a duplex as a rental property for $680,000 plus $20,300 in closing costs. Four years later, she spends $62,500 on improvements to the property, remodeling the bathrooms and the kitchens in both units. After Greene makes these capital expenditures, her adjusted basis in the duplex property is $762,800.

Maintenance expenses, such as repainting, replacing a broken window, or having the roof cleaned, aren't capital expenditures. Maintenance expenses don't affect basis.

For certain types of property, a taxpayer's initial basis is also adjusted to take into account depreciation deductions, which will be discussed later in this chapter. These deductions are subtracted from the initial basis in calculating the adjusted basis.

	Initial basis (acquisition cost)
+	Capital expenditures
–	Depreciation deductions
	Adjusted basis

Realization

Not every gain is immediately taxable. A gain isn't considered taxable income until it is **realized**. Ownership of an asset involves gain if the asset is appreciating in value. But for tax purposes, a gain is realized only when a sale or exchange occurs; the gain is then separated from the asset.

> **Example:** Referring back to the example given above, suppose that during Greene's six years of ownership property values have been increasing steadily. Her improved duplex (which she acquired for $700,300 and invested another $62,500 in) now has a market value of $895,000.
>
> Greene has enjoyed an economic gain or benefit: she now owns property that's worth $132,200 more than she put into it. However, that $132,200 isn't realized—and therefore isn't treated as income subject to taxation—until she sells the duplex.

The gain or loss realized on a transaction is the difference between the net sales price (called the **amount realized** in the tax code) and the adjusted basis of the property.

	Amount realized (net sales price)
–	Adjusted basis
	Gain or loss

In calculating the amount realized, the sales price includes money or other property received in exchange for the property, plus the amount of any mortgage debt that's eliminated. This means that if the buyer takes the property subject to the seller's mortgage or assumes it, the amount of that debt is treated as part of the sales price for tax purposes.

The selling expenses (such as the brokerage commission and the seller's other closing costs) are subtracted from the sales price to arrive at the amount realized.

	Money received
+	Market value of other property received
+	Mortgage debt disposed of
–	Selling expenses
	Amount realized (net sales price)

Recognition and Deferral

A gain is said to be **recognized** in the year it is taxed. A gain will be recognized in the same year it is realized, unless there is a specific exception in the tax code that allows the taxpayer to defer payment of taxes on the gain until a later tax year or a later transaction, or to exclude the gain from income and avoid paying taxes on it altogether. For example, the tax code permits an individual selling his rental property on an installment basis to defer taxation of part of the gain to the year in which it's actually received (rather than the year the sale takes place). The tax code provisions that allow recognition of a gain to be deferred are called "nonrecognition provisions."

Nonrecognition provisions (including the rule already mentioned concerning installment sales) and exclusion provisions are discussed in more detail later in this chapter.

Classifications of Real Property

Whether a particular type of real estate transaction qualifies for special tax treatment depends on the type of property involved. The tax code divides real property into the following classes:

1. principal residence property,
2. personal use property,
3. unimproved investment property,
4. property held for the production of income,
5. property used in a trade or business, and
6. dealer property.

Principal Residence Property. A principal residence (also called a main home) is the home the taxpayer owns and occupies as her primary dwelling. It might be a single-family home, a duplex, a condominium unit, a cooperative apartment, or a mobile home. If the taxpayer owns two homes and lives in both of them, the one in which she lives more of the time is the principal residence. A taxpayer can't have two principal residences at the same time.

Personal Use Property. Real property that a taxpayer owns for personal use, other than the principal residence, is classified as personal use property. A second home or a vacation cabin would belong in this category.

Unimproved Investment Property. Unimproved investment property is vacant land that produces no rental income. The land is held simply as an investment, in the expectation that it will appreciate in value.

Property Held for Production of Income. Property held for the production of income includes residential, commercial, and industrial property that's used to generate rental income for the owner.

Property Used in a Trade or Business. This category includes land and buildings that the taxpayer owns and uses in his trade or business, such as a factory owned by the manufacturer, or a small building the owner uses for his own retail business.

Dealer Property. Dealer property is property held primarily for sale to customers rather than for long-term investment. If a developer subdivides land for sale to the public, the lots will usually be included in this classification until they are sold.

Nonrecognition Transactions

As was explained earlier, when a nonrecognition provision in the tax code applies to a particular transaction, the taxpayer isn't required to pay taxes on a gain in the year it is realized. Recognition of the gain is deferred to a later time. The following types of real estate transactions are covered by nonrecognition provisions:

- installment sales,
- involuntary conversions, and
- "tax-free" exchanges.

Keep in mind that a nonrecognition provision doesn't completely exclude a gain from taxation, but merely defers the tax consequences to a later tax year. These aren't really "tax-free" transactions. The realized gain is simply recognized and taxed in a subsequent year.

Installment Sales

The tax code considers a sale to be an **installment sale** if less than 100% of the sales price is received in the year of sale. Nearly all seller-financed transactions are installment sales. Installment sale reporting allows the taxpayer/seller to defer recognition of part of the gain to the year(s) in which it's actually received. In effect, taxes are paid only on the portion of the profit received each year; the gain is prorated over the term of the installment contract. Installment sale reporting is permitted for all classes of property, except that dealer property is eligible only under special conditions.

Fig. 13.1 Eligibility for installment sale reporting

Installment Sale Reporting
1. Less than 100% of sales price received in year of sale 2. All classifications of real property eligible except dealer property

In installment sales, the gain recognized in any given year is calculated based on the ratio of the gross profit to the contract price. The **gross profit** is essentially the difference between the sales price and the adjusted basis.

To calculate the gross profit, take the seller's adjusted basis at the time of sale, add the amount of the commission and other selling expenses, and subtract this sum from the sales price.

Example: Once again, we'll use Greene as an example. Her adjusted basis in her duplex was $762,800. She sold the property for $895,000. She had to pay a $45,000 commission and $15,600 in other selling expenses.

$895,000	Sales price
$762,800	Seller's adjusted basis
+ 60,600	Commission and other seller expenses
$823,400	Adjusted basis plus selling expenses
$895,000	Sales price
− 823,400	Adjusted basis plus selling expenses
$71,600	Gross profit

The next step is to compare the gross profit to the contract price to arrive at the **gross profit ratio** (also called the gross profit percentage). The contract price is the total amount of all principal payments the buyer will pay the seller. In most cases, unless the buyer assumes the seller's existing loan, the contract price is the same as the sales price.

Example:

Gross Profit	÷	Contract Price	=	Gross Profit Ratio
$71,600	÷	$895,000	=	8%

The gross profit ratio is applied to the principal payments received in each year to determine how much of the principal is gain to be taxed that year. Note that the gross profit ratio isn't applied to the interest the buyer pays the seller; all of the interest payments are treated as taxable income in the year received.

If Greene, the seller in our example, received a $89,500 downpayment, $34,167 in principal installment payments, and $47,400 in interest the first year, the taxable income would be calculated as follows:

$89,500	Downpayment
+ 34,167	Installment principal payments
$123,667	Total principal payments

$123,667	Total principal payments
× 8%	Gross profit ratio
$9,893	Recognized gain
+ 47,400	Interest income
$57,293	Total taxable income

Sometimes a buyer assumes a seller's existing mortgage or deed of trust and also gives the seller a second mortgage or deed of trust for part of the purchase price. If the loan being assumed is larger than the seller's basis in the property, the excess is treated as payment received from the buyer in the year of the sale.

If the property is subject to recapture provisions because of depreciation deductions (discussed later in this chapter), the amount recaptured is also treated as a payment received in the year of sale.

Involuntary Conversions

An involuntary conversion occurs when an asset is turned into cash without voluntary action on the part of the owner: the asset is condemned, destroyed, stolen, or lost, and the owner receives a condemnation award or insurance proceeds. (A sale under threat of condemnation is also considered an involuntary conversion.) Since the award or proceeds usually represent the property's replacement cost or market value, the owner often realizes a gain on an involuntary conversion.

However, recognition of a gain on an involuntary conversion can be deferred if the taxpayer uses the money received to replace the property within the replacement period set by the IRS. Generally, the replacement period lasts for two years after the date the property was destroyed or lost (or in the case of a condemnation, two years after the end of the tax year in which the gain was realized). Recognition of the gain is deferred only to the extent that the condemnation award or insurance proceeds are reinvested in the replacement property. Any part of the gain that's used for purposes other than purchase of replacement property will be taxed as income.

"Tax-Free" Exchanges

Section 1031 of the tax code concerns property exchanges. Although 1031 exchanges are commonly called "tax-free" exchanges, they're really just tax-deferred exchanges. If unimproved investment property, income property, or property used in a trade or business is exchanged for **like-kind property**, recognition of any realized gain will be deferred. A principal residence, personal use property, and dealer property are not eligible for this type of deferral.

Tax-free exchanges are used to reduce or eliminate current tax expenses. And a taxpayer may be able to acquire property in an exchange that would have been impossible to buy with the after-tax proceeds from the sale of the old property.

The property the taxpayer receives in the exchange must be like-kind—that is, the same kind as the property given. This requirement refers to the general nature of the properties rather than their quality. Most real estate is considered to be of like kind for the purposes of the exchange deferral, without regard to whether it's improved, unimproved, residential, commercial, or industrial. For example, if a taxpayer exchanges a strip shopping center for an apartment complex, the transaction can qualify as a tax-free exchange. Both of the exchanged properties must be located in the United States to be considered like-kind property.

If nothing other than like-kind property is received in the exchange, no gain or loss is recognized in the year of the exchange. However, anything other than like-kind property that the taxpayer receives is called **boot** and recognized in the year of the exchange. In a real estate exchange, boot might be cash, stock, other types of personal property, or **debt relief**—the difference between mortgage balances.

Example: A taxpayer exchanges a property with a mortgage debt of $320,000 for one with a mortgage debt of $300,000. The taxpayer has received $20,000 in boot because of the reduction in debt (regardless of whether there has been a formal assumption of the loan). The taxpayer may be required to pay taxes on a gain of $20,000, just as if she had received $20,000 in cash along with the real property.

The following example shows how a taxpayer's actual gain and recognized gain are calculated in an exchange transaction involving boot.

Example: Taxpayer A is exchanging a small office building for Taxpayer B's commercial property. Taxpayer A's building is valued at $1,860,000 and has an adjusted basis of $1,744,000. Its mortgage has a remaining balance of $1,340,000.

Taxpayer B is giving Taxpayer A real property worth $1,804,000 with a mortgage balance of $1,305,000, plus $21,000 in cash. The debt relief for Taxpayer A is $35,000 ($1,340,000 – $1,305,000 = $35,000).

Here's how Taxpayer A's gain would be calculated:

$1,804,000	Like-kind property
35,000	Debt relief (boot)
+ 21,000	Cash (boot)
$1,860,000	Value of property and boot received
– 1,744,000	Adjusted basis of Taxpayer A's former property
$116,000	Actual (realized) gain

So Taxpayer A is receiving property and boot worth $1,860,000 and realizing a $116,000 gain on the transaction. However, only the portion of the realized gain that's attributable to boot is taxable in the year the exchange takes place. Thus, Taxpayer A's recognized gain is $56,000 ($35,000 debt relief + $21,000 cash = $56,000 total boot). Taxation of the rest of the gain ($60,000) is deferred.

Note that boot is taxable only to the extent of the gain. If the boot received exceeded the taxpayer's realized gain on the transaction, then only the amount of the gain would be taxed, not the full amount of the boot.

The taxpayer's basis in the property exchanged is transferred to the property he receives. If nothing other than like-kind property is exchanged, no adjustments are necessary. But if the exchange involved boot, the basis must be adjusted for any boot that was paid or received, and for any gain or loss that was recognized because of the boot.

Keep in mind that under certain circumstances, an exchange of real property may be a tax-deferred

Fig. 13.2 Eligibility for tax-free exchanges

"Tax-Free" Exchanges

1. Only property held for production of income, property used in a trade or business, or unimproved investment property is eligible.
2. Must be exchanged for like-kind property.
3. Any boot is taxed in the year it is received.

transaction for one of the parties but not for the other. For example, suppose Taxpayer A trades her personal residence for a rental home owned by Taxpayer B. Both A and B are planning to use their new properties as rental homes. This can't be a tax-free exchange for Taxpayer A, because a personal residence isn't eligible. But this is a tax-free exchange for Taxpayer B, who has traded one income property for another.

Originally, tax-free exchanges were limited to simultaneous transfers of ownership (trades of property). Now, however, 1031 tax deferral benefits also apply when a taxpayer sells a property to one party and then buys a like-kind property from another party in two separate transactions. Time limits apply: once the taxpayer has sold the original (relinquished) property, he has 45 days to identify a replacement property. Then, the purchase of the replacement property must close within 180 days of the sale of the relinquished property.

An agent who arranges a tax-free exchange (often referred to as a 1031 facilitator) may receive compensation from both of the parties. California law imposes bonding requirements on 1031 facilitators, in addition to other rules.

Exclusion of Gain from the Sale of a Principal Residence

We'll discuss only one exclusion from capital gains taxation, the one that will be of greatest interest to most homeowners: the exclusion of gain on the sale of a principal residence.

Until 1997, taxpayers who sold their principal residence were often eligible for the "rollover" deferral of taxation. A seller was allowed to defer taxation of the gain if the sale proceeds were used within two years to buy another residence. And a seller who was 55 or older could take advantage of a one-time exclusion of gain from the sale of the principal residence, even if the gain wasn't invested in a new residence. In 1997, both of these tax benefits were replaced with a single, less complicated exclusion from taxation.

Amount of Gain Excluded. Under current law, a taxpayer may exclude the entire gain on the sale of her principal residence, up to $250,000 if the taxpayer is filing a single return, or $500,000 if the taxpayer is married and filing a joint return.

Example:

$380,000	Amount realized (after selling costs)
– 170,000	Seller's basis in home
$210,000	Gain realized

Whether filing singly or jointly, the seller will be able to exclude the entire amount of gain—$210,000—from taxation.

If the amount of the gain on the sale of the home exceeds the $250,000 or $500,000 limit, the amount in excess of the limit will be taxed at the capital gains rate.

Example:

$475,000	Amount realized (after selling costs)
– 170,000	Seller's basis in home
$305,000	Gain realized

If the seller is filing a single return, only $250,000 of the $305,000 gain will be excluded from taxation. The seller will have to pay capital gains taxes on the $55,000 that exceeded the exclusion limit.

Eligibility. To qualify for this exclusion, the seller must have both owned and used the property as a principal residence for at least two years during the five-year period ending on the date of sale. Because of this rule, this exclusion is available only once every two years.

Note that if the sellers are married and filing a joint return, only one spouse has to meet the ownership test, but both spouses must meet the use test. If only one spouse meets both the ownership test and the use test, the maximum exclusion the married couple can claim is $250,000, even if they file a joint return.

If the seller owned and used the property as a principal residence for less than two years because of special circumstances (for example, if he sold the home after only a year because of a change in health or employment), the seller may be able to claim a reduced exclusion.

Deductions Available to Property Owners

As was explained earlier, a **deduction** is subtracted from a taxpayer's income before the tax rate is applied. The income tax deductions allowed to real property owners are a significant benefit of ownership. There are deductions for:

- depreciation (cost recovery),
- uninsured casualty and theft losses,
- repairs,
- real property taxes,
- mortgage interest,
- points paid to a mortgage lender, and
- operational losses from rental property.

Depreciation Deductions

Depreciation deductions (sometimes called cost recovery deductions) permit a taxpayer to recover the cost of an asset over a period of years. Only property used for the production of income or used in a trade or business is eligible for depreciation deductions. They can't be taken in connection with a principal residence or other personal use property, unimproved investment property, or dealer property.

Depreciable Property. In general, only property that wears out and will eventually have to be replaced is **depreciable**—that is, eligible for depreciation deductions. For example, apartment buildings, business or factory equipment, and the trees in commercial fruit orchards all have to be replaced, so they are depreciable. But land doesn't wear out, so it's not depreciable.

Time Frame. The entire expense of acquiring an asset can't be deducted in the year it's incurred (although that's permitted with many other business expenses, such as wages, supplies, and utilities). However, the expense can be deducted over a number

Fig. 13.3 Favorable tax treatment for real property

Eligibility for Favorable Income Tax Treatment			
	Installment Sale	"Tax-Free" Exchange	Depreciation Deductions
Principal Residence	Yes	No	No
Personal Use	Yes	No	No
Unimproved Investment	Yes	Yes	No
Trade or Business	Yes	Yes	Yes
Income	Yes	Yes	Yes
Dealer	No	No	No

of years; for most real estate, the recovery period is between 27½ and 39 years. The length of the recovery period is a reflection of legislative policy and has little, if any, relationship to the actual length of time that the property will be economically useful. The whole field of depreciation deductions has been subject to frequent modification by Congress.

Effect on Basis. As we said in the discussion of basis at the beginning of the chapter, any allowable depreciation deductions reduce the taxpayer's adjusted basis in the property. Note that this reduction occurs whether or not the taxpayer actually takes the deduction. If the deduction was allowable—that is, the taxpayer was entitled to take it—the basis will be reduced. By reducing the basis, these deductions affect the taxpayer's eventual gain or loss on resale of the property.

Uninsured Casualty or Theft Loss Deductions

When property is damaged or stolen and the loss isn't covered or is only partially covered by insurance, the property owner is generally permitted to deduct the uninsured loss from taxable income. To calculate the amount of the deductible loss, first subtract the estimated fair market value of the property after the loss from its estimated value before the loss. Compare this reduction in value to the owner's adjusted basis in the property. From the lower of the two figures, subtract any insurance reimbursement that the owner has received or will receive. For most types of property, the result is the amount of the deductible loss.

Example: Ramirez owned property worth $975,000, with an adjusted basis of $714,000. After the property was damaged in a flood, its value dropped to $830,000. This represented a reduction in value of $145,000.

$975,000	Value before flood damage
– 830,000	Value after flood damage
$145,000	Reduction in value

Ramirez's insurance company paid her only $110,000, so she suffered an uninsured casualty loss. To calculate how much of the loss Ramirez will be able to deduct from her taxable income, use the reduction in value ($145,000), since that figure is less than Ramirez's adjusted basis ($714,000).

$145,000	Reduction in value
– 110,000	Insurance reimbursement
$35,000	Deductible loss

For personal use property (including a principal residence), the amount of the deductible loss is reduced by some additional calculations. After going through the steps described above, subtract $100 from the loss. Next, subtract 10% of the taxpayer's adjusted gross income. The result is the taxpayer's deductible loss for personal use property.

Example: Return to the previous example, but now suppose that the property is Ramirez's home. Start where the previous calculation left off, subtract $100, and then subtract 10% of Ramirez's adjusted gross income, which is $95,000.

$35,000	Uninsured loss
100	Subtracted from loss
– 9,500	10% of adjusted gross income
$25,400	Deductible loss

Thus, Ramirez will be able to deduct $25,400 from her taxable income for this casualty loss concerning personal use property.

If a taxpayer has more than one casualty loss for personal use property in a given tax year, $100 must be subtracted from each loss. However, 10% of the adjusted gross income is subtracted from the total amount of those losses, not from each loss.

Repair Deductions

A repair expense is an expenditure incurred to keep the property in ordinary, efficient operating condition. For most types of real property, expenditures for repairs are deductible in the year paid.

However, repair expenses are not deductible for principal residences or other personal use property. This includes expenditures for maintenance, upkeep, and ordinary wear and tear, and it also includes condominium assessments.

For any type of real property, repair expenses shouldn't be confused with capital expenditures. As explained earlier, capital expenditures add to the value of the property and frequently prolong its economic life. Capital expenditures aren't deductible in the year made, but rather are added to the taxpayer's basis. The resulting increase in the basis will affect the gain or loss on the eventual sale of the property. It will also increase the allowable depreciation deductions if the property is eligible for those.

Property Tax Deductions

General real estate taxes are deductible for any type of property. Special assessments for repairs or maintenance are deductible, but those for improvements (such as new sidewalks) are not.

Mortgage Interest Deductions

For most property, interest paid on a mortgage or deed of trust is usually completely deductible. However, there are some limitations on interest deductions for personal residences (principal residences or second homes).

A taxpayer may deduct interest payments on mortgage debt of up to $1,000,000 ($500,000 for a married taxpayer filing separately) used to buy, build, or improve a first or second residence. In addition, interest on a home equity loan of up to $100,000 ($50,000 for a married taxpayer filing separately) can be deducted without regard to the purpose of the loan. When the loan amount exceeds these limits, the interest on the excess isn't deductible.

Occasionally a condominium project borrows money by mortgaging the common areas, and the unit owners are required to pay a share of the mortgage payment. In that case, a unit owner may deduct the interest portion of her share from taxable income.

The deductibility of mortgage interest is one reason why homeowners often use a home equity loan to pay off credit card debt. The interest on credit cards isn't deductible, but the interest on the home equity loan is. Currently, mortgage interest is the only type of consumer interest that is deductible.

Deductibility of Points and Other Loan Costs

The IRS considers points paid to a lender in connection with a new loan (including discount points and the origination fee) to be prepaid interest, and the borrower is generally allowed to deduct them. This is true even if the points were paid by the seller on the borrower's behalf. (The borrower's basis in the property must be reduced by the amount of the seller-paid points.)

Note that fees a lender charges to cover specific services aren't deductible, even if the lender refers to them as points. This includes, for example, appraisal fees, document preparation fees, and mortgage insurance premiums.

If a seller paying off a loan is required to pay a prepayment penalty, the amount of the penalty is usually deductible. For tax purposes, a prepayment penalty is treated as a form of interest.

Deducting Operational Losses from Rental Property

A taxpayer who owns and actively manages a rental property may deduct up to $25,000 of operational losses from his ordinary income. To understand this rule, you need to understand the distinction between ordinary income and passive income.

As a general rule, **passive income** is income a taxpayer earns from an enterprise (such as a limited partnership) that he doesn't materially participate in. However, the IRS always considers rental income to be passive income, even if the taxpayer participates in the management of the rental property.

In most cases, passive losses—losses from passive activities—can only be deducted from passive income, not from ordinary income. For instance, suppose you earned $85,000 last year at your job, but your small ownership interest in a real estate investment trust lost $7,000. You couldn't deduct the $7,000 loss (a passive loss) against your salary (which is ordinary income), because you can only deduct passive losses from passive income.

However, losses from the operation of rental property receive special treatment, as long as the taxpayer actively participates in the property's management (and meets certain other requirements). Unlike other passive losses, up to $25,000 in operational losses from rental property can be deducted from ordinary income.

Example: Woodruff, a high school teacher, owns a rental property and actively participates in managing it. Last year the property's annual operating expenses added up to $119,000 and the rental income was only $100,000. This $19,000 loss is deductible from ordinary income. That means Woodruff can take a $19,000 deduction against the $70,000 salary he earns from his teaching job.

Not every rental property owner who actively participates in management of the property can take advantage of this rule. There are several significant restrictions. For example, the taxpayer can't be involved in any other passive activities, and his adjusted gross income can't exceed a certain limit.

Don't confuse an operational loss with lost income due to rental property vacancies. If a rental property sits vacant for all or part of the year, that lost income isn't deductible. The only figure that can be deducted is the overall difference between a rental property's annual income and annual operating expenses—an operational loss.

Also, don't confuse an operational loss with a loss from the sale of a rental property. Losses from the sale of a rental property are subject to different rules, which we discussed at the beginning of this chapter.

One final point: If the taxpayer is a real estate professional who materially participates in rental property activities, those aren't considered passive activities. That means there's no $25,000 limit on the amount of operational losses that the real estate professional can deduct from her ordinary income.

Rental Payment Deductions

We should mention one deduction connected with real estate that concerns not property owners but tenants. Rent paid for property used in a trade or business is deductible as a business expense. However, rent paid for property not used in a trade or business (such as rent for a home) isn't deductible.

California Income Tax

In addition to the federal income tax, there's a California state income tax. The provisions of California's income tax laws are substantially the same as the Internal Revenue Code. For example, with limited exceptions, the California statutes simply refer to the federal law for such items as the definitions of gross income, adjusted gross income, itemized deductions, and taxable income. There's a different standard deduction under state law for those who don't itemize and, of course, the tax rates on taxable income are different.

As with federal law, the state income tax is a progressive tax with higher rates imposed on higher income levels. Income tax brackets and the standard deduction are adjusted for inflation by the California Franchise Tax Board each year based on the California Consumer Price Index.

Chapter Summary

1. Any economic benefit realized by a taxpayer is treated as part of his income, unless there's a specific provision of the tax code that excludes it from income. The tax code provides for certain deductions from income before the tax rate is applied, and also for tax credits, which are subtracted from the amount of tax owed.

2. A gain or a loss is realized when an asset is sold. A gain is recognized (taxed) in the year it is realized, unless a nonrecognition or exclusion provision in the tax code applies.

3. A taxpayer's initial basis in property is the amount she originally invested in it. To determine the adjusted basis, capital expenditures are added to the initial basis, and allowable depreciation deductions are subtracted from it. The taxpayer's gain or loss is the difference between the amount realized and the adjusted basis.

4. In the tax code, real property is classified as principal residence property, personal use property, unimproved investment property, property held for the production of income, property used in a trade or business, or dealer property.

5. The tax code's nonrecognition provisions for real property transactions allow taxation of gain to be deferred in installment sales, involuntary conversions, and "tax-free" exchanges. There's also an exclusion of up to $250,000 (or $500,000 if filing jointly) of gain allowed on the sale of a principal residence.

6. The tax deductions available to property owners include depreciation deductions (only for income property and property used in a trade or business); uninsured casualty or theft loss deductions; repair deductions (not for principal residences or personal use property); deduction of property taxes; deduction of mortgage interest; deduction of points; and deduction of operational losses for rental property. There are limits on the mortgage interest deduction for personal residences.

Key Terms

Income—Any economic benefit realized by a taxpayer that isn't excluded from income by the tax code.

Deduction—An expense that can be used to reduce taxable income.

Marginal tax rate—The tax rate that applies to the last dollar that a taxpayer earns.

Basis—A taxpayer's investment in his property.

Initial basis—The amount of a taxpayer's original investment in a property; how much it cost to acquire the property. Also called the cost basis or the unadjusted basis.

Adjusted basis—The initial basis plus capital expenditures and minus allowable depreciation deductions.

Realization—A gain or a loss is realized when it is separated from the asset; this separation generally occurs when the asset is sold.

Recognition—A gain is said to be recognized when it is taxable; it is recognized in the year it is realized, unless recognition is deferred by the tax code.

Installment sale—A sale in which less than 100% of the sales price is received in the year of sale.

Involuntary conversion—When property is converted to cash without the voluntary action of the owner, as when property is destroyed, stolen, lost, or condemned, and the owner receives insurance proceeds or a condemnation award.

Depreciation deductions—Deductions from the taxpayer's income to allow the cost of an asset to be recovered over a period of years. These are allowed only for depreciable property that's held for the production of income or used in a trade or business. Also called cost recovery deductions.

Repair expenses—Money spent on repairs to keep property in ordinary, efficient operating condition.

Capital expenditures—Money spent on improvements to property, which add to its value or prolong its economic life.

Tax-free exchange—When like-kind property is exchanged, allowing taxation of the gain to be deferred. Also called a Section 1031 exchange.

Like-kind property—In a tax-free exchange, property received that's of the same kind as the property transferred. Any two pieces of real estate are considered to be of like kind.

Boot—Something given or received in a tax-free exchange that isn't like-kind property, such as cash.

Chapter Quiz

1. A homeowner's basis in her principal residence would be adjusted to reflect:
   a) depreciation deductions
   b) expenses incurred to keep the property in good repair
   c) mortgage interest paid
   d) the cost of installing a deck

2. A married couple bought a home for $250,000. After living in the home for three years, they sold it for only $246,000. How much of this loss can they deduct on their federal income tax return?
   a) The full $4,000 loss
   b) Only $3,000
   c) Only $2,000
   d) None of it

3. Which of the following could the owner of unimproved investment property deduct on her federal income tax return?
   a) A loss on the sale of the property
   b) The depreciation of the land
   c) Depreciation deductions
   d) Any of the above

4. Which of the following exchanges could not qualify as a "tax-free" exchange?
   a) An office building for a hotel
   b) An apartment house for a warehouse
   c) Timber land for farm equipment
   d) A city lot for a ranch

5. Under the federal income tax code, income is always taxed in the year it is:
   a) realized
   b) recognized
   c) recovered
   d) deferred

6. Ortega just sold his principal residence. After subtracting his selling costs, the amount of gain realized was $163,000. Ortega will be allowed to exclude the entire amount of the gain from taxation only if:
   a) he is married and is filing a joint return
   b) he has never claimed this exclusion before, since it can only be used once in a lifetime
   c) the gain isn't a capital gain
   d) he owned and occupied the property as his principal residence for two of the previous five years

7. Torrence owns a triplex as an investment property. She paid $550,000 for it, including her closing costs. The allowable depreciation deductions for the property have amounted to $20,000, Torrence has spent $50,000 on capital improvements, and the market value of the property has risen by 15%. What is Torrence's adjusted basis?
   a) $600,000
   b) $620,000
   c) $580,000
   d) $530,000

8. Gillespie is buying a home that will be his principal residence. He is financing the purchase with a $300,000 mortgage loan. How much of the interest that he pays on the loan can he deduct from his income?
   a) All of it
   b) Up to $100,000 in interest
   c) 50%
   d) None of it

9. The Wongs are selling some property on a five-year contract. Their gross profit ratio on the sale is 15%. This year, they will receive $6,178 in interest and $4,453 in principal. With installment sale reporting, approximately how much of that will be recognized and included in the Wongs' taxable income for this year?
   a) $1,595
   b) $5,380
   c) $6,846
   d) $10,631

10. Sherrick is selling a lot for $172,000. Her adjusted basis in the property is $136,000. In addition to the 6% commission she'll be paying her real estate broker, she will also have to pay $3,500 in closing costs. For federal income tax purposes, what is the gain Sherrick will realize in this transaction?
    a) $16,230
    b) $22,180
    c) $36,000
    d) $39,500

Answer Key

1. d) The cost of installing a deck is a capital expenditure, which would be added to the taxpayer's basis. Remember that principal residences and personal use property don't qualify for depreciation deductions.

2. d) A loss on the sale of a principal residence or personal use property is never deductible.

3. a) If the owner loses money on the sale of the property, she may be able to deduct that loss. Depreciation deductions aren't allowed for unimproved investment property, because land isn't depreciable.

4. c) The like-kind property requirement means that real estate must be exchanged for other real estate.

5. b) Income is taxed when it is recognized. It is often recognized in the same year it is realized, but that isn't true if a nonrecognition provision applies.

6. d) To qualify for the exclusion from taxation, the taxpayer must have both owned and used the property as a principal residence for two of the previous five years.

7. c) The initial basis, plus the capital expenditures, less the allowable depreciation deductions, equals an adjusted basis of $580,000.

   $550,000 + $50,000 – $20,000 = $580,000

   (Ignore the increase in market value; it doesn't affect the taxpayer's basis.)

8. a) A taxpayer can deduct all of the interest paid on a loan of up to $1,000,000 used to purchase a first or second personal residence.

9. c) Multiply the principal payments by the gross profit ratio to determine the amount of principal that will be recognized this year. Then add that to the entire amount of interest received (all of the interest is taxable).

   $4,453 × 15% = $667.95 + $6,178 = $6,845.95

10. b) Sherrick will realize a $22,180 gain in the transaction. First subtract her selling expenses (the commission and closing costs) from the sales price to determine the amount realized; then subtract her adjusted basis from the amount realized to determine the gain.

    $172,000 × 6% = $10,320 commission

    $10,320 + $3,500 costs = $13,820

    $172,000 – $13,820 = $158,180 (amt. realized)

    $158,180 – $136,000 = $22,180 (gain realized)

Chapter 14

Civil Rights and Fair Housing

I. Federal Antidiscrimination Legislation
   A. Civil Rights Act of 1866
   B. Civil Rights Act of 1964
   C. Fair Housing Act
      1. Exemptions
      2. Prohibited acts
      3. Disability and familial status
      4. Enforcement
   D. Federal fair lending laws
   E. Americans with Disabilities Act

II. California Antidiscrimination Legislation
   A. Unruh Civil Rights Act
   B. Fair Employment and Housing Act
   C. Housing Financial Discrimination Act
   D. Real estate license law and regulations

III. Discriminatory Restrictive Covenants

Chapter Overview

Civil rights laws are intended to promote fairness and freedom. In the real estate context, one of the main goals of these laws is equal housing opportunity. Anyone with the necessary financial resources should be able to choose a house or an apartment in any neighborhood, regardless of race, religion, national origin, gender, or other characteristics that have historically been used as a basis for discrimination. There are also civil rights laws that affect nonresidential real estate.

Real estate agents must be familiar with both federal and state laws that prohibit discrimination in real estate transactions and related business activities. Complying with these laws—and encouraging others to comply with them—is an essential part of a real estate agent's professional duties. In this chapter, we'll look first at the federal antidiscrimination laws that affect real estate, then at the California laws.

Federal Antidiscrimination Legislation

Federal laws that prohibit discrimination in real estate transactions and related activities include:

- the Civil Rights Act of 1866,
- the Civil Rights Act of 1964,
- the Fair Housing Act,
- federal fair lending laws, and
- the Americans with Disabilities Act.

The Civil Rights Act of 1866

The Civil Rights Act of 1866 states that "all citizens of the United States shall have the same right, in every state and territory as is enjoyed by white citizens thereof to inherit, purchase, lease, sell, hold and convey real and personal property." In regard to property ownership and property transactions, the act prohibits any discrimination based on race or color.

Enacted immediately after the Civil War, this law was largely ignored for almost a century. In the 1960s, during the civil rights movement, the act was challenged as an unconstitutional interference with private property rights. But the U.S. Supreme Court upheld the act in the landmark case of *Jones v. Mayer*, decided in 1968. The court ruled that the 1866 act "prohibits all racial discrimination, private or public, in the sale and rental of property," and that it is constitutional based on the Thirteenth Amendment to the U.S. Constitution, which prohibits slavery.

Someone who has been discriminated against in violation of the Civil Rights Act of 1866 can sue in federal court. The court could issue an injunction ordering the defendant to stop discriminating or to take affirmative steps to correct the violation. This might involve an order requiring the defendant to sell or lease property to the plaintiff. The court could also order the defendant to pay the plaintiff both **compensatory damages** (to compensate for losses and suffering caused by the discrimination) and **punitive damages** (an additional sum to punish the defendant for wrongdoing).

The Civil Rights Act of 1964

The Civil Rights Act of 1964 was one of the federal government's first attempts to promote equal opportunity in housing. The act prohibited discrimination based on race, color, religion, or national origin in many programs and activities for which the federal government provided financial assistance. Unfortunately, its effect on housing was extremely limited, because most FHA and VA loans weren't covered. In fact, it's estimated that less than 1% of all home purchases were covered by this law. It wasn't until the Civil Rights Act of 1968 that major progress was made toward fair housing goals.

The Fair Housing Act

The federal Fair Housing Act is also known as Title VIII of the Civil Rights Act of 1968. This law makes it illegal to discriminate on the basis of **race, color, religion, sex, national origin, handicap**, or **familial status** in the sale or lease of residential property or in the sale or lease of vacant land for the construction of residential buildings. The law also prohibits discrimination in advertising, lending, real estate brokerage, and other services in connection with residential real estate transactions. However, unlike the 1866 Civil Rights Act, the Fair Housing Act does not apply to nonresidential transactions, such as those involving commercial or industrial properties.

Exemptions. While the Fair Housing Act applies to the majority of residential real estate transactions, four types of transactions are exempt from it.

1. The law doesn't apply to the sale or rental of a single-family home by its owner, provided that:
   - the owner doesn't own more than three such homes;
   - no real estate broker or agent is employed in the transaction; and
   - no discriminatory advertising is used.

   If the owner isn't the most recent occupant of the home, he may use this exemption only once every 24 months.
2. The law doesn't apply to the rental of a unit or a room in a dwelling with up to four units, provided that:
   - the owner occupies one of the units as her residence;
   - no real estate broker or agent is employed; and
   - no discriminatory advertising is used.

   (This is sometimes called the **Mrs. Murphy exemption**.)
3. In dealing with their own property in noncommercial transactions, religious organizations or societies or affiliated nonprofit organizations may limit occupancy to or give preference to their own members, provided that membership isn't restricted on the basis of race, color, or national origin.
4. Private clubs with lodgings that aren't open to the public and that aren't operated for a commercial purpose may limit occupancy to or give preference to their own members.

These limited exemptions apply very rarely. Remember that the 1866 Civil Rights Act prohibits discrimination based on race or color in any property transaction, regardless of any exemptions available under the Fair Housing Act. In addition, the

Fig. 14.1 Fair housing poster

U.S. Department of Housing and Urban Development

We Do Business in Accordance With the Federal Fair Housing Law

(The Fair Housing Amendments Act of 1988)

It is Illegal to Discriminate Against Any Person Because of Race, Color, Religion, Sex, Handicap, Familial Status, or National Origin

- In the sale or rental of housing or residential lots
- In advertising the sale or rental of housing
- In the financing of housing
- In the provision of real estate brokerage services
- In the appraisal of housing
- Blockbusting is also illegal

Anyone who feels he or she has been discriminated against may file a complaint of housing discrimination:
1-800-669-9777 (Toll Free)
1-800-927-9275 (TDD)

U.S. Department of Housing and Urban Development
Assistant Secretary for Fair Housing and Equal Opportunity
Washington, D.C. 20410

Previous editions are obsolete

form HUD-928.1A(8-93)

exemptions don't apply in transactions involving a real estate licensee. Furthermore, the Fair Housing Act exemptions are essentially irrelevant in states like California, where the state civil rights laws are stricter than the federal law.

Display of Poster. Regulations implementing the Fair Housing Act require a fair housing poster (see Figure 14.1) to be prominently displayed at any place of business involved in the sale, rental, or financing of dwellings. This includes real estate offices, lenders' offices, apartment buildings, condominiums, and model homes in subdivisions. If a fair housing complaint is filed against a business, failure to display the poster may be treated as evidence of discriminatory practices.

Prohibited Acts. The Fair Housing Act prohibits the following acts if they are done on the basis of race, color, religion, sex, national origin, handicap, or familial status:

- refusing to rent or sell residential property after receiving a bona fide offer;
- refusing to negotiate for the sale or rental of residential property, or otherwise making it unavailable;
- changing the terms of sale or lease for different potential buyers or tenants;
- using advertising that indicates a preference or intent to discriminate;
- representing that property is not available for inspection, sale, or rent when it is in fact available;
- using discriminatory criteria when making a housing loan;
- limiting participation in a multiple listing service or similar service;
- coercing, intimidating, threatening, or interfering with anyone on account of his or her enjoyment, attempt to enjoy, or encouragement or assistance to others in enjoying the rights granted by the Fair Housing Act.

Also prohibited are the discriminatory practices known as blockbusting, steering, and redlining.

- **Blockbusting** occurs when someone tries to induce homeowners to list or sell their homes by predicting that people of another race (or people who have certain disabilities, people with a particular ethnic background, etc.) will be moving into the neighborhood, and that this will have undesirable consequences such as lower property values. The blockbuster then profits by buying the homes at reduced prices or (in the case of a real estate agent) by collecting commissions on the induced sales. Blockbusting is also known as **panic selling** or **panic peddling**.

  Example: Right after an African-American family moves into an all-white neighborhood, real estate agents working for XYZ Realty start calling all the other homeowners in the neighborhood. The agents imply that several other black families are planning on buying homes there, and suggest that this will lead to a sharp increase in crime and a dramatic drop in property values. The agents warn the homeowners that within months it will be difficult to sell their homes at any price. Because of these calls, several homeowners immediately list their homes with XYZ Realty. XYZ and its agents are guilty of blockbusting.

- **Steering** refers to channeling prospective buyers or tenants toward or away from specific neighborhoods based on their race (or religion, national origin, etc.) in order to maintain or change the character of those neighborhoods.

  Example: The agents at PQR Realty are "encouraged" to show Latino buyers only homes in the city's predominantly Latino neighborhood. Non-Latino buyers aren't shown homes there, except by specific request. The firm's justification for this policy is that Latino buyers would be more "comfortable" living in the Latino neighborhood, and non-Latino buyers would be "uncomfortable" there. PQR Realty is guilty of steering.

- **Redlining** is the refusal to make a loan because of the racial or ethnic composition of the neighborhood in which the security property is located.

  Example: A buyer applies to Community Savings for a loan to purchase a house located in the Cherrywood neighborhood. Cherrywood is a predominantly minority neighborhood. Community Savings rejects the loan application, because it fears that property values in Cherrywood may decline in the future because of recent racial tensions in the area. Community Savings is guilty of redlining.

The prohibition against redlining is enforced through the Home Mortgage Disclosure Act, discussed later in the chapter.

Disability and Familial Status. Originally, the Fair Housing Act didn't prohibit discrimination based on disability or familial status; these classifications were added to the law in 1988.

Disability. In connection with residential property, it's a violation of the Fair Housing Act to discriminate against someone because he has a disability. A disability (called a handicap in the act) is defined as a physical or mental impairment that substantially limits one or more major life activities. This includes people with chronic alcoholism, mental illness, or HIV/AIDS. But the act doesn't protect those who are a direct threat to the health or safety of others, or who are currently using controlled substances.

A residential landlord must allow a disabled tenant to make reasonable modifications to the property at the tenant's expense, as long as the modifications are necessary for the tenant's full use and enjoyment of the premises. (The tenant can be required to restore the premises to their original condition at the end of the tenancy, however.) Landlords must also make reasonable exceptions to their rules to accommodate disabled tenants. For example, even if they don't allow pets, they can't refuse to rent to someone because she has a guide dog.

Since 1991, new residential construction with four or more units has had to comply with special wheelchair accessibility rules under the Fair Housing Act.

Familial Status. Discrimination on the basis of familial status refers to discriminating against someone because a child (a person under 18 years old) is or will be living with him or her. Parents, legal guardians, pregnant women, and those in the process of obtaining custody of a child are protected against discrimination on the basis of their familial status.

While the Fair Housing Act doesn't override local laws limiting the number of occupants permitted in a dwelling, it's unlawful to discriminate in selling, renting, or lending money to buy residential property because the applicant is pregnant or lives with a child. "Adults only" apartment or condominium complexes are forbidden, and so are complexes divided into "adult" and "family" sections.

However, the Fair Housing Act includes an exemption for properties that qualify as "housing for older persons." Children can be excluded from properties that fit into one of the following categories:

1. properties developed under a government program to assist the elderly;
2. properties intended for and solely occupied by persons who are 62 or older; or
3. properties that adhere to policies that demonstrate an intent to house persons who are 55 or older, if at least 80% of the units are occupied by at least one person who is 55 or older.

Enforcement. The Fair Housing Act is enforced by the Department of Housing and Urban Development (HUD), through its Office of Fair Housing and Equal Opportunity. An aggrieved person may file a lawsuit in federal or state court, or he may file a complaint with HUD.

A complaint must be filed with HUD within one year after the discriminatory act occurred. The agency will investigate the case and attempt to confer with the parties in order to reconcile their differences and persuade the violator to abide by the law.

If this doesn't resolve the dispute and the complainant's claims are found to have merit, an administrative hearing will be held (unless either party chooses to have the case decided in federal court instead). In an administrative hearing, HUD attorneys litigate the case on behalf of the complainant. If a case involves a "pattern or practice" of discrimination, the U.S. Attorney General can file suit in federal court.

When someone is held to have violated the Fair Housing Act, the administrative law judge or the court may issue an injunction ordering the violator to stop the discriminatory conduct or to take affirmative steps to correct a violation. The violator may also be ordered to pay compensatory damages and attorney's fees to the complainant. A federal court can order the violator to pay punitive damages to the complainant. An administrative law judge can't impose punitive damages, but can impose a civil penalty to be paid to the government; the maximum penalty ranges from $16,000 for a first offense up to $65,000 for a third or subsequent offense. In a case litigated by the Attorney General, the court can impose a civil penalty ranging from a maximum of $75,000 for a first offense up to a maximum of $150,000 for a third or subsequent offense.

In states such as California, where the state fair housing laws are very similar to the federal law, HUD may refer complaints to the equivalent state agency (in California, the Department of Fair Employment and Housing).

Federal Fair Lending Laws

As we discussed earlier, the Fair Housing Act prohibits discrimination in residential mortgage lending. It doesn't apply to other types of credit transactions, however.

The **Equal Credit Opportunity Act** (ECOA) applies to all credit transactions, including mortgage lending. The act prohibits lenders, loan originators, mortgage brokers, and others involved in financing from discriminating based on race, color, religion, national origin, sex, marital status, or age (as long as the applicant has reached the age of majority), or because the applicant's income is derived partly or wholly from public assistance.

The **Home Mortgage Disclosure Act** provides a way to evaluate whether lenders are fulfilling their obligation to serve the housing needs of the communities where they're located. The act facilitates the enforcement of federal laws against redlining.

Under the Home Mortgage Disclosure Act, large institutional lenders in metropolitan areas must submit annual reports on the residential mortgage loans (both purchase and improvement loans) that they originated or purchased during the fiscal year. The information is categorized by number and dollar amount, type of loan (FHA, VA, other), and geographic location by census tract or county. The reports may reveal areas where few or no home loans have been made, alerting investigators to possible redlining.

Americans with Disabilities Act

The Americans with Disabilities Act (ADA), which has been in effect since 1992, is a federal law intended to ensure that people with disabilities have equal access to public facilities. The ADA requires any business or other nonresidential facility open to the public to be accessible to people with disabilities.

Under the ADA, it's illegal to discriminate against anyone on the basis of disability in any place of public accommodation or commercial facility. A **disability** is defined as any physical or mental impairment that substantially limits one or more of an individual's major life activities (the same definition used for the Fair Housing Act). A **public accommodation** is a private entity with nonresidential facilities open to the public, if the operation of the facilities affects commerce. Real estate offices are considered to be public accommodations, along with hotels, restaurants, retail stores, shopping centers, banks, and the offices of attorneys, accountants, and doctors.

To ensure the accessibility of public accommodations, the ADA requires each of the following to be accomplished, as long as it is "readily achievable":

- Both architectural barriers and communication barriers must be removed so that goods and services are accessible to people with disabilities.
- Auxiliary aids and services must be provided so that no one with a disability is excluded, denied services, segregated, or otherwise treated differently from other individuals.
- New commercial construction must be accessible to people with disabilities, unless that would be structurally impractical.

For example, the owner of a commercial building with no elevator may have to install automatic entry doors and a buzzer at street level so that the customers of a second-floor business can ask for assistance. A commercial building owner might also be required to alter the height of a pay phone to make it accessible to someone in a wheelchair, add grab bars to restroom stalls, and take a variety of other steps to make the building's facilities accessible.

California Antidiscrimination Legislation

Real estate agents, sellers, landlords, and others involved in real estate activities must comply not only with the federal laws we've covered, but also with state laws that prohibit discrimination. In California, the Unruh Civil Rights Act, the Fair Employment and Housing Act, the Housing Financial Discrimination Act, and the Real Estate Law all have provisions designed to promote fairness in real estate transactions.

Unruh Civil Rights Act

Under California's Unruh Civil Rights Act, everyone is entitled to the full use of any services provided by a business establishment, regardless of sex, race, color, religion, ancestry, national origin, disability, medical condition, genetic information, marital status, or sexual orientation. In transactions related to housing, business establishments are also not allowed to discriminate based on age or familial status, except in qualified housing for senior citizens, as discussed below.

The Unruh Act prohibits real estate licensees from discriminating in the performance of their work, since a brokerage firm is a business establishment. A broker can't refuse a listing or turn away a prospective buyer for discriminatory reasons.

Apartment houses, homeowners and condominium associations, and real estate developments are also considered business establishments under the Unruh Act. Thus, the act makes it unlawful for most condominiums or apartment complexes to have a "No Children" rule. However, developments for senior citizens that fulfill certain qualifications may require at least one member of each household to be at least 55 or older and (with some exceptions) may exclude those younger than 45. Remember that this state law must be interpreted in conjunction with the federal rules concerning housing for older persons, discussed above. The state law may be applied to give more protection against discrimination than federal law, but not to give less protection.

Someone held to have violated the Unruh Act will be required to pay the injured party's actual damages and attorney's fees. In addition, the violator may have to pay the injured party up to three times the amount of actual damages or $4,000, whichever is more. In some cases, civil penalties may be imposed as well.

Fair Employment and Housing Act

The Fair Employment and Housing Act is also known as the **Rumford Act**. It generally prohibits all housing discrimination in California based on race, color, religion, sex, gender, gender identity, gender expression, sexual orientation, marital status, national origin, ancestry, familial status, disability, genetic information, or source of income (receipt of public assistance).

It's unlawful for an owner, landlord, assignee, managing agent, real estate licensee, or business establishment to discriminate in selling or renting any housing accommodation. The law specifically prohibits a seller or landlord from asking about the race, color, religion, sex, gender, gender identity, gender expression, sexual orientation, marital status, national origin, ancestry, familial status, genetic information, or disability of any prospective buyer or tenant. Landlords may, of course, request documentation to verify identity and financial qualification to rent. A real estate licensee should refuse to answer a prohibited question from a seller or landlord.

The Fair Employment and Housing Act also specifically prohibits anyone from advertising housing for sale or rent in discriminatory terms. This includes any ad that suggests a preference for a particular group, such as a landlord's ad indicating a preference for women or married couples as tenants.

Fig. 14.2 Antidiscrimination legislation

Legislation	Prohibits Discrimination
Civil Rights Act of 1866	Based on race, for any type of property
Civil Rights Act of 1964	In some federal programs
Fair Housing Act	In sale, lease, or financing of housing
Americans with Disabilities Act	In public accommodations/commercial facilities
Unruh Civil Rights Act	By any business establishment
Fair Employment and Housing Act	In sale, lease, or financing of housing
Housing Financial Discrimination Act	By lenders in residential transactions

The act also prohibits discrimination in the financing of housing. Under the act, it's unlawful for any bank, mortgage company, or other financial institution to discriminate against any person because of race, color, religion, sex, gender, gender identity, gender expression, sexual orientation, marital status, national origin, ancestry, familial status, disability, genetic information, or source of income.

There are a few exemptions. The act does not apply to accommodations operated by nonprofit religious, fraternal, or charitable organizations. It also does not apply to the rental of a portion of a single-family owner-occupied home to one boarder. And when a rental arrangement will involve shared living space, it's permissible for the advertising to state that it is available only to women, or only to men.

Housing discrimination complaints are submitted to the Department of Fair Employment and Housing (DFEH). If the DFEH determines that a complaint should be pursued, it will require the parties to participate in no-cost mediation. If mediation is ineffective, DFEH will file a lawsuit in superior court.

If found guilty, the violator may be ordered to:

- sell/lease the housing in question to the injured party, if it's still available;
- sell/lease similar property to the injured party, if it's available;
- provide financial assistance or other benefits previously denied; or
- pay damages to the injured party.

In especially serious cases, the violator may have to pay the state a civil penalty ranging from $50,000 up to $100,000.

Housing Financial Discrimination Act

The California Housing Financial Discrimination Act (which is sometimes called the **Holden Act**) requires a lender to make lending decisions based on the merits of the borrower and the security property, rather than on the fact that the property is in a particular neighborhood. The act states that it's against California's public policy to deny mortgage loans or to impose stricter terms on loans because of neighborhood characteristics unrelated to the creditworthiness of the borrower or the value of the real property. A lender can't refuse to lend money simply because the borrower wishes to purchase a home in a neighborhood where nearly all of the residents belong to a particular minority group, for example.

Under this law, financial institutions may not:

- discriminate in the provision of financial assistance to purchase, construct, rehabilitate, improve, or refinance housing on the basis of the characteristics of the neighborhood surrounding the property, unless the lender can demonstrate that such consideration is necessary to avoid an unsound business practice;
- consider the racial, ethnic, religious, or national origin composition of the neighborhood surrounding the property; or
- discriminate in the provision of financial assistance for housing on the basis of race, color, religion, sex, gender, gender identity, gender expression, sexual orientation, marital status, national origin, ancestry, familial status, source of income, disability, or genetic information.

Real Estate Law and Regulations

Both the California Real Estate Law and the Real Estate Commissioner's regulations prohibit discriminatory behavior by licensees. Licensees who engage in discriminatory behavior are subject to disciplinary action, and may have their licenses suspended or revoked. (See Chapter 16.)

Brokers have the duty to supervise their affiliated licensees and take reasonable steps to make sure they are familiar with the requirements of both federal and state laws prohibiting discrimination.

Discriminatory Restrictive Covenants

At one time in the United States it was common for a property's deed or a subdivision's CC&Rs to include a restrictive covenant prohibiting the sale or lease of the property to non-whites or non-Christians. These discriminatory restrictions were generally considered legal and enforceable until the Supreme Court decided the case of *Shelley v. Kraemer* in 1948. The court ruled that it was unconstitutional—a violation of the Fourteenth Amendment—for state or federal courts to be involved in the enforcement of racially restrictive covenants. As a result of the decision, those covenants became legally unenforceable.

Today, although discriminatory restrictive covenants still appear in some older documents, it's a violation of both federal and state laws to attempt to enforce them or comply with them. Under California law, restrictive covenants are illegal if they discriminate based on race, color, religion, sex, gender, gender identity, gender expression, sexual orientation, familial status, marital status, disability, genetic information, national origin, source of income, or ancestry.

State law imposes a requirement concerning illegal covenants on those who provide copies of recorded documents to others in the course of their work. This includes county recorders, title company employees, escrow agents, homeowners association representatives, and real estate agents. Whenever someone is given a copy of a previously recorded deed or declaration of restrictions that contains a discriminatory covenant, the person providing the copy must stamp the document or attach a cover page stating that the restriction is void and may be removed by recording a Restrictive Covenant Modification. Note that if an illegal restriction is included in a new deed, although the restriction is void and unenforceable, the conveyance is still valid.

Chapter Summary

1. Federal laws that prohibit discrimination in real estate transactions and related activities include the Civil Rights Act of 1866, the Civil Rights Act of 1964, the Fair Housing Act, the Equal Credit Opportunity Act, the Home Mortgage Disclosure Act, and the Americans with Disabilities Act.

2. The Civil Rights Act of 1866 prohibits discrimination based on race or color in all real estate transactions. The Civil Rights Act of 1964 prohibits discrimination based on race, color, religion, or national origin in some programs that receive financial assistance from the federal government.

3. The Fair Housing Act prohibits discrimination based on race, color, religion, sex, national origin, disability, or familial status throughout the United States. It applies only to transactions involving residential property, however.

4. Blockbusting, steering, and redlining are three discriminatory practices prohibited by the Fair Housing Act. Blockbusting is attempting to obtain listings or encourage sales by predicting the entry of minorities into the neighborhood and implying that this will cause a decline in the neighborhood. Steering is the channeling of buyers or renters to specific neighborhoods based on race or other protected characteristics. Redlining is the refusal to make loans on properties located in a particular area based on the racial or ethnic composition of the area.

5. The Fair Housing Act prohibits discrimination in residential lending activities. The Equal Credit Opportunity Act prohibits discrimination in credit transactions, including mortgage lending. The Home Mortgage Disclosure Act requires large lenders to submit reports that can be used to detect redlining.

6. The Americans with Disabilities Act guarantees people with physical or mental disabilities equal access to public accommodations. A disability is a physical or mental impairment that substantially limits one or more major life activities.

7. California state laws that prohibit discrimination in real estate transactions and related activities include the Unruh Civil Rights Act, the Fair Employment and Housing Act (the Rumford Act), the Housing Financial Discrimination Act (the Holden Act), and the Real Estate Law.

8. Discriminatory restrictive covenants in a deed or a subdivision's declaration of restrictions are illegal. A conveyance of property isn't invalidated by a discriminatory restriction, although the restriction is void.

Key Terms

Blockbusting—Attempting to induce homeowners to list or sell their homes by predicting that members of another racial or ethnic group, or people suffering from some disability, will be moving into the neighborhood. Also called panic selling.

Steering—Channeling prospective buyers or tenants toward or away from particular neighborhoods based on their race, religion, or national origin, in order to maintain or change the character of the neighborhoods.

Redlining—Refusing to make a loan because of the racial or ethnic composition of the neighborhood in which the security property is located.

Familial status—Refers to those who have children (under 18 years old) living with them. It also includes someone who is pregnant or is in the process of securing custody of a child.

Disability—A physical or mental impairment that substantially limits one or more major life activities. Also called a handicap.

Public accommodation—A private entity with nonresidential facilities open to the public, if operation of the facilities affects commerce.

Chapter Quiz

1. When a real estate agent channels prospective buyers away from a particular neighborhood because of their race, it's called:
   a) blockbusting
   b) steering
   c) redlining
   d) clipping

2. Rental of a room or a unit in an owner-occupied dwelling is exempt from the federal Fair Housing Act if the dwelling contains:
   a) two or more units
   b) three units or less
   c) less than five units
   d) six units or more

3. A real estate broker is helping the Jacksons sell their single-family home. Can this transaction be exempt from the federal Fair Housing Act?
   a) Yes, as long as the Jacksons own no more than three single-family homes
   b) Yes, as long as no discriminatory advertising is used
   c) No, because a real estate agent is involved
   d) No, the act applies to all residential sales transactions, without exception

4. The Gardenia Village condominium has a "No Kids" rule. This is not a violation of the federal Fair Housing Act:
   a) if the condo qualifies as "housing for older persons" under the terms of the law
   b) if no discriminatory advertising is used
   c) because the Fair Housing Act doesn't prohibit age discrimination
   d) because condominiums aren't covered by the Fair Housing Act

5. Title VIII of the Civil Rights Act of 1968 prohibits:
   a) discrimination in housing
   b) discrimination in residential lending
   c) Both a) and b)
   d) Neither a) nor b)

6. Blockbusting is an acceptable practice:
   a) only under the supervision of real estate licensees
   b) only when approved in advance by either HUD or the Justice Department
   c) only if the seller and the buyer mutually agree to it
   d) under no circumstances

7. A deed restriction created in 1920 that prohibits the sale of property to a non-white person until after 2020 is:
   a) valid until all the property owners agree to eliminate the restriction
   b) enforceable
   c) unenforceable
   d) covered by title insurance

8. The Home Mortgage Disclosure Act helps to enforce the prohibition against:
   a) redlining
   b) steering
   c) blockbusting
   d) flipping

9. To comply with the federal Fair Housing Act, a landlord is required to:
   a) permit a disabled tenant to make reasonable modifications to the property at the tenant's expense
   b) make reasonable exceptions to the landlord's rules to accommodate disabled tenants
   c) Both a) and b)
   d) Neither a) nor b)

10. Under California law, it would be permissible for a landlord to refuse to rent to a prospective tenant because the tenant:
    a) has a child
    b) is blind
    c) can't afford the rent
    d) All of the above

11. The Unruh Civil Rights Act prohibits discrimination by:
    a) lenders only
    b) real estate agents only
    c) all real estate related businesses
    d) any business entity

12. Which of the following is not covered by the federal Fair Housing Act?
    a) A commercial building leased to businesses that are open to the public
    b) An eight-unit multifamily dwelling
    c) A triplex listed for sale with a real estate broker
    d) A vacant lot intended for residential construction

13. A developer who intended to rent housing in a particular development only to persons 45 years of age or over would be in violation of the:
    a) Civil Rights Act of 1866
    b) Civil Rights Act of 1964
    c) Fair Housing Act
    d) Americans with Disabilities Act

14. Under the Americans with Disabilities Act:
    a) real estate firms are exempt
    b) real estate firms may discriminate against people with disabilities when taking listings, if appropriate
    c) real estate offices must be accessible to people with disabilities
    d) only individual real estate agents are prohibited from discriminating against people with disabilities

15. The California Housing Financial Discrimination Act prohibits:
    a) redlining
    b) steering
    c) blockbusting
    d) panic selling

Answer Key

1. b) Channeling prospective buyers or tenants away from (or toward) certain neighborhoods based on their race, religion, or national origin is called steering. It's a violation of the Fair Housing Act.

2. c) The Fair Housing Act exemption for rentals applies to owner-occupied dwellings with up to four units.

3. c) No residential transaction in which a real estate agent is employed is exempt from the Fair Housing Act.

4. a) The Fair Housing Act doesn't allow an apartment house or a condominium to discriminate on the basis of familial status unless the complex qualifies as "housing for older persons."

5. c) Title VIII of the 1968 Civil Rights Act (better known as the Fair Housing Act) prohibits discriminatory practices when selling, renting, advertising, or financing housing.

6. d) The discriminatory practice known as blockbusting is entirely prohibited by the Fair Housing Act.

7. c) A deed containing such a provision is valid, but the restriction is unenforceable.

8. a) The Home Mortgage Disclosure Act helps to enforce the prohibition against redlining by requiring large institutional lenders to file an annual report of all mortgage loans made during that year. Loans are categorized according to location, alerting investigators to areas of possible redlining.

9. c) The Fair Housing Act requires a residential landlord to allow a disabled tenant to make reasonable modifications to the property. The landlord must also make reasonable exceptions to the rules to accommodate a disabled tenant.

10. c) Rejecting a prospective tenant because he can't afford the rent is not a violation of anti-discrimination laws; rejecting him based on a disability or based on familial status is a violation.

11. d) The Unruh Civil Rights Act prohibits discriminatory activities by business entities.

12. a) The Fair Housing Act applies only to residential properties, not to commercial or industrial properties.

13. c) The developer's age limit would violate the Fair Housing Act. Housing for older persons is permitted, but 45 isn't the cutoff age.

14. c) Under the ADA, real estate firms must take reasonable steps to make their premises accessible to people with disabilities.

15. a) The Housing Financial Discrimination Act (also known as the Holden Act) prohibits redlining.

Chapter 15

Real Estate Construction, Ownership, and Investment

I. Construction
   A. Architectural styles
   B. Building codes and regulations
   C. Role of the architect
   D. Plans and specifications
   E. Wood frame construction
   F. Glossary of construction terms
II. To Rent or to Buy?
   A. Advantages of renting
   B. Advantages of buying
   C. Buying vs. renting
III. Factors to Consider When Choosing a Home
IV. Investing in Real Estate
   A. Types of investments
   B. Investment characteristics
   C. Advantages of investing in real estate
   D. Disadvantages of investing in real estate
   E. Choices when investing in real estate

Chapter Overview

In bringing a buyer and a seller together, a real estate agent must be a "jack of all trades." Not only must the agent be familiar with property values, contracts, and financing, she must also be familiar with the rudiments of residential construction, the advantages of buying a home, the elements to look for in a home, and the benefits of investing in real estate. This chapter briefly describes some aspects of residential construction, focusing on wood frame construction. Then the chapter goes on to discuss the relative merits of renting or buying a home, and the factors to consider when choosing a home—either as a residence or as an investment. The final section of the chapter is an introduction to real estate investment.

Construction

Real estate agents aren't home inspectors or architects, and they shouldn't give clients or customers the impression that they're experts in residential construction. However, California law does impose a duty on all licensees to visually inspect the homes they sell. Furthermore, most home buyers rely on their real estate agent for some advice on the structural quality of particular homes. So agents must be able to evaluate the basic soundness of a home's construction.

An agent's preliminary evaluation should be supplemented, whenever appropriate, with the opinions of professional inspectors. This is especially true with respect to structural integrity and the safety and suitability of the plumbing and electrical components of the building.

In order to evaluate the basic soundness of a home, a real estate agent should be familiar with the following aspects of residential construction:

- architectural styles,
- local building codes and regulations,
- the role of the architect,
- plans and specifications, and
- construction methods and terminology.

Architectural Styles

Homes come in a variety of architectural styles. The quality of a home's construction isn't determined by its style (although the style may affect the cost of constructing the home). No one style is inherently more desirable than another. The value of each particular style depends on the personal preference of the home buyer.

Several common architectural styles are illustrated in Figure 15.1. Of course, many homes have their own unique style, or are combinations of two or more styles. Split-level, Spanish, California ranch, and modern (sometimes called contemporary) are popular architectural styles in California.

Split-level homes have visually attractive designs and make effective use of hilly terrains. Spanish-style homes are one- or two-story homes with white or pastel stucco exteriors and red tile roofs; they look cool and comfortable in southern California's heat. Modern-style homes usually incorporate large windows and glass doors, and are

Fig. 15.1 Architectural styles

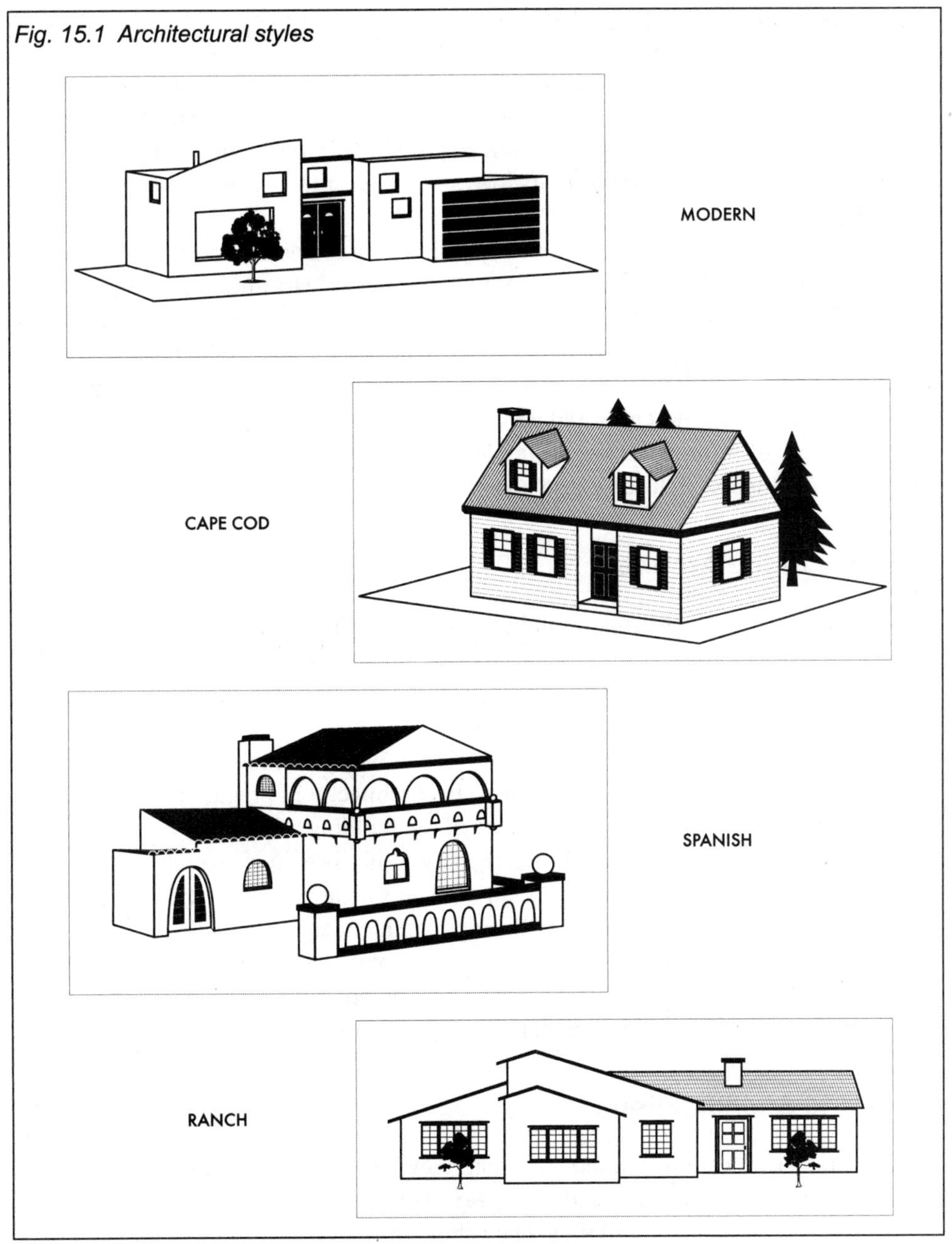

designed with an open interior. Because of the flexibility of modern home designs, they are well suited for building on hillsides or other difficult sites. California ranch homes have one story and low-pitched or flat roofs. The exterior may be wood, masonry, or stucco.

A one-story ranch home is the simplest to construct and maintain. However, it requires more land in relation to living space than a two-story or split-level home. Thus, a one-story home may be uneconomical where land is at a premium. Split-level construction is more expensive, but it's popular because it effectively utilizes land with varying topography. Two-story construction is the most economical per square foot of living space, since twice as much living space is provided with one foundation, one roof, and the same amount of land. The inconvenience of stairs and exterior maintenance on the upper story are the primary drawbacks of two-story homes.

Building Codes and Regulations

Local building codes prescribe the types of materials that must be used in residential construction, the acceptable methods of construction, and the number and placement of such items as electrical outlets, plumbing fixtures, and windows. The size and placement of a building on its lot are also governed by building codes and other local regulations.

Building codes promote some degree of uniformity in construction. Their construction guidelines also help ensure that homes meet at least minimum standards of quality. This is especially important in regard to safety issues. For example, a home's ability to resist fire or earthquake damage is of vital importance to both the homeowner and the surrounding community. (See Chapter 5 for a discussion of a local government's authority to enact and enforce building codes.)

Key sources of information regarding local regulations are local planning and building departments, architects, and construction contractors.

The Role of the Architect

The architect is the construction industry professional that a real estate agent is most likely to meet. Most people think of an architect as a person who designs buildings, but a good architect will also provide a range of other services throughout the construction process.

Under a standard contract, an architect will first work with the owner to develop a design that fulfills the owner's needs. Next, the architect will prepare more detailed drawings, describing all of the components of the building, along with an estimate of the probable cost of construction. When the design has been approved by the owner, the architect will draw up the official plans and specifications and will help the owner get bids from contractors and permits from government agencies.

Finally, the architect acts as the owner's representative throughout the actual construction phase, visiting the site to inspect the work, approving periodic payments to the contractor, and interpreting the plans and specifications.

Plans and Specifications

Plans and specifications are the technical drawings and text that explain in detail how a building is to be constructed. The **plans** are drawings of the vertical and horizontal cross-sections of the building. They show the placement of foundations, floors, walls, roofs, doors, windows, fixtures, and wiring. The **specifications** are the text that accompanies the plans, prescribing the type of materials to be used and the required quality of workmanship. Plans and specifications are usually prepared by an architect and take the form of blueprints.

Wood Frame Construction

The most common type of home construction is the wood frame building. It's popular because of its low cost, ease and speed of construction, and flexibility of design. One-story, two-story, and split-level homes can all be wood frame homes.

Because wood frame buildings are so common, this is the type of construction we will focus on here. The construction of a wood frame building is illustrated in the following diagrams, and a glossary of construction terms is provided for use in conjunction with these diagrams.

Elements of Wood Frame Construction. It's easier to judge the quality of a home with some knowledge of the elements of construction. The materials required for each element are usually specified by local building codes. The following are the basic elements of residential wood frame construction.

Foundation. Virtually all modern building foundations are made with reinforced concrete. Concrete has the advantages of low cost, plasticity, and high compressive strength. When concrete is reinforced by steel bars or mesh, it also has good tensile strength (resistance to bending or cracking).

The wider part of the base of a foundation wall is called a footing. It supports the weight of the structure. A sill plate is a board that's attached to the top of the concrete foundation. The framing of the house rests on the sill plate.

Framing. The framing is usually constructed of dimensional lumber, although the use of metal framing is becoming more common in some areas. Lumber is classified as either "green" or "dry," depending on its moisture content. Dry lumber is considered superior to green lumber for framing because it's less prone to warpage—the deformity in shape caused by uneven shrinking.

The size and length of framing members varies, depending upon their particular application as girders, joists, studs, rafters, and so on. The parallel boards used to support the load of the floor and ceiling are called joists. Vertical members called studs are attached to the sole plate, which is a horizontal board that rests on the floor joists. (See Figure 15.2.)

Walls serve two purposes. They provide structural support and they separate the interior space into individual rooms. The walls that provide support are called load-bearing walls. Load-bearing walls support a vertical load, such as a second floor or the roof. (See Figure 15.4.) Load-bearing walls are usually built to be stronger than non-load bearing walls, and they are rarely moved during remodeling.

Exterior Sheathing and Siding. Exterior sheathing is the covering applied to the outside of the frame. The most common form of exterior sheathing is plywood panels that are four feet wide by eight feet long. Plywood serves an additional function by adding shear strength to the walls. Shear strength is the capacity of a wall to resist a sideways racking force, and it's normally provided by corner bracing in the frame.

Exterior siding is the visible finish layer applied to the outside of the building. It may be plywood, boards, vinyl siding, shingles, or other materials. The

Fig. 15.2 Foundation and framing

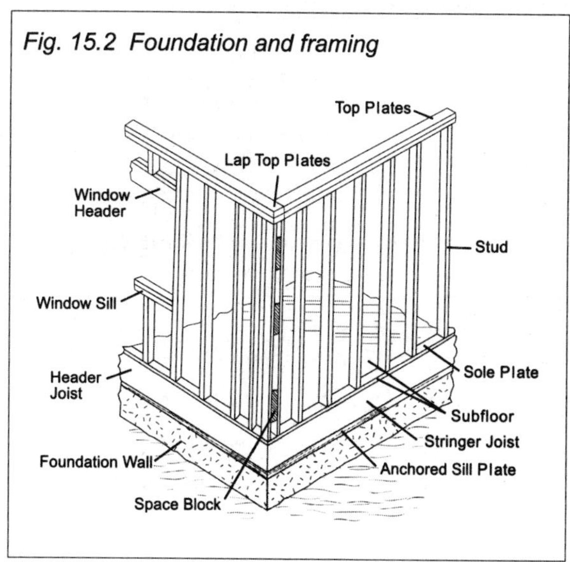

Fig. 15.3 Residential construction details

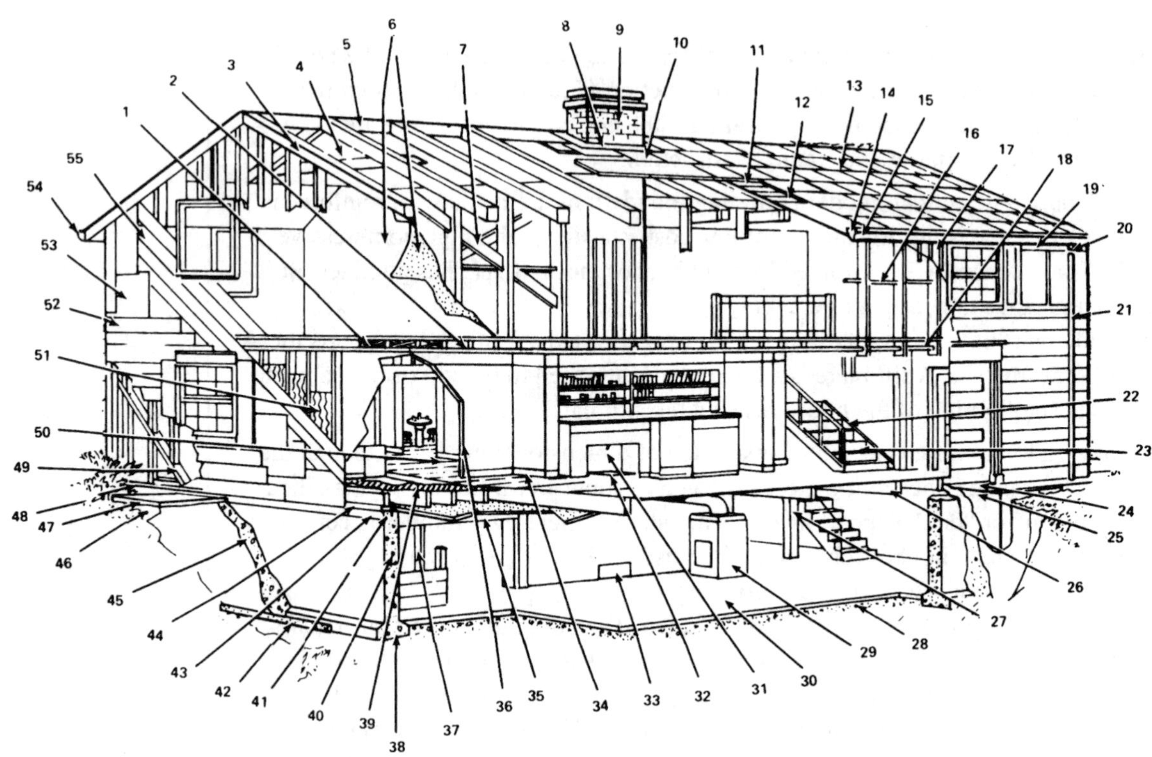

CONSTRUCTION DETAILS

1. CROSS BRIDGING
2. SECOND FLOOR JOISTS
3. ROOF RAFTERS
4. COLLAR BEAM
5. RIDGE BOARD
6. PLASTER BASE,LATH AND PLASTER WALLS
7. CROSS BRACING
8. FLASHING AND COUNTER FLASHING
9. BRICK CHIMNEY
10. TIGHT ROOF SHEATHING (ALL OTHER COVERINGS)
11. SPACED 1" x 4" SHEATHING (WOOD SHINGLES)
12. ROOFING FELT
13. FINISH ROOFING (SHINGLE)
14. SOFFIT OR CORNICE
15. FACIA OF CORNICE
16. FIRE STOPS
17. VERTICAL BOARD AND BATTEN SIDING
18. RIBBON PLATE
19. FACIA BOARD
20. LEADER HEAD OR CONDUCTOR HEAD
21. LEADER, DOWNSPOUT OR CONDUCTOR
22. STAIR STRINGER
23. MAIN STAIR TREADS AND RISERS
24. ENTRANCE DOOR SILL
25. CONCRETE STOOP
26. FIRST FLOOR JOISTS
27. BASEMENT POST
28. CINDERFILL
29. BOILER OR FURNACE
30. BASEMENT CONCRETE FLOOR
31. DAMPER CONTROL
32. ASH DUMP
33. CLEANOUT DOOR
34. BASEBOARDS
35. GIRDER
36. FRAME PARTITION
37. POST
38. FOOTING
39. SUB-FLOORING, DIAGONAL
40. FOUNDATION WALL
41. PLATE ANCHOR BOLT
42. DRAIN TILE
43. TERMITE SHIELD
44. SILL PLATE
45. GRAVEL FILL
46. GRADE LINE
47. BASEMENT AREAWAY
48. SOLE PLATE
49. CORNER BRACING
50. FINISH FLOOR
51. INSULATION, BATTS
52. WALL SIDING
53. WALL BUILDING PAPER
54. GUTTER
55. WALL SHEATHING, DIAGONAL

Fig. 15.4 Methods of roof framing

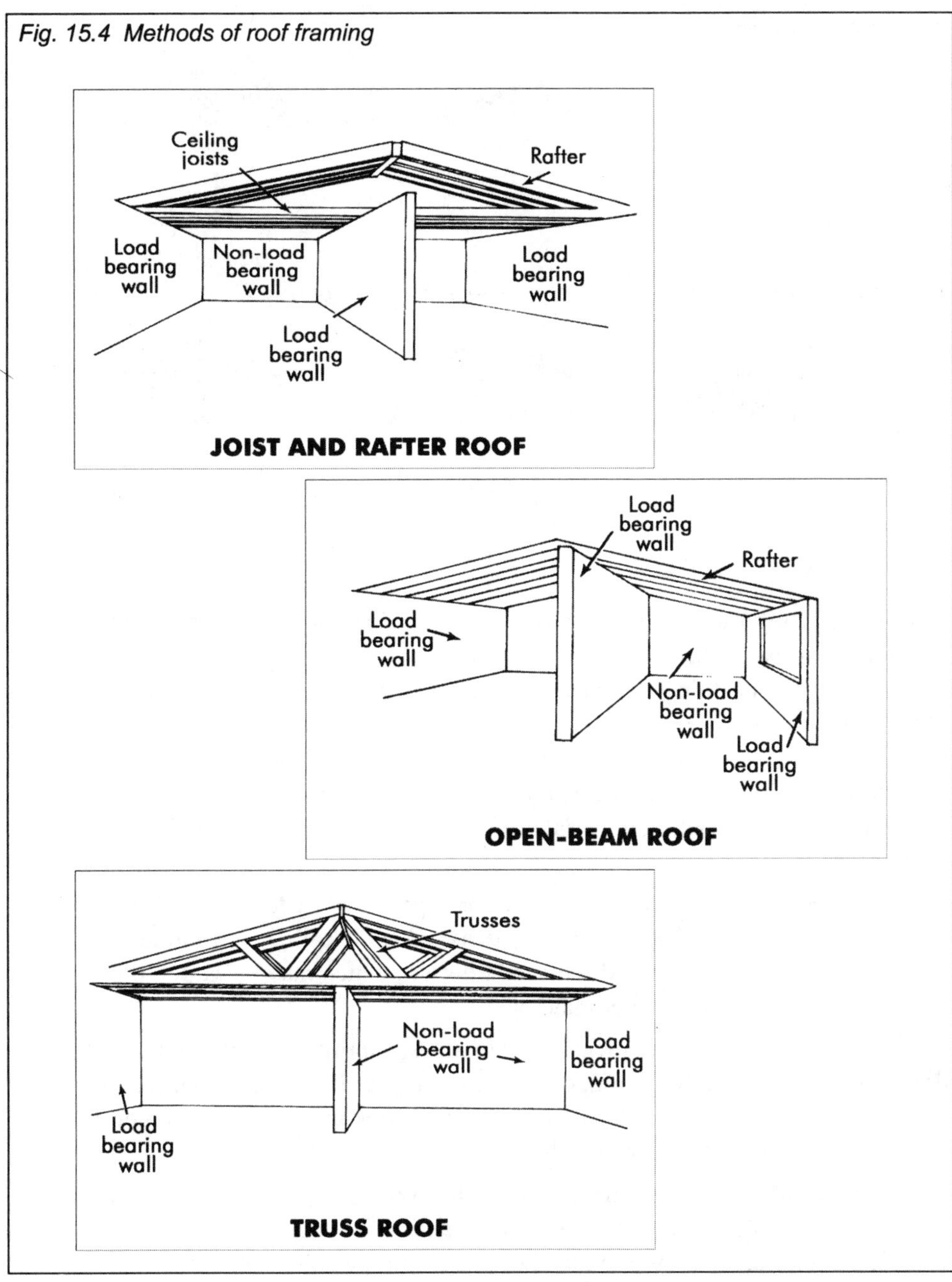

two most important characteristics of siding are its resistance to weathering and its aesthetic appeal.

Interior Sheathing. This is the covering applied to the inside of the frame, on the walls and ceilings. In the past, the most common form of sheathing was lath and plaster, a cement-like mixture applied over a matrix of wood strips attached to the frame. Modern buildings use drywall construction for interior sheathing. The term "drywall" is used because there's no need to add water to the material before application. Drywall products usually come in large sheets (like plywood) and are fastened to the frame with glue, nails, or screws. Sheetrock and wallboard are two common drywall products. The joints between panels are hidden by covering them with a strip of tape embedded in a plaster-like filler. This process is called "taping" the joints.

Fig. 15.5 Roof styles

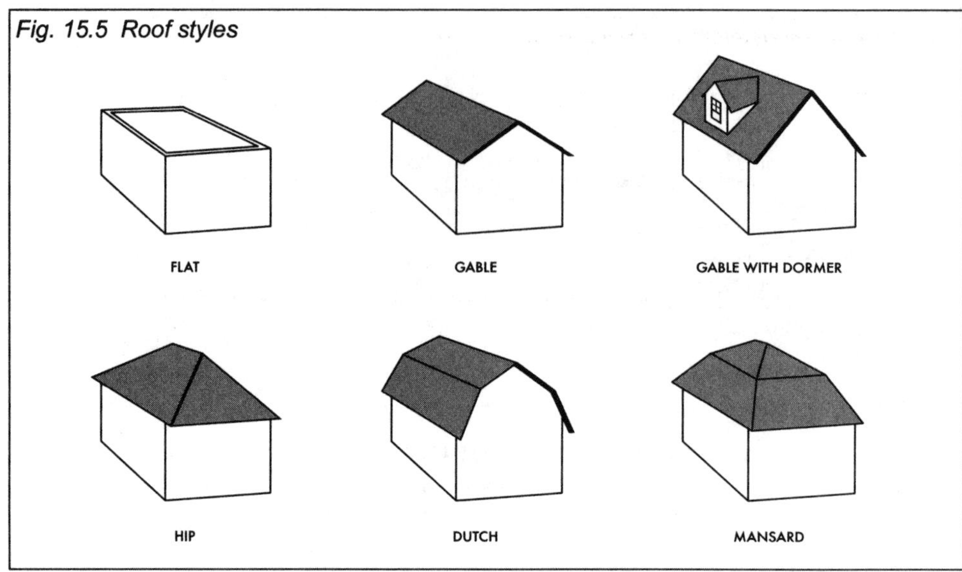

Roofing. The structural part of the roof is composed of the ridge board (the highest structural member of the house), rafters, and plywood or boards laid perpendicular to the rafters. This sheathing is then covered with a tar-impregnated paper called roofing felt. The final layer of roofing may be wood shingles, tiles, or composition roofing (tar-like shingles or rolls of material). Sometimes hot tar is simply interspersed with more layers of felt; this is called a "built-up" roof. Flashing (metal sheeting) is installed on top of the roofing material around chimneys and other openings to prevent water seepage.

Floor Covering. The strength of the floor is provided by tongue-and-groove floor boards or plywood attached to the floor joists, which is called the subflooring. The subflooring is then covered with finished flooring, which may be carpet, tile, linoleum, hardwood strips, or other material.

Plumbing. The plumbing includes drain pipes, supply pipes, and fixtures. The drain pipes are made of cast iron, concrete, or plastic. The supply pipes are made of galvanized steel, copper, or plastic. Plumbing fixtures are either cast iron or pressed steel that's coated with enamel or fiberglass.

Electrical. Most modern wiring is in the form of cable, which is an insulated cord-like material containing two or more strands of copper or aluminum wire. The electrical cables are enclosed in metal or plastic piping called conduit.

The electrical cables run in circuits from a supply source (a fuse box or, more commonly, a breaker panel) to the various outlets for plugs or light fixtures. A breaker panel is a series of circuit breakers that automatically shut off the current in a circuit under overload conditions. Most outlets supply 110 volts of power, except for certain outlets designed for major appliances (ranges, water heaters, dryers, etc.), which supply 220 volts.

Heating, Ventilating, and Air Conditioning (HVAC). These systems are composed of heating and/or cooling appliances that serve warm, cool, or fresh air to the rooms of a house through a series of galvanized sheet metal tubes called ducts. The ducts open at various places in the building called registers. The registers may be closed off independently in order to direct the heat or air conditioning to areas where it's needed.

Fig. 15.6 Construction terms

Glossary of Construction Terms

Anchor bolts—Bolts embedded in concrete, used to hold structural members in place.

Areaway—An open space around a basement window or doorway that provides light, ventilation, and access.

Beam—A principal structural member used between posts, columns, or walls.

Bearing wall or partition—A wall or partition that supports a vertical load in addition to its own weight.

Board—Lumber that is less than two inches thick.

Board foot—A unit of measurement for lumber; one foot square and one inch thick.

Bridging—Pieces fitted in pairs from the bottom of one floor joist to the top of adjacent joists, and crossed to distribute the floor load.

BTU—British Thermal Unit; a measure of heating capacity.

Built-up roof—A roof composed of several layers of rag felt, saturated with pitch or asphalt.

Cased opening—An interior opening without a door that is finished with jambs and trim.

Caulk—To seal cracks and joints to make them waterproof.

Collar beam—A beam connecting rafters at a point considerably above the wall plate.

Column—An upright supporting member, circular or rectangular in shape.

Conduit—A pipe or tube, usually metal, in which wiring is installed.

Corner braces—Diagonal braces set into studs to reinforce corners of frame structures.

Counterflashing—Flashing used on chimneys at the roof line to cover shingle flashing and prevent the entry of moisture.

Crawlspace—A space between the ground and the floor joists that is used for access.

Dimensional lumber—Lumber that is two to five inches thick and up to twelve inches wide.

Dormer—A projecting structure built out from a sloping roof.

Drywall—Materials used for wall covering that don't need to be mixed with water before application (e.g., sheetrock).

Eaves—The margin or lower part of a roof that projects over an exterior wall.

Fascia—A wooden member nailed to the ends of projecting rafters.

Fire stop—A block or stop used in a wall between studs to prevent the spread of fire and smoke.

Flashing—Sheet metal or other material used in roof and wall construction to prevent rain or other water from entering.

Flue—The space in a chimney through which smoke, gas, or fumes rise.

Footing—The spreading course at the base of a foundation wall, pier, or column.

Framing—The timber structure of a building that gives it shape and strength. It includes the wall, floors, ceilings, and roof.

Gable—That portion of a wall contained between the slopes of a roof.

Glazing—The process of installing glass into sashes and doors.

Gutter—A wooden or metal trough attached to the edge of a roof to collect and conduct water from rain and melting snow.

(Continued on next page)

Header—A horizontal structural member that supports the load over an opening, such as a window or door.

Hip roof—A roof that rises from all four sides of the building.

Interior trim—A general term for all the molding, casing, baseboards, and other trim items applied inside the building.

Insulation—Any material highly resistant to heat transmission that is used to reduce the rate of heat flow.

Jamb—The top and two sides of a door or window frame that contact the door or sash.

Joist—One of a series of parallel framing members used to support floor and ceiling loads.

Lath—Material fastened to the frame of a building to act as a base for plaster.

Molding—A narrow strip of wood used to conceal surface or angle joints, or as an ornamentation.

Partition—An interior wall that subdivides space within a building.

Pier—A column of masonry used to support other structural members.

Pilaster—A part of a wall that projects not more than one-half of its own width beyond the outside or inside face of a wall.

Pitch—Inclination or slope.

Plan—A drawing representing any one of the cross-sections of a building.

Plaster—A mixture of lime, cement, and sand used to cover inside or outside wall surfaces.

Plate—The horizontal member of a wall frame to which the studs are attached.

Rafter—One of a series of structural members of a roof.

Reinforced concrete—Concrete poured around steel bars or steel meshwork, in such a manner that the two materials act together to resist force.

Riser—The vertical stair member between two consecutive stair treads.

R-value—A measure of resistance to heat transfer.

Sheathing—Structural covering; boards or prefabricated panels that are attached to the exterior studding or rafters.

Siding—The finish covering of the outside walls of a frame building.

Sill—The lowest member of the frame of a structure, usually horizontal, resting on the foundation. Also, the lower member of a window or exterior door frame.

Specifications—A written document stipulating the quality of materials and workmanship required for a job.

Stud—One of a series of vertical wood or metal structural members in walls and partitions. In most modern frame buildings, the studs are set 16 inches apart.

Subfloor—Boards or panels laid directly on floor joists, over which a finished floor will be laid.

Timber—A piece of lumber five inches or larger in its least dimension.

Trim—The finish materials in a building (moldings, etc.).

Trimmer—The stud into which a header is framed; it adds strength to the side of the opening.

Truss—A structural unit, usually triangular in shape, which provides rigid support over wide spans.

Weephole—A small hole in the foundation wall to drain water to the outside.

HVAC systems sometimes have an energy-efficient ratio (EER) rating. The higher the EER, the more efficient the system.

Insulation is used to make HVAC systems less costly to run. Insulation is material that's resistant to the transfer of heat. It comes in batts or rolls, or in loose form, and it's inserted between wall studs and between the joists of floors and ceilings. Insulation also comes in sheets that can be secured to the sheathing of the structure. The effectiveness of insulating materials is gauged by an "R-value." The higher the R-value, the more resistant the material is to the transfer of heat, and the better it is for insulation purposes. Local building codes require insulation with a minimum R-value to be used in all new construction. When insulation is adequate, the inside surface of an exterior wall will be about the same temperature as the surface of an interior wall.

Structural Pest Problems. One major problem with wood frame buildings is their susceptibility to damage by wood-eating insects, especially termites. Several techniques are used to minimize the possibility of termite damage:

- the ground under and around the building may be treated with a chemical that keeps termites away from the foundation;
- lumber that's in contact with the soil or the foundation, such as sills or beams, may be treated with a chemical to prevent termites from gaining access to the frame of the building; and
- metal shields may be inserted between the foundation and the superstructure to physically prevent termites from reaching the wood.

When a home is for sale, it's generally a good idea to have it examined by a licensed structural pest control inspector. The inspector will provide a report on the structural soundness of the building, listing defects caused by wood-destroying insects, other pests, moisture, or fungus. In termite-prone areas (including many parts of California), a pest control report is required in any transaction financed with an FHA or VA loan. In fact, California lenders generally require a pest control report no matter what type of financing is involved. It makes sense for a home seller to order a pest control inspection when the property is first listed, before setting the listing price.

After performing a pest control inspection, the inspector must provide a written report within ten business days to the property owner and to the party who ordered the inspection. If the property is being sold, the seller must give a copy of the report to the buyer as soon as it's practical to do so and before closing. Unless the parties agree otherwise, the seller is expected to pay for having existing pest problems corrected, but not for work to prevent infestation. The buyer pays for preventive work.

Within ten days of completing an inspection, the pest control inspector must file the address of the inspected property with the state Structural Pest Control Board. If a home was inspected within the previous two years, anyone can obtain a copy of the report by submitting a request to the board.

To Rent or to Buy?

Real estate agents are often asked to discuss the relative advantages and disadvantages of renting versus buying a place to live. Some considerations are primarily emotional, such as security, pride of ownership, and the freedom to have pets or to remodel according to personal preference. These types of considerations can't be evaluated objectively by a third party; their importance can be measured only by the prospective home buyer. However, other elements of comparison are largely financial, and a real estate agent can help a prospective home buyer evaluate these elements objectively.

Advantages of Renting

The advantages of renting over buying can be briefly summarized. In comparison to buying, renting:

- requires less financial commitment and risk,
- gives a person greater mobility, and
- carries with it fewer responsibilities.

Financial Commitment. Compared to the funds necessary to buy a home, the initial cash outlay to rent a home or apartment is quite modest. In most cases, a security deposit and one or two months of prepaid rent is sufficient. Even with low-downpayment financing, the cash required to purchase a home (the amount of the downpayment, loan fees, and closing costs) normally far exceeds the cost of moving into an apartment or a rental home. Furthermore, at least for the first few years, the monthly rental payment is likely to be substantially less than a monthly mortgage payment.

Financial Risk. Renters have little financial investment in their rented premises and the neighborhood in which they live. Therefore, there's little financial risk in renting. If the property values in a neighborhood decline and the neighborhood becomes run down or otherwise undesirable, renters can simply give the required notice—or wait until the lease expires—and move away. A homeowner in the same neighborhood runs the risk of losing some or all of his investment in the property.

Mobility. It's faster, easier, and cheaper for a renter to move than for a homeowner to move. A renter can move after giving the required notice or waiting until the lease expires. Even if a renter has to leave abruptly, any deposit or rent (prepaid or owed under the terms of the lease) that may be forfeited is likely to be less than the cost of selling one home and buying another. Selling a home can be a long and expensive process, typically taking at least a few months (often much longer in a slow market) and costing about 10% of the home's value.

Maintenance and Repairs. An owner is responsible for maintaining the property and making any needed repairs. For a renter, the cost of maintenance and repairs is generally included in the rent. The renter usually has no direct responsibility for doing maintenance work and making repairs. Also, a renter doesn't face the burden of sudden large expenditures for unexpected repairs.

Amenities. Renters often enjoy the use of recreational facilities, such as swimming pools and tennis courts, that are beyond the financial reach of most homeowners.

Advantages of Buying

For many people, buying instead of renting affords both the subjective advantages of security and personal satisfaction and the financial advantages of equity appreciation and tax deductions.

Security. A homeowner enjoys a certain amount of security in knowing that he can continue to live in the home as long as the mortgage payments are made. A renter has no real security beyond the term of the lease. When the lease expires, the renter may have to find another place to live. A month-to-month tenant has even less security.

Privacy and Freedom from Restrictions. In most cases, a homeowner enjoys greater privacy than a renter and has greater freedom to use the property. An owner can redecorate or remodel the home to suit her own taste, and can keep pets or engage in other activities that are prohibited by many rental agreements.

Monthly Payments. A homeowner's monthly mortgage payment usually starts out higher than the rental payment for equivalent lodging. However, over time, rents tend to rise at a faster rate than mortgage payments. This is especially true if the mortgage has a fixed interest rate. In that case, the monthly payment increases only as the property tax and insurance portions of it increase, which usually happens quite slowly. If the mortgage has an adjustable interest rate, the payment amount may increase rapidly if interest rates rise, but it will decrease if interest rates go down. Thus, a monthly rental payment may eventually be larger than a monthly mortgage payment.

Investment Appreciation. It's impossible to predict whether or how much a particular home will appreciate in value. As a result of adverse economic conditions, neighborhood decline, or poor maintenance, it may depreciate instead. Historically, however, average home values have outpaced the average inflation rate. When a home appreciates, the homeowner typically enjoys an increase in home equity, and thus an increase in net worth. For a renter, in contrast, the appreciation of property values is likely to mean a rent increase.

Tax Advantages. For the homeowner, federal income tax laws allow tax deductions for property taxes and for mortgage interest. The interest paid on a loan secured by a personal residence is the only type of consumer interest that's eligible for deduction from federal income taxes. Also, at least part of the gain realized on the sale of most principal residences is never taxed at all. An equivalent tax benefit isn't available to someone who rents her principal residence. (See Chapter 13 for a more complete discussion of income taxes and real estate ownership.)

Comparison of Renting and Buying

Real estate agents sometimes use worksheets to compare the net costs of renting and buying for prospective customers. The comparison worksheets demonstrate how the overall cost of buying a home may be less than the cost of renting, at least in the long run. Worksheet forms take into account not only the monthly mortgage or rental payments, but also the homeowner's increases in equity and the benefit of income tax deductions.

A simplified example of a comparison worksheet is shown in Figure 15.7. This worksheet has been filled in with data for a proposed purchase of a $500,000 home, with the buyer making a 10% downpayment and obtaining a $450,000 loan at a fixed annual interest rate of 6%. Closing costs bring the total cash requirement for the purchase up to $63,000. Taxes, homeowner's insurance, the annual appreciation rate for local property values, and the buyer's income tax bracket have all been estimated. The total estimated monthly payment, including principal and interest, property taxes, homeowner's insurance, and the monthly renewal premium for private mortgage insurance, is approximately $3,406.

Fig. 15.7 Comparison of renting and buying

Comparison of Estimated Net Cost of Renting and Buying

Buying

Purchase price		$500,000
Cash required (downpayment and closing costs)		$63,000
Loan amount		$450,000
Loan term		30 years
Interest rate		6%
Property taxes		$4,740
Homeowner's insurance premium		$1,500
Property appreciation rate (estimated)		2%
Income tax bracket		28%
Out-of-pocket costs:		
Monthly payment		
Principal and interest		$2,698
Property taxes		395
Homeowner's insurance		125
Other monthly expenses (PMI)		+ 188
Total monthly payment		$3,406
less:		
Average monthly principal amortization		– 1,250
Tax benefit		
Average interest portion of payment	1,448	
Property tax portion of payment	395	
Other	+ 0	
Total deductible items	$1,843	
Monthly value of tax deduction		– 516
Effective monthly cost of ownership		$1,640
less:		
Average monthly appreciation		– 833
Monthly Net Cost of Buying		**$807**

Renting

Out-of-pocket costs:	
Monthly rent	$2,000
less:	
Monthly interest from savings not used for purchase ($63,000 @ 4%)	– 210
Monthly Net Cost of Renting	**$1,790**

The monthly cost of buying the home on these terms is compared with the cost of renting comparable housing at a monthly rent of $2,000. At first glance, a comparison of the monthly mortgage payment of $3,406 to the monthly rental payment of $2,000 would seem to give the advantage to renting, especially considering the substantial amount of cash required for the purchase—cash that could otherwise be earning interest. However, the worksheet takes into account the economic benefits of home ownership, resulting in a lower net cost for the home purchase.

To begin with, part of the monthly mortgage payment goes to amortize the loan. These payments to principal are typically recovered when the home is sold. For a $450,000 loan with a 30-year term, the average monthly amortization would be $1,250 ($450,000 ÷ 360 months = $1,250). Of course, in the early years of the loan term a much smaller portion of each payment would go to principal, and in the later years a larger portion of the monthly payment would go to principal.

Next, some portions of the payment—the interest and the property taxes—are tax deductible. In this case, the average monthly interest is $1,448 (again, in the early years a larger portion would go to interest, and in the later years a smaller portion would go to interest), and the monthly property tax payment is $395, for a total of $1,843 in tax-deductible items. If the buyer is in the 28% income tax bracket, that would represent a tax savings of about $516 per month ($1,843 × .28 = $516).

Finally, the home may appreciate in value and give the purchaser a return on his investment as well as a place to live. Even at the modest rate of appreciation used in this example, 2% per year, the appreciation return is substantial. On $500,000, it would be $10,000 per year, or about $833 per month.

After taking into account all of the economic benefits of buying, the net effective cost of buying is only $807 per month.

The monthly rental is $2,000, with no federal income tax deductions and no benefits to the renter if the property appreciates in value. The renter would be able to obtain some interest or other investment yield on the $63,000 not used for a downpayment and closing costs. In this example, a yield of 4% is used, giving the renter a monthly benefit of $210 and a net effective cost of renting of $1,790 per month.

It should be emphasized that this example is based on estimates and assumptions that are subject to debate and also subject to change. A change in interest rates, property tax rates, or the tax law would significantly alter the income tax benefits of buying. Also, the average monthly principal and interest portions would be different for a buyer who intended to own the home for less than the full 30-year amortization term. And a change in the rate of appreciation would have a great impact on the final net cost of home ownership. Even so, this type of comparison worksheet can help potential buyers understand the benefits of home ownership that can offset what first appears to be the much higher cost of buying a home.

Factors to Consider When Choosing a Home

When a real estate agent shows a home to a buyer, both the buyer and the seller often rely on the agent to point out the positive features of that home. So it's important that real estate agents understand what considerations are important to most home buyers. These features have an impact on both the property's subjective attractiveness to a home buyer and the property's objective value as estimated by an appraiser. (Appraisal is discussed in Chapter 11.)

Neighborhood Considerations

Since the surrounding neighborhood greatly influences the overall desirability of a home and also has a great impact on value, careful consideration should be given to neighborhood characteristics.

Percentage of Ownership. Are most of the homes owner-occupied, or is there a large percentage of rental properties? Neighborhoods that are predominantly owner-occupied are generally better maintained, less susceptible to loss in value, and more likely to appreciate in value.

Conformity. Values are protected if there's a reasonable degree of homogeneity in the neighborhood. This includes homogeneity of styles, ages, prices, sizes, and quality of structures.

Changing Land Use. Does the neighborhood land use appear stable, or are there indications of a transition from residential to some other type of land use?

Street and Sidewalks. Do the neighborhood streets have good access to traffic arterials? If a property doesn't front on a publicly dedicated and maintained street, the buyer should ask whether there's an enforceable road maintenance agreement signed by the property owners.

What is the condition of the driveway, street, and sidewalks? Are there street lights and fire hydrants on the block? Are there sanitary and/or storm sewers? If so, have they already been paid for, or is there a special assessment against the properties in the neighborhood?

Availability of Utilities and Public Services. Are all of the basic utilities available, including water, sewer, electricity, gas, and telephone service? Is there cable television, high-speed internet service, and good cell phone reception? Are the utility lines above ground, or is there underground wiring? Is the neighborhood adequately served by public transportation, police, and fire protection?

School District. In what primary and secondary school districts is the neighborhood located? How far away are the schools? Are they within walking distance? The quality of the local schools or school district can make a major difference in value and can be an extremely important basis for decision for many buyers with school-age children.

Social Services. Are there places of worship, hospitals or health care facilities, and other social services nearby?

Overall Neighborhood Values. Does it appear that the overall condition of homes in the neighborhood and the property values are stable, improving, or declining?

The Home

Of course, the home itself—its size, condition, and amenities—should be reviewed with a prospective buyer. Our discussion focuses on a single-family home, but most of these considerations apply to other types of housing as well.

Site/View. First, the agent should look at the lot on which the house is located. What is the size and shape of the lot? Rectangular lots are usually more desirable than odd or irregularly shaped parcels. Is the lot on the corner? Is it level, gently sloping, or steep? Unusually steep lots present a danger of soil instability. Does it appear that water runoff and drainage are good? What is the quality and extent of the landscaping? If the home is new, has any landscaping (such as the lawn, shrubbery, and trees) already been done, or will the buyer have to do it all? The cost of new landscaping can be quite a bit more than many home buyers realize.

Is there a view? In many areas, a view can add greatly to a property's appeal and increase its value substantially.

Exterior Appearance. How old is the house, and when was it last painted? What is the age and condition of the roof and flashing, gutters, downspouts, siding, windows, doors, and weatherstripping? Thin or curled shingles, cracked, blistered, or peeling paint, and rusted or sagging gutters and downspouts are indications that costly repairs may soon be needed. Does the foundation appear to be in good shape, or are there cracks or other evidence of settling? If there's no basement, are the vents and crawlspace adequate?

Plumbing and Electrical Systems. If it isn't a new home, what is the age of the plumbing and electrical systems? Is the plumbing copper, plastic, or some combination of materials? Is the water pressure adequate? Do the electrical service panel and existing outlets indicate that there's sufficient electrical service to the home? Do the electrical and plumbing systems, or as much of them as can be seen, appear to be in good condition?

Heating, Ventilating, and Air Conditioning. What type of heating system does the home have: electric, gas, or oil; forced air, floor furnaces, baseboard heaters? What is the type and size of the water heater? If there's air conditioning, is it a central system or window units? If it isn't a new home, what is the age and apparent condition of the heating, hot water, and air conditioning systems? Is the present owner aware of any problems, inadequacies, or defects?

Garage/Carport. Generally, a garage is better than a carport. What is the size of the garage or carport—single, double, or triple? Is there work or storage space in addition to space for parking? Is there an entrance, protected from the weather, directly from the garage or carport into the home?

Attic/Basement. Is there an attic or a basement? If so, what type of access is there from the rest of the home? Is there room for storage or work space? Would it be possible to convert all or part of the basement into additional bedrooms or living area?

Energy-Efficient Features. Escalating energy costs and environmental concerns have created an increased demand for energy-efficient homes. Examples of energy-efficient features include clock-controlled thermostats, insulation-wrapped water heaters, insulated ducts and pipes in unheated areas, adequate insulation for floors, walls, and attic, and weatherstripping for doors and windows. In some areas, solar energy equipment is popular.

Overall Interior Design. A real estate agent should know some of the features of a well-designed, efficient floor plan. For instance, it shouldn't be necessary to pass through the living room to reach other rooms, or to go through one of the bedrooms to reach another.

Other design considerations include the number and the size of bedrooms, closets, and bathrooms: are there enough of them, and are they large enough, considering the square footage of the home? Is there a separate dining room, or is the dining area part of the kitchen or living room? Is there sufficient work space in the kitchen and laundry room, and is there storage space for cleaning and gardening tools? Are there enough windows and natural light, especially in the kitchen and other work or recreational spaces?

Considerations for Particular Rooms. Certain features are important for the comfort and efficient use of particular rooms.

- **Living Room/Family Room.** How large are the living room and the family room (if there is one)? Is the shape of each room and the available wall space adequate for the furniture that will be placed in it?
- **Dining Room or Area.** Is the dining area convenient to the kitchen, large enough in relation to the size of the home, and able to accommodate the number of people who will be eating there?
- **Kitchen.** Is the kitchen convenient to an outside entrance and to the garage or carport? Is there adequate counter and cabinet space? What is the quality and condition of the kitchen cabinets? What is the type, quality, and condition of the kitchen floor? Are any of the appliances going to be included in the sale? If so, are they large enough, of good quality, and in good repair?
- **Bedrooms.** Is the number of bedrooms and their size adequate for the family? The size of the master bedroom is especially important. Are the bedroom closets large enough? It's better for the bedrooms to be located apart from the family room, living room, kitchen, and other work or recreational spaces.
- **Bathrooms.** There should be at least two bathrooms if the home has more than two bedrooms. In many areas, particularly in newer homes, a private bathroom off the master bedroom is standard. What is the type and condition of the tile or other wall and floor coverings? Are there windows or ceiling fans to provide adequate ventilation?

Design Deficiencies. Here's a brief list of some of the most common design deficiencies that real estate agents and home buyers should watch out for:

- the front door opens directly into the living room;
- there's no front hall closet;
- the back door is difficult to reach from the kitchen, or from the driveway or garage;

- there's no comfortable area in or near the kitchen where the family can eat;
- the dining room isn't easily accessible from the kitchen;
- the stairway to the second floor is in a room rather than in a hallway or foyer;
- bedrooms or bathrooms are visible from the living room or foyer;
- the family room (or rec room) isn't visible from the kitchen;
- there's no access to the basement from outside the house;
- the bedrooms aren't separated by a bathroom or by a closet wall (for soundproofing); and
- outdoor living areas aren't accessible from the kitchen.

Investing in Real Estate

After buying a home, many people become interested in purchasing real estate as an investment. They realize that while the value of real estate fluctuates, property that's in good condition and that's located in a good neighborhood will usually increase in value in the long run. (A word of caution: Real estate agents shouldn't act as investment counselors. They should always refer clients to an accountant, attorney, or investment specialist for investment advice.)

An investment is an asset that's expected to generate a **return** (a profit). A return on an investment can take various forms, including interest, dividends, rents, or appreciation. An asset appreciates (increases in value) because of inflation, and may also appreciate because of a rising demand for the asset. For example, a parcel of prime vacant land appreciates as land suitable for development becomes increasingly scarce.

Types of Investments

Investments can be divided into two general categories: ownership investments and debt investments. With **ownership investments**, the investor takes an ownership interest in the asset. Real estate and stocks are examples of ownership investments. The return on ownership investments usually takes the form of dividends, rent, and/or appreciation. Ownership investments are sometimes called **equities**.

A **debt investment** is essentially a loan that an investor makes to an individual or an entity. For example, a bond is a debt owed to an investor by a government entity or a corporation. The investor lends the entity money for a set period of time, and in return the entity promises to repay the money on a specific date (the maturity date), along with a certain amount of interest. An ordinary mortgage loan is another example of a debt investment.

Investors often choose to **diversify** their investments—that is, they invest in a variety of different types of investments, instead of putting all their eggs in one basket. The mix of investments that a person or a company owns, plus any cash reserves, is referred to as a **portfolio**.

Note that for tax purposes, investment income (such as interest, dividends, or rents) is usually distinguished from earned income (salary, wages, or income from self-employment).

Investment Characteristics

An investor evaluates any investment opportunity in terms of three potential advantages: safety, liquidity, and yield. (The **yield** is the investor's total return on the investment, or ROI.) These three characteristics are interrelated. Safety and liquidity tend to go together. On the other hand, for a high return an investor often sacrifices safety or liquidity, or both.

Safety. An investment is considered safe if there's little risk that the investor will actually lose money on it. Even if the investment doesn't generate the return she hopes for, the investor will at least be able to recover the money she originally invested.

Some types of investments are very safe, because they carry a guarantee. A simple example is the federal deposit insurance that protects funds (up to $250,000) in a bank account. As long as he doesn't exceed the $250,000 coverage limit, it's highly unlikely that a depositor will lose any of the money he puts into an insured bank account. On the other hand, some types of investments are inherently risky. For instance, an investor who puts his money into an uncertain venture such as a brand new company is likely to lose his investment if the company isn't a success.

Liquidity. A **liquid asset** is one that can be converted into cash (liquidated) quickly. Money in a bank account is extremely liquid: to convert it into cash, the investor has only to present the bank with a withdrawal slip or check. Mutual funds, stocks, and bonds are less liquid—they may take a little longer (perhaps a few days) to convert into cash. Other items, such as jewelry or coin collections, aren't considered liquid at all, because an investor might have to wait weeks or months to find a buyer and exchange those assets for cash. Real estate isn't a liquid asset.

As a general rule, the more liquid the asset, the lower the return. For example, the money in an ordinary savings account is very liquid, but it offers only a modest return, in the form of a low rate of interest. If you make a commitment to keep the funds deposited for a specified period (as with a certificate of deposit), you'll get a slightly higher rate. Generally, the longer the period, the higher the rate.

Liquidity is an advantage because the investor can cash in the investment immediately if the funds are needed for an unexpected expense, or because a better investment opportunity has arisen. Money in a nonliquid investment is effectively "locked up" and unavailable for other purposes. Real estate and other nonliquid assets can be excellent investments, but their lack of liquidity has consequences that a prospective investor should take into account.

Yield. Investments that are both safe and liquid tend to offer the lowest returns. In a sense, investors "pay" for safety and liquidity with a low return. To get a high return, an investor usually must take the risk of losing some or even all of the money originally invested. The investor may also have to sacrifice liquidity, allowing the money to be tied up for a while.

Of course, except with the very safest investments, the yield isn't fixed at the time the investment is made. The yield can change with market conditions, such as an increase or a decrease in market interest rates.

As a general rule, the greater the risk, the higher the potential yield needs to be. Otherwise investors won't be willing to make the investment. Investors also expect higher yields from long-term investments, as compensation for keeping their money tied up for longer periods of time.

With some types of investments, the return will be much greater if the investor can afford to keep the investment for a long time, in order to take advantage of healthy market conditions. This is true of real estate.

Example: Jeanne and Harold each buy a piece of land for $20,000 in the same year. One year later, Jeanne desperately needs some cash. The market for land has taken a downturn, and Jean is forced to sell her property at a loss. She ends up with only $17,000 of her original $20,000 investment.

Harold, on the other hand, is in no hurry to sell his property, so he can wait for optimal market conditions. He keeps the land for twelve years and then sells it at the peak of a real estate cycle, when property values are high. Because Harold could afford to choose when to sell the property, he walks away from the transaction with $60,000, an excellent return on his original $20,000 investment.

Advantages of Investing in Real Estate

People invest in real estate for many reasons. The advantages of investing in real estate can be broken down into three general categories:

- appreciation,
- leverage, and
- cash flow.

In addition, real estate investment has certain tax benefits.

Appreciation. When property appreciates, that means it is increasing in value due to changes in the economy or other outside factors. Although real estate values fluctuate, over a period of several years real estate tends to appreciate at a rate equal to or higher than the rate of inflation. As a result, real estate has traditionally been considered an effective "hedge" against inflation. And when buildable property becomes scarce, the value of properties in prime locations increases even more rapidly.

Appreciation causes a property owner's equity to increase. **Equity** is the difference between the value of the property and the liens against it, so an increase in the property's value increases the owner's equity in the property. Also, each monthly mortgage payment increases the owner's equity, by reducing the loan's principal balance. Equity adds to an owner/investor's net worth and can also be used to secure an equity loan. So even though real estate isn't considered a liquid asset, equity in real estate can be used to generate cash funds.

Leverage. Real estate investors can take advantage of **leverage**, which means using borrowed money to invest in an asset. If the asset appreciates, then the investor earns money on the money borrowed as well as the money she invested.

Example: Martha purchases a rental home for $315,000. She makes a $63,000 downpayment and borrows the rest of the purchase price. The rent generated by the property covers all the expenses of operating the property, plus the mortgage payment and income taxes. The property appreciates at 3% per year for five years. At the end of the five years, Martha sells the property for $365,000. She has made a $50,000 profit on her $63,000 investment. This averages out to a 15.8% annual return over the five-year period. The property appreciated at 3% per year, but because she invested only 20% of the purchase price, Martha was able to generate a 15.8% return on her investment.

Cash Flow. Many real estate investments generate a positive cash flow, in addition to appreciating in value. Cash flow is spendable income—the amount of money left after all the property's expenses have been paid, including operating costs, mortgage payments, and taxes. When a real estate investment generates a positive cash flow, the investor's monthly income increases. Thus, a real estate investment can increase both the investor's net worth (through appreciation) and his income (through positive cash flow).

Another way in which a property can generate cash flow is through a **sale-leaseback** arrangement. In a sale-leaseback, the owner of a building (typically a commercial property) sells the building to an investor, but then leases the property back from the investor and continues to use it. The money generated by the sale can be used for expansion, acquiring inventory, or investment elsewhere. At the same time, the seller can deduct the rent paid to lease the property from her income taxes as a business expense. Sometimes a sale-leaseback arrangement also includes a **buy-back** agreement, in which it's agreed that the seller will buy the property back for its fair market value after a certain number of years.

Investors sometimes use the term "cash on cash," which refers to a property's first year cash flow divided by the initial investment. It pinpoints the ratio between cash invested (equity) and cash received.

Tax Benefits. The tax benefits of real estate investment include reducing the amount of taxes owed with deductions for depreciation, mortgage interest, and operating expenses; and deferring payment of taxes with tax-free exchanges and installment sales. The income tax implications of real estate ownership are discussed in Chapter 13.

Disadvantages of Investing in Real Estate

Of course, real estate investments can be a mixed blessing. There are some disadvantages to real estate investments that must be considered carefully.

First of all, real estate investment often requires expert advice. Investing in real estate is typically far more complicated than putting money in a savings account or a mutual fund. It's also more time-consuming. Not only does the initial purchase take time and effort, but the property must be managed after it's purchased. Rental rates must be set, tenants found, rents collected, and maintenance and repairs completed. Even if the investor decides to hire a property manager to manage the property, there are many decisions that must be made by the investor.

As we discussed earlier, real estate investments aren't liquid. Time is required to convert real estate into cash. Furthermore, there are substantial risks involved in investing in real estate. There's no guarantee that the investor won't lose some or all of his downpayment. For instance, there's always the chance that the property's value may decline because of economic conditions (national, regional, or local).

Example: On a national scale, property values are keeping pace with inflation. However, Lumbertown relies solely on the timber industry and the local lumber mill for employment. The local mill shuts down and the town is economically crippled. Even though real estate is generally a good investment, property values in Lumbertown will decline rapidly.

Also, the income generated by a property may not be enough to cover the expenses of operating it. A negative cash flow may force the investor to sell the property in a hurry, for less than she paid for it.

Choices When Investing in Real Estate

There are basically two ways to invest in real estate. One way is to purchase property as an individual investor. The other way is to invest in real estate indirectly, by putting money into an investment syndicate, buying securities, or making or buying mortgage loans.

Buying Real Estate as an Investment. An investor who decides to purchase real estate directly must first decide what type of property to invest in, and then which particular piece of property to purchase.

Types of Properties. There are many types of real estate for an investor to choose from. There are residential properties (including single-family homes, duplexes, triplexes, four-plexes, townhouses, condominiums, and apartment buildings), office properties, retail properties, and industrial parks. Of course, an investor might choose to purchase vacant land and either develop it, or simply hold onto it to reap the benefits of appreciation.

The investor should consider whether a potential investment will require property management. A commercial property or a multifamily residential property is likely to require on- or off-site management, either by the investor or by a professional property manager.

Most real estate investors start out by purchasing residential property. The first choice is often a single-family home or duplex. There are many advantages to investing in a rental house. Rental houses are more affordable for the beginning investor than other types of income property. They are scarce in many communities, so they are often easy to rent. Single-family homes often attract stable tenants, such as single professionals or young families. Rental houses are usually easier to sell than other income property, in case the investor needs to liquidate. Also, single-family homes can be managed easily by the owner. Two- to four-unit residential properties have many of these same advantages. In addition, the investor may choose to live in one of the units of a duplex, triplex, or four-plex, which makes management even easier.

Qualities to Look For. Buying a rental property is often simpler than buying a home—it's a business decision rather than an emotional decision. When a family purchases a home, it looks for a house that fits its lifestyle and satisfies its emotional needs. On the other hand, a rental house usually has to meet only a few requirements: it should be in good condition, it should be located in a good neighborhood, it should contain enough square footage to satisfy the average tenant, and the design shouldn't be so unconventional that it would alienate the average tenant.

The location of a rental property should appeal to the people who are its potential tenants. The pool of likely renters typically includes blue collar workers, single people, people pursuing careers, elderly people, and young families. The neighborhood should have easy access to employment centers, transportation, shopping, and schools. A rental house will have extra appeal if it's located near a college, a hospital, or a shopping center.

The structural components of the property should be in good condition. This will attract better tenants and reduce the need for costly upkeep and repairs. The foundation is critical; are there any cracks, breaks, bulges, or shifts? The age and condition of the heating, wiring, and plumbing systems should be examined. Would they be expensive to maintain or repair? What about the insulation? Will the tenant be faced with large electricity or gas bills?

Once an investor has found a suitable property in a good location, he will be ready to begin managing the property (perhaps with the help of a professional property manager) and learning firsthand about how real estate investments work.

Property Management. A real estate investor may need to hire a property manager to oversee day-to-day operations of a large property. The duties of a property manager can include maintaining the property, performing repairs and periodic property inspections, handling tenant complaints, collecting rents, showing vacant units, and acting as a liaison between tenants and the owner. Under California law, a residential property with more than 15 units must have a resident manager (one who lives on the premises).

A property manager may be paid a flat fee or a commission. The commission could be a percentage of gross receipts, of new leases, or of the rent expected over the lease term.

Indirect Real Estate Investment. Instead of buying property herself, an investor could put money into a **real estate investment syndicate**. Investors purchase interests in the syndicate, which uses the investment capital to buy and develop property. A syndicate may take the form of a partnership, a joint venture, a corporation, a trust, or a limited liability company. It may be able to qualify for special tax treatment by meeting the IRS requirements for a **real estate investment trust**, or REIT (see Chapter 2).

Another alternative for investors is buying **mortgage-backed securities** issued by one of the secondary market agencies such as Fannie Mae (see Chapter 9), or by a private entity. A private entity that issues mortgage-backed securities may be organized as a **real estate mortgage investment conduit** (REMIC) in order to qualify for tax benefits.

An investor can act as a private lender, making mortgage loans that enable others to buy real estate. However, private lenders must be careful not to run afoul of legal requirements concerning usury, advertising consumer credit, and so on. Depending on the nature and extent of her activities, a private lender in California may be required to have a real estate license (see Chapter 16). Someone who buys and sells mortgage loans also may have to be licensed, either as a real estate agent or as a securities dealer, and may be subject to securities laws.

 Chapter Summary

1. To accurately assess the value of a home, a real estate agent needs to be able to judge the quality of the construction. It's important to be familiar with common construction techniques and materials, and to have some understanding of the technical systems (plumbing, wiring, heating, and cooling). Knowing how to read plans and specifications can be very useful, especially when dealing with new construction.

2. A real estate agent is often asked to compare buying a home to renting one. The advantages of renting include less financial commitment and risk, fewer maintenance responsibilities, greater mobility, and facilities a homeowner often couldn't afford. The advantages of buying include security, satisfaction in ownership, privacy, and freedom from restrictions. Although a mortgage payment is typically much larger than a rental payment, property appreciation, equity, and tax deductions can make buying less expensive than renting over the long run.

3. In addition to judging construction quality, a real estate agent helping a customer choose a home should evaluate the neighborhood, the site, and the exterior and interior design.

4. After purchasing a home, some people decide to venture into real estate investment. The advantages of real estate investment include appreciation, leverage, cash flow, and tax benefits. The disadvantages include the time required to choose and manage property, the fact that real estate investments aren't liquid, and the risk of losing some or all of the money invested.

Key Terms

Plans—Detailed technical drawings of the vertical and horizontal cross-sections of a building, used as a guide in its construction.

Specifications—Text that accompanies the plans of a building, describing the types of materials and the standards of workmanship to be used in the construction.

Investment—An asset that is expected to generate a return (a profit).

Portfolio—The mix of investments (plus cash reserves) owned by an individual or a company.

Liquidity—An asset's ability to be converted into cash quickly.

Appreciation—When an asset increases in value. Appreciation may be due to inflation, or it may occur because the asset is becoming scarcer or demand for it is increasing.

Equity—The difference between the value of a property and the liens against it.

Leverage—Using borrowed money to invest in an asset. If the asset appreciates, the investor earns money on the borrowed funds as well as the funds she invested.

Cash flow—Spendable income; the amount of money left after all of the property's expenses have been paid, including operating costs, mortgage payments, and taxes.

Real estate investment syndicate—A group of people or companies who join together to purchase and develop real estate.

Real estate investment trust (REIT)—A real estate investment business that qualifies for tax advantages if certain requirements are met.

Real estate mortgage investment conduit (REMIC)—A business entity that purchases and securitizes mortgage loans, and that qualifies for tax advantages if certain requirements are met.

Chapter Quiz

1. In building construction, standards of construction quality are assured through:
   a) the planning commission
   b) zoning ordinances
   c) building codes
   d) None of the above

2. All of the following are likely to go up eventually; which of them will probably increase most gradually?
   a) A rental payment
   b) A fixed-rate mortgage payment
   c) An adjustable-rate mortgage payment
   d) All of the above will increase at the same rate

3. All of the following lots contain the same area. Which would generally be considered the most desirable?
   a) A rectangular lot with a gentle slope
   b) A triangular lot with a steep slope
   c) A triangular lot with a gentle slope
   d) A level T-shaped lot

4. Which of the following is considered a drawback in a floor plan?
   a) A door leads directly from the kitchen to the garage
   b) The front door leads directly into the living room
   c) The separate dining room is right next to the kitchen
   d) The bedrooms are isolated from the kitchen and family room

5. The value of a home is enhanced if:
   a) there are rental properties in the neighborhood as well as owner-occupied homes
   b) there are retail businesses as well as homes on the block
   c) strict zoning laws have made the lots and houses in the neighborhood similar to one another
   d) All of the above

6. When comparing a mortgage payment to a rental payment, all of the following should be taken into account except:
   a) the landlord's equity in the rental property
   b) appreciation of the homeowner's property
   c) the federal tax deduction for mortgage interest
   d) whether the mortgage interest rate is fixed or adjustable

7. A house with many horizontal projections and vertical lines, and with large areas of glass, is classified as:
   a) contemporary
   b) ranch
   c) colonial
   d) Spanish

8. Which of the following is an advantage of renting, as opposed to owning, a home?
   a) Security and stability
   b) Appreciation
   c) Federal tax deduction
   d) Mobility

9. Which of the following isn't drywall material?
   a) Wallboard
   b) Plywood
   c) Sheetrock
   d) Plaster

10. R-value is a term used in reference to:
    a) a type of loan
    b) a zoning classification
    c) a government agency
    d) insulation

11. The mix of investments owned by an individual or a company is known as:
    a) a portfolio
    b) leverage
    c) a yield
    d) equity

12. Martinson's investments consist of $20,000 in a money market account, $7,000 in a savings account, and $52,000 in certificates of deposit. Martinson's main investment concern is probably:
   a) a high return
   b) liquidity
   c) safety
   d) Both b) and c)

13. One major disadvantage of investing in real estate is:
   a) the use of leverage to increase returns
   b) lack of liquidity
   c) uniformly low returns
   d) the fact that a constantly increasing supply decreases values

14. What do stocks, real estate, and investment in a real estate investment trust all have in common?
   a) They are all liquid investments
   b) They are all very safe investments
   c) They all provide safe, but low, returns
   d) They are all ownership investments

15. The difference between the value of real property and the liens against it is:
   a) equity
   b) leverage
   c) yield
   d) cash flow

Answer Key

1. c) Building codes are local ordinances that set standards for construction quality.

2. b) A fixed-rate mortgage payment will increase very gradually, as property taxes and insurance premiums go up.

3. a) Rectangular lots are preferred to odd-shaped lots because more of the area can be used efficiently. Steeply sloping lots are often difficult to build on and are unstable, so level land or a gentle slope is preferable.

4. b) It's a disadvantage to have the front door open directly into the living room (rather than into an entry hall), since that makes it necessary to pass through the living room to get to the rest of the house. All of the other design features listed are considered advantages.

5. c) While few people would like all of the houses on their street to be identical, a reasonable degree of conformity is considered desirable and enhances the value of the homes.

6. a) The landlord's equity in the rental property isn't likely to have much effect on the rental payment. However, appreciation, mortgage rates, and federal and state income tax deductions do affect how mortgage payments compare to rental payments.

7. a) The house described is contemporary, or modern, in design. One of the main features of contemporary houses is many large windows.

8. d) It's much easier and less expensive to move out of a rental than to sell a home and buy a new one. All of the other answers are advantages of owning a home.

9. d) Drywall material (unlike plaster) doesn't require the addition of water during construction.

10. d) R-value is a measure of insulating capacity.

11. a) A portfolio is the mixture of investments (and cash reserves) held by a person or an entity.

12. d) All of these types of investments are both relatively liquid and relatively safe.

13. b) The lack of liquidity is a serious disadvantage of investing in real estate. The use of leverage is one of the benefits of investing in real estate.

14. d) Stocks and real estate (owned either directly or through a real estate investment trust) are considered ownership investments.

15. a) The difference between the value of real estate and the liens against it is the owner's equity.

Chapter 16

California Real Estate License Law

I. Administration of the Real Estate Law
II. Real Estate Licenses
  A. When a license is required
  B. When a license is not required
  C. License qualifications
  D. License application and term
  E. Miscellaneous license provisions
  F. Special activities
  G. Business opportunities
III. Disciplinary Action
  A. Disciplinary procedures
  B. Grounds for disciplinary action
  C. Examples of unlawful conduct
  D. Real Estate Fund
IV. Trust Funds
  A. Definition of trust funds
  B. Handling trust funds
  C. Trust accounts
  D. Trust fund records
  E. Advance fees
V. Documentation Requirements
  A. Document copies
  B. Broker's review of documents
  C. Broker/salesperson agreements
VI. Advertising Regulations
  A. Licensee designation in advertising
  B. First contact solicitation materials
  C. Internet advertising
  D. Advertising loans and notes
  E. Inducements
  F. Do Not Call Registry
VII. Antitrust Laws and Real Estate Licensees
  A. Prohibited practices and activities
  B. Avoiding antitrust violations

Chapter Overview

In California, the real estate profession is tightly regulated. Both real estate licensing requirements and the day-to-day responsibilities of real estate agents are set forth in the Real Estate Law. This chapter discusses when a real estate license is and isn't required, the qualifications for a license, licensing and renewal procedures, disciplinary action against licensees, the rules for handling trust funds, and other requirements of the Real Estate Law. It also explains how antitrust laws affect the real estate business.

Administration of the Real Estate Law

California's **Real Estate Law** (also known as the license law) is contained in sections 10000 to 10580 of the Business and Professions Code. The purpose of the law is to regulate the real estate profession and protect the public from incompetent, unethical, or dishonest real estate agents.

The Real Estate Law is administered by the **California Bureau of Real Estate** (CalBRE). The law is enforced by the chief officer of the CalBRE, the **Real Estate Commissioner**.

The Real Estate Commissioner's job is to implement and enforce the provisions of the Real Estate Law in a way that will provide the maximum protection possible to members of the public who deal with real estate licensees. The Commissioner is given many broad powers to accomplish this end.

The Commissioner has the power to adopt, amend, or repeal regulations necessary to enforce the Real Estate Law. These regulations have the force and effect of law. The Commissioner's regulations can be found in sections 2705 to 3109 of Title 10 in the California Code of Regulations.

The Commissioner also has the authority to:

- investigate non-licensees alleged to be performing activities for which a license is required;
- screen and qualify applicants for a license;
- investigate complaints against licensees; and
- regulate some aspects of the sale of subdivisions, franchises, and real property securities.

In addition, the Commissioner may:

- hold formal hearings to determine issues involving a licensee, a license applicant, or a subdivider and, after such a hearing, suspend, revoke, or deny a license or stop sales in a subdivision;
- bring actions for injunctions and claims for restitution on behalf of those injured by licensees who violate the Real Estate Law; and
- bring actions to stop trust fund violations.

The Real Estate Commissioner is advised on legal matters by the state attorney general. County district attorneys are responsible for prosecuting violations of the Real Estate Law that occur in their county. Willful violations of the Real Estate Law are misdemeanors and punishable with a fine of up to $10,000 and/or up to six months in jail.

The Real Estate Commissioner is appointed by the governor and serves at his or her pleasure. To qualify for the position of Real Estate Commissioner, a person must have been a real estate broker actively engaged in business for five years in California, or must have related experience associated with real estate activity in California for five of the previous ten years. The Commissioner and CalBRE employees are prohibited from engaging in professional real estate activities, and from having an interest in any real estate firm.

Fig.16.1 Commissioner's powers and duties

California Real Estate Commissioner

- Adopts and amends regulations to implement Real Estate Law
- Screens and qualifies real estate license applicants
- Issues, renews, or denies licenses
- Investigates complaints against licensees and enforces Real Estate Law
- Regulates some aspects of subdivisions, franchises, and real property securities

Real Estate Licenses

A common way of regulating an industry or profession is to require its members to be licensed. The state can try to ensure a licensed person's competence and exercise control over his professional activities by requiring education, testing, and record-keeping, and by enforcing minimum standards of business conduct.

When a License is Required

The Real Estate Law requires anyone who is acting, advertising, or appearing to act as a real estate broker or as a real estate salesperson to have a real estate license.

Definition of Real Estate Broker. A real estate broker is a person who does or negotiates to do certain acts on behalf of another, for compensation or in the expectation of compensation. These acts include all of the following:

1. **Sales, purchases, and exchanges.** Selling, buying, or exchanging real property or a business opportunity. (Business opportunities are discussed later in the chapter.)
2. **Leases.** Leasing or collecting rents from real property or a business opportunity; or buying, selling, or exchanging leases on real property or a business opportunity.
3. **Advertising and listings.** Soliciting prospective sellers, buyers, or tenants, or listing real property or a business opportunity for sale or lease.
4. **Government lands.** Locating or filing an application for the purchase or lease of lands owned by the state or federal government.
5. **Advance fees.** Charging or collecting an advance fee to promote the sale or lease of real property or a business opportunity (by advertising or listing it, by obtaining financing, or in some other way).

6. **Mortgage loan brokerage.** Soliciting borrowers or lenders for or negotiating loans secured by liens on real property or business opportunities, or collecting payments or performing other services in connection with such loans.
7. **Selling, buying, or exchanging loans or securities.** Selling, buying, or exchanging real property securities, land contracts, or promissory notes secured by liens on real property or business opportunities, and performing services for the holders of contracts or notes.

MLO Endorsement. A real estate broker may not engage in the activities listed in paragraph 6 above, in connection with residential mortgage loans, unless the Bureau of Real Estate has added a special **mortgage loan originator endorsement** to his real estate license. The requirements for obtaining an MLO endorsement include obtaining a license through the Nationwide Mortgage Licensing System and Registry (see Chapter 10). An MLO endorsement requires prelicense and continuing education in addition to the education required for a real estate broker's license.

A real estate broker isn't allowed to accept compensation from a lender or a mortgage loan originator in a transaction involving a residential mortgage loan unless the broker has an MLO endorsement. That restriction applies even if the broker provides only real estate brokerage services (the activities listed in paragraphs 1, 2, and 3 on the list above), not mortgage loan brokerage services.

A real estate broker may still take certain steps, like providing an application form and collecting information needed to process a loan application, without triggering the MLO endorsement requirements; the MLO requirements apply only to brokers who offer or negotiate loans for compensation. For the purposes of these MLO rules, a residential mortgage loan is a loan primarily for personal, family, or household use that is secured by a dwelling with up to four units.

Making or Selling Loans as a Principal. As we said, the broker definition generally applies to acts performed on behalf of another. The broker definition also covers certain acts performed on one's own behalf, rather than on behalf of another. Specifically, it covers engaging as a principal in the business of making or selling loans secured by real property. You are considered to be "in the business" if, during the course of one calendar year, you:

- buy for resale, sell, or exchange eight or more land contracts or promissory notes secured by real property; or
- make eight or more loans secured by one- to four-unit residential property using your own funds.

Definition of Salesperson. A real estate salesperson is a person hired by a broker to do one or more of the acts listed in the broker definition given above. A salesperson's license permits real estate activity only while under the control and supervision of a broker. A salesperson can't act directly for a principal in a real estate transaction.

Furthermore, a salesperson may receive compensation only from his own broker. Neither clients nor cooperating brokers may pay the salesperson directly. Instead, they are required to pay the salesperson's broker, who then pays the salesperson.

An MLO endorsement is required for salespersons (as well as brokers) who engage in residential mortgage loan brokerage activities. A salesperson can obtain an MLO endorsement only if her broker also has an MLO endorsement.

Associate Brokers. A person licensed as a broker may choose to work for another broker instead of operating her own brokerage. Such a broker (who may be called an **associate broker** or a **broker-salesperson**) is subject to essentially the same limitations as a salesperson.

The associate brokers and salespersons who work for a particular broker are sometimes referred to as the broker's **affiliated licensees.**

Fig.16.2 Types of licensees

Broker

- Individual, corporation, or partnership
- Authorized to operate brokerage and represent clients

Salesperson

- Works with and represents broker
- Can't represent client directly

Business Entities. A real estate license can be issued to a corporation. At least one corporate officer must be designated to act as the broker under the corporate brokerage license. That officer must also be individually licensed as a broker, and can only act as a broker with respect to the corporate brokerage.

While there is no "partnership license," a partnership may perform acts for which a broker's license is required, provided that every partner through whom the partnership acts is a licensed real estate broker.

Penalties for Unlicensed Activities. For any act that requires a real estate license, the penalty for acting without a license is a fine of up to $20,000 and/or six months' imprisonment for an individual, or a fine of up to $60,000 for a corporation. The same penalties apply to acting as a mortgage loan originator without an MLO endorsement.

Note that it's unlawful for a broker to employ or compensate any unlicensed person for performing acts that require a real estate license, or to employ or compensate a licensee without an MLO endorsement for loan origination activities. The broker would be subject to disciplinary action and could have his license suspended or revoked.

On the other hand, it is not illegal for a broker to pay a referral fee (a finder's fee) to an unlicensed person who introduces a prospective buyer or seller to the broker—as long as the person doesn't perform any actions for which a license is required.

When a License Is Not Required

There are numerous exemptions from the real estate licensing requirements. The exemptions generally cover those who are acting on their own behalf, those who are regulated by another agency (such as securities brokers), and those who are performing functions that don't require expertise. All of the following, among others, are exempt:

1. Those acting on their own behalf with respect to their own property.
2. A corporate officer acting on behalf of a corporation, or a general partner acting on behalf of a partnership, with respect to property owned, leased, or to be purchased or leased by the corporation or partnership.
3. A person acting under a properly executed power of attorney from the owner of the property.
4. An attorney at law providing legal services to a client.

5. A person acting under court order (for example, a receiver in bankruptcy or a trustee).
6. A trustee under a deed of trust.
7. With respect to mortgage loan activities, an employee or representative of a financial institution, insurance company, pension fund, federally approved housing counseling service, or cemetery authority; a licensed finance lender; or a licensed residential mortgage lender or servicer.
8. With respect to activities related to business opportunities, mortgage loans, or real property securities, a licensed securities broker-dealer.
9. A person performing clerical functions and not discussing the price, terms, or condition of property.
10. A manager of a hotel, motel, or trailer park, or employees of the manager.
11. A resident apartment manager, who manages the apartment complex in which she lives, or employees of the resident manager.
12. An employee of a property management company who is supervised by a real estate licensee working for the company.
13. Film location representatives, who negotiate for the use of property for photographic purposes.

Unlicensed Real Estate Assistants. Real estate brokers and salespersons sometimes hire a real estate assistant to help them with their work. It's not necessary for a real estate assistant to have a real estate license, as long as the assistant's duties fall within the exemption for a person performing clerical functions, number 9 on the list above.

The Bureau of Real Estate has issued guidelines (currently available on the CalBRE website) explaining what unlicensed real estate assistants are allowed to do. Generally, they may provide factual information about a property to prospective buyers, but they aren't permitted to show the property or discuss the terms of a possible sale. They may prepare documents and advertising, as long as the licensee they work for reviews and approves the documents or ads before they're used.

Unlicensed Property Management Assistants. In addition to performing clerical functions, property management company employees supervised by a licensee (number 12 on the list above) are allowed to show property to prospective tenants, provide information about rental rates and lease provisions, handle rental applications, accept security deposits, and collect rents. A broker may delegate responsibility for the supervision of a property management assistant to a salesperson with at least two years of full-time experience as a real estate licensee.

License Qualifications

Applicants for real estate licenses in California must meet several qualifications. By imposing these requirements, particularly the education requirements, the state tries to ensure at least a minimum level of competence for all real estate professionals.

Salesperson's Qualifications. To obtain a salesperson's license, an applicant must:

1. be at least eighteen years old;
2. be honest and truthful;

3. pass the licensing exam;
4. apply on the prescribed form;
5. pay the license fee;
6. be fingerprinted;
7. provide her social security number to the CalBRE;
8. submit proof of legal presence (documentation showing that she is in the United States legally); and
9. complete nine semester units of education, including Real Estate Principles, Real Estate Practice, and an elective chosen from the following list: Legal Aspects of Real Estate; Real Estate Appraisal; Real Estate Financing; Real Estate Economics; General Accounting; Business Law; Escrow; Property Management; Real Estate Office Administration; Mortgage Loan Brokering and Lending; Common Interest Developments; or Computer Applications in Real Estate.

Broker's Qualifications. To obtain a broker's license, an applicant must:

1. have two years of full-time experience as a real estate licensee within the past five years;
2. be at least eighteen years old;
3. be honest and truthful;
4. pass the licensing exam;
5. apply on the prescribed form;
6. pay the license fee;
7. be fingerprinted;
8. provide his social security number to the CalBRE;
9. submit proof of legal presence (documentation showing that he is in the United States legally); and
10. complete 24 semester units (eight courses) of education, including:
    a. five required courses: Real Estate Practice; Real Estate Appraisal; Legal Aspects of Real Estate; Real Estate Financing; and either Real Estate Economics or Accounting; and
    b. three other courses chosen from this list: Advanced Legal Aspects of Real Estate; Advanced Appraisal; Advanced Financing; Real Estate Principles; Property Management; Escrow; Business Law; Real Estate Office Administration; Mortgage Loan Brokering and Lending; Common Interest Developments; or Computer Applications in Real Estate.

A broker's license applicant who takes both Real Estate Economics and Accounting has to complete only two additional elective courses, not three.

The experience requirement (item one on the list above) may be waived if the applicant either has the equivalent of two years of general real estate experience, or has a degree from a four-year college or university in a course of study that included a major or minor in real estate. In addition, the education requirements will be waived for any salesperson's license or broker's license applicant who is already licensed to practice law in California. To obtain a waiver, an applicant must submit a written petition to the CalBRE.

License Application and Term

License applicants must apply for their licenses within one year of the date they pass the exam (not the date they receive notice that they passed). Brokers' and salespersons' licenses must be renewed every four years. A mortgage loan originator endorsement for a real estate license must be renewed annually; the endorsement will expire each year on December 31.

License Renewals. Licenses are renewed by completing the continuing education requirement (discussed below), applying to the Bureau of Real Estate, and paying the appropriate fees. The licensee doesn't have to take another examination. The renewal application must be postmarked prior to midnight of the expiration date to prevent the license from expiring. However, the renewal application may not be filed earlier than 90 days before the expiration date.

Resident aliens who don't have permanent status must submit proof of legal presence in the United States to the CalBRE every time they renew their license.

Late Renewal. A license that has expired within the previous two years may be renewed without retaking the licensing examination. The licensee must file a renewal application and pay a late renewal fee. If the license isn't renewed within the two-year grace period, all license rights are lost. This means that in order to be licensed again, the former licensee must meet all the requirements for original license applicants, including passing the licensing exam again.

Continuing Education. A real estate license can't be renewed unless the licensee fulfills the continuing education requirement. A special form that confirms attendance at the required courses must accompany the renewal application.

A salesperson or broker renewing her license generally must have completed a total of 45 hours of continuing education courses during the previous four years. The specific course requirements depend on whether it's the licensee's initial renewal or a subsequent renewal.

Initial Renewal. When a salesperson or broker renews her license for the first time after it was issued, the 45 hours of continuing education must include:

1. five separate three-hour courses (15 hours total) on these mandatory subjects: ethics, agency, trust fund handling, fair housing, and risk management; and
2. at least 18 hours of courses designated as consumer protection courses.

The remaining hours may be in consumer service courses (courses covering business skills that enable licensees to competently serve customers), or the licensee may take additional consumer protection courses.

Subsequent Renewals. Each of a licensee's subsequent renewals (after the initial renewal) will also require 45 hours of continuing education within the previous four years. The specific course requirements are slightly different from the ones for the initial renewal, however. The 45 hours must include:

1. either 15 hours in separate courses on ethics, agency, trust fund handling, fair housing, and risk management; or an eight-hour survey course covering those five subjects; and
2. at least 18 hours of consumer protection courses.

As with the initial renewal, the remaining hours may be in consumer service courses or additional consumer protection courses.

70/30 Continuing Education Exemption. A licensee 70 years old or older isn't required to fulfill the continuing education requirement if he's been a real estate licensee in good standing in California for at least 30 years. (Any period during which the license was expired doesn't count toward the 30 years.) The licensee must submit proof that he qualifies for this exemption to the Bureau of Real Estate.

Continuing Education for MLO Endorsement. For the annual renewal of a real estate licensee's mortgage loan originator endorsement, the licensee is required to complete at least eight hours of continuing education every year. The eight hours must include at least three hours on federal laws, two hours on ethics issues (fraud, consumer protection, and fair lending), two hours on lending standards for nontraditional or subprime mortgage loans, and one hour on mortgage origination.

Miscellaneous License Provisions

Brokerage Offices. A real estate broker licensed in California is required to have a place of business in the state. A broker may also have one or more branch offices. A separate license must be issued for each branch office. The broker can add or cancel a branch office by filing a form with the Bureau of Real Estate.

The broker may appoint a licensee as manager of the branch office, and assign that licensee responsibility for overseeing licensed activities at that branch. The branch manager will, like the broker, be subject to discipline for Real Estate Law violations that happen at the branch. If a branch manager is replaced or terminated, the broker must immediately notify the CalBRE.

Location of Licenses. A broker is required to hold the licenses of all of her affiliated licensees. These licenses, and also the broker's own license, must be kept at the broker's main office.

Termination of Affiliation. If a salesperson quits or is discharged by his broker, the broker is required to return the salesperson's license certificate to the salesperson within three business days. The broker must notify the Commissioner of the termination by submitting a form to the Bureau of Real Estate within ten days.

If a salesperson changes brokerages with a transaction still in progress, when that transaction subsequently closes, she may be owed a commission by a broker for whom she no longer works. In this instance, the commission should be sent by the former employing broker to the new employing broker, who will then pass it to the salesperson.

Transfer of Salesperson's License. The Commissioner must also be notified when a salesperson transfers affiliation from one broker to another. The new broker is required to submit a notification form to the CalBRE within five days after the salesperson begins working for her.

Before giving his license certificate to the new broker, the salesperson is supposed to cross out the name and address of the former broker, then write the name of the new broker and the address of the new broker's main office on the back of the certificate. The salesperson should also date and initial these changes.

Discharge for Disciplinary Cause. If a salesperson is discharged for conduct that is grounds for disciplinary action, her broker must file a certified written statement of facts with the Commissioner. If the broker fails to do so, his own license could be suspended or revoked.

Termination of Broker's License. If a broker's license is suspended or revoked, the licenses of all of the broker's salespersons are automatically canceled. They may transfer their licenses to other brokers.

If a broker's license expires, the licenses of his salespersons are immediately placed on non-working status. The broker can reactivate them after renewing his own license.

Address Changes. Licensees are required to maintain current addresses on file with the Bureau of Real Estate. A broker must provide a mailing address, the address of her principal place of business, and the addresses of any branch offices. A salesperson must provide a mailing address and the address of his broker's principal place of business.

When a broker changes the location or address of her main office or a branch office, she must send written notice to the CalBRE within one business day. All licensees affected by the change should correct their license certificates by crossing out the old address and writing the new one on the back, and dating and initialing the changes.

Fictitious Names. A real estate broker may obtain a license under a fictitious business name, unless the name:

- is misleading or would constitute false advertising;
- implies a partnership or corporation that does not exist;
- violates certain statutory provisions; or
- has been formerly used by a licensee whose license has been revoked.

There are also some restrictions on fictitious business names that include the word "escrow" or imply that the broker provides escrow services.

A fictitious business name statement must be filed with the clerk of the county where the business is located. In addition, the statement must be published at least once a week for four weeks in a newspaper in the county. An **affidavit** (a written statement sworn before a notary public) indicating that the publication requirement has been fulfilled must also be submitted to the county clerk. The statement expires five years after it was initially filed.

Child Support Delinquency. The California Department of Child Support Services (DCSS) maintains a list of individuals who haven't complied with a court order concerning child support payments. The Bureau of Real Estate can't issue or renew a full-term real estate license for an applicant whose name appears on the DCSS list. Instead, the CalBRE will issue a 150-day license and notify the applicant that a full-term license will be issued only if the applicant obtains a release from the DCSS during the 150-day period.

Also, if a current licensee's name appears on the DCSS list and isn't removed within 150 days, the Bureau of Real Estate may suspend his or her license. The suspension will remain in effect until the delinquency has been cleared up.

Notification of Criminal Prosecution or Disciplinary Action. Licensees are required to notify the CalBRE if they have been indicted, charged with a felony, convicted of a crime, or had another license suspended or revoked by another licensing agency.

Special Activities

Prepaid Rental Listing Services. A prepaid rental listing service provides prospective tenants with listings of residential property available for rent. Tenants are charged a fee before or at the same time that the listing service provides the listings. The listing service isn't involved in negotiating leases or rental agreements.

Licensed real estate brokers may operate a prepaid rental listing service without an additional license or a special permit. Other individuals or companies must obtain a prepaid rental listing service license from the Bureau of Real Estate.

Mineral, Oil, and Gas Transactions. At one time, the Bureau of Real Estate issued special mineral, oil, and gas (MOG) licenses. Someone who had an MOG license could act as an agent in transactions concerning mineral, oil, or gas rights, even if he didn't have a real estate license. While some MOG licenses are still in effect, no new ones have been issued since 1994. Since then, a real estate license has been required.

Real Property Securities. One way of financing a real estate purchase or project is to form an investment syndicate, such as a limited partnership (see Chapter 2). When investors provide capital for a real estate investment but aren't actively involved in management of the property or its development, their interests are considered to be real property securities. As a general rule, someone who's involved in issuing or selling real property securities or soliciting investors must be licensed as a real estate broker or as a securities broker-dealer. (The California Department of Business Oversight regulates securities and issues securities licenses.)

Out-of-State Subdivisions. Lots that are located in a subdivision in another state may be sold or offered for sale in California only if the subdivision has been registered with the Bureau of Real Estate.

A real estate broker licensed in California may engage in transactions involving out-of-state property, as long as she remains physically in California while doing so. A California broker may also split a commission with an out-of-state broker.

Business Opportunities

A business opportunity is the sale or lease of a business, typically including inventory, fixtures, lease assignments, and goodwill. As a general rule, listing a business opportunity or representing the buyer of a business opportunity requires a real estate license, even if there's no real property involved. If shares of stock in a corporation are involved in the sale, the agent may also need a securities license.

One common type of business opportunity is a **franchise agreement**, where the purchaser (franchisee) buys the right to sell goods under a brand name and marketing system offered by the franchisor in exchange for a franchise fee. A franchise may be sold by a real estate licensee, a securities licensee, or any person registered for that purpose with the California Department of Business Oversight.

Business opportunity transactions typically involve the transfer of personal property (such as furniture and equipment used in the business), so the seller gives the buyer a bill of sale. The bill of sale must contain the names of the transferor and transferee, the location of the business, and a description of the personal property, including any trade fixtures and equipment and the trade name.

If the sale also involves real property, two purchase agreements might be used, one for the real property and one for the personal property. There will often be two separate escrows for the real property and the personal property. And, of course, the seller will give the buyer a deed as well as a bill of sale.

Sales Tax. The transfer of personal property in a business opportunity transaction is subject to sales tax. As in an ordinary purchase at a store, the buyer usually pays the sales tax to the seller, and the seller in turn pays the Board of Equalization.

There's another sales tax issue when the business being sold is a wholesale or retail business. The buyer should obtain a Certificate of Clearance from the state Board of Equalization, certifying that the seller has paid all sales tax owed on previous wholesale or retail transactions. Otherwise, the buyer may have **successor's liability** for the seller's unpaid sales tax and be required to pay it. Also, to start operating the business, the buyer will have to obtain a seller's permit from the Board of Equalization.

Bulk Sales. Business opportunity buyers must comply with the **Uniform Commercial Code**, which imposes certain requirements on bulk sales. A **bulk sale** is a sale, not in the ordinary course of the seller's business, of more than half of the seller's inventory. A buyer who's interested in a bulk sale must notify the seller's creditors by recording a notice of the transaction with the county recorder, sending a notice to the county tax collector by certified or registered mail, and publishing a notice in the local newspaper. If these requirements aren't met, the buyer may become liable to the seller's creditors.

Transfer of Liquor License. The sale of a business opportunity may include the transfer of an alcoholic beverage license, or liquor license. Liquor sales are strictly regulated, and state law limits the number of licenses that can be issued in a given county based on its population. As a general rule, an existing liquor license may be transferred from person to person or from premises to premises, subject to approval from the Department of Alcoholic Beverage Control (ABC). To obtain approval, the seller and the buyer must submit an application to ABC and post a public notice concerning the application on the premises. ABC will investigate the buyer and the proposed location before approving the transfer.

The rules governing issuance and transfer of liquor licenses vary depending on the type of establishment, the type of license, and other factors. For instance, the law generally prohibits issuance of a license to a private club that has existed for less than one year. And when a liquor license is transferred, there may be a limit on how much the seller is allowed to charge the buyer for the license, depending on what type of license it is and how long ago it was issued. For example, if a certain type of license is transferred within five years after it was issued, the seller isn't allowed to charge the buyer more than the fee originally paid to obtain the license.

Disciplinary Action

To be effective, laws must be enforced. The Real Estate Commissioner has the authority to investigate and discipline licensees who violate the Real Estate Law or the Commissioner's regulations. The Real Estate Commissioner's website must list the status of every licensee, disclosing any accusations, suspensions, or revocations.

Disciplinary Procedures

The Commissioner is required to investigate the actions of a licensee when someone submits a written complaint. The Commissioner may also investigate a licensee on his or her own motion, even when no formal complaint has been made. The investigation usually consists of getting statements from witnesses and the licensee; checking records (public records, bank records, and title company records, as appropriate); and perhaps calling an informal meeting of everyone concerned.

If, after an investigation, it appears that a violation of the law has occurred, the Commissioner may choose between:

- issuing a citation without holding a formal hearing into the matter, or
- filing an accusation and scheduling a formal hearing.

Citation. Citations are available to the Commissioner in the case of lesser violations of the Real Estate Law where the facts are not contested. A citation may include a fine of up to $2,500. It may also include an order that directs a licensee to stop an ongoing violation.

A citation is considered a disciplinary action, but is not publicly reported in the same way that a license revocation or suspension (or a monetary penalty in lieu of suspension) would be. A licensee has 30 days after receiving notice of a citation to request a formal hearing from the Bureau of Real Estate. If the licensee does not request a hearing in this timeframe, the citation is considered final.

Accusation and Hearing. If it appears that a violation of the law has occurred, an accusation is filed. An accusation is a written statement of the charges against the licensee. The accusation must be filed within three years of the allegedly unlawful act, unless the act involved fraud, misrepresentation, or a false promise. In that case, an accusation must be filed within one year after discovery by the injured party or within three years after the act (whichever is later), but in no case can it be filed more than ten years after the act.

The accusation is served on the licensee; information about the accusation is also posted on the Bureau of Real Estate's website. A date is set for an **administrative hearing**, in which an administrative law judge will consider the case. The accused licensee will also be given an explanation of her rights.

The licensee may appear at the hearing with or without an attorney. Testimony is taken under oath, and a record is made of the proceedings. Based on the hearing, the administrative law judge submits a proposed decision to the Commissioner, who may accept or reject it. The formal decision is made by the Commissioner. If the decision is adverse, the licensee may petition for reconsideration. The licensee also has the right to appeal the formal decision to superior court.

Possible Penalties After a Hearing. If the evidence at the hearing substantiates the charges against the licensee, her license may be suspended or revoked. A **suspension** lasts for a specified number of days. A **revocation** lasts indefinitely, unless the license is reinstated; the licensee may not apply for reinstatement for one year.

When it's in the public interest to do so, the Commissioner may impose a monetary penalty in lieu of license suspension. The fine can be as much as $250 for each day the license would have been suspended, up to a maximum of $10,000.

Imposition of a disciplinary penalty by the Commissioner doesn't protect a licensee from criminal prosecution or from liability in a civil suit. This criminal or civil liability would not be considered "double jeopardy."

Discipline against a real estate licensee may also lead to revocation or suspension of the licensee's mortgage loan originator license. Revocation or suspension of an MLO endorsement will be handled through the same disciplinary process.

Debarment. When a licensee has knowingly or recklessly violated the Real Estate Law or the Commissioner's regulations, has caused material damage to the public, or has been convicted of a crime or held liable in a civil action for conduct that involves dishonesty or is related to the qualifications or duties of a real estate licensee, the Commissioner can bar the licensee from any position of employment, management, or control for up to 36 months. A debarred licensee is prohibited from acting as a real estate broker or salesperson; from engaging in real estate related business activities on the premises of a brokerage; and from participating in real estate related business activities of a financial institution, a lender, an escrow company, or a title company.

Restricted Licenses. The Commissioner may issue a restricted license to replace a license that was suspended or revoked. The restricted license is, in effect, a probationary license. It may have a limited term, restrict the licensee to certain types of activities, require affiliation with a particular broker or the filing of a surety bond, or impose other limitations.

Desist and Refrain Orders. The Commissioner has the power to issue a desist and refrain order, ordering a licensee who is engaged in activities that violate the Real Estate Law to stop the violation. The licensee must stop immediately, but then may request a hearing on the matter.

Suspension Without a Hearing. If a person obtains a license through fraud, misrepresentation, deceit, or material misstatements of fact, the license can be suspended without a hearing. The Commissioner's power to do this expires 90 days after the license is issued, and the suspension is effective only until a hearing is held and the Commissioner makes a formal decision.

Grounds for Disciplinary Action

The grounds for suspending, revoking, or denying a license are set forth in the Real Estate Law; the main list can be found in Sections 10176 and 10177 of the Business and Professions Code. While licensing and license renewal requirements attempt to ensure the licensee's minimum competence, it is this list of acts or omissions that sets the standard for the licensee's day-to-day behavior.

The grounds for disciplinary action include all of the following actions and conduct:

1. Making a substantial misrepresentation (deliberately or negligently making a false statement of fact, or failing to disclose a material fact to a principal).
2. Making a false promise that is likely to persuade someone to do or refrain from doing something.
3. Embarking on a continued and flagrant course of misrepresentation or false promises.
4. Acting as a dual agent without the knowledge or consent of all of the parties involved.
5. Commingling your own money or property with money or property you received or are holding on behalf of a client or customer (trust funds).
6. Failing to put a definite termination date in an exclusive listing agreement.
7. Receiving an undisclosed amount of compensation on a transaction (a secret profit).
8. If you have a listing agreement that includes an option to purchase the listed property, exercising the option without revealing to the principal in writing the amount of profit to be made and obtaining the principal's written consent.
9. Acting in any way, whether specifically prohibited by statute or not, that constitutes fraud or dishonest dealing.
10. Getting a purchaser's written agreement to buy a business opportunity property and to pay a commission, without first obtaining the written authorization of the property owner (a listing agreement).
11. As a lender or mortgage broker, failing to disburse funds in accordance with a mortgage loan commitment.
12. Intentionally delaying the closing of a mortgage loan for the sole purpose of increasing the borrower's interest rate or other charges.
13. Knowingly or intentionally misrepresenting the value of real property, or providing an opinion of value for residential property in which you hold an interest.
14. Willfully or repeatedly failing to comply with the law that requires a real property transfer disclosure statement in certain transactions.
15. Acquiring or renewing a license by fraud, misrepresentation, or deceit.
16. Being convicted of (or pleading not guilty or no contest to) a felony charge, or a crime that is substantially related to the qualifications, functions, or duties of a real estate licensee.
17. False advertising, such as a material false statement about property offered for sale, or a misrepresentation of the licensee's credentials.
18. Willfully disregarding or violating the Real Estate Law or the Commissioner's regulations.
19. Willfully using the term "Realtor®" or any trade name of a real estate organization that you are not actually a member of.
20. Having a real estate license denied, revoked, or suspended in another state for actions that would be grounds for denial, revocation, or suspension in California.
21. Performing activities requiring a real estate license negligently or incompetently.

22. As a broker, failing to exercise reasonable supervision over the activities of your salespersons.
23. Using government employment to gain access to private records, and improperly disclosing their confidential contents.
24. Violating the terms of a restricted license.
25. Using "blockbusting" tactics: soliciting business on the basis of statements regarding race, color, sex, religion, ancestry, marital status, or national origin.
26. Violating the Franchise Investment Law, the Corporate Securities Law, or regulations of the Department of Business Oversight.
27. Violating the laws governing the sale of real property securities.
28. When selling property in which you have a direct or indirect ownership interest, failing to disclose the nature and extent of that interest to a buyer.
29. Violating or failing to comply with the state statute concerning mortgages and foreclosures.
30. Having a final judgment entered against you in a civil suit for fraud, misrepresentation, or deceit in regard to a real estate transaction.
31. As a broker, failing to notify the Commissioner in writing of the discharge of a salesperson based on her violation of the Real Estate Law or the Commissioner's regulations.
32. Committing fraud in an application for the registration of a mobile home, failing to provide for the delivery of a properly endorsed certificate of ownership of a mobile home from the seller to the buyer, or participating in the sale or disposal of a stolen mobile home.
33. Failing to indicate in an advertisement that you are a real estate licensee, or failing to include your license number in a purchase agreement or in solicitation materials such as business cards and advertising flyers.
34. As a broker, failing to notify the buyer and the seller, in writing, of the property's selling price within one month after the sale closes, unless escrow issues a closing statement.
35. Employing or compensating an unlicensed person for an act that requires a license.
36. Failing to give a copy of a contract to a party who has just signed it.
37. Accepting compensation for referring a customer to any of these types of companies: escrow, pest control, home warranty, or title insurer.
38. Undertaking to arrange financing for a transaction in which you're already acting as a real estate agent, or vice versa, without disclosing that dual role in writing to all parties within 24 hours.

In addition, Section 10087 of the Business and Professions Code authorizes the Commissioner to suspend a licensee or debar him from any position of employment, management, or control for up to 36 months if the licensee:

- knew or should have known that he was violating the Real Estate Law or the Commissioner's regulations, or has caused material damage to the public; or
- was convicted of or pleaded no contest to a crime, or was held liable in a civil action or administrative proceeding, if the matter involved dishonesty, fraud, deceit, or any other offense reasonably related to the qualifications, functions, or duties of a real estate licensee.

Examples of Unlawful Conduct

The Bureau of Real Estate's *Reference Book* lists examples of unlawful conduct that would be grounds for disciplinary action. It's divided into two parts: unlawful conduct in sale, lease, and exchange transactions, and unlawful conduct in loan transactions. This list is reprinted here in full.

Examples of Unlawful Conduct—Sale, Lease, or Exchange. In a sale, lease, or exchange transaction, conduct such as the following may result in license discipline under Sections 10176 or 10177 of the Business and Professions Code:

1. Knowingly making a substantial misrepresentation of the likely value of real property to:
   a. Its owner, either for the purpose of securing a listing or for the purpose of acquiring an interest in the property for the licensee's own account.
   b. A prospective buyer, for the purpose of inducing the buyer to make an offer to purchase the real property.
2. Representing to an owner of real property when seeking a listing that the licensee has obtained a bona fide written offer to purchase the property, unless at the time of the representation the licensee has possession of a bona fide written offer to purchase.
3. Stating or implying to an owner of real property during listing negotiations that the licensee is precluded by law, by regulation, or by the rules of any organization, other than the broker firm seeking the listing, from charging less than the commission or fee quoted to the owner by the licensee.
4. Knowingly making substantial misrepresentations regarding the licensee's relationship with an individual broker, corporate broker, or franchised brokerage company or that entity's/person's responsibility for the licensee's activities.
5. Knowingly underestimating the probable closing costs in a communication to the prospective buyer or seller of real property in order to induce that person to make or to accept an offer to purchase the property.
6. Knowingly making a false or misleading representation to the seller of real property as to the form, amount and/or treatment of a deposit toward the purchase of the property made by an offeror.
7. Knowingly making a false or misleading representation to a seller of real property, who has agreed to finance all or part of a purchase price by carrying back a loan, about a buyer's ability to repay the loan in accordance with its terms and conditions.
8. Making an addition to or modification of the terms of an instrument previously signed or initialed by a party to a transaction without the knowledge and consent of the party.
9. Making a representation as a principal or agent to a prospective purchaser of a promissory note secured by real property about the market value of the securing property without a reasonable basis for believing the truth and accuracy of the representation.
10. Knowingly making a false or misleading representation or representing, without a reasonable basis for believing its truth, the nature and/or

condition of the interior or exterior features of a property when soliciting an offer.

11. Knowingly making a false or misleading representation or representing, without a reasonable basis for believing its truth, the size of a parcel, square footage of improvements or the location of the boundary lines of real property being offered for sale, lease or exchange.
12. Knowingly making a false or misleading representation or representing to a prospective buyer or lessee of real property, without a reasonable basis to believe its truth, that the property can be used for certain purposes with the intent of inducing the prospective buyer or lessee to acquire an interest in the real property.
13. When acting in the capacity of an agent in a transaction for the sale, lease or exchange of real property, failing to disclose to a prospective purchaser or lessee facts known to the licensee materially affecting the value or desirability of the property, when the licensee has reason to believe that such facts are not known to nor readily observable by a prospective purchaser or lessee.
14. Willfully failing, when acting as a listing agent, to present or cause to be presented to the owner of the property any written offer to purchase received prior to the closing of a sale, unless expressly instructed by the owner not to present such an offer, or unless the offer is patently frivolous.
15. When acting as the listing agent, presenting competing written offers to purchase real property to the owner in such a manner as to induce the owner to accept the offer which will provide the greatest compensation to the listing broker without regard to the benefits, advantages and/or disadvantages to the owner.
16. Failing to explain to the parties or prospective parties to a real estate transaction for whom the licensee is acting as an agent the meaning and probable significance of a contingency in an offer or contract that the licensee knows or reasonably believes may affect the vacating of the property by the seller or its occupancy by the buyer.
17. Failing to disclose to the seller of real property in a transaction in which the licensee is an agent for the seller the nature and extent of any direct or indirect interest that the licensee expects to acquire as a result of the sale. (The licensee should disclose to the seller: prospective purchase of the property by a person related to the licensee by blood or marriage; purchase by an entity in which the licensee has an ownership interest; or purchase by any other person with whom the licensee occupies a special relationship where there is a reasonable probability that the licensee could be indirectly acquiring an interest in the property.)
18. Failing to disclose to the buyer of real property in a transaction in which the licensee is an agent for the buyer the nature and extent of a licensee's direct or indirect ownership interest in such real property: e.g., the direct or indirect ownership interest in the property by a person related to the licensee by blood or marriage; by an entity in which the licensee has an ownership interest; or by any other person with whom the licensee occupies a special relationship.
19. Failing to disclose to a principal for whom the licensee is acting as an agent any significant interest the licensee has in a particular entity when the licensee recommends the use of the services or products of such entity.

Examples of Unlawful Conduct—Loan Transactions. When soliciting, negotiating or arranging a loan secured by real property or the sale of a promissory note secured by real property, conduct such as the following may result in license discipline:

1. Knowingly misrepresenting to a prospective borrower of a loan to be secured by real property or to an assignor/endorser of a promissory note secured by real property that there is an existing lender willing to make the loan or that there is a purchaser for the note, for the purpose of inducing the borrower or assignor/endorser to utilize the services of the licensee.
2. Knowingly making a false or misleading representation to a prospective lender or purchaser of a loan secured directly or collaterally by real property about a borrower's ability to repay the loan in accordance with its terms and conditions.
3. Failing to disclose to a prospective lender or note purchaser information about the prospective borrower's identity, occupation, employment, income and credit data as represented to the broker by the prospective borrower.
4. Failing to disclose information known to the broker relative to the ability of the borrower to meet his or her potential or existing contractual obligations under the note or contract, including information known about the borrower's payment history on an existing note, whether the note is in default or the borrower in bankruptcy.
5. Knowingly underestimating the probable closing costs in a communication to a prospective borrower or lender of a loan to be secured by a lien on real property for the purpose of inducing the borrower or lender to enter into the loan transaction.
6. When soliciting a prospective lender to make a loan to be secured by real property, falsely representing or representing without a reasonable basis to believe its truth, the priority of the security, as a lien against the real property securing the loan, i.e., a first, second or third deed of trust.
7. Knowingly misrepresenting in any transaction that a specific service is free when the licensee knows or has a reasonable basis to know that it's covered by a fee to be charged as part of the transaction.
8. Knowingly making a false or misleading representation to a lender or assignee/endorsee of a lender of a loan secured directly or collaterally by a lien on real property about the amount and treatment of loan payments, including loan payoffs, and the failure to account to the lender or the assignee/endorsee of a lender as to the disposition of such payments.
9. When acting as a licensee in a transaction for the purpose of obtaining a loan, and in receipt of an advance fee from the borrower for this purpose, failing to account to the borrower for the disposition of the advance fee.
10. Knowingly making a false or misleading representation about the terms and conditions of a loan to be secured by a lien on real property when soliciting a borrower or negotiating the loan.
11. Knowingly making a false or misleading representation or representing, without a reasonable basis for believing its truth, when soliciting a lender or negotiating a loan to be secured by a lien on real property, about the market value of the securing real property, the nature and/or

condition of the interior or exterior features of the securing real property, its size or the square footage of any improvements on the securing real property.

As you can see, there are many grounds for disciplinary action in California. These provisions are the state's attempt to prevent unscrupulous behavior by real estate licensees. But suspending a real estate license after the fact doesn't help someone who lost money because of a licensee's unlawful actions. The injured party can take the licensee to court, but what if the licensee has no money or other assets? In that case, a judgment would be worthless. Under those circumstances, the state has provided an additional means of redress, through the Real Estate Fund.

The Real Estate Fund

All license fees go to the state treasury and are then credited to a fund called the **Real Estate Fund**. Some of the money in the Real Estate Fund is then disbursed to other accounts. Up to 8% of the money is credited to the **Education and Research Account** and used to advance real estate education and research projects. Up to 12% of the money in the Real Estate Fund is credited to the **Recovery Account**. (Monetary penalties collected by the Commissioner also go into the Recovery Account.) The purpose of the Recovery Account is to help compensate parties who have been injured by real estate licensees.

When an injured party gets a civil judgment (or arbitration award) against a licensee based on the licensee's intentional fraud, misrepresentation, or deceit, or conversion of trust funds, the injured party can apply to the Recovery Account for payment of the judgment. The injured party must be able to show that the licensee has no funds or assets that could be seized to pay the judgment.

The Recovery Account will pay up to $50,000 for losses in a single transaction and up to $250,000 for losses caused by one licensee. Once payment is made from the Recovery Account on behalf of a licensee, his license is automatically suspended as of the day of payment. The license can't be reinstated until the amount disbursed from the Recovery Account is fully repaid, with interest. Even bankruptcy doesn't release the licensee from this obligation.

Trust Funds

The most common cause of disciplinary action is the mishandling of trust funds. This is largely due to confusion about what trust funds are and what must be done with them. California law is very specific about how trust funds are to be handled, and it's imperative for licensees to be thoroughly acquainted with these rules. Even an honest mistake could result not only in a violation of the Real Estate Law, but also in a breach of the agency duties that licensees owe their clients and customers (see Chapter 8).

Definition of Trust Funds

The first step toward properly handling trust funds is learning to recognize them. Simply stated, trust funds are money or other valuables a licensee is holding on behalf of someone else. Trust funds can be cash, a check, a promissory note, or any

other item of personal property. The licensee merely holds the money or property on behalf of another party (usually a client or customer) while a real estate transaction is in progress. The CalBRE's *Reference Book* provides this definition of trust funds:

> *Money or other things of value that are received by a broker or salesperson on behalf of a principal or any other person, and which are held for the benefit of others in the performance of any acts for which a real estate license is required.*

The most common example of trust funds is the good faith deposit that a buyer gives to a broker along with the buyer's offer to purchase a listed property. The broker holds the buyer's deposit "in trust" while the seller decides whether or not to accept the buyer's offer. Another example is rent that a broker providing property management services collects from tenants and holds temporarily before passing it on to her client.

Advance fees are also considered trust funds. These are fees that a client may pay a broker in advance to defray anticipated costs, such as the advertising expenses associated with a listing, or as upfront compensation for services the broker will provide. While funds collected upfront for appraisal fees or credit report fees are not considered advance fees, they still must be treated as trust funds. (We'll discuss advance fees in more detail at the end of this section.)

Other types of funds in a broker's possession, such as general operating funds, earned real estate commissions, or rent from the broker's own real estate, aren't trust funds, because the broker isn't holding them on behalf of someone else.

Handling Trust Funds

When a real estate broker accepts trust funds from a client or customer, she must deposit them into:

1. a neutral escrow account,
2. the hands of the principal, or
3. a trust account maintained by the broker in a bank or other recognized depository.

Which of these alternatives is the appropriate one depends on the circumstances and on the broker's instructions. In any case, however, the trust funds must be deposited no later than three business days following receipt of the funds. If the funds are deposited into escrow or the hands of the principal rather than into the broker's trust account, the transfer must be noted in the broker's trust fund records.

If trust funds are given to a salesperson instead of directly to the broker, the salesperson must immediately deliver the funds to the broker, or, if so directed by the broker, to one of the three places listed above.

There is one exception to these rules. When a broker receives a good faith deposit check from a buyer, the broker can hold the check uncashed before the buyer's offer is accepted, if:

1. the check isn't negotiable by the licensee, or the buyer has given written instructions that the check isn't to be deposited or cashed until the offer is accepted; and
2. the seller is informed (before or when the offer is presented) that the check is being held.

Once the offer is accepted, the broker can continue to hold the uncashed deposit check only if he receives written authorization from the seller to do so.

Trust funds must stay in the trust account until their owner directs otherwise. While the owner of the trust funds is usually easy to identify, it should be noted that the ownership of trust funds may change as the real estate transaction progresses. For example, the ownership of a good faith deposit varies depending on whether or not the buyer's offer has been accepted. Before acceptance, the funds belong to the buyer and must be handled according to her instructions. After acceptance, however, ownership isn't so clear-cut, and the funds must be handled as follows:

- A check held uncashed by the broker before acceptance of the offer may continue to be held uncashed only on written authorization from the seller.
- The check may be given to the seller only if both parties agree to that in writing.
- No part of the deposit money can be refunded without the express written permission of the seller.

If a transaction falls through after the good faith deposit has been deposited into escrow or a broker's trust account, there may be a dispute over the money; the buyer and the seller may each feel entitled to it. In this situation, the escrow agent or broker who holds the funds in trust may file an **interpleader** action, turning the matter over to a court. The court will decide which party is the rightful owner of the funds.

Trust Accounts

The primary reason for maintaining a separate account for trust funds is to avoid **commingling**. Commingling means mixing trust funds with personal funds. A broker must never put trust funds into his general account. Likewise, the broker must never put his own funds into a trust account. This is true even if careful records are kept of the deposits and withdrawals.

Commingling shouldn't be confused with **conversion**, which is the actual misappropriation of a party's funds for the broker's own purposes. Conversion is a basis for theft charges under the California penal code. (Theft also includes wrongfully removing a piece of real or personal property, or defrauding another person of money, labor, or real or personal property.)

The prohibition against commingling makes it more difficult for a broker to "borrow" trust funds. The prohibition also protects trust funds from any legal action that might be taken against the broker.

Fig.16.3 Rules for handling trust funds

Handling Trust Funds

- Must be deposited within three days following receipt.
- Salesperson must deliver funds to broker or deposit them in compliance with broker's instructions.
- Check for good faith deposit can be held uncashed before buyer's acceptance under certain circumstances.
- Broker must not commingle personal funds with trust funds.

Example: Suppose a broker dies, or is sued by a client. The broker's general account could very well be frozen during the course of the probate or lawsuit. If trust funds were kept in the broker's general account, they would be unavailable to the owners of those funds until the probate was completed or the lawsuit concluded.

Also, if trust funds were placed in the broker's general account, a judgment creditor might be able to seize those funds along with the broker's own funds.

Shortages or Overages. The total amount of funds in the trust account must always equal the broker's aggregate trust fund liability. The process of comparing the trust fund balance to the sum of individual transactions is called **reconciliation**. When reconciled, the trust account balance must equal the total of the balances due to individual clients and customers.

If the trust account balance is less than the total liability, there is a **trust fund shortage**. Such a shortage is a violation of the Real Estate Commissioner's regulations. If the trust account balance is greater than the total liability, there is a **trust fund overage**. This is also a violation of the regulations, since non-trust funds can't be commingled with trust funds.

A broker should always make sure that a check deposited into the trust account has cleared before disbursing any funds against the check. If funds are disbursed and the check hasn't cleared, or the check bounces, a trust fund shortage will occur.

Exceptions to Commingling Rule. There are two exceptions to the rule against commingling.

1. The broker must pay the service charges on the trust account out of her general funds. The broker can have up to $200 of personal funds in a trust account for this purpose. However, a better arrangement is to have the bank deduct the trust account service fees directly from the broker's general account.
2. Sometimes a broker is entitled to deduct her commission from trust funds. In this case, the broker should promptly transfer the commission out of the trust account into her general account. If it isn't practical to transfer the commission immediately, it can stay in the trust account for no more than 25 days.

The broker should never pay personal obligations out of the trust account, even if the payments are a draw against the broker's commission. The earned commission must be transferred to the broker's general account before it can be used to pay personal obligations.

Account Requirements. A trust account must be opened in the broker's name as it appears on the broker's license, in a recognized financial institution in California. The account must be specifically designated as a trust account, with the broker as trustee. The financial institution can't require prior written notice before allowing withdrawals from the account.

The trust account can't be an interest-bearing account, with one exception: at the request of the owner of the trust funds, the broker can deposit the funds into a separate interest-bearing trust account, as long as the broker discloses how the interest is calculated, who pays the service charges, and how the interest is to be paid. The broker may not receive any of the interest or benefit from it directly or indirectly.

Withdrawals. Withdrawals from a trust account generally require the signature of the broker (or in the case of a corporation licensed as a broker, the signature of the designated broker-officer). However, a broker may also authorize the following individuals to withdraw trust funds:

1. a salesperson or an associate broker employed by the broker; or
2. any unlicensed employee, provided that he is covered by a fiduciary bond equal to the total amount held in trust.

While a broker can authorize others to withdraw trust funds, she can't delegate responsibility for the funds. The broker is always accountable for any trust fund violation, even one caused by the negligence or irresponsibility of an employee.

Trust Fund Records

It's very important to keep proper records of all trust funds, including trust fund checks that are held uncashed, trust funds that are sent directly to escrow, and trust funds that have been released to the owner. Thorough trust fund records enable the broker to prepare accurate accountings for clients, to calculate the amounts owed to clients at any given time, and to see if there's an imbalance in the trust account. The broker must reconcile his trust account records on a monthly basis.

A broker can use one of two types of accounting systems to keep track of trust funds: a simple columnar system or an alternative system that complies with general accounting practices. Regardless of which method is used, the accounting system must show the following:

1. all trust fund receipts and disbursements with pertinent details in chronological order;
2. the balance of each trust account based on all recorded transactions;
3. all receipts and disbursements affecting each client or customer's account in chronological order; and
4. the balance owing to each beneficiary based on recorded transactions.

Columnar System. If a broker chooses to use the columnar recordkeeping system, there are three types of records she must keep:

1. **A record of all trust funds received and disbursed.** This record is used to list all trust funds deposited to and disbursed from the trust account. It must include the following information:
   a. the date the funds were received;
   b. from whom they were received;
   c. the amount received;
   d. the date of deposit;
   e. for disbursements, the party to whom the funds were paid;
   f. the amount paid out;
   g. the check number and date; and
   h. the daily balance of the bank account.
2. **A record for each client/customer or transaction.** This record lists the funds received from or for each client or customer. It must include the following information:
   a. the date of the deposit;
   b. the amount of the deposit;

   c. the name of the payee or the payor;
   d. for funds paid out, the check number, date, and amount; and
   e. the daily balance of the individual account.
3. **A record of trust funds received but not deposited into the trust account.** This record must show:
   a. the date the funds were received;
   b. the form of the payment;
   c. the amount received;
   d. a description of any property received in lieu of funds;
   e. where the funds were forwarded to; and
   f. the date of disposition.

General Accounting Practices System. Instead of a columnar system, a broker may use an alternative system that complies with generally accepted accounting practices. That system must include a journal, a cash ledger, and beneficiary records for each trust account.

1. **Journal.** A journal is a daily chronological record of trust fund receipts and disbursements that shows:
   a. all trust fund transactions in chronological order;
   b. enough information to identify the transaction (e.g., date, amount received, name of payee, etc.); and
   c. the total receipts and total disbursements at least once a month.
2. **Cash ledger.** This shows, usually in summary form, the increases and decreases in the trust account and the resulting account balance.
3. **Beneficiary ledger.** A beneficiary ledger must be maintained for each client or customer, or for each transaction or series of transactions. It shows, in chronological order, the details of all receipts and disbursements relating to the individual account, and the resulting account balance.

All trust fund records are subject to inspection by the Commissioner. The broker must keep copies of all trust records (including canceled checks) for each transaction for three years. The three-year period begins on the date the transaction closes, or on the date of the listing if the transaction doesn't close.

Advance Fees

As we said earlier, an advance fee is money that a real estate broker collects from a client in advance to cover expenses she expects to incur on the client's behalf, or as upfront compensation for services she has yet to provide. Advance fees must be handled in compliance with the trust funds rules we've discussed so far. They must not be commingled with the broker's own funds, and they must be deposited into the broker's trust account within three days after receipt.

Before collecting advance fees in connection with any services, however, a broker must submit all of the materials she's planning to use in advertising or promoting those services to the Bureau of Real Estate for approval, along with the advance fee agreement she will be entering into with her clients. The CalBRE will review the materials to make sure that they give a full description of the services to be provided; state the total amount of the advance fee and when it must be paid; specify a termination date for the agreement; do not contain deceptive guarantees; and are not otherwise misleading.

Once placed in a broker's trust account, advance fees generally can't be withdrawn until they're actually expended for the client's benefit or until five days after an accounting has been sent to the client. (This may be either a quarterly accounting or a final accounting after the agency has ended.)

Documentation Requirements

In addition to the trust fund records described above, the Bureau of Real Estate also requires brokers to keep all of the documents connected with a real estate transaction. These documents include:

- listings and buyer agency agreements;
- purchase agreements;
- rent collection receipts;
- bank deposit slips;
- canceled checks;
- supporting papers for checks, such as invoices, escrow statements, or receipts;
- agency disclosure statements;
- transfer disclosure statements; and
- property management agreements.

These documents must be kept for at least three years, beginning with the date of closing (or the date of listing, if the transaction doesn't close), and they must be available for inspection by the Commissioner. If there is sufficient cause, these records may be audited.

The following documents must be kept for four years instead of three: real property security statements, and disclosure statements given to noninstitutional lenders or deed of trust purchasers.

Document Copies

Whenever a licensee prepares a document for signature, she must give a copy of the document to the person signing it when the signature is obtained. The Real Estate Law makes this mandatory for contractual documents (including listing agreements, buyer representation agreements, purchase agreements, property management agreements, all contract addenda, and any later amendments), while other laws require it for disclosure statements, settlement statements, and various other documents.

Broker's Review of Documents

Brokers are responsible for supervising their salespersons, and failure to do so is grounds for disciplinary action. The broker's supervisory responsibilities include reviewing any documents prepared by a salesperson that may have a material effect on the rights or obligations of a party to a transaction.

Broker-Salesperson Agreements

Whenever a broker hires a real estate salesperson, there must be a written agreement that documents their relationship. The broker must keep the agreement on file at the broker's office, and then retain the agreement for three years after the relationship is terminated.

Advertising Regulations

Real estate licensees need to be aware of the laws that regulate advertising—not just those that pertain specifically to real estate, but also more general rules, such as the prohibition against false advertising. A violation of state laws against false advertising is a misdemeanor; it's also a violation of the Real Estate Law.

Licensee Designation in Advertising

Advertisements published or distributed by a real estate licensee must include a licensee designation, some indication that the advertiser is a licensee. (An advertisement that doesn't fulfill this requirement is sometimes referred to as a **blind ad**.) A single word such as "broker," "agent," or "Realtor®" is sufficient, or even an abbreviation such as "bro." or "agt."

This rule generally applies to advertising concerning any matter for which a real estate license is required. There's an exception for classified ads for rental properties: if the ad gives the phone number or address of the rental property, a licensee designation isn't necessary.

A licensee designation doesn't have to be included when a licensee advertises his own property for sale or lease, since that isn't an act for which a real estate license is required.

First Contact Solicitation Materials

A licensee must include her license identification number in any solicitation materials that are intended to be the first point of contact with consumers (potential clients or customers). First contact solicitation materials include business cards, stationery, advertising fliers, and other materials designed to solicit the creation of a professional relationship with a consumer. The law specifically states that identification numbers are not required on "For Sale" signs or in ads that appear in print or electronic media.

First contact solicitation materials used by a real estate licensee who has a mortgage loan originator endorsement must include the identification number issued by the Nationwide Mortgage Licensing System and Registry, in addition to the real estate license number.

Internet Advertising

Brokers who advertise or provide information about real estate services on the Internet are required to comply with a rule concerning contact with specific customers.

There must be procedures in place to ensure that only a real estate licensee (or someone exempt from the licensing requirement) responds to inquiries from customers or otherwise contacts customers.

Advertising Loans and Notes

California imposes additional regulations on a licensee's advertisements for loans secured by real property. Any ad of this type must receive prior approval from the Bureau of Real Estate before it's published. Naturally, any ad that is misleading or deceptive won't be approved.

Ads for loans may not use a phrase like "guaranteed" without explaining how the loan is secured. They also may not imply that a loan can or will be approved over the telephone; that any government agency has endorsed the licensee's business activities; or that loans are available on terms more favorable than those generally available in the community, unless the advertiser can show that those terms would be available without undisclosed restrictions or conditions.

Similar regulations apply to ads concerning the resale of promissory notes. For instance, an advertisement may not guarantee a yield on a note other than the interest rate specified in the note, unless it also includes the note rate and the amount of the discount. (The discount is the difference between the outstanding note balance and the sales price of the note.)

Inducements

Sometimes a gift, prize, or rebate will be offered as an **inducement**, either for attending a sales presentation or for purchasing property. (Inducements are always forbidden as part of loan transactions.) If attendance at a sales presentation is required to obtain a gift, that must be disclosed in the advertisement or solicitation. Any other conditions for receiving gifts or prizes must also be disclosed. Note that if an inducement is given to one of the parties in a transaction, that's a material fact that must be disclosed to all of the parties.

Do Not Call Registry

Licensees who solicit business by making "cold calls" to strangers must comply with the Federal Trade Commission's telemarketing rules. It's against the law to make this type of call to someone whose name appears on the National "Do Not Call" Registry, so licensees must check the registry before placing calls; persons who engage in ongoing telemarketing must check the registry at least once every 31 days. There are also "Do Not Email" and "Do Not Fax" registries.

Antitrust Laws and Real Estate Licensees

In addition to the Real Estate Law, federal and state antitrust laws impose certain restrictions on a real estate agent's behavior towards clients, customers, and other agents.

At the foundation of antitrust laws is the idea that free enterprise is an important element of a democratic society, and that competition is good for both the economy and society as a whole. Antitrust laws prohibit any agreement that has the effect of creating an **unreasonable restraint of trade**. A restraint of trade is any act that prevents an individual or a company from doing business in a certain area or with certain people. When two or more business entities participate in a common scheme which has the effect of a restraint of trade, it's called a **conspiracy**.

Antitrust laws have a long history. The foremost federal law, the **Sherman Antitrust Act**, dates back to 1890. California's main state antitrust law, the **Cartwright Act**, was passed in 1907. While antitrust issues are commonly associated with big steel mills, oil companies, and telephone services, in 1950 antitrust laws were held to apply to the real estate industry as well. In a landmark case, the U.S. Supreme Court held that mandatory fee schedules, established and enforced by a real estate board, violated the Sherman Act (*United States v. National Association of Real Estate Boards*).

A real estate agent who violates antitrust laws may be subject to both civil and criminal actions. An individual found guilty of violating the Sherman Act can be fined up to one million dollars and/or sentenced to ten years' imprisonment. A corporation can be fined up to one hundred million dollars.

Prohibited Practices and Activities

Antitrust laws prohibit the following business practices and activities:

- price fixing,
- group boycotts,
- tie-in arrangements, and
- market allocation.

Price Fixing. Price fixing is defined as the cooperative setting of prices or price ranges by competing firms. To avoid the appearance of price fixing, real estate agents from different brokerages should never discuss their commission rates. (It's a discussion between competing brokers or salespersons that could violate the law. A broker can discuss commission rates with his own affiliated agents, and agents who work for the same broker can discuss rates with each other.) One exception to this general prohibition is that competing brokers involved in a cooperative sale are allowed to discuss a commission split—the division of the commission between the listing broker and the selling broker.

Even a casual announcement that a broker is planning on raising his commission rates could lead to antitrust problems.

Example: Broker Wood goes to a dinner given by his local MLS, and he's asked to discuss current market conditions. In the middle of his speech, he mentions that he's going to raise his commission rates, no matter what anyone else does. This statement could be viewed as an invitation to conspire to fix prices. If any other MLS members raise their rates in response to Wood's statement, they could be held to have accepted his invitation to conspire.

Brokers must understand that they don't have to actually consult with each other to be charged with conspiring to fix commission rates. The kind of scenario described in the previous example is enough to lead to an antitrust lawsuit.

Publications that appear to fix prices are prohibited as well. A multiple listing service or other real estate association that publishes "recommended" or "going" rates for commissions could be sued.

Group Boycotts. A group boycott is an agreement between two or more business competitors (such as real estate brokers from different firms) to exclude another competitor from fair participation in business activities.

> **Example:** Becker and Jordan are brokers from competing real estate companies. Over lunch together, they discuss the business practices of a third broker, Harley. Becker says she thinks Harley is dishonest. Jordan agrees. He says that he's decided not to do business with Harley. He avoids Harley whenever possible, and just doesn't call back if Harley calls to ask about a listed property. He suggests that Becker should do the same. Jordan and Becker could be found guilty of a conspiracy to boycott.

If a real estate broker feels that another broker is dishonest or unethical, she may choose not to do business with him. However, that broker can't encourage other brokers to follow suit.

Tie-in Arrangements. A tie-in arrangement (also called a tying arrangement) is defined as "an agreement to sell one product, only on the condition that the buyer also purchases a different (or tied) product…"

> **Example:** Brown is a subdivision developer. Tyson, a builder, wants to buy a lot. Brown tells Tyson that he will sell him a lot only if Tyson enters into a list-back agreement. In other words, Tyson must sign a contract promising that after he builds a house on the lot, he will list the improved property with Brown.

The developer's requirement in the example is an illegal tie-in arrangement. Note, however, that list-back agreements aren't necessarily illegal. A list-back agreement is illegal only if it's a required condition of the sale, creating a tie-in arrangement. Two parties may mutually agree on a list-back agreement without violating antitrust laws.

Market Allocation. Another type of business practice that violates antitrust laws is market allocation, when competitors divide up a market. It's illegal for competing businesses to agree not to sell certain products or services in specified areas, or to agree not to sell to certain customers in specified areas.

As with group boycotts, only collective action or agreement constitutes illegal market allocation. It's perfectly acceptable for an individual business to limit the market area it serves, or to limit its business to certain types of customers. So it wouldn't violate antitrust laws if ABC Realty decided to specialize in luxury homes, or if XYZ Realty decided to specialize in mid-priced homes. But it would be a violation for ABC and XYZ to enter into an agreement allocating their area's luxury market to ABC and the mid-priced market to XYZ.

Avoiding Antitrust Violations

There are several things real estate brokers can do or avoid doing in order to prevent antitrust violations. Brokers should:

- always establish their fees and other listing policies independently, without consulting competing firms;
- never use listing forms that contain preprinted commission rates;

- never imply to a client that the commission rate is fixed or nonnegotiable, or refer to a competitor's commission policies when discussing commission rates;
- never discuss their business plans with competitors;
- never tell clients or competitors that they won't do business with a competing firm, or tell them not to work with that firm because of doubts about its competence or integrity; and
- train their affiliated licensees to be aware of and avoid actions that may violate antitrust laws.

Chapter Summary

1. California's Real Estate Law requires those engaging in real estate activities to be licensed, and then regulates the actions of licensees. The purpose of the Real Estate Law is to protect members of the public who deal with real estate agents.

2. The Real Estate Commissioner implements the provisions of the Real Estate Law by enacting regulations, investigating the activities of licensees, and taking disciplinary action against those who violate the Real Estate Law.

3. The Real Estate Law determines who's required to have a real estate license and sets forth the licensing requirements for brokers and salespersons.

4. The Real Estate Law also establishes standards of lawful conduct and specifies the grounds for disciplinary action.

5. Trust funds received by a licensee generally must be deposited into a trust account or a neutral escrow, or delivered to the principal, within three business days after they are received.

6. Brokers are required to keep trust account and transaction records for at least three years.

7. Antitrust laws prohibit price fixing, group boycotts, tie-in arrangements, and market allocation agreements. Real estate brokers must be especially careful to avoid discussing commission rates with competing brokers.

Key Terms

Real Estate Law—A California statute that governs the licensing and business practices of real estate agents.

Bureau of Real Estate—The state agency that administers the Real Estate Law.

Real estate broker—A person who is licensed to represent others for compensation in real estate transactions.

Real estate salesperson—A person who is licensed to work for and represent a broker in real estate transactions.

Mortgage loan originator endorsement—A special endorsement to a real estate license that authorizes the licensee to engage in mortgage loan brokerage and origination activities for compensation.

Real Estate Fund—In the state treasury, a special account into which all license fees are placed.

Recovery Account—An account funded by license fees, used to compensate members of the public injured by the unlawful acts of real estate licensees, when other compensation isn't available.

Trust funds—Funds held by a broker on behalf of clients or customers.

Commingling—The mixing of trust funds with the broker's personal or business funds.

Trust account—A bank account that a broker uses to keep trust funds segregated from the broker's personal or business funds.

Advance fee—Money a broker receives from a client before providing services, either to cover anticipated expenses or as upfront compensation, which must be treated as trust funds.

Price fixing—The cooperative setting of prices by competing firms.

Group boycott—An agreement between two or more business competitors to exclude another competitor from fair participation in business activities.

Tie-in arrangement—An agreement to sell one product only on the condition that the buyer also purchases a different product. Also called a tying arrangement.

Market allocation—An agreement between competitors to divide up a market, in which the parties agree that one or both won't sell certain products or services in specified areas, or won't sell to certain customers in specified areas.

Chapter Quiz

1. Someone applying to renew her real estate license usually must have completed ______ hours of approved courses within the four-year period preceding license renewal.
   a) 15
   b) 20
   c) 45
   d) 90

2. A corporation may engage in the real estate brokerage business if the officer acting for the corporation:
   a) is a licensed salesperson
   b) is given the proper authority from the Commissioner of Corporations
   c) is a licensed real estate broker
   d) is the president of the corporation

3. Commingling is:
   a) the same as embezzlement
   b) mixing personal funds with trust funds
   c) any dishonest behavior related to trust funds
   d) paying a commission to a unlicensed person

4. Brokers must retain copies of all listings, purchase agreements, and trust account records for:
   a) one year
   b) two years
   c) three years
   d) four years

5. All of the following can make a withdrawal from a broker's trust account except:
   a) a salesperson in the broker's employ who has been authorized by the broker
   b) the broker's secretary, who has been authorized by the broker and is covered by a fiduciary bond
   c) a corporate officer of a corporation licensed as a broker
   d) the unlicensed, unbonded spouse of a broker who has been authorized by the broker

6. The Recovery Account will pay a maximum of ____________ per transaction.
   a) $50,000
   b) $100,000
   c) $250,000
   d) There is no limit

7. The bill of sale used in a business opportunity transaction must contain all of the following, except:
   a) names of transferor and transferee
   b) description of the personal property
   c) location of the business
   d) names and addresses of any creditors

8. A broker's trust account records:
   a) can be kept by a columnar method
   b) must be kept in a safe deposit box at a financial institution in California
   c) can be kept by the principal
   d) should be discarded one year after the transaction closes

9. A broker may keep an earned commission in a trust account for no more than:
   a) one day
   b) seven days
   c) 25 days
   d) 60 days

10. It's legal for a broker to place a good faith deposit:
   a) in a trust account
   b) in a neutral escrow
   c) in the hands of the broker's principal
   d) Any of the above

11. The maximum amount of a broker's own funds allowed in her trust account is:
   a) none
   b) $50
   c) $200
   d) $500

12. The commission rate a listing broker can charge on a sale is determined by:
    a) the Real Estate Commissioner
    b) the seller and the broker
    c) the multiple listing service
    d) the buyer and the seller

13. A broker's license:
    a) must be carried by the broker at all times
    b) should be kept in a safe place, such as a home safe or a safe deposit box at a bank
    c) must be kept in the broker's main office
    d) is kept in the field office of the Bureau of Real Estate nearest the broker's main office

14. A salesperson's license is valid for:
    a) two years
    b) three years
    c) four years
    d) five years

15. The funds that support the Recovery Account come from:
    a) interest accruing on trust accounts
    b) a surcharge on real estate developers
    c) private donations
    d) real estate license fees

16. Trust funds must be deposited into a broker's trust account:
    a) within three business days following receipt of the funds
    b) within 30 days of receipt of the funds
    c) by the broker's certified public accountant
    d) within three days after the transaction closes

17. Applicants for a broker's license must have:
    a) six years of experience as a real estate licensee
    b) 24 semester units of real estate education
    c) a sponsoring broker willing to testify to the applicant's honesty
    d) All of the above

18. A resident apartment manager who manages the apartment complex he lives in:
    a) must have a real estate salesperson's license
    b) need not have a real estate license
    c) must be supervised by a real estate licensee
    d) must register with the Bureau of Real Estate

19. All of the following are grounds for disciplinary action except:
    a) commingling
    b) failing to put a termination date in an exclusive listing
    c) negotiating with a seller to establish the commission rate
    d) failing to supervise a salesperson

20. Trust funds:
    a) are always money, never items of personal property
    b) may be put into the broker's general account, as long as scrupulous records of the deposits and withdrawals are kept
    c) can be given to the Real Estate Commissioner for deposit
    d) must never be deposited into the broker's general account

Answer Key

1. c) License renewal applicants generally must have completed 45 hours of continuing education during the four years prior to renewal.

2. c) Under a corporate license, any officer designated to represent the corporation in real estate brokerage activities must also be licensed as a broker.

3. b) Mixing personal funds with trust funds is called commingling.

4. c) Most transaction and trust account records must be kept for three years.

5. d) Withdrawals may not be made without the signature of the broker or of an authorized licensee, corporate officer, or bonded employee.

6. a) The Recovery Account will pay up to $50,000 per transaction to satisfy an unpaid judgment against a licensee.

7. d) In the sale of a business opportunity, the bill of sale must contain the names of the transferor and transferee, the location of the business, and a description of the personal property. The names and addresses of creditors are not required.

8. a) The broker's trust fund records can be kept by a columnar method.

9. c) Earned commissions should be withdrawn as soon as possible, but may remain in the trust account for up to 25 days if necessary.

10. d) A good faith deposit may be placed in a trust account or in a neutral escrow, or be given to the principal, depending on the circumstances.

11. c) A broker may keep up to $200 of her own funds in a trust account to cover service charges.

12. b) Commissions are negotiated between the broker and the client/seller.

13. c) A broker's license must be kept at the broker's main office, along with the licenses of all affiliated licensees.

14. c) A salesperson's license must be renewed every four years.

15. d) Up to 12% of all real estate license fees go into the Recovery Account. Monetary penalties for license law violations also go into the Recovery Account.

16. a) As a general rule, trust funds must be deposited in a trust account no later than three business days after receipt of the funds.

17. b) Broker applicants must complete 24 semester units (eight courses) of real estate education.

18. b) A resident apartment manager doesn't have to be licensed.

19. c) Brokers are free to negotiate their commissions with sellers. (In fact, it's grounds for disciplinary action to lead a seller to believe the commission rate is set by regulation.)

20. d) Trust funds must never be deposited into the broker's general account. That would be commingling, which is grounds for disciplinary action.

Chapter 17

Real Estate Math

I. Solving Math Problems
  A. Four-step approach
    1. Read the question
    2. Write down the formula
    3. Substitute
    4. Calculate
  B. Decimal numbers
    1. Converting fractions
    2. Converting percentages
    3. Decimal calculations
II. Area Problems
  A. Squares and rectangles
  B. Triangles
  C. Odd shapes
III. Volume Problems
IV. Percentage Problems
  A. Solving percentage problems
  B. Commission problems
  C. Loan problems
    1. Interest rates
    2. Principal balance
  D. Profit or loss problems
  E. Capitalization problems
V. Tax Assessment Problems
VI. Seller's Net Problems
VII. Proration Problems
  A. Property taxes
  B. Insurance premiums
  C. Rent
  D. Mortgage interest

Chapter Overview

Real estate agents use math constantly: to calculate their commissions, to determine the square footage of homes they are listing or selling, to prorate closing costs, and so on. Electronic calculators make all of these tasks much easier than they once were, but it is still necessary to have a basic grasp of the math involved. This chapter provides step-by-step instructions for solving a wide variety of real estate math problems.

Solving Math Problems

We're going to begin our discussion of real estate math with a simple approach to solving math problems. Master this four-step process, and you'll be able to solve most math problems you are likely to encounter.

1. Read the question

The most important step is to thoroughly read and understand the question. You must know what you are looking for before you can successfully solve any math problem. Once you know what you want to find out (for example, the area, the commission amount, or the total profit), you'll be able to decide which formula to use.

2. Write down the formula

Write down the correct formula for the problem you need to solve. For example, the area formula is *Area* = *Length* × *Width*, which is abbreviated $A = L \times W$. Formulas for each type of problem are presented throughout this chapter, and there is a complete list at the end of the chapter.

3. Substitute

Substitute the relevant numbers from the problem into the formula. Sometimes there are numbers in the problem that you will not use. It's not unusual for a math problem to contain unnecessary information, which is why it is very important to read the question first and determine what you are looking for. The formula will help you distinguish between the relevant and irrelevant information given in the problem.

In some problems you will be able to substitute numbers into the formula without any additional steps, but in other problems one or more preliminary steps will be necessary. For instance, you may have to convert fractions to decimals.

4. Calculate

Once you have substituted the numbers into the formula, you are ready to perform the calculations to find the unknown—the component of the formula that was not given in the problem. Most of the formulas have the same basic form: $A = L \times W$. The problem will give you two of the three numbers (or information to enable you to find two of the numbers) and then you will either have to divide or multiply to find the third number, which is the solution to the problem.

Whether you'll multiply or divide is determined by which component in the formula is the unknown. For example, the formula $A = L \times W$ may be converted into two other formulas. All three formulas are equivalent, but they are put into different forms depending on the element to be discovered.

1. If the quantity A (the area) is unknown, then the following formula is used: $A = L \times W$. The number L is **multiplied** by W. The product of L multiplied by W is A.

2. If the quantity L (the length) is unknown, the following formula is used: $L = A \div W$. The number A is **divided** by W. The quotient of A divided by W is L.

3. If the quantity W (the width) is unknown, the following formula is used: $W = A \div L$. The number A is **divided** by L. The quotient of A divided by L is W.

Thus, the formula $A = L \times W$ may be used three different ways depending on which quantity is unknown. For the examples below, assume the area of a rectangle is 800 square feet, the length is 40 feet, and the width is 20 feet.

$A = L \times W$	$L = A \div W$	$W = A \div L$
$A = 40' \times 20'$	$L = 800\ Sq.ft. \div 20'$	$W = 800\ Sq.ft. \div 40'$
$40' \times 20' = 800\ Sq.ft.$	$800\ Sq.ft. \div 20' = 40'$	$800\ Sq.ft. \div 40' = 20'$

After you've substituted the numbers given in the problem into the formula, you might have trouble deciding whether you're supposed to multiply or divide. It may help to compare your equation to the very familiar calculation $2 \times 3 = 6$. If the unknown component of your equation is in the same position as the 6 in $2 \times 3 = 6$, then you need to multiply the two given numbers to find the unknown.

If the unknown component is in the 2 position or the 3 position, you need to divide. You'll divide the given number in the 6 position by the other given number to find the unknown.

$? \times 3 = 6$ *becomes* $6 \div 3 = 2$	$2 \times ? = 6$ *becomes* $6 \div 2 = 3$

Now let's apply the four-step approach to an example. Suppose a room is 10 feet wide and 15 feet long. How many square feet does it contain?

1. **Read the question**. This problem asks you to find the square footage or area of a rectangular room. So you'll need the area formula for a rectangle.

2. **Write down the formula**. *Area = Length × Width*

3. **Substitute**. Substitute the numbers given in the problem into the formula. The length of the rectangle measures 15 feet, and the width measures 10 feet: $A = 15' \times 10'$.

4. **Calculate**. Multiply *Length* times *Width* to get the answer: $15' \times 10' = 150\ Sq.ft.$ Thus, $A = 150$. The area of the room is 150 square feet.

Suppose the problem gave you different pieces of information about the same room: the area is 150 square feet and it's 10 feet wide. How long is the room? Again, follow the four-step approach.

1. **Read the question**. You're asked to find the length or width of a rectangle. You'll need the area formula again.
2. **Write down the formula**. *Area = Length × Width*
3. **Substitute**. Substitute the numbers given in the problem into the formula: *150 = L × 10′*.
4. **Calculate**. The length of the rectangle is the unknown. Thus, the basic area formula is converted into a division problem to find the length: *150 Sq. ft. ÷ 10′= 15′*. The quotient of 150 divided by 10 is 15. The length of the rectangle, or of the room, is therefore 15 feet.

Decimal Numbers

To carry out a calculation, it's easier to work with decimal numbers than with fractions or percentages. So if a problem presents you with fractions or percentages, you'll usually convert them into decimal numbers.

Converting Fractions. To convert a fraction into decimal form, divide the top number of the fraction (the numerator) by the bottom number of the fraction (the denominator).

Example: To change ¾ into a decimal, divide 3 (the top number) by 4 (the bottom number): *3 ÷ 4= .75.*

Example: To convert ⅔ into a decimal, divide 2 (the top number) by 3 (the bottom number): *2 ÷ 3= .66667.*

If you don't already know them, it's useful to memorize the decimal equivalents of the most common fractions:

¼ = .25
½ = .5
¾ = .75

Converting Percentages. To solve a problem involving a percentage, you'll first convert the percentage into a decimal number, then convert the decimal answer back into percentage form.

To convert a percentage to a decimal, remove the percent sign and move the decimal point two places to the left. It may be necessary to add a zero.

Example:

98% becomes .98

5% becomes .05

32.5% becomes .325

17.5% becomes .175

To convert a decimal into a percentage, do just the opposite. Move the decimal point two places to the right and add a percent sign.

Example:

.15 becomes 15%

.08 becomes 08%, or 8%

.095 becomes 09.5%, or 9.5%

The percent key on a calculator performs the conversion of a percentage to a decimal number automatically. On most calculators, you can key in the digits and press the percent key, and the calculator will display the percentage in decimal form.

Decimal Calculations. Calculators handle decimal numbers in exactly the same way as whole numbers. If you enter a decimal number into the calculator with the decimal point in the correct place, the calculator will do the rest. But if you're working without a calculator, you'll need to apply the following rules.

To add or subtract decimals, put the numbers in a column with their decimal points lined up.

Example: To add 3.75, 14.62, 1.245, 679, 1,412.8, and 1.9, put the numbers in a column with the decimal points lined up as shown below, then add them together.

3.75
14.62
1.245
679.0
1,412.8
+ 1.9
2,113.315

To multiply decimal numbers, first do the multiplication without worrying about the decimal points. Then put a decimal point into the answer in the correct place. The answer should have as many decimal places (that is, numbers to the right of its decimal point) as the total number of decimal places in the numbers that were multiplied. So count the decimal places in the numbers you are multiplying and put the decimal point the same number of places to the left in the answer.

Example: Multiply 24.6 times 16.7. The two numbers contain a total of two decimal places.

24.6
× 16.7
410.82

In some cases, it will be necessary to include one or more zeros in the answer to have the correct number of decimal places.

Example: Multiply .2 times .4. There is a total of two decimal places.

.2
× .4
.08

In this calculation, a zero has to be included in the answer in order to move the decimal point two places left.

To divide by a decimal number, move the decimal point in the denominator (the number you're dividing the other number by) all the way to the right. Then move the decimal point in the numerator (the number that you're dividing) the same number of places to the right. (In some cases it will be necessary to add one or more zeros to the numerator in order to move the decimal point the correct number of places.)

Example: Divide 26.145 by 1.5. First move the decimal point in 1.5 all the way to the right (in this case, that's only one place). Then move the decimal point in 26.145 the same number of places to the right.

26.145 ÷ 1.5 becomes 261.45 ÷ 15

Now divide. *261.45 ÷ 15 = 17.43*

Remember, these steps are unnecessary if you're using a calculator. If the numbers are keyed in correctly, the calculator will automatically give you an answer with the decimal point in the correct place.

Area Problems

A real estate agent often needs to calculate the area of a lot, a building, or a room. Area is usually stated in square feet or square yards. The formula to be used for the calculation depends on the shape of the area in question. It may be a square, a rectangle, a triangle, or some combination of those shapes.

Squares and Rectangles

As stated earlier, the formula for finding the area of a square or a rectangle is $A = L \times W$.

Example: If a rectangular room measures 15 feet along one wall and 12 feet along the adjoining wall, how many square feet of carpet would be required to cover the floor?

1. **Read the question.** You're being asked to find the area (the square footage) of a rectangle.
2. **Write down the formula.** $A = L \times W$
3. **Substitute.** $A = 15' \times 12'$
4. **Calculate.** Since the quantity A is unknown, multiply L times W for the answer: *15′ × 12′ = 180 Sq. ft.* So 180 square feet of carpet are needed to cover the floor.

180
Sq. Feet
15'
12'

Now take the problem one step further. If carpet is on sale for $12 per square yard, how much would it cost to carpet the room?

1. **Read the question.** You're first being asked to determine how many square feet there are in a square yard, and then to determine how many square yards

there are in 180 square feet. A square yard is a square that measures one yard on each side. There are three feet in a yard.

2. **Write down the formula.** $A = L \times W$

3. **Substitute.** $A = 3' \times 3'$

4. **Calculate.** Since the quantity *A* is the unknown, multiply *L* times *W*: $3' \times 3' = 9$ *Sq. ft.*

So there are 9 square feet in a square yard. Now divide 180 by 9 to see how many square yards there are in 180 square feet: *180 ÷ 9 = 20 Sq. yd.*

Now multiply the number of square yards (20) by the cost per square yard ($12): *20 × $12 = $240 Cost to carpet room.*

Triangles

The formula for finding the area of a triangle is:

Height
× ½ Base
Area

or *Area = ½ Base × Height*

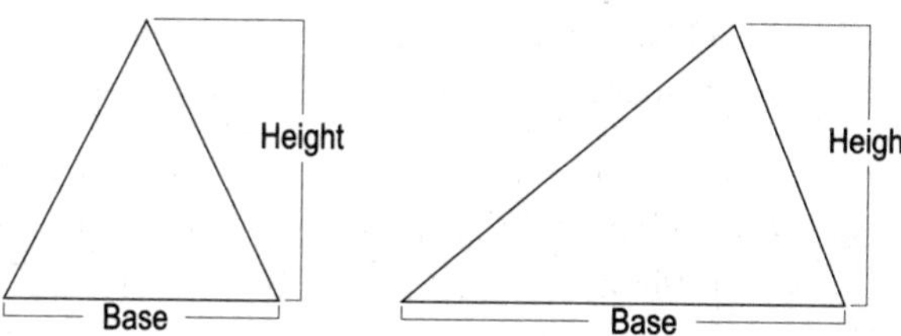

Example: If commercial building lots in a certain neighborhood are selling for approximately $5 per square foot, approximately how much should the lot pictured below sell for?

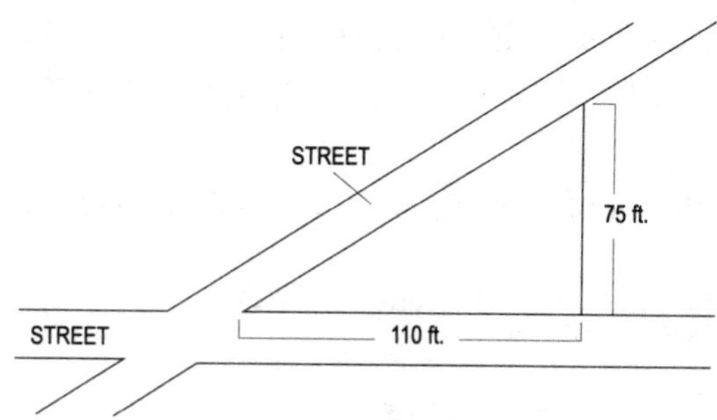

1. **Write down the formula.** $A = \frac{1}{2} B \times H$

2. **Substitute.** *Area = 55′ (½ of 110) × 75′*

3. **Calculate.** *75′ × 55′ = 4,125 Sq. ft.*

The order of multiplication doesn't matter. You can multiply 110 times 75 and then divide it in half. Or you can divide 110 by 2 and then multiply the result by 75. Or you can divide 75 by 2 and then multiply the result by 110. Whichever way you do it, the answer will be the same.

	Step 1	Step 2	Answer
a)	*110 × 75 = 8,250*	*8,250 ÷ 2 = 4,125*	*4,125 Sq. ft.*
b)	*110 ÷ 2 = 55*	*55 × 75 = 4,125*	*4,125 Sq. ft.*
c)	*75 ÷ 2 = 37.5*	*37.5 × 110 = 4,125*	*4,125 Sq. ft.*

The lot contains 4,125 square feet. If similar lots are selling for about $5 per square foot, this lot should sell for about $20,625.

4,125	*Square feet*
× $5	*Per square foot*
$20,625	*Selling price*

Odd Shapes

The best approach to finding the area of an odd-shaped figure is to divide it up into squares, rectangles, and triangles. Find the areas of those figures and add them all up to arrive at the area of the odd-shaped lot, room, or building in question.

Example: If the lot pictured below is leased on a 50-year lease for $3 per square foot per year, with rental payments made monthly, how much would the monthly rent be?

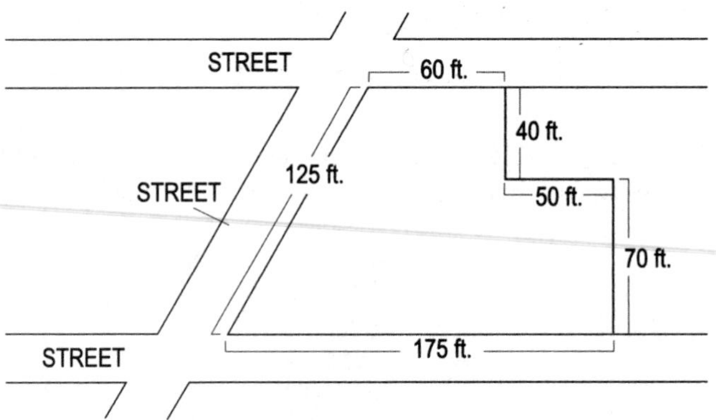

First, divide the lot up into rectangles and triangles.

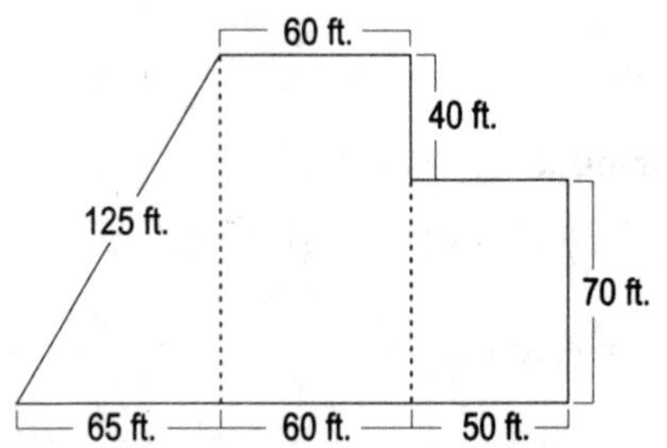

The next step is to find the area of each of the following figures. The height of the triangle is determined by adding together the 70-foot border of the small rectangle and the 40-foot border of the large rectangle, as shown above.

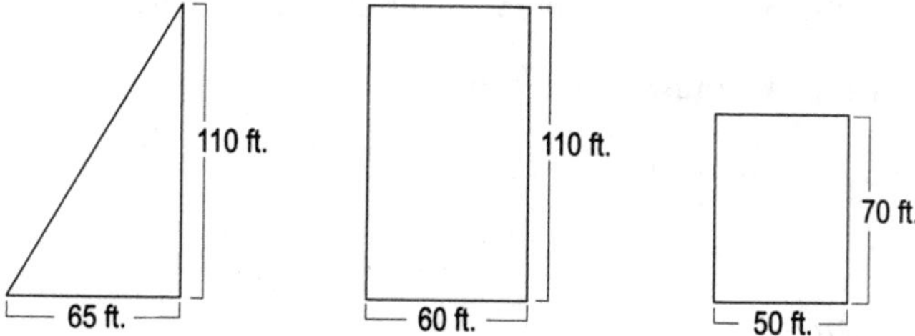

First, find the area of the triangle.

1. **Write down the formula.** *A = ½ Base × Height*
2. **Substitute.** *A = 32.5′ (½ of 65′) × 110′*
3. **Calculate.** *32.5′ × 110′ = 3,575 Sq. ft.*

Then, find the area of the large rectangle.

1. **Write down the formula.** *A = Length × Width*
2. **Substitute.** *A = 110′ × 60′*
3. **Calculate.** *110′ × 60′ = 6,600 Sq. ft.*

Next, find the area of the small rectangle.

1. **Write down the formula.** *A = Length × Width*
2. **Substitute.** *A = 70′ × 50′*
3. **Calculate.** *50′ × 70′ = 3,500 Sq. ft.*

Finally, add the three areas together to find the area of the entire lot: *3,575 + 6,600 + 3,500 = 13,675 Total square feet.*

The lot contains 13,675 square feet. At $3 per square foot per year, the annual rent would be $41,025.

13,675	*Square feet*
× $3	*Rent per square foot*
$41,025	*Annual rent*

The monthly rental payment would be one-twelfth of the annual rent: *$41,025 ÷ 12 = $3,418.75.* Thus, the monthly rental payment for this odd-shaped lot is $3,418.75.

Volume Problems

Occasionally you may need to calculate the volume of a three-dimensional space. Volume is usually stated in cubic feet or cubic yards. A formula for calculating volume can be stated as: *Volume = Length × Width × Height*, or *V = L × W × H.* It's the same as the area formula, except it has one added element: *H*, the height of the space being measured.

Example: The floor of a storage unit measures 13 feet 6 inches by 20 feet, and it has a 12-foot ceiling. What is the volume of the unit in cubic yards?

1. **Write down the formula.** $V = L \times W \times H$

2. **Substitute.** $V = 20' \times 13.5' \times 12'$

3. **Calculate.**

Step 1	Step 2
20′	*270 Square feet*
× 13.5′	*× 12′*
270 Square feet	*3,240 Cubic feet*

4. **Now convert the cubic feet into cubic yards.** As you saw earlier, a square yard measures 3 feet by 3 feet, or 9 square feet. A cubic yard measures 3 feet by 3 feet by 3 feet, or 27 cubic feet. Divide the volume of the storage area in cubic feet by 27 to find the volume in cubic yards: *3,240 ÷ 27 = 120 Cubic yards*. The volume of the storage space is 120 cubic yards.

Percentage Problems

Many real estate math problems involve percentages. This includes problems about brokerage commissions, interest on mortgage loans, property appreciation or depreciation, and capitalization.

Solving Percentage Problems

To solve percentage problems, you'll usually convert the percentage into a decimal number, calculate, and then convert the answer back into percentage form. As explained earlier, a percentage is converted into a decimal number by removing the percent sign and moving the decimal point two places to the left. If the percentage is a single digit (for example, 7%), it will be necessary to add a zero (.07). To convert a decimal number into a percentage, you reverse those steps: move the decimal point two places to the right and add the percent sign.

In a math problem, whenever something is expressed as a percentage "of" another number, that indicates that you should multiply that other number by the percentage. For instance, what is 75% of $40,000?

Step 1	Step 2
75% becomes .75	*$40,000*
	× .75
	$30,000

Basically, percentage problems ask you to find a part of a whole. The whole is a larger figure, such as a property's sales price. The part is a smaller figure, such as a broker's commission. The general formula might be stated thus: *A percentage of the whole equals the part.* This can be written as an equation: *Part = Whole × Percentage.*

Example: A house is listed for sale at a price of $172,000, with an agreement to pay the broker a commission of 6% of the sales price. The property sells for $170,000. How much is the commission?

1. **Write down the formula.** *P = W × %*

2. **Substitute.** Change the percentage (6%) into a decimal number (.06) first: *P = $170,000 × .06.*

3. **Calculate.**

$170,000	*Sales price*
× .06	*Commission rate*
$10,200	*Commission*

The broker's commission is $10,200.

In some percentage problems, the part is given and you're asked to calculate either the whole or the percentage. For those problems, you'll need to rearrange the percentage formula into a division problem. If the whole is the unknown, divide the part by the percentage: *Whole = Part ÷ Percentage.*

If the percentage is the unknown, divide the part by the whole: *Percentage = Part ÷ Whole.*

Notice that in either case, you'll be dividing the value of the part by either the whole (to determine the percentage) or by the percentage (to determine the whole).

Commission Problems

Like the example above, most commission problems can be solved with the general percentage formula: *Part = Whole × Percentage.*

The percentage is the commission rate, and the whole is the amount that the commission is based on. In most problems, this will be the sales price of a piece of property. The part is the amount of the commission.

Example: A listing agreement provides for a commission of 7% of the sales price to be paid to the broker. The broker has agreed to pay his salesperson 60% of the commission. How much will the salesperson receive if the property sells for $580,000?

1. **Write down the formula.** *P = W × %*

2. **Substitute.** Change the percentage (7%) to a decimal number (.07): *P = $580,000 × .07.*

3. **Calculate.** The part is the unknown quantity, so the percentage is multiplied by the whole.

$580,000	*Sales price*
× .07	*Commission rate*
$40,600	*Total commission*

The total commission is \$40,600. The salesperson is entitled to 60% of the total commission. Apply the percentage formula again to determine the amount of the salesperson's share.

1. **Write down the formula.** $P = W \times \%$

2. **Substitute.** Convert the percentage (60%) to a decimal number (.60): $P =$ *\$40,600 × .60.*

3. **Calculate.**

\$40,600	*Total commission*
× .60	*Salesperson's percentage*
\$24,360	*Salesperson's share*

The following example illustrates another form that commission problems can take.

Example: A listing agreement provided for a two-tiered commission based on the property's sales price. The commission would be 7% of the first \$100,000 and 5% of any amount over \$100,000. If the commission was \$8,250, what was the sales price?

1. **Read the question.** You're given the commission rates and the amount of the commission, and then asked to find the sales price. Your first step in the process is to find out how much of the commission amount is attributable to the first \$100,000 of the sales price.

2. **Write down the formula.** $P = W \times \%$

3. **Substitute,** converting the percentage to a decimal: $P =$ *\$100,000 × .07.*

4. **Calculate.** *\$100,000 × .07 = \$7,000*

So \$7,000 of the commission is based on the first \$100,000 of the sales price. Next, subtract to find the amount of the rest of the commission.

\$8,250	*Total commission*
– 7,000	*Commission from first \$100,000*
\$1,250	

Now you know that out of the total commission, \$1,250 is attributable to the part of the sales price in excess of \$100,000. You can use that figure along with the second-tier commission rate (5% of the amount over \$100,000) to determine by how much the sales price exceeded \$100,000.

1. **Write down the formula.** $P = W \times \%$

2. **Substitute,** converting the percentage to a decimal: *\$1,250 =* $W \times .05$.

3. **Calculate.** The quantity W (the whole) is the unknown. To isolate the unknown, the basic formula must be turned into a division problem. The part divided by the percentage equals the whole: *\$1,250 ÷ .05 = \$25,000.*

This shows that the portion of the sales price in excess of \$100,000 amounted to \$25,000. Thus, the total sales price is \$100,000 plus \$25,000, or \$125,000.

Loan Problems

Loan problems include interest problems and principal balance problems. These can be solved using the general percentage formula: *Part = Whole × Percentage.* Here, the part is the amount of the interest, the whole is the loan amount or principal balance, and the percentage is the interest rate.

Example: Henry borrows $5,000 for one year and agrees to pay 7% interest. How much interest will he be required to pay?

1. **Write down the formula.** *P = W × %*

2. **Substitute.** *P = $5,000 × .07*

3. **Calculate.**

$5,000	*Loan amount*
× .07	*Interest rate*
$350	*Interest*

Henry will pay $350 in interest.

Interest Rates. Interest rates are expressed as annual rates—a certain percentage per year. Some problems present you with monthly, quarterly, or semi-annual interest payments instead of the annual amount. In that case, you'll need to multiply the payment amount stated in the problem to determine the annual amount before you substitute the numbers into the formula.

Example: If $450 in interest accrues on a $7,200 interest-only loan in six months, what is the annual interest rate?

1. **Read the question.** You're asked to find the annual interest rate, but the interest amount given in the problem ($450) accrued in only six months. The annual interest amount would be double that, or $900.

2. **Write down the formula.** *P = W × %*

3. **Substitute.** For the part (the interest amount), be sure to use the annual figure ($900): *$900 = $7,200 × Percentage.*

4. **Calculate.** Rearrange the formula to isolate the unknown (in this case, the percentage). The part is divided by the whole to determine the percentage: *$900 ÷ $7,200 = .125.*

Convert the decimal number back into a percentage: .125 becomes 12.5%. Thus, the annual interest rate is 12½%.

Principal Balance. Some loan problems ask you to determine a loan's current principal balance at a certain point in the loan term.

Example: A home loan has monthly payments of $625, which include principal and 9% interest and $47.50 per month for tax and insurance reserves. If $27.75 of the June 1 payment was applied to the principal, what was the outstanding principal balance during the month of May? (Mortgage interest is paid in arrears, so the June payment includes the interest that accrued during May.)

1. **Write down the formula.** $P = W \times \%$. Once again, in this context the part is the amount of interest, the whole is the loan balance, and the percentage is the interest rate.

2. **Substitute.** First, find the interest portion of the payment by subtracting the reserves and the principal portion.

   $625.00 Total June payment
   47.50 Reserves
   – 27.75 Principal
   $549.75 Interest portion of payment

   Next, multiply the interest portion by 12 to determine the annual interest amount: *$549.75 × 12 = $6,597.*

   Now substitute the annual interest amount and rate into the formula: *$6,597 = W × .09.*

3. **Calculate.** Rearrange the formula to isolate the unknown, *W*. This is a division problem: *$6,597 ÷ .09 = $73,300.*

   The outstanding principal balance for May was $73,300.

Profit or Loss Problems

Profit or loss problems ask you to compare the cost or value of a piece of property at an earlier point in time with its cost or value at a later point. They can be solved using a variation on the percentage formula. Instead of *Part = Whole × Percentage*, the formula is stated like this: *Now = Then × Percentage.*

The *Then* spot in the formula is for the value or cost of the property at an earlier time specified in the problem. The *Now* spot is for the value or cost at a later time. The percentage is 100% plus the percentage of profit or minus the percentage of loss.

The idea is to express the value of the property after a profit or loss (*Now*) as a percentage of the property's value before the profit or loss (*Then*). If there is no profit or loss, the *Now* value is exactly 100% of the *Then* value, because the value has not changed. If there is a profit, the *Now* value will be greater than 100% of the *Then* value, since the value has increased. If there is a loss, the *Now* value will be less than 100% of the *Then* value.

Example: Bonnie bought a house five years ago for $450,000 and sold it this year for 30% more than she paid for it. What did she sell it for?

1. **Write down the formula.** *Now = Then × %*

2. **Substitute.** To get the percentage, you must add the percentage of profit to or subtract the percentage of loss from 100%. In this case there is a profit, so you add 30% to 100%, then convert it to a decimal number (130% becomes 1.30): *Now = $450,000 × 1.30.*

3. **Calculate.** *$450,000 × 1.30 = $585,000*

Bonnie sold her house for $585,000.

Example: Paul sold his house this year for $840,000. He paid $1,050,000 for it two years ago. What was the percentage of loss?

1. **Write down the formula.** *Now = Then × %*
2. **Substitute.** *$840,000 = $1,050,000 × %*
3. **Calculate.** The percentage is the unknown quantity; thus, the formula is rearranged to isolate the percentage: *$840,000 ÷ $1,050,000 = .80 or 80%.*

The *Now* value is 80% of the *Then* value. Subtract 80% from 100% to find the percentage of loss: *100% – 80% = 20% Loss.*

Paul took a 20% loss on the sale of his house.

Let's look at another example, except this time there is a profit instead of a loss.

Example: Martha bought her home six years ago for $377,400. She sold it recently for $422,700. What was her percentage of profit?

1. **Write down the formula.** *Now = Then × %*
2. **Substitute.** *$422,700 = $377,400 × %*
3. **Calculate.** Once again, the percentage is the unknown quantity; thus, the formula is rearranged to isolate the percentage: $*422,700 ÷ $377,400 = 1.12 or 112%.*

The *Now* value is approximately 112% of the *Then* value. Subtract 100% from 112%, and you determine Martha received 100% of what she paid for the house, plus a 12% profit.

Let's try to solve one last variation of this type of problem.

Example: Ken sold his duplex for $280,000, which represents a 16% profit over what he paid for it five years ago. What did Ken originally pay for the property?

1. **Write down the formula.** *Now = Then × %*
2. **Substitute.** *$280,000 = Then × 116%*
3. **Calculate.** In this instance, the unknown is the price Ken originally paid for the duplex; so you isolate the *Then* part of the equation: *$280,000 ÷ 1.16 = $241,379.31.*

The price Ken paid was $241,379.

Some profit or loss problems involve appreciation or depreciation that has accrued at an annual rate over a specified number of years. You solve this type of problem by applying the "Then and Now" formula one year at a time.

Example: A property that is currently worth $174,000 has depreciated 3% per year for the past four years. How much was it worth four years ago?

1. **Write down the formula.** *Now = Then × %*

2. **Substitute**. Because the property is worth 3% less than it was one year ago, the percentage is 97% (100% – 3% = 97%): *$174,000 = Then × .97.*

3. **Calculate**. Rearrange the formula to isolate the unknown, the *Then* value: *$174,000 ÷ .97 = $179,381.44.*

   The property was worth $179,381.44 one year ago. Apply the formula to $179,381.44 to determine the property's value two years ago. Repeat the process twice more to find the value four years ago.

   $179,381.44 ÷ .97 = $184,929.31

   $184,929.31 ÷ .97 = $190,648.77

   $190,648.77 ÷ .97 = $196,545.12

The property was worth about $196,545 four years ago.

Capitalization Problems

Capitalization problems involve the capitalization approach to value, a method of real estate appraisal that is discussed in detail in Chapter 11.

The capitalization formula is another variation on the percentage formula. Instead of *Part = Whole × Percentage*, the formula is stated like this: *Income = Value × Capitalization Rate.*

The value here is an investment property's value, or the purchase price an investor should be willing to pay for the property in order to obtain a specified rate of return.

The specified rate of return is the capitalization rate. This is the percentage of return the investor desires on the investment. The desired rate of return varies according to many factors. A higher desired rate of return will mean a higher capitalization rate and a lower value for the property.

The income in the capitalization formula is the annual net income produced by the investment property.

Example: A property produces an annual net income of $26,000. If an investor desires an 11% rate of return, what should he pay for the property?

1. **Write down the formula.** *I = V × %*

2. **Substitute.** *$26,000 = V × .11*

3. **Calculate.** Rearrange the formula to isolate *V*, the unknown quantity: *$26,000 ÷ .11 = $236,363.64.*

The investor should be willing to pay approximately $236,364 for the property.

Example: If a property is valued at $1,000,000 using an 8% capitalization rate, what would its value be using a 10% capitalization rate? First, apply the capitalization formula to determine the property's annual net income.

1. **Write down the formula.** *I = V × %*

2. **Substitute.** *I = $1,000,000 × .08*

3. **Calculate.**

$1,000,000	*Value*
× .08	*Capitalization rate*
$80,000	*Annual net income*

The net income is $80,000 annually. Now substitute that figure into the formula to find the value at a 10% capitalization rate.

4. **Substitute.** *$80,000 = V × .10*

5. **Calculate.** Rearrange the formula to isolate *V*, the unknown quantity: *$80,000 ÷ .10 = $800,000.*

So the value of the same property using a 10% capitalization rate is $800,000, compared to $1,000,000 at the 8% rate. As you can see, a higher capitalization rate applied to the same net income results in a lower value for the property.

In some problems, it's necessary to deduct a vacancy factor and operating expenses from gross income to arrive at the net income.

Example: A ten-unit apartment building has six units that rent for $800 per month and four units that rent for $850 per month. Allow 5% for vacancies and uncollected rent. Operating expenses include: annual property taxes of $7,200, monthly utilities of $2,475, and maintenance expenses of approximately $13,600 per year. The owner has an outstanding mortgage balance of $257,000 at 8% interest, with monthly payments of $2,150. If an investor requires a 7.5% rate of return, how much should she offer for the property?

1. **Write down the formula.** *I = V × %*

2. **Substitute.** Remember that the income referred to in the capitalization formula is annual net income. Thus, it's necessary to calculate the annual net income before substituting. The first step in that process is calculating the annual gross income.

   $800 × 12 months = $9,600/year × 6 units = $57,600
   $850 × 12 months = $10,200/year × 4 units = $40,800
   $98,400

   The gross income is $98,400 per year.

   Next, calculate the vacancy factor and deduct it from the gross income to find the effective gross income. The vacancy factor is 5% of the gross income.

$98,400	*Gross income*
× .05	
$4,920	*Vacancies*

   Thus, the loss to be expected from uncollected rents and vacancies is $4,920 per year.

$98,400	*Gross income*
– 4,920	*Vacancies*
$93,480	*Effective gross income*

The operating expenses must be deducted from the effective gross income to arrive at the net income. Remember, since you are trying to find annual net income, all the expenses must be annual also. The operating expenses add up as follows:

$7,200 Property taxes
29,700 Utilities (at $2,475 per month)
+ 13,600 Maintenance
$50,500 Annual operating expenses

The annual operating expenses are $50,500. (The mortgage payments are not treated as operating expenses. See Chapter 11.) Subtract the operating expenses from the effective gross income to determine the annual net income.

$93,480 Effective gross income
– 50,500 Annual operating expenses
$42,980 Annual net income

Now, substitute the net income and the cap rate into the formula *I*= *V* × %: *$42,980 = V × .075.*

3. **Calculate**. Rearrange the formula to isolate *V*, the unknown quantity: *$42,980 ÷ .075 = $573,067.*

The investor should be willing to pay approximately $573,067 for the property.

Example: Continuing with the previous example, if an investor paid $750,000 for the apartment building, what capitalization rate was used? (Assume that the property's income and operating expenses were the same.)

1. **Write down the formula.** *V* × % = *I*
2. **Substitute**. You already know the net income from the preceding problem: *$42,980 = $750,000 × %.*
3. **Calculate**. Isolate the unknown quantity, the capitalization rate: *$42,980 ÷ $750,000 = .0573 or 5.73%.*

The investor used a capitalization rate of approximately 5.7%.

A capitalization problem may give you the property's **operating expense ratio** (O.E.R.). The O.E.R. is the percentage of the gross income that is used to pay the annual operating expenses. The remainder is the annual net income.

Example: The property's annual gross income is $480,000, and its O.E.R. is 79%. If an investor wants a 10½% return, how much is the property worth to her?

1. **Write down the formula.** *I* = *V* × %
2. **Substitute**. Calculate the annual operating expenses using the operating expense ratio. Then subtract the operating expenses from the gross income to arrive at the annual net income.

$480,000 × .79 = $379,200 Annual operating expenses
$480,000 – $379,200 = $100,800 Annual net income

Now substitute the income and the cap rate into the formula: *$100,800 = V × .105.*

3. **Calculate**. Rearrange the formula to isolate *V*, the unknown quantity: *$100,800 ÷ .105 = $960,000 Value.*

The investor should be willing to pay $960,000 for the property.

Tax Assessment Problems

Many tax assessment problems can be solved using this formula: *Tax = Assessed Value × Tax Rate*. You may first have to determine the assessed value before you can carry out the rest of the calculations. Assessed value is a property's value for taxation purposes.

Example: According to the tax assessor, the property's market value is $292,300. The applicable assessment ratio is 85%. If the tax rate is 3%, how much is the annual tax amount?

1. **Multiply** the market value by the assessment ratio to determine the assessed value of the property: *$292,300 × 85% = $248,455 Assessed value.*

2. **Substitute** the assessed value and the tax rate into the formula: *Tax = $248,455 × .03.*

3. **Calculate.**

$248,455	*Assessed value*
× .03	*Tax rate*
$7,453.65	*Annual taxes*

The annual taxes for this property are $7,453.65.

In some problems, the tax rate is not stated as a percentage of the assessed value. Instead, it is expressed as a dollar amount per hundred or per thousand dollars of assessed value.

Example: A property with an assessed value of $173,075 is taxed at a rate of $2.35 per hundred dollars of assessed value. How much is the annual tax amount?

1. **Divide** $173,075 by 100 to determine how many hundred dollar increments there are in the assessed value: *$173,075 ÷ 100 = 1,730.75 or 1,731 $100 increments.* (A partial $100 increment would be taxed as one $100 increment.)

2. **Multiply** the number of hundred dollar increments by the tax rate to calculate the annual tax amount.

1,731	*$100 increments*
× $2.35	*Tax rate*
$4,067.85	*Annual taxes*

The annual tax is $4,067.85.

In other problems, the tax rate is expressed as a specified number of mills per dollar of assessed value. A mill is one-tenth of one cent (.001). Ten mills equals one cent, and 100 mills equals 10 cents.

Example: The property's market value is $310,000 and the assessment ratio is 70%. The tax rate is 21 mills per dollar of assessed value. How much is the annual tax amount?

1. **Multiply** the market value by the assessment ratio to find the assessed value.

$310,000	*Market value*
× .70	*Assessment ratio*
$217,000	*Assessed value*

2. **Multiply** the assessed value by the tax rate to determine the tax. In decimal form, 21 mills is .021.

$217,000	*Assessed value*
× .021	*Tax rate*
$4,557	*Annual tax*

The annual tax is $4,557.

Seller's Net Problems

In a seller's net problem, you're told that a seller wants to take away a specified net amount from closing, after paying the broker's commission and other closing costs. You're then asked to calculate how much the property will have to sell for if the seller is to receive the desired net.

Example: The seller wants to net $50,000 from the sale of her home. She will have to pay off her mortgage balance, which is approximately $126,500, and pay $1,560 for repairs, $2,015 for other closing costs, and a 7% broker's commission. What's the minimum sales price that will net the seller $50,000?

1. **Add** the seller's desired net to the costs of sale, excluding the commission.

$50,000	*Seller's net*
126,500	*Mortgage*
1,560	*Repairs*
+ 2,015	*Closing costs*
$180,075	*Total*

$180,075 is the amount that must be left to the seller after the commission has been paid, if she is to be able to pay all of the listed expenses and still have $50,000 left over.

2. **Subtract** the commission rate from 100%: *100% – 7% = 93%.*

3. **Divide** the total from step one by the percentage from step two. Since the commission rate will be 7% of the sales price, the seller's net plus the other costs will have to equal 93% of the sales price: *$180,075 ÷ .93 = $193,629.*

The property will have to sell for approximately $193,629 for the seller to net $50,000.

This may seem counterintuitive at first. At first glance, it may seem that you're applying the commission rate to the closing costs as well as the selling price. But you aren't. This is best understood by working backwards through the problem. By doing so, you'll see that, as in the real world closing process, the commission is subtracted from the selling price, and then the seller's closing costs are subtracted from those proceeds.

Start by calculating the cost of the 7% commission.

$193,629	*Selling price*
× .07	*Commission*
$13,554	

Now subtract the commission and the other closing costs from the gross proceeds, to find the seller's net proceeds.

$193,629	*Selling price*
13,554	*Commission*
126,500	*Mortgage*
1,560	*Repairs*
– 2,015	*Closing costs*
$50,000	*Net proceeds*

Proration Problems

Proration is the allocation of an expense between two or more parties. As was explained in Chapter 12, prorations are required in real estate closings, where a variety of expenses are prorated based on the closing date.

There are basically three steps in the proration process:

1. Calculate the per diem (daily) rate of the expense.
2. Determine the number of days for which one person is responsible for the expense.
3. Multiply the per diem rate by the number of days to determine the share of the expense that one party is responsible for: *Share = Rate × Days.*

To determine the per diem rate of an annual expense, divide the amount of the expense by 365 days, or 366 in a leap year. Some problems will instruct you to divide by 360 days instead, to simplify the calculation. (A 360-day year is sometimes referred to as a banker's year, as opposed to a calendar year.)

To determine the per diem rate of a monthly expense when you are prorating on the basis of a calendar year, divide the amount of the expense by the number of days in that particular month. Alternatively, to simplify the calculation, you may be instructed to base your prorations on a banker's year, which means that every month has 30 days, including February.

We'll present you with a series of examples concerning the proration of various expenses: property taxes, hazard insurance, rent, and mortgage interest. See Chapter 12 for more information about these expenses.

Property Tax Prorations

Property taxes are an annual expense. At closing, the taxes may or may not have been paid yet. If they've already been paid, the buyer will owe the seller a share of the taxes. If they haven't been paid, the seller will owe the buyer a share. Either way, the proration process is essentially the same.

Example: The closing date is February 3, and the seller has already paid the annual property taxes, which were $2,045. At closing, the seller is entitled to a credit for the tax amount covering the period from February 3 through June 30 (the tax year begins on July 1). The same amount will be a debit for the buyer. How much will the buyer owe the seller for the property taxes? Use a 360-day year with 30-day months for your calculations.

1. **Calculate the per diem rate** for the property taxes, using a 360-day year: *$2,045 ÷ 360 = $5.68 per diem.*

2. **Count the number of days** that the buyer is responsible for, using 30-day months.

   28 days February 3 through 30
   30 days March
   30 days April
   30 days May
   + 30 days June
   148 days

3. **Substitute** the rate and number of days into the formula ($S = R \times D$), then calculate.

   148 Days
   × $5.68 Per diem
   $840.64 Credit to seller

At closing, the buyer will be debited $840.64 and the seller will be credited $840.64 for the property taxes from February 3 through the end of the tax year.

In the following example, the taxes haven't been paid yet. You're given the seller's share of the taxes and asked to calculate the annual tax amount.

Example: The seller hasn't paid any portion of the annual taxes. The closing is scheduled for September 21. At closing, the seller will owe the buyer $663.60 for the taxes. How much was the annual tax bill? This time, use a 365-day year and exact-day months in your calculations. The buyer's responsibility for the taxes begins on the day of closing.

1. **Write down the formula.** $S = R \times D$

2. **Substitute.** First add up the number of days that the seller is responsible for.

   31 days July
   31 days August
   + 20 days September
   82 days

3. Substitute the seller's share and the number of days into the formula: *$663.60 = R × 82.*

4. **Calculate**. Rearrange the formula to isolate *R*, the unknown quantity: *$663.60 ÷ 82 = $8.09 Per diem.*

The per diem rate is $8.09. Multiply that by 365 to arrive at the annual tax amount.

365	*Days*
× $8.09	*Per diem*
$2,953	*Annual taxes*

The annual taxes were $2,953.

Insurance Prorations

A seller is entitled to a refund from the hazard insurance company for any prepaid insurance coverage extending beyond the closing date.

Example: The Morgans are selling their house, and the transaction is closing on May 12. They paid an annual hazard insurance premium of $810 that provides coverage through the end of October. If the insurance company does not charge the sellers for the day of closing, how much of the premium will be refunded to them? Base your calculations on a 360-day year.

1. **Calculate the per diem rate** for the insurance, using a 360-day year: *$810 ÷ 360 = $2.25 Per diem.*

2. **Add up the number of days** for which the sellers are owed a refund, using 30-day months.

19 days	*May*
30 days	*June*
30 days	*July*
30 days	*August*
30 days	*September*
+ 30 days	*October*
169 days	

3. **Substitute** the rate and number of days into the formula ($S = R \times D$), then calculate.

169	*Days*
× $2.25	*Per diem*
$380.25	*Credit to seller*

The insurance company will refund $380.25 to the sellers.

Rent Prorations

If the property being sold is rental property, the seller will owe the buyer a prorated share of any rent that has been paid in advance.

Example: A ten-unit apartment building is being sold, with the closing scheduled for April 23. Four of the units rent for $1,500 per month, and the other six rent for

$1,200 per month. All of the tenants paid their April rent on time. What share of the prepaid rents will the seller owe the buyer at closing?

1. **Determine the total amount** of rent owed for April.

   $1,500 × 4 = $6,000

   $1,200 × 6 = $7,200

   $6,000 + $7,200 = $13,200

2. **Calculate the per diem rate** for the month of April:
   $13,200 ÷ 30 = $440 Per diem.

3. **Determine the number of days** of rent the buyer is entitled to, beginning on the closing date. April 23 through April 30 is eight days.

4. **Substitute** and **calculate.**

$440	*Per diem*
× 8	*Days*
$3,520	*Prorated rent*

The seller will owe the buyer $3,520 in prepaid rents at closing.

Mortgage Interest Prorations

Two different types of mortgage interest prorations are necessary in most transactions, one for the seller and one for the buyer. The seller typically owes a final interest payment on the loan he is paying off.

Example: The remaining balance on the seller's mortgage is $317,550, and the interest rate is 8%. The closing date is set for July 6. Because mortgage interest is paid in arrears, the mortgage payment that the seller paid on July 1 covers the interest that accrued during June. At closing, the seller owes the lender interest covering July 1 through the closing date. How much will that interest payment be? Base your calculations on a calendar year.

1. First calculate the annual interest, using the percentage formula.

   a. **Write down the formula.** *Payment = Loan balance × Interest*

   b. **Substitute.** *P = $317,550 × .08*

   c. **Calculate.**

$317,550	*Loan amount*
× .08	*Interest rate*
$25,404	*Annual interest*

2. Next, find the per diem rate of the expense. Divide the annual rate by 365:
   $25,404 ÷ 365 = $69.60 Per diem.

3. Determine the number of days the seller owes interest for. The lender will charge the seller interest for the day of closing. Thus, the seller owes interest for six days, from July 1 through July 6.

4. Finally, substitute the numbers into the proration formula ($S = R \times D$) and calculate.

\$69.60	*Per diem*
× 6	*Days*
\$417.60	*Final interest payment*

At closing, the seller will be required to make a final interest payment of \$417.60.

The buyer also owes some mortgage interest at closing. This is prepaid interest (interim interest) on the buyer's new loan. Prepaid interest covers the closing date through the last day of the month in which closing takes place.

Example: The principal amount of the buyer's new loan is \$230,680. The interest rate is 8%. The transaction closes on June 22. How much prepaid interest will the buyer's lender require the buyer to pay at closing? Base your calculations on a 365-day year.

1. Use the percentage formula to calculate the annual amount of interest.
   a. **Write down the formula.** *Payment = Loan balance × Interest rate*
   b. **Substitute.** *P = \$230,680 × 8%*
   c. **Calculate.** *\$230,680 × .08 = \$18,454.40*
2. Find the per diem rate of the expense. Divide the annual rate by 365: *\$18,454.40 ÷ 365 = \$50.56.*
3. Determine the number of days the buyer is responsible for. In prepaid interest prorations, the buyer pays for the day of closing. There are nine days: June 22, 23, 24, 25, 26, 27, 28, 29, and 30.
4. Substitute the daily rate and number of days into the proration formula *(S = R × D)* and calculate.

\$50.56	*Per diem*
× 9	*Days*
\$455.04	*Prepaid interest*

The buyer's interest charge would be \$455.04.

Chapter Summary

Converting fractions to decimals:

Divide numerator (top number) by denominator (bottom number).

Converting percentages to decimals:

Move decimal point two places to the left and drop the percent sign.

Converting decimals to percentages:

Move decimal point two places to the right and add a percent sign.

Area formula for squares and rectangles:

Area = Length × Width

$A = L \times W$

Area formula for triangles:

Area = ½ Base × Height

$A = \frac{1}{2} B \times H$

Volume formula:

Volume = Length × Width × Height

$V = L \times W \times H$

Percentage formula:

Part = Whole × Percentage

$P = W \times \%$

Profit or loss formula:

Now = Then × %

Capitalization formula:

Income = Rate × Value

$I = \% \times V$

Proration formula:

Share = Daily Rate × Number of Days

$S = R \times D$

1. Find annual or monthly amount.

2. Find daily rate.

3. Determine number of days.

4. Substitute and calculate.

Chapter Quiz

1. Christine and Tom bought a house one year ago for $168,500. If property values in their neighborhood are increasing at an annual rate of 7%, what is the current market value of their house?
   a) $180,295
   b) $184,270
   c) $195,980
   d) $198,893

2. A home just sold for $183,500. The listing broker charged the seller a 6½% commission. The listing broker will pay 50% of that amount to the selling broker, and 25% to the listing salesperson. How much will the listing salesperson's share of the commission be?
   a) $11,927
   b) $5,963
   c) $3,642
   d) $2,982

3. A rectangular lot that has a 45-foot frontage and contains 1,080 square yards has a depth of:
   a) 63 feet
   b) 216 feet
   c) 188 feet
   d) 97 feet

4. An acre contains 43,560 square feet. What is the maximum number of lots measuring 50 feet by 100 feet that can be created from a one-acre parcel?
   a) Six
   b) Seven
   c) Eight
   d) Nine

5. Felicia sold a client's building for $80,000 and received a commission of $5,600. What was her commission rate?
   a) 6.5%
   b) 7%
   c) 7.5%
   d) 8%

6. Jake bought a lot for $5,000 and later sold it for $8,000. What was his percentage of profit?
   a) 60%
   b) 75%
   c) 80%
   d) 85%

7. Diane wants to purchase an income property that has an annual net income of $16,000. If she wants at least an 8% return on her investment, what is the most she should pay for the property?
   a) $150,000
   b) $175,000
   c) $195,000
   d) $200,000

8. George purchases a building for $85,000. The building generates a yearly net income of $5,100. What is his rate of return?
   a) 5.5%
   b) 6%
   c) 6.5%
   d) 7%

9. How many square yards are there in a rectangle that measures 75 × 30 feet?
   a) 6,750
   b) 2,250
   c) 750
   d) 250

10. Mike is purchasing an apartment building. The closing date is September 15, and the seller has already collected the monthly rents in the amount of $13,960 for September. The parties agree that Mike will receive rents for the closing day. At closing, the seller will have to pay Mike a prorated share of the September rents, which will amount to approximately:
    a) $612
    b) $931
    c) $7,445
    d) $9,035

11. A triangular lot has a 40-foot base and a 30-foot height. What is the area of the lot?
    a) 500 square feet
    b) 600 square feet
    c) 750 square feet
    d) 650 square feet

12. What is the decimal equivalent of five-eighths (5/8)?
    a) .625
    b) .0825
    c) 1.58
    d) 1.60

13. Kay has obtained a $112,000 loan at 8.5% interest, to finance the purchase of a home. At closing, the lender will require her to prepay interest for April 26 through April 30. Assuming that the closing agent uses a 365-day year for the proration, how much will that prepaid interest amount to?
    a) $64.35
    b) $104.32
    c) $130.40
    d) $1,403.84

14. The Binghams are selling their house and paying off the mortgage at closing. The remaining principal balance on the mortgage at closing will be $168,301.50. They will also have to pay interest that accrued over the 7-day period between their last mortgage payment and the closing date. If the annual interest rate on the Binghams' mortgage was 10%, how much will they have to pay in interest at closing? (Use a 365-day year for the proration.)
    a) $85.21
    b) $322.77
    c) $409.86
    d) $694.41

15. Carol has just paid $460,000 for a building that will bring her a 9.75% return on her investment. What is the building's annual net income?
    a) $34,965
    b) $36,750
    c) $41,220
    d) $44,850

Answer Key

1. a) The current market value of Christine and Tom's house is approximately $180,295. The question asks you to determine the current value of the house based on its earlier value, so the applicable formula is *Then* × *%* = *Now*. Here, the value has increased by 7%, so the appropriate percentage is 107% (100% + 7%), or 1.07 (as a decimal). *$168,500 × 1.07 = $180,295.*

2. d) The listing salesperson will get $2,982. This is a percentage question with two parts. First multiply the sales price by the broker's commission rate to determine the full commission. *$183,500 × .065 = $11,927.50.* Then multiply that number by 25% to determine the listing salesperson's share: *$11,927.50 × .25 = $2,981.88.*

3. b) The depth of the lot is 216 feet. The question asks you to determine the length of one of the sides of a rectangle, so the applicable formula is *Area* = *Length* × *Width*, *A* = *L* × *W*.

   First convert the area from square yards to square feet, so that it is in the same unit of measurement as the frontage. A square yard is a square that measures 3 feet on each side, or 9 square feet (3 × 3 = 9). Thus, 1,080 square yards is 9,720 square feet (*1,080 × 9 = 9,720*).

   Now substitute the numbers you have into the formula. *9,720 = 45 × L.* Isolate the unknown quantity, H, by changing to another version of the same formula: *L = 9,720 ÷ 45.*

   Divide the area, 9,720 square feet, by the width, 45 feet, to determine the length of the rectangle: *9,720 ÷ 45 = 216 feet.*

4. c) There are eight 50′ × 100′ lots in an acre, with one somewhat smaller lot left over. Use the area formula to determine the area of a 50′ × 100′ lot. *A = 50 × 100 = 5,000 square feet.* Thus, each lot will have an area of 5,000 square feet. Now divide the total number of square feet in the acre by the area of each lot: *43,560 ÷ 5,000 = 8.71.*

5. b) Felicia's commission rate was 7%. Use the percentage formula, *Part* = *Whole* × *Percentage, P* = *W* × *%*. You know the part ($5,600) and the total ($80,000), so switch the formula to isolate the percentage, then substitute and calculate.

   P ÷ W = %

   $5,600 ÷ $80,000 = %

   $5,600 ÷ $80,000 = .07. Thus, the commission rate was 7%.

6. a) Jake's profit on the sale of the lot was 60%. The question asks you to determine what percentage of the original price (the *Then* value) the sales price (the *Now* value) represents. So use the formula *Now* = *Then* × *%*, switching it around to isolate the unknown quantity, the percentage:

   Now ÷ Then = %

   $8,000 ÷ $5,000 = 1.60 or 160%

   The *Now* value is 160% of the *Then* value—in other words, 60% more than the *Then* value. Thus, Jake's profit on the sale was 60%.

7. d) Diane could pay \$200,000 for the property and get an 8% return on that investment. This is a capitalization problem, so use the capitalization formula, *Income = Rate × Value, I = R × V*. You know the net income (\$16,000) and the capitalization rate (8%), so switch the formula to isolate the unknown quantity, V:

   I ÷ R = V

   \$16,000 ÷ .08 = \$200,000

8. b) George has a 6% return on his investment. This problem calls for the capitalization formula again, but this time it's the rate that is unknown. Switch the formula to isolate the rate, R:

   I ÷ V = R

   \$5,100 ÷ \$85,000 = .06 = 6%

9. d) There are 250 square yards in a 75′ × 30′ rectangle. The area formula, *A = B × H,* will give you the area in square feet: *75′ × 30′ = 2,250 square feet.* Then you must convert that figure to square yards. There are 9 square feet in a square yard, so divide 2,250 by 9: *2,250 ÷ 9 = 250 square yards.*

10. c) Mike, the buyer, is entitled to approximately \$7,445 in rent for the period from the closing date through September 30. The proration formula is *Share = Rate × Days, S = R × D.* First determine the per diem rate for the rents by dividing the total amount by the number of days in the month: *\$13,960 ÷ 30 = \$465.33.* Next, determine the number of days for which the buyer is entitled to the rent: September 15 through 30 is 16 days. Finally, multiply the rate by the number of days to find the buyer's share: *\$465.33 × 16 = \$7,445.*

11. b) The area of the lot is 600 square feet. Since the lot is triangular, the appropriate area formula is *Area = ½ Base × Height, A = ½ B × H.* Here, the base is 40 feet, so ½ the base is 20 feet. *20 feet × 30 feet = 600 square feet.*

12. a) The decimal equivalent of 5/8 is .625. To determine this, divide the numerator of the fraction (the top number, 5) by the denominator (the bottom number, 8). *5 ÷ 8 = .625.*

13. c) The prepaid interest will be \$130.40. First determine the annual interest, using the percentage formula: *Part = Whole × Percentage, P = W × %.* The principal (the whole) is \$112,000 and the rate (the percentage) is 8.5%. *\$112,000 × .085 = \$9,520.* Next, divide the annual interest by 365 to determine the per diem rate. *\$9,520 ÷ 365 = \$26.08.* Multiply the per diem rate by the number of days for which Kay is responsible for this expense—five days. *\$26.08 × 5 = \$130.40.*

14. b) The Binghams will have to pay \$322.77 in interest at closing. To find the annual interest amount, use the percentage formula, *P = W × %. \$168,301.50 × .10 = \$16,830.15.* Divide that figure by 365 to determine the per diem rate: *\$16,830.15 ÷ 365 = \$46.11.* Finally, multiply the per diem rate by the number of days: *\$46.11 × 7 days = \$322.77.*

15. d) The building's annual net income is \$44,850. Use the capitalization formula, *Income = Rate × Value: .0975 × \$460,000 = \$44,850.*

Glossary

The definitions given here explain how the listed terms are used in the real estate field. Some of the terms have additional meanings, which can be found in a standard dictionary.

AAA Tenant—A nationally known tenant with the highest credit rating, whose name would lend prestige to a property.

Abandonment—Failure to occupy and use property, which may result in a loss of rights.

Abrogate—To repeal, annul, nullify, abolish, or otherwise bring to an end by official or formal action.

Absolute Fee—*See:* Fee Simple Absolute.

Abstract of Judgment—A document summarizing the essential provisions of a court judgment which, when recorded, creates a lien on the judgment debtor's real property.

Abstract of Title—*See:* Title, Abstract of.

Abut—To touch, border on, be adjacent to, or share a common boundary with.

Acceleration Clause—A provision in a promissory note or security instrument allowing the lender to declare the entire debt due immediately if the borrower breaches one or more provisions of the loan agreement. Also referred to as a call provision.

Acceptance—1. Agreeing to the terms of an offer to enter into a contract, thereby creating a binding contract. 2. Taking delivery of a deed from the grantor.

Acceptance, Qualified—*See:* Counteroffer.

Accession—The acquisition of title to additional property by its annexation to real estate already owned. This can be the result of human actions (as in the case of fixtures) or natural processes (such as accretion and reliction).

Accord and Satisfaction—An agreement to accept something different from (and usually less than) what the contract originally called for.

Accretion—A gradual addition to dry land by the forces of nature, as when waterborne sediment is deposited on waterfront property.

Accrued Items of Expense—Expenses that have been incurred but are not yet due or payable. On a settlement statement, the seller's accrued expenses are credited to the buyer.

Acknowledgment—When a person who has signed a document formally declares to an authorized official (usually a notary public) that she signed voluntarily. The official can then attest that the signature is voluntary and genuine.

Acquisition Cost—The amount of money a buyer was required to expend in order to acquire title to a piece of property. In addition to the purchase price, this might include closing costs, legal fees, and other expenses.

Acre—An area of land equal to 43,560 square feet, or 4,840 square yards, or 160 square rods.

Actual Age—*See:* Age, Actual.

Actual Authority—*See:* Authority, Actual.

Actual Eviction—*See:* Eviction, Actual.

Actual Notice—*See:* Notice, Actual.

ADA—Americans with Disabilities Act.

Addendum—A page attached to a purchase agreement or other contract that contains additional provisions.

Adjacent—Nearby, next to, bordering, or neighboring; may or may not be in actual contact.

Adjustable-rate Mortgage—*See:* Mortgage, Adjustable-rate.

Adjusted Basis—*See:* Basis, Adjusted.

Adjustment Period—The interval at which the interest rate or monthly payment for an adjustable-rate mortgage is changed.

Administrative Agency—A government agency (federal, state, or local) that administers a complex area of law and policy, adopting and enforcing detailed regulations that have the force of law. For example, the California Bureau of Real Estate is the administrative agency charged with regulating the real estate profession.

Administrative Law Judge—An official appointed to decide cases in which an individual is in conflict with the rules and regulations of an administrative agency. For example, a disciplinary hearing against a real estate agent accused of violating the Real Estate Law would ordinarily be conducted by an administrative law judge.

Administrator—A person appointed by the probate court to manage and distribute the estate of a deceased person, when no executor is named in the will or there is no will.

Ad Valorem—A Latin phrase that means "according to value," used to refer to taxes that are assessed on the value of property.

Adverse Possession—Acquiring title to real property that belongs to someone else by taking possession of it without permission, in the manner and for the length of time prescribed by statute.

Affiant—One who makes an affidavit.

Affidavit—A sworn statement made before a notary public (or other official authorized to administer an oath) that has been written down and acknowledged.

Affiliated Licensee—A real estate salesperson or associate broker who is employed by a broker.

Affirm—1. To confirm or ratify. 2. To make a solemn declaration that isn't under oath.

After-acquired Title—*See:* Title, After-acquired.

Age, Actual—The age of a structure from a chronological standpoint (as opposed to its effective age); how many years it has actually been in existence.

Age, Effective—The age of a structure as indicated by its condition and remaining usefulness (as opposed to its actual age). Good maintenance may increase a building's effective age, and poor maintenance may decrease it; for example, a 50-year-old home that has been well maintained might have an effective age of 15 years, meaning that its remaining usefulness is equivalent to that of a 15-year-old home.

Agency—A relationship of trust created when one person (the principal) grants another (the agent) authority to represent her in dealings with third parties.

Agency, Apparent—When third parties are given the impression that someone who hasn't been authorized to represent another is that person's agent, or else are given the impression that an agent has been authorized to perform acts which are in fact beyond the scope of his authority. Also called ostensible agency.

Agency, Dual—When an agent represents both parties to a transaction, as when a real estate broker represents both the buyer and the seller.

Agency, Exclusive—*See:* Listing, Exclusive Agency.

Agency, Ostensible—*See:* Agency, Apparent.

Agency Confirmation Statement—A written statement that indicates which party a real estate agent is representing. It must be signed by both the buyer and the seller before they enter into a residential purchase agreement.

Agency Disclosure Form—A form that explains the duties of a seller's agent, a buyer's agent, and a dual agent. It must be signed by both the buyer and the seller before they enter into a residential purchase agreement.

Agency Law—The body of legal rules that govern the relationship between agent and principal, imposing fiduciary duties on the agent and also imposing liability for the agent's actions on the principal.

Agent—A person authorized to represent another (the principal) in dealings with third parties.

Agent, Closing—The person who handles the closing process on behalf of the parties to a real estate transaction. This could be an independent escrow agent, an employee of the lender or the title company, a real estate broker, or a lawyer.

Agent, Dual—*See:* Agency, Dual.

Agent, Escrow—1. A third party who holds funds, documents, or other valuables on behalf of the parties to a transaction, releasing these items to the parties only when certain conditions in the escrow instructions have been fulfilled. 2. A company licensed to provide escrow services in California. 3. Any closing agent.

Agent, General—An agent authorized to handle all of the principal's affairs in one area or in specified areas.

Agent, Gratuitous—An agent who doesn't have a legal right to claim compensation for her services (such as a broker who acts on behalf of a seller without having a written contract with the seller).

Agent, Listing—A broker who has a listing agreement with a seller, or a salesperson representing the listing broker. The listing agent may or may not turn out to also be the selling agent, the one who procures an acceptable offer from the buyer.

Agent, Selling—The real estate agent who writes and presents the offer to purchase that the seller accepts. In some cases, the selling agent is the same person as the listing agent.

Agent, Special—An agent with limited authority to do a specific thing or conduct a specific transaction.

Agent, Universal—An agent authorized to do everything that can be lawfully delegated to a representative.

Agents in Production—The elements necessary to generate income and establish a value in real estate: labor, coordination, capital, and land.

Age of Majority—*See:* Majority, Age of.

Agreement—*See:* Contract.

Air Lot—A parcel of property above the surface of the earth, not containing any land; for example, a condominium unit on the third floor.

Air Rights—The right to undisturbed use and control of the airspace over a parcel of land; may be transferred separately from the land.

Alienation—The transfer of ownership or an interest in property from one person to another, by any means.

Alienation, Involuntary—Transfer of an interest in property against the will of the owner, or without action by the owner, occurring through operation of law, natural processes, or adverse possession.

Alienation, Voluntary—When an owner voluntarily transfers an interest in property to someone else, most commonly by deed or will.

Alienation Clause—A provision in a security instrument that gives the lender the right to declare the entire loan balance due immediately if the borrower sells or otherwise transfers the security property. Also called a due-on-sale clause.

All-inclusive Deed of Trust—*See:* Mortgage, Wraparound.

Allodial System—A system of individual ownership of land (as opposed to the feudal system, in which the sovereign owned all of the land).

Alluvion—The solid material deposited along a riverbank or shore by accretion. Also called alluvium.

Alquist-Priolo Act—A California law that requires applications for development of property in an earthquake fault zone to include a geologic report.

ALTA—American Land Title Association, a nationwide organization of title insurance companies. An extended coverage title policy is sometimes referred to as an ALTA policy.

Amendment—A supplementary agreement changing one or more terms of a contract, which must be signed by all of the parties to the original contract. Also called a contract modification.

Amenities—Features of a property that contribute to the pleasure or convenience of owning it, such as a fireplace, a beautiful view, or its proximity to a good school.

Americans with Disabilities Act—A federal law that requires facilities that are open to the public to be accessible to people with disabilities.

Amortization, Negative—The addition of unpaid interest to the principal balance of a loan, thereby increasing the amount owed.

Amortize—To gradually pay off a debt with installment payments that include both principal and interest. *See:* Loan, Amortized.

Annexation—Attaching personal property to real property, so that it becomes part of the real property (a fixture) in the eyes of the law.

Annexation, Actual—The physical attachment of personal property to real property, so that it becomes part of the real property.

Annexation, Constructive—The association of personal property with real property in such a way that the law treats it as a fixture, even though it isn't physically attached. For example, a house key is constructively annexed to the house.

Annual Percentage Rate (APR)—All of the charges that a borrower will pay for the loan (including the interest, origination fee, discount points, and mortgage insurance costs), expressed as an annual percentage of the amount borrowed.

Annuity—A sum of money received in a series of payments at regular intervals (often annually) over a period of time.

Anticipation, Principle of—An appraisal principle which holds that value is created by the expectation of benefits to be received in the future.

Anticipatory Repudiation—Action taken by one party to a contract to inform the other party, before the time set for performance, that he doesn't intend to fulfill the contract.

Antideficiency Rules—Laws that prohibit a secured lender from suing the borrower for a deficiency judgment in certain circumstances (for example, after nonjudicial foreclosure of a deed of trust).

Appeal—When one of the parties to a lawsuit asks a higher court to review the judgment or verdict reached in a lower court.

Appellant—The party who files an appeal because she is dissatisfied with the lower court's decision. Also called the petitioner.

Appellee—In an appeal, the party who did not file the appeal. Also called the respondent.

Apportionment—A division of property (as among tenants in common when the property is sold or partitioned) or liability (as when responsibility for closing costs is allocated between the buyer and the seller) into proportionate, but not necessarily equal, parts.

Appraisal—An estimate or opinion of the value of a piece of property as of a particular date. Also called valuation.

Appraiser—One who estimates the value of property, especially an expert qualified to do so by training and experience.

Appraiser, Fee—An independent appraiser hired to appraise real estate for a fee, as opposed to an appraiser who works for a lender, a government agency, or some other entity as a salaried employee.

Appreciation—An increase in value; the opposite of depreciation.

Appropriation—Taking property or reducing it to personal possession, to the exclusion of others.

Appropriative Rights System—A system of allocating water rights, in which a person who wants to use water from a certain lake or river is required to apply for a permit. A permit has priority over other permits that are issued later. Also called the prior appropriation system. *Compare:* Riparian Rights.

Appropriative Rights—The water rights of a person who holds a water appropriation permit.

Appurtenances—Rights that go along with ownership of a particular piece of property, such as air rights or mineral rights. They are ordinarily transferred with the property, but may, in some cases, be sold separately.

Appurtenances, Intangible—Rights that go with ownership of a piece of property that do not involve physical objects or substances; for example, an access easement (as opposed to mineral rights).

Appurtenant Easement—*See:* Easement Appurtenant.

APR—*See:* Annual Percentage Rate.

Area—1. Locale or region. 2. The size of a surface, usually in square units of measure, such as square feet or square miles.

ARM—*See:* Mortgage, Adjustable-Rate.

Arm's Length Transaction—A transaction in which there is no family relationship, friendship, or pre-existing business relationship between the parties.

Arranger of Credit—A real estate licensee or attorney who arranges a transaction where credit is extended by a seller of residential property.

Artificial Person—A legal entity, such as a corporation, that the law treats as an individual with legal rights and responsibilities; as distinguished from a natural person, a human being. Sometimes called a legal person.

Assemblage—Combining two or more adjoining properties into one tract.

Assessment—The valuation of property for purposes of taxation.

Assessor—An official who determines the value of property for taxation.

Asset—Anything of value that a person owns.

Assets, Capital—Assets held by a taxpayer other than: (1) property held for sale to customers; and (2) depreciable property or real property used in the taxpayer's trade or business. Thus, real property is a capital asset if it is used for personal use or for profit.

Assets, Liquid—Cash and other assets that can be readily turned into cash (liquidated), such as stock.

Assets, Section 1231—Properties used in a trade or business or held for the production of income (a reference to Section 1231 in the federal income tax code).

Assign—To transfer rights (especially contract rights) or interests to another.

Assignee—One to whom rights or interests have been assigned.

Assignment—1. A transfer of contract rights from one person to another. 2. In the case of a lease, the transfer by the original tenant of her entire leasehold estate to another. *Compare:* Sublease.

Assignment of Contract and Deed—The instrument used to substitute a new vendor for the original vendor in a land contract.

Assignor—One who has assigned his rights or interest to another.

Assumption—Action by a buyer to take on personal liability for paying off the seller's existing mortgage or deed of trust.

Assumption Fee—A fee paid to the lender, usually by the buyer, when a mortgage or deed of trust is assumed.

Attachment—Court-ordered seizure of property belonging to a defendant in a lawsuit, so that it will be available to satisfy a judgment if the plaintiff wins. In the case of real property, an attachment creates a lien.

Attachments, Man-made—*See:* Fixture.

Attachments, Natural—Plants growing on a piece of land, such as trees, shrubs, or crops. *See:* Emblements; Fructus Industriales; Fructus Naturales.

Attestation—The act of witnessing the execution of an instrument, such as a deed or a will.

Attorney General—The principal legal advisor for state government, including legal advisor to the Bureau of Real Estate on matters regarding the Real Estate Law.

Attorney in Fact—Any person authorized to represent another by a power of attorney; not necessarily a lawyer (an attorney at law).

Attractive Nuisance—A dangerous property feature that is inviting to children, and therefore a potential source of liability for the property owner.

Auditing—Verification and examination of records, particularly the financial accounts of a business or other organization.

Authority, Actual—Authority actually given to an agent by the principal, expressly or by implication.

Authority, Apparent—Authority to represent another that someone appears to have and that the principal is estopped from denying, although no actual authority has been granted.

Authority, Express—Actual authority that the principal has expressly given to her agent, either orally or in writing.

Authority, Implied—An agent's authority to do everything reasonably necessary to carry out the principal's express orders.

Automated Underwriting—*See:* Underwriting, Automated.

Avulsion—1. A sudden (not gradual) tearing away of land by the action of water. 2. A sudden shift in a watercourse.

Balance, Principle of—An appraisal principle which holds that the maximum value of real estate is achieved when the agents in production (labor, coordination, capital, and land) are in proper balance with each other.

Balance Sheet—*See:* Financial Statement.

Balloon Payment—A payment on a loan (usually the final payment) that is significantly larger than the regular installment payments.

Bankruptcy—1. A situation resulting when the liabilities of an individual, corporation, or firm exceed the assets. 2. Declaration by a court that an individual, corporation, or firm is insolvent, with the result that the assets and debts are administered under bankruptcy laws.

Barter—To exchange or trade one commodity or piece of property for another without the use of money.

Base Line—In the government survey system, a main east-west line from which township lines are established. Each principal meridian has one base line associated with it.

Basis—A figure used in calculating a gain on the sale of real estate for federal income tax purposes. Also called cost basis.

Basis, Adjusted—The owner's initial basis in the property, plus capital expenditures for improvements, and minus any allowable depreciation deductions.

Basis, Initial—The amount of the owner's original investment in the property; what it cost to acquire the property, which may include closing costs and certain other expenses, as well as the purchase price.

Bearer—Whoever has possession of a negotiable instrument. *See:* Endorsement in Blank.

Bench Mark—A surveyor's mark at a known point of elevation on a stationary object, used as a reference point in calculating other elevations in a surveyed area; often a metal disk set into cement or rock.

Beneficiary—1. One for whom a trust is created and on whose behalf the trustee administers the trust. 2. The lender in a deed of trust transaction. 3. One entitled to receive real or personal property under a will; a legatee or devisee.

Beneficiary's Statement—A document in which a lender confirms the status of a loan (the interest rate, principal balance, etc.) and describes any claims that could affect an interested party. *Compare:* Offset Statement.

Bequeath—To transfer personal property to another by will.

Bequest—Personal property (including money) that is transferred by will.

Betterment—An improvement to real property that is more extensive than ordinary repair or replacement and that increases the value of the property.

Bilateral Contract—*See:* Contract, Bilateral.

Bill of Sale—A document used to transfer title to personal property from one person to another.

Binder—1. An agreement to consider a deposit as evidence of the potential buyer's good faith when she makes an offer to buy a piece of real estate. 2. An instrument providing immediate insurance coverage until the regular policy is issued. 3. Any payment or preliminary written statement intended to make an agreement legally binding until a formal contract has been drawn up.

Blind Ad—An advertisement placed by a real estate licensee that doesn't indicate that it was placed by a licensee.

Block—In a subdivision, a group of lots surrounded by streets or unimproved land.

Blockbusting—Attempting to induce owners to list or sell their homes by predicting that members of another race or ethnic group, or people suffering from some disability, will be moving into the neighborhood. This violates antidiscrimination laws. Also called panic selling.

Blue Laws—Statutes or ordinances restricting the transaction of business or other activities on Sundays and certain holidays.

Blue Sky Laws—Laws that regulate the promotion and sale of securities in order to protect the public from fraud.

Board of Directors—The body responsible for governing a corporation on behalf of the shareholders, which oversees the corporate management.

Bona Fide—In good faith; genuine; not fraudulent.

Bond—1. A written obligation, usually interest-bearing, to pay a certain sum at a specified time. 2. Money put up as a surety, protecting someone against failure to perform, negligent performance, or fraud.

Bond, Completion—A bond posted by a contractor to guarantee that a project will be completed satisfactorily and free of liens. Also called a performance bond.

Bonus—An extra payment, over and above what is strictly due.

Boot—In a tax-free exchange, something given or received that isn't like-kind property; for example, in an exchange of real property, if one party gives the other cash in addition to real property, the cash is boot.

Boundary—The perimeter or border of a parcel of land; the dividing line between one piece of property and another.

Bounds—Boundaries. *See:* Metes and Bounds Description.

Branch Manager—A licensee designated by a firm's primary broker to manage the operations of a branch office.

Breach—Violation of an obligation, duty, or law.

Breach of Contract—An unexcused failure to perform a contractual obligation.

Broker, Associate—A person who has qualified as a broker, but is affiliated with another broker.

Broker, Cooperating—A broker who belongs to a multiple listing service and helps sell a property that is listed with another member of the service (the listing broker).

Broker, Designated—A corporate officer or general partner who is authorized to act as the broker for a licensed corporation or for a partnership.

Broker, Fee—A real estate broker who allows another person to use his license to operate a brokerage, in violation of the license law.

Broker, Listing—A broker who has a listing agreement with a property seller.

Broker, Real Estate—One who is licensed to represent members of the public in real estate transactions for compensation.

Brokerage—A real estate broker's business.

Brokerage Fee—The commission or other compensation charged for a real estate broker's services.

Buffer—An undeveloped area separating two areas zoned for incompatible uses.

Building Codes—Regulations that set minimum standards for construction methods and materials.

Building Restrictions—Rules concerning building size, placement, or type; they may be public restrictions (in a zoning ordinance, for example) or private restrictions (in CC&Rs, for example).

Bulk Transfer—The sale of all or a substantial part of the merchandise, equipment, or other inventory of a business, not in the ordinary course of business.

Bulk Transfer Law—A law requiring a seller who negotiates a bulk transfer (usually in connection with the sale of the business itself) to furnish the buyer with a list of creditors and a schedule of the property being sold, and to notify creditors of the impending transfer.

Bump Clause—A provision in a purchase agreement that allows the seller to keep the property on the market while waiting for a contingency clause to be fulfilled. If the seller receives another good offer in the meantime, she can require the buyer to either waive the contingency clause or terminate the contract.

Bundle of Rights—The rights inherent in ownership of property, including the right to use, lease, enjoy, encumber, will, sell, or do nothing with the property.

Bureau of Real Estate—The state government agency that administers California's Real Estate Law.

Business Opportunity—A business that is for sale.

Buydown—The payment of discount points to a lender to reduce (buy down) the interest rate charged to the borrower; especially when a seller pays discount points to help the buyer/borrower qualify for financing.

Buyer Representation Agreement—A contract in which a prospective buyer hires a real estate broker to act as her agent in locating suitable property and negotiating its purchase, or in negotiating the purchase of a property that the buyer has already found. Also called a buyer agency agreement.

California Coastal Act—A California law designed to protect and control development along the California coastline.

California Environmental Quality Act (CEQA)—A California law that is designed to protect the state's environment. It is similar to the National Environmental Policy Act.

California Veterans Farm and Home Purchase Program—A state-sponsored residential finance program designed to provide inexpensive home and farm loans to veterans. Often referred to as the Cal-Vet program.

Call—In a metes and bounds description, a specification that describes a segment of the boundary. For example, "south 15° west 120 feet" is a call.

Call Provision—*See:* Acceleration Clause.

Cal-Vet—*See:* California Veterans Farm and Home Purchase Program.

Cancellation—Termination of a contract without undoing acts that have already been performed under the contract. *Compare:* Rescission.

Cap—A limit on how much a lender may raise an adjustable rate mortgage's interest rate or monthly payment per year, or over the life of the loan.

Capacity—The legal ability or competency to perform some act, such as enter into a binding contract (contractual capacity) or execute a valid will (testamentary capacity).

Capital—Money (or other forms of wealth) available for use in the production of more money.

Capital Assets—Assets held by a taxpayer other than: 1) property held for sale to customers in the ordinary course of the taxpayer's business; and 2) depreciable property or real property used in the taxpayer's trade or business. Thus, real property is a capital asset if it is owned for personal use or for profit.

Capital Expenditures—Money spent on improvements and alterations that add to the value of the property and/or prolong its life.

Capital Gain—Profit realized from the sale of a capital asset. If the asset was held for more than one year, it is a long-term capital gain; if the asset was held for one year or less, it is a short-term capital gain.

Capital Improvement—Any improvement that is designed to become a permanent part of the real property or that will have the effect of significantly prolonging the property's life.

Capitalization—A method of appraising real property by converting the anticipated net income from the property into the present value. Also called the income approach to value.

Capitalization Rate—A percentage used in capitalization (Net Income = Capitalization Rate × Value). It is the rate believed to represent the proper relationship between the value of the property and the income it produces; the rate that would be a reasonable return on an investment of the type in question, or the yield necessary to attract investment of capital in property like the subject property. Often called the cap rate.

Capitalize—1. To provide with cash, or capital. 2. To determine the present value of an asset using capitalization.

Capital Loss—A loss resulting from the sale of a capital asset. It may be long-term or short-term, depending on whether the asset was held for more than one year or for one year or less.

Capture, Rule of—A legal rule that grants a landowner the right to all oil and gas produced from wells on his land, even if it migrated from underneath land belonging to someone else.

CAR—California Association of Realtors®.

Carryback Loan—*See:* Mortgage, Purchase Money.

Carryover Clause—*See:* Safety Clause.

Cash Flow—The residual income after deducting from gross income all operating expenses and debt service.

Cash on Cash—The ratio between cash received in the first year and cash initially invested.

Caveat Emptor—A Latin phrase meaning "Let the buyer beware." It expresses the idea that a buyer is expected to examine property carefully before buying, instead of relying on the seller to disclose problems. This was once a firm rule of law, but it has lost much of its force, especially in residential transactions.

CC&Rs—A declaration of covenants, conditions, and restrictions; usually recorded by a developer to place restrictions on all lots within a new subdivision.

CEQA—*See:* California Environmental Quality Act.

CERCLA—*See:* Comprehensive Environmental Response, Compensation, and Liability Act.

Certificate of Discharge—The document a mortgagee gives the mortgagor when the mortgage debt has been paid in full, acknowledging that the debt has been paid and the mortgage is no longer a lien against the property. Also called a satisfaction of mortgage or mortgage release.

Certificate of Eligibility—A document issued by the Department of Veterans Affairs as evidence of a veteran's eligibility for a VA-guaranteed loan.

Certificate of Occupancy—A document issued by a local government agency (such as the building department) verifying that a newly constructed building is in compliance with all codes and may be occupied.

Certificate of Reasonable Value—*See:* Notice of Value.

Certificate of Sale—The document given to the purchaser at a mortgage foreclosure sale, instead of a deed; replaced with a sheriff's deed only after the redemption period expires.

Certiorari, Writ of—A writ in which a higher court requests a transcript of proceedings that took place in a lower court, for appellate review.

Chain of Title—*See:* Title, Chain of.

Change, Principle of—An appraisal principle which holds that it is the future, not the past, that is of primary importance in estimating a property's value, because economic and social forces are constantly changing it.

Charter—A written instrument granting a power or a right of franchise.

Chattel—An article of personal property.

Chattel Mortgage—*See:* Mortgage, Chattel.

Chattel Real—Personal property that is closely associated with real property. The primary example is a lease.

Civil Law—The body of law concerned with the rights and liabilities of one individual in relation to another; includes contract law, tort law, and property law. *Compare:* Criminal Law.

Civil Rights—Fundamental rights guaranteed to individuals by the law. The term is primarily used in reference to constitutional and statutory protections against discrimination or government interference.

Civil Rights Act of 1866—A federal law guaranteeing all citizens the right to purchase, lease, sell, convey and inherit property, regardless of race or color.

Civil Rights Act of 1964—A federal law prohibiting discrimination on the basis of race, color, national origin, or religion in many programs for which the government provides financial assistance.

Civil Suit—A lawsuit in which one private party sues another private party (as opposed to a criminal suit, in which an individual is sued—prosecuted—by the government).

Civil Wrong—*See:* Tort.

Clean Air Act—A federal law intended to maintain and enhance air quality.

Clean Water Act—A federal law intended to maintain and enhance the quality of the nation's water resources.

Client—One who employs a broker, lawyer, appraiser, or other professional. A real estate broker's client can be a seller, a buyer, a landlord, or a tenant.

Closing—The final stage in a real estate transaction, when the seller receives the purchase money, the buyer receives the deed, and title is transferred. Also called settlement.

Closing Costs—Expenses incurred in the transfer of real estate in addition to the purchase price; for example, the appraisal fee, title insurance premium, broker's commission, and documentary transfer tax.

Closing Date—The date on which all the terms of a purchase agreement must be met, or the contract will terminate.

Closing Statement—*See:* Settlement Statement.

Cloud on Title—A claim, encumbrance, or apparent defect that makes the title to a property unmarketable. *See:* Title, Marketable.

Code of Ethics—A body of rules setting forth accepted standards of conduct, reflecting principles of fairness and morality; especially one that the members of an organization are expected to follow.

Codicil—An addition to, or revision of, a will.

Collateral—Anything of value used as security for a debt or obligation.

Collusion—An agreement between two or more persons to defraud another.

Color of Title—*See:* Title, Color of.

Commercial Acre—The remainder of an acre of newly subdivided land after deducting the amount of land dedicated for streets and sidewalks.

Commercial Bank—A type of financial institution that has traditionally emphasized commercial lending (loans to businesses), but which also makes many residential mortgage loans.

Commercial Paper—Negotiable instruments, such as promissory notes, sold to meet the short-term capital needs of a business.

Commercial Property—Property zoned and used for business purposes, such as a restaurant or an office building; as distinguished from residential, industrial, or agricultural property.

Commingled Funds—Funds from different sources that are deposited in the same account and thereby lose their separate character; for example, if a spouse deposits cash that is her separate property in an account with funds that are community property, the entire amount may be treated as community property.

Commingling—Illegally mixing trust funds held on behalf of a client with personal funds.

Commission—1. The compensation paid to a broker for services in connection with a real estate transaction (usually a percentage of the sales price). 2. A group of people organized for a particular purpose or function; usually a governmental body, such as a planning commission.

Commitment—In real estate finance, a lender's promise to make a loan. A loan commitment may be "firm" or "conditional"; a conditional commitment is contingent on something, such as a satisfactory credit report on the borrower.

Common Areas—*See:* Common Elements.

Common Elements—1. The land and improvements in a condominium, planned development, or other housing development that are owned and used collectively by all of the residents, such as parking lots, hallways, and recreational facilities available for common use. 2. In a building with leased units or spaces, the areas that are available for use by all of the tenants. Also called common areas.

Common Elements, Limited—In a condominium or other development, features outside of the dwelling units that are reserved for the use of the owners of particular units, such as an assigned parking space. Also called limited common areas.

Common Law—1. Early English law. 2. Long-established rules of law based on early English law. 3. Rules of law developed in court decisions, in contrast to statutory law.

Community Property—In California and other community property states, property owned jointly by a married couple, as distinguished from each spouse's separate property; generally, any property acquired through the labor or skill of either spouse during marriage.

Co-mortgagor—Someone (usually a family member) who accepts responsibility for the repayment of a mortgage loan, along with the primary borrower, to help the borrower qualify for the loan.

Comparable—In appraisal, a property that is similar to the subject property and that has recently been sold. The sales prices of comparables provide data for estimating the value of the subject property using the sales comparison approach. Also called a comp or a comparable sale.

Competent—1. Of sound mind, for the purposes of entering into a contract or executing a legal instrument (mentally competent). 2. Both of sound mind and having reached the age of majority (legally competent).

Competition, Principle of—An appraisal principle which holds that profits tend to encourage competition, and excess profits tend to result in ruinous competition.

Completion Bond—*See:* Bond, Completion.

Compliance Inspection—A building inspection to determine, for the benefit of a lender, whether building codes, specifications, or conditions established after a prior inspection have been met, before a loan is funded.

Comprehensive Environmental Response, Compensation, and Liability Act—A federal law that governs liability for environmental cleanup costs.

Comprehensive Plan—*See:* General Plan.

Concurrent Ownership—*See:* Ownership, Concurrent.

Condemnation—1. Taking private property for public use through the government's power of eminent domain. 2. A declaration that a structure is unfit for occupancy and must be closed or demolished.

Condemnation Appraisal—An estimate of the value of condemned property to determine the just compensation to be paid to the owner.

Condition—1. A provision in a contract that makes the parties' rights and obligations depend on the occurrence (or nonoccurrence) of a particular event. Also called a contingency clause. 2. A provision in a deed that makes title depend on compliance with a particular restriction.

Conditional Commitment—*See:* Commitment.

Conditional Fee—*See:* Fee Simple Defeasible.

Conditional Use Permit—A permit that allows a special use, such as a school or hospital, to operate in a neighborhood where it would otherwise be prohibited by the zoning. Also called a special exception permit.

Condominium—Property developed for concurrent ownership, where each co-owner has a separate interest in an individual unit, combined with an undivided interest in the common elements.

Confirmation of Sale—Court approval of a sale of property by an executor, administrator, or guardian.

Conflict of Interest—When an agent (or other person occupying a position of trust) is in a situation where the action that would promote his own interests conflicts with the action that would promote the interests of the principal. The agent should inform the principal of this situation and offer to withdraw.

Conforming Loan—*See:* Loan, Conforming.

Conformity, Principle of—An appraisal principle which holds that the maximum value of property is realized when there is a reasonable degree of social and economic homogeneity in the neighborhood.

Conservation—1. Preservation of structures or neighborhoods in a sound condition. 2. Preservation or controlled use of natural resources for long-term benefits.

Conservator—A person appointed by a court to take care of the property of another who is incapable of taking care of it herself.

Consideration—Anything of value given to induce another to enter into a contract, such as money, goods, services, or a promise. Sometimes called valuable consideration.

Conspiracy—1. An agreement or plan between two or more persons to perform an unlawful act. 2. Under the antitrust laws, an agreement in restraint of trade.

Construction Lien—*See:* Lien, Mechanic's.

Constructive—Held to be so in the eyes of the law, even if not so in fact. *See:* Annexation, Constructive; Eviction, Constructive; Notice, Constructive; Severance, Constructive.

Consumer Price Index—An index that tracks changes in the cost of goods and services for a typical consumer. Formerly called the cost of living index.

Consummate—To complete.

Contiguous—Adjacent, abutting, or in close proximity.

Contingency Clause—*See:* Condition.

Contour—The shape or configuration of a surface. A contour map depicts the topography of a piece of land by means of lines (contour lines) that connect points of equal elevation.

Contract—An agreement between two or more persons to do or not do a certain thing, for consideration.

Contract, Bilateral—A contract in which each party has made a binding promise to perform (as distinguished from a unilateral contract).

Contract, Conditional Sales—*See:* Contract, Land.

Contract, Executed—A contract in which both parties have completely performed their contractual obligations.

Contract, Executory—A contract in which one or both parties have not yet completed performance of their obligations.

Contract, Express—A contract that has been put into words, either spoken or written.

Contract, Implied—A contract that hasn't been put into words, but is implied by the actions of the parties.

Contract, Installment Sales—*See:* Contract, Land.

Contract, Land—A contract for the sale of real property in which the buyer (the vendee) pays in installments. The buyer takes possession of the property immediately, but the seller (the vendor) retains legal title until the full price has been paid. Also called a conditional sales contract, installment sales contract, real estate contract, or contract for deed.

Contract, Oral—A spoken agreement that hasn't been written down. Also called a parol contract.

Contract, Parol—*See:* Contract, Oral.

Contract, Real Estate—1. Any contract pertaining to real estate. 2. A land contract.

Contract, Sales—*See:* Purchase Agreement.

Contract, Unenforceable—An agreement that a court would refuse to enforce. For example, a contract is unenforceable if its contents can't be proved or if the statute of limitations has run out.

Contract, Unilateral—A contract that is accepted by performance; the offeror has promised to perform his side of the bargain if the other party performs, but the other party hasn't promised to do so. *Compare:* Contract, Bilateral.

Contract, Valid—A binding, legally enforceable contract.

Contract, Void—An agreement that isn't an enforceable contract, because it lacks a required element (such as consideration) or is defective in some other respect.

Contract, Voidable—A contract that one of the parties can disaffirm without liability, because of lack of capacity or a negative factor such as fraud or duress.

Contract for Deed—*See:* Contract, Land.

Contract Modification—*See:* Amendment.

Contract of Adhesion—A contract that is one-sided and unfair to one of the parties; a take-it-or-leave-it contract, in which the offeror had much greater bargaining power than the offeree.

Contract of Sale—*See:* Purchase Agreement.

Contractor—One who contracts to perform labor or supply materials for a construction project, or to do other work for a specified price.

Contractor, Independent—*See:* Independent Contractor.

Contract Rent—*See:* Rent, Contract.

Contractual Capacity—The legal capacity to enter into a binding contract. A person with contractual capacity is mentally competent and has attained the age of majority.

Contribution, Principle of—An appraisal principle which holds that the value of real property is greatest when the improvements produce the highest return commensurate with their cost (the investment).

Conventional Financing—*See:* Loan, Conventional.

Conversion—1. Misappropriating property or funds belonging to another; for example, converting trust funds to one's own use. 2. The process of changing an apartment complex into a condominium or cooperative.

Conversion Option—A provision in many adjustable-rate mortgages that gives the borrower the option of converting to a fixed interest rate at one or more points during the first years of the loan term; if the borrower chooses to do this, the loan will remain at that fixed rate for the remainder of the term.

Conveyance—The transfer of title to real property from one person to another by means of a written document, especially a deed.

Cooperating Agent—A member of a multiple listing service who attempts to find a buyer for a listing.

Cooperative—A building owned by a corporation, where the residents are shareholders in the corporation; each shareholder receives a proprietary lease on an individual unit and the right to use the common areas.

Cooperative Sale—A transaction in which the listing agent and the selling agent work for different brokers. *Compare:* In-House Sale.

Co-ownership—*See:* Ownership, Concurrent.

Corner Influence—The increase in a commercial property's value that results from its location on or near a corner, with access and exposure on two streets.

Corporation—An association in which individuals may purchase ownership shares, and which is treated by the law as an artificial person, separate from the individual shareholders.

Corporation, Domestic—A corporation doing business in the state where it was created (incorporated).

Corporation, Foreign—A corporation doing business in one state, but created (incorporated) in another state, or in another country.

Correction Lines—In the government survey system, adjustment lines used to compensate for the curvature of the earth; they occur at 24-mile intervals (every fourth township line), where the distance between range lines is corrected to six miles.

Correlation—*See:* Reconciliation.

Cosign—To add one's signature to a promissory note in connection with a loan made to another person, agreeing to share responsibility for repaying the loan.

Cost—The amount paid for something, in money, goods, or services.

Cost, Replacement—In appraisal, the current cost of constructing a building with the same utility as the subject property with modern materials and construction methods.

Cost, Reproduction—In appraisal, the cost of constructing a replica (an exact duplicate) of the subject property, using the same materials and construction methods that were originally used, but at current prices.

Cost Approach to Value—One of the three main methods of appraisal, in which an estimate of the subject property's value is arrived at by estimating the cost of replacing the improvements, then deducting the estimated accrued depreciation and adding the estimated market value of the land.

Cost Basis—*See:* Basis.

Cost of Living Index—*See:* Consumer Price Index.

Cost Recovery Deductions—*See:* Depreciation Deductions.

Co-tenancy—*See:* Ownership, Concurrent.

Counteroffer—A response to a contract offer, changing some of the terms of the original offer. It operates as a rejection of the original offer (not as an acceptance). Also called a qualified acceptance.

County—An administrative subdivision of the state, created by the state and deriving all of its powers from the state.

Coupon Rate—*See:* Nominal Interest Rate.

Course—In a metes and bounds description, a direction, stated in terms of a compass bearing.

Covenant—1. A contract. 2. A promise. 3. A guarantee (express or implied) in a document such as a deed or lease. 4. A restrictive covenant.

Covenant, Restrictive—A promise to do or not do an act relating to real property, especially a promise that runs with the land; usually an owner's promise not to use property in a specified manner.

Covenant Against Encumbrances—In a deed, a promise that the property isn't burdened by any encumbrances other than those that are disclosed in the deed.

Covenant of Quiet Enjoyment—A promise that a buyer or tenant's possession will not be disturbed by the previous owner, the landlord, or anyone else making a lawful claim against the property.

Covenant of Right to Convey—In a deed, a promise that the grantor has the legal ability to make a valid conveyance.

Covenant of Seisin—In a deed, a promise that the grantor actually owns the interest she is conveying to the grantee.

Covenant of Warranty—In a deed, a promise that the grantor will defend the grantee's title against claims superior to the grantor's that exist when the conveyance is made.

CPM—Certified Property Manager; a property manager who has satisfied the requirements set by the Institute of Real Estate Management of the National Association of Realtors®.

CRE—Counselor of Real Estate; a member of the American Society of Real Estate Counselors.

Credit—A payment receivable (owed to you), as opposed to a debit, which is a payment due (owed by you).

Credit Arranger—An intermediary between prospective borrowers and lenders, who negotiates loans; for example, a mortgage broker. *See also:* Mortgage Loan Originator.

Credit Bidding—In a foreclosure sale, when the lender acquires the property by bidding the amount the borrower owes.

Credit History—An individual's record of bill payment and debt repayment, as revealed in a credit report compiled by a credit rating bureau. Also called credit reputation.

Credit Score—A number, calculated based on an individual's credit history, that's used in underwriting as an indication of how likely it is that the applicant will default on the proposed loan.

Credit Union—A type of financial institution that may serve only the members of a particular group (such as a labor union or a professional association), and that has traditionally emphasized consumer loans.

Creditor—One who is owed a debt.

Creditor, Secured—A creditor with a security interest in or a lien against specific property. If the debt isn't repaid, the secured creditor can repossess the property or (in the case of real estate) foreclose on the property and collect the debt from the sale proceeds.

Creditor, Unsecured—A creditor who doesn't have a lien against or other security interest in any of the debtor's property (and who therefore is less likely to be able to collect the debt if the debtor fails to pay it as agreed).

Creditworthiness—The extent to which an individual is a good credit risk; how likely he is to repay a loan on the schedule set by the lender, or how likely to default.

Criminal Law—The body of law under which the government can prosecute an individual for crimes, wrongs against society. *Compare:* Civil Law.

Cubage—The cubic volume of an object; in the case of a building, determined by multiplying the width by the depth by the height (measuring from the basement floor to the outside surfaces of roof and walls).

Cul-de-sac—A dead-end street, especially one with a semicircular turnaround at the end.

Curable—In reference to depreciation, capable of being corrected at a cost that could be recovered in the sales price if the property were subsequently sold. (Depreciation is incurable if it can't be corrected, or if it would cost more to correct than the correction would add to the property's value.)

Cure—To remedy a default, by paying money that is overdue or fulfilling other obligations that have not been met.

Customer—From the point of view of a real estate agent, a prospective property buyer.

Damage Deposit—*See:* Security Deposit.

Damages—1. Losses that a person suffers as a result of a breach of contract or a tort. 2. In a civil lawsuit, an amount of money the defendant is ordered to pay the plaintiff.

Damages, Actual—*See:* Damages, Compensatory.

Damages, Compensatory—Damages awarded to a plaintiff as compensation for injuries (personal injuries, property damage, or financial losses) caused by the defendant's act or failure to act. Also called actual damages.

Damages, Liquidated—A sum that the parties to a contract agree in advance (at the time the contract is made) will serve as full compensation in the event of a breach.

Damages, Punitive—In a civil lawsuit, an award added to actual damages, to punish the defendant for outrageous or malicious conduct and discourage others from similar conduct.

Datum—An artificial horizontal plane of elevation, established in reference to sea level, used by surveyors as a reference point in determining elevation.

Dealer—One who regularly buys and sells real estate in the ordinary course of business.

Dealer Property—Property held for sale to customers rather than for long-term investment; a developer's inventory of subdivision lots, for example.

Debit—A charge or debt owed to another.

Debtor—One who owes money to another.

Debt Service—The amount of money required to make the periodic payments of principal and interest on an amortized debt, such as a mortgage.

Decedent—A person who has died.

Declaration of Abandonment—A document recorded by an owner that voluntarily releases a property from homestead protection.

Declaration of Homestead—A recorded document that establishes homestead protection for a property that would not otherwise receive it.

Declaration of Restrictions—*See:* CC&Rs.

Decrement—A decrease in value; the opposite of increment.

Dedication—A voluntary or involuntary gift (that is, an uncompensated transfer) of private property for public use; may transfer ownership or simply create an easement.

Dedication, Common Law—Involuntary dedication, resulting from a property owner's acquiescence to public use of her property over a long period. Also called implied dedication.

Dedication, Statutory—A dedication required by law; for example, dedication of property for streets and sidewalks as a prerequisite to subdivision approval.

Deduction—An amount a taxpayer is allowed to subtract from his income before the tax on the income is calculated (as distinguished from a tax credit, which is deducted from the tax owed).

Deed—An instrument which, when properly executed and delivered, conveys title to real property from the grantor to the grantee.

Deed, Administrator's—A deed used by the administrator of an estate to convey property owned by a deceased person to the heirs.

Deed, General Warranty—A deed in which the grantor warrants the title against defects that may have arisen before or during her period of ownership. Also simply called a warranty deed.

Deed, Gift—A deed that isn't supported by valuable consideration; often lists "love and affection" as the consideration.

Deed, Grant—A deed that uses the word "grant" in its words of conveyance and carries certain implied warranties. The most commonly used type of deed in California.

Deed, Quitclaim—A deed that conveys any interest in a property that the grantor has at the time the deed is executed, without warranties.

Deed, Sheriff's—A deed delivered, on court order, to the holder of a certificate of sale when the redemption period after a mortgage foreclosure has expired.

Deed, Special Warranty—A deed in which the grantor warrants title only against defects that may have arisen during his period of ownership.

Deed, Tax—A deed given to a purchaser of property at a tax foreclosure sale.

Deed, Trust—*See:* Deed of Trust.

Deed, Trustee's—A deed given to a purchaser of property at a trustee's sale.

Deed, Warranty—1. A general warranty deed. 2. Any type of deed that carries warranties.

Deed, Wild—A deed that won't be discovered in a traditional title search, because of a break in the chain of title.

Deed Executed Under Court Order—A deed that is the result of a court action, such as a judicial foreclosure or a partition.

Deed in Lieu of Foreclosure—A deed given by a borrower to a mortgage lender, transferring title to the property in order to satisfy the debt and avoid foreclosure.

Deed of Partition—Deed used by co-owners (such as tenants in common or joint tenants) to divide up the co-owned property so that each can own a portion in severalty.

Deed of Reconveyance—The instrument used to release the security property from the lien created by a deed of trust when the debt has been repaid.

Deed of Trust—An instrument that creates a voluntary lien on real property to secure the repayment of a debt, and which includes a power of sale clause permitting nonjudicial foreclosure. The parties are the grantor or trustor (the borrower), the beneficiary (the lender), and the trustee (a neutral third party).

Deed Release Provision—*See:* Release Clause.

Deed Restrictions—Provisions in a deed that restrict use of the property, and which may be either covenants or conditions.

Default—Failure to fulfill an obligation, duty, or promise, as when a borrower fails to make payments, or a tenant fails to pay rent.

Default Judgment—*See:* Judgment, Default.

Defeasance Clause—A clause in a mortgage, deed of trust, or lease that cancels or defeats a certain right upon the occurrence of a particular event.

Defeasible Fee—*See:* Fee Simple Defeasible.

Defendant—1. The person being sued in a civil lawsuit. 2. The accused person in a criminal lawsuit.

Deferred Maintenance—Curable depreciation resulting from maintenance or repairs that were postponed, causing physical deterioration. *See:* Deterioration, Physical.

Deficiency Judgment—*See:* Judgment, Deficiency.

Degree—In surveying, a unit of circular measurement equal to $^1/_{360}$ of one complete rotation around a point in a plane.

Delivery—The legal transfer of a deed from the grantor to the grantee, which results in the transfer of title.

Demand—Desire to own coupled with ability to afford. This is one of the four elements of value, along with scarcity, utility, and transferability.

Demise—1. A conveyance of an interest in real property through the terms of a lease. 2. The transfer of an estate or interest in property to another for years, for life, or at will.

Density—In land use law, the number of buildings or occupants per unit of land.

Department of Housing and Urban Development (HUD)—The federal cabinet department responsible for public housing programs, FHA-insured loan programs, and enforcement of the Fair Housing Act. The FHA and Ginnie Mae are both part of HUD.

Deposit—Money offered as an indication of commitment or as a protection, and which may be refunded under certain circumstances; for example, a good faith deposit or a tenant's security deposit.

Deposition—The formal, out-of-court testimony of a witness in a lawsuit, taken before trial for possible use during the trial; either as part of the discovery process, to determine the facts of the case, or when the witness may not be available during the trial.

Deposit Receipt—*See:* Purchase Agreement.

Depreciable Property—In the federal income tax code, property that's eligible for depreciation deductions because it will wear out and have to be replaced.

Depreciation—1. A loss in value (caused by physical deterioration, functional obsolescence, or external obsolescence). 2. For the purposes of income tax deductions, apportioning the cost of an asset over a period of time.

Depreciation, Accrued—Depreciation that has built up or accumulated over a period of time.

Depreciation, Age-Life—A method of estimating depreciation for appraisal purposes, based on the life expectancy of the property, assuming normal maintenance.

Depreciation, Curable—Deferred maintenance and functional obsolescence that would ordinarily be corrected by a prudent owner, because the correction cost could be recovered in the sales price.

Depreciation, Incurable—Physical deterioration, functional obsolescence, or external obsolescence that is either impossible to correct, or else not economically feasible to correct, because the cost could not be recovered in the sales price.

Deterioration, Physical—A loss in value due to wear and tear, damage, or structural defects. Physical deterioration that's curable is called deferred maintenance.

Depreciation, Straight Line—A method of calculating depreciation for income tax or appraisal purposes, in which an equal portion of a structure's value is deducted each year over the anticipated useful life; when the full value of the improvement has been depreciated, its economic life is exhausted.

Depreciation Deductions—Under the federal income tax code, deductions from a taxpayer's income to permit the cost of an asset to be recovered; allowed only for depreciable property that is held for the production of income or used in a trade or business. Also called cost recovery deductions.

Depth Table—A mathematical table used in appraisal to estimate the differences in value between lots with different depths. Frontage has the greatest value, and land at the rear of a lot has the least value.

Dereliction—*See:* Reliction.

Descent—Transfer of property by intestate succession instead of by will. A person who receives property by intestate succession is said to receive it by descent, rather than by devise or bequest.

Detached Residence—A home physically separated from the neighboring home(s), not connected by a common wall.

Developed Land—Land with man-made improvements, such as buildings or roads.

Developer—One who subdivides or improves land to achieve a profitable use.

Development—1. Any development project, such as a new office park. 2. A housing subdivision. 3. In reference to a property's life cycle, the earliest stage, also called integration.

Devise—1. (noun) A gift of real property through a will. 2. (verb) To transfer real property by will. *Compare:* Bequest; Bequeath; Legacy.

Devisee—Someone who receives title to real property through a will. *Compare:* Beneficiary; Legatee.

Devisor—A testator who devises real property in his will.

Directional Growth—The direction in which a city's residential neighborhoods are expanding or expected to expand.

Disability—A physical or mental impairment that substantially limits a person in one or more major life activities, according to the Americans with Disabilities Act and Fair Housing Act. Also called a handicap.

Disaffirm—To ask a court to terminate a voidable contract.

Disbursements—Money paid out or expended.

Disclaimer—A denial of legal responsibility.

Discount—1. (verb) To sell a promissory note at less than its face value. 2. (noun) Discount points.

Discount Points—A percentage of the principal amount of a loan that the lender collects (or withholds from the loan amount) when the loan is originated, to increase the lender's upfront yield on the loan.

Discount Rate—The interest rate charged when a member bank borrows money from the Federal Reserve Bank.

Discrimination—Treating people unequally because of their race, religion, sex, national origin, age, or some other characteristic.

Disintegration—In a property's life cycle, the period of decline when the property's present economic usefulness is near an end and constant upkeep is necessary.

Dispossess—To force someone out of possession of real property through legal procedures, as in an eviction.

Documentary Transfer Tax—*See:* Tax, Documentary Transfer.

Domicile—The state where a person has his permanent home.

Dominant Tenant—*See:* Tenant, Dominant.

Dominant Tenement—*See:* Tenement, Dominant.

Donative Intent—The intent to transfer title immediately and unconditionally; required for proper delivery of a deed.

Double-entry Bookkeeping—An accounting technique in which an item is entered in the ledger twice, once as a credit and once as a debit; used for some settlement statements.

Downpayment—The part of the purchase price of property that the buyer is paying in cash; the difference between the purchase price and the financing.

Downzoning—Rezoning land for a more limited use.

Drainage—A system to draw water off land, either artificially (e.g., with pipes) or naturally (e.g., with a slope).

Dual Agency—*See:* Agency, Dual.

Due-on-sale Clause—*See:* Alienation Clause.

Duplex—A structure that contains two separate housing units, with separate entrances, living areas, kitchens, and bathrooms.

Duress—Unlawful force or constraint used to compel someone to do something (such as sign a contract) against her will.

Dwelling—A building or a part of a building used or intended to be used as living quarters.

Earnest Money—*See:* Good Faith Deposit.

Easement—An irrevocable right to use some part of another person's real property for a particular purpose.

Easement, Access—An easement that enables the easement holder to reach and/or leave her property (the dominant tenement) by crossing the servient tenement. Also called an easement for ingress and egress.

Easement, Aviation—An easement that allows aircraft to fly through the airspace over the servient tenement (above a specified height).

Easement, Implied—*See:* Easement by Implication.

Easement, Negative—An easement that prevents the servient tenant from using her own land in a certain way (instead of allowing the dominant tenant to use it); essentially the same thing as a restrictive covenant that runs with the land.

Easement, Positive—An easement that allows the dominant tenant to use the servient tenement in a particular way. This is the standard type of easement (see the first definition of Easement, above); the term "positive easement" is generally used only when contrasting a standard easement with a negative easement.

Easement, Prescriptive—An easement acquired by prescription; that is, by using the property openly and without the owner's permission for the period prescribed by statute.

Easement Appurtenant—An easement that benefits a piece of property, the dominant tenement. *Compare:* Easement in Gross.

Easement by Express Grant—An easement granted to another in a deed or other document.

Easement by Express Reservation—An easement created in a deed when a landowner is dividing the property, transferring the servient tenement but retaining the dominant tenement; an easement that the grantor reserves for his own use.

Easement by Implication—An easement created by law when a parcel of land is divided, if there has been long-standing and apparent prior use and the easement is reasonably necessary for the enjoyment of the dominant tenement. Sometimes called an easement by necessity.

Easement by Necessity—1. A special type of easement by implication, created by law even when there has been no prior use, if the dominant tenement would be entirely useless without an easement. 2. Any easement by implication.

Easement in Gross—An easement that benefits a person instead of a piece of land. There is a dominant tenant, but no dominant tenement. *Compare:* Easement Appurtenant.

ECOA—*See:* Equal Credit Opportunity Act.

Economic Life—The period during which improved property will yield a return over and above the rent due to the land itself; also called the useful life.

Economic Obsolescence—*See:* Obsolescence, External.

Economic Rent—*See:* Rent, Economic.

Effective Age—*See:* Age, Effective.

Egress—A means of exiting; a way to leave a property; the opposite of ingress. The terms ingress and egress are most commonly used in reference to an access easement.

EIS—Environmental Impact Statement.

Ejectment—A legal action to recover possession of real property from someone who isn't legally entitled to possession of it; an eviction.

Elements of Comparison—In the sales comparison approach to appraisal, considerations taken into account in selecting comparables and comparing comparables to the subject property. They include date of sale, location, physical characteristics, terms of sale, and conditions of sale.

Emancipated Minor—*See:* Minor, Emancipated.

Emblements—Crops that are produced annually through the labor of the cultivator, such as wheat.

Emblements, Doctrine of—The legal rule that gives an agricultural tenant the right to enter the land to harvest crops after the lease ends.

Eminent Domain—The government's constitutional power to take (condemn) private property for public use, as long as the owner is paid just compensation.

Employee—Someone who works under the direction and control of another. *Compare:* Independent Contractor.

Encroachment—A physical intrusion onto neighboring property, usually due to a mistake regarding the location of the boundary.

Encumber—To place a lien or other encumbrance against the title to a property.

Encumbrance—A nonpossessory interest in real property; a right or interest held by someone other than the property owner, which may be a lien, an easement, a profit, or a restrictive covenant.

Encumbrance, Financial—A lien.

Endorsement—Assignment of a negotiable instrument (such as a check or a promissory note) to another party by the payee, by signing the back of the instrument.

Endorsement, Special—An endorsement to a specific person (as opposed to an endorsement in blank).

Endorsement in Blank—An endorsement that doesn't specify a particular holder, so that the bearer (whoever has possession of the instrument) is entitled to payment.

Enjoin—To prohibit an act, or command performance of an act, by court order; to issue an injunction.

Entitlement—The amount of the borrower's guaranty in a VA loan.

EPA—Environmental Protection Agency.

Equal Credit Opportunity Act (ECOA)—A federal law that prohibits lenders from discriminating against loan applicants on the basis of race, color, religion, national origin, sex, marital status, or age, or because the applicant's income is derived from public assistance.

Equilibrium—In the life cycle of a property, a period of stability, during which the property undergoes little, if any, change.

Equitable Interest or Title—*See:* Title, Equitable.

Equitable Remedy—In a civil lawsuit, a judgment granted to the plaintiff that is something other than an award of money (damages). An injunction, rescission, and specific performance are examples.

Equitable Right of Redemption—*See:* Redemption, Equitable Right of.

Equity—1. An owner's unencumbered interest in her property; the difference between the value of the property and the liens against it. 2. A judge's power to soften or set aside strict legal rules in order to bring about a fair and just result in a particular case.

Equity Sharing—When one person loans another money for the acquisition of property in exchange for a share in the appreciation of the property. *Compare:* Mortgage, Shared Appreciation.

Erosion—Gradual loss of soil due to the action of water or wind.

Escalation Clause—A clause in a contract or mortgage that provides for payment or interest adjustments (usually increases) if specified events occur, such as a change in the property taxes or in the prime interest rate. Also called an escalator clause.

Escheat—Reversion of property to the state when a person dies intestate and no heirs can be located.

Escrow—An arrangement in which something of value (such as money or a deed) is held on behalf of the parties to a transaction by a third party (an escrow agent) until specified conditions have been fulfilled.

Escrow Agent—*See:* Agent, Escrow.

Escrow Instructions—Directions given to an escrow agent by the parties to a transaction, setting forth the parties' obligations and the conditions for closing.

Estate—1. An interest in real property that is or may become possessory; either a freehold or a leasehold. 2. The property left by someone who has died.

Estate, Fee Simple—*See:* Fee Simple.

Estate, Periodic—*See:* Tenancy, Periodic.

Estate at Sufferance—*See:* Tenancy at Sufferance.

Estate at Will—*See:* Tenancy at Will.

Estate for Life—*See:* Life Estate.

Estate for Years—*See:* Tenancy, Term.

Estate of Inheritance—An estate that can pass to the holder's heirs, such as a fee simple.

Estoppel—A legal doctrine that prevents a person from asserting rights or facts that are inconsistent with his earlier actions or statements.

Estoppel Certificate—A document that prevents a person who signs it from later asserting facts different from those stated in the document. Also called an estoppel letter.

Et al.—Abbreviation for the Latin phrase "et alius" or "et alii," meaning "and another" or "and others."

Ethics—A system of accepted principles or standards of moral conduct. *See:* Code of Ethics.

Et ux.—Abbreviation for the Latin phrase "et uxor," meaning "and wife."

Eviction—Dispossession or expulsion of someone from real property.

Eviction, Actual—Physically forcing someone off of real property (or preventing them from re-entering), or using the legal process to make them leave. *Compare:* Eviction, Constructive.

Eviction, Constructive—When a landlord's act (or failure to act) interferes with a tenant's quiet enjoyment of the property, or makes the property unfit for its intended use, to such an extent that the tenant is forced to move out or would be justified in doing so.

Eviction, Self-help—The use of physical force, a lock-out, or a utility shut-off to evict a tenant, instead of the legal process. This is generally illegal.

Excess Land—Land that is part of a parcel that doesn't add to the value of that property. For instance, where the value of a property lies primarily in its frontage, additional depth would not increase the property's value.

Exchange—*See:* Tax-Free Exchange.

Exclusive Listing—*See:* Listing, Exclusive.

Exculpatory Clause—A clause in a contract that relieves one party of liability for certain defaults or problems. Such provisions are not always enforceable.

Execute—1. To sign an instrument and take any other steps (such as acknowledgment) that may be necessary to its validity. 2. To perform or complete. *See:* Contract, Executed.

Execution—The legal process in which a court orders an official (such as the sheriff) to seize and sell the property of a judgment debtor to satisfy a lien.

Executor—A person named in a will to carry out its provisions. (If it is a woman, she may be referred to as the executrix, but that term has passed out of use.) Also called a personal representative.

Exemption—A provision holding that a law or rule doesn't apply to a particular person or group. For example, a person entitled to a tax exemption isn't required to pay the tax.

Expenses, Fixed—Regularly recurring property expenses, such as general real estate taxes and hazard insurance. *Compare:* Expenses, Variable.

Expenses, Maintenance—In connection with income-producing property, the cost of utilities, supplies, cleaning, repairs, and services for tenants, along with administrative expenses, management fees, and building employee wages.

Expenses, Operating—For income-producing property, the fixed expenses, maintenance expenses, and reserves for replacement; does not include debt service.

Expenses, Variable—Expenses incurred in connection with property that don't occur on a set schedule, such as the cost of repairing a roof damaged in a storm. *Compare:* Expenses, Fixed.

Express—Stated in words, whether spoken or written. *Compare:* Implied.

Extender Clause—*See:* Safety Clause.

External Obsolescence—*See:* Obsolescence, External.

Failure of Purpose—When the intended purpose of an agreement or arrangement can no longer be achieved. In most cases, this releases the parties from their obligations.

Fair Employment and Housing Act—A California civil rights law that prohibits all housing discrimination in California based on race, color, religion, sex, gender, gender identity, gender expression, sexual orientation, marital status, national origin, ancestry, familial status, genetic information, source of income, or disability. Also known as the Rumford Act.

Fair Housing Act— A law that makes it illegal to discriminate on the basis of race, color, religion, sex, national origin, disability (handicap), or familial status in the sale or rental of residential property (or vacant land that will be used for residential construction). Also called Title VIII of the Civil Rights Act of 1968.

Fannie Mae—Popular name for the Federal National Mortgage Association (FNMA).

FDIC—*See:* Federal Deposit Insurance Corporation.

Feasibility Study—A cost-benefit analysis of a proposed project, sometimes required by a lender before giving a loan commitment.

Fed—*See:* Federal Reserve.

Federal Deposit Insurance Corporation (FDIC)—A federal agency that insures deposits in financial institutions.

Federal Fair Housing Act— *See:* Fair Housing Act.

Federal Home Loan Bank System (FHLB)—Twelve regional wholesale banks that loan funds to FHLB members, which are local community lenders.

Federal Home Loan Mortgage Corporation (FHLMC)—A government-sponsored enterprise that is one of the major secondary market entities; commonly called Freddie Mac.

Federal Housing Administration (FHA)—An agency within the Department of Housing and Urban Development (HUD). Its main activity is insuring home mortgage loans, to encourage lenders to make more affordable loans.

Federal National Mortgage Association (FNMA)—A government-sponsored enterprise that is one of the major secondary market entities; commonly called Fannie Mae.

Federal Reserve—The government body that regulates commercial banks and implements monetary policy in an attempt to keep the national economy running well. Often referred to as the Fed.

Federal Reserve System—The twelve Federal Reserve Banks, which make loans to member banks.

Federal Trade Commission (FTC)—A federal agency responsible for investigating and eliminating unfair and deceptive business practices.

Fee—*See:* Fee Simple.

Fee, Conditional—*See:* Fee Simple Subject to a Condition Subsequent.

Fee, Defeasible—*See:* Fee Simple Defeasible.

Fee Broker—*See:* Broker, Fee.

Fee Appraiser—*See:* Appraiser, Fee.

Fee Packing—When a predatory lender or mortgage broker charges an interest rate or fees that far exceed the norm and aren't justified by the cost of the services provided.

Fee Simple—The highest and most complete form of ownership, which is of potentially infinite duration. Often just called a fee.

Fee Simple Absolute—A fee simple estate that is not defeasible or conditional, not subject to termination. *Compare:* Fee Simple Defeasible.

Fee Simple Defeasible—A fee simple estate that is subject to termination if a certain condition isn't met or if a specified event occurs. Also called a qualified fee.

Fee Simple Subject to a Condition Subsequent—A fee simple defeasible that can be terminated by legal action if the condition isn't met, but which does not end automatically. (The only type of fee simple defeasible currently recognized in California.) Also called a conditional fee.

FHA—*See:* Federal Housing Administration; Loan, FHA.

FHLMC—*See:* Federal Home Loan Mortgage Corporation.

Fidelity Bond—A bond to cover losses resulting from the dishonesty of an employee.

Fiduciary Relationship—A relationship of trust and confidence, where one party owes the other (or both parties owe each other) loyalty and a higher standard of good faith than is owed to third parties. For example, an agent is a fiduciary in relation to the principal; husband and wife are fiduciaries in relation to one another.

Finance Charge—1. Any charge a borrower is assessed, directly or indirectly, in connection with a loan. 2. Under the Truth in Lending Act, the sum of the interest, origination fee, discount points paid by the borrower, mortgage insurance premiums, and certain other charges. Sometimes called the total finance charge.

Financial Statement—A summary of facts showing the financial condition of an individual or a business, including a detailed list of assets and liabilities. Also called a balance sheet.

Financing Statement—A brief instrument that is recorded to perfect and give constructive notice of a creditor's security interest in an article of personal property.

Finder's Fee—A referral fee paid to someone for directing a buyer or a seller to a real estate agent.

Firm Commitment—*See:* Commitment.

FIRPTA—*See:* Foreign Investment in Real Property Tax Act.

First Lien Position—The position held by a mortgage or deed of trust that has higher lien priority than any other mortgage or deed of trust against the property.

First Refusal—*See:* Right of First Refusal.

Fiscal Policy—The federal government's financial actions, including spending, collecting revenue, and borrowing; managed by the United States Treasury.

Fiscal Year—Any twelve-month period used as a business year for accounting, tax, and other financial purposes, as opposed to a calendar year.

Fixed Disbursement Plan—A construction financing arrangement that calls for the loan proceeds to be disbursed in a series of predetermined installments at various stages of the construction.

Fixed-rate Loan—*See:* Loan, Fixed-rate.

Fixed Term—A period of time that has a definite beginning and ending.

Fixture—An item that used to be personal property but has been attached to or closely associated with real property in such a way that it has legally become part of the real property. *See:* Annexation, Actual; Annexation, Constructive.

Flipping—*See:* Loan Flipping; Property Flipping.

Floor Area Ratio—A zoning requirement that controls the ratio between a building's floor space and the percentage of the lot it occupies.

Flowage Rights—The right to submerge or flood a piece of land. Also called a flowage easement.

FNMA—*See:* Federal National Mortgage Association.

Footloose Industry—An industry that isn't tied to a particular location.

Foreclosure—Sale of property initiated by a lienholder, against the owner's wishes, so that the unpaid lien can be satisfied from the sale proceeds.

Foreclosure, Judicial—1. The sale of property pursuant to court order to satisfy a lien. 2. A lawsuit filed by a mortgagee or deed of trust beneficiary to foreclose on the security property when the borrower has defaulted.

Foreclosure, Nonjudicial—Foreclosure by a trustee under the power of sale clause in a deed of trust.

Foreign Investment in Real Property Tax Act—A federal law that requires a real estate buyer to withhold funds from a seller who isn't either a U.S. citizen or a resident alien, then forward the withheld funds to the Internal Revenue Service.

Foreshore—Land between the mean high and mean low water marks. Also called foreshore land.

Forfeiture—Loss of a right or something else of value as a result of failure to perform an obligation or condition.

Franchise—A right or privilege granted by a government to conduct a certain business, or a right granted by a private business to use its trade name in conducting business.

Fraud—An intentional or negligent misrepresentation or concealment of a material fact, which is relied upon by another, who is induced to enter a transaction and harmed as a result.

Fraud, Actual—Intentional deceit or misrepresentation to cheat or defraud another.

Fraud, Constructive—A breach of duty that misleads the person the duty was owed to, without an intention to deceive. For example, if a seller gives a buyer inaccurate information about the property without realizing that it is false, that may be constructive fraud.

Freddie Mac—Popular name for the Federal Home Loan Mortgage Corporation (FHLMC).

Free and Clear—Ownership of real property free of any liens other than property tax liens.

Freehold—A possessory interest in real property that has an indeterminable duration. It can be either a fee simple or a life estate. Someone who has a freehold estate has title to the property (as opposed to someone who has a leasehold estate, who is only a tenant).

Frontage—The distance a property extends along a street or a body of water; the distance between the two side boundaries at the front of the lot.

Front Foot—A measurement of property for sale or valuation, with each foot of frontage presumed to extend the entire depth of the lot.

Front Money—The cash required to get a project or venture underway; includes initial expenses such as attorney's fees, feasibility studies, loan charges, and a downpayment.

Fructus Industriales—Plants planted and cultivated by people, such as crops. This is a Latin phrase meaning "fruits of industry."

Fructus Naturales—Naturally occurring plants ("fruits of nature").

Fugitive Substance—A substance that isn't stationary in its natural state; includes oil, natural gas, and water.

Functional Obsolescence—*See:* Obsolescence, Functional.

Gain—Under the federal income tax code, that portion of the proceeds from the sale of an asset that is recognized as taxable profit. *Compare:* Capital Gain.

Garnishment—A legal process by which a creditor gains access to the funds or personal property of a debtor that are in the hands of a third party. For example, if the debtor's wages are garnished, the employer is required to turn over part of each paycheck to the creditor.

General Agent—*See:* Agent, General.

General Lien—*See:* Lien, General.

General Plan—A comprehensive, long-term plan of development for a community, which is implemented by zoning and other laws. Also called a comprehensive plan or a master plan.

Gift Funds—Money that a relative (or other third party) gives to a buyer who otherwise would not have enough cash to close the transaction.

Ginnie Mae—Popular name for the Government National Mortgage Association (GNMA).

Good Faith Deposit—A deposit that a prospective buyer gives the seller as evidence of his good faith intent to complete the transaction, and which is forfeited if the buyer defaults. Also called earnest money.

Good Faith Improver—*See:* Innocent Improver.

Good Will—An intangible asset of a business resulting from a good reputation with the public, serving as an indication of future return business.

Government Lot—In the government survey system, a parcel of land that isn't a regular section (one mile square), because of the convergence of range lines, or because of a body of water or some other obstacle; assigned a government lot number.

Government National Mortgage Association (GNMA)—One of the three major secondary market entities, commonly called Ginnie Mae; a federal agency that is part of the Department of Housing and Urban Development.

Government-sponsored Enterprise (GSE)—A private corporation that is chartered and supervised by the federal government. The most important GSEs in the real estate industry are the secondary market entities Fannie Mae and Freddie Mac.

Government Survey System—A system of grids made up of range and township lines that divide the land into townships, which are further subdivided into sections. A particular property is identified by its location within a particular section, township, and range. Also called the rectangular survey system.

Grant—To transfer or convey an interest in real property by means of a written instrument.

Grant Deed—*See:* Deed, Grant.

Grantee—One who receives a grant of real property.

Granting Clause—Words in a deed that indicate the grantor's intent to transfer an interest in property.

Grantor—One who grants an interest in real property to another.

Gross Income Multiplier—A figure which is multiplied by a rental property's gross income to arrive at an estimate of the property's value. Also called a gross rent multiplier.

Gross Income Multiplier Method—A method of appraising residential property by reference to its rental value. Also called the gross rent multiplier method.

Group Boycott—In antitrust law, an agreement between two or more competitors to exclude another competitor from equal participation in business activities.

GSE—*See:* Government-Sponsored Enterprise.

Guardian—A person appointed by a court to administer the affairs of a minor or an incompetent person.

Guide Meridians—In the government survey system, lines running north-south (parallel to the principal meridian) at 24-mile intervals.

Habendum Clause—A clause included after the granting clause in many deeds. It begins "to have and to hold" and describes the type of estate the grantee will hold.

Habitability, Implied Warranty of—A warranty implied by law in every residential lease, stating that the property is fit for habitation.

Handicap—*See:* Disability.

Heir—Someone entitled to inherit another's property under the laws of intestate succession.

Heirs and Assigns—A phrase used in legal documents to cover all successors to a person's interest in property. Assigns are successors who acquire title in some manner other than inheritance, such as by deed.

HELOC—*See:* Home Equity Line of Credit.

Hereditament—Property (real or personal) that can be inherited.

Hereditament, Corporeal—Tangible property, real or personal, that can be inherited; property with physical substance, such as a car or a house.

Hereditament, Incorporeal—Intangible property, real or personal, that can be inherited, such as an easement appurtenant or accounts receivable.

Highest and Best Use—The use which, at the time of appraisal, is most likely to produce the greatest net return from the property over a given period of time.

Historical Rent—*See:* Rent, Contract.

HMDA—*See:* Home Mortgage Disclosure Act.

Holden Act—*See:* Housing Financial Discrimination Act.

Holder in Due Course—A person who obtains a negotiable instrument for value, in good faith, without notice that it is overdue or notice of any defenses against it.

Holdover Tenant—*See:* Tenant, Holdover.

Home Equity Line of Credit (HELOC)—A credit account secured by equity in the borrower's home, which allows the borrower to borrow up to a specified credit limit, as with a credit card.

Home Equity Loan—*See:* Loan, Home Equity.

Home Mortgage Disclosure Act (HMDA)—A federal law that requires large institutional lenders to make annual reports on residential mortgage loans. The reports disclose areas where few or no home loans have been made and alert regulators to potential redlining.

Homeowners Association—A nonprofit association made up of homeowners in a subdivision, responsible for enforcing the CC&Rs and managing other community affairs.

Homestead—An owner-occupied dwelling, together with any appurtenant outbuildings and land.

Homestead Law—A state law that provides homestead property with limited protection against judgment creditors' claims.

Housing Financial Discrimination Act—A California civil rights law that requires lenders to make lending decisions based on the merits of the borrower and the security property, rather than the neighborhood where the property is located. Also called the Holden Act.

HUD—*See:* Department of Housing and Urban Development.

Hundred Percent Location—For a retail business, a location (normally in a city's downtown business area) that is considered the best for attracting business.

Hybrid ARM—*See:* Mortgage, Hybrid.

Hypothecate—To make property security for an obligation without giving up possession of it. *Compare:* Pledge.

ILSA—*See:* Interstate Land Sales Full Disclosure Act.

Implied—Not expressed in words, but understood from actions or circumstances. *Compare:* Express.

Impound Account—*See:* Reserve Account.

Impounds—Money collected from a borrower and kept in a reserve account by a lender.

Improvements—Man-made additions to real property.

Improvements, Misplaced—Improvements that don't fit the most profitable use of the site. They can be overimprovements or underimprovements.

Imputed Knowledge—A legal doctrine stating that a principal is considered to have notice of information that the agent has, even if the agent never told the principal.

Inadvertent Dual Agency—When a real estate agent who is representing one party to a transaction unintentionally also becomes the agent of the other party (and therefore a dual agent), because her actions have led the other party to believe that she is acting as his agent.

Inchoate—Partial, incomplete, unfinished; begun but not completed, as in the case of a contract that hasn't been executed by all of the parties.

Inchoate Instruments—Documents that are not fully executed, or that are required to be recorded and have not been.

Inchoate Interest—A future interest in real estate, such as an interest a minor will receive when she comes of age.

Income, Disposable—Income remaining after income taxes have been paid.

Income, Effective Gross—A measure of a rental property's capacity to generate income; calculated by subtracting a vacancy factor from the economic rent (potential gross income).

Income, Gross—A property's total income before making any deductions (for bad debts, vacancies, operating expenses, etc.).

Income, Net—The income that is capitalized to estimate the property's value; calculated by subtracting the property's operating expenses (fixed expenses, maintenance expenses, and reserves for replacement) from the effective gross income.

Income, Ordinary—For income tax purposes, income that is not passive income; for example, wages from employment. *Compare:* Income, Passive.

Income, Passive—Income derived from an enterprise that the taxpayer does not materially participate in; for example, income a limited partner receives from a limited partnership. Also, income from the operation of a rental property is generally considered to be passive income even if the taxpayer does participate in managing the property. *Compare:* Income, Ordinary.

Income, Potential Gross—A property's economic rent; the income it could earn if it were available for lease in the current market.

Income, Residual—The amount of income that an applicant for a VA loan has left over after taxes, recurring obligations, and the proposed housing expense have been deducted from his gross monthly income.

Income, Spendable—The income that remains after deducting operating expenses, debt service, and income taxes from a property's gross income. Also called net spendable income or cash flow.

Income Approach to Value—One of the three main methods of appraisal, in which an estimate of the subject property's value is based on the net income it produces; also called the capitalization method or the investor's method of appraisal.

Income Property—Property that generates rent or other income for the owner, such as an apartment building. In the federal income tax code, it is referred to as property held for the production of income.

Income Ratio—A standard used in qualifying a buyer for a loan, to determine whether she has sufficient income. The buyer's debts and proposed housing expense shouldn't exceed a specified percentage of her income.

Incompetent—1. Not legally competent; lacking contractual or testamentary capacity. 2. Not mentally competent; not of sound mind.

Incorporeal Rights—Rights in real property that don't involve physical possession of anything, such as an easement.

Increment—An increase in value; the opposite of decrement.

Independent Contractor—A person who contracts to do a job for another, but retains control over how she will carry out the task, rather than following detailed instructions. *Compare:* Employee.

Index—A published statistical report that indicates changes in the cost of money; used as the basis for interest rate adjustments in an ARM.

Index, Tract—An index of recorded documents in which all documents that carry a particular legal description are grouped together.

Indexes, Grantor/Grantee—Indexes of recorded documents maintained by the county recorder, with each document listed in alphabetical order according to the last name of the grantor (in the grantor index) and grantee (in the grantee index).

Ingress—A means of entering a property; the opposite of egress. The terms ingress and egress are most commonly used in reference to an access easement.

In-house Sale—A transaction in which the buyer and the seller are brought together by salespersons who work for the same broker. *Compare:* Cooperative Sale.

Injunction—A court order prohibiting someone from performing an act, or commanding performance of an act.

Innocent Improver—Someone who makes an improvement on land in the mistaken belief that he owns the land. Also called a good faith improver.

Installment Note—*See:* Note, Installment.

Installment Sale—Under the federal income tax code, a sale in which less than 100% of the sales price is received in the year the sale takes place.

Instrument—A legal document, usually one that transfers title (such as a deed), creates a lien (such as a mortgage), or establishes a right to payment (such as a promissory note or contract).

Insurance, Hazard—Insurance against damage to the policy holder's property caused by fire, flood, theft, or other mishap. Also called casualty insurance.

Insurance, Homeowner's—An insurance policy that combines hazard insurance coverage for a homeowner's real and personal property with liability insurance coverage.

Insurance, Liability—Insurance against liability for negligence that injures another person or damages another person's property.

Insurance, Mortgage—Insurance that protects a lender against losses resulting from a borrower's default.

Insurance, Mutual Mortgage—The mortgage insurance provided by the FHA to lenders who make loans through FHA programs.

Insurance, Private Mortgage (PMI)—Insurance provided by private companies to conventional lenders for loans with loan-to-value ratios over 80%.

Insurance, Title—Insurance that protects against losses resulting from undiscovered title defects. An owner's policy protects the buyer (the new property owner), while a mortgagee's policy protects the security interest of the buyer's lender.

Insurance, Title, Extended Coverage—Title insurance that covers problems that should be discovered by an inspection of the property (such as encroachments and adverse possession), in addition to the problems covered by standard coverage policies. An extended coverage policy is sometimes referred to as an ALTA (American Land Title Association) policy.

Insurance, Title, Homeowner's Coverage—Title insurance for residential property with up to four units that covers many of the types of problems covered by an extended coverage policy.

Insurance, Title, Standard Coverage—Title insurance that protects against latent title defects (such as forged deeds) and undiscovered recorded encumbrances, but doesn't protect against problems that would only be discovered by an inspection of the property.

Integration—In a property's life cycle, the earliest stage, when the property is being developed. Also called development.

Interest—1. A right or share in something (such as a piece of real estate). 2. A charge a borrower pays to a lender for the use of the lender's money.

Interest, Compound—Interest computed on both the principal and its accrued interest, as in a savings account. *Compare:* Interest, Simple.

Interest, Future—An interest in property that will or may become possessory at some point in the future; a remainder or a reversion.

Interest, Interim—*See:* Interest, Prepaid.

Interest, Prepaid—Interest on a new loan that must be paid at closing; covers the interest that will accrue during the month in which the transaction closes. Also called interim interest.

Interest, Simple—Interest that is computed on the principal amount of the loan only. (This is the type of interest charged in connection with real estate loans.) *Compare:* Interest, Compound.

Interest, Undivided—A co-owner's interest, giving her the right to possession of the whole property, rather than to a particular section of it.

Interpleader—A court action filed by someone who is holding funds that two or more people are claiming. The holder turns the funds over to the court; the court resolves the dispute and delivers the money to the party who is entitled to it.

Interstate Land Sales Full Disclosure Act (ILSA)—Federal legislation designed to provide buyers with full and accurate information in regard to subdivided property that is sold or advertised across state lines.

Intestate—Without a valid will.

Intestate Succession—Distribution of the property of a person who died intestate to his heirs.

Invalid—Not legally binding or legally effective; not valid.

Inventory—A detailed list of the stock-in-trade of a business.

Inverse Condemnation Action—A court action by a private landowner against the government, seeking compensation for damage to property that resulted from government action.

Inverted Pyramid—A way of visualizing ownership of real property. In theory, a property owner owns all the earth, water, and air enclosed by a pyramid that has its tip at the center of the earth and extends up through the property boundaries out into the sky.

Investment Property—Unimproved property held as an investment in the expectation that it will appreciate in value.

Involuntary Conversion—For income tax purposes, when an asset is converted into cash without the voluntary action of the owner, as when property is condemned or destroyed and the owner receives a condemnation award or insurance proceeds.

Involuntary Lien—*See:* Lien, Involuntary.

Joint Venture—Two or more individuals or companies joining together for one project or a related series of projects, but not as an ongoing business. *Compare:* Partnership.

Judgment—1. A court's binding determination of the rights/duties of the parties in a lawsuit. 2. A court order requiring one party to pay the other damages.

Judgment, Default—A court judgment in favor of the plaintiff due to the defendant's failure to answer the complaint or appear at a hearing.

Judgment, Deficiency—A personal judgment entered against a borrower in favor of the lender if the proceeds from a foreclosure sale of the security property aren't enough to pay off the debt.

Judgment Creditor—A person who is owed money as a result of a judgment in a lawsuit.

Judgment Debtor—A person who owes money as a result of a judgment in a lawsuit.

Judgment Lien—*See:* Lien, Judgment.

Judicial Foreclosure—*See:* Foreclosure, Judicial.

Just Compensation—The compensation that the Constitution requires the government to pay a property owner when private property is taken under the power of eminent domain.

Laches, Doctrine of—A legal principle holding that the law will refuse to protect those who fail to assert their legal rights within a reasonable time.

Land—In the legal sense, the solid part of the surface of the earth, everything affixed to it by nature or by man, and anything on it or in it, such as minerals and water; real property.

Land Contract—*See:* Contract, Land.

Landlocked Property—A parcel of land without access to a road or highway.

Landlord—A landowner who has leased his property to another. Also called a lessor.

Landmark—A monument, natural or artificial, set up on the boundary between two adjacent properties, to show where the boundary is.

Land Residual Process—A method of appraising vacant land.

Latent Defects—Defects that aren't visible or apparent (as opposed to patent defects).

Lateral Support—*See:* Support, Lateral.

Latitude Lines—*See:* Parallels.

Lawful Object—An objective or purpose of a contract that does not violate any law or judicial determination of public policy.

Lease—A conveyance of a leasehold estate from the fee owner to a tenant; a contract in which one party pays the other rent in exchange for the possession of real estate. Also called a rental agreement.

Lease, Fixed—A lease in which the rent is set at a fixed amount, and the landlord pays most or all of the operating expenses (such as taxes, insurance, and maintenance costs). Also called a flat lease, gross lease, or straight lease.

Lease, Graduated—A lease in which it is agreed that the rental payments will increase at intervals by a specified amount or according to a specified formula.

Lease, Gross—*See:* Lease, Fixed.

Lease, Ground—A lease of the land only, usually for a long term, to a tenant who intends to construct a building on the property.

Lease, Net—A lease requiring the tenant to pay all the costs of maintaining the property (such as taxes, insurance, and repairs), in addition to the rent paid to the landlord.

Lease, Percentage—A lease in which the rent is based on a percentage of the tenant's monthly or annual gross sales.

Lease, Sandwich—A leasehold interest lying between the property owner's interest and the interest of the tenant in possession. For example, when the tenant in a ground lease constructs a building and rents out space in the building, she is sandwiched between the landowner's interest and the interest of her building's tenant.

Lease, Straight—*See:* Lease, Fixed.

Leaseback—*See:* Sale-Leaseback.

Leasehold—A possessory interest in real property that has a limited duration. Also called a less-than-freehold estate.

Legacy—A gift of personal property by will. Also called a bequest.

Legal Description—A precise description of a parcel of real property, one that would enable a surveyor to determine the exact location of the boundaries. It may be a lot and block description, a metes and bounds description, or a government survey description.

Legal Person—*See:* Artificial Person.

Legatee—Someone who receives personal property (a legacy) under a will.

Lender, Institutional—A bank, savings and loan, or similar organization that invests other people's funds in loans; as opposed to an individual or private lender, which invests its own funds.

Lessee—One who leases property from another; a tenant.

Lessor—One who leases property to another; a landlord.

Less-than-freehold—*See:* Leasehold.

Leverage—The effective use of borrowed money to finance an investment such as real estate.

Levy—To impose a tax.

Liability—1. A debt or obligation. 2. Legal responsibility.

Liability, Joint and Several—A form of liability in which two or more persons are responsible for a debt both individually and as a group.

Liability, Limited—When a business investor is not personally liable for all of the debts of the business, as in the case of a limited partner or a corporate shareholder.

Liability, Vicarious—A legal doctrine stating that a principal can be held liable for harm to third parties resulting from an agent's actions.

Liable—Legally responsible.

License—1. Official permission to do a particular thing that the law doesn't allow everyone to do. 2. Revocable, non-assignable permission to use another person's land for a particular purpose. *Compare:* Easement.

Lien—A nonpossessory interest in real property, giving the lienholder the right to foreclose if the owner doesn't pay a debt owed to the lienholder; a financial encumbrance on the owner's title.

Lien, Attachment—A lien intended to prevent transfer of the property pending the outcome of litigation.

Lien, Construction—*See:* Lien, Mechanic's.

Lien, Equitable—A lien arising as a matter of fairness, rather than by agreement or by operation of law.

Lien, General—A lien against all the property of a debtor, rather than a particular piece of her property. *Compare:* Lien, Specific.

Lien, Involuntary—A lien that arises by operation of law, without the consent of the property owner. Also called a statutory lien.

Lien, Judgment—A general lien against a judgment debtor's property.

Lien, Materialman's—A lien in favor of a person who supplied materials (as opposed to labor) for a construction project; a type of mechanic's lien.

Lien, Mechanic's—A lien against property in favor of a person who provided labor or materials to improve the property. Also called a construction lien.

Lien, Mello-Roos—A lien for an assessment imposed under the Mello-Roos Community Facilities Act.

Lien, Property Tax—A specific lien on property to secure payment of property taxes.

Lien, Specific—A lien that attaches only to a particular piece of property, not to all of the debtor's property. *Compare:* Lien, General.

Lien, Statutory—*See:* Lien, Involuntary.

Lien, Tax—A lien on property to secure the payment of taxes.

Lien, Voluntary—A lien placed against property with the consent of the owner; either a deed of trust or a mortgage.

Lienholder, Junior—A secured creditor whose lien is lower in priority than another's lien.

Lien Priority—The order in which liens are paid off out of the proceeds of a foreclosure sale.

Lien Theory—The theory holding that a mortgage or a deed of trust doesn't involve a transfer of title to the lender, but merely creates a lien against the property in the lender's favor. *Compare:* Title Theory.

Life Estate—A freehold estate that lasts only as long as a specified person (referred to as the measuring life) is alive. Also called an estate for life.

Life Tenant—Someone who owns a life estate; the person entitled to possession of the property during the measuring life.

Like-kind Exchange—*See:* Tax-free Exchange.

Limited Common Elements—*See:* Common Elements, Limited.

Limited Liability—*See:* Liability, Limited.

Limited Liability Company —A form of business entity that offers both limited liability for its owners and certain tax benefits.

Limited Partnership—*See:* Partnership, Limited.

Lineal—Relating to a line; having only length, without depth. A lineal mile is 5,280 feet in distance.

Liquidated Damages—*See:* Damages, Liquidated.

Lis Pendens—A recorded notice stating that there is a lawsuit pending that may affect title to the defendant's real estate.

Listing—1. Putting property up for sale through a real estate broker. 2. A written agency contract between a seller and a real estate broker, stipulating that the broker will be paid a commission for finding (or attempting to find) a buyer for the seller's property. Also called a listing agreement.

Listing, Exclusive—Either an exclusive agency listing or an exclusive right to sell listing.

Listing, Exclusive Agency—A listing agreement that entitles the broker to a commission if anyone other than the seller finds a buyer for the property during the listing term.

Listing, Exclusive Right to Sell—A listing agreement that entitles the broker to a commission if anyone—including the seller—finds a buyer for the property during the listing term.

Listing, Net—A listing agreement in which the seller sets a net amount she is willing to accept for the property. If the actual selling price exceeds that amount, the broker is entitled to keep the excess as his commission.

Listing, Open—A nonexclusive listing, given by a seller to as many brokers as he chooses. If the property is sold, a broker is only entitled to a commission if she was the procuring cause of the sale.

Listing Agreement—*See:* Listing.

Littoral Land—Land that borders on a stationary body of water (such as a lake, as opposed to a river or stream). *Compare:* Riparian Land.

Littoral Rights—The water rights of an owner of littoral land, in regard to use of the water in the lake.

LLC—*See:* Limited Liability Company.

Loan, Amortized—A loan that requires regular installment payments of both principal and interest (as opposed to an interest-only loan). It is fully amortized if the installment payments will pay off the full amount of the principal and all of the interest by the end of the repayment period. It is partially amortized if the installment payments will cover only part of the principal, so that a balloon payment of the remaining principal balance is required at the end of the repayment period.

Loan, Bridge—*See:* Loan, Swing.

Loan, Called—A loan that has been accelerated by the lender. *See:* Acceleration Clause.

Loan, Carryback—*See:* Mortgage, Purchase Money.

Loan, Conforming—A loan made in accordance with the underwriting criteria of the major secondary market entities, Fannie Mae and Freddie Mac, and which therefore can be sold to those entities.

Loan, Construction—A loan to finance the cost of constructing a building, usually providing that the loan funds will be advanced in installments as the work progresses. Also called an interim loan.

Loan, Conventional—An institutional loan that isn't insured or guaranteed by a government agency.

Loan, Equity—A loan secured by the borrower's equity in property she already owns.

Loan, FHA—A loan made by an institutional lender and insured by the Federal Housing Administration, so that the FHA will reimburse the lender for losses that result if the borrower defaults.

Loan, Fixed-rate—A loan on which the interest rate will remain the same throughout the entire loan term. *Compare:* Mortgage, Adjustable-rate.

Loan, Fully Amortized—*See:* Loan, Amortized.

Loan, Gap—*See:* Loan, Swing.

Loan, G.I.—*See:* Loan, VA-Guaranteed.

Loan, Guaranteed—A loan in which a third party has agreed to reimburse the lender for losses that result if the borrower defaults.

Loan, Home Equity—A loan secured by the borrower's equity in a home he already owns.

Loan, Institutional—A loan made by a financial institution or a mortgage company, as opposed to a loan made by a seller or other private party.

Loan, Interest-only—1. A loan that allows the borrower to pay only the interest during the loan term, so that the entire amount borrowed (the principal) is due at the end of the term. 2. A loan that allows the borrower to pay only the interest during a specified period at the beginning of the term, with the principal amortized over the remainder of the term.

Loan, Interim—*See:* Loan, Construction.

Loan, Jumbo—A loan for an amount that exceeds the conventional loan limits set annually by Fannie Mae and Freddie Mac.

Loan, Partially Amortized—*See:* Loan, Amortized.

Loan, Participation—A loan in which the lender receives some yield on the loan in addition to the interest, such as a percentage of the income generated by the property, or a share in the borrower's equity in the property.

Loan, Permanent—*See:* Loan, Take-Out.

Loan, Rollover—A loan in which the interest rate is periodically renegotiated, typically every three years or every five years.

Loan, Seasoned—A loan with an established record of timely payment by the borrower.

Loan, Swing—A loan that enables the borrower to purchase a new house without waiting for her old house to be sold; the loan is secured by the borrower's equity in the old house, and it will be paid off out of the sale proceeds. Also called a bridge loan or a gap loan.

Loan, Take-out—Long-term financing used to replace a construction loan (an interim loan) when construction has been completed. Also called a permanent loan.

Loan, Underlying—*See:* Mortgage, Wraparound.

Loan, VA-guaranteed—A home loan made by an institutional lender to an eligible veteran, where the Department of Veterans Affairs will reimburse the lender for losses if the veteran borrower defaults.

Loan Broker—*See:* Mortgage Broker.

Loan Correspondent—An intermediary who arranges the loan of an investor's money to a borrower, and then services the loan.

Loan Fee—A loan origination fee or assumption fee.

Loan Flipping—When a predatory lender or mortgage broker encourages a homeowner to refinance repeatedly in a short period, when there's no real benefit to doing so.

Loan Origination—Making a loan, including processing the application, underwriting the loan, and giving the loan funds to the borrower. *Compare:* Loan Servicing.

Loan Servicing—Collecting payments from a borrower and otherwise administering a loan after it has been made. This may be done by the same entity that originated the loan, or by a different entity, in exchange for servicing fees from an investor that has purchased the loan. *Compare:* Loan Origination.

Loan Term—The length of time a borrower is allowed for repaying a mortgage. Also called the repayment period.

Loan-to-value Ratio (LTV)—The relationship between the loan amount and either the sales price or the appraised value of the property (whichever is less), expressed as a percentage.

Lock-in Clause—A clause in a promissory note or land contract that prohibits prepayment before a specified date, or prohibits it altogether.

Longitude Line—*See:* Meridian.

Lot—A parcel of land; especially, a parcel in a subdivision.

Lot and Block Description—The type of legal description used for platted property. It states the property's lot number and block number (if any) and the name of the subdivision, indicating the plat map recorded in the county where the property is located. Sometimes called a recorded plat description.

Love and Affection—The consideration sometimes listed on a deed when real estate is conveyed between family members with no money exchanged. The law recognizes love and affection as good consideration (as distinguished from valuable consideration, which is money, goods, or services).

LTV—*See:* Loan-to-Value Ratio.

MAI—Member of the Appraiser's Institute. The initials identify a member of the American Institute of Real Estate Appraisers of the National Association of Realtors®.

Majority, Age of—The age at which a person becomes legally competent; generally, 18 years old.

Maker—The person who signs a promissory note, promising to repay a debt. *Compare:* Payee.

Maps and Plats—*See:* Lot and Block Description.

Margin—In an adjustable-rate mortgage, the difference between the index rate and the interest rate charged to the borrower.

Marginal Land—Land that is of little economic value and barely repays the cost of working it.

Marketable Title—*See:* Title, Marketable.

Market Data Approach—*See:* Sales Comparison Approach.

Market-oriented Industry—An industry that requires appropriate transportation facilities for delivery of raw materials and distribution of the finished product.

Market Price—1. The current price generally being charged for something in the marketplace. 2. The price actually paid for a property. *Compare:* Value, Market.

Market Value—*See:* Value, Market.

Master Plan—*See:* General Plan.

Master/Servant Relationship—A legal term for a standard employer/employee relationship.

Material Fact—An important fact; one that is likely to influence a decision.

Maturity Date—The date by which a loan is supposed to be paid off in full.

Measuring Life—*See:* Life Estate.

Meeting of Minds—*See:* Mutual Consent.

Megalopolis—An extensive, heavily populated, continuously urban area, including any number of cities.

Megan's Law—A law that requires law enforcement authorities to maintain a database concerning registered sex offenders and make the information available to the public.

Mello-Roos—*See:* Lien, Mello-Roos.

Merger—1. Uniting two or more separate properties by transferring ownership of all of them to one person. 2. When the owner of a parcel acquires title to one or more adjacent parcels.

Meridian—An imaginary line running north and south, passing through the earth's poles. Also called a longitude line.

Meridian, Principal—In the government survey system, the main north-south line in a particular grid, used as the starting point in numbering the ranges.

Meridians, Guide—In the government survey system, lines running north-south (parallel to the principal meridian) at 24-mile intervals.

Metes—Measurements.

Metes and Bounds Description—A legal description that starts at an identifiable point of beginning, then describes the property's boundaries in terms of courses (compass directions) and distances, ultimately returning to the point of beginning.

Mill—One-tenth of one cent; a measure used to state property tax rates in some cases. For example, a tax rate of one mill on the dollar is the same as a rate of one-tenth of one percent of the assessed value of the property.

Mineral Rights—Rights to the minerals located on or beneath the surface of a piece of property.

Minimum Property Requirements (MPR)—A lender's requirements concerning the physical condition of a building, which must be met before a loan can be approved.

Minor—A person who hasn't yet reached the age of majority; generally, a person under 18.

Minor, Emancipated—A person under the age of majority who has contractual capacity, because he is or has been married, has served in the military, or has been emancipated by court order.

MIP—Mortgage insurance premium; especially a premium for an FHA-insured loan.

Misrepresentation—A false or misleading statement. *See:* Fraud.

MLO—*See:* Mortgage Loan Originator.

MLS—*See:* Multiple Listing Service.

Monetary Policy—The federal government's management of the availability and cost of borrowed money; overseen by the Federal Reserve.

Monopoly—Exclusive control over the production or sale of a product or service by a single entity or group.

Monument—Any fixed, visible marker (natural or artificial) used in a survey or a metes and bounds description to establish a point on or near the boundary of a piece of property.

Mortgage—1. An instrument that creates a voluntary lien on real property to secure repayment of a debt. In contrast to a deed of trust, a mortgage ordinarily does not include a power of sale, and so can only be foreclosed judicially. The parties are the mortgagor (borrower) and mortgagee (lender). 2. The term is often used more generally, to refer to either a mortgage or a deed of trust. *See:* Mortgage Loan.

Mortgage, Adjustable-rate (ARM)—A loan in which the interest rate is periodically increased or decreased to reflect changes in the cost of money. *Compare:* Loan, Fixed-rate.

Mortgage, Balloon—A partially amortized mortgage loan that requires a large balloon payment at the end of the loan term.

Mortgage, Blanket—A mortgage that covers more than one parcel of property.

Mortgage, Budget—A loan with monthly payments that include a share of the property taxes and insurance premiums, in addition to principal and interest. The lender places the money for taxes and insurance in a reserve account.

Mortgage, Chattel—An instrument that makes personal property (chattels) security for a loan. In states that have adopted the Uniform Commercial Code (including California), the chattel mortgage has been replaced by the security agreement.

Mortgage, Closed—A loan that can't be paid off early.

Mortgage, Closed-end—A loan that doesn't allow the borrower to increase the balance owed; the opposite of an open-end mortgage.

Mortgage, Direct Reduction—A loan that requires a fixed amount of principal to be paid in each payment. The total payment becomes steadily smaller, because the interest portion becomes smaller with each payment as the principal balance decreases.

Mortgage, First—The mortgage on a property that has first lien position; the one with higher lien priority than any other mortgage against the property.

Mortgage, Graduated Payment—A mortgage which allows a borrower to make smaller payments at first, and larger payments as the borrower's earnings increase.

Mortgage, Growing Equity—A fixed-rate mortgage with scheduled increases in the monthly payment amount, so that the loan is paid off more quickly.

Mortgage, Hard Money—A mortgage given to a lender in exchange for cash, as opposed to one given in exchange for credit.

Mortgage, Hybrid—An adjustable-rate mortgage with an initial adjustment period that's significantly longer than the subsequent adjustment periods, so that it's like a fixed-rate mortgage during the first years of the loan term. For example, with a 5/1 hybrid ARM, the first interest rate adjustment occurs five years into the loan term, and there are annual rate adjustments after that.

Mortgage, Junior—A mortgage that has lower lien priority than another mortgage against the same property. Sometimes called a secondary mortgage.

Mortgage, Level Payment—An amortized loan with payments that are the same amount each month, although the portion of the payment that is applied to principal steadily increases and the portion of the payment applied to interest steadily decreases. *See:* Loan, Amortized.

Mortgage, Open—A mortgage without a prepayment penalty.

Mortgage, Open-end—A loan that permits the borrower to reborrow the money she has repaid on the principal, usually up to the original loan amount, without executing a new loan agreement.

Mortgage, Package—A mortgage that is secured by items of personal property (such as appliances or carpeting) in addition to the real property.

Mortgage, Purchase Money—1. When a seller extends credit to a buyer to finance the purchase of the property, accepting a deed of trust or mortgage instead of cash. Sometimes called a takeback or carryback loan. 2. In a more general sense, any loan the borrower uses to buy the security property (as opposed to a loan secured by property the borrower already owns).

Mortgage, Reverse—A mortgage that provides a source of income for an older person who owns a home free and clear; in exchange for a mortgage against the equity in the home, the lender sends the homeowner monthly payments. Also called a reverse equity or reverse annuity mortgage.

Mortgage, Satisfaction of—*See:* Certificate of Discharge.

Mortgage, Secondary—*See:* Mortgage, Junior.

Mortgage, Senior—A mortgage that has higher lien priority than another mortgage against the same property; the opposite of a junior mortgage.

Mortgage, Shared Appreciation—A mortgage in which a lender is entitled to a share of the increasing value of the property as it appreciates. Sometimes called an equity sharing arrangement.

Mortgage, Subprime—A loan made to a borrower who would not qualify for an ordinary mortgage loan (often, but not necessarily, because her credit history doesn't meet the standards for a prime loan). A subprime lender typically charges higher interest rates and fees to offset the extra risks the loan entails.

Mortgage, Wraparound—A seller financing arrangement in which the seller uses part of the buyer's payments to make the payments on an existing loan (called the underlying loan). The buyer takes title subject to the underlying loan, but does not assume it. When the security instrument used for wraparound financing is a deed of trust instead of a mortgage, it may be referred to as an all-inclusive deed of trust.

Mortgage-backed Securities—Securities that have pools of mortgage loans as collateral, issued by Fannie Mae, Freddie Mac, and other secondary market entities.

Mortgage Banker—*See:* Mortgage Company.

Mortgage Broker—An intermediary who brings real estate lenders and borrowers together and negotiates loan agreements between them, but does not originate or service loans. Also called a mortgage loan broker.

Mortgage Company— A residential real estate lender that originates mortgage loans either for resale on the secondary market or on behalf of large investors, and that may also service loans on behalf of investors. Also called a mortgage banker.

Mortgagee—One who accepts a mortgage from a property owner as security for payment of a financial obligation; a mortgage lender. *Compare:* Mortgagor.

Mortgage Fraud—Using deception to obtain a mortgage loan by defrauding the lender.

Mortgage Loan—Any loan secured by real property, whether the actual security instrument used is a mortgage or a deed of trust.

Mortgage Loan Broker—*See:* Mortgage Broker.

Mortgage Loan Broker Law—A California law that limits the size of the fees and commissions that can be charged by a mortgage broker in certain transactions, and that requires a broker to give a disclosure statement to her customers. Also called the Necessitous Borrower Act or the Real Property Loan Law.

Mortgage Loan Originator (MLO)—1. A loan officer, mortgage broker, or real estate licensee who helps a prospective borrower apply for a mortgage loan. 2. Under the SAFE Act, any individual who, for compensation or gain, takes a residential mortgage loan application or offers or negotiates the terms of a residential mortgage loan.

Mortgaging Clause—A clause in a mortgage that describes the security interest given to the mortgagee.

Mortgagor—A property owner (usually a borrower) who gives a mortgage to another (usually a lender) as security for payment of a financial obligation. *Compare:* Mortgagee.

Multiple Listing Service (MLS)—An organization of brokers who share their exclusive listings.

Mutual Consent—When all parties freely agree to the terms of a contract, without fraud, undue influence, duress, menace, or mistake. Mutual consent is achieved through offer and acceptance; it is sometimes referred to as a "meeting of the minds."

Mutual Water Company—A company formed by property owners in a community for the purpose of obtaining a supply of water at reasonable rates. Stock in the company is issued to the members.

NAR—National Association of Realtors®.

Narrative Report—A detailed appraisal report in which the appraiser summarizes the data and the appraisal methods used, to convince the reader of the soundness of the estimate; a more comprehensive presentation than a form report.

National Environmental Policy Act (NEPA)—Federal legislation that regulates development by federal agencies and private development that requires federal approval or involves federal funding.

Natural Person—A human being, an individual (as opposed to an artificial person, such as a corporation).

Natural Servitude, Doctrine of—A legal principle which holds that a property owner is liable for any damage caused by diverting or channeling flood waters from his property onto someone else's.

Navigable Waters—A body of water large enough so that watercraft can travel on it in the course of commerce.

Necessitous Borrower Act—*See:* Mortgage Loan Broker Law.

Negative Amortization—*See:* Amortization, Negative.

Negligence—Conduct that falls below the standard of care that a reasonable person would exercise under the circumstances; carelessness or recklessness.

Negotiable Instrument—An instrument containing an unconditional promise to pay a certain sum of money to order or to bearer, on demand or at a particular time. It can be a check, promissory note, bond, draft, or stock. *See:* Note, Promissory.

Neighborhood Analysis—The gathering of data on home sizes and styles, topography, features, and amenities in a neighborhood, as part of the appraisal or property management process.

NEPA—*See:* National Environmental Policy Act.

Net Income—*See:* Income, Net.

Net Listing—*See:* Listing, Net.

Net Spendable—*See:* Income, Spendable.

Net Worth—An individual's personal financial assets, minus her personal liabilities.

Nominal Interest Rate—The interest rate stated in a promissory note. Also called the note rate or coupon rate. *Compare:* Annual Percentage Rate.

Nonconforming Loan—A loan that doesn't meet the underwriting criteria of the major secondary market entities. *Compare:* Loan, Conforming.

Nonconforming Use—A property use that doesn't conform to current zoning requirements, but is allowed because the property was being used in that way before the present zoning ordinance was enacted.

Nonpossessory Interest—An interest in property that doesn't include the right to possess and occupy the property; an encumbrance, such as a lien or an easement.

Nonrecognition Transaction—A transaction for which a taxpayer is not required to pay income taxes in the year the gain is realized.

Notarize—To have a document certified by a notary public.

Notary Public—Someone who is officially authorized to witness and certify the acknowledgment made by someone signing a legal document.

Note—*See:* Note, Promissory.

Note, Demand—A promissory note that is due whenever the holder of the note demands payment.

Note, Installment—A promissory note that calls for regular payments of principal and interest until the debt is fully paid.

Note, Joint—A promissory note signed by two or more persons with equal liability for payment.

Note, Promissory—A written promise to repay a debt. It may or may not be a negotiable instrument.

Note, Straight—A promissory note that calls for regular payments of interest only, so that the entire principal amount is due in one lump sum at the end of the loan term.

Note Rate—*See:* Nominal Interest Rate.

Notice, Actual—Actual knowledge of a fact, as opposed to knowledge imputed by law (constructive notice).

Notice, Constructive—Knowledge of a fact imputed to a person by law. A person is held to have constructive notice of something when he should have known it (because he could have learned it through reasonable diligence or an examination of the public record), even if he didn't actually know it.

Notice of Cessation—A notice recorded when work on a construction project has ceased (although the project is unfinished), to limit the time allowed for recording mechanic's liens.

Notice of Completion—A notice recorded when a construction project has been completed, to limit the time allowed for recording mechanic's liens.

Notice of Default—A notice sent by a secured creditor to the debtor, informing the debtor that she has breached the loan agreement.

Notice of Nonresponsibility—A notice that a property owner may record and post on the property to protect his title against construction liens, when someone other than the owner (such as a tenant) has ordered work on the property.

Notice of Sale—A notice stating that foreclosure proceedings have been commenced against a property.

Notice to Quit—A notice to a tenant, demanding that she vacate the leased property.

Notice of Value (NOV)—A document issued in connection with the appraisal for a transaction financed with a VA-guaranteed loan. Formerly called a Certificate of Reasonable Value.

Notice to the World—Constructive notice of the contents of a document provided to the general public by recording the document.

Novation—1. The withdrawal of one party to a contract and the substitution of a new party, relieving the withdrawing party of liability. 2. The substitution of a new obligation for an old one.

Nuisance—A use of property that is offensive or annoying to neighboring landowners (a private nuisance) or to the larger community (a public nuisance).

Obligatory Advances—Disbursements of construction loan funds that the lender is obligated to make when the borrower has completed certain phases of construction.

Obsolescence—Any loss in value (depreciation) due to reduced desirability and/or usefulness.

Obsolescence, External—A loss in value resulting from factors outside the property itself, such as proximity to an airport. Also called economic obsolescence or external inadequacy.

Obsolescence, Functional—A loss in value due to inadequate or outmoded equipment, or as a result of a poor or outmoded design.

Offer—The action of one person (the offeror) in proposing a contract to another (the offeree). If the offeree accepts the offer, a binding contract is formed.

Offer, Illusory—An offer that isn't a valid contract offer, because it requires something more than simple acceptance in order to create a contract.

Offer, Tender—*See:* Tender.

Offeree—One to whom a contract offer is made.

Offeror—One who makes a contract offer.

Officer—In a corporation, an executive authorized by the board of directors to manage the business of the corporation.

Offset Statement—A document in which a borrower confirms the status of the loan (the interest rate, principal balance, etc.) and describes any claims that could affect an interested party. *Compare:* Beneficiary's Statement.

Off-site Improvements—Improvements that add to the usefulness of a site but are not located directly on it, such as curbs, street lights, and sidewalks.

Open Listing—*See:* Listing, Open.

Open Market Operations—The Federal Reserve's manipulation of the money supply through the purchase and sale of government securities.

Option—A contract giving one party the right to do something, without obligating him to do it.

Optionee—The person to whom an option is given.

Optionor—The person who gives an option.

Option to Purchase—An option giving the optionee the right to buy property owned by the optionor at an agreed price during a specified period.

Option to Renew—A lease provision that gives the tenant the right to renew the lease on specified terms when it expires.

Ordinance—A law passed by a local legislative body, such as a city council.

Ordinary Income—*See:* Income, Ordinary.

Orientation—The placement of a house on its lot, with regard to its exposure to the sun and wind, its position in relation to a view, privacy from the street, and protection from outside noise.

Origination—*See:* Loan Origination.

Origination Fee—A fee a lender charges a borrower upon making a new loan, intended to cover the administrative costs of making the loan. Also called a loan fee.

"Or More"—A provision in a promissory note that allows the borrower to prepay the debt.

Ostensible Agency—*See:* Agency, Apparent.

Outlawed—Barred by the statute of limitations.

Overimprovement—An improvement that is more expensive than is justified by the value of the land.

Overlying Right—A landowner's right to use percolating or diffused ground water.

Ownership—Title to property, dominion over property; the rights of possession and control.

Ownership, Concurrent—Shared ownership of one piece of property by two or more individuals, each owning an undivided interest in the property (as in a tenancy in common or joint tenancy, or with community property). Also called co-ownership or co-tenancy.

Ownership in Severalty—Ownership by one individual.

Panic Selling—*See:* Blockbusting.

Par—1. The accepted standard of comparison; the average or typical rate or amount. 2. Face value. For example, a mortgage sold at the secondary market level for 97% of par has been sold for 3% less than its face value.

Parallels—Imaginary lines running east and west, parallel to the equator. Also called latitude lines.

Parcel—A lot or piece of real estate, especially a specified part of a larger tract.

Partial Reconveyance—The instrument given to the borrower when part of the security property is released from a blanket mortgage under a partial release clause.

Partial Release Clause—*See:* Release Clause.

Partial Satisfaction—The instrument given to the borrower when part of the security property is released from a blanket mortgage under a partial release clause.

Partition—The division of a property among its co-owners, so that each owns part of it in severalty. This may occur by agreement of all of the co-owners (voluntary partition), or by court order (judicial partition).

Partner, General—A partner who has the authority to manage and contract for a general or limited partnership, and who is personally liable for the partnership's debts.

Partner, Limited—In a limited partnership, an investor who isn't personally liable for the partnership's debts.

Partnership—An association of two or more persons to carry on a business for profit. The law regards a partnership as a group of individuals, not as an entity separate from its owners. *Compare:* Corporation.

Partnership, General—A partnership in which each member has an equal right to manage the business and share in the profits, as well as an equal responsibility for the partnership's debts. All of the partners are general partners.

Partnership, Limited—A partnership made up of one or more general partners and one or more limited partners, organized in compliance with the Limited Partnership Act.

Partnership Property—All property that partners bring into their business at the outset or later acquire for their business.

Party Wall—A wall located on the boundary line between two adjoining parcels of land that is used or intended to be used by the owners of both properties.

Passive Activity—An investment or other enterprise that may result in a financial gain for a taxpayer without the taxpayer's active participation. *See:* Income, Passive.

Passive Income—*See:* Income, Passive.

Passive Loss—A financial loss to a taxpayer that results from a passive activity.

Patent—The instrument used to convey government land to a private individual.

Payee—In a promissory note, the party who is entitled to be paid; the creditor or lender. *Compare:* Maker.

Payment Shock—When the amount of the monthly payment on a loan increases so sharply that the borrower struggles to pay it or is unable to pay it.

Percolation Test—A test to determine the ability of the ground to absorb or drain water; used to determine whether a site is suitable for construction, particularly for installation of a septic system.

Per Diem—Daily.

Periodic Tenancy—*See:* Tenancy, Periodic.

Personal Property—Any property that isn't real property; movable property not affixed to land. Also called chattels or personalty.

Personal Representative—*See:* Executor.

Personalty—Personal property.

Personal Use Property—Property that a taxpayer owns for her own use (or family use), as opposed to income property, investment property, dealer property, or property used in a trade or business.

Petitioner—*See:* Appellant.

Physical Deterioration—A loss in value resulting from wear and tear, damage, or structural defects. Curable physical deterioration is often called deferred maintenance.

Physical Life—An estimate of the time a building will remain structurally sound and capable of being used. *Compare:* Economic Life.

Plaintiff—The party who brings or starts a civil lawsuit; the one who sues.

Planned Development—A residential development with lots that are owned separately and common areas (common elements) that are co-owned by all of the lot owners.

Planning Commission—A local government agency responsible for preparing the community's general plan for development.

Plat—A detailed survey map of a subdivision, recorded in the county where the land is located.

Plat Book—A large book containing subdivision plats, kept at the county recorder's office.

Platted Property—Subdivided property.

Pledge—The transfer of possession of property by a debtor to the creditor as security for repayment of the debt. *Compare:* Hypothecate.

Plot Plan—A plan showing lot dimensions and the layout of improvements (such as buildings and landscaping) on a property site.

Plottage—The increment of value that results when two or more lots are combined to produce greater value. Also called the plottage increment.

PMI—*See:* Insurance, Private Mortgage.

Point—One percent of the principal amount of a loan. *See:* Discount Points.

Point of Beginning (POB)—The starting point in a metes and bounds description; a monument or a point described by reference to a monument.

Points—*See:* Discount Points.

Police Power—The constitutional power of state and local governments to enact and enforce laws for the protection of the public's health, safety, morals, and general welfare.

Possession—1. The holding and enjoyment of property. 2. Actual physical occupation of real property.

Possessory Interest—An interest in property that includes the right to possess and occupy the property. The term includes all estates (leasehold as well as freehold), but does not include encumbrances.

Potable Water—Water that is safe to drink.

Power of Attorney—An instrument authorizing one person (the attorney in fact) to act as another's agent, to the extent stated in the instrument.

Power of Sale Clause—A clause in a deed of trust giving the trustee the right to foreclose nonjudicially (sell the debtor's property without a court action) if the borrower defaults.

Preapproval—A process that allows a prospective borrower to submit a loan application to a lender and get approved for a loan before beginning the home-buying process.

Predatory Lending—Lending practices that unscrupulous lenders and mortgage brokers use to take advantage of (prey upon) unsophisticated borrowers. Real estate agents, appraisers, and home improvement contractors sometimes participate in predatory lending schemes.

Predatory Steering—Steering a buyer toward a more expensive loan when the buyer could qualify for a less expensive one.

Prepayment—Paying off part or all of a loan before payment is due.

Prepayment Penalty—A penalty charged to a borrower who prepays the loan.

Prepayment Privilege—A provision in a promissory note allowing the borrower to prepay.

Prescription—Acquiring an interest in real property (usually an easement) by using it openly and without the owner's permission for the period prescribed by statute.

Price Fixing—The cooperative setting of prices by competing firms, in violation of antitrust laws.

Prima Facie—At first sight; on the face of it.

Primary Market—The financial market in which mortgage loans are originated, where lenders make loans to borrowers. Also called the primary mortgage market. *Compare:* Secondary Market.

Prime Rate—The interest rate a bank charges its best customers (those with the most assets and best credit ratings).

Principal—1. One who grants another person (an agent) authority to represent him in dealings with third parties. 2. One of the parties to a transaction (such as a buyer or a seller), as opposed to those who are involved as agents or employees (such as a broker or an escrow agent). 3. In regard to a loan, the amount originally borrowed, or the portion of that amount that remains to be repaid, as opposed to the interest.

Principal Meridian—*See:* Meridian, Principal.

Principal Residence Property—Real property that is the owner's home, his main dwelling. Under the federal income tax laws, a person can only have one principal residence at a time.

Prior Appropriation—*See:* Appropriative Rights System.

Private Mortgage Insurance—*See:* Insurance, Private Mortgage.

Probate—A judicial proceeding in which the validity of a will is established and the executor is authorized to distribute the estate property; or, when there is no valid will, in which an administrator is appointed to distribute the estate to the heirs.

Probate Court—A court that oversees the distribution of property under a will or intestate succession.

Procuring Cause—The real estate agent who was primarily responsible for bringing about a sale.

Profit—A nonpossessory interest; the right to enter another person's land and take something (such as timber or minerals) away from it.

Progression, Principle of—An appraisal principle which holds that a property of lesser value tends to be worth more when it is located in an area with properties of greater value than it would be if located elsewhere. *See:* Regression, Principle of.

Promisee—Someone who has been promised something; someone who is supposed to receive the benefit of a contractual promise.

Promisor—Someone who has made a contractual promise to another.

Promissory Note—*See:* Note, Promissory.

Property—1. The rights of ownership in a thing, such as the right to use, possess, transfer, or encumber it. 2. Something that is owned.

Property Flipping—Purchasing property and then reselling it very soon at a much higher price. This is generally legal, but it's illegal if fraudulent means were used to deceive the original seller about the value of the property.

Property Held for Production of Income—*See:* Income Property.

Property Manager—A person hired by a property owner to administer and maintain property, especially rental property.

Property Tax—*See:* Tax, Property.

Property Used in a Trade or Business—Property such as business sites and factories used in a taxpayer's trade or business.

Proposition 13—A ballot initiative that amended California's state constitution in 1978, imposing limits on property taxation.

Proprietorship, Individual or Sole—A business owned and operated by one person.

Proration—The process of dividing or allocating something (especially a sum of money or an expense) proportionately, according to time, interest, or benefit.

Public Record—The official collection of legal documents that individuals have filed with the county recorder in order to make the information contained in them public.

Public Use—A use that benefits the public. A condemnation action is constitutional only if the property is taken for a public use.

Puffing—Superlative statements about the quality of a property that should not be considered assertions of fact.

Purchase Agreement—A contract in which a seller promises to convey title to real property to a buyer in exchange for the purchase price. Also called a purchase and sale agreement, deposit receipt, sales contract, or contract of sale.

Purchaser's Assignment of Contract and Deed—The instrument used to assign the vendee's equitable interest in a land contract to another.

Pure Competitive Market—A market in which prices rise and fall in response to supply and demand without outside restrictions.

Qualified Acceptance—*See:* Counteroffer.

Qualifying Standards—The standards a lender requires a loan applicant to meet before a loan will be approved. Also called underwriting standards.

Quantity Survey Method—In appraisal, a method of estimating the replacement cost of a structure. It involves a detailed estimate of the quantities and cost of materials and labor, and overhead expenses such as insurance and contractor's profit.

Quiet Enjoyment—Use and possession of real property without interference from the previous owner, the landlord, or anyone else claiming an interest. *See:* Covenant of Quiet Enjoyment.

Quiet Title Action—A lawsuit to determine who has title to a piece of property, or to remove a cloud from the title.

Quitclaim Deed—*See:* Deed, Quitclaim.

Range—In the government survey system, a strip of land six miles wide, running north and south.

Range Lines—In the government survey system, the north-south lines (meridians) located six miles apart.

Ratify—To confirm or approve after the fact an act that was not authorized when it was performed.

Ready, Willing, and Able—A buyer is ready, willing, and able if he makes an offer that meets the seller's stated terms, and has the contractual capacity and financial resources to complete the transaction.

Real Estate—*See:* Real Property.

Real Estate Commissioner—The head of the Bureau of Real Estate, who is responsible for implementing and enforcing the Real Estate Law.

Real Estate Contract—1. A purchase agreement. 2. A land contract. 3. Any contract having to do with real property.

Real Estate Fund—A special account into which all real estate license fees are credited.

Real Estate Investment Trust (REIT)—A real estate investment business that qualifies for tax advantages if certain requirements are met.

Real Estate Law—A California statute that governs the licensing and business practices of real estate agents.

Real Estate Settlement Procedures Act (RESPA)—A federal law that governs residential real estate closings, prohibiting kickbacks from settlement service providers, requiring lenders to make disclosures concerning closing costs to loan applicants, and requiring closing agents to prepare a uniform settlement statement.

Realization—When a gain is separated from an asset, and therefore becomes taxable.

Real Property—Land and everything attached to or appurtenant to it. Also called realty or real estate. *Compare:* Personal Property.

Real Property Loan Law—*See:* Mortgage Loan Broker Law.

Realtor®—A real estate agent who is an active member of a state or local real estate board that is affiliated with the National Association of Realtors®.

Realty—*See:* Real Property.

Reasonable Use Doctrine—A limitation of water rights, holding that there is no right to waste water.

Recapture—Recovery by an investor of money that was invested; a return of the investment, as opposed to a return on the investment (a profit).

Recapture Clause—1. A provision in a percentage lease that allows the landlord to terminate the lease and regain the premises if a certain minimum volume of business is not maintained. 2. A provision in a ground lease that allows the tenant to purchase the property after a specified period of time.

Receiver—A person appointed by a court to manage and look after property or funds that are involved in litigation.

Reconciliation—The final step in an appraisal, when the appraiser assembles and interprets the data in order to arrive at a final value estimate. Also called correlation.

Reconveyance—Releasing the security property from the lien created by a deed of trust, by recording a deed of reconveyance.

Recording—Filing a document at the county recorder's office, in order to have it placed in the public record.

Recording Numbers—The numbers stamped on documents when they're recorded, used to identify and locate the documents in the public record.

Recovery Account—A special account funded by real estate license fees, which is used to compensate people who have been injured by the unlawful acts of real estate licensees and who would otherwise go uncompensated.

Rectangular Survey System—*See:* Government Survey System.

Redeem—To buy something back, or otherwise reclaim possession of something.

Redemption—When a defaulting borrower pays the full amount of the debt, plus costs, to avoid the loss of his property due to foreclosure.

Redemption, Equitable Right of—A borrower's right to redeem property prior to a foreclosure sale.

Redemption, Statutory Right of—A borrower's right to redeem property after a foreclosure sale.

Redlining—Refusal by a lender to make loans secured by property in a certain neighborhood because of the racial or ethnic composition of the neighborhood.

Reformation—A legal action to correct a mistake, such as a typographical error, in a deed or other document. The court will order the execution of a correction deed.

Regression, Principle of—An appraisal principle which holds that a valuable property surrounded by properties of lesser value will tend to be worth less than it would be in a different location; the opposite of the principle of progression.

Regulation Z—The Federal Reserve Board's regulation that implements the Truth in Lending Act.

Reinstate—To prevent foreclosure by curing the default and resuming repayment of the loan.

Release—1. To give up a legal right. 2. A document in which a legal right is given up.

Release, Lien—A document removing a lien, given to the borrower once a mortgage or deed of trust has been paid off in full.

Release Clause—1. A clause in a blanket mortgage or deed of trust which allows the borrower to get part of the security property released from the lien when a certain portion of the debt has been paid or other conditions are fulfilled. Often called a partial release clause. 2. A clause in a land contract providing for a deed to a portion of the land to be delivered when a certain portion of the contract price has been paid. Also known as a deed release provision.

Reliction—The gradual receding of a body of water, exposing land that was previously under water. Also called dereliction.

Remainder—A future interest that becomes possessory when a life estate terminates, and that is held by someone other than the grantor of the life estate. *Compare:* Reversion.

Remainderman—The person who has an estate in remainder.

Remaining Economic Life—*See:* Economic Life.

Remise—To give up; a term used in quitclaim deeds.

Rent—Compensation paid by a tenant to the landlord in exchange for the possession and use of the property.

Rent, Contract—The rent that is actually being paid on property that is currently leased.

Rent, Economic—The rent that a property would be earning if it were available for lease in the current market.

Rent, Ground—The earnings of improved property that are attributed to the land itself, after allowance is made for the earnings attributable to the improvement.

Replacement Cost—*See:* Cost, Replacement.

Replevin—Legal proceedings undertaken by a tenant to recover possession of personal belongings that have been unlawfully confiscated by a landlord (usually for nonpayment of rent).

Reproduction Cost—*See:* Cost, Reproduction.

Rescission—Termination of a contract in which each party gives anything acquired under the contract back to the other party. (The verb form is rescind.) *Compare:* Cancellation.

Reservation—A right retained by a grantor when conveying property. For example, mineral rights, an easement, or a life estate can be reserved in the deed.

Reserve Account—A trust account maintained by a mortgage lender for payment of property taxes and insurance premiums on the security property. The lender deposits money collected from the borrower (typically at closing and/or as part of the monthly loan payments) into the account, and then pays the expenses out of the account when they become due. Also called an impound account or an escrow account.

Reserve Requirements—The percentage of deposits commercial banks must keep on reserve with the Federal Reserve Bank.

Reserves for Replacement—For income-producing property, regular allowances set aside to pay for the replacement of structures and equipment that are expected to wear out.

Resident Manager—A manager of an apartment building or complex who resides on the property. Unlike a property manager, a resident manager isn't required to have a real estate license.

Residual—1. The property value remaining after the economic life of the improvements has been exhausted. 2. Commissions in the form of delayed payments (when a part of the commission is paid with each installment on an installment sales contract, for example) are referred to as residuals.

Residual Income—*See:* Income, Residual.

RESPA—*See:* Real Estate Settlement Procedures Act.

Respondent—*See:* Appellee.

Respondeat Superior, Doctrine of—A legal rule holding that an employer is liable for torts (civil wrongs) committed by an employee within the scope of her employment.

Restitution—Restoring something to a person that he was unjustly deprived of.

Restriction—A limitation on the use of real property.

Restriction, Deed—A restrictive covenant in a deed.

Restriction, Private—A restriction imposed on property by a previous owner, a neighbor, or the subdivision developer; a restrictive covenant or a condition in a deed.

Restriction, Public—A law or regulation limiting or regulating the use of real property.

Restrictive Covenant—*See:* Covenant, Restrictive.

Retainer—A fee that a client pays a professional before services are provided, and which is usually applied to any compensation later earned.

Return—A profit from an investment; a yield over and above the amount originally invested.

Reversion—A future interest that becomes possessory when a temporary estate (such as a life estate or a leasehold estate) terminates, and that is held by the grantor or her successors in interest. *Compare:* Remainder.

Rezone—An amendment to a zoning ordinance, usually changing the uses allowed in a particular zone. Also called a zoning amendment.

Right of First Refusal—A right to have the opportunity to purchase or lease a particular property before anyone else, in the event that the property becomes available.

Right of Way—An easement that gives the holder the right to cross another person's land.

Riparian Land—Land that is adjacent to or crossed by a body of water, especially flowing water such as a stream or a river. *Compare:* Littoral Land.

Riparian Rights—The water rights of a landowner whose property is adjacent to or crossed by a body of water. *Compare:* Appropriative Rights System.

Risk Analysis—*See:* Underwriting.

Rule of Capture—*See:* Capture, Rule of.

Rumford Act—*See:* Fair Employment and Housing Act.

Running with the Land—Binding or benefiting the successive owners of a piece of property, rather than terminating when a particular owner transfers his interest. Usually said in reference to an easement or a restrictive covenant.

SAFE Act—The Secure and Fair Enforcement for Mortgage Licensing Act, a federal law that imposes licensing and registration requirements on mortgage loan originators nationwide.

Safety Clause—A clause in a listing agreement providing that for a specified period after the listing expires, the broker will still be entitled to a commission if the property is sold to someone the broker dealt with during the listing term. Also called an extender clause or carryover clause.

Sale-Leaseback—A form of real estate financing in which the owner of industrial or commercial property sells the property and leases it back from the buyer. In addition to certain tax advantages, the seller/lessee obtains more cash through the sale than would normally be possible by mortgaging the property, since lenders won't often lend 100% of the value.

Sales Comparison Approach—One of the three main methods of appraisal, in which the sales prices of comparable properties are used to estimate the value of the subject property. Also called the market data approach.

Sales Contract—*See:* Purchase Agreement.

Salesperson—A licensee who is authorized to represent a broker in a real estate transaction.

Satisfaction of Mortgage—*See:* Certificate of Discharge.

Savings and Loan Association—A type of financial institution that traditionally specialized in residential mortgage loans.

Savings Bank—A type of financial institution that traditionally emphasized consumer loans and accounts for small depositors.

Scarcity—A limited or inadequate supply of something. This is one of the four elements of value (along with utility, demand, and transferability).

Secondary Financing—Money borrowed to pay part of the required downpayment or closing costs for a first loan, when the second loan is secured by the same property that secures the first loan.

Secondary Market—The market in which investors (including Fannie Mae, Freddie Mac, and Ginnie Mae) purchase real estate loans from lenders. Also called the secondary mortgage market. *Compare:* Primary Market.

Secret Profit—A financial benefit that an agent takes from a transaction without informing the principal, in violation of the agent's fiduciary duties.

Section—In the government survey system, a section is one mile square and contains 640 acres. There are 36 sections in a township.

Section 1031 Exchange—*See:* Tax-Free Exchange.

Securities—1. Shares in an enterprise that represent an ownership interest but not managerial control. 2. Stocks, bonds, and similar investment instruments.

Security Agreement—Under the Uniform Commercial Code, a document that creates a lien on personal property being used to secure a loan.

Security Deposit—Money a tenant gives a landlord at the beginning of the tenancy to protect the landlord in case the tenant fails to comply with the terms of the lease. The landlord may retain all or part of the deposit to cover unpaid rent or repair costs at the end of the tenancy.

Security Instrument—A document that creates a voluntary lien to secure repayment of a loan. For debts secured by real property, it is either a mortgage or a deed of trust.

Security Interest—The interest a creditor may acquire in the debtor's property to ensure that the debt will be paid.

Security Property—The property that is serving as collateral for a loan or an extension of credit, which can be retained, repossessed, or foreclosed on if the debt is not paid.

Seisin—Actual possession of a freehold estate; ownership.

Seller Financing—When a property seller extends credit to the buyer for part of the purchase price, accepting a mortgage, a deed of trust, or a land contract to secure payment.

Separate Property—Property owned by a married person that is not community property; includes property acquired before marriage or by gift or inheritance after marriage.

Servant—*See:* Master/Servant Relationship.

Servicing—*See:* Loan Servicing.

Servient Tenant—*See:* Tenant, Servient.

Servient Tenement—*See:* Tenement, Servient.

Setback Requirements—Provisions in a zoning ordinance that don't allow structures to be built within a certain distance from a property line.

Settlement—1. An agreement between the parties to a civil lawsuit in which the plaintiff agrees to drop the suit in exchange for money or the defendant's promise to do or refrain from doing something. 2. Closing.

Settlement Statement—A document that presents a final, detailed accounting for a real estate transaction, listing each party's debits and credits and the amount each will receive or be required to pay at closing. Also called a closing statement.

Severalty—*See:* Ownership in Severalty.

Severance—1. Termination of a joint tenancy. 2. The permanent removal of a natural attachment, fixture, or appurtenance from real property, which transforms the item into personal property.

Severance, Constructive—When a landowner enters into a contract to sell an appurtenance or natural attachment, the contract constructively severs the item from the land—making it the personal property of the buyer—even before the buyer has actually removed it from the land.

Shareholder—An individual who holds an ownership share in a corporation and has limited liability.

Sheriff's Deed—The document conveying title to the person who purchased a foreclosed property at a sheriff's sale, given at the end of the statutory redemption period.

Sheriff's Sale—A foreclosure sale held after a judicial foreclosure. Sometimes called an execution sale.

Sherman Antitrust Act—A federal law that prohibits any agreement in restraint of trade.

Short Plat—The subdivision of a parcel of land into four or fewer lots.

Short Sale—When a homeowner who's facing foreclosure sells the property for less than the remaining balance on the mortgage, and the lender agrees to accept the sale proceeds and fully discharge the debt.

Sinking Fund—Money set aside to accumulate (including accrued interest) so that some obligation can be satisfied or some asset can be replaced at the end of a predetermined period.

Site Analysis—Gathering and evaluating data about the physical characteristics of a property and other factors affecting its use or title, as part of the appraisal process.

Special Agent—*See:* Agent, Special.

Special Assessment—A tax levied only against the properties that have benefited from a public improvement (such as a sewer or a street light), to cover the cost of the improvement; creates a special assessment lien.

Special Exception Permit—*See:* Conditional Use Permit.

Specific Lien—*See:* Lien, Specific.

Specific Performance—A legal remedy in which a court orders someone who has breached a contract to actually perform as agreed, rather than simply paying damages to the other party.

Square Foot Method—In appraisal, a method of estimating replacement cost by calculating the square foot cost of replacing the subject home.

SRA—A member of the Society of Real Estate Appraisers.

Stable Monthly Income—A loan applicant's gross monthly income that meets the lender's tests of quality and durability.

Statute—A law enacted by a state legislature or the U.S. Congress.

Statute of Frauds—A law that requires certain types of contracts to be in writing and signed in order to be enforceable.

Statute of Limitations—A law requiring a particular type of lawsuit to be filed within a specified time after the event giving rise to the suit occurred.

Steering—Channeling prospective buyers or tenants to or away from particular neighborhoods based on their race, religion, national origin, or ancestry.

Straight Note—*See:* Note, Straight.

Subagent—A person to whom an agent has delegated authority, so that the subagent can assist in carrying out the principal's orders; the agent of an agent.

Subcontractor—A contractor who, at the request of the general contractor, provides a specific service, such as plumbing or drywalling, in connection with the overall construction project.

Subdivided Lands Act—A California law that requires a subdivider to disclose certain information to all lot buyers.

Subdivision—1. A piece of land divided into two or more parcels. 2. A residential development.

Subdivision, Common Interest—A subdivision in which an individual owner owns or leases a separate lot or unit and also has an undivided interest in the development's common areas or common elements; for example, a condominium. *Compare:* Subdivision, Standard.

Subdivision, Standard—A subdivision in which each owner owns a separate parcel of land and does not share ownership of common areas or common elements with other lot owners. *Compare:* Subdivision, Common Interest.

Subdivision, Undivided Interest—A subdivision in which individual owners own undivided interests in a parcel of land and have a nonexclusive right to use and occupy the property; for example, a recreational vehicle park.

Subdivision Map Act—A California law that gives cities and counties the power to regulate subdivisions in order to ensure that the subdivisions comply with the local general plan.

Subdivision Plat—*See:* Plat.

Subdivision Regulations—State and local laws that must be complied with before land can be subdivided.

Subjacent Support—*See:* Support, Subjacent.

Subject to—When a purchaser takes property subject to a deed of trust or a mortgage, she isn't personally liable for paying off the loan. In case of default, however, the property can still be foreclosed on.

Sublease—When a tenant transfers something less than her entire leasehold estate to someone else (a subtenant); this could be the right to possession of only part of the leased property, or it could be the right to possession of the entire leased property, but for only part of the remainder of the lease term. *Compare:* Assignment.

Subordination Clause—A provision in a mortgage or deed of trust that permits a later mortgage or deed of trust to have higher lien priority than the one containing the clause.

Subprime Lending—*See:* Mortgage, Subprime.

Subrogation—The substitution of one person in the place of another with reference to a lawful claim or right. For instance, a title company that pays a claim on behalf of its insured, the property owner, is subrogated to any claim the owner successfully undertakes against the former owner.

Substitution, Principle of—A principle of appraisal holding that the maximum value of a property is set by how much it would cost to obtain another property that is equally desirable, assuming that there would not be a long delay or significant incidental expenses involved in obtaining the substitute.

Substitution of Liability—A buyer wishing to assume an existing loan may apply for the lender's approval; once approved, the buyer assumes liability for repayment of the loan, and the original borrower (the seller) is released from liability.

Succession—Acquiring property by will or inheritance.

Sufferance—Acquiescence, implied permission, or passive consent through a failure to act, as opposed to express permission.

Supply and Demand, Principle of—A principle holding that value varies directly with demand and inversely with supply. That is, the greater the demand, the higher the value; and the greater the supply, the lower the value.

Support, Lateral—The support that a piece of land receives from the land adjacent to it.

Support, Subjacent—The support the surface of a piece of land receives from the land beneath it.

Support Rights—The right to have one's land supported by the land adjacent to it and beneath it.

Surplus Productivity, Principle of—A principle of appraisal which holds that the net income that remains after paying the proper costs of labor, organization, and capital is credited to the land and tends to set its value.

Surrender—Giving up an estate (such as a life estate or a leasehold) before it has expired.

Surveying—Accurately determining the precise location of the boundaries of a piece of property.

Survivorship, Right of—A characteristic of joint tenancy; surviving joint tenants automatically acquire a deceased joint tenant's interest in the property.

Syndicate—An association formed to operate an investment business. A syndicate isn't a recognized legal entity; it can be organized as a corporation, partnership, limited liability company, or trust.

Tacking—Adding together successive periods of use or possession by more than one person to make up the statutory period required for prescription or adverse possession.

Taking—When the government acquires private property for public use by condemnation, it's called "a taking." The term is also used in inverse condemnation lawsuits, when a government action has damaged private property.

Tax, Ad Valorem—A tax assessed on the value of property.

Tax, Documentary Transfer—A state tax levied on every sale of real estate. Also called the real estate excise tax.

Tax, Excise—*See:* Tax, Documentary Transfer.

Tax, General Real Estate—An annual ad valorem tax levied on real property.

Tax, Improvement—*See:* Special Assessment.

Tax, Progressive—A tax, such as the federal income tax, that imposes a higher tax rate on a taxpayer who earns a higher income.

Tax, Property—1. The general real estate tax. 2. Any ad valorem tax levied on real or personal property.

Tax Credit—A credit that is subtracted directly from the amount of tax owed. *Compare:* Deduction.

Tax Deed—*See:* Deed, Tax.

Tax-free Exchange—A transaction in which one piece of property is traded for another piece of like-kind property. If the property involved is held for investment or the production of income, or used in a trade or business, tax on the gain may be deferred. Also called a 1031 exchange.

Tax Sale—Sale of property after foreclosure of a tax lien.

Tenancy—Lawful possession of real property; an estate.

Tenancy, Joint—A form of concurrent ownership in which the co-owners have equal undivided interests and the right of survivorship.

Tenancy, Periodic—A leasehold estate that continues for successive periods of equal length (from week to week or month to month, for example), until terminated by proper notice from either party. Also called a month-to-month (or week-to-week, etc.) tenancy. *Compare:* Tenancy, Term.

Tenancy, Term—A leasehold estate that lasts for a definite period (one week, three years, etc.), after which it terminates automatically. Also called an estate for years or a tenancy for years.

Tenancy at Sufferance—A situation in which a tenant (who entered into possession of the property lawfully) stays on after the lease ends without the landlord's consent.

Tenancy at Will—A leasehold estate that results when a tenant is in possession with the owner's permission, but there's no definite lease term; as when a landlord gives a holdover tenant permission to remain on the premises until another tenant is found.

Tenancy by the Entirety—A form of joint ownership of property by husband and wife (in some states that don't have a community property system).

Tenancy for Years—*See:* Tenancy, Term.

Tenancy in Common—A form of concurrent ownership in which two or more persons each have equal or unequal undivided interests in the entire property, but no right of survivorship. *Compare:* Tenancy, Joint.

Tenant—Someone in lawful possession of real property; especially, someone who has leased property from the owner.

Tenant, Dominant—A person who has easement rights on another's property; either the owner of a dominant tenement, or someone who has an easement in gross.

Tenant, Holdover—A lessee who remains in possession of the property after the lease term has expired.

Tenant, Life—Someone who owns a life estate.

Tenant, Servient—The owner of a servient tenement; that is, someone whose property is burdened by an easement.

Tender—An unconditional offer by one of the parties to a contract to perform his part of the agreement. If made when the offeror believes the other party is breaching, it establishes the offeror's right to sue if the other party doesn't accept it. Also called a tender offer.

Tenement, Dominant—Property that receives the benefit of an easement appurtenant.

Tenement, Servient—Property burdened by an easement. In other words, the owner of the servient tenement (the servient tenant) must allow someone who has an easement (the dominant tenant) to use the property.

Tenements—Everything of a permanent nature associated with a piece of land that is ordinarily transferred with the land. Tenements are both tangible (buildings, for example) and intangible (air rights, for example).

Tenure—The period of time during which a person holds certain rights with respect to a piece of real property.

Tenure, Allodial—A system of real property ownership in which an individual's ownership may be complete or absolute (except for those rights held by the government, such as eminent domain and escheat). *Compare:* Tenure, Feudal.

Tenure, Feudal—A system of land ownership in which the sovereign owns all the land and grants lesser interests to others in return for services; the dominant system in Europe during the Middle Ages. *Compare:* Tenure, Allodial.

Term—A prescribed period of time; especially, the length of time a borrower has to pay off a loan, or the duration of a lease.

Term Tenancy—*See:* Tenancy, Term.

Testament—*See:* Will.

Testamentary Capacity—The legal ability to make a valid will. This generally requires sufficient mental competence to understand the nature of a will, remember the extent of one's property, and recognize the relatives who would ordinarily be expected to benefit (often referred to as "the natural objects of one's bounty").

Testate—Refers to someone who has died and left a will. *Compare:* Intestate.

Testator—A person who makes a will. (At one time, a woman who made a will was referred to as a testatrix, but that term has fallen out of use.)

Third Party—1. A person seeking to deal with a principal through an agent. 2. In a transaction, someone who isn't one of the principals.

Thrift Institution—A savings and loan association or a savings bank.

Tie-in Arrangement—An agreement to sell one product, only on the condition that the buyer also purchases a different product.

Tight Money Market—A situation in which loan funds are scarce, resulting in high interest rates and discount points.

TILA—*See:* Truth in Lending Act.

Time is of the Essence—A clause in a contract that means performance on or before the exact dates specified is an essential element of the contract. Failure to perform on time is a material breach.

Timeshare—In a timesharing arrangement, buyers purchase the exclusive right to possession of the property (usually a resort condominium) for a specified period each year.

Title—Lawful ownership of real property. Sometimes also used to refer to the deed or other document that is evidence of that ownership.

Title, Abstract of—A brief, chronological summary of the recorded documents affecting title to a particular piece of real property.

Title, After-acquired—Title acquired by a grantor after he attempted to convey property he didn't own.

Title, Chain of—1. The series of deeds (or other documents) that transferred title to a piece of property from one owner to the next, as disclosed in the public record. 2. A chronological listing of the recorded documents concerning a particular piece of real property; more complete than an abstract.

Title, Clear—A good title to property, free from encumbrances or defects; marketable title.

Title, Color of—Title that appears to be good title, but which in fact is not; commonly based on a defective instrument, such as an invalid deed.

Title, Equitable—1. A claim to property that a court would recognize as a matter of fairness, although legal title is held by another party. 2. The interest held by someone who is in the process of acquiring property, even though someone else still holds the legal title; for example, the vendee's interest under a land contract. 3. The interest held by someone who has transferred legal title to another party as security for a loan. Also called an equitable interest.

Title, Legal—1. A valid claim of property ownership. 2. The interest in property that is held by the owner when another party is in the process of acquiring the property; for example, the vendor's interest under a land contract. 3. The interest held by the lender when title to property has been transferred only as security for a loan. Also called naked title.

Title, Marketable—Title free and clear of objectionable liens, encumbrances, or defects, so that a reasonably prudent person with full knowledge of the facts would not hesitate to purchase the property.

Title, Slander of—Disparaging or inaccurate statements, written or oral, concerning a person's title to property.

Title Company—A title insurance company.

Title Insurance—*See:* Insurance, Title

Title Report—A report disclosing the condition of the title to a particular piece of property, prepared by a title company before the actual title insurance policy is issued. Sometimes called a preliminary title report.

Title Search—An examination of the public record to determine all rights, claims, and interests affecting title to a piece of property.

Title Theory—The theory holding that a mortgage or deed of trust gives the lender legal title to the security property while the debt is being repaid. *Compare:* Lien Theory.

Topography—The contours of the surface of the land (level, hilly, steep, etc.).

Torrens System—A system of land registration used in some states, which allows title to be verified without the necessity of a title search. Title to registered land is free from all encumbrances or claims not registered with the title registrar. (In California, the Torrens system is no longer in use.)

Tort—A breach of a duty imposed by law (as opposed to a duty voluntarily taken on in a contract) that causes harm to another person, giving the injured person the right to sue the one who breached the duty. Also called a civil wrong (in contrast to a criminal wrong, a crime).

Total Finance Charge—*See:* Finance Charge.

Township—In the government survey system, a parcel of land six miles square, containing 36 sections; the intersection of a range and a township tier.

Township Lines—Lines running east-west, spaced six miles apart, in the government survey system.

Township Tier—In the government survey system, a strip of land running east-west, six miles wide and bounded on the north and south by township lines.

Tract—1. A piece of land of undefined size. 2. In the government survey system, an area made up of 16 townships; 24 miles on each side.

Trade Fixtures—Articles of personal property annexed to real property by a tenant for use in her trade or business, which the tenant is allowed to remove at the end of the lease.

Transferability—If an item is transferable, then ownership and possession of that item can be conveyed from one person to another. Transferability is one of the four elements of value, along with utility, scarcity, and demand.

Transfer Disclosure Statement—A form on which a seller is required to disclose information about the property to prospective buyers, in transactions involving residential property with up to four units.

Trespass—An unlawful physical invasion of property owned by another.

Triggering Terms—Under the Truth in Lending Act, a loan term which, if stated in an advertisement for consumer credit, "triggers" the requirement of full disclosure of repayment terms. Triggering terms include the amount of any finance charge, loan payment, or required downpayment, or the repayment period or number of payments.

Trust—A legal arrangement in which title to property (or funds) is vested in one or more trustees, who manage the property on behalf of the trust's beneficiaries, in accordance with instructions set forth in the document establishing the trust.

Trust Account—A bank account, separate from a real estate broker's personal and business accounts, used to segregate trust funds from the broker's own funds.

Trust Deed—*See:* Deed of Trust.

Trustee—1. A person appointed to manage a trust on behalf of the beneficiaries. 2. A neutral third party appointed in a deed of trust to handle the non-judicial foreclosure process in case of default.

Trustee in Bankruptcy—A person appointed by the court to handle the assets of someone in bankruptcy.

Trustee's Sale—A nonjudicial foreclosure sale under a deed of trust.

Trust Funds—Money or things of value received by an agent, not belonging to the agent but being held for the benefit of others.

Trustor—The borrower in a deed of trust. Also called the grantor.

Truth in Lending Act (TILA)—A federal law that requires lenders to make disclosures concerning loan costs to applicants for consumer loans, including any mortgage loan that will be used for personal, family, or household purposes; also requires certain disclosures in advertisements concerning consumer credit.

Underimprovement—An improvement that, because of deficiency in cost or size, is not the most profitable use of the land; not the highest and best use.

Underwriting—In real estate lending, the process of evaluating a loan application to determine the probability that the applicant would repay the loan, and matching the risk to an appropriate rate of return. Sometimes called qualifying or risk analysis.

Underwriting, Automated (AU)—Loan underwriting carried out by a computer program; the program generates a recommendation that a human underwriter uses in deciding whether to approve the loan. *Compare:* Underwriting, Manual.

Underwriting, Manual—Underwriting carried out in the traditional fashion by a human being, without the aid of an automated underwriting system.

Underwriting Standards—*See:* Qualifying Standards.

Undivided Interest—*See:* Interest, Undivided.

Undivided Interest Subdivision—*See:* Subdivision, Undivided Interest.

Undue Influence—Exerting excessive pressure on someone so as to overpower the person's free will and prevent him from making a rational or prudent decision; often involves abusing a relationship of trust.

Unearned Increment—An increase in the value of a property that comes about through no effort on the part of the owner, such as one resulting from a population shift or favorable zoning changes.

Unenforceable—*See:* Contract, Unenforceable.

Uniform Commercial Code—A body of law adopted in slightly varying versions in most states (including California), which attempts to standardize commercial law dealing with such matters as negotiable instruments and sales of personal property. Its main applications to real estate law concern security interests in fixtures and bulk transfers.

Uniform Standards of Professional Appraisal Practice (USPAP)—A set of guidelines adopted by the Appraisal Foundation, which appraisers are required by law to follow in certain appraisals.

Uniform Settlement Statement—A settlement statement required for any transaction involving a loan that is subject to the Real Estate Settlement Procedures Act (RESPA).

Unilateral Contract—*See:* Contract, Unilateral.

Unilateral Offer of Subagency—A provision that used to be standard in listing agreements used by multiple listing services, which made any member of the MLS who found a buyer for the property a subagent of the seller.

Unit-in-place Method—In appraisal, a method of estimating replacement cost by estimating the cost of each component (foundation, roof, etc.), then adding the costs of all components together.

Unjust Enrichment—An undeserved benefit; a court generally will not allow a remedy (such as forfeiture of a land contract) if it would result in the unjust enrichment of one of the parties.

Unlawful Detainer—A summary legal action to regain possession of real property; especially, a suit filed by a landlord to evict a defaulting tenant.

Unruh Civil Rights Act—A California civil rights law that guarantees the right of all persons to use the services provided by any business establishment.

Useful Life—*See:* Economic Life.

Use Value—*See:* Value, Utility.

USPAP—*See:* Uniform Standards of Professional Appraisal Practice.

Usury—Charging an interest rate that exceeds legal limits.

Utility—The ability of an item to satisfy some need and/or arouse a desire for possession; one of the four elements of value, along with scarcity, demand, and transferability.

VA—Department of Veterans Affairs.

Vacancy Factor—A percentage deducted from a property's potential gross income to determine the effective gross income, estimating the income that will probably be lost because of vacancies and tenants who don't pay.

Valid—The legal classification of a contract that is binding and enforceable in a court of law.

Valuable Consideration—*See:* Consideration.

Valuation—*See:* Appraisal.

Value—The present worth of future benefits.

Value, Assessed—The value placed on property by the taxing authority (the county assessor, for example) for the purposes of taxation.

Value, Market—The most probable price which a property should bring in a competitive and open market under all conditions requisite to a fair sale, the buyer and seller each acting prudently and knowledgeably, and assuming the price is not affected by undue stimulus. (This is the definition used by the federal financial institution regulatory agencies.) Sometimes called value in exchange. Compare: Market Price.

Value, Utility—The value of a property to its owner or to a user. Also called use value or value in use.

Value in Exchange—*See:* Value, Market.

Value in Use—*See:* Value, Utility.

Variable Interest Rate—A loan interest rate that can be adjusted periodically during the loan term, as in the case of an adjustable-rate mortgage.

Variance—Permission (from the local zoning authority) to build a structure in a way that violates the strict terms of the zoning ordinance.

Vendee—A buyer or purchaser; particularly, someone buying property under a land contract.

Vendor—A seller; particularly, someone selling property by means of a land contract.

Vicarious Liability—*See:* Liability, Vicarious.

Void—Having no legal force or effect.

Voidable—*See:* Contract, Voidable.

Voluntary Lien—*See:* Lien, Voluntary.

Voucher System—In construction lending, a system in which the general contractor gives subcontractors vouchers (instead of cash) for services rendered. The vouchers, which are statements attesting to the sum owed, are then presented to the construction lender for payment.

Waiver—The voluntary relinquishment or surrender of a right.

Warehousing—When a mortgage company or other lender borrows money on a short-term basis and uses it to originate loans, then sells the loans to permanent investors on the secondary market.

Warrant System—In construction lending, a system in which bills are presented to the lender for direct payment to the supplier or laborer.

Warranty, Implied—In a sale or lease of property, a guarantee created by operation of law, whether or not the seller or landlord intended to offer it.

Warranty of Habitability—*See:* Habitability, Implied Warranty of.

Waste—Destruction, damage, or material alteration of property by someone in possession who holds less than a fee estate (such as a life tenant or a lessee), or by a co-owner.

Water Rights—The right to use water from a particular body of water. *See:* Appropriative Rights System; Littoral Rights; Riparian Rights.

Water Table—The level at which water may be found, either at the surface or underground.

Wholesale Lender—A large lender that makes loans through intermediaries such as mortgage brokers or loan correspondents, instead of dealing directly with borrowers.

Wild Deed—*See:* Deed, Wild.

Will—A person's stipulation regarding how her estate should be disposed of after she dies. Also called a testament.

Will, Formal—A will that meets the statutory requirements for validity. As a general rule, it must be in writing and signed in the presence of at least two competent witnesses.

Will, Holographic—A will written entirely in the testator's handwriting, which may be valid even if it wasn't witnessed.

Will, Nuncupative—An oral will made on the testator's deathbed; valid in some states (although not in California) as to bequests of personal property worth under $1,000.

Without Recourse—A qualified or conditional endorsement on a negotiable instrument, which relieves the endorser of liability under the instrument.

Wraparound Financing—*See:* Mortgage, Wraparound.

Writ of Attachment—*See:* Attachment.

Writ of Execution—A court order directing a public officer (such as the sheriff) to seize and sell property to satisfy a debt.

Writ of Possession—A court order issued after an unlawful detainer action, informing the tenant that he must vacate the landlord's property within a specified period or be forcibly removed by the sheriff.

Yield—The return of profit to an investor on an investment, stated as a percentage of the amount invested.

Zone—An area of land set off for a particular use or uses, subject to certain restrictions.

Zoning—Government regulation of the uses of property within specified areas.

Zoning Amendment—*See:* Rezone.

Index

A

B

C

D

E

F

G

H

I

J

K

L

M

N

O

Y

Z